# THE POLITICS OF PATRIOTISM

Between the 1830s and 1880s European problems had a profound impact on British politics. In *The Politics of Patriotism* Jonathan Parry examines the effect on the British Liberal movement of the most significant of these, including the 1848 revolutions, the unification of Italy, the Franco-Prussian War and the Eastern question. Dr Parry argues that these European problems made patriotism a major political question: governments were judged not only by their success in promoting British interests abroad, but also by the purity, potency and 'Englishness' of the political values they represented. *The Politics of Patriotism* makes a major contribution towards understanding three important aspects of nineteenth-century British history: British attitudes to Europe, contemporary notions of national identity, and the nature and dynamic of British Liberalism. Setting foreign and domestic policy discussions in a patriotic framework, Dr Parry offers a new analysis of the ideas that influenced the Liberal Parliamentary coalition and the turning-points that affected its vigour and unity as a political movement.

In two previous books Dr Parry has re-examined many of the central tenets of Victorian Liberalism, and its operation as a political force. *The Politics of Patriotism* takes this reinterpretation of the British Liberal movement significantly further, as well as offering a stimulating and original demonstration of the variety of ways in which European events affected British political debate. For both reasons it will be of interest to a wide range of scholars and students of British history.

JONATHAN PARRY is Reader in Modern British History at the University of Cambridge and Fellow of Pembroke College. A Fellow of the Royal Historical Society, Dr Parry is also the author of *Democracy and religion: Gladstone and the Liberal party, 1867–1875* (Cambridge, 1986) and *The rise and fall of Liberal government in Victorian Britain* (New Haven, 1993).

# THE POLITICS OF PATRIOTISM

*English Liberalism, National Identity and Europe,*
*1830–1886*

JONATHAN PARRY

CAMBRIDGE
UNIVERSITY PRESS

CAMBRIDGE UNIVERSITY PRESS
Cambridge, New York, Melbourne, Madrid, Cape Town, Singapore, São Paulo

Cambridge University Press
The Edinburgh Building, Cambridge CB2 2RU, UK

Published in the United States of America by Cambridge University Press, New York

www.cambridge.org
Information on this title: www.cambridge.org/9780521839341

© Jonathan Parry 2006

First published 2006

Printed in the United Kingdom at the University Press, Cambridge

*A catalogue record for this publication is available from the British Library*

*Library of Congress Cataloguing in Publication data*

ISBN-13    978-0-521-83934-1 hardback
ISBN-10    0-521-83934-3 hardback

'And Do You Find, Sir,' pursued Mr Podsnap, with dignity, 'Many Evidences that Strike You, of our British Constitution in the Streets Of The World's Metropolis, London, Londres, London?'

The foreign gentleman begged to be pardoned, but did not altogether understand.

'The Constitution Britannique,' Mr Podsnap explained, as if he were teaching in an infant school. 'We Say British, But You Say Britannique, You Know' (forgivingly, as if that were not his fault). 'The Constitution, Sir . . . We Englishmen are Very Proud of our Constitution, Sir. It Was Bestowed Upon Us By Providence. No Other Country is so Favored as This Country.' . . .

'And other countries,' said the foreign gentleman. 'They do how?'

'They do, Sir,' returned Mr Podsnap, gravely shaking his head; 'they do – I am sorry to be obliged to say it – *as* they do.'

'It was a little particular of Providence,' said the foreign gentleman, laughing; 'for the frontier is not large.'

'Undoubtedly,' assented Mr Podsnap; 'But So it is. It was the Charter of the Land. This Island was Blest, Sir, to the Direct Exclusion of such Other Countries as – as there may happen to be. And if we were all Englishmen present, I would say', added Mr Podsnap, looking round upon his compatriots, and sounding solemnly with his theme, 'that there is in the Englishman a combination of qualities, a modesty, an independence, a responsibility, a repose, combined with an absence of everything calculated to call a blush into the cheek of a young person, which one would seek in vain among the Nations of the Earth.'

Charles Dickens, *Our mutual friend* (1864–5), book 1, chapter 11

The English [political] system has too precarious a foot-hold in reason . . . is too penetrated through and through with fiction, for any great contest in the western world to be indifferent either to those who revere, or to those who despise and hate it. There is sure to be some side of such a contest with a lesson or a warning for England. We thus fight our battles vicariously in other countries, and hence the otherwise unaccountable warmth and sincerity with which foreign concerns are discussed by the keenest English politicians.

John Morley, 'England and the war', *Fortnightly Review*, 8 (1870), 479–80

# Contents

vii

# Acknowledgments

Perhaps it is fitting that this study, of the insularity that underlay nineteenth-century British international aspirations, owes a very great deal to one small town in East Anglia. It could not have been written without the help of the librarians of the Cambridge University Library. It has benefited enormously from the stimulus provided over the years by the Cambridge University students who took my third-year course on 'The British and Europe, 1815–1906' and more recently my jointly run Special Subject, 'Culture wars in mid-Victorian England, 1848–1859'. My colleagues in the History Faculty, and our graduate seminar, have thrown up many stimulating ideas. The Master, Fellows, staff and students of Pembroke College have provided the ideal environment in which to work, though, perhaps conscious of that generosity, they have also given me a large number of opportunities for administrative distraction from this project. Richard Fisher of the Cambridge University Press has been a magnificently supportive editor.

I am very grateful to the Arts and Humanities Research Council for granting me a term of Research Leave in which to complete the typescript. I am also grateful to the Royal Historical Society for permission to republish some excerpts from an article that I previously published in its *Transactions*, 6:11 (2001). In addition I must thank the Hartley Institute, Southampton, for permission to republish passages from an essay of mine which is appearing in *Palmerston studies*, ed. D. Brown and M. Taylor (2 vols., forthcoming) and Oxford University Press for permission to republish several passages from an essay of mine in *Liberty and authority in Victorian Britain*, ed. P. Mandler (2006).

I have incurred many individual debts. For general help and specific insights and information, I should like to thank Derek Beales, David Bebbington, Duncan Bell, Eugenio Biagini, Clyde Binfield, Joe Bord, Roderick Braithwaite, Richard Brent, Arthur Burns, Peter Clarke, David Craig, Martin Daunton, Richard Drayton, Jane Duncan, Stephen Evans, Richard Gaunt, Peter Ghosh, Lawrence Goldman, Peter Gray, Bendor Grosvenor,

Tim Harper, Tony Hopkins, Theo Hoppen, Tony Howe, Mark Jackson, Patrick Jackson, Max Jones, Stuart Jones, Alan Kahan, Bruce Kinzer, Jon Lawrence, Bill Lubenow, Allan MacColl, Roy Macleod, Peter Mandler, Phillips O'Brien, James Raven, Richard Shannon, Stephen Taylor, James Thompson, John Thompson, Karina Urbach and John Vincent – and Mark Kaplanoff and Colin Matthew, whose help, unfortunately, I can call on no more.

I have learned a lot from my current and former research students, John Bew, Michael Ledger-Lomas, Paul Readman and Kathryn Rix, and from discussions with others in and beyond PhD vivas, especially Ben Griffin, Pandeleimon Hionidis, Tristram Hunt, Matthew Roberts and Emma Winter. I am particularly grateful to Michael and to Ben for reading and commenting so helpfully on the whole typescript, and to Paul for help with chapter 7.

Michael Bentley and Miles Taylor provided exceptionally useful critical comments on an earlier draft, from which the current version has benefited incalculably. Boyd Hilton performed a similar service for a large portion of the typescript, but that is merely a small part of what I have gained from his insight, help and repartee over the years. And I owe more than I can say, personally and historically, to Chris Clark, Patrick Higgins, Julian Hoppit, Joanna Lewis, Miri Rubin and Gareth Stedman Jones.

It was always my intention to dedicate this book to Maurice Cowling, who died in August 2005. One of its aims is to consider how historians can best capture the complex dynamic of political history and especially the relation between political tactics, languages and ideas. Anyone who was taught by him or became a colleague of his – and I fell into both categories – will know that these issues preoccupied him enormously and that his approach to them was distinctive and sophisticated. In fact it was more sophisticated than he usually managed to convey in print. I have dedicated this book to his memory, partly because he inspired me to tackle these issues, but also, as is often the case in a pupil–teacher relationship, because I really wanted to come up with something that would satisfy him. Maurice was not an easy person to please, and this could be disconcerting to the thin-skinned. Sadly I shall never know what he would have made of it. It has taken me a long time to realise that, for all his trenchant and usually unprintable criticisms of other approaches to political history, he almost certainly never worked out an entirely satisfactory answer to these problems himself. It has taken me even longer to realise that probably there is no entirely satisfactory answer. Still, one can but try.

# Introduction

This book has two main objectives. The first is to consider why European events had such an impact on nineteenth-century British Liberal policy and politics. The core of the book is the five chapters in Part II, which explore the domestic effect of particular continental episodes. Chapter 4 considers the 1848 revolutions and their consequences to 1854. Chapter 5 discusses the impact through the 1860s of the unification of Italy, and chapter 6 the crisis of 1870–1, including the Franco-Prussian War, the Paris Commune and the Vatican Council. Chapter 7 examines the Eastern question as it developed from the Bulgarian agitation of 1876 through to the occupation of Egypt in 1882, and its ramifications for African and imperial policy in the 1880s. Part II also contains an introductory chapter on the period 1830–47. This focuses on four approaches taken at that time by influential Liberals – Russell, Palmerston, Cobden and the leaders of radical evangelical Dissent – to the question of how to struggle against the powerful forces of European illiberalism. Each of these had lasting effects on the party.

These chapters cover those European events that had the most important political ramifications at home (with one exception).[1] They trace the interrelationships between these discussions and the development of ideas of Englishness in Liberal argument. Therefore, the book is also a contribution to the now substantial literature on national identity in the nineteenth century. The overwhelming bulk of this work has been cultural rather than political in scope, though some important studies have discussed the place of patriotism in popular and Radical politics.[2] This book argues that one of the major themes of nineteenth-century *elite* politics was the image of itself

---

[1] As noted below, p. 35, I have not provided much coverage of free-trading themes, because these are worth a book to themselves – which has already been written. See A. Howe, *Free trade and Liberal England, 1846–1946* (Oxford, 1997).

[2] E.g. H. Cunningham, 'The language of patriotism, 1750–1914', *History Workshop Journal*, 12 (1981), 8–33; M. Taylor, *The decline of British Radicalism, 1847–1860* (Oxford, 1995); M. C. Finn, *After Chartism: class and nation in English Radical politics, 1848–1884* (Cambridge, 1993); G. Claeys, 'Mazzini, Kossuth and British Radicalism, 1848–1854', *Journal of British Studies*, 28 (1989), 225–61; J. F. Kutolowski,

that Britain should project – whether on the diplomatic stage, in its self-presentation *vis-à-vis* the continental powers, or in internal affairs. Foreign, imperial and Irish debates turned on the purposes and values that Britain should assert, much more than on attitudes to specific overseas peoples. Foreign policy was not just an exotic or minority pursuit concerned primarily with the details of diplomacy; when it was politically important, it raised general issues which had significant connotations for domestic policy. The claim is *not* that foreign affairs were more important than the big domestic political issues and social tensions, but rather that studying debates about foreign policy crucially illuminates Victorian politics in general.

The second objective, therefore, is to contribute something to the debate on the nature and development of British Liberalism as a political movement, and to offer a fresh conceptual perspective to explain the rhythms of Liberal politics. A similar book could be written about Conservatism, for the Liberals certainly did not have a monopoly of patriotic language. The focus here, however, is on Liberal politics, because this was a period of Liberal political dominance. It is the last of a trilogy of books which have attempted to shed light on the political strategies and ideological profile of the Victorian Liberal party. The ultimate purpose is to show that domestic, foreign, imperial and Irish issues all involved similar underlying themes – of the responsibility of political leaders and the political nation to forge a strong and beneficent national community on healthy principles. As a result, the outcomes of apparently disparate crises in these diverse areas, occurring simultaneously, usually followed similar patterns, and this allows us to understand the shifts and turns in Liberal politics over time. Though the book argues for significant continuities in Liberal rhetoric, it also stresses the importance of key turning-points in Liberal history, when politicians' assumptions were forced to change.

The conclusion summarises the book's contribution on this second front. The two chapters in Part I are designed to help towards it: they are general essays about important aspects of Liberal *domestic* political argument and how these changed over time. Naturally, patriotic themes were central to much of Liberal domestic as well as foreign political discussion and could be treated at far greater length than they are here. These chapters focus on constitutional and ethical issues. To some extent they draw on more detailed work that I have published earlier. In particular, my second book, *The rise*

'Mid-Victorian public opinion, Polish propaganda, and the uprising of 1863', *Journal of British Studies*, 8 (1969), 86–110; R. McWilliam, *Popular politics in nineteenth-century England* (London, 1998).

*and fall of Liberal government in Victorian Britain*, offers a more narrative account of Victorian Liberal politics, for those who need it.[3] Chapters 1 and 2 aim instead to provide a broad-ranging analytical overview. They are written so as to emphasise the significance of national identity in Liberal domestic argument, thus facilitating comparison with the chapters in Part II. Most of this introduction, like Part II, focuses on the book's first objective.

## THE POLITICS OF FOREIGN POLICY

Foreign affairs were bound to loom large in nineteenth-century British politics. It was generally assumed that Britain was the greatest power in the world, owing to its worldwide naval and trading presence. This book focuses on the European element of those affairs – though it will be necessary from time to time to refer also to Liberal attitudes to the United States and to the empire, particularly in order to shed light on Liberal assumptions about constitutionalism and race. It focuses on Europe partly because European countries offered the most obvious comparisons in discussions about national identity, and because nineteenth-century elites were more familiar with the Continent and had many more ties to European political, intellectual and cultural movements than with any other places. The continental focus is also explained by the fact that the European powers remained Britain's major rivals all over the world. In particular, the problem of balancing the threats from France and Russia, its two major competitors, could never be ignored for long. Europe was more politically contentious in this period than empire. The colonies became a political problem either when other powers threatened them or when their governance raised questions of English identity and character that had already been argued out in other contexts.

Despite Britain's global status, modern historical accounts tend to confine nineteenth-century foreign questions to a compartment, separate from

---

[3] *The rise and fall of Liberal government in Victorian Britain* (New Haven, 1993). See also *Democracy and religion: Gladstone and the Liberal party, 1867–1875* (Cambridge, 1986). *Rise and fall* includes a detailed appendix of biographical information on leading Liberals, whereas in this book I have merely provided some very basic information in the index. It may be helpful to record a significant error in the table on pp. 336–7 of the paperback edition. Three lines from the hardback edition were omitted by the typesetter after the final proof. The lines:

'**New boroughs created**

In London:  5 2-member 1832
        2 more 2-member 1867'

should appear at the top of p. 337. They form the beginning of the second part of the table, and naturally p. 337 makes little sense without them.

the main political dramas of the time. Partly this has been because the field
has been left mostly to specialist diplomatic historians, who have well-
defined but restricted approaches to the task of writing about international
crises and have tended not to consider their domestic dimensions.[4] On the
other hand, domestic political historians have tended to concentrate on
issues that appeared central to voters, and it has generally been accepted
that foreign policy was not a major electoral issue. This book, however,
is concerned with Parliamentary and elite politics rather than elections,
and it argues that, considered in the right context, foreign issues are very
illuminating.

For a start, it was politically important to use the international stage to
project an image of Britain as a particular kind of regime, a community
upholding desirable constitutional and ethical values. Foreign tensions were
very frequently presented in ideological terms: between a Britain which
stood for constitutionalism, law, inclusiveness, conscience and humanitarianism, and various alternative continental regimes – usually autocratic,
sometimes republican – which were threatening and 'un-English'. The most
basic Liberal assumption, until the 1860s, was that a successfully inclusive
British political community was at odds with an overwhelmingly autocratic Continent. This provided a comprehensible and uplifting narrative
by which foreign crises could be explained to a domestic audience and the
politicians involved cast in a virtuous and patriotic light. The projection
of these values could be useful in foreign affairs themselves, because the
suggestion that the British people as a whole supported a particular policy
could often add to diplomatic effectiveness. The notion that broad Parliamentary and popular support made Britain more steadfast and powerful
in international disputes than regimes which lacked popular legitimacy
was an important part of Palmerston's strategy in 1840 and 1853–4. But
the domestic audience was usually the more important. For example, as
a number of historians have argued, Palmerston's self-conscious encouragement of constitutionalism abroad was designed, in part, to advertise to
Radicals the soundness and virtue of his constitutional principles at home.[5]

---

[4] Laudable exceptions include M. Swartz, *The politics of British foreign policy in the era of Disraeli
and Gladstone* (London, 1985) and D. Brown, *Palmerston and the politics of foreign policy 1846–55*
(Manchester, 2002). It is striking that the most brilliant diplomatic historian of nineteenth-century
Europe has always been scathing about the role played by British Liberal politicians in the system,
apparently not appreciating the domestic constraints on them. See P. W. Schroeder, *Austria, Great
Britain and the Crimean War: the destruction of the European Concert* (Ithaca, NY, 1972) and *The
transformation of European politics, 1763–1848* (Oxford, 1994).

[5] M. Taylor, *British Radicalism*; Brown, *Palmerston and foreign policy*; A. Taylor, 'Palmerston and
Radicalism, 1847–1865', *Journal of British Studies*, 33 (1994), 157–79.

A major element of Radical patriotism had long been a critique of institutional corruption and exclusiveness, and successful Liberal politicians needed to avoid such criticism.[6] The 'England' that Liberals claimed to be defending was one that they identified with the inclusive constitutional tradition.

A second issue was the defence of the realm, which was always complicated by domestic considerations. Defence had not been a major issue in the 1830s and early 1840s. This subsequently gave rise to a prominent myth – peddled assiduously by a well-connected military lobby – that it had been sidelined by the increasing political influence of the commercial middle classes, selfishly concerned to reduce their taxes. From the mid-1840s there were periodic public panics about the inadequacy of Britain's defences: in 1845–8, 1851–3, 1859–60, 1871 and 1882–5. One cause of these was fear that France might use technological developments – steam and then iron-clad ships – to reduce Britain's historic naval lead, especially given the navy's increasing need to protect British commerce across the globe. But a more important reason was a combination of political and psychological anxieties about the vulnerability of a Parliamentary regime in the face of the continental standing armies. In the 1850s Palmerston's brand of Liberalism benefited from these panics because feeble minority Conservative governments and Cobdenite commercial Radicals bore the brunt of the blame for them. The effect was to add to the perception that the vigorous pursuit of constitutional liberalism was a necessary element of national strength. However, after 1870 Gladstone's first two Liberal governments were badly wounded by further defence panics and became associated with penny-pinching commercialism. The latter panics reflected, firstly, a perceived inability to influence European affairs after the Franco-Prussian War, and then, after the occupation of Egypt in 1882, greatly expanded commitments in the Mediterranean and around the African coast. Chapter 7 argues that the occupation of Egypt blew a major hole in Victorian fiscal policy.

In some ways, then, British debates about world affairs were insular. However, the outward-looking aspects should not be understated. Britain's destiny to play a strong world role and the responsibility of politicians to safeguard that strength were persistent themes in political discussion. Maintaining national vigour and power and applying that vigour to honourable

---

[6] Cunningham, 'Language of patriotism'; M. C. Finn, '"A vent which has conveyed our principles": English Radical patriotism in the aftermath of 1848', *Journal of Modern History*, 64 (1992), 637–59; P. Harling, *The waning of 'Old Corruption': the politics of economical reform in Britain, 1779–1846* (Oxford, 1996).

purposes had long been seen – certainly in the eighteenth century – as among the most important duties of the politician, whose place in history would depend on his conduct in this respect. Failure to project a confident, influential presence on the European stage was seen as a mark of weakness and irresponsibility. It was interpreted as playing into the hands of powerful rivals, since most foreign policy issues, however apparently narrow or exotic, ultimately raised questions of Britain's standing *vis-à-vis* France or Russia – the Don Pacifico affair in Greece in 1850 being a good example. In the circumstances of the day, it was all but impossible politically for Gladstone not to stand up to the French in Egypt in 1882 or to the Russians at Pendjeh in 1885. Moreover, the perception of strength and success internationally carried with it a host of political advantages. It allowed an association with desirable values such as energy and manliness. It was generally popular commercially. It was also one of the most effective ways in which politicians could talk the language of common national purpose, which was important in the urgent quest for social unity at a time of rapid change.

Naturally, politicians' defence of British interests abroad was hard-headed and unsentimental. However, the justification of this defence was usually couched in constitutional and humanitarian rhetoric, and these were not just empty words, even if they were sometimes hypocritical ones. It was in fact a staple of Liberal argument that there was no incompatibility between 'British interests' and the general interests of world progress: the spread of constitutional regimes, free trade and peaceful relations between states. Grant Duff suggested in 1880 that since 1848 the whole course of European events had been 'playing the game of England, if only England is wise', by advancing 'the principle of freedom'.[7] When Disraeli's government of 1874–80 started defining 'British interests' in terms of mere territorial acquisition in Asia, without reference to these other aspirations, it was roundly condemned as selfish, materialistic, reactionary and ignorant of the true dynamics of global development.[8] The general foreign-policy aim in the nineteenth century was to uphold national power by following principles of restraint, equilibrium and peace abroad. Britain had nothing to gain from continental war; indeed it was important for it to avoid specific territorial commitments on the Continent which would be expensive and would reduce future freedom of manoeuvre in maintaining a power balance. Britain's global strength depended on international trade,

---

[7] M. E. G. Duff, *Foreign policy* (London, 1880), pp. 15–16.     [8] See pp. 331–40 below.

the avoidance of major conflict and the maintenance of a balance between the powers. This would prevent any state from threatening the current international status quo – thus safeguarding Britain's worldwide commercial and naval dominance and colonial possessions. Given time and peace, the socialising progress of commerce might well encourage British-style constitutional liberalism abroad, and reduce the influence of the feudal-military blocs which propped up European autocracies. Peace would also underpin the low tax regime at home. These foreign-policy objectives fitted neatly with the Liberal aristocracy's strategy for maintaining its political power at home, through responsible public service, an alliance with commerce, and the judicious pursuit of a policy of low taxes on all classes. The international vision paralleled the domestic one.

It was essential to maintain the freedom to play the powers off against each other and to prevent them from ganging up against Britain throughout the world. As Palmerston famously said, Britain had no eternal allies and no perpetual enemies, just eternal interests.[9] Britain relied for diplomatic influence in Europe on the maintenance of a balance between the powers, and on its ability to use its naval supremacy in the Mediterranean to show its strength. Nearly all of the European disputes in which it was a major participant involved seaboards – Iberia, Italy, Greece, the Dardanelles, Egypt, Belgium. If the European balance was awry, or the major international tensions were in landlocked parts of Europe, Britain's influence would be minimal – and the public would complain that the world's 'leading power' was being humiliated.

France and Russia were the two greatest threats to Britain, but neither, by itself, was 'the enemy', in either the Foreign Office or the political imagination. Paradoxically, often the only way of exercising the degree of European influence that domestic public opinion expected was for Britain to undertake an informal, or occasionally formal, alliance with the French. When this happened, as in the Spanish Civil War of the 1830s or the Crimean War of 1854–6, Britain might hope to cut a dash in Europe.[10] A French entente offered the best chance of preventing the Continent – and perhaps the United States – from ganging up to challenge Britain's global naval strength.[11] Until the late 1850s French support was a counterweight to the influence of the 'Northern' or 'Eastern' combination of Russia,

[9] *Hansard*, 97:122, 1 Mar. 1848.
[10] Clarendon, 1864, in J. K. Laughton, *Memoirs of the life and correspondence of Henry Reeve* (2 vols., London, 1898), vol. ii, p. 103.
[11] Clarendon feared this, to Granville, 12 Mar. 1856, in Sir H. Maxwell, *The life and letters of George William Frederick fourth earl of Clarendon* (2 vols., London, 1913), vol. ii, p. 119.

Austria and Prussia, which was widely seen by liberals as a universal anti-liberal force headed by Russia. And in the Mediterranean it was essential for the British fleet not to be at odds with both France and Russia. A policy of working with the former against the latter whenever the opportunity arose would check the Russian threat and also ensure that France won no strategic benefits that Britain did not also win, thus perpetuating the restraints on France's power. Cooperation emphatically did not mean trust: Palmerston argued that Britain should choose its allies according to the threat that they posed in war, and that action together with France was necessary in order to frustrate the latter's 'vast schemes of extension and aggression'.[12] He did not doubt that France's greatest goal was 'the humbling of England, the traditional Rival of France, and the main obstacle to French supremacy in Europe and all over the world'.[13] In Spain in the 1830s and again in the East in the 1850s a military alliance with France was undertaken as much to prevent France gaining undue advantage in those areas as to check Russia. Similarly it was the French threat to Northern Italy as much as the Austrian presence there which determined Britain's Italian policy for over twenty years. Reeve described the aim of the alliance well when he compared France to a man who married a woman with a great fortune but was prevented from getting his hands on a penny of it.[14]

In presenting these joint ventures for public consumption, the role of the French was downplayed and the ideological element emphasised. The Spanish policy of the 1830s was portrayed as a virtuous crusade against the forces of reaction abroad, to match the one at home in that decade. And victory against Russia in the Crimean War encouraged a perception that the march of civilisation, headed by Britain, was banishing the absolutist shadow from southern and eastern Europe. Confidence about this reached its apogee with the successful diplomatic and popular struggle to rid Italy of Austrian and French influence in 1859–61. In other words, British interventions on the Continent were usually projected as interventions on behalf of cherished ideals. This was partly a matter of educating the public out of its insularity, and disguising decisions taken for strategic reasons in language more palatable to taxpayers. However, it was also sometimes the

---

[12] M. F. Urban, *British opinion and policy on the unification of Italy 1856–1861* (New York, 1938), pp. 355–6; D. F. Krein, *The last Palmerston government: foreign policy, domestic politics, and the genesis of splendid isolation* (Ames, IA, 1978), pp. 21–2.

[13] 1863: R. Millman, *British foreign policy and the coming of the Franco-Prussian War* (Oxford, 1965), p. 116.

[14] 23 Feb. 1856, Laughton, *Reeve*, vol. I, p. 359.

case that the political potency of these ideals and their simultaneous resonance in domestic policy required politicians to take them into account diplomatically. For example, in 1853–4, a policy of assertion in the eastern Mediterranean was necessary for strategic reasons, but public clamour for a vigorous opposition to autocracy, operating on a divided cabinet, escalated that policy into a declaration of war. Similarly, over Italy in 1859 and over Egypt in 1882, popular and political pressures led to a more active policy against European rivals than was dictated by underlying strategic objectives. Moreover, as chapter 3 argues, policy-makers themselves saw the struggles against Russia and France partly in terms of values as well as strategy: the promotion of constitutional monarchy or an open trading system had real advantages for Britain.

All the points made so far demonstrate the limits to the political acceptability of ideas of non-intervention abroad. Whenever there was a defence panic, the selfishness of the materialist taxpaying commercial classes was blamed, and equated with a doctrine of irresponsible and unrestrained *laissez-faire* at home. The role of non-interventionism in nineteenth-century Britain, like that of *laissez-faire*, has been exaggerated. A *tendency* to non-interventionism abroad was a long-standing tradition, since Britain sought to keep the peace, had no territorial aspirations on the Continent and shunned entangling alliances and the old diplomatic system. A majority in most Liberal cabinets was primarily concerned with keeping Britain out of international trouble, which would help to maintain low taxes and to pacify the Commons. There was an assumption, for most of the period, and especially in the late 1850s and 1860s, that English values were so powerful and progressive that they would win out in Europe without recourse to war. There was a hostility, particularly among Radicals, to any British participation in efforts by the great powers to suppress the 'natural' growth of liberal movements. There was therefore a powerful consensus against too much continental meddling at all times after 1815. And there was a critique of 'imperialism', though this was defined mainly in constitutional terms, to mean a Napoleonic perversion of political liberties for the pursuit of glory; it was not a refusal to accept imperial responsibilities.

But none of this implied a doctrine of non-intervention. Patriotic celebration was so central a feature of domestic political life that it was inconceivable to admit weakness abroad. No politician could be successful who suggested that Britain was not a very great power in the world. There was, at least, a notion that England should work with other powers for the preservation of peace, stability and independence: in 1879 Hartington declared that alliances of this sort had 'always . . . in the main' been Liberal policy.[15] Moreover, any peace that appeared dishonourable to the values with which the British liked to identify was likely to be severely criticised, and any politician irresponsible enough to make such a peace severely condemned. And any vigorous international activity in line with liberal patriotic ideas, to check reactionary or perfidious foreign aspirations, would be strongly supported as 'manly'. In 1856 Aberdeen observed: 'An English Minister must please the newspapers, and the newspapers are always bawling for interference. *They* are bullies, and they make the Government bully.'[16] From time to time Liberals could be found muttering that prestige was a foreign word, redolent of Napoleonic Caesarism. Nonetheless it was politically necessary to assert the strength of Britain against other powers, especially when autocracy was strong in the 1830s or early 1850s, or once European rivalry developed an imperial angle in the 1870s and 1880s. Demands for non-intervention were at their height in the mid-1860s, but, as chapter 5 shows, they were a product of an unusual *lack* of threats: of British arrogance about the direction of world progress. Even then, as we shall see, many Liberals found it demeaning and materialistic to put low taxes ahead of notions of national global duty. This denied Britain's God-given global destiny, implied an insular selfishness at odds with the increasing communion between peoples and set a bad moral example to the domestic electorate. A vigorous policy could be presented as a Providential one on behalf of oppressed peoples, or as beneficial to English commerce. In fact there was, if anything, an increasing willingness to take bold measures abroad as confidence in the democratic accountability of the state increased, as long as the activity in question could be defended on ethical as well as patriotic grounds. By the 1880s, as chapter 7 makes clear, the most influential Radicals in the party were urging a stronger international policy and were blaming the failure to promote one on aristocratic effeteness in the Foreign and Colonial Offices.

Though the Conservative party also attempted to project itself as a patriotic and inclusive party – stressing particularly its attachment to traditional institutions and to Protestant ideals – it was not usually able to do so as effectively as its opponents. The Liberals presented themselves as the more reliable interpreters of the historic English constitution, the sounder defenders of popular liberties, and the more zealous enemies of anti-social

---

[15] At Manchester, 24 Oct. 1879, in marquess of Hartington, *Election speeches in 1879 and 1880* (London, 1880), p. 56.

[16] M. C. M. Simpson, *Many memories of many people* (London, 1898), p. 253.

threats to them. And they were generally more successful at making a strong foreign policy look compatible with economy and disinterested government. They claimed that a fair and open attitude to the constitution underpinned and reinforced an effective, assertive promotion of British interests abroad. Liberalism worked best when it managed to suggest that the successful deployment of Britain's international power was intimately connected with the coherence of the domestic political community and the vitality and international relevance of Britain's values. This may have been an illusion, but it was a very potent one in the years around 1854, 1859 and 1880, for example.

One reason why it worked so well was because it was usually easy to accuse the Conservative party of lacking both confidence in the people and competence at disinterested economic management. This twin failure, Liberals alleged, worked in conjunction with Tory aristocratic effeteness, and deafness to liberalising trends in Europe, to explain Tories' unwillingness to undertake a bold liberal policy abroad. The vulnerable status of Conservative governments – usually lacking a Parliamentary majority – added to this perception of weakness in 1830, 1852 and 1859. As Geoffrey Hicks has recently argued, mid-Victorian Conservatives tended to have a different approach to foreign affairs, stressing support for the status quo against republican innovation, and a quietist policy of cooperation with other powers, rather than moral constitutionalist arguments.[17] Under Wellington, Peel, Aberdeen and Derby, the Conservatives rarely mastered the politics of foreign policy, and they suffered for it. Even Disraeli did not succeed as much as is often assumed, as chapter 7 argues. By contrast, Liberals claimed that their domestic policies allowed them to rest on popular confidence and to tap national energies in pursuit of vigour abroad, a natural policy for a party that represented the true manliness of the English character. This, they said, was not a warmongering policy: on the contrary, a stance of responsible activity in Europe would prevent the need for war, ensuring, in a way that Conservative inability to interpret the trend of European opinion did not, that national resources would not be squandered in conflict. Despite differences of tone on foreign policy, both Palmerston and Gladstone tended to make these points about their domestic opponents. In the first half of the period, any suggestion of Conservative sympathy with the Holy Alliance or other forms of continental autocracy was ruthlessly exploited. In the second, the Liberals were presented, in Disraeli, with an

---

[17] G. Hicks, 'Don Pacifico, democracy, and danger: the Protectionist party critique of British foreign policy, 1850–1852', *International History Review*, 26 (2004), 515–40.

opponent made in heaven (or perhaps not) when it came to debates about true English character values.

However, on several occasions in this period the Liberal coalition became fractured or disorientated; its dynamic faltered. All political visions, however ostensibly inclusive, are flawed: they antagonise some groups or classes. Moreover, this period predated the professionalisation of political life, and the primary task of political leadership was therefore to galvanise and discipline a body of MPs who were independently minded, independently wealthy and often complacent and lazy. This might be achieved for a few years at a time, but never permanently, and so coalitions regularly needed to be reforged, especially as external circumstances changed.

There were three particular ways in which the politics of patriotism could fail to work for the Liberals. One, as noted above, was that it was not always possible to project a successful image in Europe or a resolute defence policy. Secondly, class and religious tensions inevitably arose within the Liberal party, and though the exemplary content of patriotic political language partly aimed at smoothing over these internal tensions, this was not always possible. Indeed patriotism was itself not simply a normative term; expressions of national identity involved all sorts of historical and ideological baggage.[18] Definitions of national character or national purpose varied in ways that subtly reflected different class or denominational agendas. In the 1830s and 1840s many Radicals objected to Whig government essentially on class or religious grounds, and many Tories also objected to it on the latter; talk of Whig 'un-Englishness' on educational policy, as outlined in chapter 3, was one way of expressing that concern, but should not disguise its underlying nature. Many Radicals continued to be uneasy at the elitist or complacent nature of Liberal leadership after 1848, even though they never managed to mount an effective challenge to it. At the root of the discernible unease expressed by some propertied voters at developments in Liberalism after 1867 was a sense that the Liberal party was increasingly being swayed by pressures that they disapproved of rather than by their own social and denominational priorities. The Liberal party's ability to rally supporters around an English national mission waxed and waned depending on the latter's willingness to believe that the 'England' which the Liberal elites represented was broadly compatible with their own.

Thirdly, there was always scope for tension between the assertion of English global greatness and the more cosmopolitan elements within the

[18] M. Taylor, 'John Bull and the iconography of public opinion in England, c 1712–1929', *Past and Present*, 134 (1992), 93–128.

Liberal mind. Celebration of British power and success was a natural political instinct; it strengthened public support and reflected a genuine self-confidence among the elite, especially after 1850. Yet almost all leading Liberals thought in international terms, one way or another, as noted in the next section. It was difficult to be a reformer without pointing to practices elsewhere from which the British could benefit. Elite Liberal culture was sufficiently cosmopolitan to be knowledgeable about other civilisations – especially classical, French, German and American ones. Russell was a typical Whig in maintaining that a political leader needed a broad understanding of continental cultures, in order to be sensitive to the distinctiveness of the English while avoiding a narrowly insular inflexibility.[19] Surely a genuine patriot should seek to prick stupid native complacency and improve his community, including by importing civilised ideas from abroad? Yet it could equally be argued that true patriotism involved reasserting traditional values which the country had neglected, to its disadvantage, in favour of damaging alien ones. Therefore while there was one tendency in Liberalism to look abroad, for instance to improve educational and social practices, there was another tendency which associated the Continent with a materialistic culture from which Britain must urgently be purified. So it was always possible for some Liberals to attack others for their continentalism. In different ways, Russell, Palmerston, Cobden and Gladstone could all be accused of being too 'un-English'. At various times this damaged them and contributed to division and weakness in Liberal politics.

## ENGLISHNESS, NATION AND RACE

Any book on relations abroad needs to engage briefly with some general questions about English attitudes to foreign peoples, in view of the enormous amount of recent writing on themes of national identity and race. This section argues two main points, as far as *political* debate is concerned. The first is that the focus in those debates was insular, in that it was nearly always on the benefits or threats to *English (or British)* interests and values, and on the responsibility that the *English (or British)* state and people had in dealing with the issue. (I tend to use 'English' and 'British' interchangeably, as explained at the end of the Introduction.) There was much less interest in the relative merits of, and nice distinctions between, the *other* nations or races involved, and the political historian should not spend much energy on making these distinctions. The second point is that, once that primary

---

[19] Lord John Russell, *Essays, and sketches of life and character* (London, 2nd edn, 1821), pp. 128–36.

theme is accepted, we can nonetheless observe a change over time in general English perceptions of the extent to which other cultures were backward or improvable. The two points together support this book's broader argument, since they allow us to see that the underlying issues in foreign, imperial, Irish and domestic policy were usually very similar. They revolved primarily around the nature of *British* responsibility, but also around the extent to which progress would occur naturally and how far it was necessary or fruitful to use the power of the *state* to assist it.

The historian of the politics of foreign policy does not need to worry too much about Victorian attitudes to particular nationalities and cultures (though there was a broader sympathy for Protestant than Catholic regimes). It is misleading to reduce the story of British attitudes to Europe to notions of 'Russophobia' or 'Francophobia'.[20] There is no puzzle in the fact that public opinion switched so rapidly from a neurotic obsession with the threat from Napoleonic France in 1852 to a virulent campaign against Russia in 1853–4 which was fought in (uneasy) alliance with the French. In both cases the collective recoil was against the same thing: an ideologically alien regime with expansionist, threatening intentions. At times when politicians presented Russia, France or Austria as a threat to Britain, the similarities in the presentation of each outweighed the differences; the emphasis was on *general* stereotypes of bureau and barrack at odds with English liberty. Russell explained to the Queen that the popularity of the anti-Austrian Hungarian agitator Kossuth was because he was seen as 'the representative of English institutions against despotism'.[21] Palmerston argued that only Britain could promote real liberalism abroad and that this meant the successful adoption of the British constitutional model.[22]

As chapters 5 and 7 show, events in Italy, Greece and Bulgaria between the 1850s and 1870s were significant in British politics not, in the main, because of what the British thought about the Italians, Greeks and Bulgarians, which was distinctly flexible depending on context. Rather, debate turned on the ideals that the British should promote there, and about the dangers of Austrian, French, Russian and Turkish illiberalism. The Bulgarian agitation was powered much less by humanitarian sympathy with the Bulgarians than by genuine or politically motivated guilt at the role of previous and present British governments in maintaining Turkish oppression over them.

---

[20] See e.g. J. H. Gleason, *The genesis of Russophobia in Great Britain: a study of the interaction of policy and opinion* (Cambridge, MA, 1950).

[21] 24 Oct. 1851, *LQV 1837–61*, vol. II, p. 325.

[22] F. L. Müller, *Britain and the German question: perceptions of nationalism and political reform, 1830–1863* (Basingstoke, 2001), p. 208.

Dreams of progress in Italy and then Greece in the 1860s were founded on the hope that both countries were falling under the influence of Britain rather than alternative powers.[23] We cannot get very far in explaining these British attitudes by reference to specific racial preconceptions. It was not the notion of ethnic nationalism but that of constitutional liberty against oppressive alien regimes that powered Liberal commitment to the struggles for Greek or Italian independence. Optimism about the receptiveness of both peoples to British liberal ideas was at its height in the early 1860s, at the same time as pessimism was mounting about the French capacity to receive them. Most Liberals did not think that the French were inherently inferior to the Italians or Greeks, just that Frenchmen's political education had been in the wrong hands for too long.

The idea that British governments needed to pursue an active foreign policy was frequently called into question in the twenty years after 1846, essentially because of a *general* suspicion of bureaucratic and aristocratic meddling, and an optimism about global progress if such interference came to an end. Chapters 3 and 4 argue that in the 1840s there was a reaction against the liberal activist foreign policy of Palmerston, initially owing to its cost and to a Radical distrust of Whig aristocrats. Cobden's argument, that state diplomatic activity obstructed rather than assisted true commercial and political progress, gained supporters. As chapter 1 shows, there was a similar rejection of an activist role for the state in domestic policy in the late 1840s. But in foreign affairs this anti-statist mood was challenged in the early 1850s by Palmerston's ability to recast his activist policy in a patriotic light, helped by the alarming return of autocracy in Europe after the failed revolutions of 1848, and by the emergence of an apparently illiberal regime in France, headed by Napoleon III.

However, at this stage, suspicion of a high-taxing interventionist state was still very strong, and Palmerston was able to pursue his policy only by reaching an understanding with those Liberals and Radicals who insisted on the principle of low and equitable taxation and tariffs. Gladstone, Chancellor of the Exchequer 1852–5 and 1859–66, was seen as the key defender of this latter position. For most of the 1850s and early 1860s this uneasy alliance between the two policies held, crucially strengthening Liberal government. Had the Liberals appeared interested only in a selfishly 'commercial' tax-cutting policy then they would have lost much support from advocates of an 'honourable' and 'vigorous' policy. But had they appeared sympathetic to

---

[23] See, for example, *The Times*' view that in offering the Greek throne to Queen Victoria's second son, the Greeks were expressing their desire to develop 'institutions like our own': 2 Dec. 1862, p. 8.

extravagant vested-interest finance then confidence in their fairness between classes would have been greatly reduced. Then the apparent defeat of continental autocracy by the early 1860s raised afresh the question of the future basis of national policy. Was it still necessary to rely on power assertion and gunboats? Would the extension of constitutionalism and free commerce not happen naturally? Would a more humanitarian and subtle approach to dealings with local cultures not be more appropriate for a liberal power? By the mid-1860s there was quite a debate about these issues. Towards the end of the decade anxieties re-emerged about British power abroad, and more voices urged an assertive policy. At roughly the same time, Liberals accepted the need for a more active policy of social intervention at home, following the 1867 Reform Act, as chapters 1 and 2 demonstrate.

In imperial policy, the emphasis was also usually on the political and ethical duties of the British state and people, rather than the particular virtues or vices of the locals. For example, the first major ethical crusade of nineteenth-century Liberalism was that of 1829–33 against slavery in the empire, which united Whig humanitarians with politicised evangelical Dissenters and Anglicans – often nicknamed 'Saints' – in a common cause which had significant echoes in several of the later episodes discussed in this book.[24] But one of the fundamental concerns of the evangelicals in this coalition had been their strong sense of the sin afflicting British society and the need to atone in God's eyes for past national errors, including the ill-treatment of those creatures of God who were former slaves. And the other, particularly marked among the Jamaican missionaries themselves, had been the sense that with God's guidance they would create a new and virtuous society on the island, superior to that both of the planters and of the amoral Anglican aristocracy that still ruled in Britain in the 1830s and 1840s.[25] The subsequent weakening of these two imperatives powerfully altered the balance of opinion – assisted by a change in attitudes to native peoples, considered below. By the 1850s both atonement-oriented pessimism about Britain's standing before God and strong distrust of the ruling elite had waned in the face of a much more optimistic attitude towards British economic progress and political power. And already in the turbulent 1840s it was generally said that political purification at home was more urgent than the welfare of freed slaves thousands of miles away. After 1850 there was less interest at home in native protection. This can be seen from the

---

[24] A. D. Kriegel, 'A convergence of ethics: Saints and Whigs in British antislavery', *Journal of British Studies*, 26 (1987), 423–50.

[25] C. Hall, *White, male and middle-class: explorations in feminism and history* (Cambridge, 1992), ch. 9.

decline of Parliamentary interest in Britain's duty physically to protect the Maori from exploitation by the New Zealand settlers, or the South African Griqua and Basuto from attacks by the Boers. These issues seemed much less weighty than the promotion of self-government in both places, which avoided interminable squabbling and cut costs for the domestic taxpayer. The move towards self-government in New Zealand, together with the abandonment of claims to police the Transvaal and the Orange river territory in 1852–4, were celebrated at home in standard political terms, as the properly 'English' constitutional solution, rejecting the 'slough of dominion'. Protests from the enfeebled evangelical lobby were drowned out.[26]

At first sight the power of anti-statist argument immediately after 1848 suggests that there was a serious threat of dismantling the empire. There was a strong and successful movement in the Commons in favour of self-government for the white settler colonies, amid much condemnation of the Colonial Office for attempting to keep them under control. Yet this was a manoeuvre to pander to general prejudices strongly held in *British* politics at this time, in favour of self-government and low taxes rather than autocratic 'over-government'. It was a movement to make the colonies more 'British', releasing their inhabitants' vigour so that they could contribute to global progress, in contrast to the fettered societies of Europe. They would be symbols of the dynamism of the British character. Throughout the 1850s and early 1860s it was sometimes assumed that these colonies would naturally progress to complete independence, and there seemed little alarm at the prospect. This was part of the contemporary assumption that British political, economic, cultural and moral influence would increasingly bestride the world, irrespective of formal territorial links. There was so much optimism that Britain's influence would be spread naturally by opinion and example, that force and political conquest seemed superfluous.

But this was the language of superiority, not non-intervention, as became apparent whenever British influence was threatened, as in India, or in Canada in the early 1860s. Any challenge to British honour, by natives or by another power, must be resisted as a potential humiliation. In English eyes, the defining event of the Indian Mutiny of 1857 was the massacre of over two hundred white women and children at Cawnpore, a barbarous crime against the innocent that had to be avenged in the name of law and civilisation, and, in some eyes, of Providence as well. Initial reactions

---

[26] *The Times*, quoted in S. Stembridge, *Parliament, the press and the colonies, 1846–1880* (New York, 1982), pp. 76–9.

to the Mutiny also included a reprise of the traditional Radical critique of supine, blundering, aristocratic officialdom. Characteristic of the late 1840s, this critique had resurfaced powerfully but briefly in the early stages of the Crimean War.[27] But, as in the Crimean War, there was also a view, which became increasingly prominent, that Britain was now a mature self-governing polity, and, if the essence of Englishness was communal self-reliance, then the political nation should take some responsibility for good imperial government rather than put all the blame on an elite. The effect was to place commitment to the imperial project on a broader footing.[28] Major-General Havelock, who had saved many English lives in the Mutiny but then died a martyr's death of dysentery, was presented as the model British soldier, a new Cromwell, fearless, self-disciplined and energetic. He was portrayed both as a representative of truly national virtues of manly individual courage and decisiveness against the old caricature of the bumbling aristocratic officer, and as a man guided at every step by his deep and firm religious faith.[29] Either way, his spirit set an example for future rulers in India, military and civil. Indeed the cult of Havelock, following on from the image overhaul towards the end of the Crimean War, assisted in the rebranding of the army as a socially responsible, representative and patriotic institution rather than a threat to popular liberties.[30] The Mutiny encouraged an intensified loyalty to the state as a Christian entity, particularly among Nonconformists, and led some Liberals to redefine Britain's imperial mission in the same virtuous, manly and communal terms that were coming to the fore at home.[31] But above all it led to a realisation that India must be held, in order to maintain Britain's prestige among the great powers.[32]

Similarly, the repression of a revolt in Jamaica in 1865 by the British governor Eyre was a *cause célèbre* primarily because it led to an impassioned debate about the values that Britain should project at home and abroad, at a time when, as we saw, there were already different views about its future mission. Martial law was introduced and over four hundred natives

---

[27] G. Dawson, *Soldier heroes: British adventure, empire and the imagining of masculinities* (London, 1994), pp. 109–10.

[28] B. Stanley, 'Christian responses to the Indian Mutiny of 1857', in W. J. Sheils (ed.), *The Church and war: Studies in Church history, volume 20* (Oxford, 1983), pp. 277–89.

[29] Dawson, *Soldier heroes*, chs. 4–5.

[30] O. Anderson, 'The growth of Christian militarism in mid-Victorian Britain', *English Historical Review*, 86 (1971), 46–72.

[31] Stanley, 'Christian responses'.

[32] Clarendon to Elgin, in D. Hurd, *The Arrow War: an Anglo-Chinese confusion 1856–1860* (London, 1967), p. 99. See also Stanley, 'Christian responses', p. 283.

executed, including the respected black Baptist minister G. W. Gordon, in many cases without adequate evidence of wrongdoing. Many Liberals saw this as a violation of English laws and the honour of England's name. Arbitrary justice could no more be justified in a colony than at home. It sullied England's reputation abroad and was condemned even by 'continental despotisms'.[33] T. H. Huxley, no admirer of the black man, would not accept that English law allowed 'good persons' to strangle 'bad persons'.[34] The more optimistic Liberals argued that English laws and liberties always had the potential to advance civilisation, and therefore that civil disorder derived from misgovernment by a sectional clique of prejudiced planters who had failed to offer equal justice and compulsory education. On the other side, defenders of Eyre said that his decisive action had saved the lives and honour of the English women and children in Jamaica and had re-established order. Though some of his supporters did assume that the natives were racially backward and would only respond to firm treatment, their emphasis on order also reflected the return of widespread anxieties about the need for strong government at home, in general and over the working classes in particular, in view of the expectation of an impending Reform bill. There was a particular critique of the foolishness of *bienpensants* who insisted on denying the importance of state authority and the fragility of civilisation; the imposition of law, not missionary humbug and naïveté, must be the basis of English government of other cultures.[35] Moreover, supporters said, Eyre had reasserted English prestige internationally. The Jamaican uprising was an embarrassment because it exposed the complacency of the general view of the early 1860s that, in flagrant contrast to the embattled United States, Britain knew how to bring stability and progress to a mixed-race society. It therefore stung British pride – more than the Indian Mutiny, according to *The Times*.[36] The simultaneous re-emergence of a powerful United States in the region, threatening Canada, added to the need to assert British strength.

From the later 1860s it became clearer than ever that the retention of imperial territory was a strategic and political necessity, essential in order

[33] Anon., 'Public affairs', *Fortnightly Review*, 3 (1865–6), 362. See D. A. Lorimer, *Colour, class and the Victorians: English attitudes to the negro in the mid-nineteenth century* (Leicester, 1978), p. 196; C. Bolt, *Victorian attitudes to race* (London, 1971), pp. 84–5.

[34] Lorimer, *Colour*, p. 191.

[35] For reactions to the Eyre case, see B. Semmel, *The Governor Eyre controversy* (London, 1962), Bolt, *Victorian attitudes*, ch. 3, and C. Hall, '"From Greenland's icy mountains . . . to Africa's golden sand": ethnicity, race and nation in mid nineteenth-century England', *Gender & History*, 5 (1993), 225.

[36] Bolt, *Victorian attitudes*, pp. 77–8, 105.

to uphold the British name. Interest in imperial consolidation stemmed in part from the passage of Parliamentary reform, which made some commentators keen to urge a more vigorous and responsible national policy and anxious about democratic ignorance of global priorities. Then, after 1870, British influence was embarrassingly weakened in a German- and Russian-dominated Europe, while the European powers decisively extended their rivalry to the extra-European sphere. The Russian threat to India grew, while France and later Germany eyed territories on the African coastline, previously informally dominated by the Royal Navy. There is no question that it was the threat from other European powers that made African questions increasingly significant in British politics. A mini-crisis about the Gambia in 1870 showed that talk of the climatic unsuitability of the tropics for English settlement was easily brushed off once a French threat emerged to the territory. The main driver of policy was naked rivalry, bolstered by considerations of strategy (not least naval bases) and pressure from commercial opinion on the Liberal benches in the 1880s. Though there might be less easy optimism about prospects for the rapid improvement of natives under British rule, it was still maintained that the British had the power to do more good than the French and the Germans – and that French control of the African coast would be a blow to free trade. Moreover the religious-humanitarian anxiety about Britain's responsibility to the natives returned, in the guise of hostility to the slave trade, particularly as practised by Arab traders. The prime issue was British responsibility, not native improvability. The struggle to cleanse the Continent of the slavers' immorality could be seen as consistent with the long-term strategy of 'Africa for the Africans'.[37] But, fundamentally, as chapter 7 argues, the main reason why empire resonated in British politics in the 1870s and 1880s was continental competition. In foreign politics, Europe was always at the centre of the plot, even when the action was set somewhere else.

So in political discussion about Britain's relations with other peoples, the precise characteristics of those peoples was hardly ever the issue. The English were much more interested in themselves. Politics was nearly always dominated by questions of British power and British responsibilities. However, Liberal attitudes were also, to a lesser extent, influenced by more abstract ideas about civilisation, progress and race.

It was a Liberal commonplace that all peoples had the potential for improvement and civilisation (and yet that barbaric passions lay quite close

[37] Ibid., p. 113.

to the surface of society even in the most civilised nations). These views were based on the assumption that human nature was fundamentally similar everywhere, and in the eyes of God. Societies had developed to very different degrees, owing to climate, the distribution of natural resources, and the institutionalisation of particular social habits and customs, not least commercial and religious ones. But they were malleable: in principle they could all evolve in a more civilised direction. Indeed there were many reasons to assume that that was the will of the Creator, with the ultimate hope of the unity of mankind.[38] It was the responsibility of advanced societies to set a good example, both to primitive peoples and to other advanced ones, since the latter could learn from each other. Civilisation involved breaking down vested interests and narrowness and establishing more common ground, toleration, communication and commerce among peoples. Thus large units were potentially more civilised than small ones, and a powerful country had the opportunity and the duty to spread civilisation over the greatest extent possible. Though peoples should be allowed the benefits of constitutional and decentralised government once they had reached political maturity, there was no merit in encouraging them to separate from a larger liberal constitutional power. National risings were justifiable on constitutional grounds – against foreign or militarist oppression and in pursuit of liberty and the rule of law. But separatist ethnic or racial nationalism was regrettable. Liberal Britain's task included the constitutional integration of its British and Irish Catholics and its Jews (allowed to sit in Parliament in 1829 and 1858). Britain was strong because it had absorbed ethnic differences in a higher political unity. In 1862 Acton described this 'English system' of combining different nations in one state, and preserving the liberties of each, as a 'necessary . . . condition of civilised life'.[39]

This 'civilisational' philosophy was inherently transnational, rooted in European Enlightenment thinking. One of the themes of Liberal thought in the 1850s and 1860s was that the progress of civilisation required a synthesis of the best of existing cultures in a higher ideal, and that even a country as advanced as Britain could learn lessons from other societies. Indeed, most of the thought-systems that influenced the Victorian Liberal mind – classical republicanism, Enlightenment commercialism, idealist organicism – were international movements of universal applicability. The ultimate aim of Christianity, and of the most influential secular Radical alternatives, was

---

[38] P. Mandler, ' "Race" and "nation" in mid-Victorian thought', in S. Collini, R. Whatmore and B. Young (eds.), *History, religion, and culture: British intellectual history 1750–1950* (Cambridge, 2000), pp. 225–8.
[39] J. E. E. D. Acton, 'Nationality', *Home and Foreign Review*, 1 (1862), 15–17.

the unity of man, transcending national boundaries. It was not unusual to deny any contradiction between patriotism and internationalism: both were ultimately about the love and improvement of one's fellow-man, the creation of God. The Congregationalist Robert Vaughan, writing in 1843, commented that 'the love of country is one of our moral instincts implanted by the Divine hand, but the same may be said of the love of mankind, and commerce carries with it a tendency to bring these passions into harmony with each other'.[40] By spreading constitutionalism and free commerce, Britain would be promoting progress everywhere.

However, from the 1840s assumptions changed to some degree. There was still a general acceptance that human nature was elementally the same everywhere, but there was increasing awareness that in practice differences between more advanced peoples and others were becoming so great that there was little chance of rapid improvement of the latter. This was the result of Britain's astonishing economic progress, and the sense that politically Britain was now much more mature than even most other European countries. After 1848 it was widely said that the difference between the progressive and backward parts of Europe was growing. Indeed one impetus for support for Italian liberalism was the belief that northern Italy now fell in the former camp while its Austrian oppressors were stuck in the latter. Sometimes the lack of dynamism in eastern Europe was blamed primarily on autocratic political structures, and sometimes on the backward culture of the Slav peoples.[41] It became a real question, in the middle of the century, how malleable and progressive in practice different nationalities and races currently were, and intellectual interest in racial differentiation and classification grew. In general, as chapter 1 argues, the effect of 1848 was to disillusion those who had believed that constitutions by themselves would bring progressive stability; more emphasis was placed on the need to change character, necessarily a much slower process.

This shift had two effects. First, it strengthened British self-satisfaction at the advanced state of its own public opinion, relative to any other country, with the partial exception of the other peoples schooled in the Anglo-Saxon cultural tradition, such as the Americans. It allowed the emergence of what one speaker at the British Association in 1863 jokingly described as an Englishman's favoured stereotype, that in theory 'all men are morally and

---

[40] R. Vaughan, *The age of great cities: or, modern society viewed in relation to intelligence, morals, and religion* (London, 1843), p. 262. For F. D. Maurice on a similar theme, see H. S. Jones, 'The idea of the national in Victorian political thought', *European Journal of Political Theory*, 5 (2006), 17–18.

[41] For the latter, see, for example, George Dawson's 1849 lectures on Europe, discussed in Hall, 'From Greenland's icy mountains', 220.

intellectually alike' but that in practice they were all 'equally inferior to himself'.[42] Even the Francophile J. S. Mill became depressed at the failure of the French to hold to their republican tradition after 1852 and at their love affair with Napoleon III's superficial charms; he became more pessimistic that they could be educated out of their irresponsible materialism.[43] Secondly, it strengthened the argument that the key to social progress was the slow process of altering opinion and habits rather than the simple one of changing laws. This simultaneously increased confidence about the naturalness of progress in the right conditions, and increased doubts about the value of making zealous efforts to improve peoples who were particularly far below English standards. On the whole it was assumed that most European societies were sufficiently advanced to fit the first category, however far behind Britain they might be, but that much of the rest of the world was in the second. This explains the rapid growth of the assumption that Turkey was unimprovably decadent and 'un-European', which though to some extent delayed by the propaganda necessities of the Crimean War, burst into full flood thereafter.

The effect was particularly striking on views towards 'primitive races' in the tropics. Ever since the high mortality rate of a philanthropic expedition of 1841 to the Niger, enthusiasm for English attempts to settle and civilise the tropics had been waning. The English, surely, could do more to advance civilisation in the temperate zones for which the Anglo-Saxon race was suited.[44] The failure of the West Indian sugar industry after the removal of protection strengthened the stereotype that the black man was too lazy, backward and effete to prosper commercially. By the early 1860s there was undoubtedly less interest in the 'negro question' than twenty years before.[45] This also meant that, despite the shock of the Mutiny, Liberal interest in India never became very strong; it did not fit Liberal assumptions well, since it was a more difficult society to improve than the utilitarian reformers of the 1820s and 1830s had hoped. Despite considerable indignation at Governor Eyre, there was little effective resistance to the idea that the black Jamaicans were unfit for self-government, justifying the imposition of Crown Colony status by the Conservatives in 1867. The claim that Britain was more an Asiatic than a European power was made by Disraeli for the Conservatives as early as 1866, but, like so many of his observations, it was designed to

---

[42] Professor Flower: Bolt, *Victorian attitudes*, pp. 4–5.
[43] G. Varouxakis, *Victorian political thought on France and the French* (Basingstoke, 2002), pp. 81, 153–4.
[44] See e.g. Somerset, 1862, in Lorimer, *Colour*, p. 124, and A. Trollope, *The West Indies and the Spanish Main* (1859; 1968 edn), pp. 82–4.
[45] Lorimer, *Colour*, pp. 114–24; Bolt, *Victorian attitudes*, pp. 104–5.

offend Liberal pieties rather than to reflect a consensus.[46] As chapter 7 shows in particular, by the 1860s and 1870s most Liberals preferred to focus on an Anglo-Saxon idea of Britain's ethical global mission, very often including the United States on a par with the white settler colonies. However, it was never acceptable to deny completely the possibility of native improvement, or to disavow altogether Britain's continuing responsibility for its non-white empire – particularly when challenged by other powers.

This increasingly conscious recognition of racial differences undoubtedly had an impact on policy. But this was not in all circumstances negative. In the 1860s scholarly interest in ethnic social and cultural differences was manifested in a historicist interest in traditional customs and the emerging science of anthropology, and these approaches could shape policy construc-tively where there was a political will to take them into account. As we see in chapter 5, a more active interventionist policy was pursued in Ireland in the late 1860s, taking more notice of local 'Celtic' characteristics. This was driven by a felt need to uphold Britain's responsibility to maintain the Union against foreign threats.

Therefore, with qualifications, this book shares the approach of Peter Mandler, who has stressed the dominance of the 'civilisational' approach in mid-Victorian England and has criticised the recent tendency among historians of empire to depict British attitudes as essentially ethnic and racialist. As chapter 1 demonstrates, Liberals paid much more attention to political frameworks than to ethnic peculiarities in explaining the success and progressiveness of nations. They believed that acceptance of the rule of law and the terms and conditions of citizenship had shaped English character the most, not innate racial differences. The main reason why they argued that rapid progress could not be expected in Italy or Greece in the 1860s was because of the previous backwardness of their *institutions* – the legacy of bad government and priestcraft.[47]

Nonetheless, Mandler's implication, that because English thinkers embraced the 'civilisational' perspective, they did not have a strong concep-tion of national character, needs to be revised. It was in fact common for writers to trace and celebrate the ways in which historical development had shaped national consciousness.[48] Moreover, political definitions of exem-plary 'Englishness' frequently ran institutional and ethnic characteristics

---

[46] W. F. Monypenny and G. E. Buckle, *The life of Benjamin Disraeli earl of Beaconsfield* (6 vols., London, 1910–20), vol. IV, p. 467.
[47] See chapter 6 below, and e.g. Dickens to Chorley, 3 Feb. 1860, in G. Storey *et al.* (eds.), *The letters of Charles Dickens* (12 vols., Oxford, 1965–2002), vol. IX, p. 207.
[48] H. S. Jones, 'Idea of the national', 14–15.

together, particularly from 1848; in March of that year, for example, Earl Grey could not 'help thinking that there is a difference in the capability of the Anglo Saxon race for self Govnt from that of the other European races'.[49] Similarly, the Liberal critique of Disraeli's 'un-Englishness' in the late 1870s mixed the two components. In view of the amount of superiority about English characteristics that was expressed from the middle of the century, it would have been surprising had an element of English nationalism not surfaced. Mandler's claim that the writers that he studies were unable to 'think . . . about the English as a nation' because their view that elites shaped progress required them to maintain class distinctions seems questionable.[50] In any case, this book deals in political argument, which relied on appeals to and invocations of 'the people'. In politics, arguments about the greatness of national character were undoubtedly compatible with the idea of improvement from above. Many Liberals genuinely wished to extend citizenship well into the lower classes. But this did not imply that the values of all citizens were equally attractive; that was why state activity was necessary to mould them. Similarly, efforts to integrate Irish Catholics and Jews into the political system did not imply that Catholic or Jewish character qualities were all meritorious. The inclusiveness of constitutional rhetoric paralleled and indeed justified a renewed effort to privilege some values over others, with the aim of creating a more coherent and congenial nation.

On the other hand, this book is at odds with several influential scholars in the anti-Mandler camp who have argued that the Governor Eyre affair was a turning-point in British attitudes to race, and that the 1860s saw a hardening of racial attitudes on more rigidly 'biological' lines.[51] As far as Liberal attitudes are concerned, one significant step – the waning of zeal for quick improvement – had already happened in the 1840s and 1850s, while after 1865 there continued to be a general acceptance of Britain's liberal responsibility to act as a trustee superintending the slow and steady development of native peoples. The Liberals brought back constitutional government in Jamaica in 1884 in order to symbolise their commitment to that idea. To the extent that the spread of scientific textbooks peddling

---

[49] Grey to Elgin, 22 Mar. 1848, in Sir A. G. Doughty (ed.), *The Elgin–Grey papers 1846–1852* (4 vols., Ottawa, 1937), vol. I, p. 125.

[50] Mandler, 'Race and nation', p. 232.

[51] Bolt, *Victorian attitudes*, ch. 3; R. Hyam, *Britain's imperial century, 1815–1914: a study of empire and expansion* (2nd edn, Basingstoke, 1993), pp. 155–66. Hyam's discussion is very suggestive but surely anticipates the emergence of a pessimistic reading of Darwin (and of fully-fledged muscular Christianity) and ignores the more upbeat sentiments so prominent in the 1860s. A more convincingly nuanced approach is taken by Lorimer, *Colour*, pp. 60–6, 203ff.

Darwinian notions helped to popularise the idea that racial distinctions were unalterable and biological, their main impact was not until the late 1870s and beyond. The effect was to bolster a much more hard-headed, essentially Tory language of empire in the 1880s and 1890s, which put Liberalism on the defensive. And what was true of Liberal attitudes to European and native imperial peoples was also, necessarily, true of attitudes to the Irish.

## IRELAND: BRITISH, EUROPEAN OR COLONY?

Every chapter in Part II also includes a large section on Ireland. This is because the best way to understand the politics of the Irish question is to see it in a similar light to the other issues under discussion – that is, in terms of the interplay between 'English' and 'un-English' values. Ireland was part of the United Kingdom, but appeared problematically different, culturally and socially. Was it British? Was it, instead, more European? Was it more properly a white settler colony? Or was Ireland best treated as a subjugated possession inhabited by an inferior race, another India? Much of the historiography of Ireland asserts the last, but without much evidence, as Stephen Howe has recently pointed out.[52] It is true that comparisons were frequently made between Irish and Indian agricultural problems and needs, and that some Irish land policy was shaped accordingly[53] – though the influence of the *continental* historicist tradition was also significant in the move to give greater respect to Irish tenurial customs in the 1860s. However, this book is not concerned with the detail of land policy but with broader approaches to government, and it argues that Liberals' *political* strategy for Ireland was no more (or less) affected by racial assumptions than were their attitudes to Europe already discussed. For the reasons set out in the previous section, Victorian Englishmen very often declared themselves superior to the Irish and used demeaning stereotypes to caricature them.[54] But in dealing with Ireland, Liberal politicians were severely

---

[52] S. Howe, *Ireland and empire: colonial legacies in Irish history and culture* (Oxford, 2000). The ambiguity of Ireland's status within the empire is well caught by A. Jackson, 'Ireland, the Union, and the empire, 1800–1960', in K. Kenny (ed.), *Ireland and the British empire* (Oxford, 2004), pp. 123–53.

[53] S. B. Cook, *Imperial affinities: nineteenth century analogies and exchanges between India and Ireland* (London, 1993); R. D. C. Black, 'Economic policy in Ireland and India in the time of J. S. Mill', *Economic History Review*, 2nd ser., 21 (1968), 321–36.

[54] There is now an impassioned debate about how racialist English attitudes to the Irish were. See L. P. Curtis, *Apes and angels: the Irishman in Victorian caricature* (Newton Abbot, 1971); S. Gilley, 'English attitudes to the Irish in England, 1780–1900', in C. Holmes (ed.), *Immigrants and minorities in England* (London, 1978), pp. 81–110; R. F. Foster, *Paddy and Mr Punch: connections in Irish and*

constrained by their own political values: it was impossible for the party ever to agree on a *non*-constitutionalist strategy for ruling it. To treat it as an imperial dependency was out of the question. It was the most intractable of political problems because it raised fundamental and insoluble questions about British identity. Irish issues were usually seen in terms of British responsibility: to impose just law, to defeat 'alien' threats (Ultramontane or republican), or to extend aspects of 'English' governing principles in the name of progress. At some times, there was more scope to argue that the Irish had similarities with continental peoples and that British policy in Ireland should follow European practice – though those advocating these 'continental' solutions argued that they were the most patriotic, since they would promote the true Liberal ideal of the United Kingdom as the model of a society which would promote civilisation and progress by synthesising disparate values in a higher unity. The tension about Liberal Irish strategy often concerned the extent to which this semi-'continental' strategy would itself be unacceptably 'un-English'. Moreover, attacks on governments for unpatriotic policies in Ireland tended to be made in conjunction with similar attacks in other policy spheres. So the way to a better understanding of the twists and turns of Liberal Irish policy is through seeing them in the context of the deeper rhythms of Liberal politics that this book sets out.

At root, Liberalism was concerned with political integration through the implementation of a liberal constitution. Liberal notions of British national identity were constitutionalist and religiously pluralist, never narrowly Protestant. Hardly any issue was more fundamental to Liberalism than Catholic Emancipation, passed in 1829 in order to end Irish Catholics' continuing sense of alienation from Britain after the Union of 1801. In 1839 Russell asserted that Irish disorder was the consequence of past misgovernment, not a flaw in the character of the people.[55] Commitment to liberal governing practices in order to secure and enhance the Union was arguably the leading principle of the Liberal party as it developed from 1835. No Liberal government could sit happily with the charge of oppressing Ireland, however attractive the idea of a benevolent dictatorship was to licensed thinkers like Macaulay.[56] If coercion was introduced, it was always politically necessary, at every point between the 1830s and 1880s, for it to be accompanied by improving reform. On a more mundane level, as a

---

*English history* (London, 1993), pp. 171–94; S. Howe, *Ireland and empire*, p. 50; M. de Nie, *The eternal Paddy: Irish identity in the British press* (Madison, WI, 2004); G. K. Peatling, 'The whiteness of Ireland under and after the Union', *Journal of British Studies*, 44 (2005), 115–34; L. P. Curtis, 'Comment: the return of revisionism', *Journal of British Studies*, 44 (2005), 134–45.

[55] *Hansard*, 47:14, 15 Apr. 1839.     [56] Parry, *Rise and fall*, p. 107.

party of 'outsiders', the Liberals were friends of Irish Catholics as well as British Nonconformists. The votes of Irish MPs were frequently essential for the survival of Liberal governments and, in the O'Connell era at least, patronage was used on a large scale to woo them. Though Irish (and to a lesser extent Scottish) electoral reform proceeded on a different basis to that in England until 1885, reflecting political traditions and social circumstances, the principles were not radically different. And in 1884–5 there was finally an acceptance (after some dissent) that the same franchise arrangements should apply throughout the United Kingdom. One reason why some Radicals opposed Home Rule in 1886 was because, in their view, the United Kingdom had only just been born as a fully functioning political community, capable of taking the interests of all groups properly into account.

Yet it was not so easy to agree on the detail of governing Ireland under the Union. There was general acceptance of the classic liberal principle that larger political units, if enjoying good constitutions, could extend freedom and civilisation further and better than small ones. There was an equally general assumption that the Irish were economically and socially backward and were prime candidates to receive this improving government from London. Though condescending, this view can hardly be seen as imperialist, since it was also widely held about the working classes (and to some extent all classes) in Britain. There was a good deal of comparison with continental Catholic peoples, and a hope that the Irish would develop like those of Switzerland or Germany rather than like those of Spain. The task of integrating Roman Catholics had been faced by other governments of mixed populations. So an important strand of Liberal thought wished Irish religious and land policy to be shaped by European precedent. But there was another, more doctrinaire view, that certain principles admired by the English, such as political economy, were generally beneficial and should be applied there. And many, particularly in the 1850s, argued that the Irish character could be improved only by social change rather than by force of law, and that the best strategy was merely the preservation of order in the hope of attracting capital for economic development. In reality, policy was a complex mixture of the three views.[57] But we are more interested in political controversy, and much of the Irish controversy of the 1830s and 1840s arose because Liberal ministers became identified with a distinctively 'continental' religious policy of state encouragement for all sects – a sharp and contentious break from Tory Protestant Little Englandism. Russellite

---

[57] R. D. C. Black, *Economic thought and the Irish question, 1817–70* (Cambridge, 1960).

Liberal Anglicanism sought to combine pluralism and moralism in Ireland just as it fused constitutionalism and ethical guidance on the mainland.

Hostility to the 'continental' strand in Liberal Irish thinking then ensured a patriotic reaction within the party after 1848, part of the general rejection of apparently overbearing, illiberal statism. Though at one level an element of a political game, this was also a serious statement about the basis on which a British state should react to pressure from the papacy. One problem after 1848 was an enhanced anxiety about Ultramontane influence in Irish politics, which threatened to undermine the Catholic loyalty to the state that Liberal constitutional policy had been designed to secure. However, the result, in the post-1848 climate, was a decisive rejection in Parliament of state endowment of Catholicism, as inconsistent with British values. In the medium term, by the 1860s, the Liberal consensus view moved towards the alternative strategy of checking papal interference, the policy of general disestablishment and disendowment in Ireland. This move was enormously assisted by the example of Italy, which in the early 1860s seemed to be following an attractively progressive and pro-British path. Though Liberal support for Italian unification, itself partly inspired by hostility to the papacy, began by alienating the bulk of Irish Catholics, it ended, in the late 1860s, with an alliance with them in support of disestablishment of the Anglican Church in Ireland. On Church and land issues, the policy of the Gladstone government of 1868 aimed to combine sensitivity to Irish cultural peculiarities with a strong opposition to Ultramontane and foreign republican tendencies in Irish politics. It sought to forge an ethical union of Britain and Ireland on a pluralistic but patriotic basis, just as it sought to integrate the classes in Britain by an improving social policy.

However, as chapter 6 shows, this new approach was wrecked by the continental dramas of 1870–1. This was partly because these dramas damaged liberal optimism about the scope for global progress under British leadership, which had consequential effects for confidence about progress in Ireland. Moreover, the Vatican Council raised the spectre of the Ultramontane threat in a more strident form, strengthening the feeling that papal influence in the United Kingdom must be checked. The effect was that powerful groups of Liberals became determined to resist concessions to Catholicism in Irish and British educational policy, shattering the alliance with Irish Catholics and falling back on a specifically British definition of national political purpose.

All these events demonstrate that in political crises the temptation was always to discuss Irish issues in terms of British identity and responsibilities, much more than in terms of specific Irish virtues or vices. Indeed Gladstone, generally seen as the Liberal prime minister most sympathetic to Ireland, took care to avoid giving Irish MPs much influence over policy – part of his general determination to govern on a national rather than sectional basis. By the 1880s the main context of Irish debates was not the papal threat but British global power, prestige and image. Gladstone felt that persistent coercion was damaging the liberal image of the British state and preventing the education of the Irish into political citizenship. But his critics saw his proposal of Home Rule as a dangerous, enfeebling step that risked the break-up of the empire. This was a greater concern for most Unionists than the future government of Ireland itself, about which they often lacked ideas. Nonetheless, they tended still to assert either the Whiggish idea of responsible trusteeship for Ireland, or the Chamberlainite notion that a vigorous democratic government could solve the grievances of its Irish as well as its British citizens. Unionists hardly ever saw Ireland itself as a colony.[58] Gladstone talked more about colonial comparisons, but in the context of the mid-Victorian battle for white settler self-government – and with the same aim, as in 1848–51, of purifying *British* and imperial politics as much as Irish. He saw Home Rule as a virtuous reassertion of the proper relationship between British government and the English-speaking peoples overseas, which was becoming corrupted at every level by alien principles.

## ASSUMPTIONS AND APPROACHES

In its broader objectives, this is a book about the political strategies, tactics and languages pursued by Liberals of the Parliamentary class, and their consequences for the health, dynamism, breadth and unity of the Liberal coalition of propertied men that dominated British politics for most of the period under review. It focuses on political debate as conducted in Parliament and in the high-to-middle-brow media. All politics is the art of compromise between the establishment of a broad coalition of support and the pursuit of particular aims. Parties need to develop inclusive policies, ideas and myths to rally their supporters, to establish their political centrality and to provide points of attack on opponents. They need to surmount the many obstacles that events constantly throw up in the way of maintaining broad support. In the nineteenth century there was also a persistent concern to stabilise the state while building a larger political

---

[58] S. Howe, *Ireland and empire*, p. 67. See, for example, the emphasis of Robert Lowe on this point: colonies could be abandoned, but Ireland was an integral part of the realm: 'What shall we do for Ireland?', *Quarterly Review*, 124 (1868), 259.

community – a task in which the British governing classes succeeded well. Political leadership, then, is a great art. This book aims to contribute to an understanding of its successes and failures in the nineteenth century. In order to do so, it looks at the conventional political elite, but also at a clerisy, writers in newspapers and periodicals who forged arguments and myths which played important parts in influencing opinion.

There are of course a number of valid ways of writing political history. Though the approach followed here is by no means unique, it seems, at first sight, to follow some different assumptions from the two most celebrated types of writing about Victorian politics to have flourished over the last forty years. Firstly, in its emphasis on the role of ideas and concepts, it appears at odds with the 'high politics' school of the 1960s and 1970s, which is generally taken to be sceptical about the relationship between ideals and political practice.[59] In fact the 'high politics' school is better seen as part of a larger historical movement at that time to inject professionalism and sophistication, and to reject the pieties of earlier generations of nineteenth-century scholars – an approach which has culminated in the magisterial *New Oxford History*.[60] To see it as concerned to empty politics of ideological content is a falsely reductionist view. It was aware that politicians used issues for personal advantage, and that the real reasons why those issues were controversial were often different from surface appearances, and both these insights are central to this book. But it was also aware that politicians have a national leadership function, in which ideals and doctrines are essential.[61] Indeed the main methodological objective of this book is to attempt to rework the traditional 'high political' approach on a broader canvas, marrying a properly sophisticated account of political practice with a due attention to the importance of contemporary ideas and values. It tackles the longer period rather than the day-to-day level – on the basis that the need in Victorian political history is not more detail but better perspective and conceptualisation of what we know. It takes ideas seriously, while trying to avoid overidealising politicians' intentions, imposing ahistorical

---

[59] M. Cowling, *1867: Disraeli, Gladstone and revolution, the passing of the Second Reform Bill* (Cambridge, 1967); A. Jones, *The politics of Reform, 1884* (Cambridge, 1972); A. B. Cooke and J. R. Vincent, *The governing passion: cabinet government and party politics in Britain, 1885–6* (Brighton, 1974).

[60] The classic works of this type of the 1960s included R. Blake, *Disraeli* (London, 1966), P. Smith, *Disraelian Conservatism and social reform* (London, 1967) and R. T. Shannon, *Gladstone and the Bulgarian agitation 1876* (London, 1963). K. T. Hoppen's volume in the *New Oxford History*, *The Mid-Victorian generation 1846–1886* (Oxford, 1998), is particularly good as a synthesis of the work of the last two generations of scholars for that period. It is now complemented by B. Hilton, *A mad, bad, and dangerous people? England 1783–1846* (Oxford, 2006).

[61] See particularly P. Williamson, *Stanley Baldwin: Conservative leadership and national values* (Cambridge, 1999).

modern assumptions on them, or reducing politics to an oversimplified scheme driven by class, race or gender stereotypes. Politics was, as Gladstone wrote, 'at once a game and a high art', and a properly sophisticated account should appreciate their intricate interaction rather than trying to privilege one over the other.[62] Political conflict was not just a matter of plotting at Westminster but of engaging more successfully with mainstream rhetorical traditions than one's rivals, within and outside the party, in order to command the immediate situation and to provide national leadership.

In fact this book is part of a trend: other political and intellectual historians have become increasingly aware, over the last twenty years, of the need to conceptualise Victorian politics more accurately. The result has been an enormous increase in the scope and sophistication of discussion of Victorian political language, from which these pages benefit significantly. It is no longer enough to define Liberalism in terms of the Manchester school and meritocracy, or by yet more scrutiny of Mill and Gladstone. Of course, some will think that this sophistication makes it foolhardy to try to generalise about the relationship of politics and ideas over time, as this book tries to do.

Secondly, by concentrating on elite politics and opinion, this survey provides a different perspective from that of the most stimulating work of the last decade, which has focused on extra-Parliamentary Radicalism and on the relationship between popular politics and the electoral process.[63] This book is not concerned with the gaining of mass popularity or the winning of elections. One reason for that is that Parliamentary politics before 1885 was not concerned with electoral appeals and benefits to anything like the extent that became routine during the twentieth century. Governments worried about control of Parliament infinitely more than about voter approval. Before the Third Reform Act, national issues were less important in determining the outcome of elections than alliances of local interest groups. Between 1846 and 1885 the Liberal Parliamentary coalition normally expected to win elections as long as it demonstrated a decent degree of unity and focus. Of course some national issues had a major role to play in the Liberal electoral appeal, most crucially low taxation and tariffs,

---

[62] Gladstone to M. Müller, 25 Nov. 1872, Müller papers, Bodleian Library, d 170, f.183.
[63] See e.g. J. Lawrence and M. Taylor (eds.), *Party, state and society: electoral behaviour since 1820* (Aldershot, 1997); J. Lawrence, *Speaking for the people: party, language, and popular politics in England, 1867–1914* (Cambridge, 1998); E. F. Biagini, *Liberty, retrenchment and Reform: popular Liberalism in the age of Gladstone, 1860–1880* (Cambridge, 1992); J. Vernon, *Politics and the people: a study in English political culture, c. 1815–1867* (Cambridge, 1993); P. Joyce, *Democratic subjects: the self and the social in nineteenth-century England* (Cambridge, 1994).

Parliamentary reform and Dissenting grievances. At local level these often operated in a hard-headed and practical way, suggesting a somewhat different image for Liberalism to the ones on which this book concentrates. However, these images were not incompatible, and the ability of the party to project them all merely indicates how complex and skilful a business politics is.

Nevertheless, it is almost certainly the case that at various times, the strategies detailed here satisfied many extra-Parliamentary Radicals, helped to woo voters and contributed to Liberal electoral success. The principal sources for this book are columns in *Hansard*, newspaper reports of speeches, and articles in the national periodical press. All were widely read. As Jon Lawrence has argued, there is significant scope to make more connections between Parliamentary and popular politics.[64] However, there was never a complete fit: each world had its own cultures, traditions and priorities, and effective connections can be made between them only once historians are clear what these were. This book aims to assert the importance of elite Liberal political argument (after all, interest in politics there was much more continuous than it was at the grass-roots), and to illuminate it better. A different study would be needed to demonstrate with any plausibility the reach of the arguments discussed here at popular level. Nonetheless, in writing this book, I have been stimulated by recent work on extra-Parliamentary Radicalism and I hope that historians of that Radicalism can find something useful in it, which might help to extend the amount of common ground.

One argument particularly associated with recent work on Victorian popular politics is that the 'triumph of party' at local electoral level should not be exaggerated, since there continued to be considerable suspicion of both party leaderships as elitist or sectional organisations.[65] This argument suggestively restates a more traditional theme in the literature on Victorian Liberalism: the difficulty of imposing unity on the Liberal party, and its tendency to quarrel. Colin Matthew once contended that even in Gladstone's day the Liberals were not a party.[66] At first sight, then, it would appear perverse to write about Liberalism as a more or less coherent movement

---

[64] J. Lawrence, 'Political history', in S. Berger, H. Feldner and K. Passmore (eds.), *Writing history: theory and practice* (London, 2003), p. 196.

[65] Lawrence and M. Taylor, *Party, state and society*, pp. 16, 81, 95–6.

[66] J. Vincent, *The formation of the Liberal party, 1857–1868* (Harmondsworth, 1972 edn); D. A. Hamer, *Liberal politics in the age of Gladstone and Rosebery: a study in leadership and policy* (Oxford, 1972) and *The politics of electoral pressure: a study in the history of Victorian reform agitations* (Hassocks, 1977); H. C. G. Matthew, *Gladstone 1809–1874* (Oxford, 1986), p. 191.

from the 1830s onwards, as this book does. But the claim is certainly not that the Liberals were always united: they were obviously divided on several levels at the time of their defeat in 1874, and throughout this period tension between different strands of Whig and Radical opinion was rarely absent. Politics is an endlessly fluid process in which no unity, no victory is ever final. Moreover, party in its modern, nationally organised, large-scale form only developed owing to the stimulus of the 1867 and 1884/5 Reform Acts. However, this does not mean that party was not important beforehand. At electoral level, after all, most voters acted fairly consistently on party lines, while Victorian Liberal politicians were concerned with the integration of the political nation as they defined it. They were very aware of the power of party in galvanising and disciplining energies for political purposes.

Since the eighteenth century, Whigs had believed that fidelity to party spirit was the best guarantee of honourable and principled behaviour, by protecting MPs from the tempting faction, flattery and benefits of court politics. After 1832 Liberals continued to argue that party spirit was a crucial safeguard against the excessive influence of the court and its 'Continental Advisers', a particular concern during, and beyond, Prince Albert's hey-day.[67] It was one of the guarantors of English constitutionalism against the threat of continental Caesarism. Meanwhile, the 1832 Reform Act and 1835 Municipal Corporations Act entrenched party divisions in the localities. The younger Whigs of Russell's generation emphasised the role of party at Westminster as the best way of securing and balancing elite authority and orderly popular participation. It would improve ministerial accountability and Parliamentary discipline, thus maintaining aristocratic leadership of a broad coalition of support and allowing a potentially fractious Parlia-ment to enact necessary measures in the people's name. It educated MPs into thinking in broad and patriotic terms, checking corruption and self-ishness.[68] This idea of party as a stimulating but also disciplinary force remained central to Russell's Liberalism in the 1860s. For his successor Gladstone, party was even more instrumental, a means of channelling pop-ular energies to achieve a virtuous set of political outcomes. Radicals were right to be suspicious of the disciplinary function of party, since this was one of its main objectives. Therefore it is no surprise to find them com-plaining about the priorities of party leaders. The important question is not whether the discontented set out any alternative agendas, which they naturally did, but whether these alternatives were widely held enough to be

---

[67] See Wodehouse journal, 7 June 1863, 26 May 1864, in *Kimberley*, pp. 99, 136.
[68] H. Reeve, 'Earl Grey on Parliamentary government', *Edinburgh Review*, 108 (1858), 277–8, 281–2.

capable of derailing the party's course and threatening national political stability. Maintaining party solidarity was never easy and required painstaking effort at central and local level, but in essence both main party leaderships managed it, thus sustaining elite political dominance.

This book argues that a number of broad ideas and arguments were available to leading politicians, from which they could try to fashion a successful political language for the Liberal Parliamentary party. These fell into three main categories. The first were the constitutional themes considered in chapter 1, emphasising liberty under the rule of law, 'self-government', and the importance of keeping the constitution free from vested-interest pressures and ensuring that it represented the nation effectively, accountably and harmoniously. The second, closely connected, were arguments for low taxes on all social classes, and the abolition of those restrictions on freedom of trade which would tend to favour particular sectional interests. Though the latter are mentioned in chapter 1, this book does not place particular emphasis on them, mainly because the role of free trade in Liberal discourse, especially on international affairs, has already been so well covered recently, particularly by Anthony Howe.[69] The third were arguments about moral improvement and the development of the moral conscience, through social and educational reform, the encouragement of religious activity, and attacks on un-Christian or inhumane forces, which are discussed in chapter 2. It is important to appreciate the skill with which successful political leaders were capable of drawing on elements of these three approaches, and the variety of ways in which they could be woven together, in order to fashion a political agenda. For example, Gladstone was usually able to do this despite his Peelite lack of sympathy with aspects of the Whig tradition. A nuanced treatment of his leadership needs to reflect both his strengths and his occasional weaknesses in this endeavour.[70]

All three sets of values were attractive not least because Liberals generally believed them to have contributed significantly to the historical development of an English national identity. In political argument, English identity was most commonly defined in terms of deep-rooted institutions, practices and laws which had won wide respect and loyalty. British self-confidence and success were attributed mainly to the way in which these political structures had strengthened liberty and self-discipline, suppressed intolerance and dogmatism, and encouraged enterprise, Protestantism and individual

---

[69] A. Howe, *Free trade and Liberal England*. Another fine contribution in a related area is P. Marsh, *Bargaining on Europe: Britain and the first common market, 1860–1892* (New Haven, 1999).

[70] See *Note on previous work* on pp. 38–9.

responsibility. Therefore all three strands of argument remained attractive throughout the period; indeed, one implication of this book is that the politics of the two decades after 1867 make most sense when they are placed in the context of earlier years, rather than viewed as entirely a new era. The Bulgarian agitation cannot be understood in isolation from the Crimean War; the problems Gladstone faced in defence policy after 1870 and 1882 are best seen in the context of the invasion scares of 1852 and 1859; there were important links between his move for Irish Home Rule and the colonial and Irish debates of 1848–53. Similarly, I have suggested elsewhere that Disraeli's later career enthusiasms, for example on the colonies and on social reform, are best seen in the light of his views of the 1840s, rather than as precursors of an innovative Tory popular political appeal.[71]

However, as chapters 1 and 2 show, these languages could also create division within the Liberal coalition, as some elements within it were accused of preferring their self-interest to the promotion of the right ideals. These divisions were intensified by a persistent suspicion that many who promoted the cause of 'party' were in reality encouraging factionalism and sectionalism. Definitions of these 'factions' varied: some people objected to the power of aristocratic Whig cliques over the Liberal agenda, while others were increasingly alarmed at the influence of organised popular pressure groups and the caucus. So there were always limits to enthusiasm for party. Even in the 1870s and 1880s it was accepted that there were many issues (including most social reform proposals) which were best treated in a cross-party spirit, and that MPs were men of dignity and standing whose independence of expression should be valued.[72] The Liberal party particularly, believing itself to represent popular forces, had a tradition of avoiding a *dirigiste* approach to party whipping and instead expecting a continuous process of internal debate, allowing the reconciliation of Parliamentary and extra-Parliamentary pressures.[73] And Palmerston's leadership of Liberal opinion, in the 1850s and early 1860s, placed significantly less emphasis on notions of party and creed than Russell had done, and instead projected a deliberately 'national' approach which appealed to many Radicals – among others – partly because it appeared less factional.

Even those Liberal leaders who took a more partisan approach than Palmerston tended to define party objectives in broadly integrative or uplifting terms rather than as a precise programme or interest group agenda.

[71] J. P. Parry, 'Disraeli and England', *Historical Journal*, 43 (2000), 699–728.
[72] For Gladstone's argument at Greenwich in 1871 that social reform was 'non-political legislation', see *Bassett*, p. 415.
[73] See e.g. Parry, *Rise and fall*, p. 131.

This was one reason why patriotic language could be so effective politically, especially since it could often embrace more specific constitutional or economic points as well. Association with an improving, ethical ideal implied that Liberalism was more than a narrowly partisan affair. Such appeals also helped to head off campaigns by interest groups within the party to develop their own alternatives. For example, the discovery of an uplifting foreign-policy purpose around which the party could organise helped to marginalise Nonconformist pressure for disestablishment, both in 1850–1 and after 1876. In 1868 an Irish issue, similarly remote from most voters' material preoccupations, achieved the same effect. Emphasis on national success and inculcation of patriotism also helped in the task of political integration. The moralising, missionary aspect of nineteenth-century politics should not be understated. Most elite politicians regarded the inculcation of civic responsibility, of public spirit, as a significant duty. Bagehot argued that the Commons should 'teach the nation what it does not know'.[74]

Perhaps political parties which dominate an era always succeed in projecting an above-party identity at the same time as managing the more humdrum task of satisfying the material aspirations of many voters. At any rate, at times when Liberals were successful in the nineteenth century, it was because they managed to occupy the political centre ground and to appear to speak for the majority of the political nation.

Finally, it should be pointed out that though this book highlights various national identity themes in Liberal politics, it is not suggesting that these were the only ways in which English national identity could be defined in the nineteenth century. National identity is a diffuse and abstract concept, about which generalisation is dangerous. However, that is not to say that it is a bogus or shallow one. Therefore, though the book shows national identity themes being manipulated for political benefit, it is not implying that the themes themselves were an 'invention', a 'construction', or a false consciousness imposed by an elite. In fact, they were attractive because they resonated deeply with very many people and had deep historical roots. The challenges of politics created the disagreements that this book covers, rather than something rotten at the heart of national identity.

Moreover, because it is not a book about national identity as such, it does not deal with the question of a separate Scottish or Welsh identity. Since its focus is on the effect of European affairs on elite politics, rather

---

[74] W. Bagehot, *The English constitution*, ed. M. Taylor (1867; Oxford, 2001 edn), p. 101; see Earl Grey, *Parliamentary government considered with reference to Reform* (London, 1864 edn), p. 37.

than on the constituencies, it has not seemed necessary to consider the extent to which these issues might have played differently in Scotland or Wales. This is in no way to deny the influence of non-English themes on British Liberalism. The influence of the Scottish universities enhanced the cosmopolitanism of Whiggery. The party always relied heavily on Scottish and Welsh support. This strengthened its emphasis on the quest for national unity through decentralised government recognising the civil liberties and interests of diverse groups. In the 1880s growing Liberal interest in Scottish devolution and Welsh disestablishment should be seen as an element of the debate about how to reconcile an expanding empire with principles of participatory government. Such issues were seen as constitutional in the sense of being an antidote to over-government and a way of renewing the legitimacy of executive power. But they also involved an appeal to local patriotism within a broader national framework, just as much Welsh and Scottish politics had previously done.[75] As Matthew Cragoe has recently shown for Wales, tracing the interaction of local and national identity themes requires subtlety, and it would be counterproductive to generalise about it here, in what is already a long book. In the end, I have chosen a title that refers to 'England' rather than 'Britain'.[76] However, the main reason for doing this is because contemporaries – including Carlyle and Livingstone – almost invariably used the word 'England' to mean the British state and nation. I have done the same very frequently in these pages, especially when attempting to set out contemporary notions of national purpose.

*Note on previous work*

My second book, *The rise and fall of Liberal government*, is sometimes seen as dominated by criticism of Gladstone's influence on the party. Though indeed it was critical of him in various ways, this was intended as a subordinate theme. The book's main aims were in fact to stress the vitality and coherence of Liberal traditions before Gladstone, to suggest that these had been undervalued in the literature and to argue that they continued to be more influential on Liberal policy during Gladstone's leadership than was generally understood. It also argued that the strength of these traditions helps to explain the severity of the split of 1886, for which Gladstone must undoubtedly bear considerable responsibility. Moreover, it started from the position, which I had argued in *Democracy and religion*, that Gladstone's religious priorities posed problems for many Liberals. So it sought to

---

[75] See M. Cragoe, *Culture, politics and national identity in Wales, 1832–1886* (Oxford, 2004), G. Morton, *Unionist nationalism: governing urban Scotland, 1830–1860* (East Linton, 1999), and M. Pittock, *Scottish nationality* (Basingstoke, 2001), ch. 3.

[76] As indeed I intended for *Rise and fall*, though I was persuaded to adopt 'Britain' by my American publisher.

qualify the overwhelmingly central role usually given to Gladstone in post-1867 Liberalism, and it suggested that in some ways he was an odd Liberal. I continue to believe that these points are important ones, and the last, in particular, has since been argued with incomparably more vigour by R. Shannon, *Gladstone: heroic minister, 1865–1898* (London, 1999). However, *Rise and fall* was self-consciously a revisionist book, and in the process of revisionism the organisation of the last section, particularly chapter 11, placed more emphasis on Gladstone's idiosyncrasies than I would do if I were to rewrite the book now, so it is not surprising if some readers have fastened too exclusively on this point. In fact, chapter 10 made it clear that there is a lot more to Liberalism after 1867 than points of difference between Gladstone and Whig-Liberals. Moreover, chapter 11 argued that Gladstone was in general an admired leader – if not as universally loved as some accounts would suggest – and that his strategy was not principally responsible for the defeat of 1874 (pp. 260, 272). One advantage of writing the current book is to place (even) more emphasis on the external and structural problems facing the Liberal party in 1870–4 and 1880–5, which, it should be stressed, were the main reasons for its difficulties before 1886, rather than the priorities of Gladstone. Another advantage is that, whereas both of my first two books focused on areas of policy in which Gladstone's idiosyncrasies were manifest, this one emphasises those themes of foreign policy and finance which allowed him to work effectively within Liberal traditions, helping to explain his appeal. Even here, however, my earlier points still apply, as I hope chapters 5–7 reveal: the idea of a national global mission was very common in Liberalism, and not specifically 'Gladstonian', while Gladstone's conception of that mission was in some ways unusual, influenced by a particularly intense sense of Providential destiny. Gladstone undoubtedly had difficulties in relating to the Liberal tradition, but that tradition was so diffuse that other potential leaders also had problems, and any book seeking to make sense of the ideological currents flowing through Liberalism between 1830 and 1886 must recognise that they were many and varied, and interacted in complex ways. When I wrote *Rise and fall* I was particularly struck by his difficulties, but this book tries to show the fuller, more complex picture, as clearly as it can. *Rise and fall* was in fact deliberately under-conceptualised, aiming mainly to provide a high-level analytical narrative, because it seemed more important to provide the latter than to go too deeply into these complexities.

# PART I

# *English Liberalism and national identity*

# CHAPTER I

# The English constitution and the liberal state

At the heart of nineteenth-century Liberalism was a liberal, inclusive reading of the English constitution. Liberals presented themselves as the only true defenders of the people, the only force energised by the moral power of public opinion, the only party able to uphold England's identity as a land of liberty. At several points, they stressed their commitment to constitutional reform in order to create a more effective national politics. Then they argued that Reform was in the English political tradition, which aimed at preventing oppression of popular liberties by ending vested-interest domination of politics. Reform, they said, would ensure the successful integration of the political nation and prevent class division.

But Reform would also legitimise the power of the state. Each of the three great nineteenth-century Reform Acts was followed by a strong Liberal push for a bold legislative programme. This reminds us that though constitutional, religious and economic liberty were all vital themes in Victorian politics, so was concern with the authority of the state to act on behalf of the national interest. Strong government could check the power of vested interests and could also improve national morals – by which was meant lower-class morals in particular, since Parliament was an overwhelmingly propertied body in this period. Within limits, the assertion of state power for these two purposes could be justified all the more easily as the nineteenth century wore on, since the claim that the state now represented 'the people' became stronger with each successive franchise extension.

However, many Whigs and Radicals continued to articulate a libertarian suspicion of a strong state, and one of the great difficulties of Liberal politics was to reconcile this suspicion with the exercise of state authority. A Liberal politician might run the risk of being accused of either illiberalism or irresponsibility. This was a constant tension within the party. Hostility to state intervention was at its peak in the late 1840s and 1850s, almost the only time in this period when there was so much optimism about British success and stability that the disciplinary effect of the rule of law was not a major element in Liberal politics. In the early 1870s those who were still hostile were also able to damage the Liberal agenda.

Liberal confidence in the liberal constitutional tradition and Liberal suspicion of a strong state were both encouraged by comparisons with continental countries. Though constitutional liberty won some successes, particularly in France and Belgium in the 1830s, the standard myth, until the 1860s at least, was that the major European regimes were autocratic, heavily centralised and – owing to the presence of large standing armies – militaristic.[1] Representative assemblies and local authorities seemed to have little authority there. Secret police activities, restrictions on press freedom, and the dominant position of an intolerant (usually Catholic) priesthood ensured that political and religious liberty was at a discount. Rhetoric of this kind allowed Liberals to exploit their patriotism for political gain through-out the period. They could tar Tories with the anti-patriot brush and accuse them of sympathy with autocratic continentalism. Within the party, also, disputes about the necessity for further Parliamentary reform often invoked the national heritage. Those who pressed for it could present their proposals in a reassuringly traditional and patriotic light. Those who sought to frus-trate further change pointed to the contrast with the Continent as evidence that Britain had already secured the necessary popular freedoms. In fact, for most of this period, further Reform was not a priority for the average Liberal MP, not least because of complacency at the stability and success of British constitutional arrangements.

This chapter provides a rapid general analytical overview of changing Liberal attitudes to constitutional issues, with particular reference to themes of national identity. More detail is available elsewhere.[2] It focuses on the main turning-points thrown up by the three Reform Acts of 1832, 1867 and 1884, and the equally important crisis of 1848–51, when calls for further Reform were frustrated.

## THE DEFENCE OF THE LIBERAL CONSTITUTION

As one Liberal writer noted in 1867, it was an English commonplace that 'misgovernment, such as has frequently existed for generations in all conti-nental countries, has in England been always unknown', and that this was because of the ability of its Parliamentary institutions to unite the nation

---

[1] B. Porter, '"Bureau and barrack": early Victorian attitudes towards the Continent', *Victorian Studies*, 27 (1983–4), 407–33.

[2] Chapters 1 and 2 complement the detailed narrative that I offered in *Rise and fall*.

harmoniously.[3] Well before 1830 it was a staple of constitutional argument that Parliament played the crucial part in the success of the British political system by allowing a great variety of national interests scope to express their grievances peacefully, smoothing tensions, and checking potential executive overcentralisation. The Bill of Rights of 1689 had prevented the monarch from imposing taxes without Parliamentary consent, and from interfering in elections, dismissing judges or maintaining a standing army. Accountability of government to the taxpayer, together with the dissemination of much power to the localities, seemed to ensure relatively wide participation in public affairs, while the checks and balances operating in the system protected the character of the governing elite from too many charges of venality. According to the national constitutional myth, the preservation of these freedoms had helped to underpin the individual responsibility and entrepreneurship that had allowed the English genius to flourish, and the nation to grow in political and economic power. Divine Providence was frequently invoked to justify the system: the sovereign should govern in accordance with the will of Parliament because the British people and British constitution were marked out by God for a great destiny. True patriotism expressed itself in the disinterested struggle to maintain English virtue, energy and freedom against corruption. Historically, empires had fallen because they had failed to do this, allowing vested interests to rule at the expense of the public. To avoid this fate, vigorous and independent political leadership was needed both at national and local level. Defending the legal and fiscal liberties of Englishmen was seen as a patriotic endeavour. MPs for populous seats, town and county, were usually to the fore in protesting against high taxation.

In some form British politicians of all colours subscribed to this set of constitutional nostrums by 1800: that was why Pitt the Younger called himself a Whig even while becoming the first hero of the nascent Tory party. Therefore the questions of how far the constitution needed amending and what constituted a vested interest were vexed ones, on which much disagreement was possible. The Whigs who were out of power almost continuously between 1783 and 1830 held together by projecting themselves as the real patriots in politics. Their party organised itself by claiming that under George III Parliament was once again being neutered by Crown influence and corruption. The executive was learning how to abuse its power

---

[3] A. O. Rutson, 'Opportunities and shortcomings of government in England', in *Essays on Reform* (London, 1867), pp. 281–2. Rutson felt that this standard view was too complacent: Parliament had contributed, but lack of invasion was the main reason, and had disguised the fact that Parliament did not yet fulfil its harmonising potential owing to its class bias.

through heavy taxation, the enlargement of an unaccountable civil and military bureaucracy, the invasion of civil rights by repressive legislation, and discrimination against Catholic and Protestant religious minorities. These alleged Tory practices were often compared with the abuses of continental regimes. Opposing the large army estimates of 1816, the young Lord John Russell asserted that they were part of the process of converting Britain 'from a naval into a military nation, and, instead of continuing a mighty island, she was to be changed into a petty continental state'.[4] In 1822 he alleged that ministers' reliance on large standing armies, coercion and patronage to secure social order diminished 'the ancient privileges of Englishmen' and stemmed from their unwillingness to modernise the constitution by enlarging the representation.[5]

When Russell and the other Whigs came into power in 1830 and passed the 1832 Reform Act, they set themselves up as the only true guardians of the libertarian tradition. The Reform Act was presented as a purifying assault on extravagance, corruption and oppressive legislation, powered by the increasing moral force of public opinion. The Whigs grabbed the patriotic mantle and attempted to redefine politics as a virtuous constitutional struggle. They claimed to offer 'the people' a properly responsible and accountable political system, making a blunt contrast with an *ancien régime*. The most immediate and important purpose of the Whigs' coup was to smash the basis of Tory power by disfranchising 143 'rotten borough' seats, practically destroying the inbuilt Tory advantage that had kept them in opposition. The Municipal Corporations Act of 1835 similarly sought to overhaul municipal government, undermining Tory control in most towns by instituting a general ratepayer franchise, and labelling the Tories as defenders of stagnant and oligarchical corporations who had misapplied public revenues and brought discord into local life. Patronage distribution would be legitimised by making it subject to voter choice rather than elite conspiracy. From the late 1820s the Whigs had been proposing a policy of economy and lower taxation, a rejection of 'Old Corruption', and the more complete integration of Nonconformists and Catholics into the political system. In the 1830s all these agendas were pursued vigorously: the criminal-law system was overhauled, the rights of religious minorities were extended and in 1834 public expenditure reached its low point for the nineteenth century. The Reform Act undoubtedly increased the accountability of the state.

Meanwhile the government Whigs of the 1830s drew on a strategy shared by their Whig predecessors and by the Liberal Tories of the 1820s,

---

[4] *Hansard*, 1st ser. 32:845, 26 Feb. 1816.     [5] *Hansard*, 2nd ser. 7:74–5, 25 Apr. 1822.

namely that comparison with the autocratic excesses of the major continental regimes was a particularly good way to demonstrate the virtue of
the English constitution. Canning had publicised his battles with the Holy
Alliance; Fox had committed the Whigs to the promotion of 'civil and
religious liberties all over the world'.[6] Brought together in government
after 1830, their heirs, Palmerston and Grey, projected an image of Britain
crusading for the extension of constitutional liberalism through Europe,
particularly in Spain and Portugal. Europe was one stage on which the
battle for liberal principles could be fought after 1830, particularly because
of the 1830 revolution in France which, like the British events of that year,
seemed to demonstrate that respectable public opinion was now a beneficent force which could be marshalled for the promotion of constitutional
progress. Ireland was another, after the passage of Emancipation in 1829,
since Liberals argued for integrating Ireland into the United Kingdom
through constitutional and religious reform, dismantling Tory Protestant
exclusiveness. The word 'Liberal' had entered British politics in the 1810s
and 1820s in the context of the debates about Spanish and Irish constitutional reform. Significantly, it became a useful rallying-cry for the new
party which emerged in the post-Reform landscape. After the political crisis of 1834–5, which purged the Reform coalition of those members least
comfortable with the increased accountability of politicians to public opinion, the various groups of Whigs, Reformers and Radicals that made up
that coalition were increasingly labelled a 'Liberal party'.[7] Liberalism was a
useful word because it implied a commitment to civil and religious liberties
everywhere and to inclusiveness and development at home, in contrast to
stagnant and exclusive aristocratic and clerical Toryism. However, it was
helpful not least to those many Liberals who were lukewarm about further
constitutional reform in Britain. By his Iberian policy – and his later policies in Italy and elsewhere – Palmerston tried to suggest that Britain had
an attractive combination of global reach, nobility of vision, and awareness
of the power of liberal ideas. He sought, like Canning before him, to use
these struggles to imply – to Radicals, and to public opinion – that Britain
was so genuine a supporter of the spread of liberal ideas and institutions
that its own constitutional arrangements did not require further inspection
and amendment.

The defence of national civil and religious liberties against enemies at
home and abroad remained the most potent of all rallying-cries for Liberals

---

[6] J. Parry, 'Past and future in the later career of Lord John Russell', in T. C. W. Blanning and D.
Cannadine (eds.), *History and biography: essays in honour of Derek Beales* (Cambridge, 1996), p. 147.
[7] Parry, *Rise and fall*, p. 131; J. Coohill, 'Parliamentary guides, political identity and the presentation
of modern politics, 1832–1846', *Parliamentary History*, 22 (2003), 278–81.

up to at least the 1880s. In that decade Gladstone claimed that his slogan of 'Trust the People' was the principle of Althorp and Russell in the 1830s.[8] Robert Lowe wrote in 1878 that 'the history of the English constitution is a record of liberties wrung and extorted bit by bit from arbitrary power'.[9] The history of Parliament was the symbol of resistance to an overbearing executive: to William Harcourt, it was the most authentic expression of English spirit.[10] The campaign against 'Beaconsfieldism' in 1879–80 was so successful in reuniting the party – for its last great common crusade – because it spoke clearly to this tradition, in a determination to defeat the 'un-English' unconstitutionalism of Disraeli's Conservative government of 1874–80. As chapter 7 shows, Liberals claimed that his foreign policy was illiberal, secretive and jingoistic. Vested financial interests distorted foreign policy to their selfish ends, while government recklessly frittered away taxpayers' money in defiance of the class-free and accountable fiscal system established by Liberals since the late 1840s. Moreover, Disraeli practised 'personal government' at home, ignoring Parliament and increasing the influence of the court.

How had this alien system triumphed? Not by the popular will – the Liberals had retained a majority of the popular vote at the 1874 election. The first Liberal defeat since 1841 had surely been achieved by unnatural means: by the influence of over-mighty Tory landlords in the counties. In 1880, in revenge, the Liberals sought to introduce properly 'English' institutions and principles of accountability there. Central to their 1880 election campaign was a three-pronged programme of franchise reform, elected county government and land reform, with a view to liberalise county life, on 'national' rather than 'class' lines: to extend the old English art of local self-government to parts of the country which still suffered from landlord dictation. In 1885 the leading Radical Charles Dilke maintained that the object of the local government reforms was to 'revive and restore the old English Constitution', 'undoing the Norman Conquest', which had degraded the 'Saxon township . . . into the French feudal manor'.[11] Like the 1832 Reform Act, the proposed constitutional changes of the 1880s would have a double appeal: they would benefit the party electorally and would breathe into stagnant, complacent county politics the invigorating Liberal principles of participation, openness and responsibility. This was a domestic mission on behalf of the superior political, economic and moral values of the town.

---

[8] 'The history of 1852–60, and Greville's latest journals', *English Historical Review*, 2 (1887), 281.
[9] R. Lowe, 'Imperialism', *Fortnightly Review*, 24 (Oct. 1878), 463.
[10] A. G. Gardiner, *The life of Sir William Harcourt* (2 vols., London, 1923), vol. I, p. vii.
[11] At Chelsea, *The Times*, 7 Oct. 1885, p. 10.

Boroughs increasingly had effective drainage and schools, bathhouses and art galleries, mostly provided at modest cost to ratepayers; why were the counties so lacking in these symbols of integrated community purpose and yet so inefficient in their financial administration? Replacing irresponsible magistrates with elected authorities would make rural local government more accountable, more competent and more active, thereby improving standards of education and health and increasing popular respect for the propertied classes. Land reform would broaden ownership, modernise the rural economy and reconcile tenants' rights with those of landlords, introducing into the countryside some of the harmony and dynamism that had made urban Britain so politically and economically successful.

The limited land reforms of 1880–5 and the inconclusive wrangles within the party over county government subsequently took the edge off this uplifting rhetoric. Nonetheless the Liberals were united behind the extension of household franchise to the counties in the 1884 Reform Act: indeed the vote on its second reading in the Lords saw the last great rally of Liberal peers. This is not surprising, because the Act spoke so powerfully both to Liberal self-interest and to Liberal principle. It would not have reached the statute book but for the depressing defeat of 1874, but it was presented in forms that had become traditional in Liberal argument: as a way to smooth class tensions and divisions and to replace sectional and exclusive politics with a properly national and inclusive system. The enfranchisement of labourers would establish justice between them and farmers by ensuring that Parliament responded equitably to the grievances of each.[12] It might weaken the grip of the Tory squirearchy, but it would not damage the stature of propertied MPs who sought to be responsive representatives, and indeed it might bolster legitimate propertied influence. Chamberlain suggested that after 1885 there would for the first time be 'a full expression of the national will'.[13]

### THE WHIGS, STATE AUTHORITY AND ELITE RESPONSIBILITY

There was no tension in the eyes of the Whigs of 1832, or of most other nineteenth-century Liberals, between the defence of constitutional liberty and the strengthening of state authority and social morality. Citizenship involved accepting the restraints and responsibilities of the rule of law. Liberty was seen as complementary to order and justice. It was not to be

---

[12] G. O. Trevelyan, *Hansard*, 217:816–17, 23 July 1873.
[13] 29 Jan. 1885, in C. W. Boyd (ed.), *Mr Chamberlain's speeches* (2 vols., London, 1914), vol. 1, p. 152.

confused with licence, with 'doing as one likes'. It was 'the right of being ruled according to stable and just laws'.[14]

Government authority was a major issue for the Whig Reformers of the 1830s. Though they were genuinely committed to further economy, the Liberal Tories' cuts in taxation and patronage in the 1820s had made the more extreme old Whig-Radical rhetoric about Crown tyranny over Parliament look tired and outdated. Political assumptions were shifting. By the late 1820s the younger Whigs such as Russell placed more emphasis on the weakness, sloth and unpredictability of the executive government, its inability to respond effectively and systematically to public grievances. The Reformers' main charge against Wellington in 1830 was less his oppression than his feebleness and sectionalism. It was the incompetence of Tory government, especially in failing to respond adequately to the depression and unrest of 1829–30, that led to its downfall and allowed Whig Reformers to take power. They claimed that Wellington's premiership was inactive because it doubted its popular standing.[15] This attitude implied a new consciousness of the moral power of public opinion and the need for politicians to engage with it. Traditionally many Whigs had tended to take a pessimistic view of progress, assuming that the governmental threat to liberty was always potentially increasing and that only a minority of enlightened men of virtue could resist this. Now there was more emphasis on the dynamic evolution of an intelligent and patriotic public opinion, as a result of economic and social change. The role of public sentiment in the fall of Wellington in 1830 added strength to the argument that executive power could be maintained only by responding to that evolution and harnessing it.[16]

Reformers hoped that by the enfranchisement of the £10 occupiers in the boroughs in 1832, the state could reflect the morality and dynamism of the wider political nation. This, not least, would strengthen its own authority. A more uniform franchise, a stronger party system and a purified Parliament would create a more orderly and more national political arena and give the impression of popular support for government acts. By increasing confidence in the state and in its propertied leaders, which the Whigs' theatrical self-projection would then entrench, it would secure 'general acquiescence' in the rule of law.[17] As Russell said in 1831: 'it is upon

[14] *Nonconformist*, 4 Oct. 1848, p. 754; E. R. Conder, *Liberty: an address delivered . . . April 8th, 1879* (Leeds, 1879), pp. 3–4.

[15] Parry, *Rise and fall*, pp. 67, 77–8.

[16] See D. Wahrman, *Imagining the middle class: the political representation of class in Britain, c. 1780–1840* (Cambridge, 1995), pp. 307–8, for the invocation by Grey and Jeffrey of a respectable middle class, recently created by industrialisation and urbanisation.

[17] Parry, *Rise and fall*, p. 89.

law and government, that the prosperity and morality, the power and intelligence, of every nation depend'.[18] Once the Reform Act had legitimised executive rule, its authority could and should grow. In fact the Reform government of 1830 was founded on a general anxiety in the propertied classes to remedy the weakness of government and the fragility of the rule of law. From the beginning, Liberalism set itself up against sectional aristocratic effeteness. Nothing like the New Poor Law, imposing a controversial administrative structure across the nation, could have been passed under the unreformed system. Its passage was helped by urgent pressure from elements of propertied opinion, ever since the depression of the late 1820s, for reform of the poor and criminal laws in order to improve popular moral discipline. It signified the executive's concern to demonstrate the national reach of the state, and to force local gentry to behave more responsibly in their attitude to poor relief. The Reform government was the first to pass *national* legislation on a major scale. Several of its ministers and officials shared a fascination with statistical enquiry and 'useful knowledge', in the hope of understanding the state of the nation in the mass, and undertaking rational reform of society around the principle of the greater social good. As chapters 2 and 3 show, Russell and colleagues had a particular commitment to moralistic activity to shape popular character through educational reform.

The Whigs also argued that Reform would strengthen the authority of the governing classes, by making them more accountable and forcing them to be more virtuous and zealous. The natural condition of a healthy society was for the propertied classes to rule, but their failure to do so with sufficient efficiency, vigour and earnestness had begun to divide the country on unnatural and alarming class lines. Social tensions, as in the late 1820s, were evidence of political failure: the 1832 Act would force 'the proudest aristocracy in the world' to learn their political duties in order to maintain their position.[19] Russell argued that the bill did not damage the aristocracy, merely those aristocrats 'who do not live among the people, who know nothing of the people, and who care nothing for them – who seek honours without merit, places without duty, and pensions without service'. An invigorated elite leadership would make popular movements 'at once salutary and safe'. Adequate representation for the large manufacturing towns would give their inhabitants more political responsibility. The fact that London had representation was held to explain the absence of rioting there for fifty years; Russell blamed the Peterloo riots in Manchester

---

[18] *Hansard*, 4:345, 24 June 1831.
[19] J. Clive, *Macaulay: the shaping of the historian* (New York, 1975 edn), p. 230.

on the fact that 'there was no authority to which [the populace] could conform, or from which they could derive instruction'.[20]

In their emphasis on improving the public spirit of the governing elite, Whig thinking was crucially influenced by the terrible example of the French Revolution. This was not because they feared imminent revolution in Britain without Reform, but because recent French history showed the consequence of rule by a decadent governing class. The French model of government had led to bloody anarchy, followed by autocracy, between 1789 and 1815. Russell's *Causes of the French Revolution* (1832) blamed the Revolution on the corruption of the eighteenth-century French court and the erosion of its members' ideals of honour and glory. Public interests had been sacrificed to private ones, while the prevailing values had been infidelity and materialist philosophical ideas rather than pure religion, with the result that 'the passions' and 'wickedness of man' had grown out of hand.[21] Whereas Tories reacted to the Revolution by arguing that the British should cling to their own constitution as a guarantor of stability, morality and freedom, earnest Whigs like Russell saw the fate of France as a warning against allowing the virtuous activism of the ruling classes to lapse. In this he was typical of many moralist reformers, most famously Thomas Carlyle and Thomas Arnold, for whom the Revolution was a divine judgment on a corrupt society and a demonstration of the unstoppable dynamism of history, which it was positively un-Christian to oppose.[22] To Russell and other Liberal Anglican Whigs, it showed the need for Christian political leadership to promote organic unity in society, reconciling class and sectional tensions in a common acceptance of the rule of law and of morally improving state activity.

The very different form taken by French revolution in 1830 – the people's refusal to allow Charles X and Polignac to dissolve the newly elected liberal chamber – gave the Whigs encouragement in two ways. It strengthened the argument that *anciens régimes* like those of Charles X and Wellington were feeble and doomed. Wellington's reading of the events in France – that moderate Reform in Britain must be resisted – seemed perversely inappropriate and convinced middle-ground British MPs that a change of government and a Reform Act were necessary for stability.[23] Secondly, the 1830 revolution reinforced the idea that a reformed constitutional monarchy

---

[20] Parry, *Rise and fall*, pp. 87, 81.
[21] Lord John Russell, *The causes of the French Revolution* (1832), pp. 80–1. See R. Brent, *Liberal Anglican politics: Whiggery, religion and reform, 1830–1841* (Oxford, 1987), pp. 56–7.
[22] Letters, 1 Nov. 1830, 6 May 1833, in A. P. Stanley, *The life and correspondence of Thomas Arnold* (2 vols., London, 1880 edn), vol. I, pp. 249, 307–8.
[23] R. Quinault, 'The French revolution of 1830 and Parliamentary reform', *History*, 79 (1994), 377–93.

was a model to which all educated Europeans could aspire, inspired by liberals both in Britain and beyond. In this way the Whigs showed that their patriotism was more cosmopolitan than the Tories' – reflecting their links with propertied liberals in other countries, particularly France.[24] In December 1830 the Tory leader Peel protested that the tricolour, as well as the national flag, had been sighted during a procession of the trades to the King in support of Reform. But Althorp and Russell both insisted that this was not an insult to the Sovereign but an appropriate expression of admiration for the 'great and glorious and successful struggle for liberty' in France in July; the tricolour (which Louis Philippe had adopted as the new regime's flag) no longer symbolised the crime and bloodshed of the 1790s.[25]

So law, authority and public-spirited leadership were crucial elements of early Victorian Liberalism, as was the Christianity which justified and sanctified them. Government in the British as opposed to the French revolutionary tradition was defended as wise and indeed Providential, as long as it modernised itself by judicious Reform. The English constitution allowed a compromise between the idea of authority descending from above and the need to gain consent from below. The intermeshing of executive and Parliament forced MPs to take some responsibility for the maintenance of legitimate authority. In a republic, by contrast, delegates were answerable only to their constituents and could be swayed more directly by their passions, yet the regime was also potentially tyrannical because it made a claim to absolutism, in the name of the people.[26] The descent of the French revolutionary republic of the 1790s into factionalism and bloodshed underlined these points.

The Whigs therefore claimed that a strictly constitutional or Parliamentary monarchy was the best form of government, balancing authority and liberty. It was a peculiarly English compromise. On the one hand, the most fundamental principle of Whiggism was that the exercise of Crown and Court influence had the potential to damage liberty and good government. Whigs defended party as a necessary instrument to check the natural tendency of monarchs to restrict the independence of Parliament and the liberties of the people. This suspicion of monarchical power survived throughout the period, particularly in relation to foreign policy, not least because of the Germanic Court's blatant sympathies for autocratic

[24] L. G. Mitchell, *Holland House* (London, 1980), chs. 8–10. Russell, for example, travelled extensively on the Continent as a teenager and lived in France for much of the 1820s.

[25] *Hansard*, 1:988–94, 10 Dec. 1830.

[26] Earl Grey, *Parliamentary government considered with reference to Reform* (London, 1864 edn), p. 27; H. Reeve, 'Earl Grey on Parliamentary government', *Edinburgh Review*, 108 (1858), 277–8, 281–2.

continental regimes. Exploiting Liberal hostility to Victoria and Albert's attempts to influence foreign policy contributed a lot to Palmerston's popularity in 1849–53. One reason for Russell and Palmerston's determination to pursue an assertive policy over Italy in 1859–60, and for Liberals' anxiety to resuscitate party vigour in the 1860s, was to check powerful royal pressure in this area.[27] As chapter 7 shows, the apparent success of Victoria's pretensions to influence affairs in 1877–9 played a major part in the Liberal alarm at 'Beaconsfieldism'.

But, kept within bounds by the vigorous application of constitutional principle, the monarchy was invaluable, and its public standing and reputation must be safeguarded. It offered a visible representation of the rule of law in the way that no republic could, and a human representation of the particular form of balanced government that had secured British stability and progress. After 1837 Melbourne hoped that Victoria's purity and youth would underpin the Whigs' claim to monopolise the language of virtue and improvement, especially as – in contrast to her uncle – she entered with spirit into the inclusive symbolism of Whig politics, purposefully greeting the Irish Catholic leader Daniel O'Connell and his family at a levee with a 'very smiling face', and taking pleasure in bestowing the first Jewish knighthood on Moses Montefiore.[28] Many Liberals subscribed to ideas of political participation and public virtue that were drawn from the classical republics and can be called civic republicanism.[29] However, this was entirely compatible with the preservation of a monarchy that was subservient to the spirit of the constitution. Indeed Liberal foreign policy urged constitutional monarchy as the model for Europe, because it offered a balance of authority, liberty and progress which was clearly superior to autocracy or republicanism and acted as a proxy for the extension of British influence and values on the Continent.

### LIBERTARIAN REVOLUTION, 1848–51

Despite general Liberal enthusiasm for the 1832 Reform Act, the Whigs' commitment to a party system led by an elite, and to a strong state, led to considerable tension with Radicals throughout the 1830s and 1840s. This

---

[27] *Kimberley*, pp. 99, 126, 130–1.

[28] Victoria to King Leopold, 22 Feb. 1838, in *LQV 1837–61*, vol. 1, p. 106; E. Longford, *Victoria R.I.* (London, 2000 edn), p. 78.

[29] For a distinction between civic and constitutional republicanism, see B. Worden, 'Republicanism, regicide and republic: the English experience', in M. van Gelderen and Q. Skinner (eds.), *Republicanism: a shared European heritage* (2 vols., Cambridge, 2002), vol. 1, pp. 309–10.

culminated in a political crisis between 1848 and 1851, transforming the image of Liberalism. The Whigs' concern with aristocratic leadership and moralistic state policy combined with their cosmopolitanism to make it possible for Radicals to argue that they did not have enough respect for English liberties.

Many Radicals, like many Whigs, tended to legitimise their argument for Parliamentary reform on patriotic grounds by reference to the 'ancient constitution' of England: the Anglo-Saxon folkmoots, or the broad suffrage of the fourteenth century. But this argument was attractive to them not least because it suggested that political freedoms did not need to be dispensed by elites; they were deeply rooted, and since the aristocracy had played a crucial role in removing them, it was unwise to trust their leadership. In the eighteenth and early nineteenth centuries the Radical patriot tradition had been very critical of factional politics at Westminster. Governments were regularly accused of abusing their patronage powers, frittering taxpayers' money away corruptly by giving jobs to aristocratic connections in order to cement support in Parliament or simply from class or sectional favouritism. To Radicals inured to criticism of authority, Whig ideas of party in the 1830s and 1840s seemed to reprise Walpole's *Venetian* factionalism rather than a patriotic defence of *English* taxpayers' rights. This policy made it easy for disappointed place-hunters, angry Radicals, or young meritocrats to mock Whig cabinets as a 'mere family party'.[30]

Both in the 1830s and again in power after 1846 under Russell the Whig governments were indeed dominated by aristocratic networks. In 1846 he included eight peers (including his father-in-law), an Irish peer and an heir to an earldom in his cabinet of sixteen. This was because he felt that aristocratic leadership was the only way of upholding the Whig conception of party. Whigs had long believed in party because in opposition it was a virtuous bond protecting the honour of politicians from the temptation of place-hunting, while in government it prevented anarchy and feebleness. Their determination to keep charge of the direction of the Liberal party themselves was redoubled by the effects of the Reform Act. It increased the prospect of pressure from activist constituency-based lobbies such as Nonconformists, Anti-Corn Law Leaguers and O'Connellites, while Anglican and propertied fear of the political effects of this sectional extra-Parliamentary pressure generated a Tory revival. Whigs believed that maintaining the authority of a propertied political leadership and disciplining Liberal-Radical factional lobbies were essential if they were to resist that

[30] Parry, 'Past and future', p. 143.

revival. Their coolness to Canadian pressure for self-government in 1839–41 resulted not from dislike of devolution, but instead from their distrust of the sectional effect of party spirit in places which lacked active benevolent elites (particularly but not only in potentially separatist French-speaking Canada).[31]

Moreover, in the awkward conditions of the late 1830s, the Whig attachment to monarchy also raised doubts about their constitutionalism and patriotism. Their continuation in office after 1839 was embarrassingly dependent on Victoria's assertion of her royal prerogative: Peel declined the attempt to form a government after she refused to change her Whig ladies of the bedchamber. There was much negative comment on the undue influence at Court enjoyed by foreigners like Baron Stockmar and Baroness Lehzen. Tories and Radicals made great play of the excessive allowance proposed by ministers for Albert of Saxe-Coburg on his marriage to Victoria in 1840, and they managed to reduce it.[32]

In addition, the Whig belief in state activity on social and religious issues became very divisive owing to the deep depressions and social turbulence of the 1838–48 period. In various contexts in the late 1830s and early 1840s Radicals and Chartists accused the Whig government, and then the Tory ministry of 1841–6, of excessive taxation, a dictatorial centralism, military repression, an oppressive and cruel poor-law policy, a desire to impose Established Church teaching in the factory districts, and, above all, class government in favour of the aristocracy. In a climate of class tension, hostility to government expenditure could easily intensify into a campaign against parasites who lived off the state without contributing to its wealth, and who used its police powers to attempt to bolster their privileged position. Carlyle's *Past and present* (1843), the most influential reform polemic of the early 1840s, inveighed against aristocratic dilettantes and fops who were incapable of the work ethic required in a successful commercial society. A strong sense of the unpredictability of the market and the unfriendliness of the aristocratic state underpinned the Radical anxiety to bolster the economic independence and self-reliance of working-men: Samuel Smiles's *Self-help*, often seen as the greatest celebration of mid-Victorian complacency, in fact originated in lectures to working men in the mid-1840s aiming

[31] P. Buckner, *The transition to responsible government: British policy in British North America, 1815–1850* (Westport, CT, 1985), pp. 335–8.

[32] Longford, *Victoria*, pp. 111–13; D. Thompson, *Queen Victoria: gender and power* (London, 2001 edn), pp. 31–8. For one extraordinary Conservative attack on the Queen, by the MP Bradshaw, see *The Annual Register 1839* (London, 1840), pp. 311–12.

at this goal.[33] Moreover social anxiety inspired religious Radicals, particularly evangelical Nonconformists, to urge the purification of politics, the demolition of sham assumptions and the replacement of corrupt and feeble leaders in state and Church by truly virtuous patriots. This was work for a new Cromwell, given heroic treatment by Carlyle's book of 1845.

In the mid-1840s, therefore, the Whigs cut a poor figure in Radical eyes, firstly because of their inability to agree on a repeal of the Corn Laws in 1845, and secondly, as chapter 3 demonstrates, owing to their support for 'oppressive' Church establishments and education systems. The return of economic depression in 1847–8 ensured a revival of extra-Parliamentary unrest and of Radical assertiveness in the Commons. This was all the more potent because Russell's Whig government lacked a majority. By now there was nearly as much apocalyptic Radical anger at the political establishment, and pressure for a reformation of manners and morals, as in 1829–30. The Whig elite's claim to represent the national interest was being seriously questioned.

This struggle culminated in 1848–9 in a concerted drive to purge the polity of its impurities, especially its 'aristocratic' and authoritarian elements. Radicals campaigned against high taxation and expenditure and for Parliamentary reform as a way of increasing taxpayers' power to check the executive. In April 1848 the Radical MPs declared themselves a separate party in order to take forward their agenda. Joseph Hume brought in his 'Little Charter' – of household suffrage, the ballot, triennial Parliaments and fairer representation of large towns – in June. Meanwhile Nonconformists demanded voluntarism and disestablishment. Many Liberal and Peelite MPs, realising the importance of strengthening public confidence in the state by dissociating it from economic vested interests, sought more tariff and tax cuts with the intention of denying that any class or group was able to manipulate policy to its own benefit. Some of these were also motivated by an evangelical impulse to remove obstacles to the natural functioning of the economic and social mechanism.[34] Between 1848 and 1851, several cathartic battles were fought over key policy issues, including economic Protection, high-profile social reform, and the colonial, Irish and fiscal questions discussed in chapter 4. In each case the argument was that sectional and autocratic influences in the British polity must be

---

[33] R. J. Morris, 'Samuel Smiles and the genesis of self-help: the retreat to a petit bourgeois Utopia', *Historical Journal*, 24 (1981), 89–108.

[34] B. Hilton, *The age of atonement: the influence of evangelicalism on social and economic thought 1785–1865* (Oxford, 1988), ch. 6.

marginalised in order to preserve English liberties and purify political values. These can be seen as the last of a series of struggles, punctuating the 'age of atonement', to purge the state of misgovernment, corruption and complacency. Before 1850 few people were cheerful about the long-term stability and benignity of the political and economic climates.[35]

But by 1851 there was a significant shift of tone. The result of the policy battles was a definitive rejection of protectionism, patronage networks and other glaring evidence of a vested-interest state. This had an important stabilising effect. The various fiscal reforms of the 1846–53 period, particularly the repeal of the Corn Laws in 1846 and the repeal of the Navigation Laws in 1849, made it much more difficult for Radicals to argue that the state was controlled by particular classes or economic groups. By disclaiming so many responsibilities, the post-1850 state appeared more and more disinterested as between the classes. As chapter 4 argues, self-government became seen as the natural outcome in the English settler colonies, while there was a revulsion against 'continental' policies – on concurrent endowment and land – and state activism in Ireland. State activity became unfashionable altogether: high-profile interventionist social legislation became very difficult to pass, and plans for a nationwide education system were blocked.[36] On becoming Prime Minister in 1846, Russell had set out a public manifesto favouring 'great social improvements' in education, sanitation, criminal justice and Ireland, part of the agenda of moral reform discussed in chapter 2.[37] The Whig social-reform activist Morpeth, similarly, told his constituents of ministers' aim to make 'government the object of love, and law the helpmate of virtue'.[38] But in these years social reform was always vulnerable to an alliance of defenders of local rights and Radicals who portrayed statism as oppressive elite jobbery. Morpeth's Health of Towns Bill, introduced in 1847, was destroyed by such pressure, and in 1848 a milder version, excluding London, encountered similar criticism. David Urquhart opposed it as 'un-English and unconstitutional' because it destroyed 'local self-government' and increased taxation and government patronage. The

---

[35] In emphasising this apocalyptic sentiment, feeding off dislike of continental political developments, my reading is rather different to that of Leslie Mitchell, whose view of British reactions to the 1848 revolutions is that complacent self-satisfaction always predominated. This view seems to me to be too one-dimensional. See L. Mitchell, 'Britain's reaction to the revolutions', in R. J. W. Evans and H. Pogge von Strandmann (eds.), *The revolutions in Europe 1848–1849: from reform to reaction* (Oxford, 2000), pp. 83–98.

[36] P. Mandler, *Aristocratic government in the age of reform: Whigs and Liberals, 1830–1852* (Oxford, 1990), ch. 7; Parry, 'Past and future', pp. 158–60.

[37] S. Walpole, *The life of Lord John Russell* (2 vols., London, 1889), vol. 1, p. 429.

[38] Mandler, *Aristocratic government*, p. 239.

fate of 'the late Government of France . . . should be a warning to the would-be centralisers in this country. Was it not corruption which had produced the revolution in France?'[39] The 1848 Public Health Bill conceded enough to the localist lobby to pass, but it was only after the 1867 Reform Act that central government felt confident enough to be able to force localities to appoint a Medical Officer of Health.

The years 1846–50 were a major turning-point in nineteenth-century politics. Whatever commentators had thought about the earlier state of affairs, by 1851 the vast majority agreed that English libertarian values had won out. To some extent a real struggle against important foes, principally the tariff system, had taken place. But several decades of tax and tariff revisions and attacks on political and ecclesiastical patronage had in fact previously removed nearly all of the reality of 'Old Corruption'. Not much of the substance of British government needed to change in order to achieve this new image. The political crisis of these years should be seen as a theatrical attack on alien principles, presented in exaggerated form in order to demonstrate the virtue of those politicians who attacked them most vigorously. As Urquhart's remark suggested, the drama was heightened particularly by the events that were simultaneously taking place on the Continent. In 1848–9 Europe was a battleground between repression and revolution, autocracy and socialism. When the dust cleared, Russian power seemed to cast a shadow across the East, while a new Napoleon had emerged in France. The effect was to highlight the various political errors of the Continent. The crusade to purify British politics was both an assertion of the values urgently needed to protect national vigour and, increasingly, a celebration of national distinctiveness and success, which contributed to the greatly improved optimism of the 1850s once economic stability had returned.

## 1848, ENGLISHNESS AND LIBERAL POLITICS

From a British perspective the 1848 revolutions had started encouragingly, instilling the hope that they would result in the export of Britain's own constitutional liberalism. The peoples of central Europe seemed to be stirring from their sloth, shaking off government repression and embracing activity, improvement and 'the spirit of the age'.[40] On 25 March *The Times*

---

[39] *Hansard*, 98:713, 5 May 1848.
[40] R. Monckton Milnes, *The events of 1848, especially in their relation to Great Britain: a letter to the marquis of Lansdowne* (London, 1849), p. 67; Palmerston on the spirit of the age, 10 Mar. 1848,

marvelled that 'the Emperor of Austria and the Pope are simultaneously engaged in copying the British M. P. for the use of their realms'.[41] The fall of Louis Philippe in February was widely explained in terms of his rejection of liberalism and the English entente and his recourse to reactionary sentiments and allies. *The Times* noted with great satisfaction that as he fled, disguised, 'fatigued and careworn' to exile in England, he seemed finally to understand the superiority of the British way: '"Thank God, I am on British ground."'[42] But the revolutions then turned nasty, veering towards un-English extremes of socialism and then autocratic repression. English commentators fastened on one particular aspect of the Paris Revolution: the share in power given to Louis Blanc and his socialists, and the violent consequences which seemed to follow from Blanc's establishment of National Workshops on the principles of fraternity and cooperative association. The closure of the Workshops led to a socialist rebellion and a bitter four-day battle between them and the troops commanded by Cavaignac, who restored order at a high price in lives. This was a turning-point, and not just in France. The socialist experiment and its bloody conclusion horrified British middle-class opinion, because of both the seductive unsoundness of the economic values propagated and the fact that French excesses had provided another example of the terrors to which revolutions led. It raised the question of the spread of socialism and republicanism to Britain, especially in light of Smith O'Brien's attempted rebellion in Ireland. In May 1848 the government briefly restored the legislation of the 1790s allowing government to expel any alien threatening the peace, in order to prevent the spread of 'republican principles' and 'the interference of foreigners in the affairs of this country' – the only time between 1824 and 1905 that the free passage of immigrants was restricted by law.[43] The French and Irish parallels weakened middle-class sympathy for the British Chartists, who were increasingly perceived as un-English in their willingness to consider physical force. The tricolour and the cap of liberty were frequently seen at Chartist meetings.[44] By June, perceptions of physical-force activity at

---

quoted in E. de Groot, 'Contemporary political opinion and the revolutions of 1848', *History*, 38 (1953), 143.

[41] *The Times*, 25 Mar. 1848, p. 4.    [42] *The Times*, 4 Mar. 1848, p. 8.

[43] George Grey, *Hansard*, 98:560, 1 May 1848; B. Porter, *The refugee question in mid-Victorian politics* (Cambridge, 1979), p. 86.

[44] J. Belchem, 'Britishness, the United Kingdom and the revolutions of 1848', *Labour History Review*, 64 (1999), 143–58; J. Belchem, '1848: Feargus O'Connor and the collapse of the mass platform', in J. Epstein and D. Thompson (eds.), *The Chartist experience: studies in working-class Radicalism and culture, 1830–60* (London, 1982), pp. 278–9; E. Kamenka and F. B. Smith (eds.), *Intellectuals and revolution: socialism and the experience of 1848* (London, 1979), p. 105. The *Nonconformist* was

home and abroad were stimulating a middle-class reaction against Reform. It was assisted by increasing press emphasis on the damage that revolution abroad was doing to British trade with Europe.[45]

The revolutions nearly all ended in disappointment for continental liberals, culminating in Louis Napoleon's *coup d'état* of 1851. In Britain his regime, illiberal, democratic and materialist, became widely seen as the antithesis of a well-run state. But already by the end of 1848 many praised Britain's political achievement by contrasting it with the instability and extremism in Europe.[46] *Punch* produced two cartoons, 'John Bull showing the foreign powers how to make a constitutional plum pudding' and 'There is no place like home', which graphically illustrate this sentiment.[47] The first volumes of Macaulay's *History of England*, published in that year, extolled the virtues of the mixed constitution established in 1688, which, as the Whig cabinet minister Charles Wood remarked, provided a great lesson for 'all lovers of truth, all lovers of liberty, all lovers of order and of civilised freedom' in other European countries.[48]

What 1848–51 really seemed to reveal was that other nations lacked the qualities of the British character. It appeared that whenever the French or Austrians secured free institutions they used the power to select 'busybodies' to 'fetter [their] liberty'.[49] The French did not understand what 'real liberty means'; they lacked the character to build a stable liberal regime.[50] They lacked the self-discipline and experience to govern themselves, and therefore they were prey to the dangers of socialism and Caesarism. The years 1848 and 1851, following on from 1789 and 1799, created a consensus among English commentators that a major French problem was overcentralisation. Their passion for wild conceptions was strengthened by their lack of experience and education in self-government. Nearly all

---

confident that Chartists, with their 'strain of ranting and Irish braggadocio', did not represent the 'manly sentiments of English operatives': 12 Apr. 1848, p. 254.

[45] Greville, 5 July 1848, in C. C. F. Greville, *A journal of the reigns of King George IV, King William IV and Queen Victoria*, ed. H. Reeve (8 vols., London, 1896 edn), vol. VI, p. 209. The *Nonconformist* was critical of this general and selfish tendency to put questions of credit and commerce ahead of liberty: 'there are interests higher than those of the shop': 6 Sept. 1848, p. 675.

[46] See e.g. S. Laing, *Observations on the social and political state of the European people in 1848 and 1849* (1850); *Manchester Guardian*, 1851, quoted in A. Briggs, *Victorian people: a reassessment of persons and themes, 1851–67* (Harmondsworth, 1965 edn), pp. 57–8; Palmerston, *Hansard*, 112:443, 25 June 1850; Albemarle, *Hansard*, 119:5–6, 3 Feb. 1852; Reeve, 'Earl Grey on Parliamentary government', 272. There is a detailed and stimulating discussion of the cultural impact of 1848 on Britain in F. Bensimon, *Les Britanniques face à la révolution française de 1848* (Paris, 2000).

[47] *Punch*, 23 Dec. 1848, p. 267, and 20 Jan. 1849, pp. 27–30.

[48] G. O. Trevelyan, *The life and letters of Lord Macaulay* (1876; Oxford, 1978 edn), vol. II, p. 171.

[49] W. R. Greg, 'Difficulties of republican France', *Edinburgh Review*, 92 (1850), 523–4.

[50] 'The French revolution of 1848 – its causes and consequences', *Fraser's Magazine*, 37 (1848), 372.

classes in France lacked a 'due regard for the rights of others'. They could be attracted by material bribes, sensation or talk of military glory and failed to see through utopian dogma. So politicians either advocated abstract and unworkable general principles or appealed to the average avaricious Frenchman's lust for national grandeur and the seizure of property. French politics were thus dominated by passion rather than reason and by the clash of irreconcilable economic principles.[51]

It was commonly argued, by contrast, that the English constitution had worked because of Englishmen's inherited respect for law, authority and self-discipline. Contrasts between English vigour, energy and independence, and continental bureaucracy, lassitude and dependence, became commonplace. From the time of the Great Exhibition onwards it was almost universally agreed that energy, self-reliance, determination and practical common sense had marked the English out for success. The English had made the most global progress because they had learned how to govern themselves. Individual conscience, civic virtue, hard work, enterprise and respect for law had made England a great commercial power and saved it from socialism, plunder and anarchy.

These complacent assumptions were possible because of growing economic prosperity stemming from the global dominance of Britain's manufacturing products. Free trade and low taxation were generally assumed to be crucial factors in Britain's economic and political success. The language of economic liberty became and remained an incontestable article of faith in the Liberal party – a process that was strengthened by the eventual adherence of most leading Peelites to the party. All non-Protectionist MPs could agree on the correctness of free-trade principles. The repeal of the Navigation Acts in 1849 was a valuable rallying-cry for all Liberals and Peelites in Parliament, as was the brief revival of the Protectionist threat in 1849 and 1850 owing to the fall in wheat prices.[52] Protectionism implied a return to working-class discontent and agitation which would end in radicalising the political order. In contrast, free trade seemed an equitable, natural and peaceful regulator of social relationships which demonstrated the government's determination to avoid bias to particular social classes and vested interests. The economic revival after 1849

[51] Sarah Austin, 1848, in J. Ross, *Three generations of Englishwomen: memoirs and correspondence of Mrs John Taylor, Mrs Sarah Austin, and Lady Duff Gordon* (2 vols., London, 1888), vol. I, p. 218; Greg, 'Difficulties of republican France', 504–33, and Greg in *Economist*, 1 Apr. 1848, cited in Varouxakis, *Victorian political thought*, pp. 68–70; Laing, *Observations*, ch. 7; Sir James Stephen, *Lectures on the history of France* (2 vols., London, 1851), Lect. 24: N. St John Stevas (ed.), *The collected works of Walter Bagehot: Volume VIII* (London, 1974), p. 183.

[52] Lord Broughton, *Recollections of a long life* (6 vols., London, 1911), vol. VI, p. 246.

and particularly the benign climate of the 1850s encouraged much high-flown language about the benefits of 'committ[ing] ourselves to the general laws of Providence', and the progressive improvement that derived from that.[53]

On the day the Great Exhibition opened in 1851 Macaulay claimed: 'There is just as much chance of a revolution in England as of the falling of the moon.'[54] To the British press, the Exhibition seemed to demonstrate the reality of class harmony and of Britain's worldwide trading power. There was much comment about the lack of social unrest among the six million who came during the five and a half months that 'the people's palace' was open, and what this said about the national polity and character.[55] Continental courts were said to be particularly struck by the success of the opening ceremony, in which the Queen walked unprotected in front of thousands. The Turin Embassy commented that this was 'an inspiration to liberalism'.[56] She certainly intended her visits to strengthen the popularity of the monarchy by identifying it with the people. Russell told her: 'No republic of the Old or New World has done anything so splendid or so useful.'[57] The Exhibition's second perceived effect was to project the greatness of Britain's economic power. It suggested that Britain was leading the world, spreading ideals of commercial intercourse and technological innovation, increasing wealth and international harmony, in a Providential enterprise: after the opening ceremony, Victoria wrote that God's 'blessing seemed to pervade the whole undertaking'.[58]

Ironically, it had not been planned in a spirit of complacency – indeed it was a result of the anxiety of the late 1840s about Britain's economic health. The organisers hoped that it would educate provincial British manufacturers out of their insularity and worship of 'cheapness' evident in the mass manufacture of utilitarian and often ugly produce. They felt that in an era of over-competition, Britain would prosper only if it learned to compete with the better standards of industrial design achieved on the Continent, especially in France. In fact the very idea of holding a large-scale exhibition to exchange manufacturing ideas, treated with suspicion by many provincial employers when mooted in 1849–50, was borrowed from abroad. However, the atmosphere of national superiority generated by the Exhibition meant that their hopes were not realised. Indeed the arrival of so many foreign

---

[53] Parry, *Rise and fall*, p. 168.		[54] 1 May 1851, Trevelyan, *Macaulay*, vol. II, p. 226.
[55] J. Auerbach, *The Great Exhibition of 1851: a nation on display* (New Haven, 1999), pp. 158, 166–7.
[56] C. R. Fay, *Palace of industry, 1851: a study of the Great Exhibition and its fruits* (Cambridge, 1951), p. 25.
[57] Ibid., p. 70.		[58] Ibid., p. 47. For Russell's comments, see Auerbach, *Great Exhibition*, p. 162.

visitors in 1851 encouraged derogatory press and popular stereotyping. Much fun was had with the idea that their personal hygiene was suspect.[59] G. A. Sala's satire portrayed the top of the Crystal Palace transept as an ideal place for 'the administration of the justice of all nations', with Chinamen, Indians and black men hanging from it and an eastern European whipping a nubile girl.[60]

Politics for much of the 1850s continued to be dominated by these libertarian themes and continental comparisons. It remained easy to make political capital by using comparisons with continental autocracy to warn against interventionist proposals at home. The Crimean War of 1854, a war against Russia and the whole spirit of autocracy, created a particularly suitable climate for this. The powers of the General Board of Health were substantially weakened, and Toulmin Smith's Anti-Centralization Union won greater independence for local vestries to take action against insanitary conditions themselves.[61] The wartime mood strengthened all who sought to stand firm against the corrupting consequences of alien statist values. When Russell introduced resolutions calling for a 'general and compulsory' system of national education in 1856, claiming that the education system in England was backward compared with 'the other enlightened nations of the world', he was decisively rebuffed on account of his lack of patriotism. Dissenters, Peelites and Tories all attacked him for betraying the values that had made England great. Edward Baines claimed that he was advocating the despotism of Berlin and Vienna. Gladstone alleged that he wished to endanger Britain's 'national character' by substituting mere 'technical instruction' and an 'alien and foreign' dependence on the state for 'real education' based on the 'sacred interests' of true religion. Disraeli was sure that Russell had 'mistaken . . . the character of his countrymen'.[62] Anything touched by Russell was liable to the same complaint of 'un-Englishness': even the Italian refugee Panizzi's appointment that year as chief librarian of the British Museum, which he supported, was abused as an 'affront to British genius and character' by several newspapers and MPs.[63] Hostility to the corrupting effects of foreign moral habits played a part in MPs' attempt to curb Sunday trading (the 'French Sunday') in 1855, and the successful

[59] E.g. the *Punch* cartoons at 26 Apr., 10 May 1851, pp. 174, 185.

[60] G. A. Sala, *The great glass house opened: the Exhibition wot is!!* (1851).

[61] O. Anderson, *A liberal state at war: English politics and economics during the Crimean War* (London, 1967), pp. 134–9.

[62] Parry, 'Past and future', pp. 159–60. Quotations are at *Hansard*, 140:1955, 6 Mar. 1856; 141:892–3, 952–8, 912, 11 Apr. 1856; 144:797, 18 Feb. 1857. For un-Englishness, see N. Mitford (ed.), *The Stanleys of Alderley: their letters between the years 1851–1865* (London, 1939), p. 136.

[63] E. Miller, *Prince of librarians: the life and times of Antonio Panizzi of the British Museum* (London, 1967), pp. 215–20; *Hansard*, 141:1344, 21 Apr. 1856.

Parliamentary and press campaign for legislation to check obscene publications in 1857.[64] There was strong media outrage at the idea that Britain should bow to foreign regimes' pressure to restrict the rights of radicals who had sought asylum, culminating in the Orsini affair of 1858. This was not because of particular sympathy for the refugees, but from a horror that continental autocracies might tamper with British constitutional freedoms.[65]

Though many of these Parliamentary debates involved serious issues, a prolonged political game was also being played, in which politicians sought to outbid each other in patriotic sentiment and to attack their rivals for lacking it. The fundamental fact about British politics after 1846 was the breakdown of the old two-party system after the repeal of the Corn Laws. The Protectionist Conservatives formed a large bloc in opposition, but it was difficult for other groups to consider working with them. Therefore the first need was to secure a majority by rallying non-Conservatives behind an attractive banner, and the second was to win the battle for advantage within that non-Conservative coalition. Palmerston and several leading Peelites and free-trade Liberals adopted libertarian language in order to win Radical votes and to smear not only Protectionist Conservatives but also Russell and the Whig elite with the charge that they were authoritarian and sectional rather than representative spokesmen for a liberal nation. Tories and Whigs were exposed to the charge that their interest in an interventionist social policy was merely a divisive attempt to pervert taxpayer resources towards men of their own class or interests. Between 1848 and 1852 this charge was a very successful one, not only on the domestic issues mentioned above but also on the colonial and Irish ones discussed in chapter 4. Russell countered, not entirely successfully, by attempting to rally public opinion against a perceived continental threat to British liberty, in the shape of the 'Papal Aggression' of 1850. He then underwent a series of tussles with Palmerston to see who could most vigorously defend British constitutional values at home and promote them overseas. As chapter 4 shows, their enthusiasm to match each other in asserting that Britain had a global mission to defend constitutional liberalism against Russia helped to lead a divided cabinet down the slope to war in the Crimea in 1853–4. In the second half of the 1850s the struggle between Palmerston and Russell for Liberal leadership continued; the issue was whether Palmerston's bluff foreign policy and

---

[64] B. Harrison, 'The Sunday trading riots of 1855', *Historical Journal*, 8 (1965), 219–45; M. J. D. Roberts, 'Morals, art, and the law: the passing of the Obscene Publications Act, 1857', *Victorian Studies*, 28 (1985), 609–29. When Marochetti's monument to the Crimean heroes was unveiled in May 1856 at Sydenham, there was much criticism of the use of a foreign sculptor.

[65] Porter, *Refugee question*, pp. 117–19.

chauvinistic rhetoric was more attractive than Russell's commitment to constitutional reform and state activism.

These high political wrangles are a reminder that, though the shift in political tone in 1848–51 was dramatic, it was much less radical than it appeared at first sight, for two reasons. Firstly, these disputes – some serious, some mere posturing – took place within a fairly secure elite political culture: this was a game with well-understood rules, played by propertied politicians who were able to keep serious external threats to their core values at bay. It was, in fact, a classic high political crisis, though it has never been systematically analysed as such. For example, a small number of leading Peelites were among the political winners of this game because they cast themselves as modern, efficient politicians worthy of an important place in a Liberal coalition by virtue of offering a more inclusive political agenda than the old Whigs. But they were in most respects very conservative. After Peel's death in 1850 they were headed by an earl (Aberdeen) who had lifelong friendships with the two most notorious conservatives in Europe (Tsar Nicholas and Metternich). They were suspicious of Parliamentary reform and two of them, Gladstone and Sidney Herbert, were not yet even convinced that their future lay with the Liberal rather than with a revived Conservative party. Their elder statesman, Sir James Graham, who had been one of the most authoritarian Conservative Home Secretaries of the century, was still an alarmist about political and social disorder and was convinced that only strict economy in government would avert it.

Secondly, though the rhetoric used in the crisis encouraged the notion of major divisions between Whigs and Radicals, which has to some extent been perpetuated by historians ever since, differences between them were in fact confined within narrow parameters. That was why it is right to talk of a common Liberalism throughout this period, for all the practical problems faced by the party system. Few Whigs – certainly not Russell – were permanently marginalised by the shift in tone, because very little of the political culture of the 1850s was unacceptable to their principles. 'Improving' state activity in social and educational policy continued, only much more discreetly. Substantial increases in both health and education expenditure were achieved by stealthy executive action.[66]

One reason for the decline in Whig–Radical tension was the increasing marginalisation of the movement for further Parliamentary reform. In

---

[66] Parry, *Rise and fall*, pp. 202–7; R. Lambert, *Sir John Simon, 1816–1904, and English social administration* (London, 1963), pp. 325–8, 413–14, 450–2.

the face of increased confidence that Britain had an accountable, inclusive and decentralised polity, Radicals' ability to press for it quickly waned. In January 1853 Cobden declared that he was 'sick of the everlasting attempt out of doors to give the semblance of an agitation which does not exist'.[67] There was still considerable grass-roots desire for franchise extension, but the sense of injustice at current arrangements was too enfeebled to sustain an organised agitation. As Miles Taylor has argued, there was little Radical interest in continental socialism.[68] Those pundits who argued in 1848–9 that it was the robustness of national character and morals that had ensured British stability, not abstract constitutional arrangements, usually made these arguments in order to oppose those movements, like Chartism, which prioritised the principle of Parliamentary reform.[69] These arguments became very fashionable, leading to a paradox. The logic of Britain's escape from revolution suggested that British working men in steady employment who supported their households in respectability were upright citizens possessing the manly self-governing qualities that would justify receipt of the franchise. This created something of a consensus in Liberal circles that good character rather than restrictive property qualifications should now be the main determinant of the right to vote. But at the same time, complacency about the stability of the political order justified delaying Reform for the foreseeable future and indeed condemning those like Russell who sought to bring forward the issue prematurely, risking exciting the public mind unnecessarily.[70] The trajectory of the continental revolutions seemed to show the dangers of over-hasty change, especially on abstract principles, and led instead to a veneration of the 'common sense' practicality of the British compromise. Moreover, Napoleon III's eventual emergence as French Emperor damaged the cause of Reform because the success of his histrionic appeal could be blamed on the system of universal suffrage. Far better, moderate Liberals and Peelites said, to continue with tax cuts and administrative reform in order to remove sources of taxpayer grievance.[71]

---

[67] N. C. Edsall, *Richard Cobden: independent Radical* (Cambridge, MA, 1986), p. 213.

[68] M. Taylor, *British Radicalism*, pp. 113–14.

[69] See Greg, 'Difficulties of republican France', 507–10; [C. Kingsley, J. M. Ludlow *et al.*,] *Politics for the people* (1848; New York, 1971 edn), pp. 214, 253–4; W. Bagehot, 1852, in Varouxakis, *Victorian political thought*, pp. 116–17.

[70] R. E. Quinault, '1848 and Parliamentary reform', *Historical Journal*, 31 (1988), 831–51; George Grey, 1852, quoted in N. McCord, 'Some difficulties of Parliamentary reform', *Historical Journal*, 10 (1967), 382; C. S. Parker, *Life and letters of Sir James Graham* (2 vols., London, 1907), vol. II, pp. 134–7, 156–9, 204–5.

[71] For Gladstone in 1854 on administrative reform as an alternative to Parliamentary reform, see J. Morley, *The life of William Ewart Gladstone* (3 vols., London, 1903), vol. I, p. 511.

Therefore, though many Liberal MPs continued to support Reform in principle, the weakness of the agitation for it ensured that no Reform Bill was successful until 1867. There was a brief but powerful explosion of discontent at the management of the Crimean War during the stalemate of 1855.[72] However, that attack on elite institutional misgovernment was weakened by progress in the war, and by the sense – articulated by Samuel Morley, for example – that British political problems could no longer just be blamed on the governing classes and that the real need was for 'the people themselves' to take a more responsible attitude towards public affairs.[73]

A second element of potential tension within the Liberal coalition could also be defused fairly easily, since after 1850 there was less strident anti-aristocratic sentiment among Radicals. The tax and tariff reforms of the late 1840s and 1850s appeared to show that the governing classes were, on the whole, accountable to the taxpayer. It was increasingly difficult to claim that urban and commercial interests were politically marginal. The civilising function of the town community was a major emphasis of Liberal argument, deriving from classical republicanism and the Enlightenment project. Influential early Victorian writers like the Congregationalist historian Robert Vaughan maintained that commercial and social interchange in an urban environment stimulated beneficial social qualities – reason, tolerance, industry, sociability, morality, culture. Urban life facilitated progress by encouraging the exchange of knowledge and commercial competition. Through 'good laws, liberal arts, and letters' and 'spontaneous efforts in the cause of public morals', cities built up 'enlightened patriotism' based on 'Christian principles'.[74] In some Radical hands, such as Cobden's, these arguments about commercial society were used to try to challenge aristocratic claims to political dominance. They implied that towns were no more artificial than the land; they suggested that political wisdom derived from economic progress rather than requiring the teaching of an aristocracy. But celebration of urban values was perfectly compatible with propertied dominance at Westminster. Many advocates of a middle-class or urban politics confined themselves to the local sphere, not least with a view

---

[72] O. Anderson, 'The Janus face of mid-19th century English Radicalism: the Administrative Reform Association of 1855', *Victorian Studies*, 8 (1965), 231–42.

[73] At Drury Lane: *The Times*, 14 June 1855, p. 12. For the disputes about whether the ministry or the nation was more to blame for misgovernment, see O. Anderson, 'The reactions of Church and Dissent towards the Crimean War', *Journal of Ecclesiastical History*, 16 (1965), 217–19. See also the comments on the Indian Mutiny in the Introduction, p. 18.

[74] R. Vaughan, *The age of great cities: or, modern society viewed in relation to intelligence, morals, and religion* (London, 1843), pp. 1–8.

to strengthening order, loyalty and the development of citizenship in the more challenging circumstances of the nineteenth-century industrial town, through official and voluntary civic association.[75] Meanwhile, a number of Whig leaders, including Russell and Palmerston, had no doubts about the virtue of commercial society, not least on account of their Scottish university education. From 1841 most leading Whigs sat – from choice or necessity – for urban seats. Morpeth and Wood spoke for the manufacturers of the West Riding; Russell, MP for the City of London, was a poor younger son whose idea of an estate was Pembroke Lodge in Richmond Park, granted to him by the Queen in 1847 and now a municipal café. In the year that Morpeth succeeded to the broad acres of Castle Howard he still travelled to Windsor for a meeting with the Queen on top of an omnibus.[76] Whig confidence in the virtue and dynamism of the middle-class electorate had already been seen in the Municipal Corporation Act of 1835, which sought to reinvigorate and purify urban leadership and tighten civic bonds and fiscal accountability. There was strong agreement that participation in local institutional politics had played a crucial part in training the English – the foremost commercial society in the world – in self-government. Praise for the civilising qualities of the town allowed a stark contrast to be drawn with the repressive, warlike feudal landed culture which was still so powerful in many parts of Europe.[77]

Another element in 1850s culture also allowed a reconciliation between different classes of Liberal politician: the emphasis on 'manliness' as an exemplary ideal in a public figure.[78] It was widely agreed that the model Englishman valued self-reliance, not 'petticoat government' or 'grandmotherly government'. Manliness usually suggested qualities of earnestness, integrity, self-discipline, rationality and public spirit, though there was a vigorous debate about which were its most important elements, as chapter 2 suggests. However, one issue on which most advocates of manliness were agreed was that it was a set of qualities that transcended class. It became a cliché that one did not need to be an aristocrat to be a gentleman:

[75] R. J. Morris (ed.), *Class, power and social structure in British nineteenth-century towns* (Leicester, 1986); R. J. Morris and R. H. Trainor (eds.), *Urban governance: Britain and beyond since 1750* (Aldershot, 2000); J. Seed, 'Unitarianism, political economy and the antinomies of liberal culture in Manchester, 1830–50', *Social History*, 7 (1982), 1–25.

[76] Mrs Hardcastle, *Life of John, Lord Campbell* (2 vols., London, 1881), vol. II, p. 250.

[77] Vaughan, *Age of great cities*, pp. 88–96.

[78] N. Vance, *The sinews of the spirit: the ideal of Christian manliness in Victorian literature and religious thought* (Cambridge, 1985); J. Tosh, 'Gentlemanly politeness and manly simplicity in Victorian England', *Transactions of the Royal Historical Society*, 6:12 (2002), 455–72.

Anthony Trollope, Tom Hughes and Samuel Smiles all said so.[79] All classes of Englishmen were potentially virtuous, and by the 1860s the increasing prominence of John Bright and Mill in the Liberal pantheon was designed to show that an inspirational political figure did not need to be a man of property. Some Radical politicians portrayed their manliness in distinctly anti-aristocratic terms. This was true not just of Bright but of Henry Layard who self-consciously contrasted his activist explorer courage with upper-class conventionality and nepotism. This might suggest that the no-nonsense commercial man was now the only true representative of the nation, in contrast to the privileged aristocrat. John Tosh has recently argued that mid-Victorian politics deliberately celebrated manly simplicity as a contrast with earlier aristocratic political culture.[80] Yet this contrast can easily be over-drawn; it is better to recognise the skill with which many propertied politicians adjusted to fit the new image, playing on their representativeness and their rank at the same time. None succeeded more than Palmerston, the politician who defined the 1850s; he certainly projected an image more vigorous and populist than the older Whigs, but it is difficult to believe that most people did not still see him as an aristocrat. Criticism of aristocratic privilege or feebleness remained one theme in Radical rhetoric, to which the Liberal party needed to nod if they were to stay a successful and broad coalition. But Liberal aristocrats could easily escape this criticism by projecting an image of disinterested activity and zeal. Russell did so in the late 1850s, as he had in the 1830s.[81]

In fact the emphasis on manliness after 1850 allowed the Liberal aristocracy a new lease of life. Liberal party leaders until the 1890s took care to give prominent political roles to earnest public-spirited peers: Spencer, Ripon, Kimberley (and a duke's son, Hartington). These men were not typical of the aristocracy as a class, but they presented a Liberal ideal of aristocratic leadership: hard-working, plain-spoken, of good character. They reinvigorated the traditional Whig idea of public service by associating it with the more trusted and meritocratic reformed civil service of the second half of the century. They helped to perpetuate the notion that the Liberal party was an alliance of property, intellect, character and conscience which could supply moral leadership. In the 1850s young Liberal aristocrats also tended to be enthusiasts for the militia and the Volunteers, and thus to project an

---

[79] Vance, *Sinews of the spirit*, ch. 1; A. Trollope, *The New Zealander*, ed. N. J. Hall (unpub. 1856; Oxford, 1972 edn), pp. 20–8; S. Smiles, *Self-help: with illustrations of character and conduct* (London, 1859), ch. 13. This is also a central theme of Dickens's *Great expectations* (1861).

[80] Tosh, 'Gentlemanly politeness'.      [81] Parry, 'Past and future'.

image of manly military vigour – an image which was reinforced by the cult of the beard, which came in with the militia in 1852 and suggested qualities of 'courage, daring, energy, firmness, determination'.[82] Very many Liberals, especially those anxious to uphold order and the rights of property, looked to a virtuous propertied class to supply political leadership and claimed that they were the natural leaders of an ethical civic and national community. The future Liberal MP Thomas Hughes, for example, though a Christian Socialist Radical, celebrated the landed rootedness of the gentry as a key element in their patriotism, in the opening chapter of *Tom Brown's school-days* (1857). As a result of the reworked image of the aristocracy, the scope for anti-aristocratic rhetoric lessened by the late 1860s: the Radical Frederic Harrison had no difficulty in arguing, in 1871, that unlike in Prussia, the aristocracy was not a separate caste in Britain but had been 'modernised and transformed to the uses of a democratic society'.[83] Of course it was much easier to argue this because the Liberals were in power almost continuously until 1874, so that Tory grandees posed little political threat.

LIBERTY, THE STATE AND REFORM, 1850–67

The triumph of free trade, together with the appearance of class har-mony under an apparently disinterested government, created great opti-mism about the beneficial impact of 'freedom'. This optimism moved well beyond the trade sphere, into the realm of ideas, owing to a convergence of political, theological and scientific assumptions. In the 1850s the influence of evangelicalism on the political elite waned in the face of liberal theology. Englishmen, it seemed, were becoming fuller, freer men, as God intended that his creatures should do; they were using their divinely bestowed and inspired energies to lead the evolution of the world towards a higher politi-cal and economic state. In some quarters an optimistic Lamarckian view of the evolution of the inanimate and animate worlds even became fashion-able, stressing the gradual, smooth and beneficent transmutation of species rather than a jerky, brutal or apocalyptic development.[84] Confidence in the naturalness of the evolutionary process and in the peaceful stability of English public life encouraged the idea that government and law would

---

[82] David, *The beard! Why do we cut it off?* (London, 1854), pp. 4, 6. See Gladstone's comment of 1886 on the beard and the militia: W. C. Lubenow, *Parliamentary politics and the Home Rule crisis: the British House of Commons in 1886* (Oxford, 1988), p. 330.

[83] F. Harrison, 'The effacement of England', *Fortnightly Review*, 9 (1871), 161–2.

[84] Hilton, *Age of atonement*, chs. 7–8. For George Eliot's initial misreading of Darwin through Lamar-ckian spectacles, see G. Beer, *Darwin's plots: evolutionary narrative in Darwin, George Eliot and nineteenth-century fiction* (London, 1983), p. 157. I owe this reference to Boyd Hilton.

become progressively less necessary, because public opinion was becoming a more and more beneficent and natural engine of social progress. Journalism, statistical enquiry and public meetings were seen as forces of immense power which would improve the public mind more thoroughly than law ever could, because this was a natural rather than a forced process. By contrast with French despotism, press freedom was a glory of England; the status and vocation of the 'fourth estate' rose markedly in the 1850s, particularly once the repeal of the stamp duties in 1855 broadened its potential market. Society was stronger than government.[85] In 1854 Barbara Leigh Smith claimed that thinkers now generally argued that 'the tendency of progress is gradually to dispense with law'.[86] H. T. Buckle's *History of civilisation* (1857), strongly influenced by anti-statist Radical nostrums, asserted that intellect and knowledge rather than government or priests were the driving forces of progress and that England's greatness was due to the fact that the power of these obstructive forces had been kept to a minimum.

The enormous rhetorical weight placed on the idea that an autocratic and sectional state was the antithesis of English national identity ensured that freedom from potential state oppression continued to be a resonant theme in Liberal politics, capable of flaring up whenever liberties seemed threatened. However, it is important not to exaggerate the intensity and deep-rootedness of those libertarian and *laissez-faire* arguments. They were so dominant in the early 1850s, firstly because of the widespread desperation to purge impurities in the 1840s, and subsequently as a symbol of national success, once the economy recovered and British global power became so visible. Once the drive to rid politics of vested interests had run its course, it was not surprising that, in the 1860s, anxiety about strengthening the authority of law and government revived. Even in the 1850s some influential Liberals had loathed the rhetoric of *laissez-faire* as irresponsible and materialist, as chapter 2 shows. And the idea that the evolution of life-forms did not involve struggle and decay also soon waned – though even in the 1850s, similarly, many already criticised it or merely paid rhetorical lip-service to it.[87]

After all, the real object of celebration in the 1850s was British greatness and British character rather than mere liberty itself. Palmerston's domestic

[85] Parry, *Rise and fall*, p. 169; for Herbert on society and government, see *Hansard*, 154:334, 10 June 1859.

[86] B. Leigh Smith, *A brief summary in plain language of the most important laws concerning women* (1854), cited in H. D. Jump (ed.), *Women's writing of the Victorian period, 1837–1901: an anthology* (Edinburgh, 1998), p. 76.

[87] See e.g. M. Pattison, 'History of civilization in England', *Westminster Review*, 68/12 (1857), 396–9.

and foreign policies were both rooted in chauvinistic self-satisfaction. His political supremacy depended on a celebration and exploitation of national potency at home and abroad, keeping the revival of a party-oriented Liberalism in check. The triumph of anti-statism was caused not by the dominance of a coherent party-political creed but by the absence of one. It was not freedom as such but the desire to maintain an effective national political community and to develop the right virtues in the nation that was at the heart of nineteenth-century Liberalism. The underlying elements of the earlier Radical attack on state power – the hostility to vested interests, and the emphasis on disciplining and building national character – could in other circumstances encourage and justify state action. In the 1860s a more balanced view of the political community and of the responsibility of political leaders emerged, emphasising once again the need for legislation to enhance social inclusiveness, restrain anti-social behaviour, and improve Parliamentary vigour. The Whig tradition of inclusive constitutional reform and state activism was reasserted. Therefore demands for state involvement in education, and particularly for Parliamentary reform, became more prominent.

When, after Palmerston's death in 1865, the Liberals sought once again to function and develop as a party, a rough consensus emerged around the idea of Parliamentary reform. Russell had tried to take it up in 1849, 1851, 1854 and 1860 in order to restore his reputation after the Radical criticism that he had received since 1846, to vindicate the evolutionary Whiggish model of the British constitution against the Chartist alternative, and to retain his backbench following in the internal leadership struggle against Palmerston.[88] When he became Prime Minister again in 1865, he committed himself to Reform, not only for those reasons, but also to make the Liberal party a proper party again, and to galvanise Parliament, inactive in the early 1860s, to a general policy of legislative activity on educational, Irish and social issues, as in the 1830s. Many backbench MPs, especially those sitting for sizeable borough seats, had also been backing Reform consistently from at least 1857, pressured by lobbying from constituency artisans.[89] They argued that the character qualities of respectable working men – common sense, self-discipline, restraint and concern for others – were those of true Englishmen and entitled them to membership of the political community. However, deciding which working men qualified as respectable became a moot and divisive point in the discussions about the Reform bills of 1866–7.

---

[88] Parry, *Rise and fall*, pp. 175, 211.    [89] Ibid., pp. 209–11.

An important additional argument for Reform came from Liberals concerned with national unity. Liberal arguments of the 1820s about integrating the classes within the political nation were updated to reflect new circumstances. It was said that enfranchisement would integrate the working classes into the political nation and prevent them from thinking as a separate class. It would abolish what R. H. Hutton called 'class patriotism' in favour of a reassertion of Parliament's duty to reconcile social tensions. Academic Liberals hoped that Reform would establish the mythical community of sentiment between brains and numbers that they believed had arisen in Britain over the American Civil War.[90] This anxiety about the 'isolation of classes' was not founded on a sense of immediate social crisis: had this existed, there might well have been more resistance to Reform. It was largely a product of a very general Liberal concern about a lack of social unity, an inadequate appreciation of nationhood, and the growing power of wealth.[91] There was considerable criticism of penny-pinching ratepayers refusing to tackle insanitary local conditions and sheltering behind the rhetoric that such *laissez-faire* protected English character against continental bureaucracy.[92] George Dawson, Birmingham's celebrated Nonconformist pastor, lamented the decay of public virtue – of civic and national patriotism – since his youth and urged commercial leaders to take public office and ratepayers to tolerate higher council spending.[93] As chapter 5 shows, this discussion was bolstered by increasingly unsettling comparisons with continental societies – which, some argued, were more civic-minded and less self-indulgent and materialist. The uplifting patriotism of men like Mazzini, urging nation-building as a route towards greater mutual respect between men, was an influence here, as were the efforts to build a nation in Italy and to rebuild one in the United States. Working men's admiration for Garibaldi, or the Swiss, or for the cause of American unity, in the 1860s seemed to be evidence of their interest in patriotic political movements. Gladstone's famous declaration in favour of franchise reform, in May 1864, was clearly swayed by Garibaldi's visit and the warm reception for it in all

---

[90] A. Kahan, *Liberalism in nineteenth-century Europe: the political culture of limited suffrage* (Basingstoke, 2003), pp. 124–5; C. Harvie, *The lights of Liberalism: university Liberals and the challenge of democracy 1860–86* (London, 1976), pp. 113–14, 149–50.

[91] See J. Bryce, 'The historical aspect of democracy', in *Essays on Reform* (London, 1867), p. 277.

[92] Complaints of the selfishness of the commercial and ratepaying classes were a theme of Tennyson (see e.g. 'The third of February' *1852* (1852) and 'Maud' (1854)), of the Christian Socialists (see e.g. T. Hughes, 'The Volunteer's catechism, with a few words on butts', *Macmillan's Magazine*, 2 (1860), 193, and J. M. Ludlow, 'The reconstitution of England', *Contemporary Review*, 16 (1871), 507) and of J. A. Froude (see 'England's war', *Fraser's Magazine*, 3 (1871), 140, 147).

[93] W. Wilson, *The life of George Dawson* (Birmingham, 1905), pp. 150–1.

classes. He seemed awed by the moral power of humanity in the round.[94] Reform, therefore, could help to develop a stronger sense of social unity, transcending class.

Of course such high-minded notions were not all as idealistic as they seemed. Though they suggested an abstract confidence in the power of the constitution to absorb any potential threat to national solidarity, they also revealed a wariness about separate working-class organisation, particularly in trade unions, and a concern to use the law to regulate them – which became one of the priorities of Parliament after 1867. And many Liberals upheld the wariness without the internationalist high-mindedness. Though most MPs were willing to extend the borough franchise as testimony to the political maturity of the upper working classes, they could not agree on how to adjust the franchise in order to draw the line between men of good and bad character, or on the wisdom of raising working-class expectations by attempting a far-reaching reform. Most did not think that far-reaching alterations were necessary, because they were not fundamentally unhappy with the openness and balance of the existing constitution. In the mid-1860s there was still enormous confidence that the English, more than any other nation, already formed a successfully integrated political community.[95] The ironic consequence was that the Liberal party was incapable of agreeing on a Reform measure in either 1866 or 1867. Even Russell's moderate 1866 Reform Bill was defeated by Liberal dissidents, leading to his resignation and a Conservative government. And the party was clearly divided in its response to the more radical aspects of Disraeli's bill of 1867. Disraeli took great delight in pointing up the distance between the grandiose inclusivity of Liberal rhetoric and the anxiety of so many Liberal MPs in practice to exclude large numbers of working men from the franchise.

The drama of 1867 resulted in a substantial extension of the borough franchise. This was a crucial moment in Liberal and British history. One reason for this was that it satisfied (in principle) the most common traditional Radical demand, for male household suffrage, and thus seemed to answer the main query about the legitimacy of state authority. It recognised the citizenship of the bulk of the urban working classes and joined up two long-standing theories of the constitution. Radical themes of popular sovereignty were reconciled with the view that authority descended from

---

[94] D. Beales, 'Garibaldi in England: the politics of Italian enthusiasm', in J. A. Davis and P. Ginsborg (eds.), *Society and politics in the age of the Risorgimento: essays in honour of Denis Mack Smith* (Cambridge, 1991), pp. 212–14.

[95] See chapter 5 below, and, e.g. for Bagehot on America and France, Varouxakis, *Victorian political thought*, pp. 10–11, 91.

the Crown. On entering the cabinet in December 1868, the Radical John Bright told his constituents that the time had come when an honest man might enter the service of the Crown and yet not feel it necessary to 'dissociate himself from his own people'.[96] The 1867 Act definitively reinforced the assumption, partially but never fully accepted since 1848, that the British state now reflected the will of 'the people' rather than merely the views of threatening, over-assertive vested interests.

### REFORMED POLITICS AND THE STATE, 1867–74 AND BEYOND

But what did this mean for government authority? The Second Reform Act encouraged some Radicals to continue with their well-worn agenda motivated by suspicion of state power. In particular, they urged reductions in government spending, and Church disestablishment. This implied a traditional view that liberty meant freedom from state oppression. J. A. Froude wrote in 1870: 'The age of monopolies is gone. England belongs to herself. We are at last free.' But he was satirically mimicking traditional Radicals, mocking the narrowness of their conceptions of freedom. For Froude, instead, the logic of 1867 was more state interference to protect people's health, sanitation and legal rights.[97] After all, as Bagehot wrote in that year, English suspicion of the executive was illogical and regrettable, for 'freedom means that the nation, the political part of the nation, wields the executive'. Indeed he, like others later, warned against using the rhetoric of local independence to obstruct government power: local self-government should be subordinated to 'the paramount rights and duties of national self-government'.[98]

So for many Liberals the effect of 1867, just like 1832, was to increase their interest in state activity, particularly in extending the rule of law into the lives of the poor, as evidenced by the 1870 Education Act, the 1872 Licensing Act and the reforms to the Poor Law of 1869. As chapter 2 demonstrates, many moralistic Liberals, whether they approved of household suffrage or not, intended to use the increased authority that the government would gain through Reform to introduce legislation to raise the moral standards of the nation.

In the long run, the combination of 1850s liberal patriotic fervour and franchise extension in 1867 changed the emphasis of Liberalism, by

---

[96] 21 Dec. 1868, G. M. Trevelyan, *The life of John Bright* (London, 1914), p. 398.
[97] J. A. Froude, 'On progress', *Fraser's Magazine*, 2 (1870), 682.
[98] W. Bagehot, *The English constitution*, ed. M. Taylor (Oxford, 2001 edn), pp. 187–9; see also G. C. Brodrick, 'What are Liberal principles?', *Political studies* (London, 1879), p. 220.

strengthening respect for the institutions of state that traditional Radical-ism had most vigorously criticised for their cost, maladministration and exclusiveness. For the purpose of this book, the most important of these institutions was the army, once generally regarded as an arm of oppres-sion and a taxpayer-funded aristocratic bolthole. Positive press coverage in the later stages of the Crimean War and during the Indian Mutiny, the war scares of 1859 and 1871, and increasing cooperation between the regular army and the civilian Volunteer forces, all gradually facilitated the view that the army was a national institution deserving of the country's full support.

A first stage had been the war of 1854–6. Despite initial savage press crit-icism of its inept aristocratic leadership, the war eventually benefited the army: Cobden ruefully remarked that 'the aristocracy has gained immensely since the people took to soldiering'.[99] This was partly simply a reflection of satisfaction at a victory won at remarkably little cost to domestic and international business, and partly a recognition that the troops had per-formed well despite inadequate taxpayer support for many years before-hand. But the army also benefited greatly from wartime propaganda. Ast-ley's Amphitheatre and the Surrey Zoological Gardens staged immense and very popular re-enactments of Crimean military engagements, rewritten as simple heroics commanded by dashing officers in dazzling uniforms. Massive press coverage of Florence Nightingale's hospital missions repre-sented the soldiers as fallen, suffering patriots, pathetic objects of a grateful nation's Christian philanthropy. The Queen knitted clothes for the men, visited many hospitals and then presided at a pomp-laden thanksgiving ser-vice for those returning after the war.[100] In 1857 she inaugurated the award of the Victoria Cross, pointedly to be given to ordinary soldiers as well as officers in order to underline the army's national status. The war made the army appear a more respectable and even a Christian institution, though the rapidity of the change can be exaggerated.[101]

The Volunteer forces formed in response to the 1859 invasion scares then played a crucial part in the slow education of the British people into accepting the army as a national institution.[102] They sprang from initiatives within the local community, by gentry, employers, university students or

---

[99] Cobden to Wilson, 23 Sept. 1856, in N. McCord, 'Cobden and Bright in politics, 1846–1857', in R. Robson (ed.), *Ideas and institutions of Victorian Britain: essays in honour of George Kitson Clark* (London, 1967), p. 114.

[100] U. Keller, *The ultimate spectacle: a visual history of the Crimean War* (Amsterdam, 2001), pp. 55–70, 180–92.

[101] Anderson, 'Christian militarism'.

[102] H. Cunningham, *The Volunteer Force: a social and political history 1859–1908* (London, 1975), pp. 86–7, 95–6.

philanthropists. Initially they were popular because they were the very opposite of a threatening standing army maintained by overbearing taxation
imposed by a centralised state. Enthusiasm for local participatory defence
in 1859–60 was an assertion of pride in the constitutionalism and inclusiveness of the English political regime, and its basis in local freedoms. The
very fact that Volunteers were allowed to keep rifles in their homes spoke
volumes. The Liberal MP George Melly hoped that the movement would
train people to habits of self-government and thus to 'a real Liberalism'.[103]
Many Liberals who headed Volunteer corps saw them as a crusade against
materialism and in favour of civic communitarianism, uniting the social
classes in a common patriotism. Young aristocrats who were to play a large
part in Liberal cabinets in future – such as Spencer and the future Lord
Ripon – were active in them. Ripon's Christian Socialist colleague Tom
Hughes hoped that the Volunteers would 'bind the nation together again'
after the money-grubbing of recent years had weakened social ties and
higher aspirations.[104] The corps visibly upheld the cause of law and order,
strengthened respect for the military life and in most cases demonstrated
the continuing importance of hierarchy in English society. Representatives
of the local gentry often put themselves at the head of corps, allowing
middle-class Volunteers to enjoy the privilege of estate hospitality – a toad-
yism to local gentry which depressed the anti-militarist Radicals Cobden
and Bright.[105] Initially, despite their lack of training, the popularity of the
Volunteers encouraged a complacency about national security, which
seemed to underline the regular army's marginal significance in home
defence. But the government – all too aware of the Volunteers' inadequacy –
was anxious that they should train with the regular army.

Then the awesome performance of the Prussian army in the field in 1866
made it impossible to continue to ignore army reform.[106] Two reserves were
set up in 1867, and the 1870 Army Enlistment Act introduced twelve-year
enlistment, six with the colours and six with the reserve. Also, using the
Prussian model as a basis, line regiments were linked to militia battalions
and Volunteers, though somewhat half-heartedly. These changes required
the control of militia and Volunteers by the Crown rather than lord lieu-
tenants of counties, achieved by an Act of 1871, which helped to bring
Volunteers under military discipline. This package of army reform, culminating in the abolition of purchase in 1871 (covered in chapter 6), can be

---

[103] Though he felt that it would also strengthen Conservatism in Parliament: *Stanley*, p. 164.
[104] Hughes, 'Volunteer's catechism', 193.     [105] Parry, *Rise and fall*, pp. 210–11.
[106] Millman, *Franco-Prussian War*, p. 45.

seen as an attempt to reform the military wing of the aristocracy, tackling an idler culture and imposing a more virtuous professionalism. Further army reform by the Liberal government of 1880–5 was designed to strengthen local attachment to the military by building up the territorial regimental system, as well as by establishing further links with the Volunteers.

However, it would be too simplistic to say that the position of the army, or of the other institutions of state, was *immediately* boosted in the few years after 1867 by the increased legitimacy of the polity as a result of franchise extension. In fact almost the opposite happened, in the short term. In 1867–9 the general assumption was that the strengthening of democracy would allow traditional Radicalism to direct future political movement, away from the *ancien régime* vested-interest state and towards its ideal of lower spending and rigorous scrutiny of political institutions. In these years the Radical agenda was dominated by calls for reduced expenditure on the army, the navy and the colonies, by attacks on patronage and vested interests, and by calls for the disestablishment of the Church in England as well as in Ireland. This agenda was potentially seriously at odds with moralistic Liberal pressure for state social and educational reform to improve the conditions and morals of the poor.

The result of this difference of approach was that after the initial enthusiasm for the Irish reforms of the Liberal government had faded, after 1869–70, Liberal opinion became badly divided and confused about the role of the state. This was fundamentally because of the tension and suspicion caused by the unexpectedly large increase of the franchise, both among Radicals not yet ready to surrender their traditional assumptions about government power, and among propertied groups alarmed at the potential for working-class political dominance. Each feared that the power of the state would be used in uncongenial ways. These tensions were exacerbated by the crisis into which the Continent plunged in 1870–1. In 1871, once again, it seemed overrun by misgovernment: a rampantly aggressive authoritarian Prussia; a prostrate France, enfeebled by materialism, imperialism and, in the Commune, democratic socialism; a revived, intolerant papacy, confronting an increasingly powerful secularism. As in 1848–51, this generated a tendency to contrast British political culture with that of the continental powers. Whenever any group wanted to warn against what they saw as an emerging illiberal tendency within British politics, they could point to events abroad for confirmation of the evil consequences of taking that step. Controversial questions, usually at heart involving class or sectional tensions, were *argued* largely in terms of liberty and national identity – in terms of protecting the values that had traditionally preserved British power and virtue. Once again, as in 1848–51, this was to some extent a political game, played by MPs taking their chance to exploit the weakness of a government that had been unusually active and was running out of steam. These issues contributed to the paralysis that overcame Gladstone's first government between 1870 and 1874, the international aspects of which are discussed in chapter 6. It was no coincidence that discipline within the Liberal party broke down in early 1871. The government was simultaneously weakened by the sense that it had failed to protect English interests abroad and by charges that it was behaving unpatriotically at home. In late April 1871, shortly after the Black Sea crisis and at a time of great tension with the Americans, and the crisis over the budget, there were also squabbles over the Army Purchase Bill, the Licensing Bill and the people's rights in Epping Forest. Two Parliamentary diarists both recorded that Gladstone had lost his hold on the Commons by the end of the 1871 session.[107]

One complaint that emerged at this time was the traditional Radical one that an over-powerful state was increasing its scope to oppress popular liberties. This complaint was very visible in the criticism of one key element of the moralistic statist agenda, licensing reform. The 1871 Licensing Bill proposed a special police inspectorate for public houses, to be appointed by the Home Office. The old Chartist J. R. Stephens claimed that this was a French-style government spy system designed to restrict the liberties of Englishmen. It was condemned so strongly on the Liberal benches that it never even reached second-reading stage. The milder version of the Bill which became law in 1872, which put the special police inspectorate under local not central control and again restricted opening hours, inspired protests from working men at which 'Rule Britannia' was sung, placing 'particular emphasis on "Britons never shall be slaves."'[108] Similarly, the government's attempt to sell off most of the remaining Crown land in Epping Forest, which was a very popular spot for working-class East Enders' recreation, created an outcry and was defeated by a Liberal backbench revolt in April 1871.[109] In 1872 the libertarian backbencher Harcourt protested successfully against new regulations brought in by the junior minister A. S. Ayrton restricting the right of public meeting and speaking in the London Royal Parks – claiming that even French working men had

[107] T. A. Jenkins (ed.), 'The Parliamentary diaries of Sir John Trelawny, 1868–73', *Camden Miscellany*, 32 (1994), 435; *Derby diary 1869–78*, p. 88.
[108] B. Harrison, *Drink and the Victorians: the temperance question in England 1815–1872* (London, 1971), pp. 267, 276.
[109] Parry, *Rise and fall*, p. 235.

more rights.[110] Other major Radical complaints about an over-mighty state were made against the Contagious Diseases Acts, which are considered in chapter 2, and the government's sympathy for the Church in its education policies, discussed in chapter 6. On all but the last of these issues, most of the blame fell on the hapless Home Secretary H. A. Bruce, who forfeited the confidence of the Commons because he appeared too dirigiste and illiberal, and he was eventually removed to the Lords in 1873. One Radical claimed that the government aimed at 'the perfectionment of the spy system in England . . . the trammels of which will prove as dangerous and demoralizing' to liberty here as under 'the despotic Governments of the Continent'.[111]

But many other Liberals took the view that the greater danger now came from the assertiveness of a *democratic* state, suppressing the freedom, rights and individuality of minorities in order to elevate the mass, the machine and a uniform mediocrity. Gladstone's attempt to drive an unprecedented amount of executive-sponsored legislation through Parliament began to cause great resentment and to be counterproductive, since the bills were widely said to be ill-considered and a higher proportion than usual had to be withdrawn.[112] The main complaint was that legislation was being framed to catch the will-o'-the-wisp of popular sentiment. One seminal moment was the withdrawal of the match tax after a protest by match girls, requiring a recasting of the 1871 budget and higher income taxes on the propertied classes. The apparent courting of the American democracy over the Alabama affair, together with the republican sentiments expressed by Dilke, added to the sense of a drift towards a democratic tone. Hard-headed rational intellects such as Froude, W. R. Greg, Grey and Fitzjames Stephen lamented the tendency of modern political leaders to prioritise sentimental or polemical issues because these were the ones on which a party cry could be mounted. They felt that there was an urgent need instead for scientific, considered interventionist legislation, framed by experts in a non-partisan manner to deal with unfashionable but important issues like law, army, navy and colonial reform.[113] Intellectual Radical MPs like Walter Morrison attempted to revive the idea of proportional representation, earlier

[110] Gardiner, *Harcourt*, vol. 1, pp. 236–9.
[111] Samuel Blackstone, 'Paternal government: whither are we drifting?', *The Saint Pauls Magazine*, 12 (1873), 725.
[112] Parry, *Rise and fall*, pp. 254, 271; Shannon, *Gladstone 1865–1898*, pp. 95, 97, 102n, 108.
[113] W. R. Greg, 'Cost of party government', *Quarterly Review*, 126 (1869), 394–413; J. F. Stephen, 'Parliamentary government', *Contemporary Review*, 23 (1873–4), 1–19, 165–81; J. A. Froude, 'Political prospects', *Fraser's Magazine*, 5 (1872), 1–16; 3rd Earl Grey, *Hansard*, 211:1429–30, 10 June 1872.

mooted by Thomas Hare and Mill, in an attempt to preserve the influence of independent-minded thinking against what they saw as the deadening weight of democratic pressure.[114] Others, sensing that there was no longer so much scope for the independence of thought and action that they had always associated with being a Liberal or Radical Parliamentarian, criticised the increasing power of the constituency party machine, like Edward Akroyd, or left British politics altogether in despair, like Layard.[115]

So the Liberals lost their way on domestic issues between 1870 and 1874, paralleling a simultaneous confusion about the nature of Britain's global mission, and defence expenditure needs, which are both discussed in chapter 6. The large-scale Conservative revival of 1871–4 was triggered to some extent by working-class lack of interest in the Radical-Liberal agenda, but above all by an active propertied and middle-class rejection of it. Now that popular mistrust of the polity had been weakened by the decisive extension of the franchise, and by the reform of the civil service and the army in 1870–1, it became apparent that there was much less mileage in the old arguments about the wickedness of the income tax, the Church Establishment, the army and the other weapons of a formerly aristocratic state. And it was particularly easy to persuade middle-class citizens that, on the contrary, these weapons should be valued as symbols of law and of national identity, and that it was Radical attacks on them that were unpatriotic. In 1871–4 the Conservatives worked hard to associate themselves with the Church, the monarchy and the British empire, all of which they claimed were under attack from Radicals.[116]

Their success in doing so was a significant moment for Liberalism. The increasing impotence and irrelevance of the traditional Radical critique of the over-powerful vested-interest state helped the process whereby, after 1874, the Liberal party slowly and rather hesitantly came to agree on a more positive role for the state, well before the so-called 'New

---

[114] Parry, *Democracy and religion*, p. 251.
[115] Ibid., pp. 116–21. See E. Akroyd, *On the present attitude of political parties* (London, 1874), and the Layard–Gregory correspondence in Layard Papers, British Library, Add. Mss 38949.
[116] For the Church, see J. P. Parry, 'Nonconformity, clericalism and "Englishness"; the United Kingdom', in C. Clark and W. Kaiser (eds.), *Culture wars: secular–Catholic conflict in nineteenth-century Europe* (Cambridge, 2003), pp. 152–80. For the monarchy, see J. P. Parry, 'Whig monarchy, Whig nation: the representative function of modern monarchy since 1780', in A. Olechnowicz (ed.), *The monarchy and the British nation, 1780–2005* (Cambridge, forthcoming, 2007). For the effect of the Northcote–Trevelyan reforms of the 1850s in strengthening the position of a propertied aristocracy of talent in the civil service, see, for example, G. R. Searle, *Entrepreneurial politics in mid-Victorian Britain* (Oxford, 1993), pp. 123–4. For the political effect of the move to competitive examinations from 1870, see H. J. Hanham, 'Political patronage at the Treasury, 1870–1912', *Historical Journal*, 3 (1960), 75–84. For the colonies, see chapter 6 below.

Liberalism' of the twentieth century. There was nothing in principle controversial about Joseph Chamberlain's claim, in 1885, that a government chosen by the people should have more power than former regimes controlled by a small class.[117] In the 1870s and 1880s nearly all Liberals abandoned freedom of contract principles on Irish and Scottish land issues (adopting historicist principles instead) and in legislating on the game laws and agricultural holdings. Most accepted the public-utility argument for limited state intervention, claiming that the state had always intervened on those principles – in education, factory reform, and the Poor Law.[118] In 1885 the Whig Arthur Elliot and the Radical G. O. Trevelyan both maintained – thinking of the abolition of slavery in 1833 and the debates about Irish Church appropriation in 1834–5 – that it had been standard Liberal doctrine that Parliament could always interfere with private property subject to compensation, and that all public endowments were public property subject to public inquiry.[119] T. H. Green suggested that the Liberals had for fifty years been fighting 'the same old cause of social good against class interests'.[120] Modern Liberalism, G. W. E. Russell wrote in 1883, viewed the state as 'the nation in its collective and corporate character . . . the one sovereign agent for all moral, material, and social reforms'.[121]

Naturally this embrace of the state did not go too far, as chapter 2 shows. There were always those fearful of illiberal over-activity. For example, in the alarmist climate of the mid-1880s there was scope for railway magnates to be worried by Chamberlain's language at the Board of Trade, or Whig landlords to be concerned about land bills. Herbert Spencer criticised the 1880–5 government's interference with individual liberty – though he admitted that the main reason for the growth of coercive legislation was that the state was now seen as a 'responsible power'.[122] But these tensions did not significantly divide the party. Though a Liberty and Property Defence

---

[117] R. Harcourt Williams (ed.), *Salisbury–Balfour correspondence: letters exchanged between the third marquess of Salisbury and his nephew Arthur James Balfour 1869–1892* (Ware, 1988), p. 137.

[118] Parry, *Rise and fall*, pp. 244–5. In 1877 G. C. Brodrick denied that *laissez-faire* was a Liberal principle, in his pamphlet published by the Liberal Central Association, 'What are Liberal principles?', p. 220. In 1870 Lowe remarked that the principles of political economy were violated every day: E. D. Steele, *Irish land and British politics: tenant-right and nationality 1865–1870* (Cambridge, 1974), p. 306. On Ireland and Scotland, see C. Dewey, 'Celtic agrarian legislation and the Celtic revival: historicist implications of Gladstone's Irish and Scottish Land Acts, 1870–86', *Past and Present*, 44 (1974), 30–70.

[119] See A. R. D. Elliot, 'Three Reform bills', *Edinburgh Review*, 161 (1885), 583–4.

[120] T. H. Green, *Lectures on the principles of political obligation, and other writings*, ed. P. Harris and J. Morrow (Cambridge, 1986 edn), p. 196.

[121] G. W. E. Russell, 'A protest against Whiggery', *Nineteenth Century*, 13 (1883), 925. The first phrase was a quotation from Burke.

[122] H. Spencer, 'The new Toryism', *Contemporary Review*, 45 (1884), 164.

League was established in 1882 to protest against interference with freedom of contract, few of its members were active Liberals. In so far as it was a political lobby rather than a business one, its inclinations were Tory; the libertarian Radical MP Peter Taylor, for example, refused to have anything to do with it as a result.[123] The Liberal party never clung to a narrowly individualist social or economic policy, nor was the split of the party in 1886 primarily about the role of the state: Liberal Unionists did not vote significantly differently to Gladstonians on land reform issues after it.[124] It was difficult for Liberals to argue that the new electors of 1885, whom after all they themselves had enfranchised with enthusiasm, would not be reliable citizens capable of rising above narrow class concerns.

Liberal politics were inherently fractious, but this reflected an emphasis on MPs' freedom of judgment and a lack of dirigiste party whipping. It did not mean that Liberalism lacked ideological coherence. Liberalism was a political movement, concerned mainly with the inclusiveness and balance of the constitution. It was never about doctrinaire individualist anti-statism. Inevitably, there were rigid political economists in the Liberal party, some of whom were influential. But it is striking that the leading politicians of this stamp, from Lansdowne in 1827 and Charles Wood in 1845–6 to Lowe in 1866 and George Goschen in 1886, were those most easily tempted by the idea of cross-party coalitions in defence of economy and *laissez-faire*. To varying degrees, doctrinaires of this type sat loose to party; they lamented the compromises of economic principle that party political activity required. The Liberal *party* was necessarily a political concept, thinking in terms of a national political community, of responding to and integrating public opinion.

Liberals had a natural tendency to advocate constitutional reform, in order to increase accountability and legitimacy, to extend political participation and to check class separation in favour of integration under the rule of law. In all these ways they had a constitutional definition of the national interest and claimed to promote it by updating the historic principles of English Parliamentary government. But there was always an ambivalence about the need for Reform, not least because of this same admiration for the way that the constitution had preserved stability, order and liberty. The quadrupling of the electorate in less than twenty years after 1866 was

[123] E. Bristow, 'The Liberty and Property Defence League and individualism', *Historical Journal*, 18 (1975), esp. 770–3.
[124] G. D. Phillips, 'The Whig lords and Liberalism, 1886–1893', *Historical Journal*, 24 (1981), 169–70.

effected on Liberal constitutional principles, though it was the result of a series of political accidents and manoeuvres and executed with a rapidity and completeness that left many Liberals alarmed.

The second theme of this chapter has been the inherent tension about the role of the state. Suspicion of its power to oppress and to favour sectional groups was deeply ingrained, and there was a strong tendency in both Radicalism and evangelical Nonconformity to purify politics of these anti-social tendencies. Between 1847 and 1849 this purifying crusade came to dominate the Liberal agenda. From this crisis British politics moved seamlessly into the more optimistic and stable 1850s, when the same rhetoric was used to celebrate Britain's distinctness and its political and economic superiority over the Continent in a decade when it was generally assumed that Britain was the greatest power in the world. The triumph of this language, which was intimately bound up with national self-satisfaction, can easily disguise the early stages of a crucial shift: the waning of the old apocalyptic hostility to the state. By the 1860s it was clearer that another theme in Liberalism had never died out: the traditional Whiggish/utilitarian interest in using state power to supply firm and apparently disinterested government and to shape the morals and character of the people. It was influential in the reshaping of the party in 1865–8. Yet between 1869 and 1873 there was a clash between this moralistic interventionism and traditional Radical libertarianism. Just as in 1848, the political arguments fused real domestic tensions with rhetoric about what was needed to defend the purity and vigour of English political and moral life. Anxieties about an overbearing state were particularly strong at these times. After 1874, though only slowly, the case for interventionism became more accepted, as there seemed less and less chance that the state could be dominated by small groups of vested interests.

At every point, therefore, Liberal domestic political debate was affected by considerations of national identity. One staple of Liberal argument was that the state of the national character, more even than the conditions of the franchise, would determine the health of the political nation, while much of the anxiety to increase state authority rested on a concern to improve that character. The tone of popular morals was, therefore, another crucial yardstick by which British and European political culture could be compared and national vigour sustained.

# CHAPTER 2

# Character, morals and national identity

For most propertied and intellectual Liberals a crucial issue in the franchise debates was whether certain virtues – morality, self-restraint, public spirit, manliness, conscience – could be spread sufficiently widely to make a success of a broad suffrage. On the whole, they claimed to be optimistic about this, even if many of them were not always optimistic enough to agitate for an immediate further extension of the suffrage. Between 1850 and the 1880s there were many celebratory statements about the self-reliance and self-discipline of English national character. The general view was that the English talent for self-government had been shaped by generations of conditioning from a respected system of law and institutions. The common recognition of a *patria*, a community of structures, practices and values, had helped to train human faculties to accept civic responsibility. However, this praise of the English character should not be taken strictly at face value. Most of the discussions about the qualities necessary for good government were themselves intended partly to educate people into those characteristics – to teach virtue by example, and to create a national debate about the best qualities to instil. One significant concern of Liberal government was the improvement of character, and its protection from corrupting elements, many of which were seen as alien.

The main purpose of this chapter is to discuss some of the most influential Liberal approaches to the role that politics should play in sustaining the nation's morals. It focuses on attitudes to educational and social reform, and the relationship of the state with religious denominations. Like chapter 1, it is very general. Its main aims are to introduce a few of the various schools of thought within the party, to help in the identification of major turning-points in Liberal history within this period, and to trace the connections and distinctions that were made *vis-à-vis* Europe. There is a more detailed consideration of education issues in chapters 3, 5 and 6.[1]

---

[1] And in *Rise and fall*, pp. 126–7, 138–9, 201–3, 237–8, 262–5.

The emphasis in this chapter, as in chapter 1, is on the role of the state, and the responsibility of politicians, in dealing with these issues, because this was usually at the heart of the *political* controversy about them. But some clarification is needed about precisely what is being said here. The argument is *not* that any Liberals saw social and moral questions mainly in terms of central government activity. Like all Victorians, they placed relatively more emphasis on the contributions that private philanthropy, the agencies of civil society, and local authorities could make to tackling them.[2] Indeed the starting-point of all discussion on these themes was the importance of liberty from central state oppression, which, as chapter 1 showed, played a key role in Liberal and indeed all Victorian political argument. This was particularly the case in relation to *economic* issues; hostility to 'socialism' was a theme of Liberal rhetoric, on financial, libertarian and moral grounds, and involved some continental comparisons.[3] On *educational, religious and social* issues, however, there was more scope for debate about the relative role of the state in relation to private agencies. One unavoidable question was what to do about the political and social power of an existing institution, the Church of England; another was the responsibility of politicians for the moral and social state of the country. Here the instinctive libertarianism of many Liberals was at odds with concerns both for social order and for human development. It was certainly possible to argue that private philanthropic activity offered the best chance of improving morals. Most of those Liberals who were hostile to state activity in the fields discussed in this chapter remained anxious about moral improvement. The concern in this chapter, however, is to identify important schools of Liberal argument that made the question of *state* responsibility for that moral improvement impossible to ignore at certain points in the period 1830–86.

Most 'improving' activity was directed at working-class morals. But another preliminary point worth making is that the poor were not the only targets of Liberal social criticism. There was a persistent interest in the reformation of middle- and upper-class morals, especially in the sense of urging these classes to understand their civic responsibility better. Chapter 1 showed that Liberals expected elites to demonstrate social and ethical virtues. Many were intensely critical of traditional aristocratic political

---

[2] For a recent recognition of the 'centrality of locality', see P. Harling, 'The centrality of locality: the local state, local democracy, and local consciousness in late-Victorian and Edwardian Britain', *Journal of Victorian Culture*, 9 (2004), 216–34.

[3] These themes have repeatedly been covered in the literature. For an intelligent modern discussion of the complexity of Victorian attitudes to the economic and moral problems of the marketplace, see G. R. Searle, *Morality and the market in Victorian Britain* (Oxford, 1998).

behaviour: the narrow-minded patronage-guzzlers who gave the state a bad name in Britain and Ireland before 1830; the gentry who misgoverned the counties through to the 1880s; their complacent relations in regimental messes and country vicarages who obstructed the army and Church reform that was needed to meet national needs. Correcting the apathy, aloofness and apartness of the governing classes was a major aim of the 1832 and 1884 Reform Acts. Moreover, among the more zealous Liberal ministers and commentators, as well as Radical MPs and Nonconformist crusaders, there was fairly regular criticism of the apathy and selfishness of Parliament – including of the less assiduous Liberal MPs, of whom there were many. Russell claimed in 1850 that Britain's escape from revolution and epidemic in 1848–9 suggested that the nation had been blessed by Providence, and that its leaders must act with responsibility if they hoped for these blessings to continue.[4] Indeed a major reason why the Liberal party could never function effectively as a party of *laissez-faire* was the continued influence of the notion that political leaders were liable to censure if they failed to take responsibility for national interests. In the 1850s and 1860s the greatest desire in this respect was that the emerging cadre of urban leaders should show less selfish acquisitiveness and more public spirit.[5] Britain had traditionally looked to Protestantism and a public-service aristocracy to supply moral leadership but was now an intensely and increasingly commercial society. While some were alarmed by middle-class preference for commercial gain instead of public service, Radicals like Cobden and Bright were more concerned by middle-class deference to the traditional governing classes – 'tuft-hunting' – which perpetuated social stratification and snobbery and encouraged imitation of the worst habits of the aristocracy.[6] This focus on the quality of local leadership was all the more pronounced because of the decentralised nature of the British state.

So Liberalism can be seen as a movement to improve morals and to smooth class tensions, and one that adopted a different strategy towards these ends from the conventional Tory approach, which venerated Anglican Christianity and social hierarchy. One shorthand phrase which was frequently used by moralists to describe the failings that were identified in the various social classes was materialism, the elevation of selfish lower

---

[4] *Hansard*, 109:1183, 19 Mar. 1850.
[5] E.g. (Nassau Senior, 1855) Simpson, *Many memories*, p. 186. See the reference to George Dawson above, p. 74. NB the lack of voluntary support for a plan for a free hospital to thank God for British stability amid continental turbulence in 1848: Kamenka and Smith, *Intellectuals and revolution*, p. 119.
[6] See e.g. Coleridge to Heathcote, 19 Aug. 1860, in E. H. Coleridge, *Life and correspondence of John Duke Lord Coleridge* (2 vols., London, 1904), vol. I, pp. 259–60.

interests over public and humane ones, weakening the moral cement necessary to hold society together. Upper- and middle-class selfishness and irresponsibility were one manifestation of it; another was the prevalence of vice, crime and sensuality in the lower orders. Materialism appeared to depress and demoralise the conscience, the soul, the potential of man. It undermined a sense of society and it privileged the wrong values. Arguments for state activity in improving morals rested fundamentally on anxieties for social order, but there was also a genuine and significant ethical element to them. Surely the ultimate purpose of man's activity was to develop the divine spark implanted in all human creatures: to develop the full humanity of man, his energies, his powers of reason, conscience and self-government; to make him a man, not a machine or a beast. It is not too gross a generalisation to say that most of the Liberals discussed here broadly agreed that the exercise of individual mental and spiritual faculties would lead to a deeper understanding of God's purposes in shaping the world and a closer communion with the divine will. They attached great importance to the pursuit of truth and progress through reason and freedom of conscience. Though the party could not afford to identify itself with Protestantism as overtly as the Tories – not least because of the need to develop its inclusive constitutionalist philosophy in Ireland – it was nonetheless suffused with it in the sense of upholding humanity's duty and responsibility to interpret the biblical message for itself. Moreover, this emphasis on individual conscience did not imply an anti-social philosophy. A greater understanding of God's purposes for the world would bring men closer to God and to each other. Unity was God's ideal for mankind. Inclusiveness in religion as in politics was a seminal Liberal theme, though not everyone meant the same thing by it. Pursuit of a living, truthful religion involved rejecting the shams and dogmas that created division and impoverished the spirit. Unthinking adherence to religious dogma for its own sake, together with some priests' arrogant claims to dictate the meaning of the divine message, was also materialist in that sense.

Hostility to materialism was an important element in moralist Liberal discourse. But this is only a helpful generalisation up to a point, since the idea could be applied in so many diverse ways. When Liberals differed in their definitions of social or religious behaviour that was unattractively materialist, this was often because of their class, ideological or theological background. As a political movement, the most striking fact about Liberalism was the great variety of approaches to moral issues subsumed within it. This is not surprising given that the core elements of Liberal identity were constitutional and fiscal. Moreover, there were many aspects of modern commercial society of which almost all Liberals approved. At local and indeed Parliamentary levels, many Liberal politicians were first and foremost hard-headed commercial men. As chapter 1 noted, most maintained that commercial society created a superior civilisation and morality. Hard work was seen as beneficial, resulting in a satisfying national prosperity; cartoon representations of John Bull stressed both values.[7] The Reform Club, the nearest that the Liberal party possessed to a national headquarters, was a temple to well-upholstered comfort and modernity, not least in its famous kitchens. For most commercial men, few manifestations of materialism were worse than excessive state activity, sapping individual responsibility and giving some groups special economic favours – in other words, 'socialism'.

In practice, in order to be politically dominant, Liberals needed to satisfy the commercial instincts of their core middle-class constituency while also assuring swathes of propertied and intellectual opinion that they had higher ideals than mere worship of money. The successes and failures of this balancing-act form one of the themes of Part II, since the issues discussed there were crucial in the attempt to achieve it. One purpose of the moralising language and tone considered in this chapter was to disguise the importance of the commercial constituency to the Liberal party, in order to achieve a broader national appeal.

Perhaps inevitably, though many Liberals were naturally drawn to high-minded moral arguments, these were often counterproductive politically. The greatest single problem for Liberals in asserting their national reach and patriotism as a political party was the ability of the Conservatives to charge that they were unfriendly to institutional Anglicanism, the national Church. This was a – perhaps the – major cause of the only two Liberal electoral defeats of this period, in 1841 and 1874, and the party's failure to win an overall majority in 1885. It stemmed from the primacy of constitutionalism and pluralism in Liberal thinking. Since early in the century the Whig party had been committed to improving the political rights of religious minorities and dismantling the Tory *ancien régime*. It never accepted that Protestant Nonconformists and Roman Catholics should not have political representation, and, once this was achieved in 1828–9, there was unstoppable pressure within the party to support at least some of the subsequent grievances of these sects. Liberals were instinctively sympathetic to allegations of oppression by the socially and politically powerful Church Establishment, with its Tory connections. By the late 1850s nearly all Liberal

---

[7] M. Taylor, 'John Bull'.

MPs had come round to advocating the abolition of Church rates. Non-conformist freedom to take degrees at Oxford and Cambridge was secured by the Liberal legislation of 1854, 1856 and 1871. Suspicion of the Church's capacity to use its privileged position to prevent true liberty of religious teaching, and to benefit the Conservative party in the process, was one of the main causes of the Nonconformist unhappiness with some provisions of the 1870 Education Act.[8] Even in 1880, an incoming Liberal government could still find a legitimate Nonconformist grievance to rectify, with the Burials Act.

So it was easy to accuse the Liberal party of hostility to the Church of England, which most Anglicans regarded as a crucial agency for moral instruction of a rapidly expanding and potentially threatening population. At local level the core of Liberalism was usually Nonconformist, in entrenched opposition to a Church party. At policy level, the persistent efforts of some Liberals to supersede Church domination of the educational network by a more systematic and inclusive national system was bound to create an Anglican reaction. Some Liberals had heterodox beliefs; Liberal enthusiasm for state intervention could easily look like an essentially irreligious and utilitarian policy of national improvement. Indeed mid-century politics was profoundly shaped by an attack, mounted by Tories, Tractarians and moral pundits (but also Nonconformists, as we shall see), on what appeared to be the Whigs' overly cold and secular approach in the 1830s, running parallel to the critique of their aristocratic narrowness.

Moreover, in such a pluralistic and individualistic party there was ongoing tension, particularly about attitudes to the state's religious remit. These mirrored the tensions discussed in chapter 1, because the different elements all considered themselves to have the best solution to the problem of how to realise a national moral community. The Whiggish elements advocated a close link between the state and a reformed Church Establishment capable of speaking to the nation. But they could easily be accused of wishing to oppress private judgment – at the taxpayer's expense. Nonconformist hostility to the Church Establishment was culturally affiliated to Radical suspicion of the authority of the secular state. In their hostility to materialism and to the repression of liberty of thought, Nonconformists regarded themselves as intensely patriotic – in a way that has hardly been discussed by historians. Equally worthy of fresh study is the timing of changes in their attitudes to politics. It is argued here that their suspicion of the state flared up intensely between 1870 and 1874, in a restatement of their traditional

---

[8] Parry, 'Nonconformity, clericalism', pp. 159–65.

anxiety about oppression. But the rationale of their arguments was shifting, and once the smoke had cleared a greater acceptance of state legitimacy was apparent – following the pattern of the secular Radical attitude to the state traced in chapter 1.

Finally, Liberal moral argument was open to charges of 'un-Englishness' because it was powerfully shaped by various schools of continental thought. Many Liberal thinkers argued that it was important to wage war on the supercilious selfishness of insular Englishmen and that the British must develop a stronger sense of society by learning from continental habits; the true values of communal patriotism were international. Some elements of Liberalism were always self-consciously hostile to narrow nationalist triumphalism. Not surprisingly, these arguments were particularly strongly held in the 1850s and 1860s, in reaction to the dominant consensus that was traced in chapter 1. They contributed to the reassertion of confidence in the state and social reform in the latter decade. But this also helped to create intra-party division as well as to justify the Tory argument that Liberals lacked real patriotism.

So religious and educational issues were often damaging for the party. On the other hand, as the above points imply, Liberal moralists were, in their various ways, concerned with establishing a more effective national community and were sometimes able to overcome the various obstacles to doing so, by finding points of agreement. One fairly continuous backdrop was the French 'other'. The continuing prevalence of materialism, sensuousness and decadence in France provided a persistent comparative dimension to Liberal moral argument. Nothing offered a more pregnant example of social calamity than the French Revolution of 1789. The sinful qualities in human nature – private vice, luxury and decadence – had come to the fore at the expense of the moral. It was commonly argued that such decay could be staved off only by religious purity, because of its positive effects on economic, political and moral vigour, social harmony, and justice.[9] Comparisons of British morality with its enfeebled state in France were common, particularly during Napoleon's Second Empire and then the 1871 Commune. The moral and hence political failings of the French character were blamed for the defeat of 1870 and for recurring social instability. Indeed, this opened the way for periodic panics about a *cultural* invasion of materialist and amoral habits from across the Channel, complementing anxieties about *military* invasion.

[9] R. Vaughan, *The age of great cities: or, modern society viewed in relation to intelligence, morals, and religion* (London, 1843), pp. 353–65; Parry, *Democracy and religion*, pp. 83–4.

## WHIGGISM, LIBERAL ANGLICANISM AND THE CRISIS
### OF 1846–51

The Whig governments of the 1830s dealt vigorously and systematically with what was generally seen by the propertied classes to be a moral and social crisis at the end of the 1820s. They claimed to offer a rigorous policy to tackle vice, crime and pauperism on a national footing for the first time. Lord John Russell described the government's role as to introduce 'system, method, science, economy, regularity, and discipline'.[10] Reformers rallied behind an emphasis on utilitarian state activity for the common good through the maintenance of law and the introduction of measures to extend rational and self-disciplined behaviour. They shared a commitment to a coordinated national policy to reduce the capacity of 'booby lords and squires' and sectional and reactionary Tory Churchmen to damage good government.[11] This approach had profound social effects and, not surprisingly, stirred up controversy. Government social policy, particularly the New Poor Law, acquired a reputation for meanness and uncaring dictation from the centre. Meanwhile, 'godless' state power was asserted in several areas of national life – among them, grants to non-Anglican schools, a secular system of marriage registration, and the appropriation of pauper bodies for anatomy lessons.[12] In these ways, and in its pluralist Irish and British religious policy, Liberalism seemed to threaten traditional religious and moral values. Many leading Liberals were sceptical erastian anti-clericals; some were Benthamite utilitarians. Since the party also rested increasingly on Nonconformist support at constituency level, the result was a vigorous reaction by Anglican and Tory interests, made worse by the beginnings of anxiety about the threats to orthodox religion from German theology. This reaction produced a Tory victory at the 1841 election, as well as invigorating the Oxford Movement and the campaign to build more Anglican schools and teacher-training colleges. By 1841, government Liberalism could be portrayed as haughty, socially unsympathetic, and irreligious.

These charges have tended to stick, with the result that the secular and centralising strains in 1830s Liberalism have both been exaggerated. Most legislation of the 1830s sought to galvanise reformed local government institutions to take responsibility for social ills rather than to impose central diktats on them; local activity was always an important aspect of

---

[10] Parry, *Rise and fall*, p. 114, and ch. 5 more generally.
[11] Given as 'bobby': Holland, 1826, in Mitchell, *Holland House*, p. 174.
[12] See e.g. U. R. Q. Henriques, *Before the Welfare State: social administration in early industrial Britain* (London, 1979); R. Richardson, *Death, dissection and the destitute* (London, 1987).

Liberalism. Similarly, Whig policy sought to bolster, not undermine, the religious conscience. As Leader of the Commons between 1835 and 1841, Russell's great contribution to Liberalism was to fuse Whig constitutionalism with the moralism of the earnest young Whigs of his generation who, owing to their engagement with the work of extra-Parliamentary writers such as Thomas Arnold, are usually called Liberal Anglicans. The civil servant James Stephen described Russell's as the only 'dominant soul' among the politicians with whom he had worked. Gladstone praised him for his 'inexhaustible sympathy with human suffering' and for 'identif[ying] political with personal morality', while Bagehot thought that he 'perhaps alone . . . has succeeded . . . in the oratory of conviction'.[13] Russell was a Foxite Whig, alert to repression in a number of forms, particularly the repression of freedom of belief. No group of men, he argued, had exclusive understanding of religious truth or the right to impose it on others. Revelation was progressive; most religious dogma had been invented in periods of inferior morality and was no longer suitable. The principal historical function of doctrines like damnation, transubstantiation or predestination had been to divide man from man and to justify war, torture and slavery in the name of a God who had preached the duty of forgiveness, tolerance and eternal love.[14]

However, deeply affected by the French Revolution, Russell rejected a merely utilitarian idea of the state: neither Benthamism nor Manchester school Liberalism offered a basis for a properly ethical society. Government was not just a law-enforcement agency; it was a divinely ordained agency for the promotion of a humanitarian morality. The 'duty of a State is [to] inculcate religion and morality among the great body of the people'.[15] Government must raise the 'energy', 'tone' and 'moral character' of the population, must act on 'the great mass of vice and misery' in the country's midst and must build a nation of people 'deriving their strength, deriving their conduct, deriving their loyalty, from enlightened religious and moral principles'.[16] Firm government action – for example over policing and prisons – was needed to repress the 'evil . . . passions' in man and reform human depravity. But if the state merely meted out punishment, it would fail to win hearts and minds and would invite rebellion. It had responsibilities to improve the education of the people and to offer them

[13] C. E. Stephen (ed.), *Sir James Stephen: letters* (pr. pr. 1906), p. 99; W. E. Gladstone, 'The Melbourne government: its acts and persons', *Nineteenth Century*, 27 (1890), 54–5; W. Bagehot, 'The character of Sir Robert Peel', in *Biographical studies*, ed. R. H. Hutton (London, 1907 edn), p. 30.
[14] Parry, 'Past and future', p. 147.     [15] *Hansard*, 33:1277, 1 June 1836.
[16] Parry, 'Past and future', pp. 167, 172; (1837) Walpole, *Russell*, vol. 1, p. 284.

social and legal reform.[17] As Home Secretary between 1835 and 1839, Russell was responsible for the government's social, legal, policing and prison reforms. In particular he was committed to educational legislation on the basis of Christian principles and morals. The spread of 'sound, moral, and religious instruction' would lead men to love God with heart, soul and mind, redeeming their sins; it would teach them to love their neighbours and the principles of humanity and philanthropy; and it would lead them to apply their God-given energies to useful work and to attack vice.[18]

Through Liberal Anglicanism particularly, Liberalism became influenced by the international early-nineteenth-century organicist reaction against the secular, egalitarian, universalist revolutionary threat of the 1790s. This reaction inspired a search for a coherent nationally based organic society around principles that built on the respect for humanity that the French Revolution exemplified, but combined it with attachment to religion, ethics and order. This movement was particularly evident in Germany and then among Englishmen, like Coleridge, attracted by German thought. Coleridge influenced both Liberal Anglicanism and Christian Socialism (considered below) by stressing the un-Christian, worthless and selfish nature of a life focused on material concerns, and the connection between the awakening of the divine light within each man, and social unity. He suggested that sectarianism in politics and religion encouraged human vanity, conflict and narrowness rather than cooperation and a common willingness to embrace progress. He maintained that the narrow mechanistic superficiality of Paleyite philosophy (influential on older Whigs) trivialised religion by confining it to externals and the reasoning process. A dry literal belief in every word of the Bible, divorced from an understanding of its context, was equally unenlightening. Dogmatic political economy worshipped the profit motive and treated humans as machines. Secular rights-based Radicalism peddled the false belief that external political machinery could transform the inward nature of man; it had goaded animal passions and lusts until they broke out in the Terror. All these worldly ideologies were materialist. In contrast, Liberal Anglicans and Christian Socialists sought to Christianise the humanitarian principles of the French Revolution in order to confront and defeat its malevolent effects. More valuable than political reconstruction was the task of spreading an undoctrinal and humane Christianity to the largest number of people. Important particularly was a

---

[17] Parry, 'Past and future', pp. 150–1.
[18] Ibid., pp. 147–8. There is a large literature on these reforms; they are also treated in Parry, *Rise and fall*, ch. 5.

moral and spiritual education, going beyond narrow utilitarian reason. It was not just the clergy, themselves tainted by sectionalism, but a national moral leadership, a clerisy embracing the political and intellectual elites, who should take on this task. They were best suited to understand and communicate the progressive revelation of the living truths of religion. Then the superior capacity of the English to understand true Christianity would allow England to do God's work in taking the lead in preserving human societies from the destruction unleashed in France. This was a global anti-revolutionary mission, but it was first and foremost a patriotic concern, emphasising the integrative role of the nation-state.[19]

Liberal Anglicanism offered one solution to the great problem of how to reconceptualise the relations between religion and the state after the major constitutional changes of 1828–32. Liberal Anglicans believed in the moralising power of the Church Establishment but wanted to ensure that it acted for the good of the nation as a whole rather than a narrow sect. In both the political and ecclesiastical spheres, they argued, Tories were spokesmen for a blinkered oligarchy. Tory Anglicanism was damaging the chance of a Christian nationhood, owing to its outdated concern with defining national religion in narrowly and divisively sectional terms, and its broader complacency, laziness and narrow dogmatism. This was surely a disastrous policy to pursue – all the more obviously so in the great social convulsions of 1829–30 and 1838–41. Arnold called Toryism the spirit that crucified Christ.[20] The answer was to reform the Anglican Church Establishment and improve national education. This aim fitted in with broader Whig political concerns. On the right basis, the Church Establishment was invaluable. It was a body with a national reach: it supplied a moral teacher in every parish and an institutional confirmation of the Christian and Protestant principles that were so intimately bound up with the nation's past progress. In its bishops and clergy it had the spiritual equivalent of the propertied classes in politics: an intermediate layer between divine authority and popular passion, which had a duty to behave responsibly and accountably. The clergy were to teach men how to think spiritually yet sensibly, to temper excess zeal and to galvanise the lazy. Yet they should be subject to the guidance of Parliament – of the representatives of the people. This was crucial because it provided a check on the potentially intolerant or reactionary views of clergymen, and on clerical abuses such as plurality and non-residence. It guaranteed

---

[19] C. R. Sanders, *Coleridge and the broad church movement* (Durham, NC, 1942); B. Knights, *The idea of the clerisy in the nineteenth century* (Cambridge, 1978); H. S. Jones, *Victorian political thought* (Houndsmills, 2000), chs. 1, 2. For Liberal Anglicanism, see Brent, *Liberal Anglican politics*.

[20] 1833, to Bunsen, Stanley, *Arnold*, vol. 1, p. 307.

the layman's right of private judgment; it helped the Church to remain a representative body in harmony with the evolution of opinion, rather than clinging to meaningless formularies reflecting the superstitions of less progressive times. For the Whigs, Parliamentary influence over the Church Establishment, replacing dependence on the arbitrary foreign power of the papacy, was one of the greatest symbols of English political culture. The passage of the 1832 Reform Act strengthened the idea that a truly national Parliament could check the potentially sectional behaviour of the largely Tory clergy.

Liberal Anglican moralism helped the Whigs to assert that it was really Toryism which was un-Christian and unpatriotic. No doubt this was genuinely felt. But such rhetoric was also useful politically in tackling the biggest difficulty of Liberal politics. On the one hand, Liberals needed to rally a pluralist religious coalition and to keep non-Anglican voters content. On the other, they had to check the Tory reaction by advertising their commitment to religion and morality. This was a balancing-act that did not succeed in the divided and panicky social conditions of the late 1830s and 1840s. Anglican voters clung desperately to their traditions and interpreted Liberal critiques of the Church as simple unfriendliness, while Nonconformists and Radicals were suspicious of the links between what seemed a patronage-ridden Church Establishment and a patronage-ridden state. For all that, Liberal Anglican ideas were too powerful and attractive ever to surrender their place as a great bulwark of Liberal ethical politics. The argument that the state should support a broad moralising religion remained at the heart of elite Liberalism. This underpinned the Anglican Establishment, especially once broad-church ideas came to dominate among the governing classes after 1850. It also facilitated the emergence of a national education system on an essentially undenominational religious basis after 1870.

The reason why aristocratic Whiggism briefly came to look irreligious and alien was because the ten years after 1838 were the decade of greatest public moral anxiety in the nineteenth century. Evangelicals, Tractarians and Nonconformists all demanded a national turning to God and a purging of false elements in the country's religious life.[21] Evangelicals intensified their critique of popery, while the Oxford Movement tried, controversially, to find a proper historic foundation for a national doctrinal Anglican religion. Nonconformists urged the rooting out of sinful national legislation

---

[21] For Ashley's critique of Whiggish politics and society in 1844, see P. Mandler, 'Cain and Abel: two aristocrats and the early Victorian Factory Acts', *Historical Journal*, 27 (1984), 83.

(the Corn Laws) and international practices (the slave trade). The Tory revival of the late 1830s and the middle-class Radicalism of the early and mid-1840s were both based on an urgent desire to rid public life of its amoral elements and to place government on stronger and purer foundations – though they differed greatly on what this entailed. Carlyle became a celebrated prophet, preaching the need for work, truthfulness and earnestness and to attack shams and superficiality. In 1841 and again in 1845 his writings on Oliver Cromwell promoted the idea of a godly man who had purified national politics of effete luxury, extravagance and idol-worship, and suggested that a contemporary Cromwell was needed. Though there was still much unease at the eventual execution of Charles I, it came to be more generally appreciated that the revolt of 1640–2, more than the mere constitutional transformation of 1688, was the crucial moment in national history because it demonstrated the inner strength and resolution of the national character and its determination to defeat absolutism.[22] Carlyle maintained that the English were better suited to the task of creating a virtuous society than any continental race because of their practical genius – though he was increasingly convinced that only great men, with particular divinely inspired insights and an unusually developed sense of responsibility, could lead a nation to purification.[23]

However, from around 1850 the prevailing tone of public discourse became less pessimistic. This reflected the growing recognition, traced in chapter 1, that the political nation was founded on a stable and broad basis. England was set fair to be a success story, as long as it held to certain important principles. Just as autocracy was deemed un-English, so too was elitism in any sphere: the basis of an effective national life was the spread of inclusive Christian, as of constitutional, ideals, and there was no reason to doubt the ultimate success of this in Britain. One casualty of this mood was a narrowly atonement-based evangelicalism, with its emphasis on a chastising God and its divisive emphasis on the potential for eternal punishment in hell for the unrighteous. A more optimistic incarnational emphasis on the immanence of the divine spark in all members of the nation became fashionable.[24] Surely the proper basis of Christianity was to help others in

---

[22] See B. Worden, 'The Victorians and Oliver Cromwell', in S. Collini, R. Whatmore and B. Young (eds.), *History, religion, and culture: British intellectual history 1750–1950* (Cambridge, 2000), pp. 117–19.

[23] *Past and present* (London, 1843), bk 3, ch. 5. Carlyle himself put more faith in Peel, despite his *laissez-faire* views, on account of his potential to offer heroic leadership: J. Morrow, 'The paradox of Peel as Carlylean hero', *Historical Journal*, 40 (1997), 97–110.

[24] Hilton, *Age of atonement*, chs. 7–8.

this life, following the example of Christ, the ideal of manliness, rather than to be preoccupied with one's own salvation in the next? Secondly, there was a recoil from the doctrinal rigour, traditionalism and unworldly mysticism of the Oxford Movement, in favour of a desire to reconnect Christianity to the mundane, the familial and the onward progress of humanity. The power of these two warring ecclesiastical belief systems had helped to crush Liberalism in the 1830s, but after 1850 the liberal reaction against them in turn was strong. It paralleled a simultaneous attempt to transcend the class- or doctrine-based *political* sectarianism of the 1840s, which was associated with effete aristocrats, selfish businessmen and threatening mobs, and with Benthamite and socialist ideologues.

The emphasis of progressive thinkers in the 1850s, instead, was that the national community should be conceived in humane, cross-class, optimistic language. The Great Exhibition of 1851 was widely seen as a memorial to the dignity of work and working men, and a lesson about the merits of class integration. It aimed to make people of all classes, not least the propertied establishment, more aware of the operation and significance of machinery and the importance of science and industry to the future of the country. Henry Mayhew called it 'the first attempt to dignify and refine toil'.[25] Ford Madox Brown's painting, *Work*, begun in 1852, implied that workers, the middle classes and intellectuals were all contributing to the progress of society and should learn to appreciate each other's contribution. Other Pre-Raphaelite paintings – Millais's *Christ in the house of His parents* (1850), or Madox Brown's *Jesus washing Peter's feet* (1852) – showed Christ as an ordinary worker, an exemplary figure for all. By the mid-1850s there was a great desire to believe that the class tensions within British society could be smoothed by disinterested leadership and increased mutual respect. After all, the glories of English natural scenery were already accessible to all classes of the nation, as Madox Brown's *An English autumn afternoon* and *Walton-on-the-Naze* sought to portray.

The need to make Christian values relevant to ordinary men and to the public sphere was the main reason for the interest in promoting an exemplary manliness in the 1850s, celebrating, in various proportions, God-given physical energy, pluck and virility, and the gentle spirituality of Christ. Though Carlyle's assault on materialism and social irresponsibility continued to be a powerful influence on public debate, the implication of his works on heroic leadership – that the mass of men were incapable of

---

[25] H. Mayhew, *1851*, quoted in A. M. Burton (ed.), *Politics and empire in Victorian Britain: a reader* (Basingstoke, 2001), p. 88.

anything more than being set to socially useful work by their moral superiors – became seen as unacceptably inhumane and demeaning, because it denied the capacity of all men, formed in the image of Christ, to become heroic. In 1849 Robert Vaughan argued that Carlyle was a bad political guide, since the 'great duty' of every humanitarian was 'to diminish the power of great men as far as possible, by endeavouring to diffuse as much greatness as may be through society at large'.[26] A. H. Clough ruefully remarked that Carlyle 'has led us out into the desert – and has left us there'.[27] The clash between Carlyle and Mill on 'The Negro Question' in 1849–50 defined the difference between the two anti-materialist schools. Mill – a great admirer of the humanitarian and republican tradition of the French Revolution – insisted that the hallmark of a civilised society was to treat all humanity, irrespective of race and class, with respect, cultivating men's moral faculties.[28] Thereafter, the strong Carlylean strain, with its emphasis on firm leadership and government by a virtuous elite, seemed increasingly outdated to Liberals: a residual Puritanism, religious or secular.

However, in a milder form the belief in the need for strong moral leadership continued to have an influence, especially after the return of anxiety about the consequences of the extension of democracy at home in the mid-1860s.[29] In many cases, these anxieties were obviously connected to insecurities about class and property, and increasingly to doubts about the intellectual capacity of democracy as well. And even in the 1850s Liberals emphatically continued to believe in the need for elite intellectual leadership to shape moral progress. In fact, the mid-Victorian liberal intelligentsia attached more weight than ever to the idea of a clerisy to provide guidance. Both alternatives – Tory Anglicanism and middle-class commercialism – seemed insular and narrowing. The university reform movement of the 1850s can be seen as an urgent attempt to raise the standards of British intellectual life: to assert 'the national character and genius', as H. H. Vaughan urged in 1852.[30] Fifteen years later J. R. Seeley lamented that, instead of 'overrunning the Continent with our ideas, as in the days of Locke, Newton and Bentley', French and German scholars had taken the intellectual high ground. 'In the warfare of thought we have hoped to resist regular troops by Volunteers.' University reform was a 'defence' of the 'intellectual rank

---

[26] R. Vaughan, 'Thomas Carlyle', *British Quarterly Review*, 10 (1849), 36.
[27] A. L. Le Quesne, *Carlyle* (Oxford, 1982), p. 82.
[28] J. S. Mill, 'The Negro question' (1850), *CWM*, vol. XXI, pp. 85–95.
[29] See the discussion of the Governor Eyre controversy in the Introduction, pp. 18–19.
[30] Knights, *Clerisy*, p. 205.

and character' of our country, just as military expenditure was needed to protect the coasts.[31]

In the 1860s and 1870s, Liberal moral argument was made up of various strands of thought, all of which, in different ways, placed enormous emphasis on themes of conscience and humanity. One of them, evangelical Nonconformity, considered later, was increasingly influential on Liberalism in the localities. Meanwhile, broad-church Christianity was powerful in the political and social establishment, not least at Court, and individual Liberal Anglicans and Christian Socialists – A. P. Stanley, Charles Kingsley – became household names. Liberal Anglicans approved of the changes in the Church since the 1830s: the attack on complacency and sinecures and the promotion of social work and scholarship. This allowed them to claim that it was now a more truly national institution, doing good work in the inner cities. They argued that the state connection checked priests' natural tendency towards dogmatism and narrowness by imposing the force of Parliamentary law on them. This view was strengthened by the revival of ritualism, which conjured up notions of authoritarian priests skilfully manipulating weak-minded parishioners around the time of the extension of the electorate in 1867. Broad churchmen argued that Establishment kept the Church and therefore the nation in touch with the progress of humanity, including ideas of scientific and biblical criticism. A dogmatic Anglo-Catholic Church, or insular and separatist Nonconformity, could not achieve the same.[32] Those who opposed Church Establishments were criticised for wishing to reduce the nation to 'a union for material interests'; as a divine institution it was entitled to 'the same kind of reverent service [as] the Church'. A Christian nation should publicly confess its Christianity in order to make national life 'wider, stronger, and higher in tone and aspiration'.[33] This would moderate class tension and forge stronger links between elite and mass culture, the prerequisite for a strong national character – which was itself the prerequisite of the 'Christian unity of mankind'.[34] However, most Liberals looked not just to an idealised Church, but also to other branches of the clerisy – the universities and the higher journalism as well as Parliament – to direct the nation's thought and progress. The Church needed to accommodate to the nation; the nation's life was too broad to be restrained by the needs of the Church. Liberals certainly

---

[31] In F. W. Farrar (ed.), *Essays on a liberal education*, quoted in Knights, *Clerisy*, p. 206.

[32] Parry, *Democracy and religion*, pp. 91–5.

[33] J. L. Davies, 'The voluntary principle', in W. L. Clay (ed.), *Essays on Church policy* (London, 1868), pp. 84–5.

[34] J. R. Seeley, 'The Church as a teacher of morality', in Clay, *Essays*, pp. 276–80.

tended to be very critical of the Church as it actually existed in the counties and small towns, where it usually supported landlordism and Toryism.

Anglican, Nonconformist and freethinking Liberals were all aware of the disciplinary function of politics in shaping communal values, despite their differences about practical issues of state–Church relations. One of the major themes of Gladstonian Liberalism after 1867 was that a key attribute of a well-ordered national community was its respect for the moral conscience in both its individual and collective forms. In both domestic and foreign policy, the humanity of man must be venerated. Gladstone's stress on humanity incorporated both a religious and a post-religious element, reflecting the fact that many advanced Liberals conceived of it in essentially secular terms by the 1880s. But though this language was frequently couched in the language of 'trusting the people', in practice it incorporated alarm at the potential amorality of a secular democracy and sought to use the political process to spread ethical and moral principles. The increasing interest of Nonconformity in social reform should also be seen as a bid to moralise the people. The remaining sections of this chapter look at the most significant of these movements of the post-1848 period.

### CHRISTIAN SOCIALISTS AND UNITARIANS – A COUNTER-CULTURAL PATRIOTISM

Soon after 1848 British *political* stability was generally acknowledged, but there was much more difference of opinion as to how *socially* united Britain already was. As chapter 1 suggests, there was a very widespread, complacent and chauvinistic belief that the nation was Providentially favoured and that the principles of *laissez-faire* and low rates and taxes were the acme of political morality. The Great Exhibition turned into a narrow-minded nationalistic celebration. British political achievement suggested to many people that Britain already formed an effective moral community – that national character was set along the right lines and that the importance in it of values like individual responsibility was so great that moralistic state action would probably damage rather than improve it. The problem was not that Liberalism had lost its interest in national morals, but that very many people now believed that an over-mighty state threatened morals more than it supported them. As a result, there was no longer any consensus behind an effective *political* movement for moral reform.

However, among moralists there was a strong tendency to criticise these self-satisfied responses as insular and utilitarian, and to argue that in order to create a true national community a much greater degree of social unity and mutual obligation was needed. Carlyle's assaults on *laissez-faire* and money-grubbing cast a long shadow. Most Liberal moral argument in the 1850s started from the notion that commercial materialism, together with continuing evidence of aristocratic privilege, was still a serious obstacle to true nationhood. Such, for example, was the warning given by Henry Layard in 1855, during his critique of government and national complacency over the Crimean War effort.[35] Layard, at that moment a prominent Radical politician, was a strong enemy of unmanly aristocratic feebleness but also of commercial insularity and routine, and he believed that to be a successful political and social community England needed to learn from foreign cultures. Similarly, Ford Madox Brown, like Layard born and bred in Europe, remained a critic of the continuing paralysing influence of family influence and of materialist greed in Britain and felt that affairs were managed with more justice and improvement abroad despite greater political instability.[36] The promoters who moved the Crystal Palace to Sydenham in 1854 hoped to use the building to expand the cultural horizons of Englishmen in a way that the original Crystal Palace had not done. The artistic director, Owen Jones, a friend of Layard, had urged the need for a permanent Palace in 1852 in order to improve understanding between the classes and cultivate 'refined artistic instincts' in all ranks – as access to nature and art allowed the Spaniards, for example, to do. Otherwise, he feared, 'England, in the midst of her material greatness [would] become a byword and a reproach amongst nations'.[37] The new Palace displayed a variety of Fine Arts courts reconstructing historic architectural styles, so that the English could learn how to create an art in harmony with nature, morality and contemporary means of production, which Jones felt that the great Moslem civilisations had done.[38] The Palace directors also sought to elevate the musical taste of England by exposure to uplifting continental works, particularly the German music admired by the musical director August Manns and the secretary George Grove.

Throughout the 1850s a significant minority view can be discerned, that Britain could only escape from its materialist philistinism by developing a stronger sense of society in the ways encouraged by French and German thinkers. As chapter 5 explores in more detail, writers as diverse as John Stuart Mill, Matthew Arnold, George Eliot, and the positivist

---

[35] 'The influence of education upon character', in P. J. Anderson (ed.), *Rectorial addresses delivered at the universities of Aberdeen 1835–1900* (Aberdeen, 1902), pp. 73–91.
[36] K. Bendiner, *The art of Ford Madox Brown* (University Park, PA, 1998), pp. 88, 99–100.
[37] *Lectures on the results of the Great Exhibition of 1851, second series* (London, 1853), pp. 299–300.
[38] O. Jones, *The grammar of ornament* (London, 1856; 1986 edn), pp. 2, 77–8.

circle around Richard Congreve argued that in comparison the English were socially impoverished. For example Mill, anxious not to strengthen 'the already ample self-conceit of John Bull', berated the ignorance and narrow-mindedness displayed by those who demonised republicanism and socialism. These were logical causes for continental reformers to adopt; it was Englishmen's incapacity to marry up theory and practice which blinded them to this. In theory, republicanism was more logical than constitutional monarchy, which legitimised rank and privilege in ways that sat oddly with the representative system. The 'socialism' to which the British responded so hysterically merely meant an attempt by the state to guarantee to ordinary people the moral right of subsistence (as the British had tried to do in Ireland). It was a protest against the maldistributive effects of unfettered capitalism, by encouraging the establishment of cooperatives, in order to allow a fairer spread of industrial produce.[39]

These movements were of the age in embracing ideas of humanity and conscience, but counter-cultural in criticising the complacency of British attitudes to national moral health. One of the most significant of them, as far as the rising generation of Liberal politicians was concerned, was the Christian Socialist movement led by F. D. Maurice, Charles Kingsley, Thomas Hughes and J. M. Ludlow. Its rallying-cry was hostility to materialism of all sorts. One sort was social and theological sectarianism in all its forms: believers should instead follow their conscience and search for truth. Another was uncritical worship of the principles of *laissez-faire* and material progress: Maurice denied that unrestricted competition promoted manliness and energy of character. Competition was a 'hateful, devilish' doctrine destroying 'our English life' because it argued that 'land, goods, money, labour [are] the basis of society' instead of 'human relations'.[40] It prevented the cultivation of individual manliness and common interests in society, yet these were God's two great purposes for human existence, as exemplified by Christ's life and by God's fatherly relations to Christ and to all mankind. Christian Socialism's interest in cooperative workshops was inspired by the associationist movement in France in 1848 and by horror at the London sweatshops publicised by Mayhew's 1849 articles on London Labour and the London Poor in the *Morning Chronicle*. This was part

---

[39] 'Vindication of the French revolution of February 1848' (Apr. 1849), *CWM*, vol. xx, pp. 319–63. The John Bull quotation is from 'England and Ireland' (May 1848), *CWM*, xxv, 1096. John Morley followed Mill in criticising Englishmen's dislike of political logic; hence his criticism of the 'English system' quoted at the front of this book.

[40] 21 Mar. 1852, F. Maurice, *The life of Frederick Denison Maurice, chiefly told in his own letters* (2 vols., London, 1884), vol. ii, p. 113; F. D. Maurice, *The reformation of society* (London, 1851), pp. 18–23.

of a call for the wealthy to take more interest in the slums where men like Kingsley's fictional hero Alton Locke had their God-given energy and health sapped by social conditions. It was not surprising, Kingsley argued, that such working men rejected God and turned to political Radicalism. They would only be convinced of God's benevolence if the propertied classes took up their religious and social responsibilities. For Maurice, the 'means of averting an English political revolution and of bringing what is good in foreign revolutions to know itself' was an 'English theological reformation', recovering our sense of a living God.[41] Working men needed to be claimed as true men, 'living portions of a living and united society', with 'a common life and a common object'.[42] This was a social message but also a theological one, in that it was a call for the projection of a socially concerned, undoctrinaire, living religion. It stood both against fierce evangelicalism, with its emphasis on eternal punishment – for contesting which, Maurice was removed from King's College London in 1853 – and against the unmanliness associated with Catholicism and Tractarianism. Through sexual and family relationships man expressed his energies, reproduced the race, created a divinely sanctioned microcosm of social unity and developed a sense of the common interest uniting him to past and future generations.

Therefore, with the exception of Ludlow, the Christian Socialists were only 'socialist' in the limited sense that they took their stand against 'the unsocial Christians and the unChristian Socialists'.[43] In practice they argued that socialism, Chartism and moderate Parliamentary reform were all superficial distractions from the true reformation of values that was required. Their major contribution was the effect that their work among the poor – and the belief that Maurice had actually discovered a way of communicating Christian principles to them – had on the upper- and upper-middle-class conscience. Large numbers of guilty, socially concerned propertied young men fell under the Christian Socialist spell in the 1850s, including subsequent leading Liberal politicians such as Bruce, Spencer and Goderich (the future Ripon). One reason why both Kingsley and Maurice were made professors at Cambridge in the 1860s was because of the perceived success of their appeal to the young. They contributed to the process by which the Liberal elite was recast intellectually and revitalised politically after the onslaught of 1848–50.

---

[41] To Ludlow, 24 Mar. 1848, Maurice, *Maurice*, vol. I, p. 459.
[42] Maurice, *Reformation of society*, p. 37.
[43] Maurice to Ludlow, 1850, Maurice, *Maurice*, vol. II, p. 35.

In the shorter term, however, Christian Socialism was generally regarded with some suspicion because of its criticism of English social practices. For example, Ludlow (educated in France, at the Collège Bourbon) adopted French ideas of communal organisation. In the 1850s most counter-cultural Liberal intellectuals, like the Christian Socialists, laid themselves open to attack by more insular critics. But it should not be assumed that they were not patriots. On the whole, they were concerned, as chapter 5 argues, with Britain's political and intellectual duty to lead the way to a synthesis, a higher unity, out of different national characters and customs. Most of them thought that French and German culture was flawed in one direction at least as strongly as English culture was lacking in the other. Maurice was certainly critical of German intellectual abstraction. Indeed he was a devoted patriot for whom the Church, the nation and the family were the three parts of the 'spiritual constitution': the Church's role was to lead the other two in their common task of 'healing the strife of classes'.[44] The nation was a sacred symbol of universal brotherhood, the largest which most men could imagine, and its actions, at home and abroad, should reflect the teaching of Christ.[45] Kingsley's patriotism was even more intense: he was delighted that officers from the Aldershot barracks attended his sermons at Eversley and returned his hospitality.[46]

Another significant group in the counter-cultural camp were the elite Unitarians who contributed so much to the cultural, theological and political world of the major provincial towns in the early Victorian period. In casting aside the Trinity, Unitarians believed that they were paring Christianity down to those essentials that were compatible with the exercise of reason. They rejected ideas of eternal punishment and believed that progress towards the perfection of humanity envisaged by God could be achieved through education, intellectual discovery, socialisation and the application of wealth to social improvement through humanitarian civic activity. So they had a tradition of local political commitment.[47] However, in practice the old Unitarian communities often tended towards rationalism, complacency and materialism. The turn towards idealism in Unitarian thought from the 1830s and 1840s, responding to trends in German and American thinking, checked that complacency and thus reinvigorated Unitarian community values. Preachers like James Martineau, J. J. Tayler and J. H. Thom were less interested in external evidences and literal scripturalism

---

[44] Ibid., vol. I, p. 306 (1841), vol. II, p. 376 (1860).    [45] See H. S. Jones, 'Idea of the national'.
[46] S. Chitty, *The beast and the monk: a life of Charles Kingsley* (London, 1974), p. 196.
[47] See R. Watts, *Gender, power and the Unitarians in England, 1760–1860* (London, 1998).

than in man's spiritual wants and indwelling divinity. They placed emphasis on the development of conscience, soul and mind as a way of reaching a fuller, continuously evolving and dynamic relationship with God. They valued German ideas of free enquiry and progressive education of the spirit, believing that they would help to create a common social consciousness. Respect for and obligation to one's fellow-men was a step towards reconciliation with God, individually and collectively. Before 1850 Unitarians were significant in their own communities but very conscious of being at odds with mainstream religious culture, still strongly evangelical or high church. But then the theological climate became more propitious, and preachers like Martineau developed a wider following. In 1858 he commented that Unitarian doctrinal beliefs had become much less controversial. The problem, he went on, was self-satisfied complacency, which had frustrated the social consequences – the greater sense of brotherhood – that should follow. 'The old arrangements, the old divisions of class, remain and rule exactly as before.' The Church Establishment's social power and the pull of materialism were as strong as ever.[48]

Unitarians were to the fore in the most important ethical political movement arising from this counter-cultural dislike of social philistinism and *laissez-faire*: the drive for a national education system. Poverty, degradation and ignorance should not be passively justified by evangelical arguments about man's free will; nor was the improvement of character a simple affair of following particular laws and principles, as early-century utilitarians had argued. Character was shaped by many social factors, and considerable effort was needed to train the human faculties in order to develop the full man – and woman. In 1850 a largely Unitarian Lancashire pressure group developed into the National Public Schools Association (NPSA), which lobbied for a national system of free rate-supported schools teaching secular subjects. Its leading lights were Cobden (not a Unitarian) and W. J. Fox, and it held up the United States and particularly Massachusetts as a model to follow. Cobden told the NPSA that secular education in New England had strengthened American morality, by bolstering the enlightened private judgment on which Protestantism rested, and that a similar system in Britain would 'purify the moral atmosphere of the State'. Moreover, despite the generally held 'comfortable delusion that we are placed at . . . an unmeasurable height above all other races', the Great Exhibition had revealed British inferiority and, particularly, the economic threat from

---

[48] 31 Dec. 1858, J. E. Carpenter, *James Martineau, theologian and teacher: a study of his life and thought* (London, 1905), p. 403. I owe this reference to Boyd Hilton.

America.[49] It was important for educational activists to deny the conventional libertarian claim that national education systems were necessarily tools of despotic governments – by pointing out that they were founded, as in Prussia and Scotland, on Protestant zeal to make the biblical message understood.[50] In the gloomy circumstances of the late 1840s the Lancashire Anglican Liberal Joseph Kay also looked abroad, to Germany, Switzerland, Holland and Scandinavia, to show the benefits of a systematic popular education, though he wanted more safeguards for religious education than the NPSA. He argued that the English, 'one of the most pauperised, demoralised, and worst educated people in Europe', would not otherwise be able to absorb the Protestant morality that alone could save the country from unrest, democracy and economic decline.[51]

Divisions among educational reformers about the respective roles of state and Church, and the terms on which religion should be taught, ensured that the cause of state education made very slow progress in the 1850s, until the appointment of the Newcastle Commission in 1858. Nonetheless it was generally agreed by them that the Church lacked the necessary national reach to offer an adequate education, and that the state must act in some form. Maurice, for example, underwent a crucial shift of attitude after 1848. In 1839–40 he had seen the state as a sinister utilitarian vested interest; his fulminations against the irreligion of the Whigs' education scheme had made him a darling of the Anglican establishment and had led to his appointment as a standard-bearer for Anglicanism at King's College London. By 1851 he was defending the policy of Russell's government, that the state should work with schools of different denominations, against the obstructive policy of an influential party in the Anglican National Society headed by Archdeacon Denison.[52]

In the 1860s, education policy played a central role in the rediscovery of Liberal domestic vigour after the Parliamentary apathy that had characterised Palmerston's premiership. Education was generally seen as the first thing necessary to create a sounder community and stronger national character, as part of a more general emphasis on the need for social interventionism.[53] Liberal reformers paid attention to the elementary,

---

[49] Mrs Salis Schwabe, *Reminiscences of Richard Cobden* (London, 1895), pp. 113, 141–3, 164–5, 170–4. In 1838 Cobden, on a trip to Germany, had been very impressed with the social effects of the Prussian education system: J. Morley, *The life of Richard Cobden* (2 vols., London, 1896 edn), vol. I, pp. 130–1.

[50] A. J. Mundella, *Hansard*, 202:1730, 8 July 1870.

[51] Joseph Kay, *The social condition and education of the people in England and Europe* (2 vols., London, 1850), vol. II, pp. 506–11.

[52] Maurice, *Maurice*, vol. I, pp. 273, 277, 546–7, vol. II, pp. 60–1.

[53] See, for example, the great success of the satirical story *Ginx's baby* (1870), by the future Liberal MP Edward Jenkins, which went through thirty-six editions in six years. It concerned the short

middle-class and university level. For example, the movement for the abolition of clerical tests at Oxford and Cambridge was a movement to create a truly national culture, by making the universities more attractive, not just to Nonconformists, but also to all social classes. This would help to elevate the intellectual horizons of future urban leaders as well as broadening Churchmen's minds and ensuring that England could compete with continental thought.[54] Assisted by the findings of the Royal Commissions of the 1860s, Gladstone's first government of 1868–74 reformed middle-class schools in 1869, the elementary system in 1870 and the universities in 1871. This was part of a general burst of activity for social and moral improvement, against vice, crime, ignorance and pauperism. The Licensing Bills of 1871 and 1872 sought to regulate the number of licences, reduce public-house opening hours and increase policing there. The 1870 Married Women's Property Act was a response to a fear that drink was preventing working-class husbands from protecting the living standards and respectability of their families, and it sought to give the wife limited control over her own property, as a check against family indebtedness.[55] Public health legislation of 1871 and 1872 created a comprehensive network of local sanitary authorities, each with specific obligations and a medical officer. In 1869 the government tightened the workhouse test in order to reduce the poor-rate burden and strengthened its power of arrest over frequently offending criminals in the Habitual Criminals Act.[56] In the same year was passed the last of the three Contagious Diseases Acts, under which prostitutes in eighteen protected districts around garrison stations who were suspected of carrying venereal disease could be incarcerated in special hospitals on the orders of a salaried permanent official staff. These Acts were promoted by an alliance between medical opinion concerned with the spread of disease and degeneracy, and the War Office, anxious about efficiency and hygiene in the army. Some Radical intellectuals supported them: the Millite John Morley hoped that they would protect the 'health and vigour' of the next generation by disciplining the 'permanently brutalised natures' of the underclass.[57]

and unhappy life of an unwanted child, 'God's work', for whom the law did nothing except create obstacles, because the tone of the country was unsympathetic to legislation, while religious denominations and philanthropists squabbled and split hairs rather than displaying real religious spirit.

[54] Parry, *Rise and fall*, p. 228; Harvie, *Lights of Liberalism*, pp. 145–6.

[55] For these reforms in general, see Parry, *Rise and fall*, ch. 10. For gender issues, see B. Griffin, 'Class, gender, and Liberalism in Parliament, 1868–1882: the case of the Married Women's Property Acts', *Historical Journal*, 46 (2003), 59–87.

[56] Parry, *Rise and fall*, pp. 236–41.

[57] F. B. Smith, 'Ethics and disease in the later 19th century: the Contagious Diseases Acts', *Historical Studies: Australia & New Zealand*, 15 (1971), 119–25. For another Millite, Amberley, see 1 Jan. 1870,

These measures clearly reflect the influence of three traditions of inter-ventionist Liberalism: Russell's Whig moralism, utilitarianism (significant for the new Chancellor, Robert Lowe), and Christian Socialism. Gladstone's government included the Christian Socialists Bruce, as Home Secretary, and Ripon and W. E. Forster as the two ministers with responsibility for education. All three had entered politics in the hope of doing something for the condition of the people and were strong opponents of *laissez-faire*.[58] Other cabinet ministers in favour of strong executive leadership included Kimberley, who had disliked the feebleness of the Home Office in the early 1860s, and Hugh Childers, who pined for the development of a French-style 'administration'.[59] One aim of Gladstone's was that a packed programme of 'gigantic' bills would also discipline Parliament and prevent the danger that a newly Radical body might make factional attacks on property, indi-viduals or classes.[60] Meanwhile, earnest and civic-minded northern MPs such as Forster (Bradford) and A. J. Mundella (Sheffield) saw Parliamentary activity as demonstrating the virtuousness of the political process.

Many MPs – Conservative and Liberal – felt that, just as after the pre-vious Reform Act in 1832, the state could use its enhanced legitimacy to intervene to preserve social order and to improve moral and educational standards in the new electorate – for example by tackling working-class drunkenness. The Christian Socialist commentator Ludlow attacked the immorality of non-interventionism at home and abroad as 'freedom to do everything and bear everything for the sake of gain; freedom to trade away truth, honour, self-respect, the lives of others, ay, and one's very own life, to-morrow, in order to fill one's purse to-day' instead of feeling that 'all Englishmen throughout the world' were 'members one of another'.[61] J. A. Froude, editor of *Fraser's Magazine* and a disciple of Carlyle, claimed that drunkenness and vice flourished in the cities and that armies of profes-sional burglars ruled the streets, but the 'universal root of the disorders which are preying upon us' was 'the all-pervading, all-devouring love of money', driving the mistaken 'thing which we call self-government' but was really 'anarchy and no government at all'.[62] Liberal advocates of state

to F. Newman, in B. Russell and P. Russell (eds.), *The Amberley papers: the letters and diaries of Lord and Lady Amberley* (2 vols., London, 1937), vol. II, p. 316. Mill opposed the Acts.

[58] See e.g. A. Denholm, *Lord Ripon 1827–1909: a political biography* (London, 1982), pp. 49–53 for their interest in industrial arbitration as well as education.

[59] To Gavan Duffy, 19 April 1872, in S. Childers, *The life and correspondence of the right hon. Hugh C. E. Childers 1827–1896* (2 vols., London, 1901), vol. I, p. 209.

[60] To Spencer, 16 July 1870, *Red Earl*, vol. I, pp. 85–6.

[61] J. M. Ludlow, 'The reconstitution of England', *Contemporary Review*, 16 (1871), 507–8.

[62] 'England's war', *Fraser's Magazine*, 3 n.s. (1871), 140, 147.

intervention usually insisted that a wise state could help men to help themselves, without damaging liberty, private philanthropy, or political economy principles.[63] The idea of a science of society was popularised by the annual conferences of the Social Science Association (SSA), which produced a vast body of information about social trends and urged legislative responses in each of its five areas of expertise: legal reform, education, penal reform, public health and social economy.[64]

The SSA also publicised foreign legislation which could act as a good model. So did the Royal Commission inquiries of the late 1850s and 1860s; Matthew Arnold, for example, was sent by the Newcastle Commission to report on elementary schools in France, Switzerland and Holland.[65] The Contagious Diseases Acts were strongly influenced by the example of France and Prussia, where the regulation of prostitution was well established and seemed to have improved public hygiene and military efficiency. Admiration for the perceived domesticity, sobriety and morality of the German lower and middle classes was a repeated theme of commentators and contributed to the pressure for education legislation in 1869–70.[66]

But just as in the political field, this Liberal ethical statism was to be badly checked between 1870 and 1874. It fell foul of another reaction against state interference with the individual moral conscience. Statism was said to be materialist and un-English; the health of England could only be protected by liberating that conscience. When, in 1870, compulsory school attendance was unsuccessfully advocated in the Commons, the Radical MP Leatham accused its main supporter, Mundella, of 'for ever casting a longing glance at the ways and institutions of the Continent, Continental notions of government, and Continental notions of liberty', instead of the principles 'under which our country has grown great'.[67] Several policy disputes stimulated this reaction, but two – education and contagious diseases – are particularly significant, because of the damage that they did to Liberal party unity, and because they demonstrated the political power of the most important component of ethical Liberalism not yet discussed: orthodox Nonconformity. However, this was arguably the last hurrah for anti-statist Nonconformity. The evolving views of evangelical Dissenters

---

[63] Parry, *Democracy and religion*, pp. 112–15, summarises a number of articles to this effect.
[64] L. Goldman, *Science, reform, and politics in Victorian Britain: the Social Science Association 1857–1886* (Cambridge, 2002).
[65] M. Arnold, *The popular education of France, with notices of that of Holland and Switzerland* (London, 1861).
[66] Parry, *Democracy and religion*, p. 113.      [67] *Hansard*, 202:1724, 8 July 1870.

on the relation between state, conscience and patriotism are crucial to understanding the strains of Liberal moral politics.

## EVANGELICAL NONCONFORMITY: DEFENDING THE CITADEL OF VIRTUE

In 1871–3 three pressure groups felt so strongly about aspects of Liberal legislation that they put up a number of by-election candidates against official Liberals to make their case. All three were determined to assert the supremacy of conscience over party whipping: they demanded that MPs should pledge to support moral causes if their constituents so demanded, rather than meekly following the party line. These campaigns, in which orthodox evangelical Nonconformists were heavily involved, reflected a determination that the morality of the virtuous voter should shape politics in the post-1867 era, rather than the enfeebled morality of the Westminster elite. All three, and particularly the last two, were also motivated by hostility to continental regulation, which seemed to have rotted conscience and true morality. Alien habits, secularist and materialist, must not be allowed to take root in England. If zeal was sufficient, the country could be preserved as a true community of spirit, a land of moral conscience, and virtuous values could be extended to the new electorate.

One of these campaigns, that for temperance by the United Kingdom Alliance, reflected a probably misplaced confidence that if given the choice, a moralised electorate would wish to tighten restrictions on the sale of alcohol.[68] A second, the campaign for disestablishment and for the withdrawal of state support for religious teaching, was the most important and revealing of the three and is discussed in chapter 6 because of its Irish dimensions. It was motivated by Dissenting anxiety to protect English morals from the threats of secularism at home and Ultramontanism in Ireland. Many Nonconformists argued that the only way to preserve both freedom and equality of conscience in the ecclesiastical and educational arenas across the United Kingdom was for the state to abandon any religious affiliation. This was the culmination of Nonconformist pressure for disestablishment in England.

The third was the agitation against the Contagious Diseases Acts. The extension of the Acts' system to eighteen large districts, in 1869, was the catalyst for the opposition to them mounted by Josephine Butler and a coalition of evangelicals, libertarian Radicals and feminists, which was finally

---

[68] B. Harrison, *Drink and the Victorians*, ch. 13; Hamer, *Politics of electoral pressure*, pp. 179–99.

successful in the 1880s. This campaign is much discussed in modern historiography as an assertion of women's equality before the law, and rightly so, since many of the leaders were Unitarian or Mazzinian advocates of women's entitlement to humanitarian treatment by the state. But it was also an attempt to secure those rights in face of a threat, a 'Continental system of legislating on behalf of vice and against women',[69] which had 'found a footing in our land'. The campaigners against the legislation insisted that it violated the basic principles of the English constitution, by denying an equal moral and legal standard for men and women. The repealers argued that 'the Napoleonic system' removed guarantees of personal security for women, put their freedom and reputation in the hands of the police and threatened to brutalise them. At the same time, state regulation of prostitution made 'the path of evil . . . more easy to our sons'. Here was another example of 'centralization' and 'police espionage'. It raised the prospect that the standards of the infamous Morals Police of Paris, widely said to be an agency of corruption and bribery, would be imported into Britain. And it deprived individual citizens of their Christian duty to patrol moral standards themselves, thus weakening the sense of individual responsibility and humanity without which a virtuous polity could not exist. Butler claimed that Prussia's aggressive military expansion of 1864–70, endangering European peace, was the result of the enfeeblement of the once-mighty German Protestant conscience by an over-mighty state.[70] All in all, an 'evil thing' was 'threatening our land', and 'a practical repentance' was necessary from Parliament and government.[71] Butler felt that the campaign was inspired by a special charge from God to reassert the principles of the 'Divine government of the world' against the threat from 'gross materialism and the most cruel and oppressive despotism'.[72] Because of that certainty the activists rejected the compromise proposed by the government in 1872, with Mill's assistance, which would have abolished the Acts but retained the certified hospitals and allowed voluntary examination (which many prostitutes would have welcomed).

These agitations of the early 1870s can therefore be seen in the context of Dissenting anxiety to maintain the distinctiveness of the English character, in the face of the 1867 Reform Act and of the collapse of France, the

---

[69] J. L. Paton, *John Brown Paton: a biography* (London, 1914), p. 133. Paton was Principal of the Congregational Institute.

[70] G. Petrie, *A singular iniquity: the campaigns of Josephine Butler* (London, 1971), pp. 127–8.

[71] G. W. and L. A. Johnson (eds.), *Josephine E. Butler: an autobiographical memoir* (Bristol, 1909), pp. 88–90, 94–6, 113–24.

[72] [J. Butler,] *The constitution violated: an essay* (Edinburgh, 1871), pp. 175–6.

Pope's assertion of power at the Vatican Council, and the rise of Prussian state autocracy. They reflected a traditional and intense Nonconformist suspicion of elitist state immorality. Yet they also revealed a trend in Nonconformity towards engaging the people in a moralistic politics of conscience, which could then harness the power of the state for good. This was the case over temperance legislation, for example. Therefore, though Dissenting anti-statism was superficially very powerful in 1870–4, it was being undermined by changing attitudes to politics. Even on the disestablishment question, where it seemed very virulent, the grounds for action were increasingly different from those which had animated the movement in the 1840s and 1850s.

Intensely aware of sin and materialism, orthodox Nonconformists – by which we mainly mean Congregationalists and Baptists – were concerned above all with liberating the believer's individual conscience and securing his right to a personal relationship with God. State authority, like the priesthood, denied that freedom and undercut Christ's authority. Liberty for the regenerate soul meant accepting subordination to God in a personal relationship. The principles of Christianity were universal, but the Establishment set man apart from man because it was a mere human organisation, constructed on a geographical rather than a doctrinal basis. The alliance with the state corrupted the Church's purity and spiritual zeal; the search for a national appeal led it to fudge doctrinal truth.[73] Disestablishment would bring it back to basics. All sects could work to tackle the sin and sorrow in the world, and to restore man to harmony with God. England without its Established Church would be more religious, not less.[74]

These beliefs were genuinely held, but they could easily remain abstract principles. Independency was fundamental to Congregationalists but did not force them to impose their vision on Anglicans. In order to become involved in a major political campaign for disestablishment, Nonconformists needed to be goaded to feel that the Church–state connection was an unacceptable evil. It was no accident that Radical Nonconformists took up disestablishment as a cry in the 1840s, at the time when political Radical suspicion of the oppressiveness and sectionalism of the state was at its height, and the need for national spiritual purification in the face of depression and social affliction seemed most urgent. It was easy to portray the Anglican Church as seduced from its evangelising duties by its extensive patronage structure, which gave material benefits to the same propertied class that controlled the state. At this time, provincial Nonconformists,

---

[73] Parry, *Democracy and religion*, pp. 202–5.
[74] R. W. Dale, *The politics of Nonconformity: a lecture* (Manchester, 1871), pp. 31–2.

convinced that purity did not extend far outside their own spiritual communities, typically looked on the metropolitan political world as effete and un-Christian. The moralising power of religion seemed to keep provincial bourgeois England morally superior to that of the aristocracy, despite its commercialism. In the 1840s, Whig interest in extending state endowment to Catholicism, in Ireland and in English schools, was another stimulus to Nonconformists' campaign to cut the links between politics and religion. It led them into a vigorous agitation against a national system of state-supported education, and in favour of voluntaryism, which is discussed in chapter 3. It was widely held that only Nonconformists had secured the religious purity of Britain in the seventeenth century; probably only they could be relied on to do it again.[75]

In the anti-statist political culture of the 1850s, enthusiasm for disestablishment was naturally sustained. It was presented as the natural tendency of a liberal political society, rather than just a bitter attack on Church privilege: hence the decision to change the name of the disestablishment lobby group from the British Anti-State Church Association to the Liberation Society in 1853.[76] Nonconformists argued that the 1848 revolutions demonstrated the error of the German policy of state control of religion. Political repression led able students and teachers to develop contempt for churches which worked in league with the state. State officials lacked the spiritual energy to 'train . . . the will to religious submission'. This checked the development of the individual conscience and encouraged rationalism and 'indifference to religion', which strengthened the tendencies to both absolutism and anarchy.[77] Some orthodox Nonconformists were also suspicious of German theological enquiry. In 1851 J. A. James thought that German scepticism and mysticism was a much greater threat to true religion than popery.[78] Even Edward Miall, the prominent journalist and politician, who was more sympathetic, blamed the haziness of German theology on 'universal smoking', which left nothing clearly visible.[79]

Yet the European comparison also made Nonconformists reflect on British national history and their place in it. Their task was to protect the spiritual purity of the community against a variety of threats to it, not

---

[75] Parry, 'Nonconformity, clericalism', pp. 156–8.

[76] T. Larsen, *Friends of religious equality: Nonconformist politics in mid-Victorian England* (Woodbridge, 1999), pp. 83–4.

[77] *Nonconformist*, 4 Oct., 11 Oct., 15 Nov. 1848, pp. 754, 767, 865–6. These remained standard themes: see R. W. Dale, 'The conference of Nonconformists', *British Quarterly Review*, 55 (1872), 520–2 (on training the will).

[78] 18 Sept. 1851, to Dr Sprague, in R. W. Dale, *The life and letters of John Angell James* (London, 1861), p. 545.

[79] 29 Sept. 1849, to J. M. Webb, in A. Miall, *Life of Edward Miall* (London, 1884), p. 162.

just from state oppression or corruption at home, but also, perhaps more pressingly, from popery and loose thinking abroad. The panic about papal aggression in 1850 had a profound effect on them, leading many to make a declaration of their loyalty to the British state against the threat from an over-mighty Catholic priesthood (see chapter 4). Identification with the historic national struggle against Catholicism – 'one of the chief bonds of our national unity'[80] – was very strong within Nonconformist communities. Nonconformists' place in history was reiterated in 1862 with the bicentenary celebrations of the ejection of nearly two thousand ministers from the Church of England in 1662 because their consciences would not permit them to accept the spiritual intolerance necessary to create uniformity in the national Church. By acting on their conscience, and following the will of God as they saw it, the men of 1662 had made spiritual and temporal tyranny in Britain impossible, ensured that a Parliamentary Church could never be coexistent with the nation and had ensured that, whatever the corruptions of political leaders, spirituality and freedom of conscience had prospered and the moral fabric of the country had not rotted away.[81] The celebrations reinforced an interest in theological scholarship on Puritan spiritual traditions which might revive the zeal and intensity of the 'heroic men who belonged to the times of the Commonwealth'.[82] And Cromwell was now generally seen as a statesman of conscience and an exemplary Englishmen – a serious, energetic, devout fighter against sensuality and luxury. In new northern town halls – such as Rochdale and Leeds – he was portrayed in a line of English rulers, as a symbol of the nation's civic republicanism. He had selflessly punctured the Tory notion of monarchy: Maguire's painting of *Cromwell refusing the Crown* was wildly praised on a tour of northern cities in 1859–61.[83]

By the 1860s and 1870s evangelical Nonconformists were happy to see themselves as a crucial force in national history, 'English of the English', who had secured 'civil and religious freedom' against 'royal and ecclesiastical imperiousness'.[84] Their loyalty to constitutional monarchy was undoubted;

---

80   R. W. Dale, *Protestantism: its ultimate principle* (London, 1874), pp. 10–11.
81   See the sermons featured in the *Nonconformist* between 13 Aug. and 3 Sept. 1862.
82   A. W. W. Dale, *The life of R. W. Dale of Birmingham* (London, 1898), p. 108.
83   R. Samuel, 'The discovery of Puritanism, 1820–1914: a preliminary sketch', in J. Garnett and H. C. G. Matthew (eds.), *Revival and religion since 1700: essays for John Walsh* (London, 1993), pp. 214, 220; Worden, 'Victorians and Cromwell', pp. 124–5.
84   Dr Kennedy, Chairman of the Congregational Union, at its Nottingham meeting: *Nonconformist*, 16 Oct. 1872, p. 1055; E. Miall at Manchester, in *Nonconformist*, 15 Jan. 1873, p. 59; Henry Vincent at Manchester, in *Report of the General Conference of Nonconformists, held in Manchester, January 23, 24, and 25, 1872* (Manchester, 1872), pp. 203–5.

indeed they could take the credit for the establishment of the House of Hanover.[85] Their religious communities were becoming less insular and more willing to appreciate the moral virtue of other elements in national life. Their perception of the Church Establishment improved, as a result of its inner-city philanthropy and a number of liberal evangelical appointments to senior positions. One Nonconformist claimed in 1862 that Dissenters' example had helped to make the Church 'more spiritual, more earnest'. Even so, many still felt oppressed by Church privilege and social superiority, reflecting a widespread sense in the early 1860s that Establishment culture was too complacent.[86] The resulting campaign against Church rates was driven by anger at the continuing materialism and power of the Church, especially in rural areas. But it was also increasingly clear that further Parliamentary reform would decisively improve Nonconformist political strength, and Church-rate abolition immediately followed the 1867 Reform Act.[87] Nonconformists' suspicion of the political process was being weakened by pride at the communal achievements of urban local authorities, as well as the changing image of the state discussed in chapter 1. Moreover, most Nonconformists had never been entirely comfortable with the old Radical strategy of blaming aristocratic politicians for national failures. They felt that it was the responsibility of each member of a Christian community to help to maintain its own virtue, rather than simply to pin the fault on elites. Voters should be taught by example the importance of taking responsibility for the ethical state of the nation.

In the 1850s and 1860s, as noted in chapter 1, there were already signs of Nonconformists accepting that a popular state could act for a Christian purpose and that they should take part in the struggle to infuse it with righteousness.[88] They were divided about the Obscene Publications Acts of 1857: the *Nonconformist*, as a politically Radical paper, still adopted the line that it was an illiberal increase of police power by an untrustworthy Establishment, but others welcomed it as a safeguard of respectability, and the libertarian opposition to it fizzled out.[89] As suspicion of the oppressiveness of the state began to wane, that side of Nonconformity which had a strong attachment to ideas of law and nationhood could express itself

---

[85] Revd G. Gould, *Nonconformist*, 3 Sept. 1862, p. 748.
[86] J. T. Brown, J. G. Miall, *Nonconformist*, 3 Sept. 1862, pp. 752, 749. Robert Vaughan claimed that the Church still persecutes us by 'many forms of social disparagement': *English Nonconformity* (London, 1862), p. 472.
[87] J. P. Ellens, *Religious routes to Gladstonian Liberalism: the Church rate conflict in England and Wales, 1832–1868* (University Park, PA, 1994).
[88] Stanley, 'Christian responses', pp. 283–9.     [89] Roberts, 'Obscene Publications Act', 623.

with less ambivalence. For R. W. Dale, and Eustace Conder, the 'social and political order of the nation' was 'a Divine institution'.[90] Though Nonconformists denied the national claims of a particular Church organisation, they assumed that the nation could and should be a religious community, suffused by the politics of conscience. In 1863 Dale expressed the hope that, if 'statesmen come from the sanctity of private communion with God to the great tasks of legislation and of diplomacy . . . without any formal profession of a national faith the national acts will be harmonious with the will of God'.[91]

The passage of Reform in 1867 and the settlement of the Church rates issue in 1868 were the most important factors in reconciling Nonconformists to the virtuousness and necessity of national politics. The number of Protestant Nonconformist MPs doubled between 1865 and 1868, to seventy. A significant indication of increased Radical Nonconformist trust of the state came in October 1867 when Miall, formerly a leading supporter of voluntary schools, accepted government interference in education explicitly because, he said, control of the state was passing from one class to another, so that there were no grounds for working-class suspicion of it.[92] The most prominent voluntaryist, Edward Baines, renounced it at the Congregational Union meeting in the same month. He realised from his experience on the Taunton Commission that educational efficiency could be achieved without a Prussian suppression of liberty. Moreover, he noted that public opinion was now strongly in favour of educating those in whose hands 'the safety of the empire' now rested.[93] Fear of atheism and a secularised democracy contributed enormously to this shift of view. Dale and Baldwin Brown talked of religion, together with intelligence, as crucial 'counter-balancing centrifugal forces' to the 'menacing . . . centripetal force in Democracy' which posed a 'terrible danger to the higher freedom and life of mankind'. They aimed instead to turn democracy into Christian paths, thus allowing it to fulfil its 'sacred mission'.[94]

The substantial franchise extension of 1867 thus brought home to local Nonconformist leaders the possibility and duty of shaping a moral society. One theme in the campaign for disestablishment in 1871–3 was Nonconformist confidence about the ability of private evangelical vigour to do this. This spiritual and political vision now motivated the disestablishment

---

[90] Parry, *Democracy and religion*, p. 202; E. R. Conder, *Liberty: an address delivered . . . in Sheffield, April 8th, 1879* (Leeds, 1879), p. 5.

[91] A. W. W. Dale, *Dale*, pp. 375–6.    [92] Miall, *Miall*, p. 273.

[93] E. Baines, *National education: address* (London, 1867), p. 8.

[94] J. Baldwin Brown, 'The English Church and Dissenters', *Contemporary Review*, 16 (1871), 320.

campaign more than a critique of the Church's oppressiveness – though the continued power of Anglican priests in rural areas was still a concern, as was the false teaching given by the rising number of ritualist priests. This was part of an anxiety that the Established Church was not very effective in defending personal religion, owing to the inability of a necessarily latitudinarian institution to check the development of unsound advanced speculation of the sort associated with *Essays and reviews*. 'Laxity of subscription' was 'injurious to public morals'.[95] These justifications ensured that the disestablishment movement was strongly supported between 1870 and 1873. However, none of these arguments were unchallengeable. It was a moot point whether it was wise to focus efforts on overthrowing a nationwide system of moral instruction at just the time that the democracy urgently needed education. Many Nonconformists, like Samuel Morley and Spurgeon, argued that this was certainly not a priority, and attached a higher importance to works of practical evangelicalism in cooperation with other Churches. Morley resigned from the Liberation Society in 1868. As a result, the most basic reason for the potency of disestablishment in 1870–3 lay elsewhere: with the Irish problem, as chapter 6 demonstrates. Disestablishment and secular education seemed the only proper bases on which to safeguard religious freedoms throughout the United Kingdom, and bind Ireland to Britain on equal terms, while frustrating the Ultramontane (and Anglican ritualist) revival. The threat from continental Catholicism, combined with sympathy for Irish political grievances, pushed very many Nonconformists into this position in the early 1870s; the secular strategy should be seen as primarily a political and ethical solution to a problem of integrating a nation. In other words, the major concern was now with equality of citizenship. And once the Irish and educational issues lost their intensity in 1873–4, the more fundamental doubts about whether disestablishment should be a priority resurfaced.

The priority, instead, now seemed to lie with building up the morality of politics and the morality of the poor, especially in the inner cities. On the first count, the Bulgarian agitation of 1876 and the campaign against Disraeli's unconstitutional and unethical imperialism in 1879–80 appeared to establish the principle that conscience rather than official and elite convenience should determine foreign policy. As chapter 7 shows, these movements asserted the responsibility of each voter to demand that those in charge of the state behaved in an appropriately Christian spirit – of which

---

[95] H. Allon, 'Why Nonconformists desire disestablishment', *Contemporary Review*, 17 (1871), 397; Parry, *Democracy and religion*, pp. 204–5.

Liberals believed 'Dizzi-ben-Dizzi' quite incapable. In 1879–80 the Liberal party welded the two things it cared for most – conscience and constitutionalism – into a grand synthesis of patriotic righteousness which swept it back into power. Nonconformity was now bound to the party, and to the political process, by the conviction that Liberalism could raise the ethical tone of politics. By contrast, the disestablishment movement waned after 1876 as soon as the Bulgarian agitation supplied an alternative vehicle for Nonconformist religious patriotism. In the 1880s, in England (but not Scotland or Wales where it was becoming associated with nationality issues), disestablishment of the Church was increasingly seen as a *distraction* from the business of defending the morality of the community, rather than an avenue to achieving it. In 1885 it was the Conservatives who were keenest to make a scare story about the 'Church in danger'; English Liberals were generally lukewarm about the disestablishment issue.[96] Therefore, to Liberal Anglican relief, it was never a front-line issue again. Thus were the two main Liberal strategies for the Christianisation of society reconciled.

More worryingly, by the 1880s, there were many signs that Christian morality cut less ice in national life. This was politically as well as spiritually troubling for Nonconformist preachers like Conder who believed that those who denied God were unable to 'provide any basis for public law or private freedom which does not substitute power for authority and expediency for justice'.[97] The anxiety about atheism was great enough for one evangelical Nonconformist, Samuel Morley, to oppose the admission to Parliament of the atheist Bradlaugh in 1880 – though for the vast majority of the Liberal party the Bradlaugh affair was not about morality but about the constitution, so they mounted a traditional Liberal defence of Parliament's inclusiveness.[98] How, then, could the morality of the community be defended against the threats posed by the fashionable, complacent elites and by the masses?

In the 1880s Nonconformity was affected by a panic about the maintenance of national moral purity, culminating in 1885 – the year of a further dramatic extension of the electorate. After a major petitioning effort in 1882–3, the Contagious Diseases Acts were suspended in 1883 and repealed

---

[96] A. Simon, 'Church disestablishment as a factor in the general election of 1885', *Historical Journal*, 18 (1975), 791–820.

[97] Conder, *Liberty*, p. 5.

[98] W. L. Arnstein, *The Bradlaugh case: a study in late Victorian opinion and politics* (Oxford, 1965), p. 135.

in 1886, a victory for those who regarded state regulation of prostitution as a morally unacceptable retreat into 'materialistic utilitarianism'.[99] However, repeal did nothing to solve the prostitution problem. The consequence was the channelling of moralist concerns into a number of activist campaigns against social evil, such as the social purity societies set up both by the Church and by Dissenting denominations from 1883. One of those activists, Andrew Mearns of the London Congregational Union, drew attention to the horrifying extent of child prostitution and incest in working-class London in his pamphlet, *The bitter cry of outcast London*, describing London as a vast mass of moral corruption, misery and godlessness. Mearns's publication had far-reaching consequences, mainly because it was publicised by the campaigning Liberal Dissenting journalist W. T. Stead in the *Pall Mall Gazette* in late 1883. The revelations about the moral state of London created unstoppable momentum for a high-profile Royal Commission on the Housing of the Working Classes the following year, which made so much more shocking information available that from now on the social question would be difficult for politicians to ignore. By the time of the Trafalgar Square riots of 1886 and 1887 there was a manifest propertied concern in London about a 'mighty mob . . . physically, morally, politically dangerous', likely to teach a lesson similar to that that 'the mob has tried to teach now and again in Paris'.[100] This helped to heighten permanently the profile of social reform issues.

In the short term, however, it was still issues of character and vice that most concerned Liberal activists. In 1885 Stead continued the campaign against inner-city vice with a sensational series of articles in the *Pall Mall Gazette* on the extent of juvenile prostitution in London, the 'modern Babylon', leading to the raising of the age of consent to sixteen in the 1885 Criminal Law Amendment Act. This panic took several forms. The National Vigilance Association was founded in 1885 after the passage of the Criminal Law Amendment Act, to assist the reformation of child prostitutes, to prevent them being procured to meet apparently insatiable demand for them on the Continent, and to close brothels. It was a forum for small-town moralists to protect the purity of their locality against infection from either London or abroad; by 1888 it had formed three hundred local branches. In the period up to 1914 the annual number of prosecutions of brothels

---

[99] *Methodist Protest*, 1876, cited in D. W. Bebbington, *The Nonconformist conscience: chapel and politics, 1870–1914* (London, 1982), p. 40.

[100] G. R. Sims (1889), cited in G. S. Jones, *Outcast London: a study in the relationship between classes in Victorian society* (New York, 1984 edn), pp. 224–5.

averaged over twelve hundred.[101] It also fought indecency in other forms: its most famous case came in 1888 and 1889 when, after a further outburst by Stead against 'foreign trash', it prosecuted the publisher Henry Vizetelly for his translations of Emile Zola's realist novels into English. These translations had been controversial since they began in 1885, leading among other protests to a famous one from Tennyson, in *Locksley Hall sixty years after* (1886), about the polluting effects of his approach on the morals of the young. In 1888 Gladstone claimed that 'the French novel was never so bad a dissolvent as it is now of all that binds a people into a progressive nation'.[102] Also in 1885 a marked increase in the number of nudes exhibited by young painters at the Royal Academy and the Grosvenor Gallery led to a vehement debate sparked off by a letter to *The Times* from 'a British matron', who saw in them a threat to morals and national stability.[103] And there was hostility to the idea of the French Sunday, especially when flamboyantly enjoyed by self-conscious modernising secularists. When a Secularist Cricket Club, wearing Bradlaugh's political colours, attempted to play cricket on Sunday in Leicester in 1885, their opponents tore up the wickets and threw the ball into the river.[104]

These campaigns said much about the spirit of small-town middle-class Liberalism in the 1880s. Dissenting Liberals were increasingly preoccupied with defending the idea of an ethical patriotic community against threats to it both at home and abroad. This struggle affected their approach to both social and foreign policy. The heart of their politics was not the struggle against the state or its Church but the development and defence of a moral nationhood.

Dealing with issues of state and Church posed problems for the Liberal mind, given its concern with elite guidance on the one hand but with protecting individual liberty from oppression on the other. Generalising about the Liberal ethical agenda is thus difficult. However, we can discern a hostility to complacency and prejudice in the Church, to domineering and old-fashioned priestcraft and to practices and habits that left human beings in thrall to ignorance and drunkenness. There was an impetus to develop morality and conscience, which was driven by a concern with social

---

[101] E. J. Bristow, *Vice and vigilance: purity movements in Britain since 1700* (Dublin, 1977), pp. 105–18, 154, 207–8.

[102] Quoted in E. Crawford, 'Emile Zola', *Contemporary Review*, 55 (1889), 94.

[103] 20 May, cited in A. Smith (ed.), *Exposed: the Victorian nude* (London, 2001), pp. 122–3.

[104] E. Royle, *Radicals, secularists and republicans: popular freethought in Britain, 1866–1915* (Manchester, 1980), p. 139.

order, but also by an anxiety to create an effective political citizenry and, for many, a properly Christian community as well. Working-class morals were objects of particular attention – and relatively easy subjects on which to get Parliament to pass legislation, especially in the years after the passage of Reform Acts. Middle- and upper-class behaviour was more difficult to legislate on, but politics is about setting a tone as well as producing statutes, and there were certainly enough influential voices in Parliament and the media urging a reformation of manners. Criticism focused on aspects of Victorian society which looked materialistic: its money-worship, its moral superficiality, its social hypocrisy.

Alarm at the potential tyranny of state and Church never disappeared, and was particularly intense in the late 1840s and early 1850s, and, to a lesser extent, in the early 1870s. Nonetheless, on the whole, suspicion of both waned as confidence in the moral power of the collective conscience grew, particularly from the 1860s. By the 1870s and 1880s even many freethinkers appreciated the ethical power of the Church Establishment: T. H. Green felt that disestablishment would make the clergyman a mere priest or preacher, instead of a leader in useful social work; T. H. Huxley wanted the Church to preach class reconciliation by setting before men's minds 'an ideal of true, just, and pure living'.[105] And even in the early 1870s many Liberals and Conservatives argued that state social reform, within limits, was immensely valuable, not least in warding off the dangers of Commune-style socialism by demonstrating that communal beneficence was compatible with the maintenance of individual responsibility.[106] After the depressing Liberal defeat of 1874, there was more acceptance of the need for educational and social reform to build a more united society, wage war on the residuum and offer a constructive politics. The pursuit of practical social legislation as an antidote to negative sectionalism in the party was the policy advocated by Forster and Mundella, and Forster's good showing in the leadership election of 1875 shows how much support there was for it in the Liberal party.[107] In the same way, Disraeli and his ministers were very aware of its attractiveness as a positive, relatively non-partisan and non-contentious cry.

One crucial reason for Liberal willingness to accept state social reform was the emphasis placed on the role of local government, participation

[105] 1871, in L. Huxley, *Life and letters of Thomas Henry Huxley* (2 vols., London, 1900), vol. I, p. 309.
[106] See e.g. duke of Northumberland, President of the Social Science Association, in *Illustrated London News*, 1 Oct. 1870, p. 342; D. Steele, *Lord Salisbury: a political biography* (London, 1999), pp. 79–81.
[107] P. Jackson, *Education Act Forster: a political biography of W. E. Forster (1818–1886)* (Madison, NJ, 1997), ch. 10. For Rosebery in 1874 on the need for legislative measures to tackle social division, see L. McKinstry, *Rosebery: statesman in turmoil* (London, 2005), p. 63.

and community in implementing it. A good example was education: by the 1880s most Liberals – even those Nonconformists originally most suspicious of state intervention – had become warm supporters of the idea of communal responsibility for education, through school boards, compulsory attendance, and local authority control. Talk of building up local powers in partnership with central government usefully stressed the state's grass-roots legitimacy at a time when central politics was still largely controlled by elites. It suggested a degree of popular sovereignty; it claimed to educate voters into political life and the exercise of individual responsibility, checking materialism; it prevented sectional 'faddists' from imposing a potentially unpopular policy on the whole country. One of the points on which Hartington and Chamberlain were agreed in the 1880s was that the extension of popular self-government was a cardinal Liberal principle.[108]

Arguments that England formed an effective political and ethical community, in which the powers of state, locality and individual were well balanced, were bolstered by comparison with the moral failings of France and other continental societies. Alarm at the supposedly enfeebling effects of continental materialism contributed to Liberal debates on a great range of subjects, appropriate and inappropriate, from religious education to contagious diseases, the Volunteer Force, and the Sabbath. As Gladstone said at Aberdeen in September 1871, 'the French nation, probably never would have undergone the frightful calamities which it has been destined to experience during the last 15 months' had its people acquired 'that kind of personal and individual self-reliance by which the people of this country are so largely distinguished'. England's 'national greatness' derived from 'the sense of individual responsibility for public matters, and the facility of combination in our local community'.[109]

In the 1880s the perception that socialism was making waves on the Continent strengthened these comparisons. By 'socialism' was usually meant a value system that did not respect individual responsibility and conscience and that instead believed that the state should be merely concerned with the distribution of material goods. Gladstone warned that the practice of giving 'large doles of public money' was inconsistent with the 'habits of self-government' that had protected the British from the problems that had afflicted foreign countries.[110] In 1885 Earl Cowper opined that outside Britain democracy had often led to a passive, degenerative Caesarism,

---

[108] Parry, *Rise and fall*, p. 241.      [109] *The Times*, 27 Sept. 1871, p. 6.
[110] At Dublin, *The Times*, 8 Nov. 1877, p. 7.

as in the French Second Empire, and that constitutional monarchy and patriotic and libertarian values were the best antidotes to it.[111] Frederic See-bohm, writing in 1880 about the threats posed globally to Liberal values by imperialism and socialism, believed that England – and its empire – stood the best chance of avoiding authoritarianism because the Liberal party was influenced by 'Christian spirit', which could guide democracy away from socialism by teaching the real meaning of individual responsibility and the brotherhood of man.[112] George Brodrick considered it necessary to carry 'the spirit of Christianity, democratic as it is . . . into political life' if we are to maintain 'a high national character'.[113]

In the early 1880s, then, Liberal commentators were still preoccupied with the problem of how to secure a distinctively ethical national community, based on moral – usually Christian – ideas and on a marriage of localist participation with elite guidance. This was certainly an anxiety for Gladstone, as it was for Nonconformists, as noted above. So it was for Liberal intellectuals like Seeley, who attached enormous significance to the strong nation-state both as an object of popular allegiance and as a means of projecting England's Providential destiny abroad. He envisaged that a national education system and moralised universities could bolster national confidence and coherence against cosmopolitan democratic and autocratic evils, just as Stein's reforms had consolidated Prussia against the Napoleonic threat.[114] Writers such as Green and Toynbee who could not accept orthodox Christian doctrines thought instead in terms of ethical humanist variants on it and justified interventionist social legislation in terms of bolstering the 'moral and material well-being' of the individual conscience against degrading poverty, atheism or amoral bureaucracy.[115] A successful Liberal language had to be ethical: supporters often described the party's mission in terms of making a nation, or improving the world, by freeing body and soul to do God's purpose, or creating a spiritual brotherhood of man which would override distinctions of class or race.[116]

---

[111] Earl Cowper, 'Caesarism', *Contemporary Review*, 17 (1885), 1–14. See also Sidgwick on fears of Caesarism and socialism in 1886: W. C. Lubenow, 'The Liberals and the national question: Irish Home Rule, nationalism, and their relationship to nineteenth-century Liberalism', *Parliamentary History*, 13 (1994), 134.

[112] F. Seebohm, 'Imperialism and socialism', *Nineteenth Century*, 7 (1880), 732–3.

[113] G. C. Brodrick, 'The progress of democracy in England', *Nineteenth Century*, 14 (1883), 923–4.

[114] R. Shannon, 'John Robert Seeley and the idea of a national Church', in R. Robson (ed.), *Ideas and institutions of Victorian Britain: essays in honour of George Kitson Clark* (London, 1967), pp. 240–55.

[115] T. H. Green, *Lectures on the principles of political obligation, and other writings*, ed. P. Harris and J. Morrow (Cambridge, 1986 edn), p. 204.

[116] See e.g. the various contributions in A. Reid (ed.), *Why I am a Liberal* (London, 1885), pp. 11, 27, 32, 59, 78, 83.

One reason for this preoccupation was concern about the nation's moral and political health. In the early 1880s another far-reaching Reform Bill beckoned; Conservatism was reviving, by exploiting class-based insecurities and materialism; atheism and socialism were gaining converts at home as well as abroad. In the same way, the Liberals' attempt to define an international ethical agenda for the 1880 government, discussed in chapter 7, was motivated not least by question marks about the continued purchase of English Liberal principles abroad in the face of rising international rivalry and protectionism. There is no doubt that domestic and external threats to Liberal values created great concern in the 1880s, and that in retrospect they were to prove extremely formidable.

On the other hand, nor had the Liberal ethical agenda at any previous time lacked powerful enemies. In the late 1830s and the early 1870s Liberals had been overwhelmed by a powerful Tory revival based on Anglican and propertied defensiveness. Materialism and apathy had been a constant problem in and outside Parliament. Liberals had often been divided on religious, educational and other moral issues, and groups within the party had accused their opponents of favouring 'un-English' values. For all the anxiety, in 1880 there were also reasons to be cheerful about the potency of Liberal ideals of citizenship, conscience and freedom – and about Britain's ability to assert its ideals abroad. These two sets of arguments were closely linked, as they had always been. The construction and defence of an effective political community and the preservation of its values against alien threats were themes as relevant to foreign as to domestic affairs.

PART II

*Europe and Liberal politics*

# CHAPTER 3

# Liberalism and the Continent, 1830–1847

As will already be clear from Part I, the Whig governments of the 1830s left an ambivalent legacy. They laid many of the foundations of nineteenth-century Liberalism, but the strategies they adopted also opened them to severe criticism from Radicals and others, especially in the 1840s. The principal components of this criticism were their preference for giving cabinet posts to aristocrats, their coolness to further constitutional reform, their enthusiasm for a sweepingly interventionist and national social policy, their belief in spending taxpayers' money on endowing religion in Britain and Ireland, and their failure to stop expenditure rising in the late 1830s. To many Chartists and other Radicals their poor-law and prison policies seemed offensively illiberal and hypocritically moralistic; yet both Anglicans and Nonconformists found their educational and religious policies insufficiently respectful of true religion and alarmingly heterodox, utilitarian or flippant. The result was a very powerful double shift of mood in the 1840s, away from 'aristocratic' and centralising government on the one hand, and in search of a moral reformation on the other. Whig patriotism was severely questioned.

Many themes of the 1830–47 period had an international context. This chapter confines itself to those issues which are most useful in understanding later Liberal politics. It considers, firstly, the fate of the two elements of Liberal strategy in the 1830s which had the clearest 'continental' relevance, each of them identified with one of the two leading Liberals of the next thirty years, Russell and Palmerston. Secondly, it reviews the two main Radical critiques of them in the 1840s, formulated by Cobden and by evangelical Nonconformity. All four approaches claimed to have a particular idea of England's mission and remained extremely significant for the party thereafter; but all also had an Achilles' heel which allowed their opponents to accuse them of being 'un-English'. These accusations contributed to the serious divisions in the Whig–Radical coalition by 1847.

One underlying reason for these tensions was insecurity about the strength of Liberalism, both at home and abroad. Its subsequent successes in Britain should not obscure its weak position in 1830. Whigs and Radicals had been in opposition for decades; the Reform coalition of 1830 was unwieldy and unstable; economic and political tensions remained massive. One consequence of this weakness was that the Whigs needed to look to the Continent for policy assistance. They lamented the effects of Tory insularity, which they felt had failed either to satisfy Irish Catholics or to fight Britain's corner in Europe. Russell's strategy to pacify Ireland required Britain to borrow from continental practices and to cooperate with the papacy. So did his educational policy for England. In Europe the Eastern powers were still formidable. To gain status abroad, Britain needed to work with a liberal France; it also needed to assert its naval and imperial power. Both of these strategies were controversial, especially the second in the economic depression of 1839–41. Palmerston's foreign policy was more effective in resisting the charge of lack of patriotism than Russell's Irish policy (or than Russell's variant on foreign policy). Indeed in 1840 he began to thrash his way towards the stance that would win him such political popularity between 1849 and 1853, by casting himself as a vigorous foe of autocracy. Even so, his high expenditure and attachment to the aristocratic diplomatic game seemed of a piece with the Whigs' governing tone, generating a lot of criticism in the mid-1840s. But the Radical alternatives to these foreign and Irish policies turned out to be equally problematical for Liberal unity and popularity.

### RUSSELL, EDUCATION, IRELAND AND EUROPE

The Whig governments' Irish and religious policy between 1834 and 1841 was the feature that most distinguished them from the Conservative party. On the one hand, it bound together an emerging 'Liberal party'; on the other, it contributed enormously to its electoral defeat in 1841. It was based on two principles. One was the commitment to constitutionalism, the attack on powerful vested interests and the integration of underprivileged groups which as a general Liberal theme was traced in chapter 1. The other was the emphasis on the moral duty of the state to defuse sectarian bitterness and educate children of all sects in the principles of religion, morality and toleration. This led to an interest in principles of appropriation and of concurrent endowment of Irish religions, as well as mixed education.

The Whigs had come to be strong upholders of the Union with Ireland. Victory over France in 1815 and Canningite optimism about Britain's global influence in the 1820s had established a climate of national pride in which Repeal would have been unacceptable – especially if suggested in 1830 by an untried government which had supplanted Britain's greatest military hero by promising stronger national leadership. But the Whigs went further, arguing that a responsible and active government which treated Catholics as 'the free subjects of a free country' could pacify Catholic discontents and solve the Irish question. Catholic Emancipation, achieved in 1829, would be the crucial first step to this. Giving them representation in the legislature would help to remove Catholics' legitimate suspicion of Irish government, which had been dominated by Protestant landlords – the 'miserable monopolising minority' who had ruled Ireland for generations without providing 'for the welfare of the people'.[1] The 1829 Act also required Catholic office-holders to swear loyalty to the Crown and renounce any conflicting allegiance to Rome. There would be no scope for 'foreign affections, and foreign intrigues'.[2] Constitutional liberalism would now constrain the power of the Roman Catholic Church.

A further stage in this strategy developed after the crisis of 1834–5. Emancipation created great turmoil in the Reform coalition because it led to the emergence in Irish politics of a strong O'Connellite lobby for further benefits for the Catholics. The tithe war had demonstrated the depth of Catholic hostility to the bloated Anglican Established Church. Many Reform MPs felt that the implication of the 1832 Reform Act was that Parliament had to listen to Catholic representatives and could not rule Ireland merely by coercion. As Howick said, if Britain would not govern Ireland by the 'consent of the people . . . you are not fit to govern her at all'.[3] The Reform government divided badly in 1834–5 on the question of responding to and working with Irish Catholics. When the Whigs returned to office in 1835 it was on the basis that they would willingly do so. Pragmatism and constitutional principle both dictated this. The government now required Irish support to survive in Parliament. But the more advanced Whigs also appreciated that to recognise O'Connell as the leading tribune of the Irish people would help to secure Irish support for the Union.

One significant theme of Whig Irish policy after 1835 was reliance on patronage politics to build a coalition with Irish Catholic MPs. State money was spent accordingly: ministers appointed at least six Catholics to political office, reformed the Irish political force, bringing in many Catholics,

---

[1] Russell, *Hansard*, 36:221, 7 Feb. 1837, and 47:17, 15 Apr. 1839. The alliterative phrase was borrowed from Fox.
[2] H. G. Ward, *Hansard*, 27:418, 30 Mar. 1835.    [3] *Hansard*, 29:947, 22 July 1835.

and removed large numbers of Protestant magistrates. Equally characteristic of Whiggery was the symbolically inclusive leadership posturing of
the Lord-Lieutenant Mulgrave.[4] The Whigs claimed that England and Ireland must be treated as one nation; Spring Rice wished to rename Ireland
'West Britain'.[5] Municipal reform, in 1840, opened the city of Dublin to
Catholic leadership (O'Connell was elected Lord Mayor in 1841), though
the House of Lords greatly limited the radical consequences for Ireland as
a whole. The government's various legislative and administrative initiatives
suggested that it was 'conquering the "anti-Saxon" Spirit of Ireland', in
O'Connell's words.[6] The strategy of cooperation with Catholic representatives and engagement with Catholic opinion seemed to be working. The
number of MPs advocating repeal of the Union fell sharply between 1835
and 1841.

The Whigs' Irish strategy was also founded on a high notion of the state's
responsibility to promote popular morals, and especially moral education,
as a support for stability and progress. Their policies were based on the
principle that the state was in practice more capable of diffusing morality
and religious understanding to the Irish people than a Church Establishment which was alien to the majority, and that the best instrument was
education, which was crucial for 'moral control'. Church Establishments
existed for 'the moral and religious instruction of the people', and endowments for that purpose must be made beneficial to the entire population
rather than just a minority: hence the call for appropriation of the Church
of Ireland's surplus revenues.[7] This was an extension of the Whig strategy
of forging political alliances with Catholic forces. It rested on the idea of
working with all the Churches, including the Catholic priests, to spread
morality. This was primarily a political rather than a theological strategy.
However, it was supported by various religious justifications. Some Whigs
argued from the Paleyite view that religion was a matter of private judgment
and that the state should support religion on the basis of its social utility,
not on some notion of divinely ordained truth. It was asserted that the
state should concentrate on an undogmatic education based on elementary
Christian precepts, because these would do most to make the Irish better
Christians. Surely it was pointless to squabble about the teaching of dogma,
all the more so since methods of biblical and historical enquiry pioneered in
Germany had confirmed that most Christian dogma was a human accretion

---

[4] Parry, *Rise and fall*, p. 139.
[5] Brent, *Liberal Anglican politics*, p. 51 (Mulgrave). Spring Rice, *Hansard*, 22:1193–4, 23 Apr. 1834.
[6] P. Scherer, *Lord John Russell: a biography* (Selinsgrove, 1999), p. 97.
[7] Russell and Morpeth, *Hansard*, 24:797, 749, 23 June 1834.

for irreligious purposes. And some were also confident that any education that promoted powers of reasoning and enlightenment would strengthen Protestantism and loyalty to England in the long run.[8]

Ireland was thought to be particularly suitable for an assertive government policy since the Irish Catholics, like many other Europeans, respected strong authority and firm leadership. In England the materials out of which progress grew – industry, diffusion of property, developed institutions, the emphasis on self-government and self-discipline – were inherent in civil society; in Ireland they were not. Over the Irish Sea, therefore, as Cornwall Lewis wrote in 1836, 'improvement and civilisation must . . . descend from above'.[9] Moreover in the absence of an advanced English-style public opinion, a strong state was needed to keep over-mighty landlord vested interests in check.[10] In 1848 Russell observed that 'the Irish are fashioned more like our continental neighbours than ourselves – that instead of detesting Government control they cannot well do without it – and that we cannot change the nature of a nation in this respect'.[11]

To govern Ireland well, therefore, continental models of state partnership with the various Churches would be useful. In most north-west European states, more than one religion was recognised and supported by the state, and laws were in place encouraging the education of children together while tolerating their right to be instructed in different religious opinions. The aim was to strengthen state power in the aftermath of revolution, using law and political pressure to discipline potentially destabilising religious fervour. Following Napoleon's policy, concordats with the Pope were signed after 1815 in a number of European states (in Italy, Germany, Switzerland and the Netherlands) which had substantial Catholic populations, regulating their constitutional position. The Prussian government, meanwhile, aimed in its Church Union policy of 1817 to increase state influence over the local Protestant clergy while bolstering the Church's position against possible Catholic proselytism.[12]

Prussian reformers in the 1810s also aimed to increase the number of non-confessional schools, teaching children of different sects together. In

---

[8] Howick, *Hansard*, 27:449, 29:935–6, 30 Mar., 22 July 1835; Russell, *Hansard*, 29:1054–5, 22 July 1835. On the older Whig view, see G. F. A. Best, 'The Whigs and the Church Establishment in the age of Grey and Holland', *History*, 45 (1960), 103–18.

[9] G. C. Lewis, *On local disturbances in Ireland; and on the Irish Church question* (London, 1836), p. vi.

[10] Russell, Apr. 1846, quoted in P. Gray, *Famine, land and politics: British government and Irish society, 1843–1850* (Dublin, 1999), p. 142.

[11] 21 May 1848, Gray, *Famine, land and politics*, p. 207.

[12] See C. Clark, 'The Napoleonic moment in Prussian Church policy', in D. Laven and L. Riall (eds.), *Napoleon's legacy: problems of government in Restoration Europe* (Oxford, 2000), pp. 217–35.

fact, this policy softened in the 1820s in the face of Protestant and Catholic criticism of the anti-clerical fervour with which the state seemed to be pursuing this policy. As a result, in most areas in Prussia, and in many other states, there were at least two different schools in each locality, run by different sects, so that separate education was the norm rather than the exception. Nonetheless, the principle of supporting joint education where possible remained alive, both in Prussia and in Catholic Belgium under Dutch rule before 1830. The idea that all schools should offer some general religious education, to which all sects could relate, was held up as a model by British advocates of reform.[13] The Irish Catholic Liberal MP Thomas Wyse argued from continental examples that, even if children of different faiths were given their denominational instruction separately, there were still great benefits for 'public morals' in a national system of integrated general instruction.[14]

Continental example seemed to suggest that state support for religious sects and for undenominational religious teaching had assisted social integration in areas of diverse religious loyalties. In the Catholic provinces of the Rhineland, for instance, each denomination was entitled to state endowment, an arrangement established by Napoleon's Concordat and continued by the Prussians when they took it over. Several Whigs became intrigued by the Rhineland and other examples.[15] Cornewall Lewis, one of the government commissioners appointed in 1834 to inquire into the affairs and property of the Anglican Church in Ireland, argued that concurrent endowment, now so widespread in European states of mixed religion, had reduced sectarian tension and removed religion from politics in the Rhineland.[16] He and Palmerston felt that an adaptation of this policy in Ireland might produce 'the same happy results, in the absence of religious discord among the people, and the general good will of all persuasions towards the Government'.[17]

Why, therefore, should the state not offer endowment to Catholics and Ulster Presbyterians as well as Anglicans? This would put the policy of institutional support for Protestantism on a more defensible footing, make the Catholic clergy financially independent of their flock, and, crucially, enhance their loyalty to the state. It would be the ecclesiastical equivalent of

---

[13] See e.g. Ward, *Hansard*, 29:965, 23 July 1835.　　[14] *Hansard*, 48:544–5, 19 June 1839.
[15] See e.g. Littleton on Holland, Belgium and Saxony, *Hansard*, 27:584–5, 1 Apr. 1835.
[16] Lewis, *Local disturbances in Ireland*, pp. 425–8.
[17] *Papers relating to the Ecclesiastical Establishments of Prussia*, P. P. (1836), vol. XL, 315, p. vi. In a letter of 7 Nov. 1834, published in the report (p. 1), Palmerston considered that Prussia was a 'model for the imitation of other countries in such matters'.

the Whig policy of integrating Catholics by patronage politics. Clergymen would be better able to give spiritual and moral leadership independent of unabated popular zeal, political and religious, while the establishment of a patronage relationship with the state would encourage not just gratitude but mutual sympathy. Concurrent endowment would increase the state's hope of influencing the Catholic clergy, but would also demonstrate the state's impartiality, inclusiveness and benevolence, and facilitate a process of discussion and negotiation between sects. Moreover, concurrent endowment seemed the best basis on which to govern a global liberal empire. The Whigs acknowledged – much more readily than their Tory predecessors – that there was already a diversity of endowment of religion there. Prime Minister Melbourne argued in 1835 that Britain's 'great and mighty empire', the largest since the downfall of Rome, could only be upheld and governed well if 'you legislate according to the interests and feelings which prevail in every constituent part'.[18] Religious toleration and the civilising imperative seemed a central pillar of England's global moral power.

The most basic point at issue between Whigs and Tories, especially after 1834, was whether to govern Ireland on traditional Protestant principles or with an eye to 'civilised' practice in other European countries. It was a badge of pride and common sense for the Whigs to choose the latter. They charged that the Tories were responsible for the flagrant misgovernment of Ireland, most recently in resisting Catholic Emancipation. In clinging to a narrowly Protestant conception of national identity, they were doing great damage to Irish stability, contentment and prosperity. In 1836 the Tory peer Lyndhurst said that the majority of the Irish people were 'alien to Englishmen', a statement that Russell quickly denied and condemned.[19]

From these ideas, Whig ministers developed three policies for Ireland. Firstly, there was education, which was as important to the Whig strategy of Union as it was for the Prussians in building a sense of nationhood after 1807. In 1831 they imposed the system of providing secular and moral education to children of all sects together, with the possibility of additional separate denominational instruction. The subsidy which the pre-1830 Tory government had given to the Kildare Place Society – suspect to Catholics because it used the Protestant Bible – was now reallocated to the new system. Crucially, most of the Catholic bishops, led by Archbishop Murray, supported the government's proposal that the moral teaching should include daily school readings of biblical extracts which had been agreed

---

[18] *Hansard*, 30:728–9, 20 Aug. 1835. For a similar sentiment, see Russell, *Hansard*, 79:1010, 18 Apr. 1845.
[19] Lyndhurst, *Hansard*, 33:734, 9 May 1836; Russell, *Hansard*, 33:1288, 1 June 1836.

between leaders of the denominations. This was a major breakthrough, previously suggested by Spring Rice on the basis of a similar arrangement in France and Italy.[20] However, the consequence – that the Protestant Bible would not be taught in schools in its entirety – led to much Protestant anger, particularly in Ulster. Tories soon alleged that in practice the system was being dominated by the Catholic Church, especially since in southern Ireland many schools were attached to Catholic churches.

Secondly, between 1834 and 1838 British politics revolved around Russell's declaration of 1834 in favour of appropriation of the surplus revenues of the Established Anglican Church in Ireland. This was a political question, frequently related to questions about the Reformed Parliament's right to act on behalf of the whole nation. Supporters argued that everywhere else in Europe states had asserted their rights to deal with Church property in ways acceptable to, and of benefit to, the majority of the people; the British were uniquely backward.[21] It was particularly 'preposterous' for a state so proud of its Reformation to assert that Church property was inalienable.[22] In 1835 the Radical MP John Bowring also explicitly linked the Commons' support of appropriation with the moves being made by Britain's allies, the new liberal Portuguese and Spanish governments, to reallocate surplus clerical revenues to national purposes. In other words, these were the policies that Palmerston's interventionist liberal foreign policy would assist, striking a blow against exclusive clericalism.[23]

Thirdly, the refusal of the Tory-dominated Lords to accept the principle of appropriation led the Irish ministers in the Whig government to consider the full continental idea of state 'concurrent endowment' of the Catholic and Protestant religions, in the light of Lewis's report. This idea had in fact been mooted by previous governments at various times, but it was awkward since, if carried to its logical conclusion, it would, as Morpeth acknowledged, 'shake the whole framework of society'.[24] Russell had proposed it in October 1833, as part of a comprehensive Irish initiative, and it was raised on a number of occasions in the debates of 1834–5.[25] But in 1836–7, the cabinet again rejected it.

The reason why appropriation was never implemented and concurrent endowment was never even introduced was that the Whig strategy quickly

---

[20] T. Spring Rice, 'Education of the Irish poor', *Edinburgh Review*, 43 (1825), 222–3.
[21] Ward, *Hansard*, 23:1390, 27 May 1834; Bowring, *Hansard*, 27:821, 3 Apr. 1835.
[22] Shiel, *Hansard*, 33:1409, 2 June 1836.
[23] *Hansard*, 27:821, 3 Apr. 1835.    [24] *Hansard*, 33:219, 25 Apr. 1836.
[25] On 1833, see Brent, *Liberal Anglican politics*, pp. 88–9.

encountered extraordinarily strong opposition. This was because of a powerful religious reaction among both Protestants and Catholics in the late 1830s. As chapter 2 noted, this reaction was fuelled by a panic about morals at a time of social anxiety, and by the suspicion that the Whigs were unfriendly to real religion. It also reflected a trend across Europe – which was driven largely by alarm about anti-clerical tendencies in politics and in the field of thought. Over the next few years these developments all but destroyed Russell's strategy and the Whig government which was trying to implement it. In Britain the Conservative party benefited greatly from the sense that Anglicanism was under threat from erastian Whiggery, utilitarianism and politically active Dissent. Tories opposed appropriation on the ground that the Anglican Church was charged with the propagation of divine truth and that it was impious and dangerous to attack its property, especially at a time of Radical resurgence and social unrest. They also tapped Protestant and nationalist sentiment. They tended to deny that Europe could teach the British how to govern Ireland. Hardinge, for example, did not want Britain to follow the Belgian policy of giving state support to Jewish synagogues.[26] One young Tory, Gladstone, argued that the Rhineland analogy was inappropriate because the British would not tolerate the degree of state control over religious doctrine practised in Prussia.[27] O'Connell thundered that the Tories' insularity made them 'the laughing stock and the contempt of Europe'.[28] But it did them no harm among the English electorate.

Just as significant were growing indications of Catholic hostility to state entanglements which compromised their independence. In 1837 the Pope gave private support to the Irish bishops' resistance to concurrent endowment.[29] Across Europe the revival of Catholic Ultramontanism in the late 1830s reflected a widespread interest in spiritual devotion and mystical religious experience. Religious houses, missions and pilgrimages proliferated. Moreover interest in spirituality was also strong in neo-pietist Protestant circles. This movement across the religious denominations helped the Churches to challenge the attempts of post-revolutionary continental states to control religion through state policy. They were able to reverse the latitudinarian tendencies of Prussian educational policies and to achieve more safeguards for their own religious teaching, by claiming that state teacher-training seminaries were disseminating amoral Pestalozzian

[26] Hardinge, *Hansard*, 27:586, 1 Apr. 1835. See Bateson, *Hansard*, 29:971, 23 July 1835.
[27] *Hansard*, 33:1315–19, 1 June 1836.    [28] *Hansard*, 27:725, 2 Apr. 1835.
[29] D. A. Kerr, *Peel, priests and politics: Sir Robert Peel's administration and the Roman Catholic Church in Ireland, 1841–1846* (Oxford, 1982), p. 65.

educational ideals.[30] This religious reaction also benefited from growing
alarm at the rationalist movements in the universities, particularly in the
Germany of Feuerbach and Strauss.

In Ireland the Catholic backlash was led by Archbishop MacHale of
Tuam, who denounced the national education system in 1838. He disliked
the extent of government control and the latitudinarian content of the textbooks approved for classroom use, such as Whately's *Lessons on the truth
of Christianity*. He was also alarmed by talk in Whig circles of reforming
the Irish universities on German lines, with mixed education (but Protestant and Catholic theological faculties). MacHale, a strong Irish patriot,
felt that continental universities spread atheism and immorality: 'we have
heard enough about foreigners'.[31] Over the next two years he worked with
Paul Cullen, Rector of the Irish College at Rome, to try to persuade the
Vatican to denounce the national system. His attitude was controversial in
Ireland, since the national system was generally popular; the threat of out-
right condemnation was eventually staved off. Nonetheless, for the British
government this was a new and disturbing development in Irish politics.
The Whigs used diplomatic channels to try to influence the Vatican in
favour of the national system, claiming that it promoted 'habits of morality
and order' in Ireland. Indeed they also used the diplomatic entente with
the liberal French government – an entente to which Russell was particularly attached, as the next section shows – to help to make this point at
Rome.[32]

Ultramontane Catholic assertiveness quickly began to cause alarm in
Protestant circles in Europe and Britain. In the Rhineland the new Catholic
archbishop of Cologne, supported by the Pope, challenged the Prussian
state's policy on the religious instruction of children of mixed marriages.
The archbishop suspected that the Prussian state was seeking to use its
legal power to drive forward the Protestantisation of the Rhineland. He
demanded freedom for Catholic priests to refuse to approve mixed marriages under terms of which they disapproved. When he was arrested in
November 1837, the Pope supported him. The Prussian government eventually had to allow the Church a freer hand on the issue. British evangelical

---

[30] For pietist and separatist movements in Prussia, see C. M. Clark, 'The politics of revival: pietists,
    aristocrats, and the state Church in early nineteenth-century Prussia', in L. E. Jones and J. Retallack
    (eds.), *Between reform, reaction, and resistance: studies in the history of German conservatism from 1789
    to 1945* (Oxford, 1993), pp. 31–60. On schooling see K. A. Schleunes, *Schooling and society: the politics
    of education in Prussia and Bavaria 1750–1900* (Oxford, 1989), pp. 91–5.
[31] J. J. Auchmuty, *Sir Thomas Wyse 1791–1862: the life and career of an educator and diplomat* (London,
    1939), p. 167.
[32] Brent, *Liberal Anglican politics*, pp. 225–7.

Protestants feared that this Catholic vigour presaged a papal challenge to the law in most of northern Europe. One of them, the young Tory Lord Ashley, co-wrote an article in the *Quarterly Review* arguing that Roman Catholic aggression was on the rise in Europe, not least in Ireland.[33] His argument was helped by the strongly anti-Catholic and anti-erastian Prussian diplomat Bunsen, who was now in England. Ashley, like many other Protestants, believed that the only real answer to Catholic assertiveness was a vigorous revival by the Anglican Church.

This combination of vigorous Tory Anglicanism, and more general anxiety about Ultramontane Catholic revival, explains the vehemence of the opposition to the Whig government's education scheme for *England*, which Russell introduced in 1839. It seemed to contain all the offending elements of previous policies: state interference, restrictions on Anglican privileges and freedom, and benefits to Catholicism. To introduce such a scheme was politically risky, given the government's precarious position in Parliament by 1839, but Russell considered it important both for his own honour and in view of the social situation.

Russell was personally committed to measures to 'raise the character of the people' by making them aware of 'their religious and moral duties'.[34] This was, not least, in light of the Chartist agitation and the unprecedented amount of information about social conditions produced by the Poor Law Commissioners' reports. He acknowledged that a continental degree of state control in education would 'shock the civil and political feelings of the country'.[35] But the development of national education schemes abroad made it all the more imperative not to neglect education in Britain: it was a question of economic and social prudence and Christian responsibility.[36] How could the state deny its duty to give the benefits of religion to the poor, while continuing to impose heavy criminal penalties for misbehaviour? Education was also the best check against the spread of Ultramontane superstition and proto-Catholic perversions of Anglican doctrines. Russell did not believe that the Church, left to its own devices, had the vigour to meet the educational need, especially not in the cities.

Economic depression made many other Liberals keen to support an education bill in 1839. The difficulty, however, was that a statist approach would be awkward politically, raising interconnected fears of anti-clericalism, secular Radicalism and continental despotism. Some of the highest-profile

---

[33] A. McCaul and Lord Ashley, 'Papal conspiracy – Archbishop of Cologne etc', *Quarterly Review*, 63 (1839), 88–120.

[34] *Hansard*, 91:1221, 22 Apr. 1847; 43:730, 14 June 1838.

[35] *Hansard*, 39:394, 30 Nov. 1837; 45:275, 12 Feb. 1839.     [36] *Hansard*, 45:284, 12 Feb. 1839.

advocates of state education were utilitarian Radicals concerned to disseminate secular 'useful knowledge'. Utilitarian ideas of educational centralisation also smacked of the unpopular and dictatorial New Poor Law. When one Radical MP, Roebuck, introduced his planned scheme in 1833, he emphasised the importance of training the individual to be a useful and virtuous citizen. He praised the compulsory nature of the Prussian system, and the decision of France, in that year, to introduce a national scheme: these were 'the two most enlightened countries in Europe'.[37] He won almost no support in the Commons. Anti-continental rhetoric was already being used to oppose state intervention.[38]

However, utilitarians were able to make their continental comparisons more effectively in other contexts. A Select Committee of 1835, the result of backbench Liberal pressure, focused attention on the superior artistic education provided for artisans in Germany and France, arguing that British ornamental metalwork and fine textiles were suffering in the market owing to their inferior design. This persuaded the Board of Trade in 1836 to establish a School of Design, on the Bavarian and Prussian model. Between 1842 and 1852 twenty-one similar institutions were created or subsidised in the provinces.[39]

These arguments were part of a more general interest among reformers in continental approaches to the task of civilising society. In 1830 Russell's brother William, in Geneva, expressed admiration for the new ideas circulating about 'the amelioration of mankind'. 'I should like to see England start from its lethargy & take a lead, as it is, like a bad hound, we are lagging behind.'[40] Most advocates of state education, like Edward Lytton Bulwer and Sarah Austin (who translated Cousin's report on Prussian schooling, the basis of the French reform of 1833), argued that the continental systems taught not just secular knowledge but also moral and aesthetic qualities, elevating the mind and conscience and eroding class selfishness and materialism.[41] British promoters of national education focused on the orderliness, industry and sobriety of Switzerland, Holland and Prussia. They also relied on a cascade of statistics – that novel but potentially devastating polemical device – to show that school attendance in Britain was significantly

---

[37] *Hansard*, 20:139, 147, 30 July 1833.
[38] William Cobbett abhorred the government's introduction of a small education grant in 1833 as a 'French' and 'Doctrinaire' plan to 'force education': *Hansard*, 20:735, 17 Aug. 1833.
[39] Q. Bell, *The schools of design* (London, 1963), pp. 68, 101.
[40] To Holland, 29 Dec. 1830, in G. Blakiston (ed.), *Lord William Russell and his wife, 1815–1846* (London, 1972), p. 227.
[41] E. L. Bulwer, *England and the English* (1833; Chicago, 1970 edn), bk 3, ch. 3; V. Cousin, *Report on the state of public instruction in Prussia*, trans. S. Austin (London, 1834), pp. xv–xvii.

lower than in other Northern European countries.[42] In 1837, 80 per cent of Prussian children were apparently attending.[43] Liberal educational reformers were anxious to dissociate their ideas from the whiff of continental autocracy. They pointed out that the system of a school in each parish was general to Europe, including Scotland, and to the United States, and had been built up by communal civic consciousness more than by central dictation. Even so, it was impossible for them not to suggest that the continental systems were better than the British. Indeed, some took pride in pointing out that England was not, as it boasted, 'the first country in Europe in point of civilization', but among the most backward in terms of general diffusion of knowledge, with lamentable consequences for agriculture, industry, morality and social harmony.[44]

Russell personally favoured a rate-aided national system, which was too controversial for the government to consider.[45] But the Tories found it easy to argue against the scheme that he introduced in 1839, of a system of grants for schools, administered by a government agency (a Committee of the Privy Council) in return for acceptance of inspection. They claimed that this betrayed the nation's religious and constitutional principles, in three ways. First, that the plan was un-English in its application of despotic central state power. The establishment of a Committee of Privy Council, with power over education grants, raised fears of a second Poor Law Commission trampling over local rights, and the prospect of a powerful cabinet minister directing national education after the manner of the Prussian *Kulturministerium*. This was an effective charge principally because of the proposal for a normal school, based on the example of the Prussian teacher-training seminaries praised by Cousin, which aimed to assemble guidance on good teaching methods for dissemination to schools.[46] The Tories alleged that power over the religious education of the people was being given to an 'irresponsible' government board which would use it to accrue patronage power.[47] It might decide to assist schools of any religion and none; it might set out a new official religion and dominate 'the youthful mind of the country'.[48] In contrast, they defended the vigour and independence of the National Society, the Church's educational arm, which had

[42] Lansdowne, *Hansard*, 48:1260–3, 5 July 1839.    [43] Schleunes, *Schooling and society*, pp. 108–9.

[44] Wyse, *Hansard*, 48:532–3, 19 June 1839.

[45] D. G. Paz, *The politics of working-class education in Britain, 1830–50* (Manchester, 1980), ch. 6.

[46] Russell indeed suggested that the aim of the normal school was to lay down model 'modes of education' for grant-aided schools to follow, borrowing from the example of 'foreign establishments' as well as domestic ones: *Hansard*, 45:281, 12 Feb. 1839.

[47] Stanley, *Hansard*, 48:232–4, 14 June 1839.    [48] Ashley, *Hansard*, 48:270, 14 June 1839.

formed diocesan Boards of Education in the late 1830s. This appeal to ideas of private action and religious freedom struck a chord with many Radicals and Dissenters. Indeed one youthful Tory with Radical leanings, Disraeli, claimed that, under pressure from irreligious philosophers in the Central Society for Education, the Whigs were betraying England's 'happy system of self-government' in favour of the sort of education system that Austria, 'the China of Europe', and Prussia used to ensure 'implicit obedience', and that would benefit the Catholic Church.[49]

Linked to this criticism was a claim that the religion taught in the normal school and attached model school, which by implication might be disseminated across the country in future, was bogus and un-English. The government plan made a distinction between general and special religious education. All pupils were to receive a general biblical education: Anglicans and Dissenters would get this together, though Catholics could choose to receive readings from their own Bible instead. More doctrinal teaching could be provided by the sects separately. Russell was attached to this idea of common education in order to counter sectarianism, especially as between Church and Dissent. The alternative, of different normal schools for each denomination, was rejected. Prime Minister Melbourne, no fool, had from the beginning felt that the attempt to establish a combined system was doomed.[50] The implication that the government wished to disseminate a toothless general Christianity gave the Tories an open goal. It could be blamed on the influence of the Central Society for Education, which was widely alleged to prefer a completely secular scheme. Where, the Tories asked, was the state's commitment to teach Christian truth? Ashley considered the Whig scheme 'hostile to revealed religion' since it drew a false distinction between basic Christianity and dogma.[51] Education must reach to the heart. Gladstone reiterated his argument that the state had a conscience and a duty to provide the people with truth, and its denial of this responsibility would destroy 'the national character which had hitherto been the boast of England'.[52] Graham claimed that the scheme undermined the Church and the nation's defences against popery and rationalism. He and Peel argued that mixed education had failed to protect Protestant interests in Ireland and was on the wane in Prussia, where the denominations were now mainly taught separately.[53] In other words, the Tories

---

[49] *Hansard*, 48:580, 583–4, 20 June 1839.
[50] J. Murphy, *The religious problem in English education: the crucial experiment* (Liverpool, 1959), p. 157.
[51] Ashley, *Hansard*, 48:276–9, 14 June 1839.      [52] *Hansard*, 48:627, 632, 20 June 1839.
[53] *Hansard*, 48:646–55, 673–5, 20 June 1839. Another young Tory, Acland, said that mixed education was also under attack in Holland: *Hansard*, 48:569, 19 June 1839.

were aware (owing to Bunsen's information) of the recent collapse of the Prussian erastian state policy. Melbourne felt that Bunsen and his young and intensely Protestant Tory friends were setting the country against the Whigs.[54]

Therefore Tories argued, thirdly, that the attempt to pursue the chimera of combined education would benefit Catholicism in England, as it had in Ireland.[55] Bunsen felt that the Whigs were 'in O'Connell's hands'.[56] The plan for the normal school involved the taxpayer paying for the cost of training Catholic teachers and of reading the Catholic Bible in the school. At a popular level this was the Tories' main weapon in stirring up petitions against the scheme. The campaign against the bill was so strong that the government was forced to weaken its proposals by dropping the plan for the normal and model schools and giving religious agencies more power over inspection of their own schools. Important in this campaign were the Wesleyans, mainly on anti-Catholic grounds: on 21 May they declared the scheme 'a direct violation of the first principles of the Protestant constitution'.[57]

So in Tory eyes the oppressiveness of the Whig scheme threatened to damage Protestant vigour and play into Catholic hands: in all respects it fell foul of 'English' values. One cabinet minister, writing anonymously, reflected that given John Bull's 'antipathy to all foreign inventions', any future government scheme must avoid appearing to advocate them.[58] The Tories' strong defence of Anglicanism contributed decisively to their victory at the 1841 election. This victory appeared to be a triumph for Church, land and roast beef, the best of old England. In fact, old England had had its last hurrah. The years 1846 and 1848 were to underline how far British politics was changing. Significantly, it was not just Tories who were critical of Whig government, both on religious policy and generally, by 1840. The reaction against the 1839 bill was assisted by Nonconformist and Wesleyan unease about the Whigs' political and religious principles. As the events of 1847–9 were to prove once and for all, the Russellite Irish and educational strategy was unacceptable to too many elements in the polity. The idea of a strong state in institutional alliance with a Catholic Church was increasingly rejected – all the more so since that Church itself was increasingly hostile to modernising, erastian Whiggery and reluctant to make compromises with British governments.

---

[54] F. Bunsen, *A memoir of Baron Bunsen* (2 vols., London, 1868), vol. 1, p. 499.

[55] Jackson, *Hansard*, 45:285–7, 12 Feb. 1839.    [56] Bunsen, *Bunsen*, vol. 1, pp. 507–8.

[57] Murphy, *Religious problem*, p. 182n.

[58] T. Spring Rice, 'Ministerial plan of education', *Edinburgh Review*, 70 (1839), 157–8.

However, it was far from clear what replacement principles would work in Ireland. That was one reason why the Whigs were so anxious about its situation in 1840–1.[59] By the end of 1840 O'Connell was already beginning to mobilise for Repeal, in anticipation of a Tory government. Between 1839 and 1841 the Whigs clung to their strategy of attempting to integrate Irish Catholicism through institutional and patronage alliances, and to face down attempts by Ultramontane influences in the Catholic Church to interfere with their policy. Melbourne appointed two of the most prominent Irish Catholics, Sheil and Wyse, as junior ministers in August 1839, while the Lord Lieutenant warned the Archbishop of Dublin that the government would not tolerate 'despotic interference' by papal forces in Irish politics.[60] When Russell returned as Prime Minister in 1846, this strategy of seeking clerical cooperation developed further: his father-in-law Lord Minto was dispatched on an eventually unsuccessful mission to the Pope in 1847, in order to pursue an informal concordat. The hope was that he would make plain his support for social order in Ireland, and his blessing for Russell's policies of concurrent endowment and mixed universities. This was the apogee of the Russellite mission to civilise Ireland.

The urgency of seeking papal assistance in governing Ireland was something on which Russell and Foreign Secretary Palmerston agreed at this time.[61] They saw it as crucial not just in pacifying the country but also in maintaining Britain's influence in Europe. Disunity and fear of disorder in Ireland weakened Britain's international prestige and tied down British soldiers: in 1843 Russell complained that 'France and Russia may do as they please East and West, while O'Connell hangs on the rear of our forces.'[62] Ireland was never just a problem in isolation; it always impacted on British standing and policy abroad. More positively, a concordat might benefit Italy as well as Ireland, if it encouraged the Pope and other Italian rulers to undertake constitutional changes. These might pacify reformers and prevent the two extremist outcomes in the Italian peninsula that the Whigs feared: a Radical uprising for unification on republican principles, and Austrian or French intervention in an attempt to repress this. An active diplomatic policy could do as much for Britain's continental standing as a policy of institutional alliances could do for Ireland.

---

[59] See Lord William Russell's comment, 2 Feb. 1841, in *Gooch*, vol. 1, p. 33.
[60] Brent, *Liberal Anglican politics*, p. 227.
[61] Palmerston to Russell, 19 Aug. 1847, *Gooch*, vol. 1, pp. 172–3.
[62] To Melbourne, quoted in J. Prest, *Lord John Russell* (London, 1972), p. 193.

## PALMERSTON AND LIBERAL FOREIGN POLICY

The foreign policy of the governments of the 1830s was influenced by three different – though not incompatible – policy traditions. The first emphasised economy and peace. Most Whigs had usually been uneasy about the wars of 1776–1815. There was a tendency to see them as foolish crusades against national aspirations in America and France, whose principal domestic consequences had been the perpetuation of existing political abuses, increased jobbery, and the creation of a massive national debt. As a result, the cry of military non-interference in the domestic affairs of other countries became a staple of progressive politics in the 1820s and 1830s. Defence expenditure and national-debt interest payments threatened to overwhelm taxpayers; the need for spending reductions was obvious, and the passage of Reform in 1832 increased the pressure. Between 1830 and 1835 government spending was cut by 10 per cent to £48.9 million, including reductions of over £3 million in military expenditure. Many assumed that a Whig- and Radical-dominated Commons would not vote supplies for a war in Europe. Peace seemed vital for British commercial interests and for the spread of civilisation and enlightened principles. Cabinet plans to intervene in Portugal in January 1834 were scuppered by the opinion of the fervently anti-militaristic Althorp, the Leader of the Commons, that Parliament would probably refuse to support them.[63]

The tricky question, however, was how to square disapproval of military interference with the other great Foxite principle of 'the cause of civil and religious liberty all over the world'. Napoleon had tried to crush liberty in the Iberian peninsula, prompting nationalist uprisings from 1808, which were encouraged by Britain. After 1815 the 'Holy Alliance' continued the attempt at suppression, in Spain and Italy. Should Britain assist these uprisings? This question caused a long-running tension within Whiggery between a large party that favoured peace and the more interventionist group led by Russell's mentor Holland (Fox's nephew) and later by Russell himself. Russell was to accuse the Whig leaders Grenville and the 2nd Earl Grey of betraying the Foxite cause by failing to support the Spanish after 1808.[64] Such an allegation maligned Grey, but its real target was probably Grey's son Howick, the 3rd Earl Grey from 1845, who was a much more

---

[63] A. D. Kriegel (ed.), *The Holland House diaries 1831–1840: the diary of Henry Richard Vassall Fox, third Lord Holland* (London, 1977), p. 248.
[64] John, Earl Russell, *Recollections and suggestions 1813–1873* (2nd edn, London, 1875), pp. 5–9.

consistent advocate of non-intervention.[65] As a youth, the ardently patriotic Russell visited the battlefields of Spain three times, in 1810, 1812 and
1813, and was personally conducted along the lines of Torres Vedras by
General Hill.[66] Puny Lord John was a soldier manqué; he loved military
metaphors in his speeches and commanded a company of the Bedfordshire
militia.[67] In late 1854 he was to become obsessed by the desire to take charge
of the mismanaged war effort and save the situation in the Crimea.[68] Russell argued that nations, like individuals, displayed their honour by their
disinterested defence of liberty, and that it was England's mission to act up
to this ideal. He also believed that Britain's imperial responsibilities – for
example in Canada – could only be upheld by decisive vigour, which he
aimed to supply as Colonial Secretary in 1839–41.[69] However, he was also
very conscious of the duty to preserve peace, which he saw as the ideal of
a true Christian, patriot and Foxite. At several moments in his career he
identified himself emotionally against bombastic warmongering: one, in
1840, is considered below. In 1855, he made himself look unpatriotic and
inconsistent by favouring peace at Vienna, had to resign and then presented himself as a 1790s Whig marginalised by the nation's bloodthirsty
spirit.[70] Similarly in 1857 he criticised the attack on Canton, believing it to
be motivated by talk of 'prestige', a foreign word, instead of the character
and honour of England, on which its greatness was founded.[71] But honour
was more vital than peace: in September 1853 he sent the most famous
phrase in diplomatic history echoing down the generations when he said
in a speech that 'if peace cannot be maintained with honour, it is no longer
peace'.[72] And he was not above talking of prestige himself.[73]

    In other words, though the Whig party was predisposed to a pacific
and economical policy, a second strand was willing to consider bold intervention to promote the cause of liberty and to defend ideals of honour
and responsibility. The balance of power between the two was decisively
affected by the impact of a third approach, upheld by the former Canningite Palmerston. Appointed Foreign Secretary in 1830, he made the post his

---

[65] See E. A. Smith, *Lord Grey 1764–1845* (Oxford, 1990), pp. 166–73.
[66] Prest, *Russell*, pp. 12–14.      [67] S. J. Reid, *Lord John Russell* (London, 1895), p. 16.
[68] Ibid., p. 243; O. W. Hewett '. . . and Mr. Fortescue': a selection from the diaries of Chichester Fortescue, Lord Carlingford, 1851–62* (London, 1958), p. 68.
[69] Parry, 'Past and future', p. 152.      [70] Prest, *Russell*, p. 377; Parry, 'Past and future', p. 161.
[71] *Hansard*, 144:1476, 26 Feb. 1857.      [72] At Greenock: Walpole, *Russell*, vol. II, p. 190.
[73] *Hansard*, 148:1048, 9 Feb. 1858, professing shock that, over the Conspiracy to Murder Bill, Palmerston should think the favour of a foreign power of more value to England than 'the maintenance of her ancient prestige'. Palmerston seems to have been less worried about using the word, for example in urging a policy on the Conservatives in 1852: Brown, *Palmerston and foreign policy*, p. 138.

own – despite frequent protests – in every Liberal government until December 1851. Like Canning, he focused on strengthening Britain's diplomatic and strategic position by making it an arbiter of European affairs in order to prevent any other power dominating the Continent, and he presented that strategy as a principled stand against despotism. He did so from a hard-headed concern to advance British interests, strengthened by an element of genuine ideological commitment, and an awareness of its domestic political benefits. In his later career the main benefit was extra-Parliamentary popularity. In the 1830s and 1840s, however, the major advantage of this strategy was to strengthen his hand in the Whig coalition by allying him with the Russellite tradition against the non-interventionists. Though there were frequently important differences between Palmerston's and Russell's approaches to foreign policy – Russell tended to be keener on preserving good relations abroad, particularly with ideologically friendly powers such as Orleanist France and America – they tended to stand together against those economising cabinet colleagues whom Palmerston derisively called the 'Broadbrims', in a reference to Quaker pacifism.[74] No cabinet in this period contained a majority in favour of a policy of assertiveness: there was a preference for economy, caution, peace and not upsetting other powers, for a host of domestic and foreign reasons. Palmerston and Russell ensured that that majority was usually defeated; indeed as Foreign Secretaries in the late 1840s and early 1860s, both tried to ignore the cabinet as much as possible. For this alliance to work, it was crucial for Palmerston to talk the language of liberalism, and for Russell, as the ideological heir of Fox, to interpret Palmerston's policy in terms with which Whigs could identify.

Palmerston was pragmatic in asserting Britain's interests by playing France and Russia off against each other. He had a psychological need to be the spider at the centre of world affairs, manipulating all he surveyed from the Foreign Office. But his talk of promoting liberalism was not just a rhetorical construct to hide his strategic objective. As befitted a child of the Enlightenment and a former undergraduate at Edinburgh University, he perceived an ongoing world-historical struggle between progressive British and autocratic values. He saw Europe divided into two camps, one relying on physical repression and the other gaining strength from the power of public opinion.[75] In 1836 he said that Britain could no longer work with the

---

[74] D. Southgate, '*The most English minister . . .*': *the policies and politics of Palmerston* (London, 1966), p. 243. I have discussed the differences between Palmerston and Russell's foreign strategy further in 'Palmerston and Russell', in D. Brown and M. Taylor (eds.), *Palmerston studies* (2 vols., Southampton, forthcoming), vol. 1, ch. 7, where some of this material is repeated.

[75] *Hansard*, 2nd series, 21:1668, 1 June 1829.

Eastern powers because 'their views and opinions are nowadays the reverse of ours'.[76] Constitutional states, meanwhile, were 'natural allies'.[77] Constitutional values were likely to triumph in the end, but it was Britain's interest and duty to join the struggle for them. Global progress moved in fits and starts, always at risk in the short term from brute force or the eruption of passions; Britain should promote it internationally, just as government had a responsibility to assist social improvement at home. Such progress was in line with God's will; it was military repression by the autocracies to prevent the spread of commerce and constitutionalism that was un-Christian. Commercial and social evolution would benefit England's own interests – peace and stability.[78] More liberal trading arrangements and a reluctance to make war for dynastic purposes would follow the establishment of stable constitutional governments in Europe.[79] In the 1830s he felt that Anglo-French pressure in Spain and Portugal had a great moral effect, suggesting that the triumph of constitutionalism was inevitable – and helping Britain to put pressure on Russia in the East, where Britain had been too weak since 1828.[80]

Constitutional monarchy was England's trademark; its spread would assist England's prestige and psychological dominance in Europe. Palmerston and Russell viewed the battle over European forms of government as the equivalent of military warfare. Every gain for autocracy was a gain for Austria, Russia or the 'Holy Alliance'; every republican regime might become a vehicle for propagating the ideas of the French Revolution. Palmerston considered that 'large republics seem to be essentially and inherently aggressive'.[81] Either way, internal and external stability was unlikely. Victories for constitutional monarchies, on the other hand, demonstrated that Europe was following the Providential path to a higher civilisation – to England's advantage.

So Britain's policy should not be 'non-intervention' – which in any case 'was not an English word'. It should only be 'non-interference' in the sense of not using force of arms to alter other countries' internal affairs.[82] It

---

[76] Southgate, *Most English minister*, p. 161.  [77] *Hansard*, 14:1045, 2 Aug. 1832.
[78] *Hansard*, 2nd series, 21:1669, 1 June 1829.
[79] Constitutional states were 'less likely to go to war than despotic governments because money will not be voted lightly' by their Parliaments: K. Bourne, *Palmerston: the early years 1784–1841* (London, 1982), p. 626.
[80] Sir H. L. Bulwer, *The life of Henry John Temple, Viscount Palmerston* (2 vols., London, 1870), vol. II, p. 197.
[81] Palmerston to Normanby, 28 Feb. 1848, in E. Ashley, *The life of Henry John Temple, Viscount Palmerston: 1846–1865* (2 vols., London, 1876), vol. I, p. 81.
[82] *Hansard*, 14:1067, 2 Aug. 1832.

should involve 'intermeddling in every way . . . short of actual military force' in Portugal and other places where England's security was affected.[83] And elsewhere England's interest lay in 'interfering by friendly counsel and advice', to 'maintain the liberties and independence of all other nations', to 'throw her moral weight into the scale of any people who are spontaneously striving for . . . rational govt, and to extend as far and as fast as possible civilization all over the world'.[84] Russell, similarly, squared his support for 'intermeddling' with the old Foxite tradition of not interfering in the internal affairs of other countries, by arguing that it was Austria, not Britain, which was behaving irresponsibly in Italy and should be opposed. In 1848 Palmerston and Russell both took the line that while England should not tear up the Treaty of Vienna, it should encourage Austria to abandon Lombardy and Venetia, because the political and intellectual awakening among northern Italians – the progressive movement of public opinion – was making it too difficult for Austria to govern them effectively any more.[85]

Of course some of this was rhetorical puff. In particular, in the 1820s and 1840s, the combined weight of the continental autocracies was stronger than Palmerston implied. This justified caution as well as activism; Britain lacked the strength to promote constitutionalism everywhere. To focus on resisting a few specific foolish attempts by other powers to reach beyond their grasp, especially in areas bordering the sea, maximised chances of success. Palmerston and Russell were in fact conservatives on the major issues of European politics. The British sought no territories there; British interest lay in peace and hence good trading conditions; the existing balance of power offered stability; good diplomatic relations had to be maintained with other powers. The number of occasions on which a naval power like Britain could give effective practical support to the development of liberal governments was small, and liberalism was always a relative term. British interests lay in the establishment of stable constitutional monarchies in Europe which were not in the pockets of France or Russia; they did not lie in destabilising Europe in pursuit of principle. If change seemed likely to lead to the destruction of international order, to Radical republican anarchy, or to a counter-revolution strengthening the grip of autocracy, then the status quo was the best solution. This can be seen by looking at Palmerston's attitude to Germany in 1848–9. In principle, he liked the

---

[83] *Hansard*, 2nd series, 21:1646, 1 June 1829.
[84] *Hansard*, 14:1067, 2 Aug. 1832, and (1838) Bourne, *Palmerston*, p. 627.
[85] Memorandum, 1 May 1848, in Walpole, *Russell*, vol. II, pp. 40–2.

notion of a consolidation of German regimes into a stronger unit, as long
as this unit favoured constitutionalism and followed a liberal tariff policy.
That would benefit British trade and would prevent instability in the region
which France or Russia might exploit. On the other hand, most proposals
for change looked likely to increase that instability, because they lacked
substance. The subsequent reaction would either strengthen the hands
of Austria and Russia in Germany or promote the cause of republicanism,
which would be unacceptable both strategically (creating a Franco-German
rapprochement) and ideologically. In practice, therefore, he was a stabilising
influence on events.[86]

But if Palmerston's assertiveness was qualified in practice, it still offered an
uplifting contrast to the position of anti-interventionist Conservatives. In
the 1830s particularly, his stance against the continental autocracies allowed
him to attack the Conservative opposition at home, in a way that built on
the Liberals' domestic arguments. Good government, Liberals said, meant
active, national government assisting constitutionalism and moral progress;
bad government was the feeble and complacent acceptance of autocratic
rule in Europe. What made Palmerston a Liberal was the realisation that
the maintenance of British global power was incompatible with a passive
Tory approach to foreign policy. Britain's constitutionalism was a point
of distinctness and a major asset in European diplomacy. Britain's arguments had added weight because they appeared to rest on the loyalty of
the taxpaying electorate. Moreover, assertiveness was the only way forward
for Britain, because the power of the reactionaries was greater in Europe
than it was at home, and potentially damaging to British interests. After
serving for many years under Lord Liverpool and Canning, in 1828 Palmerston set himself up in opposition to Wellington's Tory government for
withdrawing Canning's troops from Portugal and recognising the clerical
Miguel's regime there. He claimed that Wellington had given way to the
Holy Alliance, in Portugal and the East, rather than disciplining Miguel
and forcing Turkey to settle with Greece. This had betrayed constitutional
values and demeaned Britain's standing among the 'improving nations of
civilized Europe'. Because Wellington's government had no respect for public opinion and foolishly believed that the continental powers' strategy of
repressing constitutionalism could work, it lacked the vision, the 'energy
and promptitude', the 'vigour and decision', to look after Britain's interests
in Europe.[87] Similarly, for Wellington to resort to 'sword & bayonet' to

---

[86] Müller, *Britain and the German question*, esp. pp. 16–19, 24–5, 52–4, 72, 114.

[87] *Hansard*, 2nd series, 21:1659–60, 1663, 1667–8, 1 June 1829; and Palmerston to Sulivan, 14 Aug. 1828,
in K. Bourne (ed.), *The letters of the third Viscount Palmerston to Laurence and Elizabeth Sulivan
1804–1863* (London, 1979), p. 213.

govern Ireland in the late 1820s undermined Britain's foreign standing and prestige, by tying down its troops, revealing its disunity to other powers and sacrificing the constitutionalism on which its reputation rested.[88] There was, therefore, nothing hypocritical about Palmerston's committed membership of the Reform cabinet in 1830. He believed that in all departments of government the Tories were too effete. In the 1840s, again, he and Russell argued that the foreign and Irish policy of Peel and Aberdeen in 1841–6 was an inglorious sequel to that of Wellington: a lack of 'energy and boldness' in Europe, which would cost money in the long run, and which was exacerbated by the failure to pacify Ireland.[89] Thus the foreign policy of the two men was a mirror of Whig domestic policy, founded on the belief that an alliance with the evolving power of public opinion would strengthen the authority of ministers to govern in line with enlightened principles and would prevent the autocracies of the Continent from frustrating them.

There were other domestic political benefits of a policy of selective strength, relying on naval power and projecting a powerful international image. It was easier to generate domestic interest in foreign policy if the focus was on specific ill-deeds by other powers. And if public confidence in Britain's global position was bolstered, the danger of popular panics about inadequate defence would be minimised. The more vigour Britain showed in keeping continental illiberalism at bay, the less public insecurity about defence there would be. This would allow government to keep naval expenditure under control and thus pacify the taxpayer. Canning had pulled off this trick in the 1820s, though, as it happened, the severe depressions of 1838–41 and 1847–8 made Palmerston's military expenditure controversial in any event.

In all these ways, therefore, Palmerston and Russell sought to project a strong liberal image. But the greatest difficulty in the 1830s and 1840s was how to make an impact on European affairs, when liberalism was weak and autocracy strong. Here the key was France: a French entente allowed Britain to punch above its weight in continental affairs, kept its two main rivals apart and prevented the Continent from closing ranks against it. French support was invaluable to Palmerston in securing the independence of Belgium in 1831 and in creating the Quadruple Alliance of 1834 which finally drove Miguel out of Portugal. This alliance with liberal regimes in Spain and Portugal gave the impression that Britain's values were making headway throughout the Iberian peninsula, a marked contrast to the triumph of the Holy Alliance in Spain in 1823. Palmerston exaggerated

---

[88] See the various letters of Sept.–Oct. 1828 in Bourne, *Letters to Sulivan*, p. 217.
[89] On Europe, see Russell to Lady Holland, 7 Aug. 1842, *Gooch*, vol. I, p. 56.

the extent of Russian and Austrian involvement in Iberia in order to show their defeat by liberal principles.[90] An entente with liberal France also gave opportunities for idealistic rhetoric in the Commons, encouraged the general sense of global progress and created common ground between Palmerston and the Francophile wing of the Whig party, led by Holland and Clarendon.

But Palmerston also saw the entente as the best way of keeping tabs on France, preventing France from challenging Britain for naval parity, which would make the latter 'a dependency of France'.[91] France was England's age-old rival and perpetual threat, with a notorious expansionary appetite. Making Belgium an independent and neutral state was a check on French aggression as much as on that of Holland or Russia. The Quadruple Alliance aimed to prevent France from stealing a march on Britain in Spain and winning a special advantage. Palmerston pursued a similar strategy when he unsuccessfully proposed to the cabinet a French alliance in Italy in 1848, claiming that French intervention in northern Italy was better for European progress and stability than Austrian control there, as long as it was 'subjected to the consent of Great Britain'.[92] It was crucial to prevent successful French expansion, and politically essential not to show weakness towards France.

Therefore the great problem which emerged in 1839–40, splitting the cabinet, was how to handle French ambitions in the Near East. Since the Napoleonic era, France had had a vision of asserting itself in Egypt – still nominally part of the Ottoman empire – in order to establish a gateway to the East. The French had conquered Algiers in 1830 and were building up the naval base at Toulon. The restlessness of the Pasha of Egypt, Mehemet Ali, now came to their aid. Having thrown off his vassalage to the Sultan, he occupied Syria in spring 1839. The French encouraged Mehemet Ali, assuming that Britain's need for allies against Russian designs on Constantinople would force it to tolerate an increase of French influence in the area. But this was optimistic in view of Britain's past intolerance of French plans to control the Middle Eastern trade routes – plans destroyed by Nelson's victory over Napoleon at the Battle of Aboukir Bay in 1798. Moreover an Egyptian challenge to Ottoman territorial integrity would make the Sultan more dependent on Russia, increasing the latter's influence in the Near East. Thus in Palmerston's eyes both France and Russia would

---

[90] Schroeder, *Transformation of European politics*, pp. 723–5.
[91] Palmerston to Russell, 4 July 1840, *Gooch*, vol. 1, p. 6.
[92] Southgate, *Most English minister*, pp. 219–20.

benefit from an inactive British policy. France was unwilling to consider a solution that did not give Mehemet Ali control of much of Syria. Eventually the threat of Franco-Egyptian success forced the other four major European powers to sign a series of agreements on the Near East in July 1840, but the French still refused to give way. A revolt in Lebanon then showed that Mehemet Ali's position in Syria was weaker than he claimed. From September to November 1840 the British navy took the initiative under Palmerston's guidance, supplying the Lebanese insurgents with weapons, capturing Beirut after a decisive naval engagement and then successfully bombarding Acre. Mehemet Ali's army was forced to withdraw to Egypt. The French could not risk an escalation of the conflict by direct intervention, and Thiers resigned in embarrassment.

Throughout the crisis, the British cabinet was split. The diehard supporters of a liberal alliance with the French in the West made common cause with the pacific economising party against Palmerston. Holland had an ideological interpretation of European politics, in which countries were rated in terms of their constitutionalism.[93] He also valued peace as a Foxite principle. Until his death in October 1840, he leaked cabinet secrets to Guizot, thereby strengthening the French misjudgment that the British government was too divided to press for military action.[94] Clarendon was opposed to a potentially expensive foreign intervention at a time of domestic economic crisis. Palmerston had to marginalise these two cabinet ministers in particular, and the many MPs outside the cabinet who agreed with them, particularly in view of the government's poor financial situation.

In the early stages of the crisis Russell, as Leader of the House of Commons and Holland's protégé, played the vital role in supporting Palmerston and persuading the sceptical cabinet to sign the July agreements. The alternative, he said, was that France would have 'bullied and crowed'.[95] However, he was also a strong supporter of the French alliance and of the preservation of peace, and he was hostile to Russia. Therefore, when it became necessary to contemplate force, and military cooperation with Russia, to eject the Egyptians from Syria in late 1840, Russell and other cabinet centrists wavered, urging the renewal of talks with France in order to avert the possibility of a major war. He complained that Palmerston would not take a French peace plan seriously enough. As Leader of the Commons he feared the economic cost of a conflict, and the prospect of government defeat. As a liberal Francophile he disliked the alternative of forcing the French

[93] Mitchell, *Holland House*, ch. 8.     [94] Ibid., p. 299.
[95] Russell to Holland, 27 Aug. 1840, *Gooch*, vol. 1, p. 9.

government into a humiliating climb-down, thus weakening the entente
and strengthening Russian influence. As a defender of propertied government at home and abroad he was alarmed that if the French liberal
monarchy fell, republican principles would sweep across Europe.[96] These
may have been sensible fears, but in giving vent to them Russell revealed a
tendency to vacillation, and then to histrionics owing to jealousy at losing
influence over the development of policy. These were early signals of the
character weaknesses that were to plague his later career. He also failed
to see the point on which Palmerston's strategy rested, that the French
would not go to war because French public opinion knew that it would
be counterproductive.[97] Not surprisingly, Palmerston increasingly pursued
his diplomacy and naval operations without consulting cabinet. Owing to
the success of the naval bombardments, he got away with that strategy.

Britain had achieved an international triumph without depending on any
rival. Palmerston's victory established him as a serious figure in domestic
politics, with a strong public profile: press support strengthened his hand
during the crisis.[98] In the climate of 1839–40, when there was already great
Radical criticism of governing-class selfishness, it was easy to portray those
who opposed vigorous action as unpatriotic. The cabinet came across as
chinless and feeble, Palmerston as a man of determination and judgment,
radiating manly vigour. The 1840–1 crisis was a step on the long road
that made him, in the *Daily Telegraph*'s famous obituary phrase, 'the most
English minister that ever governed England'.[99]

Palmerston's Near Eastern policy had two other supports. It was popular in many commercial circles because of the widespread interest in
developing new markets for British goods in the Near East. It built on
the Anglo-Turkish Convention of 1838, which reduced tariffs, gave Britain
most-favoured-nation status and resulted in dramatically increased British
exports to Turkey, especially cotton, over the next fifteen years. Secondly,
it appealed to an important section of Protestant opinion. This was not
just because anti-Catholicism was an element in the popular suspicion of
France. It was also because of evangelical Protestant interest in the conversion of the Jews to Christianity, in line with prophecy, and the spread of
true religion in the Near East. Lady Palmerston felt that the swiftness of
the British military triumph at Acre – as swift as the collapse of the walls
of Jericho – portended 'something miraculous', and that the British had

[96] Ibid., pp. 12, 18.
[97] See Palmerston to the Queen, 11 Nov. 1840, in *LQV 1837–61*, vol. I, pp. 246–8.
[98] See Bourne, *Palmerston*, pp. 605, 617.     [99] Southgate, *Most English minister*, p. xxviii.

perhaps been Providentially chosen to be the agents of 'the restoration of the Jews and fulfilment of the Prophecies'.[100] The new Prussian king, Frederick William IV, and Bunsen, now the Prussian ambassador to Britain, were delighted at the settlement of the Eastern question in 1841, frustrating French and Russian expansion in the region. This opened the prospect of a Concert of Europe working for Godly objectives. Their next step would be a Protestant bishopric in Jerusalem, to be maintained jointly by British Anglicans and German Lutherans. This would strengthen British and Prussian influence in the region, promote conversions and lead the way to a more comprehensive and united Reformed Church. The Jerusalem bishopric project was strongly supported not just by British evangelicals but also by Palmerston, influenced by Ashley, his stepson-in-law. For Ashley, the collaboration would 'curb France, . . . nullify the Pope . . . and defy all the malignity of Sin, Satan, and Sedition throughout the whole world'.[101] Palmerston's zeal pushed the arrangement through as one of the Whig government's last official acts.[102] By 1850–1 it was widely held that Palmerston was a particularly vigorous Protestant.[103] His activities in the Near East, his opposition to Austria and the papacy in Italy in 1848, and his hostility to the international slave trade probably all contributed to that.

It is clear that Palmerston's assertive foreign policy was more generally attractive than Russell's pro-Catholic strategy in Ireland. However, its attractiveness at this stage should not be exaggerated. It did not make him a national hero; nor did it save the Whig government from defeat in 1841. Indeed the particular circumstances that made it so popular after 1848 did not yet apply. For most of the 1840s, opinion within the Liberal party on foreign strategy was deeply divided, and those who wanted to cut costs and keep Britain out of risky foreign entanglements had great influence. In 1840 economic conditions were so dire that any policy which risked the spending of more money was highly controversial. The greatest complaint against the Whig government after 1838 was its financial extravagance in the context of the severe depression, and Palmerston carried part of the blame for the cost of the wars in China and Afghanistan, which were criticised as a hubristic attempt to overburden the taxpayer and the economy in pursuit of greatness. In 1840 the first fresh taxation since 1832 caused particular embarrassment: most customs and excise duties were increased by 5 per cent. Peel, who had criticised the Whigs' interventionism in Spain and increases

---

[100] 3 Dec. 1840, in T. Lever (ed.), *The letters of Lady Palmerston* (London, 1957), p. 243.
[101] G. Battiscombe, *Shaftesbury: a biography of the seventh earl 1801–1885* (London, 1988 edn), p. 139.
[102] See R. W. Greaves, 'The Jerusalem bishopric, 1841', *English Historical Review*, 64 (1949), 328–52.
[103] See e.g. Brown, *Palmerston and foreign policy*, pp. 123, 128; Prest, *Russell*, opp. p. 390.

in naval estimates as far back as 1836, took power in 1841 on a mission to cut taxes, make peace with France and restore efficient business-like government without bluster or ideological posturing.[104] Though Palmerston frequently attacked his foreign policy for weakness, he made little headway. When Russell returned as premier in 1846, dependent on Peelite support, the climate was still unpropitious for Palmerstonianism. Most of the leading Peelites were quietists: Aberdeen told Russell that in supporting his government they expected it to be 'a Ministry of Peace'.[105] The Queen and her husband preferred to maintain the European status quo and not to rock any diplomatic boats. Altogether there was a lot of pressure for what Russell's father-in-law Minto disparagingly called a 'low and narrow policy'.[106]

This was because there were also two centres of opposition to a vigorous foreign policy within the Liberal party itself. On the Liberal front bench, the leader of the 'Broadbrims' was Grey's son, the 3rd Earl. Grey, a dogmatic political economist, spun his father's Foxite foreign policy legacy in a strictly *laissez-faire* direction. He was usually supported by his brother-in-law Charles Wood, and by Clarendon. Grey and Wood argued that peace and good relations with France were vital if British finances were to cope with the severe economic depressions of the 1840s. They also feared that Palmerston was too hostile to the United States. They became the most forceful Liberal advocates of the French entente, the policy which Peel and Aberdeen were also pursuing, and by 1845–6 were sympathetic to a rapprochement of free traders in both parties, a Liberal–Peelite coalition on broadly *laissez-faire* lines.[107] When Peel's government collapsed in December 1845, Grey (without Wood) attempted to block Palmerston's return to the Foreign Office. But Russell demurred, telling Grey that Palmerston was 'the person in the United Kingdom best fitted for that department'.[108] In the ensuing stalemate, the Liberals lost the chance to repeal the Corn Laws. When Russell finally won back power in 1846, not only did Palmerston return to the Foreign Office, but he also put supporters of assertiveness in crucial positions, particularly Auckland at the Admiralty. Anglesey, hero of Waterloo, and a keen advocate of increased defence works, was appointed Master-General of the Ordnance, where he could press for them.[109]

---

[104] *Hansard*, 31:42–4, 4 Feb. 1836.    [105] Aberdeen to Russell, 17 Nov. 1846, *Gooch*, vol. I, p. 130.

[106] Minto to Russell, 3 Jan. 1852, *Gooch*, vol. II, p. 95.

[107] F. A. Dreyer, 'The Whigs and the political crisis of 1845', *English Historical Review*, 80 (1965), 524–5, 536.

[108] Russell to Grey, 21 Dec. 1845, Walpole, *Russell*, vol. I, p. 416.

[109] Marquess of Anglesey, *One-leg: the life and letters of Henry William Paget first marquess of Anglesey* (London, 1961), pp. 322–4.

Palmerston immediately adopted a robust policy towards France over the Spanish Marriages affair, underlining his view that the Peel–Aberdeen policy had lowered the reputation of the country. In the late 1840s he saw the Peelites and their Liberal friends as particular political threats.[110]

Secondly, and most awkwardly, Cobden and other Radicals, fresh from the great victory over the Corn Laws, were appealing vigorously to tax-cutting sentiment. The rest of this chapter considers two Radical arguments of the 1840s that became powerful critiques of the Palmerstonian and Russellite strategies discussed above. These were Cobden's alternative proposals for defence and diplomatic policy, and the adoption of disestablishment and educational voluntaryism by evangelical Nonconformity. Both played central roles in the vehement Radical rejection of 'aristocratic' political culture in the late 1840s. Both castigated British governing-class failings, comparing them closely to the dominant aristocratic and clerical values of continental Europe, which they felt must be purged from domestic affairs.

### COBDENISM, FREE TRADE AND FOREIGN POLICY

All governments of the 1840s were severely criticised by Radicals for excessive spending on defence and diplomatic initiatives. In large part this criticism arose naturally from the constitutional and fiscal concerns discussed in chapter 1. But there was also a broader international perspective on these issues, which was particularly associated with Richard Cobden. Cobdenism became a crucial facet of Liberalism, albeit always a minority one in high politics. It was especially important in the years 1846–52, when its hostility to aristocracy and autocratic state structures struck chords in many quarters and offered an alternative international philosophy to that of Palmerston.

The son of an impoverished Sussex yeoman farmer, Cobden was an enemy of landlord power in Britain and the world, which he believed was holding back a more virtuous and munificent state of society.[111] His vision, inspired by Enlightenment thinking, was of small-scale industrial and agricultural producers trading harmoniously with each other across the globe, distributing God's resources efficiently and therefore maximising their productiveness. God's ultimate destiny for man was 'to unite and mingle in one common stream', and peaceful commerce would play a key role in that

---

[110] Parry, 'Palmerston and Russell'.

[111] This brief discussion of Cobdenism owes a lot to three treatments: P. J. Cain, 'Capitalism, war and internationalism in the thought of Richard Cobden', *British Journal of International Studies*, 5 (1979), 112–30; A. Howe, *Free trade and Liberal England*; M. Taylor (ed.), *The European diaries of Richard Cobden, 1846–1849* (Aldershot, 1994).

process.[112] To struggle for this state of affairs was, as one follower of the Anti-Corn Law League put it, the 'politics of equitable benevolence' and 'piety'.[113] The League's enemies were the vested interests who had arrogated these resources to themselves. Traditional human society was feudal and militaristic, based on principles of aggression, conquest, bloodshed and social division. That had held these societies back. War had done particular damage, causing bloodshed, incurring vast military expenditure and debt and creating a permanent climate of suspicion between states, fuelled by a manipulative network of aristocratic diplomats. To fund these large military and diplomatic establishments, the productive resources of society had been highly taxed. Tariffs and other indirect taxes were particularly favoured by the governing classes to pay off these debts, because they protected their rent rolls at the expense of consumers. The abolition of tariffs would remove the European feudal class's artificial benefits and place more of the tax burden on the classes that were responsible for military and other government expenditure. Tariffs and militarism were thus intimately linked; between them they had left most of humanity suffering poverty, social division and economic backwardness.

Cobden felt that most European regimes could still be described in those terms. Their excessive expenditure was the greatest obstacle to the spread of virtuous commercial society. With lower military spending, they would not need tariffs; they could improve their transport systems, to the benefit of agricultural producers, admit more goods from abroad (especially from Britain) and generate more internal consumption and prosperity. Russia's large standing army spawned the twin evils of the maintenance of feudalism at home and the ratcheting up of defence budgets in Russia's rivals. Commercial success had allowed Britain to loosen feudal shackles more than most countries, but its economy and society were still handicapped by excessive aristocratic influence. The United States, lacking an aristocracy and blessed with many natural resources, set a better social example and indeed offered a clear long-term threat to Britain's economic superiority. Britain could learn much from the United States. In some important respects – on education and land issues – Britain could also learn from continental societies. Since the 1830s Cobden had admired the moral and social condition of the Swiss, which he attributed to the subdivision of land, generating prosperity for smallholders.[114] He looked with envy to the better

---

[112] Cobden to the Frankfurt Peace Congress, 1850, quoted in Schwabe, *Cobden*, p. 119.
[113] Pye Smith, Aug. 1841: A. Prentice, *History of the Anti-Corn-Law League* (2 vols., London, 1968 edn), vol. I, pp. 237–8.
[114] Morley, *Cobden*, vol. I, pp. 27–8.

standards of education provided in Scotland, and above all in Prussia and Switzerland, which he visited several times in the 1830s and 1840s. In 1838 he wrote a remarkable paean to the 'simple and economical' Government of Prussia, 'so deeply imbued with justice to all, and aiming so constantly to elevate mentally and morally its population', in sad contrast to the British regime. Believing that national popular education was the best way to raise the moral consciousness of the people, it seemed to him that, by his keenness for it, the 'good and just' Prussian King had 'shattered the sceptre of despotism even in his own hand'.[115]

In the late 1830s Cobden was gloomy about Britain's prospects, because of the growing power of aristocratic Toryism, the timidity of the Whigs and the lack of 'public spirit' among the manufacturing elite of the northern towns. More middle-class political virtue and self-confidence seemed to be necessary if aristocratic power was to be challenged. The battle which he entered against the Corn Laws was a fight against the aristocratic and military system which they propped up. The Anti-Corn Law League presented tariffs as a sectional imposition, against the common interest. They increased the cost of industry and made it difficult for Britain to sell the exports necessary to fund its national expenditure. Their abolition would lower prices and increase Britain's industrial competitiveness, to the benefit of the middle and working classes. It would make European agriculture more profitable and increase the continental market for English industrial products. Other European powers, anxious that their agriculturalists should remain profitable, would lower their tariffs so that farmers could buy imports cheaply and thus keep down their own costs. Corn Law reform would sound the trumpet against protective tariff walls all over the world and help to dismantle aristocratic and military power.

The League's electoral strategy, refined in 1843–4, aimed to attack landlord influence, by encouraging urban voters to take up their entitlement to register for a vote in the counties, which the Tories had dominated in 1841. After 1846 Cobdenites continued to attack that influence, by extending the registration initiative and campaigning against primogeniture and the other legal devices that kept large landed estates intact. Abroad, meanwhile, free trade would encourage the division of labour between countries, bringing them into a mutually beneficial and harmonious relationship. It would produce 'the greatest revolution that ever happened in the world's history': it would thrust aside the 'antagonism of race, and creed, and language', abolish the desire and motive for 'large and mighty empires; for

---

[115] Ibid., p. 130.

gigantic armies and great navies' and place government across the globe on 'something like the municipal system'.[116]

In 1842 Cobden remarked that free trade and peace were the same cause.[117] After 1846 he became a propagandist for both. He argued that, as international commercial links developed between countries, they would pursue a more peaceful policy. Manufacturers and industrialists had a vested interest in peace. It was the necessary pre-condition of great change in the economic and social condition of Europe; it would make possible the emancipation of the Russian serfs and the development of capitalism in Russia. In 1849 he presented his first Parliamentary motion to urge the government to advocate the principles of international arbitration to solve disputes, while between 1848 and 1853 he was a major player in the six international congresses held to promote arbitration and press for disarmament. The hope was that the emergence of such a movement, across Europe, would lead to a reduction in international tension and a diversion of resources away from military expenditure to the consumer.

Domestically, his main concern after 1846 was to reduce Britain's expenditure on defence, diplomacy and the colonies. This, he suggested, was a disastrous drain on national resources which added to international tension rather than protecting British wealth. The large diplomatic establishment maintained in order to protect Britain's corner in European quarrels and to secure benefits for British trade was a waste of money, a sectional benefit for sons of aristocrats and a contributor to international tension. The defence of Ottoman integrity was an example of a pernicious idea which would only increase the chance of war; it was an attempt to prop up a regime which lacked the necessary wealth and enterprise to govern effectively and so would inevitably decay. And there was no real threat to Britain from Russia, because even if the latter advanced into the Ottoman empire and the Mediterranean with the idea of blockading British trade, the cheapness of British goods would always ensure a market.[118] In 1851 he argued that it was pointless to press for a constitutional regime in Naples before an education system was established there, since education, not British naval influence, was its only reliable basis.[119] At home, he maintained that the invasion scares of 1845–60 were whipped up by alarmists, increasing

---

[116] Cobden at Manchester, 15 Jan. 1846: R. Cobden, *Speeches on questions of public policy* (2 vols., London, 1870), vol. 1, p. 363.

[117] Cobden to Ashworth, 12 Apr. 1842, Morley, *Cobden*, vol. 1, p. 230.

[118] See the discussion in Cain, 'Capitalism', 236–7; Schwabe, *Cobden*, pp. 199–200.

[119] Schwabe, *Cobden*, pp. 155–6.

expenditure unnecessarily, risking war and benefiting the military classes.[120] And he campaigned for a reduction of the colonial commitment on similar grounds: that colonial posts did nothing more useful than sustain 'the costly appendages of aristocratic life'.[121]

Cobden's attack on diplomatic and military expenditure in the mid- and late 1840s relied on the same pillars as the struggle against the Corn Laws: the fervour of economising Radicals and the moral earnestness of Dissent. Dissenting spokesmen tended to agree that a biased state had imposed tariffs in order to obstruct for sectional purposes the machinery designed by Providence to spread resources fairly among God's peoples. Nonconformist participation had helped the League to moralise political economy, countering the charge that it was merely a manufacturers' movement for higher profits. It had given the campaign a crusading, millennial, global dimension. The same seemed possible in the case of Cobden's subsequent campaign for economy, peace and disarmament. In 1846–8 he seemed best placed to shape the future of Radicalism, harnessing the mood for national and global purification.

### EVANGELICAL NONCONFORMITY, CATHOLICISM AND THE ATTACK ON WHIGGERY

Nonconformity played an important part in the Anti-Corn Law League: 645 Dissenting ministers met in Manchester in August 1841 to hear Cobden tell them to spread the word that the Corn Laws were 'anti-scriptural and anti-Christian'.[122] But this was in fact just part of an increasing political engagement by the main evangelical Nonconformist sects in this period. The aim was to purify state and society of their ungodliness and corruptions, with a zeal made more urgent by the severe economic depression of 1838–41. The Peace Society, driven by anger at the wars and tensions of 1839–41 over France, Spain, Afghanistan and China, began a new, more political strategy of petitioning the Commons, calling for international arbitration of disputes in 1839 and for mediation in the Chinese dispute in 1840.[123] The campaign to abolish Church rates became more intense; a number of Dissenters refused to pay them. Initiating this bout of political activity had been the successful petitioning campaign of 1838, mounted by Joseph Sturge, George Thompson and others, for the immediate end of the

---

[120] R. Cobden, *The three panics: a historical episode* (3rd edn, 1862).
[121] Cain, 'Capitalism', 236.      [122] Prentice, *History*, vol. I, p. 240.
[123] S. Conway, 'The politicization of the nineteenth-century Peace Society', *Historical Research*, 66 (1993), 274–6.

apprenticeship system in the British West Indian colonies, which had seemed to be perpetuating slavery. The British and Foreign Anti-Slavery Society had been formed in that year to stimulate an international movement of opinion against the slave trade, and a World Anti-Slavery Convention was held in London in 1840. The Dissenting magazine the *Eclectic Review* claimed that the apprenticeship agitation taught us our 'power as the depositaries of a *moral influence* adequate to direct and control the national mind'.[124]

These years thus marked a shift in the balance of power within Dissenting politics, which had previously depended on a small cadre of Unitarians. Historically, most of the evangelical Dissenting congregations had seen themselves as Christian communities much more than political ones. They were conscious that their morality was superior to that of the world outside. They lacked enthusiasm for the sordidness of political activity and agitation. Though most of them recognised that the 1832 Reform Act would facilitate a virtuous political struggle against aristocratic vested interests that assisted irreligion, they were sceptical that it would do much to purify national spiritual life – not least because of their suspicion of the more secular, rationalising trends within Liberalism. However, the Act facilitated virtuous political campaigns and seemed to increase the responsibility of citizens to shape the public mind. Concern at national irreligion, together with a desire to avert divine punishment for it, increasingly impelled them to act.

So in the ten years after 1838 many evangelical Dissenters became much more continuously engaged in political affairs. In 1844 the British Anti-State Church Association (BASCA) was formed to advocate the disestablishment of the Church of England. By 1847, political Nonconformity was identified also with the cause of educational voluntaryism – the rejection of state involvement in elementary education in favour of private effort. These twin assertions that the state had no right to interfere with the nation's religious culture caused immense difficulties for the Whig–Radical coalition, especially in the late 1840s. Though Nonconformists were on principle opposed to state Churches, this did not necessarily mean that they should campaign for their removal. Increasing interest in doing so reflected a widespread concern to improve national morality at a time of social turbulence, which, as noted in chapter 2, also spawned the revolt against foppish Whiggery and cold utilitarianism, the admiration for Carlyle and Cromwell, the burgeoning Oxford Movement, and the desperate Tory adherence to paternalist

---

[124] 1838, quoted in A. Tyrrell, 'The "Moral Radical Party" and the Anglo-Jamaican campaign for the abolition of the Negro apprenticeship system', *English Historical Review*, 99 (1984), 499.

values. It was part of the Radical critique of the 'aristocratic' state, though one that, in contrast to secular Radicalism, placed more emphasis on its ethical than its constitutional failings. But it was also a reaction to the drift of the Whigs' and then Peel's Irish policy towards the principle of state endowment for Catholicism. Fear that the state was adding to the power of priesthood and doctrinal error crucially intensified the urgency of the Nonconformist revolt – and by the late 1840s made Whig policy on Ireland almost unworkable.

One great stimulus to Nonconformist political activity was the Tory revival and victory at the 1841 election – greatly assisted by the power of the Anglican Church. Church pressure had already enfeebled the Whig government, forcing it to abandon its pursuit of Church-rate reform after the Tory gains at the 1837 election.[125] This abandonment cooled relations with orthodox Dissenters, some of whom concluded by 1840–1 that no men in office could be trusted.[126] However, they feared Tory government much more than they feared the Whigs.[127] The spirit of Toryism was the spirit of priesthood, of the oppressive squire–parson alliance in the countryside and of hostility to urban values. Cobden claimed in 1842 that Tory government was 'supported by the violation of morality and religion'.[128] Thus the Church–state alliance was bound to become an issue for Dissenters.

In Dissenting eyes the two main enemies to the spread of evangelical religion were state interference and priestly oppression. Congregationalists and Baptists started from the basis that a true Church was a body of believers accepting Christ as its sole head, and searching for a personal relationship with God. They believed that the notion of a national Church, open to those of any belief or none, would pollute the evangelical purity of the religious life, while the Anglican Establishment gave power to bishops, priests and secular rulers to dictate a religious policy to citizens. Dissenting critics argued that priestly pretensions, abuse of wealth, lack of evangelising zeal and massive political bias made the Church Establishment 'anti-christian, unscriptural, and corrupt'.[129] It was a 'terrible scourge to the nation' and an 'aristocratic engine'.[130] The withdrawal of state interference and state patronage would raise the level of public morality and create the conditions

---

[125] R. Brent, 'The Whigs and Protestant Dissent in the decade of reform: the case of Church rates, 1833–1841', *English Historical Review*, 102 (1987), 887–910.

[126] Ibid., 906–7.

[127] G. I. T. Machin, *Politics and the Churches in Great Britain 1832 to 1868* (Oxford, 1977), pp. 73–4.

[128] June 1842: N. McCord, *The Anti-Corn Law League 1838–1846* (London, 1968 edn), p. 122.

[129] Foster to Cottle, Mar. 1830, J. E. Ryland, *The life and correspondence of John Foster* (2 vols., London, 1846), vol. II, p. 178.

[130] Miall, *Miall*, p. 30 (1839); *Nonconformist*, 1 Mar. 1848, p. 125.

for more effective cooperation between Protestant Churches in spreading the gospel of a vital saving Christianity. The voluntaryist movement was also stimulated by the example of the United States, and by an influx of Scottish Presbyterians.[131]

However, the idea of a campaign for disestablishment was extremely controversial, not least because it might well be politically counterproductive. When it was first mooted in 1833–4, many Dissenters argued that, while indisputable as a principle, to adopt it as a cry would 'delight and strengthen the Tories'.[132] In the Chartist-influenced and fevered climate of the late 1830s, similarly, to challenge the notion that British politics should have a religious character would play into Conservative hands. Moreover, many Dissenters were conscious of the level of social ignorance and vice, and the challenge that this posed to all religions. When BASCA was set up in 1844, John Angell James, the leading Birmingham Congregationalist, and most London ministers did not affiliate to it, and when the *Eclectic Review* supported the new organisation, the moderates saw the need for a new journal, the *British Quarterly Review*, founded in 1845 by the former London university professor Robert Vaughan. Such men argued that it was both spiritually desirable and politically necessary to spread evangelical religion further among the people by effective preaching and education, before beginning such a campaign. The *British Quarterly* deliberately sought to demonstrate the evangelical purity and social and cultural respectability of Dissent. For similar reasons, men like James and Vaughan disapproved of the way in which Radical Dissenting leaders like Miall and the evangelical Quaker Sturge combined their religious campaigns with secular agitations such as the Complete Suffrage Union. These social anxieties were felt even more strongly in the largest evangelical sect, the Wesleyan Methodists, who, despite attacking Anglican complacency and excessive wealth, retained an instinctive attachment to the idea of the Church–state connection and hence remained aloof from mainstream Dissenting politics.

The major stimulus to the establishment of BASCA and the introduction of educational voluntaryism was Dissenting hostility to the educational clauses of the Conservative government's 1843 Factory Bill. The bill proposed a powerful *ex officio* Anglican presence on the board of trustees of the rate-supported schools which were to be set up to educate factory children. Other safeguards for Anglican teaching were also included. This

---

[131] W. R. Ward, *Religion and society in England 1790–1850* (London, 1972), pp. 130–2.
[132] R. W. Dale, *James*, p. 167; J. Wilson, 1833, quoted in Brent, 'Whigs and Protestant Dissent', 897–8.

scheme managed to unite most Dissenting sects in opposition to it, ensuring its defeat. Petitions with over two million signatures were submitted against the first bill, and nearly as many against a revised version. Yet the general anxiety about the social state of the industrial districts made it likely that similar proposals for rate-funded education would recur, which would also favour the Church, given its social presence and political clout. This would be bound to create a 'new Establishment'. Andrew Reed told a packed Exeter Hall that state bias in religion and concurrent endowment in education were wrong, and that, far from needing to follow the Prussian example, 'the death of our liberties will witness also the death of our country'.[133] Accordingly, a 'voluntaryist' position emerged: that Dissenters should oppose the extension of the Privy Council grants begun in 1839, should not accept any state money for their own schools and should instead aim to build a network of educational establishments funded by Dissenting congregations. Edward Baines of Leeds became the leading voluntaryist. In 1843 he persuaded the Congregational Union to establish a central fund to provide school buildings attached to Congregational churches; by 1853, 453 schools were established under the aegis of a Congregational Board of Education, and by 1859 £173,000 had been raised.[134] The voluntaryist movement depended on a confidence – articulated by Baines in 1843 – that civic communities were being moralised by 'spontaneous zeal and Christian principle' and were more virtuous than the metropolis or the countryside.[135]

However, it was initially restricted to a fairly small range of provincial opinion. Many of the Dissenting protests against the 1843 Factory Bill had not come from Radicals and were not based on voluntaryist principles but on the other great concern of Nonconformists – hostility to priestly pretensions. Many Congregationalists were associated with schools which had accepted state grants in the 1830s, and they remained ambivalent about the voluntaryist project. The Wesleyans certainly had no difficulties with the principle of state funding for religious education: in 1847 they gladly accepted state money which they needed for their 395 day schools. What drove their objection and that of moderate Congregationalists to the 1843 proposals was the more specific fear that the bill gave too much influence

---

[133] A. Reed and C. Reed, *Memoirs of the life and philanthropic labours of Andrew Reed* (London, 1863), pp. 210–12.

[134] Larsen, *Friends of religious equality*, p. 166; C. Binfield, *So down to prayers: studies in English Nonconformity, 1780–1920* (London, 1977), p. 85.

[135] See A. Lees, *Cities perceived: urban society in European and American thought, 1820–1940* (Manchester, 1985), p. 44.

in the schools to the episcopate and to dogmatic as opposed to scriptural teaching – rather than to lay opinion.[136]

In other words, Dissenters tended to be even more anxious about priestly influence over the individual conscience than about the principles of state–Church relations. One particular reason for this was the spectre of Tractarianism at home and Roman Catholicism abroad. The Oxford Movement was the best-publicised religious movement of the day, emphasising the ancient, divinely inspired foundations of Anglican doctrines in a deliberate attempt to restore the authority of the Church at a time of bewildering flux, and specifically to challenge the latitudinarian and erastian ideas of the Whigs. Though aiming to draw out the national historic qualities of the Anglican religion, its interest in pre-Reformation doctrines and especially in the creeds of the early Fathers ensured that it offended many self-consciously Protestant Englishmen, as did its stress on the idea of the universal Church catholic. Moreover some Tractarians felt that, once Anglicanism had surrendered its independence to modernising politicians, it had denied its purpose, and that the true Christian should take refuge in Romanism, the most famous example being John Henry Newman in 1845. At home and abroad, it seemed impossible to deny the growing power of the Roman Catholic Church itself.

In 1845 evangelical Protestants – Anglican and Dissenting – became obsessed by the threat posed to the liberties of Englishmen by Catholicism and proto-Catholicism. One background was the first French invasion scare in 1844–5, after Louis Philippe's son suggested that the French could take advantage of the advent of steam power to neutralise British naval power and claim supremacy at sea. For the first time since 1815 the British Isles seemed physically threatened by the French. The Tories' much-lauded entente with France broke down when the French annexed Tahiti and imprisoned the British consul, a Protestant missionary, to the anger of evangelicals. On the Continent the Catholic Church seemed to be intimately involved in a powerful conservative reaction, typified by the Austrian suppression of the Italian liberal movement. But the main problem came in Ireland. In 1843 O'Connell, frustrated by the reintroduction of Tory principles in the government of Ireland, mounted a campaign for Repeal of the Union that was supported by many Catholic priests and not countermanded by the Pope. In this context, in 1845, the Peel government extended and made permanent the grant to the Catholic priestly seminary at Maynooth in

---

[136] See Binfield, *So down to prayers*, p. 85; D. Hempton, *Methodism and politics in British society 1750–1850* (London, 1984), pp. 171–2.

Ireland – subsidising Catholic error in the minds of evangelical Protestants. In March 1845 a number of Anglican and Dissenting evangelicals joined forces on the Central Anti-Maynooth Committee to fight this proposal. For the leading Anglican evangelical Ashley, the Maynooth proposal showed the government's 'haughty contempt of the deep, solemn Protestant feeling in the hearts of the British people'.[137]

The emergence of the Catholic issue, in conjunction with Corn Law repeal, ensured the radicalisation of evangelical non-Wesleyan Dissenters. In arguing against Maynooth, it was politically essential to separate their arguments from the 'no-popery' of evangelical Anglicans – with the result that cooperation between the two groups soon broke down. This was all the more the case after the great polarisation in politics caused by the repeal of the Corn Laws in 1846, and the emphasis placed on both Maynooth and English educational funding at the 1847 election. These events impelled Dissenters to base their ecclesiastical and educational arguments on the same linguistic basis of general freedom that the League had adopted. Language that had made possible one popular struggle against a feudal monopoly could similarly galvanise a campaign against the Church Establishment.[138] Most Dissenters argued that they opposed the Maynooth grant not, as evangelical Tories did, because of the evils of Catholicism, but because the state had no right to support particular favoured belief systems.[139] In October 1848, discussing the enthusiasm with which Dissenters agitated against a concurrent endowment policy in Ireland, on voluntaryist rather than narrowly no-popery grounds, the *Nonconformist* noted that four years ago that spirit had hardly existed.[140]

The great benefit of this position, apart from making clear their distance from the Tories, was that it allowed Dissenters to construct a sound basis for an Irish policy on the principle of denying financial aid to all religious sects. On the one hand, this protected the taxpayer from having to contribute to the cause of religious error; on the other, it saved religious ministers from becoming paid lackeys of the state. This viewpoint meant an aggressive rejection of the policy of the Russell government as a policy of patronage and control. The Radical John Bright claimed not to want the Irish clergy to become 'as tame as those of Suffolk and Dorsetshire'.[141] Irish

---

[137] Diary, 7 Apr. 1845, E. Hodder, *The life and work of the seventh earl of Shaftesbury* (3 vols., London, 1886), vol. II, p. 101.

[138] *Nonconformist*, 16 Feb. 1848, p. 97.

[139] See the declaration of the Dissenters' Parliamentary Committee, in Machin, *Politics and the Churches*, p. 190.

[140] *Nonconformist*, 4 Oct. 1848, p. 746.     [141] Machin, *Politics and the Churches*, p. 175.

grievances on Church and land should not be repressed by a domineering government. In February 1848 Miall alleged that Russell planned to endow Irish Catholicism, in order to control the thoughts of the poor. 'Without removing the grievances of the people, [this would] remove from them the opportunity of giving expression to them', making 'religion an instrument for political and aristocratical, and often unjust purposes'.[142] Only disestablishment could remove the disastrous division in Ireland created by the Protestant ascendancy mentality. Similarly, only disendowment would salve the consciences of the British public when they contemplated the Union. Britain's government of Ireland must be founded on Christian principles of justice, tolerance and liberty. If these principles predominated, in Ireland or anywhere else, all would be well.[143]

This rapid change of heart led Dissenting leaders into a self-conscious rejection of the Whigs' latitudinarian statist policy, in three areas. One was Maynooth itself, since it was Whig support for the extended grant that had enabled Peel to get it through. The second, as we shall see in chapter 4, was Russell's attempt to resolve religious tensions in Ireland after the famine by bringing in concurrent endowment of the three major Churches. The third concerned education in England, the heart of Russell's moralist strategy. When he returned as Prime Minister in 1846, he made it clear that the extension of state support for education would be a major priority. In 1846–7 the educational grant was extended to include money for trained teachers (thus increasing their salary) and for subsidising their training and increasing the powers of the inspectorate, as well as money for the purchase of books and educational apparatus. Eligibility for educational grants was opened to Wesleyans and, after the 1847 election, to Catholics. This was the most significant development in educational policy before 1870. The amount spent by the state subsequently increased inexorably, from £75,000 in 1845 to £1.3 million in 1862.[144]

By no means all Dissenters were voluntaryists: some, for example, advocated state funding of the secular component of education.[145] However, the atmosphere of 1847 made it much easier to argue for the former option. Voluntaryists set up a separate organisation in 1847, the Dissenters' Parliamentary Committee, because they considered both main political parties to be elitist, reactionary, irreligious and unpatriotic. Twenty-six MPs were returned apparently pledged to disestablishment and sixty more who would oppose further state endowments.[146] The activist Dissenters charged that

[142] *Nonconformist*, 16 Feb. 1848, p. 97.
[143] For this general optimism, see Larsen, *Friends of religious equality*, pp. 121–2.
[144] Parry, *Rise and fall*, p. 202.      [145] Larsen, *Friends of religious equality*, pp. 158–60.
[146] Machin, *Politics and the Churches*, p. 192.

the Whigs, like the Tories, were seeking to use force and taxpayers' money in a regressive policy to prop up religious institutions as mechanisms of social control. In contrast, they claimed to be able to set the people free to evangelise and create a true moral community. It was essential to avoid the errors of continental State-Churchism, which had destroyed the purity of the early Reformation, and fomented the excesses of the French Revolution in the 1790s, because it blunted the individual's moral conscience.[147] In Britain the vigour of conscience had been protected much better, principally by the Free Churches. It was progressive to rely on the 'individual sense of obligation' for the spread of education, a general sense of duty towards 'the claims of our fellow-countrymen'. It was backward to seek to found a policy for the inculcation of religious duties not on those moral foundations but on physical force instead, on the cold steel of the law.[148] The Whigs' attempt to bribe the schoolmaster was a mere utilitarian attempt to perpetuate aristocratic and bureaucratic rule. Edward Baines claimed that state-paid teachers and inspectors would create a system of 'universal espionage', suggesting that government had been infected by the 'police spirit that characterizes the statesmen of Germany'.[149] To the Revd Wells, 'state power' in religion and education, 'reaching over England' was 'against liberty, against national spirit'.[150] Unsurprisingly, the educational dispute gave further impetus to the disestablishment movement: Baines and some other leading Leeds Congregationalists, for example, now affiliated to BASCA.[151] The latter was further helped by Russell's appointment of the supposedly heterodox scholar Hampden to the bishopric of Hereford: the *Nonconformist* claimed that this showed that the aristocracy, not the orthodox laity, ran the Church.[152]

The *Nonconformist* saw the 1847 election as giving Nonconformity a great increase in 'moral power', the result of a combination of events brought about by 'an all-wise Providence'. 'Revealed truth' had triumphed at the expense of 'party trickery', weakening both of the old aristocratic factions.[153] On the eve of the 1848 revolutions Whig–Nonconformist relations could hardly have been worse.

Between 1846 and 1848 Russell's Liberal government was badly divided and dispirited on foreign policy, defence, educational and Irish issues. The

---

[147] *Nonconformist*, 11 Oct., 15 Nov. 1848, pp. 767, 865–6.    [148] *Nonconformist*, 8 Mar. 1848, p. 147.
[149] Feb. 1847, in Larsen, *Friends of religious equality*, p. 144. See his father's similar warning, 17 Mar. 1847: E. Baines, *The life of Edward Baines late MP for the borough of Leeds* (London, 1851), p. 334.
[150] 1847: D. Roberts, *Victorian origins of the British Welfare State* (New Haven, 1960), p. 69.
[151] Larsen, *Friends of religious equality*, p. 83.    [152] *Nonconformist*, 19 Jan., 16 Feb. 1848, pp. 30, 95–6.
[153] *Nonconformist*, 5 Jan., 23 Feb. 1848, pp. 1, 109.

entente with France had collapsed, made worse by Palmerston's controversial attack on France over the Spanish Marriages affairs in 1846. Louis Philippe seemed to have ended his affair with liberalism and thrown in his lot with the Eastern powers, forming a threatening phalanx against liberal principles: France worked with the Eastern powers to suppress the Polish rising at Cracow in 1846 and in the Swiss crisis of 1847. After these developments, and the invasion scare of 1844–5, Palmerston urged more spending on the navy, in order to reassert Britain's dominance and prestige and to prepare it against attack.[154] In 1845 he had told the Commons that, because of steam power, the Channel was 'no longer a barrier', merely 'a river passable by a steam bridge'.[155] On four occasions in 1846 and 1847 Palmerston and Russell joined forces to ask the cabinet to reconstitute the militia. Each time it demurred at the cost and unpopularity entailed.[156] Wood, as Chancellor of the Exchequer, led the opposition, arguing that enough was being done and that extra spending would further antagonise supporters in the provinces, already angered by the government's religious and educational policy.[157] Radical pressure for low taxes was too great to ignore.

Meanwhile the Nonconformist revolt over Ireland and education threatened to paralyse policy in both areas. Evangelical zeal to spread truth and righteousness, and banish godlessness, engendered a distrust of Tory and Whig politics as oligarchical, repressive and continental, particularly under the impetus of Corn Law repeal. However, the growth of voluntaryism was also inspired by an intense hostility to Catholicism and priesthood at a time of great anxiety about the preservation of a moral community. The voluntary solution seemed the only way of putting Irish and United Kingdom politics on a proper religious footing, ensuring political rights for all. The shrillness of Nonconformist criticism of Whiggery in 1847–8 was the result of a unique conjunction of circumstances.

To add to the political difficulties of Liberalism, the education issue drove a wedge between Cobden and the Radical Nonconformists, in and after 1847. Cobden attached great importance to a continental-style universal system of education, as the 'first step to Radicalism'.[158] Though himself an undogmatic Anglican, he worked closely with the Unitarians, especially

---

[154] See *Gooch*, vol. 1, pp. 117–19, 248–54.       [155] *Hansard*, 82:1224, 30 July 1845.
[156] M. S. Partridge, *Military planning for the defense of the United Kingdom, 1814–1870* (New York, 1989), pp. 128–31.
[157] *Gooch*, vol. 1, pp. 243–5. There was also a problem, as there was to be in 1851–2, about the most effective terms on which to organise it.
[158] 1838, Morley, *Cobden*, vol. 1, p. 127.

in Manchester, for this goal. The failure to create an education system also damaged Radical prospects in another way, in that – again like many Unitarians – Cobden was reluctant to promote the cause of Parliamentary reform in the absence of an educated workforce likely to use its vote rationally. He thus disappointed many secular Radicals. His priority was the campaign for international peace and low military spending. But, once the earnest religious rhetoric in which it was couched was disregarded, this was also easily criticised, as the strategy of a self-interested commercial class interested only in penny-pinching economy. In addition, Cobden lacked common ground with the Irish MPs, to whom he felt 'a complete antagonism and repulsion'.[159]

These intense Liberal divisions were ultimately all related. They were caused by anxiety, primarily about social tension at home, but also about the future of liberal principles at home and abroad. Ever since the late 1830s, confidence in the ability of the classes to work together had been failing. The Whigs' gestures had not been able to preserve social unity. Division between town and country, Church and Dissent, Protestant and Catholic, defined British politics. Nor had liberalism made much headway abroad against continental extremes. In Britain and Europe there had been a reaction against it, in search of authority and morality structures. The Whigs were doubly damaged by this reaction. Nonconformists, like many Anglican Tories, sought a more Christian and Protestant politics than the secular progressives of the 1830s had offered. Meanwhile Radicals itched at signs of the continued dominance of the forces of aristocracy, patronage and militarism in Europe and, to a greater or lesser extent, in Britain as well. This weakened Liberal unity, not least because the shortcomings of the governing classes, Whig and Tory, were magnified by the tendency to compare them to continental elites. Accusations of elite lack of patriotism stemmed from a combination of genuine alarm and tactical politics. Even Palmerston was accused of conniving with Russia against constitutional principles – by Julian Harney on the hustings at Tiverton in 1847, and then by Thomas Anstey and Urquhart in the Commons, who brought a motion for his impeachment in February 1848.[160] After the inspirational but also unsettling outbreak of revolution in Europe in the same month, Radical attacks on Whig un-Englishness intensified.

---

[159] K. T. Hoppen, 'Riding a tiger: Daniel O'Connell, Reform, and popular politics in Ireland, 1800– 1847', *Proceedings of the British Academy*, 100 (1999), 138.
[160] See *Hansard*, 96:291–311, 1132–1242, 8 and 23 Feb. 1848.

# CHAPTER 4

# The 1848 revolutions and the triumph
# of liberal patriotism

In February 1848 violent demonstrations in Paris forced Louis Philippe to abdicate and flee to England, while a republic was proclaimed in France. By mid-March, the Pope and the rulers of Naples, Tuscany and Piedmont-Sardinia had all granted constitutions, and agitation in Vienna had forced the fall of Metternich. In Lombardy and Venice there were risings against Austrian rule, while Hungary achieved virtual independence. Berlin was in ferment and talk of German unification under a liberal constitution was rife. The events of spring 1848 ushered in a year of great drama in continental Europe, which initially galvanised the forces of liberalism and nationalism but ended in their large-scale defeat. Liberation for Lombardy, Venetia and Hungary proved impossible to sustain, while, after a brief experiment with socialism, Paris turned to Louis Napoleon to restore order. By the early 1850s, especially after Louis Napoleon's *coup d'état* in 1851, it seemed to most British observers of continental events that several years of turbulence, violence and bloodshed had generally ended in the restoration of autocratic regimes.

As chapter 1 showed, the absence of a revolution in Britain encouraged in retrospect the myth that it had been blessed with a unique degree of political harmony and stability, owing to a combination of its liberal constitution and the nature of the English character. In 1858 Earl Grey maintained that Parliamentary government had not worked anywhere else – except, very recently, in the British-protected regimes in Belgium and Piedmont.[1] Celebrations of English superiority and peculiarity became integral to the political culture of the 1850s and necessarily involved many flattering comparisons with the Continent. Yet this sense of superiority only became rampant in the early 1850s. In 1848–50 the atmosphere was more apocalyptic. There was a concerted attack on the idea of aristocratic politics, which was both an echo of the continental turbulence, and a sometimes desperate attempt to impose

---

[1] Earl Grey, *Parliamentary government considered with reference to Reform* (London, 1864 edn), p. 15.

the values that would ensure that Britain escaped it. The *Nonconformist* declared that the 'English oligarchy', like its continental counterparts, was doomed. Henry Vincent called on the middle and working classes to come together to create a great 'moral and intellectual power', a movement for truth, justice, economy and spiritual enlightenment based on the principles of true religion.[2] In April 1848 Samuel Morley welcomed propertied-class fear at the turn of events, because only that fear would induce 'the aristocracy [to] give up the prey on which they have always been disposed to fatten'.[3] To read Radical newspapers for the first half of 1848 is to be thrust back into the world of 1830, when – also assisted by a revolution in France – the forces of reform and ethical earnestness in all classes had seemed to unite against effete and sectional misgovernment. It suited many political figures to suggest that Russell and his ministers – the allies of the Radicals in 1830 – were now no better than Wellington and the old Tories.

The effect of that attack was to alter the tone of British politics significantly. 'Whiggism', which was caricatured as an exclusive system of government by a small clique of Whig families, was declared slain in favour of the more open style of mid-Victorian Liberalism – a style appropriate for a commercially, institutionally and intellectually progressive country. Russell's government was easy prey for its enemies. Its lack of a majority made it very vulnerable to Parliamentary criticism. Its cabinet appointments and its social, religious, Irish and colonial policy all played into the hands of those who wished to portray it as concerned essentially with the defence of patronage on behalf of a governing caste. Russell and Grey were generally seen as the heads of the two great family connections in the government, and were singled out for particular attack; Grey never held office again. Russell compounded his reputation for social exclusiveness because of his shyness and taciturnity, which made him seem abrupt, proud and self-centred. Whiggism seemed too class-bound and too similar to the aristocratic and autocratic political traditions of the Continent. Other politicians – free-trading Liberals, Peelites, Radicals and Palmerston – fell over each other to proclaim that their own values, by contrast, were distinctly English and modern, capable of appealing to businessmen and indeed all classes.

The resulting political makeover contributed to a national shift of attitude towards a celebratory libertarianism – a shift that was underpinned, more fundamentally, by increased optimism about the effectiveness and superiority of the British economy and polity. In the 1850s innumerable

[2] *Nonconformist*, 3 May 1848, 19 Apr. 1848, pp. 314, 287.
[3] 9 Apr. 1848, E. Hodder, *The life of Samuel Morley* (London, 1887), p. 109.

celebrations of British stability and progress emphasised the fairness of the constitution, the self-discipline of the national character and the importance of liberty in allowing free enterprise and opinion to develop. Vigorous manly energy, liberated from elitist political obstruction, seemed capable of generating economic, social and intellectual progress. The old Whig–Tory stress on the responsibility of elites to provide moral government in order to avoid social division and divine judgment waned in the face of growing complacency about the ability of a British polity rooted in popular confidence to lead the progress of the world towards God's ideal. The effects of the collapse of the party system dovetailed with this mood, by exacerbating the difficulty of agreeing on legislative proposals and encouraging politicians to celebrate national strength and dominance instead. Such conditions were ripe for the neglect of domestic issues and concentration on foreign affairs, which offered the prospect of a national battle against autocracy elsewhere in Europe. In 1849 the conflict with continental statism seemed a life-or-death challenge for English values; by 1853 trigger-happy ebullience engendered a dangerous mood of invincibility.

This chapter starts with the working out of the Radical struggle to harness the energies unleashed on the Continent in 1848 for some productive purpose in British politics. The first three sections focus on three major areas of controversy: Ireland, the colonies, and defence and finance. In these areas, Russell–Grey aristocratic moralism was vigorously attacked. However, in each case the resulting change was less far-reaching in practice than it appeared. Once superficial adjustments had been made, a consensus emerged that British governing practice was now admirably liberal and accountable, so each issue turned into a medium for celebrating British superiority. In the last three sections we see how the major Liberal politicians – including Russell himself, but more specifically Palmerston and Gladstone – managed to cultivate and exploit this mood of superiority. A new emphasis on manly strength abroad combined with disinterested finance and firm liberal Protestantism at home suggested that Britain had sloughed off aristocratic effeteness and was fit to combat alien continental movements and domestic foreign conspiracies. The result was a drift into the Crimean War in 1854. Meanwhile, the emergence of the politics of national identity in so marked a form assisted the maintenance of propertied political influence and allowed the governing classes to see off the internal Radical threat. In areas where it proved effective, Radicalism was revealed as innocuous, compatible with the British political tradition. Where it was more challenging, it was the Radicals who ended by looking subversive and un-English. They were the real victims of a very bloodless coup by one set of propertied politicians against another.

THE ATTACK ON ARISTOCRATIC POLITICS: IRELAND

When Russell became Prime Minister in 1846 he hoped it would inaugurate a 'golden age for Ireland'.[4] He planned to settle Irish animosities by achieving two aims which the Tories could not: granting the Catholics full political and religious equality and using the power of the state to check landlords' abuses of their powers over tenants. Between 1848 and 1852 his Irish policy was destroyed. Mostly responsible was the great tragedy of the Irish famine, the political consequences of which have been traced elsewhere.[5] But Irish debates were affected also by the general determination to attack the 'aristocratic' and 'continental' approaches that Russell seemed to exemplify, and to assert 'English' liberal values in their place. Together, these trends had two effects. They strengthened distrust of Irish landlords' ability to milk the British taxpayer for their own gain, but also of Russell's land reform plans. And they heightened the suspicion of Russell's intentions to give state funding to all three major Irish religious sects, to the point that it became politically unacceptable to do so. The result of both developments was a rejection of the 'Whig' policy of positive state interference to regulate Irish society, and a growing confidence instead in the superiority of free-market principles, in economics and religion.

Irrespective of the famine, many British Liberals and Radicals wanted to reduce the influence of landlords in Ireland, on the grounds that they lacked a sense of social responsibility or a commitment to political economy principles. The Whigs had introduced the Poor Law into Ireland in 1838 in order to make the landlords responsible for poor relief and thus force them to invest in agriculture in order to minimise their relief burdens. By 1846–7 reports abounded in England that selfish landlords were failing to give adequate help in their localities, and they, together with indolent labourers, were widely blamed for Ireland's economic problems. This made famine relief schemes unpopular if they involved pouring taxpayers' money into landlords' pockets. A reconstruction of Irish society on the principles of self-help and free enterprise seemed imperative for the good of the people; the famine demonstrated the consequences of disobeying natural laws. Further

[4] Gray, *Famine, land and politics*, p. 143.
[5] Ibid.; D. A. Kerr, *'A nation of beggars'? Priests, people, and politics in famine Ireland, 1846–1852* (Oxford, 1994).

subsidy could be seen as thwarting God's will: *The Times* commented that Providence was dissolving the previously corrupt state of Irish society.[6] The banking crisis, economic depression and income-tax agitation of 1847–8 made the tone of the Commons even less generous in 1848. Charles Wood, who as an economising Chancellor was no great fan of largesse himself, noted in April 1848 that in Britain 'there is the very strongest determination not to pursue the old system of buying the landlords to keep down the people'.[7]

However, reform proposals that sought to check the social power of landlords fared no better, because they could be linked to un-English principles of socialism. For example, in the winter of 1847–8 Russell suggested the extension of tenant right, compensation for improvements and, later, a Prussian system of land banks to encourage owner-occupation, allowing small farmers to mortgage their land cheaply. Appalled by the number of evictions and the operation of 'lynch law', he wanted landlords to show greater responsibility to their tenants.[8] Some Radicals, like Cobden, desired a far-reaching redistribution of land towards small tenants, on the Swiss-German model. However, especially in the context of the Parisian revolution, such ideas appeared to threaten property rights. Smith O'Brien's attempted rebellion of July 1848 added to the assertions that the Irish were wrong-headed, ungrateful for British assistance, and keener on violence than self-improvement.[9] So reform faltered, and Russell had little other than coercion to propose for Ireland in 1848 and 1849, to his embarrassment. Hence the emergence of the Irish Tenant League, arguing for tenant right, in 1850. There was a further small Parliamentary grant, and a rate-in-aid, in 1849, as well as a loan in 1850, but even these were met with allegations of 'communism'.[10] In February 1849 Russell commented that the reason why a generous relief policy had failed 'lies deep in the breast of the British people'.[11] The only policy on which cabinet and Parliament could agree was one that was critical of landlordism in a way more acceptable to 'English' and enlightened notions of property rights and obligations. The Encumbered Estates Acts of 1848 and 1849 established a court with powers to order the sale of estates encumbered by mortgages and other debts, so that the debts could be paid off and the land resold more cheaply, it was

---

[6] P. Gray, 'National humiliation and the Great Hunger: fast and famine in 1847', *Irish Historical Studies*, 32 (2000), 193–216; Gray, *Famine, land and politics*, p. 282.
[7] Gray, *Famine, land and politics*, p. 284.
[8] Ibid., pp. 183–4, 192, 207; Kerr, *Nation of beggars*, p. 137.
[9] Gray, *Famine, land and politics*, p. 305.    [10] *Stanley*, p. 11, 30 June 1849.
[11] Kerr, *Nation of beggars*, p. 198.

hoped to enterprising farmers (British or Irish) who would sink capital in regenerative improvements. These Acts ushered in a period in which political economy principles dominated in Irish land policy. Men of property liked the defence of freedom of contract, while Radicals, Nonconformists and Peelites approved of the idea of 'business principles' and 'entrepreneurship'. Throughout the 1850s a rhetoric of freedom and political economy justified a lack of action on Irish economic policy. Reformism went out of fashion.

The 1847–9 period also saw the collapse of Russell's Irish religious policy. His first aim had been, in contrast to the Tories, to give Catholics equality of political patronage, so that they felt confidence in the state: as he called it, 'Ireland for the Irish'.[12] Once this was done, it would be possible to introduce concurrent endowment by the state of the Catholic and the Presbyterian Churches along with the existing Established Church – because assistance for their priests would no longer be seen as a bribe. By concurrent endowment, the Catholic Church would be recognised as the major spiritual and popular force in Ireland. The priesthood would gain financial security, and with it the enhanced status that would encourage responsible political behaviour. This would be all the more useful if, as a result of land reform, the number of Catholic proprietors greatly increased.[13] Cornewall Lewis felt that state assistance to the Catholic Church would not only pacify Ireland and save money on army and police, but would also bring 'prestige abroad'.[14] In spring and again in autumn 1848 Russell urged this policy on the cabinet – in the form of a tax on landlords which would allow glebes to be bought for clergymen. But, though it was seriously considered between October and December 1848, and again in late 1849, it was never introduced to Parliament, because of hostility from British Protestants and from the Irish hierarchy.

From a British perspective, 1847–8 was the worst imaginable time to consider concurrent endowment. The 1847 Parliament, elected on an Anglican and Nonconformist tide of anxiety about Maynooth, was the most 'Protestant' of the century. Lewis gloomily reflected in 1848 that the depressing condition of Ireland was the price that England paid for its Protestant zeal.[15] Anti-Catholic feeling in Parliament frustrated Russell's attempt to restore diplomatic relations with the Pope in 1848. Nonconformists opposed

[12] To Lansdowne, 19 July 1843, *Gooch*, vol. I, pp. 64–5; Hardcastle, *Campbell*, vol. II, p. 193.

[13] Kerr, *Nation of beggars*, pp. 178, 194.

[14] To Sir E. Head, 24 Nov. 1848, Sir G. F. Lewis (ed.), *Letters of the right hon. George Cornewall Lewis, Bart, to various friends* (London, 1870), p. 190.

[15] Kerr, *Nation of beggars*, p. 5.

concurrent endowment as a Whig strategy for the 'enslavement of the people', the preservation of landlord power and the re-establishment of popery.[16] Fearing that Russell would introduce the policy in the 1849 session, and galvanised by the excitements of 1848, BASCA organised a major campaign of meetings against it in the autumn of 1848. Nonconformists forced the Whig candidate at the West Riding by-election to step down because of his support for the idea, and replaced him with a voluntaryist – who was then defeated by a Conservative.[17] They felt that their opposition had played an important part in the abandonment of concurrent endowment, and this heightened their drive for the abolition of their major immediate grievance, Church rates (an abolition bill was introduced in 1849 and subsequent sessions) and their opposition to state-supported education in England.

But the increasingly intransigent opposition of the Catholic bishops was even more problematical. Russell hoped that the 1848 rebellions in Ireland and Europe would persuade them of the need to work with the state against infidelity and communism. But most bishops felt that it would be embarrassing for them to take state money at the very time when so many of their parishioners resented the inadequacy of state aid during the famine; the latter would feel betrayed and probably less loyal to the Church.[18] There was also a growing Ultramontane feeling among Catholic leaders that the revivified papacy could do more for Irish Catholicism than the government in London and Dublin. Moreover, after 1848 it was more important for the Pope to strengthen the authority of the Church against secularist threats. His earlier liberalism had been all but destroyed by the Italian revolutions of 1848–9, culminating in his own flight from Rome and then the reimposition of order in the peninsula by Austrian, Neapolitan and French troops. In Ireland, the most obvious route to the goal of defending mass loyalty to Catholicism against secular liberalism was by retaining the allegiance of the poor.

The growth of papal and episcopal obstinacy alarmed the government, both because it suggested a rising clerical assertiveness against liberal forces, and, more immediately, because it made Irish government much more difficult. This was evident not just over concurrent endowment but also in Russell's failure to get episcopal support for his policy of encouraging lay Catholics to use the new undenominational Queen's University (founded

---

[16] *Nonconformist*, 16 Aug., 20 Sept., 11 Oct. 1848, pp. 614–15, 709–10, 766–8.
[17] F. M. L. Thompson, 'Whigs and Liberals in the West Riding, 1830–60', *English Historical Review*, 74 (1959), 233.
[18] Kerr, *Nation of beggars*, pp. 181–5; *Nonconformist*, 18 Oct. 1848, p. 788.

by his government in 1850). He hoped that through university reform an enlightened Catholic middle class might develop, capable of leading Irish opinion – against excessive clerical influence. There was considerable support for the Colleges from lay Catholics and a large minority of bishops led by Archbishop Murray. But at the Synod of Thurles in autumn 1850, the Irish bishops declared, by a majority of one vote, that this 'godless' system of university education was injurious to the faith and morals of Catholics. The leadership of the new Primate, Archbishop Cullen, a fierce Ultramontane and Roman resident for thirty years, was crucial in this decision, and the Pope subsequently reaffirmed his hostility to mixed education. Cullen argued that few of the initial professorial appointments at the Colleges went to Catholics, and that it was essential to preserve the independence and vigour of Church teaching – by establishing a separate privately funded Catholic University, for which he then worked tirelessly. Russell saw these developments as a victory for an Ultramontane party against Irish lay opinion and the more compliant Murray. It was a foreign and ecclesiastical interference in politics and a declaration of contempt for the government.[19] It was all the more worrying for Irish policy since after the death of O'Connell in 1847 no lay politician had come to the fore to take up his role as a respected leader with whom the Whigs could negotiate effectively.

At this point, in October 1850, came the announcement that the Pope intended to establish a hierarchy of Catholic bishops in England, with territorial titles. This long-planned change aimed to service the Catholic population (rapidly growing in the 1840s, primarily because of Irish immigration) better than the old system of vicars-apostolic could do. The re-establishment of the hierarchy made little practical difference, certainly not to the safety of the state, to which all Catholic officeholders had to swear an oath of allegiance under the terms of the 1829 Emancipation Act. If anything, the new departure encouraged a spirit of self-government, independent of Rome, among English Catholics. However, the announcement of the establishment of a papal hierarchy was anathema to excited Protestant opinion; *The Times* labelled it a 'papal aggression'. The resulting popular furore marked the high point of Victorian anti-Catholicism. It chimed perfectly with the strong self-satisfaction in Britain at the moral virtues that derived from Protestantism, further exacerbated by the criticism of the political failings of Catholic continental countries in 1848–9 and by post-famine Irish immigration. This Protestant clamour was perhaps the

[19] *Hansard*, 114:188–90, 7 Feb. 1851.

most notable of the various British assertions of the need to defend home values at a time of European turbulence after 1848. There were violent scenes on Guy Fawkes night, and county and other meetings were held to petition against the new arrangements: by December 1850, 5 per cent of the population had participated. Asked for his views by the Anglican bishop of Durham, Russell wrote a famous reply condemning the Pope's action.[20] The Durham letter was an abstract but forceful declaration of his erastian views, and became a major event in British politics because it led the government into introducing an Ecclesiastical Titles Bill in 1851, which allowed the government to prosecute and fine clerics outside the Established Churches who assumed a territorial title without its consent.

Russell's response to the papal aggression reflected both his own intense religious emotion and his insecurity about his political position, in Britain and in Ireland. He was angry at the mounting Radical allegations of his lack of patriotism over Irish, colonial and social policy; he was also aware that Palmerston, through his foreign policy, was engaging with the post-1848 tone of national distinctiveness better than he was. He was by now a beleaguered Prime Minister and wanted to recover the initiative and redeem his popularity. But the affair also engaged his fundamental principles – which is why it is so odd that his response is sometimes seen as unprincipled, hypocritical or intolerant. His aims should not be confused with the visceral Tory or evangelical Protestant protests. Russell was an erastian constitutionalist, concerned to assert the authority of the liberal state over ecclesiastical bodies, in Britain and in Ireland. (The letter included criticism of the English Tractarians who were refusing to accept state leadership on Church of England matters and who were threatening the unity, breadth and national efficacy of the Church.) He was angry at the papacy's failure to recognise the Crown's supremacy in English ecclesiastical matters, so fundamental to Whiggish notions of English history and good government. The Pope's act was invalid until approved and regulated by the state, and an 'insult to this country'.[21] To protest about it was on a par with Palmerston's simultaneous robust assertion of Britain's international diplomatic position: indeed Palmerston himself was outraged at the 'insolent and ostentatious' manner of the papal announcement and felt the question was political, not religious.[22]

Russell also intended to lay down the law to the Irish bishops. As long as they had been willing to negotiate constructively with the government,

---

[20] 4 Nov. 1850, Prest, *Russell*, pp. 429–30.    [21] *Hansard*, 114:501, 12 Feb. 1851.
[22] To W. Temple, 27 Jan. 1851, Ashley, *Palmerston*, vol. 1, pp. 246–50.

he had not cared whether bishops used territorial titles – and in practice the British state and courts had recognised the bishops' status and rights for many years. But now he wanted to make it clear to them that the only hope of progress in Church–state affairs in Ireland was for them to reject Ultramontanism in favour of an institutional relationship with a British government. Russell, as a staunch Protestant anti-clerical, believed that the lesson of European history was that powerful ecclesiastical bodies were always a threat to lay liberties and must be checked by national governments.[23] His lifelong principle was that the way to protect the people against the Church was by maintaining 'the supremacy of Parliament as the great lay tribunal'.[24] The papacy's failure to give formal notice to the government about the introduction of a hierarchy seemed to confirm Rome's unwillingness to restart the necessary dialogue over Irish policy. Moreover, the Irish Catholics already enjoyed less government superintendence than their co-religionists almost anywhere in Europe. In introducing the Ecclesiastical Titles Bill, Russell argued that continental states would find his proposals unexceptional: 'no Roman Catholic power . . . would permit any bull to be brought into the country without the previous sanction of the civil authority'.[25] His outbursts were a defiant restatement of his view that the Catholic Church could only gain concessions from the British state by entering into a partnership, accepting Whig leadership. In the heated anti-Catholic climate of 1851, this was probably correct.

Nonetheless, the Ecclesiastical Titles Bill was a political mistake; indeed it was a trap set by the opposition. The Protestant agitation and the Durham letter created very strong pressure for a legislative response, which was bound to antagonise some of Russell's fragile coalition of Protestant and Catholic supporters whatever form it took. The Conservatives, alleging that government negotiations with the Catholic Church in Italy and Ireland had encouraged the Pope to this act of arrogance, pressed the government for a bill. It passed by very large majorities. But it was a dead letter from the outset: Russell did not intend to fine bishops or seek to have their titles removed, just to make an abstract statement about the nature of the British polity. And it deeply divided the Liberal party, badly weakening the already shaky government by alienating Irish MPs and Peelites. Most Irish MPs representing Catholic constituencies opposed the Act; fifteen subsequently

---

[23] *Hansard*, 114:190, 194, 7 Feb. 1851.
[24] John, Earl Russell, *A letter to the right hon. Chichester Fortescue, MP on the state of Ireland* (2nd edn, London, 1868), p. 73.
[25] *Hansard*, 114:197–8, 7 Feb. 1851.

voted in the successful motion to bring down the Russell government in February 1852; a significant, though as it turned out not very long-lived, independent Irish party was formed to contest the 1852 election, with unprecedented support from the Catholic Church. Irish Catholics could argue that the Bill was an offensively anti-Catholic police-state measure. Russell's declaration that he sought to govern Ireland on the principles employed in Prussia and France allowed the Irish MP G. H. Moore to allege that he was following the 'despotic' continental policy of suppressing opinions rather than the one followed by constitutional governments such as the United States.[26]

Many British Liberals – especially Radicals, Nonconformists and the leaders of the Peelite group – also criticised it vehemently, especially on Irish but also on more general grounds, as an intolerant return to penal enactments against religion which demonstrated an arrogant Whig desire to use official power to curtail religious liberties. Joseph Hume, for example, claimed that an alternative policy of 'free trade in religion' was more suited to Englishmen.[27] Many denied that the Pope was so great a threat – England was now too strong politically and intellectually. Indeed, Gladstone argued that the establishment of a national hierarchy might well make the Catholic Church in England more national, not more Ultramontane.[28] In any case, Nonconformists claimed, it was not by institutional means that the Protestantism of the national character could be defended, certainly not by upholding the patronage-ridden Established Church.[29] The measure was sinister because it justified repressive state attacks on the internal organisation of other Churches. W. J. Fox raised the possibility of regulation of Nonconformity, while Gladstone was worried that Russell's anti-Tractarian rhetoric in the Durham letter presaged a further Whig assault on the liberties of worship in the Church of England itself.[30]

The papal aggression controversy confirmed many Nonconformists, Radicals and Peelites in their suspicions of Whig statism. Indeed the slow emergence of the policy of Irish Church disestablishment came out of this crisis; it was adopted by BASCA's successor, the Liberation Society, in 1853 and taken up by its Parliamentary spokesman Edward Miall in 1856. The aim was not to give a sectional benefit to the Irish. Rather it seemed a more acceptably *British* proposal than Russell's apparently *continental* alternative, a better way of governing on behalf of the whole United Kingdom.

---

[26] *Hansard*, 114:235–6, 7 Feb. 1851.   [27] *Hansard*, 114:493, 12 Feb. 1851.
[28] *Hansard*, 115:591–2, 25 Mar. 1851.   [29] Bright, *Hansard*, 114:242–56, 7 Feb. 1851.
[30] Fox, *Hansard*, 115:370, 21 Mar. 1851, Gladstone, *Hansard*, 115:565–97, 25 Mar. 1851.

However, it took many years for this policy to gain widespread support; it was too radical for the 1850s. Russell, equally, saw his proposal as the properly patriotic one, both in allowing the good government of Ireland, and in asserting Whig constitutionalism and Protestantism in a British context. And he was far from alone. One of his most significant supporters was Britain's premier Catholic, the 13th duke of Norfolk, who converted to Anglicanism, arguing that Ultramontanism was incompatible with allegiance to the sovereign.[31] Moreover, most Nonconformists in fact supported legislation in principle, despite the vocal opposition of some of their number. Those who accepted the Ecclesiastical Titles Act asserted that in this instance the royal supremacy did not imply state control of religion, but, rather, was another term for national sovereignty and independence. The issue was one of patriotism, loyalty and political liberties, not the subordination of religion to state authority. By March–April 1851 this view was clearly in the ascendant among Dissenters.[32] The *British Quarterly Review* reminded its readers that the nation had 'no deadlier foe' than Catholicism and that if it were to 'resume its ancient sway over Britain . . . her liberties will be scattered to the wind'.[33] The affair was in fact very awkward for Dissenters, since, unlike evangelical Tory Anglicans, they did not want a strong act regulating the position of the Catholic Church, but nor could they accept a priestly claim to be above the law of England. The crisis revealed Nonconformist pride in national distinctness and the fact that the intensity of their hostility of 1845–8 to the state had been exceptional. Disestablishment certainly remained an ideal, but the need to purge the political order of its corruption seemed less urgent. At the 1852 election BASCA decided not to press candidates to pledge to religious equality, on the grounds that free trade and Reform were more important issues.[34]

The effect of such a strong demand for an *English* policy, both in response to the Catholic threat, and in dealing with Irish economic problems, meant that there was no possibility of an effective engagement with Irish political opinion in the 1850s. The lack of initiatives in Irish policy lasted through the decade. Those who argued that the Irish economy needed *laissez-faire* and freedom of contract retained ascendancy, because in an atmosphere of

---

[31] Machin, *Politics and the Churches*, p. 219.
[32] For much evidence on this point, see ibid., p. 222, and Larsen, *Friends of religious equality*, pp. 233–41, though Larsen claims that this was an unusual event, when Dissent did not 'live up to its own noble principles'.
[33] W. L. Alexander, 'Popery – its rise and development', *British Quarterly Review*, 14 (1851), 543.
[34] Larsen, *Friends of religious equality*, pp. 117–18.

rampant celebration of English political, economic and Protestant vigour, and with Irish Catholic MPs divided into factions, it was the only acceptable policy. In religious affairs, meanwhile, the endowment of Catholicism had become politically unacceptable. Russell himself came round to the consensus position, declaring against it in 1853 on the grounds that the Catholic Church, 'acting under the direction of its head, himself a foreign sovereign, has aimed at political power', both in the United Kingdom and elsewhere in Europe, challenging Crown authority and 'the general cause of liberty'.[35] His volte-face has been much criticised, but it was not inconsistent in his own eyes. If the Catholic hierarchy would not accept terms of engagement with the state, it could expect no benefits. Since the state's role was to support 'the religious liberties and civil rights of mankind', there was no point in it working with a papacy which was not willing to make concessions towards these goals.[36]

Russell, dogged by accusations of elitism, had failed to build a policy capable of tapping national loyalties for the benefit of the Liberal party. But nor had the opponents of his religious and Irish policies: there was as yet no agreement on Irish Church disestablishment. This was, not least, because the urgency of the voluntaryist campaign was on the wane. In a climate of growing national self-satisfaction, it was ceasing to be a priority. The cathartic rejection of 'aristocracy' after 1848 had petered out; further intense self-examination was unnecessary. In that sense, Russell's anti-papal appeal was not such a failure. His invocation of the spirit of British Protestantism had led large numbers of Nonconformists to declare their loyalty to the state, reflecting a shift in tone since the bitter criticisms of 1847–8. Though the episode showed that he was a much less effective political leader for the time than Palmerston, it also indicated how significant patriotic politics had become.

### THE ATTACK ON ARISTOCRATIC POLITICS: THE COLONIES

In 1848 the colonial issue was also used by the government's critics in order to extend the virtuous struggle against aristocratic misgovernment. This struggle was led by the 'colonial reformers', most of whom came together in the Society for the Reform of Colonial Government established in 1849. Core reformers included the Radicals Molesworth and Charles Buller (until his death in 1848), together with young Whigs such as Wodehouse (the future cabinet minister Kimberley) and some Conservatives such as Walpole

---

[35] *Hansard*, 127:945–6, 31 May 1853.     [36] Quotation to Clarendon, 1 Oct. 1850: Prest, *Russell*, p. 320.

and Adderley. The reform movement was also supported by Radicals such as Cobden and Hume, and by Peelites such as Lincoln, Gladstone and Graham. A few of these were instinctive supporters of the independence of the colonies, on financial grounds. The majority, meanwhile, believed in strengthening the empire. But the tensions between the two positions hardly surfaced in 1848–9 as reformers responded to the recent dismantling of imperial protection by demanding a review of the nature of the connection with the colonies and attacking domineering Whig over-government of them. In July 1848 Molesworth introduced the first of several motions on the issue. He condemned the 'weak and ignorant despotism' of the Colonial Office as 'hateful and odious' to 'men of our race' in the colonies, who were 'intelligent and energetic Englishmen' and deserved greater liberty. The Office, he claimed, ran a giant patronage system rather than an efficient and rational policy for forty communities scattered worldwide. Self-government would relieve the taxpayer significantly: the colonial army could be cut by 22,000 men, to 10,000, by a series of policy changes including the renunciation of the Falkland Islands.[37] The *Nonconformist* complained at Colonial Office attempts to impose bishops and concurrent endowment on colonies, replicating the evils of Anglicanism. This was 'Whig Guizotism', which sought to 'perpetuate the power of the aristocracy by the arts of corruption', just as the July monarchy had failed to do in France.[38] The extent of the criticism suggested to Elgin, one member of the colonial elite, that 'our masters, the middle classes' now felt that the colonies were an irritating burden.[39]

Great changes occurred in the following seven years. Responsible government was granted to New South Wales and New Zealand in 1855 (and in Prince Edward Island in 1851 and Newfoundland in 1855), following on from the major North American territories (Nova Scotia, New Brunswick and Canada itself) which had received it in 1846–8. The pace of movement towards responsible government in Australia and New Zealand was increased after 1852, because it became seen as the consensual view, assisted by the absence of any great strategic threat to Australia from another power. By 1861 universal manhood suffrage was the norm in the Australian colonies. The Cape and Jamaica received constitutional reform, but not responsible party government, in 1853 and 1854. Strikingly, the Colonial Office itself became anxious to hurry on responsible government wherever it was more or less appropriate, even before there was much local demand

---

[37] *Hansard*, 100:816, 836, 849, 25 July 1848.   [38] *Nonconformist*, 8 Mar, 10 May 1848, pp. 145, 326.
[39] Stembridge, *Parliament*, pp. 56–7.

for it.[40] In 1857 John Bright claimed that colonial reformer pressure had been responsible for a 'revolution in opinion'.[41] The influence of the aristocratic deadweights preventing this liberation, particularly Earl Grey, Colonial Secretary 1846–52, had apparently been shaken off. Colonial reformers entered the political mainstream after 1852: Lincoln (now duke of Newcastle) was influential as Colonial Secretary in developing policy on Australasia, and Molesworth was also in the Aberdeen cabinet. Once more, a tacit alliance between Radicals and Peelites seemed to have superseded Whig illiberalism.

In fact this perception was wide of the mark. The real differences between Newcastle and Molesworth on the one hand, and Grey and Russell on the other, were slight. Russell and Grey were influential in the shift towards self-government, while the Colonial Office had long preferred it where practicable. Just before becoming Colonial Secretary in 1846, Grey had talked of the need to extend to the colonies 'the privilege of self-government', 'the dearest right of Englishmen'.[42] Indeed the two men took crucial early steps towards it in Canada. In 1841 Russell, then Colonial Secretary, implemented the Durham Report in uniting Upper and Lower Canada, and made the executive (that is, the British-appointed governor and his advisers) accountable to the elected assembly on a day-to-day basis. He recognised that this was the best way to strengthen government (since a lack of accountability had made the assemblies reluctant to grant the executive revenue) and to retain British influence at little cost. However, this was not full 'responsible government' in that, in a classically Whig outcome, the governor retained control of substantial patronage, with which he sought to keep political influence – allowing Radicals continuing scope to abuse Russell. Russell felt that governor power over patronage was necessary in order to check destructive partisanship and potential republicanism in the Assembly, especially but not just among the French minority. This was also Peel's view. However, when the Whigs returned to power in 1846, Grey changed the policy, granting responsible government in the sense of accepting that party strength in the assembly should dictate the composition of the ministry, just as in Britain in 1841 and 1846, and that the governor should cede his patronage to the ministry. This was a response to opposition victories in elections in Nova Scotia in 1846 and Canada in 1847. Grey and Prime Minister Russell felt that to acquiesce in majority rule was the best way of lancing the boil of the minority French separatist movement.

[40] J. M. Ward, *Colonial self-government: the British experience* (London, 1976), ch. 9.
[41] To Cobden, 16 Apr. 1857, Morley, *Cobden*, vol. II, pp. 194–6.      [42] *Hansard*, 86:1310, 28 May 1846.

The turbulence of 1848, raising the risk of French and Irish nationalist uprisings in Canada in sympathy with European republicanism, made both men grateful that the Canadian government now included French representatives. The ease with which order was maintained in Canada in 1848 was a defining moment in policy. Indeed it led to expressions of pride at the superiority of Canadian institutions to those of the United States. In 1849 Grey agreed that the imperial Parliament would not attempt to veto Canadian measures of purely local importance. Paradoxically, the measure in question was an indemnity for the property losses suffered by Frenchmen in the 1837 rebellion – and some colonial reformers, led by Gladstone, charged that the government was behaving unpatriotically in allowing rebels to qualify for the compensation. Gladstone claimed that this betrayed 'national honour', meaning 'the honour of the Crown' and the 'most sacred duties of Government'. This was a very revealing moment, demonstrating that Grey's critics did not lack chauvinism, or at least opportunism.[43]

Despite all this, it suited Radical and Peelite colonial reformers to portray Grey as an overbearing meddler, and it was possible to do so on a number of counts. He was severely criticised for his dictatorial treatment of the Governor of the Cape, Sir Harry Smith, for failing to fight the 7th Frontier War with sufficient vigour – especially since the costly war was unpopular in Parliament. The Russell government would probably have fallen on Grey's South African policy in early 1852 had it not been defeated on the militia issue.[44] And he was reluctant to move to responsible government in Australia as quickly as the colonial reformers demanded, so his compromise Australian government bills of 1849 and 1850 encountered fierce opposition from Radical and Peelite MPs. His hesitation was partly because he felt that his opponents were enemies of the imperial connection, partly because of his hostility to the excessive factionalism of small colonial communities, which militated against the establishment of workable consensus by more independent elites, and partly because of his sense of duty.[45] Grey believed in the idea of a steady progress to self-government, but, as an evangelical, he also believed that Britain had a 'responsibility of the highest kind' to use 'the power and the advantages entrusted . . . by Providence' to diffuse 'the blessings of Christianity and civilization' to its imperial

---

[43] The best account of the process of Canadian reform is Buckner, *Transition to responsible government*. This paragraph relies heavily on chs. 7 and 8. For Elgin's reports of the perceived superiority of the Canadian to the United States' constitution (1853), see Ward, *Colonial self-government*, pp. 296–7. For Gladstone's attack in 1849, see *Hansard*, 106:223, 14 June 1849.

[44] Stembridge, *Parliament*, pp. 75–6; Matthew, *Gladstone 1809–1874*, p. 75.

[45] Stembridge, *Parliament*, pp. 7–8; Grey, *Parliamentary government*, pp. 335–9.

lands.[46] This would be done best by securing the maintenance of free trade, the protection of native minorities, and the leadership of an educated elite. For example, he discerned in Australian party behaviour a regrettable and sectional desire by speculators to grab Crown lands for private benefit rather than ordered emigration. Moreover, deeply concerned about lawlessness and the inadequacy of police and prisons in Britain, he was anxious to continue transportation to some of the eastern Australian colonies, which most of his colleagues felt was incompatible with responsible government.[47]

Both his alarm about disorder and his anxiety to do the will of Providence reflected his concern to learn lessons from the 1848 revolution in France. An important component of Whig colonial policy was the urgent sense of responsibility for colonial good government and global progress, as a Providential duty. Both Russell and Palmerston in 1850 also expressed this sense, when resisting the Radical–Peelite motion demanding the abolition of the African Squadron, which was attempting (without much success) to prevent the continuation of the West African slave trade. There was so much opposition within the Liberal coalition to funding the squadron, on grounds of economy and the Dissenting belief that an international crusade mounted by virtuous public opinion would kill the trade more effectively, that Russell made the issue a vote of confidence, to the fury of many MPs.[48] Russell and Palmerston shared a lifelong commitment to the idea of the British state's duty to attack the slave trade, as a symbol of Britain's honour and the Christian beneficence of its naval power.[49] Russell told the Commons that unless Britain continued to do its duty against slavery, it would be betraying its 'high . . . moral, and . . . Christian character' and would no longer have the right to expect the continuation of the divine blessing which had allowed Britain to escape revolution in 1848.[50] But his success in the vote was a pyrrhic victory, as the strength of the squadron was much reduced thereafter.

By 1852 there was a clear shift of political opinion away from such moralism and in favour of self-government and economy. The assumption was that representative government was so self-evidently the appropriate policy for 'British' colonies that other concerns should be marginalised. As a

[46] Earl Grey, *The colonial policy of Lord John Russell's administration* (2 vols., London, 1853), vol. I, pp. 13–15.
[47] J. M. Ward, *Earl Grey and the Australian colonies, 1846–57: a study of self-government and self-interest* (Melbourne, 1958), esp. ch. 8.
[48] See Greville, *Journal*, vol. VI, p. 332.
[49] See Palmerston's comments in Southgate, *Most English minister*, p. 151 (1864) and D. B. Davis, *Slavery and human progress* (New York, 1984) p. xviii (1846).
[50] See Walpole, *Russell*, vol. II, pp. 106–7 for this and Palmerston's note of congratulation.

result, attempts to write in safeguards for free trade in the colonies were given up. And there was less interest in protecting the natives. The Maori problem was all but forgotten when New Zealand was given responsible government in 1855 – leading to their war with the European settlers over land rights from 1860, to Grey's deep disappointment.[51] Taxpayer and Radical pressure forced successive British governments, from 1850 onwards, to abandon the policy of the 1840s to protect tribal land rights beyond South Africa's Orange River; the annexation of 1848 was reversed in 1854. Evangelical notions of Britain's responsibility to rescue the natives, spiritually and politically, seemed to be losing their power. This reflected a declining fear of divine judgment and an increasing assumption about English superiority to all other peoples.[52] Some Radicals articulated a shrill progressivism: Roebuck opined that the natives must be exterminated in the name of progress, Molesworth that they were incapable of civilisation.[53] More positively, there was also a sense that the best chance of racial integration was through economic progress and free political institutions rather than expensive military action. When representative institutions were granted at the Cape in 1854 the British insisted on a colour-blind (but not wealth-blind) franchise.

So the two major pressures on colonial policy in the early 1850s were domestic taxpayer concern with economy, and a widespread confidence in the natural global triumph of liberal principles without government assistance. In theory this suggested the impending end of the formal colonial connection, in line with other departures from *ancien régime* ideals. In the 1830s it had been widely assumed that self-government would logically lead to separation, on the United States model. The fall of the old protectionist colonial system in the 1840s seemed to challenge the value of a formal empire even more. Cobden was 'as anxious as anyone that the English race should spread itself over the earth', but he believed that this colonisation was done better by vigorous entrepreneurship and the natural ties of religion, race and language than by a costly political apparatus.[54] The settler colonies were increasingly seen as fertile and dynamic symbols of English vigour and of the benefits of the free flow of resources – since they were storehouses of raw materials. Their Anglo-Saxon values would ensure that their success would match that of the United States, which, for many Radicals, bore testament to the vigour and independence of settler life. The removal of tariffs would increase informal British power: in 1846 one MP called free trade a benevolent principle by which 'foreign nations would

---

[51] Grey, *Parliamentary government*, pp. 357–9.    [52] See Introduction, pp. 16–17, 22–3.
[53] Stembridge, *Parliament*, pp. 76–8.    [54] *Hansard*, 70:205, 22 June 1843, and 115:1443, 10 Apr. 1851.

become valuable Colonies to us, without imposing on us the responsibility of governing them'.[55] Colonial independence, sooner or later, seemed logical, and there was a general recognition – agreed by the Liberal cabinet as far back as 1836 – that it would be un-English to *resist* a colonial movement for separation if it arose.[56]

However, these high-flown sentiments had no practical importance, because there *was* no colonial movement for separation. The underlying significance of the debates of 1848–51 was in fact very different: to strengthen British pride in the colonies as symbols of healthy national values. The Russell–Grey idea of using state power to protect the natives and free-trade arrangements was defeated by a chauvinist assumption that the right values would be spread anyway. Liberals could agree in celebrating the end of the old Tory colonial preference system. The white empire was a convenient symbol of the British commitment to inclusive and constitutional, rather than exclusive and aristocratic, political ideals. It seemed a dynamic and progressive force, which provided further evidence of the success of English constitutional and religious values compared to the autocracy, protectionism and civil strife of the Continent. In 1852 Reeve compared the failure of liberalism in Europe with the movement to 'free states' in Australia and Canada. 'Whatever may be the fate of Europe, if these efforts are successful, the general cause of liberty and civilisation will not suffer.'[57] Radicals liked to see the colonies as embodying English values in a purer form than in the home country, weighed down as it was by old wealth and privilege and feudal hangovers.[58] Others saw them in a more conservative light. Gladstone, for example, wanted to strengthen their religious institutions: he was involved with the Anglican religious groups who had founded colonies (as at Canterbury in New Zealand) and colonial bishoprics. He hoped that these territories would be the equivalent of the satellite city-states of ancient Greece, colonising new lands with the civilised values of the parent state. Differences between these ideals had little political significance at the time: from the mid-1850s the white colonies ceased to be controversial issues. Indeed, as exemplars of British practices, it began to be considered unpatriotic to criticise the cost of their upkeep as freely as in the 1848–50 period. Then, the imperial nexus could be portrayed as a scam run by aristocratic and protectionist vested interests; now, to challenge colonial expenditure could easily appear grubby and materialistic, concerned with money rather

---

[55] Edward Buller, *Hansard*, 83:1399–1400, 23 Feb. 1846.     [56] See Bourne, *Palmerston*, pp. 624–5.
[57] To de Tocqueville, 23 May 1852, in Laughton, *Reeve*, vol. 1, p. 261.
[58] E.g. *Nonconformist*, 19 July 1848, pp. 534–5.

than the pursuit of liberal and patriotic values.[59] Cobden made the mistake of telling the Commons in April 1851 that he regarded the colonial issue as 'very much a pecuniary question'.[60] Molesworth's motion for cuts in imperial expenditure was easily defeated. Both men were attacked by the self-proclaimed defenders of national pride. Ironically, colonial wars and local tensions made it difficult to reduce military expenditure substantially.[61] Cobden quickly saw that convincing popular opinion of the futility of the colonial system would be an uphill struggle.

## THE ATTACK ON ARISTOCRATIC POLITICS: DEFENCE AND FINANCE

The threat to the maintenance of the imperial connection and the African Squadron were two Radical–Liberal challenges that Palmerston and Russell stood together to resist in the late 1840s. A third concerned national defence; as noted in chapter 3, the cabinet demurred at the cost and unpopularity of their plans of 1846–7 to reconstitute the militia. All three issues became battlegrounds in the struggle for the control of Liberalism against the forces of economy and the 'low and narrow party'. In common with many military men, Palmerston was genuinely worried about the likelihood of invasion owing to the advent of steam power. The argument ran that, while Britain's financial reserves were generally deemed to be very impressive, the nation was much more vulnerable to a surprise attack. It lacked seamen and battle-worthy large ships, owing to persistent naval economies and a preponderance of small vessels built to protect commerce instead.[62] In the 1840s, on average, over a thousand men left the service each year. Thirty years of peace and an absence of naval challenges had left the Commons reluctant to vote large sums for the navy. The veteran general Sir George Murray alleged that the majority of the population was 'so besotted in the gathering of riches' that their moral and patriotic fibre had rotted.[63] It was no accident that the invasion scare of the mid-1840s coincided with the greatest triumph of middle-class consumer principles, the overthrow of the Corn Laws. The demand for extra spending to combat the French

---

[59] See the criticisms of Cobdenism quoted in Stembridge, *Parliament*, pp. 50–5.
[60] *Hansard*, 115:1443, 10 Apr. 1851.
[61] M. Taylor, 'The 1848 revolutions and the British empire', *Past and Present*, 166 (2000), 179.
[62] C. J. Bartlett, *Great Britain and sea power 1815–1853* (Oxford, 1963), pp. 139–40; Partridge, *Military planning*, p. 10.
[63] Bartlett, *Britain and sea power*, p. 194.

was a response by the military elites to yet more public enthusiasm for tax reductions.

Moreover, for Palmerston, Parliamentary concern with economy was an obstacle to an effective international policy. He considered defence spending crucial diplomatically, because it frustrated French attempts to assert an equality of defensive strength with Britain, which in turn would risk another Napoleonic war. Yet these arguments were not widely appreciated. One reason for raising a scare about defence, and indeed increasing the profile of foreign policy generally, was simply to educate the public and Parliament out of their unawareness of military weakness and unwillingness to spend money rectifying it. Had Palmerston had to beg Parliament for more money to support the navy in the eastern Mediterranean in 1840, as he very nearly did, it would have badly delayed and endangered his strategy there.[64]

Wariness about Parliament's reliability over defence led Palmerston – and many military men – to urge a particular concentration on the kind of investment that would give permanent rather than transitory security. This meant a re-embodiment of the militia, but above all defensive fortifications around the major naval ports. These could be built bit by bit as money allowed, and engendered no scruples about a threat to civil liberties. They would help to guard against a snap attack at a time when the navy was scattered and undermanned. The French could do great damage to Britain's maritime power by striking at the dockyards; it would take fifty years to recover.[65] Fortifications were intended as the first level of a warning to the French that invasion would not be worthwhile. Their greatest merit was not their actual effectiveness against one – on which opinions differed – but the statement they made, that an attack on the south coast would be bitterly resisted.

Despite all this, restricting defence spending was an ideal issue for Radicals, especially in the economic depression of 1847–8. In February 1848, an insistent Russell and Palmerston finally overcame cabinet objections to asking for defence expenditure increases.[66] Russell himself introduced the government's budget, requesting an extra £385,000 for the army, navy and ordnance estimates and £150,000 to lay the foundations of a militia. This was despite a forecast deficit of nearly £1 million, which the government proposed to tackle by continuing the income tax (intended as temporary

[64] Bourne, *Palmerston*, p. 617.
[65] Palmerston to Gladstone, 15 Dec. 1859, quoted in M. J. Salevouris, *'Riflemen form': the war scare of 1859–1860 in England* (New York, 1982), p. 256.
[66] Diary, 9 Feb. 1848, Broughton, *Recollections*, vol. VI, pp. 201–2; Bartlett, *Britain and sea power*, p. 250.

in 1842) and indeed raising it from 7d to 1s in the pound, for two years. The timing could not have been worse. Predictably, Radicals denounced the 'war budget'. They portrayed the proposals as a sectional benefit for the military classes, an attempt to strengthen the 'oligarchy' at a time when all classes were suffering and extra taxation could not be afforded.[67] There were popular protests against the income tax.[68] The Protectionist Conservative opposition, still bitter at the abolition of tariffs and the consequences for tax policy, also announced their opposition.

The outbreak of the French revolution in the last week of February then swung the argument decisively against the ministry. The revolution replaced Louis Philippe with a weak republican government, raising Liberal–Radical hopes that a progressive French administration would work with Britain, as in the 1830s, for the extension of constitutional principles elsewhere in Europe. The unrest also inspired large-scale popular meetings against government expenditure, and for Parliamentary reform, in late February and early March. Indeed it was one of those meetings, in London, led by Cochrane and Reynolds, that forced O'Connor to summon a Chartist convention and mass demonstration for 10 April, in order to reassert his control over the Chartist movement.[69] From the beginning it was obvious that the government could not get a majority for the income tax increases and they were abandoned at the end of February. Fortunately, by the summer it became clear that the new French government had no scope for aggressive behaviour – its own defence budget was cut by 20 per cent in July 1848 – while its republicanism greatly lessened the risk of joint Franco-Russian activity and so, as Russell said, only a one-power naval standard was needed. In August, in the last of four budgetary statements that session, the government announced that it had revised its military spending downwards so far that the deficit was now reduced to £292,000.[70]

The events of 1847–8 were very unfortunate for the government's reputation for economic efficiency. They reinforced the view that the 'aristocratic' and 'effete' Whigs could not manage financial policy, and that official claims of a defence crisis were hollow. Cobden and his allies sought to build on the Radical momentum of February 1848 by pressing for further economical reform in order to lift excessive burdens on productive industry and the taxpayer. He used the select committee on defence expenditure to urge increased Parliamentary control over the estimates and a drastic reduction

---

[67] *Nonconformist*, 23 Feb. 1848, pp. 115–17; Bright and Cobden in *Hansard*, 96:1077, 1088, 22 Feb. 1848.
[68] Kamenka and Smith, *Intellectuals and revolution*, p. 107.    [69] Ibid., pp. 107–9.
[70] Bartlett, *Britain and sea power*, pp. 251–6; S. H. Northcote, *Twenty years of financial policy* (London, 1862), pp. 112–13.

of them. In his 'National Budget' unveiled in February 1849 he demanded that government expenditure be reduced by £10 million, to the level of 1835, principally by cutting defence spending.[71] Army, ordnance and navy expenditure did in fact fall appreciably, from an annual average of £17.1 million in 1846–9 to £14.5 million in 1849–52, but was still higher than at any point between 1830 and the first invasion scare of 1845. Though Cobden and fellow-economisers like Hume were not the major influences on this reduction – the disarray of French politics counted for more – they were nonetheless influential in setting the tone of Parliament which a weak government had to respect. In 1851, for example, the government was defeated on a motion on official salaries.

More positively, these debates showed that government and Parliament were accountable to public opinion and Radical pressure, unlike the continental autocracies.[72] Moreover, by 1851 government enjoyed a financial surplus, and thus more room for manoeuvre. It endured a series of difficult wrangles with Parliamentary groupings about the relative merits of income tax differentiation, rate relief for agriculture, debt reduction, house and window taxes, and other strategies. But it was difficult for Radicals and Protectionists to work together on these issues, and this blunted the force of Radical demands for cuts. An inquiry into the income tax, in 1851, revealed how essential it had become as a permanent revenue-raiser, especially after the abolition of most import duties. By now there was less political mileage in a campaign against it. Instead, an opportunity emerged to forge a new fiscal consensus, justifying the income tax by making it part of a balanced package with elements acceptable to all classes. Both Disraeli and Gladstone, in turn, sought to do this when Chancellor of the Exchequer in 1852–3. As explained below, this was a key moment in financial policy.

However, Russell's Whigs got no benefit from these developments. The search for a new national compromise on taxation, like much of the rest of the politics of the early 1850s, was based on a rejection of the image of both Tory protectionism and old Whiggery. Instead of their 'aristocratic' bumbling of 1835–41 and 1846–50, it seemed essential for government to adopt a different style – what the *Nonconformist* called the 'careful detail of the man of business'. In 1848 *The Times* demanded 'practical men' and the *Manchester Examiner* a 'bold, energetic and business-like' manner.[73] In view of Peel's own fiscal reputation, the Peelites were best equipped to bid for the lead of the popular forces on a 'middle-class policy'. They

[71] *Hansard*, 102:1218, 26 Feb. 1849.     [72] M. Taylor, *British Radicalism*, pp. 128–43.
[73] *Nonconformist*, 8 Mar., 15 Mar., 19 July 1848, pp. 156, 176, 529.

continued his strategy of wooing public opinion away from the theatrical rhetoric and policy of Whig grandees by offering sound, cheap and efficient government. Many of their beliefs were shared by administratively minded, unflamboyant centrist Whigs like Clarendon, George Grey and Charles Wood, for whom it was also important for the government to give the impression of being 'prudent, steady' people, reflecting the 'industrial mind and conservative progress of the country'.[74] All these men were aware that a great prize awaited those politicians who could portray themselves as un-aristocratic, inclusive and economical. As Gladstone put it later in the 1850s, a Peelite policy of retrenchment, financial equilibrium, 'resistance to abuses' and constitutional conservatism was 'going a-begging', and he intended to be the man to promote it.[75]

### PALMERSTON AND FOREIGN POLICY, 1848–52

The hopes of European liberals in the spring of 1848 were dashed over the following two years. Paris suffered harrowing bloodshed and turned to a Bonaparte to secure order, Austrian power was restored throughout its territories, Prussian liberalism lost its chance, Russian influence cast a darkening shadow in eastern Europe, and the Pope returned to Rome supported by French troops. To British Liberals, similarly, these developments were dispiriting. But they allowed Palmerston to become the most high-profile Foreign Secretary of the nineteenth century, the most popular of contemporary elite politicians and the great winner of the political game. Palmerston presented his foreign policy as a battle against autocracy abroad and sympathisers with autocracy at home. It was a secular and more successful version of Russell's campaign against the papal aggression. His ability to oppose himself to continental 'despotism' demonstrated that his patriotism was superior to that of the Court, the Conservatives, and the 'aristocratic' Whigs and Peelites who were bidding with him for the lead in the post-1846 Liberal coalition. His focus on foreign policy exploited Radical alarms about aristocratic influence but neutralised them in the pursuit of national community; it also exploited but neutralised the instability created by the collapse of the old two-party system.

From 1848 Palmerston's main foreign-policy concerns were to check isolationist sentiment at home and to prevent France or Russia from dominating the Continent, either strategically or by the triumph of the republican

---

[74] Parry, *Rise and fall*, pp. 170, 172.
[75] Gladstone to Graham, 2 Dec. 1856, Parker, *Graham*, vol. II, pp. 295–6.

and autocratic ideologies which they now represented. He also maintained that, in a progressive era, it was necessary to recognise the 'spirit of the age' in order to secure stability. The way to achieve all these ideals was to promote the 'English' solution of constitutional monarchy wherever practicable. In 1848 the best chance of doing this was in northern Italy. The outbreak of the European revolutions made the Austrian occupation of Lombardy and Venetia a vexed international question. Britain had sanctioned that occupation in 1815 in order to protect northern Italy from French expansion and therefore had responsibility for the outcome. Rebellions in Milan and Venice in early 1848 convinced Palmerston and Russell that the occupation was no longer viable, not least because a newly republican France might oppose it and conquer northern Italy for the revolutionary cause. Substantial independence for Lombardy and Venetia would allow Austria to concentrate its energies on reinforcing its hold on its territories north of the Alps, which was threatened by risings in Hungary and Prague. A strong Austrian counterweight to France and Russia at the centre of Europe remained vital for Britain's interests, but for Austria Italy had become 'the heel of Achilles, and not the shield of Ajax'.[76]

For Palmerston, the most desirable outcome would be a monarchical northern Italian buffer-state ruled by Charles Albert, King of Piedmont-Sardinia. But when Charles Albert declared war on Austria for Northern Italy in late March, the Austrians were forced to counter-attack, successfully. This led Palmerston to argue that the best way of securing peace and a new Italian settlement would be by joint action with the French, simultaneously restraining them and sending a 'moral' and 'political' message to Austria.[77] Yet the cabinet and the Queen refused his suggestion of a military alliance, hardly surprisingly given the crisis over defence and tax, and the importance of avoiding a general European war. Informally, however, British cooperation with France continued throughout 1848–9. The two powers attempted, without much effect, to mediate between the King of Naples and his Sicilian rebels. The cabinet also divided badly on the question of military assistance for the latter, Grey and the non-interventionists getting their way. The upshot was that Britain and France helped to prevent the war from spreading but failed to stop the Austrians from reconquering Lombardy and Venetia, while Charles Albert was defeated and abdicated. Meanwhile the French took advantage of the Austrian recovery to get a

---

[76] Palmerston to Leopold of Belgium, 15 June 1848, Ashley, *Palmerston*, vol. 1, p. 98.
[77] Palmerston to Russell, 30 Aug. 1848, *Gooch*, vol. 1, pp. 340–1.

foothold in Italy themselves, by occupying Rome in July 1849 in order to safeguard the Pope.

Hindered by cabinet division and extreme domestic pressure for economy, British policy up to that point cannot be deemed successful. However, the autocratic revival in Europe soon benefited Palmerston's position. In order to suppress the Hungarian uprising of 1849, Austria obtained substantial military help from Russia, maintaining its pre-1848 empire at the expense of becoming more reliant on Britain's great rival. It seemed to many Englishmen that in this, as in its behaviour in Italy and its suppression of the radical movement in Vienna itself, Austria demonstrated an increasingly reactionary outlook. Repressed Hungary, like Poland, became a symbol of liberal constitutional values in opposition to Austria *and* Russia, encouraging the perception that the East was in the grip of autocracy. In the autumn of 1849 Palmerston exploited this feeling by successfully applying 'manly firmness', in conjunction with the French, to protect Turkey from Russo-Austrian pressure to expatriate four thousand refugees from the repressed Hungarian uprising: ships were sent to the eastern Mediterranean.[78] Perceptions of the state of central and eastern Europe were visibly altering; the West, and specifically Britain, seemed to be moving ahead, while more feudal and autocratic regimes languished. Britain represented 'the spirit of the age', Austria an attempt to deny it. Palmerston compared Austria to a 'European China'.[79] Monckton Milnes suggested that the 'German' minority in that country, representing a 'higher civilization', had been crushed under the 'Slavonian heel'.[80] Few British commentators now doubted the truth of this distinction between the progressive and reactionary parts of Europe: the only question was how viable the repression of popular opinion in the latter would be in the longer run.

Austrian hostility to Palmerston's actions was well known and quickly led to claims that the Eastern powers wanted to interfere in British politics in order to change its policy. This became a highly convenient argument for Liberals. In February 1849 the Conservative opposition, led by Stanley, nearly defeated the government in the Lords on a motion complaining at its interventions to 'foment the spirit of disaffection' in Europe, particularly its informal alliance with republican France in Italy. Macaulay

[78] Palmerston to Russell, 29 Sept. 1849, *Gooch*, vol. II, p. 9.
[79] To Abercromby, 28 Dec. 1848, in Ashley, *Palmerston*, vol. I, pp. 112–13.
[80] R. M. Milnes, *The events of 1848, especially in their relation to Great Britain: a letter to the marquess of Lansdowne* (London, 1849), pp. 37–8.

felt that behind the opposition intrigue was 'the spite of foreign powers'.[81]
In July 1849, in a debate on the suppression of the Hungarian rebellion,
Palmerston attacked prominent Austrian sympathisers in Britain, implic-
itly including his Conservative and Peelite opponents. They defended
Austria, he said, not from a reasonable concern to secure its just position
in the balance of power, but as a 'great symbol of the opinions which they
entertained [in] resistance to improvement, political and social'.[82] In his
Don Pacifico speech in 1850, Russell explicitly linked Aberdeen's 'unjust'
attacks on his government's foreign policy to the promptings of 'foreigners'.[83] Aberdeen's long-standing friendly relations with Tsar Nicholas and
Metternich were notorious, as was his desire for good relations with Louis
Philippe when Conservative Foreign Secretary in 1841–6. To attack the Peelites as supporters of continental autocracy might reduce their attractiveness
to Radicals; to level the charge of autocratic sympathies at Stanley and the
Protectionist Conservatives was a counter-blast to the revival of Protectionist sentiment in 1848–9. Palmerston, like many others, was alarmed
that if the Protectionists returned to power, their foolish policies or threats
would provoke a strong backlash and eventually a Radical government.[84]
An attractive foreign policy offered the best strategy for keeping the Russell
government in power and staving off a real radicalisation of British public
life.

Palmerston particularly blamed the emigré circle around Princess Lieven,
together with his opponents on *The Times*, for a 'foreign conspiracy' against
him.[85] In the popular press, however, it was widely assumed that the major
channel of foreign interference in policy was the Court – just as when
George IV's 'cottage coterie' had opposed Palmerston's mentor Canning in
the 1820s. Both Victoria and Albert had extensive correspondence networks
with European crowned heads, including the Spanish and Portuguese roy-
als whose governments Palmerston enjoyed berating. Both were especially
sympathetic to Austrian policy in southern Europe; both rejected Palmerston's view that his own strategy was in Austria's best interests. Both felt
that he behaved improperly to foreign courts; he wrote dispatches in the
Queen's name that expressed opinions they detested in language that they

---

[81] Stanley, *Hansard*, 102:39, 42, 46, 1 Feb. 1849; diary, 3 Feb. 1849, G. O. Trevelyan, *Macaulay*, vol. II,
   p. 186.

[82] *Hansard*, 107:809–10, 21 July 1849.       [83] *Hansard*, 112:697, 28 June 1850.

[84] For Graham's fears, see Greville, *Journal*, vol. VI, p. 201 (24 June 1848) and Graham to Peel, 23 Dec.
   1849, C. S. Parker, *Sir Robert Peel from his private papers* (3 vols., London, 1899), vol. III, p. 527. See
   also Lewis to Sir E. Head, 10 June 1849, in Lewis, *Letters of Lewis*, p. 206.

[85] Southgate, *Most English minister*, p. 268.

considered peremptory. He did not always show them to her in advance or, if he did, did not take notice of her or Russell's criticisms of them. The royal pair's attempts to weaken Palmerston's policy became widely known.

But Albert's political interventions were meat and drink to the Radical press. From his arrival in Britain, he had been stereotyped as a pauper German prince in search of gullible taxpayers off whom to sponge. His political ambitions and his criticisms of party spirit aroused suspicion. So did the building of a balcony at the front of Buckingham Palace (1846–52), which suggested an attempt to cultivate a Napoleonic popular following. For most of the 1840s and 1850s these sentiments were subordinated in the public mind to admiration for the middle-class domestic values that Victoria and Albert were seen to represent. But those values were attractive precisely to the extent that they suggested that the royal family had renounced the autocratic excesses of the Hanoverians and in their domesticity and probity had become role models for a nation governed by middle-class values. Any suggestion that the monarchy still had aspirations to propagate continental and autocratic ideas in British politics would create ill-feeling. In the post-1848 climate many papers did not miss the chance to treat the ongoing battle between Albert and Palmerston as a war between alien and British policies.[86]

In Palmerston's famous speech on the Don Pacifico affair in June 1850, the passage which won him the loudest cheer was his scarcely veiled rebuke to those who were engaged in a 'foreign conspiracy' against a minister upholding 'the dignity and interests of his own country'.[87] Clarendon felt that at the heart of the issue was British freedom of action; had the government not won the Don Pacifico debate, 'foreign governments' would have become 'arrogant and *exigeants* towards us'.[88] Palmerston had ordered warships to Piraeus to seize Greek ships as ransom, to put pressure on the Greek government to compensate Don Pacifico (a British subject though a Portuguese Jew of Gibraltar) for his apparent loss of money at the hands of a local mob. This aggressive action was an instalment of Palmerston's long-standing policy to increase Britain's influence in Greek politics, particularly compared to that of its rivals, France and Russia. He was annoyed

---

[86] For contemporary views on Albert, see R. Williams, *The contentious Crown: public discussion of the British monarchy in the reign of Queen Victoria* (Aldershot, 1997). For his political interventions, see C. H. Stuart, 'The Prince Consort and ministerial politics, 1856–9', in H. R. Trevor-Roper (ed.), *Essays in British history presented to Sir Keith Feiling* (London, 1964), pp. 247–69.

[87] *Hansard*, 112:422, 25 June 1850.  [88] To Reeve, 6 July 1850, Laughton, *Reeve*, vol. 1, p. 228.

that France had recently increased its power at Athens at British expense. From his perspective, Greek public life was riddled with incompetence and corruption; instead of promoting an 'English' policy of constitutionalism and balanced budgets, the Greeks had overspent and had repeatedly defaulted on their obligation to pay Britain and the other powers interest on their guaranteed loan of 1832.[89] Albert, however, was furious at Palmerston's behaviour in Greece, because it showed no respect for the ordered Concert by which the powers were supposed to regulate European affairs and placed Britain in a dangerously exposed and isolated position. Claiming that Britain was now 'universally detested, mistrusted and treated with insult', he demanded Palmerston's removal.[90] When the Lords censured Palmerston's policy, the establishment appeared to have turned their backs on him.

But Palmerston turned his defence into a triumph by his Commons speech, which surveyed his whole policy, portraying it as a manly and patriotic endeavour to defend British interests all over the world against foreign threats. He won a great victory over the Court, the Conservatives and his Cobdenite and Peelite critics. Lady Palmerston was given a portrait by 120 MPs; 250 members of the Reform Club held a dinner for him.[91] Lady Clarendon observed that the cabinet were 'now tied hand and foot to Lord P. and his policy'.[92]

His peroration also made it clear that England's title to assert justice and civilisation abroad rested on its achievement of class harmony at home, reconciling order and liberty in ways that other powers had failed to do.[93] Domestic and foreign strength, he suggested, were intimately connected. Moreover, he portrayed his vigorous interventions as in the interest of the whole political nation. Radicals had sometimes portrayed his 'meddling' as mere aristocratic intrigue in the affairs of courts and 'petty sovereigns' which was irrelevant or costly to ordinary voters.[94] But in Greece he had intervened on behalf of a merchant's assets, indicating the willingness of the navy to protect Britain's commercial interests worldwide – thus offering a reminder of the benefits of all those ships on foreign stations. In addition, he was making a protest against the Greeks' failure to pay the British taxpayer

---

[89] J. V. Kofas, *Financial relations of Greece and the Great Powers, 1832–1862* (Boulder, CO, 1981), pp. 29–46.
[90] Albert to Russell, spring 1850, in B. Connell, *Regina v. Palmerston: the correspondence between Queen Victoria and her Foreign and Prime Minister 1837–1865* (London, 1962), pp. 114–17.
[91] Southgate, *Most English minister*, p. 277.
[92] Diary, 30 June 1850, Maxwell, *Clarendon*, vol. I, pp. 311–12.
[93] *Hansard*, 112:443–4, 25 June 1850.   [94] *Nonconformist*, 3 May 1848, p. 315.

the interest due on the state loan.[95] The *Manchester Guardian* supported his position on Greece, reflecting the views of the wealthier, export-oriented Manchester merchants.[96] His speech also coincided with a great expansion in interest in foreign travel by middle-class Englishmen, who welcomed an assurance that Britain's power would protect them. One commentator remarked that the average Englishman defined the Don Pacifico issue in terms of whether Brown or Jones might be defrauded of his Worcester sauce amid the ice of Siberia, or of his pale ale in the Mountains of the Moon.[97] The speech was generally applauded by the anti-establishment press – the more respectable parts of which Palmerston was now courting – assisted by their determination to paint their rival *The Times* as unpatriotic for its criticisms of him.

In these years, therefore, Palmerston became associated with the idea that the British nation was united and stable and that this gave it the opportunity and ability to defend civilisation and progress against despotism. He managed this despite his carefully limited support for the cause of constitutionalism across Europe in 1848–9. Apart from the sentiment that 'opinions are stronger than armies' and would ultimately triumph, he had given no support to the Hungarian rebellion against the Austrian empire, which he felt might easily destabilise central Europe.[98] But his subsequent stand with Turkey against the repatriation of the rebels had suggested a sympathy with them and their leader Kossuth, which was widely shared in Britain owing to the latter's noble lineage and constitutional views.[99] On his visit to Britain in 1851, Kossuth addressed audiences of 200,000, from middle-class intellectuals to artisan Radicals. Robert Vaughan wrote that he was the advocate of 'principles and institutions' which the English regard as their 'great treasure and birthright'.[100] It was just after this visit that Palmerston offended the Court by telling a pro-Hungarian Radical deputation from Finsbury that he was 'extremely flattered and highly gratified' by their

---

[95] Kofas, *Financial relations*, chs. 1 and 2. This was not the only case of British commerce benefiting from the government's policies. Minto maintained that British exports to Sicily had risen by 51 per cent between 1847 and 1848 after the Sicilians, with British help, had rediscovered independent constitutional government: *Hansard*, 107:689–90, 20 July 1849. Palmerston frequently lectured foreign governments on the need to pay their financial debts to British citizens; this should not be confused with a policy of actually intervening to ensure payment, which would not have been popular at home or abroad: see L. H. Jenks, *The migration of British capital to 1875* (London, 1963 edn), pp. 115–25.
[96] 29 June 1850, quoted in Brown, *Palmerston and foreign policy*, pp. 110–11.
[97] Southgate, *Most English minister*, p. 272. [98] *Hansard*, 107:813, 21 July 1849.
[99] See e.g. B. Osborne's speech, *Hansard*, 107:786–93, 21 July 1849.
[100] R. Vaughan, 'Louis Kossuth and Lord Palmerston', *British Quarterly Review*, 14 (1851), 544. See also Russell's remark to the Queen quoted in the Introduction, p. 14.

congratulatory address, in which they described the rulers of Austria and Russia as 'odious and detestable assassins'. In the previous autumn, a similar incident had arisen during the visit to England of the Austrian General Haynau, who had been demonised by the British Radical press as General Hyena for his excesses in suppressing the Hungarian rebellion. When he was on a private visit to a Southwark brewery, his presence was discovered by the workforce, who, wielding brooms, chased him and pushed him into a refuse-heap. The Radical press celebrated the encounter as demonstrating the pluck of the British working man. When the Austrians demanded that his attackers be prosecuted, Palmerston pointed out that this would be counterproductive as it would give renewed publicity to Haynau's deeds in Hungary.[101]

In the highly charged circumstances of the time, Palmerston could be excused for doing little to deflate the admiration that he received for this posturing. It made him the most popular figure in an unpopular cabinet; it helped to prop up the government and the political order. Yet it also made him vulnerable. His strongly worded dispatches to British diplomats abroad and his hectoring of foreign courts were disliked by most of the political establishment – by the majority of the cabinet, by Victoria and Albert, and by most of the politicians out of office whose alliance could at any time have brought down the Russell ministry. They felt that by alienating other countries he risked damaging trade and isolating Britain, potentially risking war and requiring much higher defence spending at a time when the domestic economy and polity were still fragile.[102] The conservative-minded also felt that he played to the Radical gallery and encouraged disrespect for the crowned heads of Europe. It was rational for a minority government to adopt a safety-first approach to foreign policy if it wished to prevent attacks from an alliance of economisers and conservatives. And, though generally approving of his policy, Russell too had doubts about Palmerston's willingness to irritate other powers. Despite his instinctive hostility to Austria's presence in Italy, he tried to rein in Palmerston's verbal attacks in 1849, fearing that they would drive Austria into Russia's hands and facilitate the latter's advance into 'the heart of Europe'.[103] Though he condoned Palmerston's assertiveness in Greece in 1850, he also believed in working with the French, whose attempts to mediate Palmerston had

---

[101] Palmerston to G. Grey, 1 Oct. 1850, Ashley, *Palmerston*, vol. 1, pp. 239–41. For the Haynau visit and its consequences, see *The Times*, 5 Sept. 1850, p. 4 and 11 Sept. 1850, p. 5.

[102] See e.g. Graham to Peel, 30 Apr. 1848 and 3 Apr. 1850, Parker, *Peel*, vol. III, pp. 495, 536; Clarendon to Russell, 22 Jan. 1852, *Gooch*, vol. II, pp. 97–9.

[103] Russell to Palmerston, 13 Apr. 1849, *Gooch*, vol. I, p. 358.

ignored. Just before the Don Pacifico affair, he told him that he would be moved out of the Foreign Office at the end of the session because Britain could not afford such international hostility.[104] The debate forced him to retract that threat, but Palmerston's opponents continued to demand that his independence be restrained, and Russell himself became more desperate to reassert his authority over government and party. His Durham letter and his attempt to reintroduce Parliamentary reform in 1850–1 were attempts to do that. Palmerston's intransigence was bound to lead to a break-up.

Moreover, when Russell finally removed him from office in December 1851, it was inevitable that those responsible for the dismissal would be portrayed as unpatriotic elitists in the popular press, even though the immediate ground for it was Palmerston's unlicensed expression of approval for the French coup. Russell had to deny the press claim that the dismissal was the work of the now notorious 'foreign conspiracy'. Albert was blamed in particular, as a stooge of continental courts – a view that was strengthened by the news that the Austrian foreign minister Schwarzenburg had held a ball at Vienna to celebrate Palmerston's dismissal.[105] Russell's speech inadvertently added to speculation about Court pressure by publicly emphasising Victoria's demand that Palmerston should not deviate from policy previously approved by her.[106] Both Russell, yet again, and the new Foreign Secretary Granville inevitably suffered in public estimation by being seen as puppets of the Palace. Whereas Palmerston was 'the true English mastiff', Granville was described as 'my lady's lapdog'.[107] The irony was that in fact economising liberal pressure in cabinet had much more to do with Palmerston's removal than royal influence; Court hostility arguably made Palmerston's tenure of his post more secure. And Russell, that hereditary opponent of Crown power, did not intend to make his policy any less liberal to please the Queen, making it clear to her in 1850 that the purpose of moving Palmerston would be to 'continue the same line of foreign policy without giving the same offence' abroad.[108]

The dismissal made little difference to Palmerston's popularity. He was now generally portrayed in cartoons as a man of the people, with a straw in his mouth rather than a peer's coronet. He epitomised one version of the fashionable idea of straightforward bluff manliness. He described his role

[104] Russell to Palmerston, 22 May 1850, Walpole, *Russell*, vol. II, pp. 60–1.
[105] Williams, *Contentious Crown*, pp. 99–102, 161–3.
[106] *Hansard*, 119:89–91, 3 Feb. 1852.     [107] Mandler, *Aristocratic government*, pp. 273–4.
[108] Walpole, *Russell*, vol. II, pp. 60–1. Russell made the same point to Albert: Connell, *Regina v. Palmerston*, pp. 119–20.

as that of 'judicious bottleholding' in the European boxing contests – an image quickly immortalised by *Punch*.[109] He was also seen as a Protestant hero, defending the independence of the land from foreign dictation of all sorts, papal, Russian and Albertian. Ironically Russell, despite the Durham letter, could be portrayed as a closet Catholic sympathiser because of the earlier links made between his aristocratic image and Irish policy.[110]

Palmerston's dismissal strengthened his image as the symbol of British resistance to the misdeeds of continental autocracy and of 'aristocratic' faction at home. He received much favourable popular press coverage, though it cannot quite be said that he became a Radical hero, in view of his opposition to Reform and the continuing Cobdenism of many Radicals and Liberals.[111] Indeed division, both within Radicalism and between the other political factions, was the most striking element in the politics of the early 1850s. The more important reason for his political rise over the next few years was that his patriotism made him the most popular of establishment politicians at a time when the party system had broken down. By standing aloof from the factions that appeared to be replacing it, and identifying with unifying national causes, he became the most indispensable man in any future successful political combination at Westminster. His image, like Gladstone's later, took on a life of its own. The Leeds Nonconformist Edward Baines came to admire him because he represented 'the intercommunication of classes'.[112]

Foreign affairs seemed better able to shore up a cross-class domestic politics than Reform or Ecclesiastical Titles. It was very revealing that one of the most promising younger Peelites, Gladstone, came round to the idea of Britain's international mission to promote justice and good government at this time. In the Don Pacifico debate he appeared to deny this idea, in a great attack on Palmerston. But it was in fact the arrogance and pride of the Don Pacifico policy to which he objected; he acknowledged that Britain sometimes had a 'duty' to encourage liberal institutions abroad.[113] Then, on a visit to Naples, he saw the conditions under which intellectual liberal dissidents from the Bourbon regime were gaoled. He became convinced that Britain had a responsibility to make an international protest against

---

[109] *LQV 1837–61*, vol. II, p. 329n; *Punch*, 6 Dec. 1851, pp. 244–7. The cartoon depicted Palmerston as bottle-holder in the prospective fight between the Russian Tsar and 'Young Europe' – favouring the latter, but doubting that the fight would come to much as the former did not have the 'constitution'.

[110] Brown, *Palmerston and foreign policy*, pp. 127–8; Prest, *Russell*, opp. p. 340 (Plate 9).

[111] Brown, *Palmerston and foreign policy*, pp. 36–7, suggests that Palmerston became a Carlylean hero, but in fact by the 1850s most Radicals were suspicious of Carlyle's brand of hero-worship.

[112] 1860: E. D. Steele, *Palmerston and Liberalism, 1855–1865* (Cambridge, 1991), p. 177.

[113] *Hansard*, 112:582, 585–6, 27 June 1850.

these 'illegal' and 'tyrannical' acts, and in 1851 he published a hyperbolic condemnation of the Naples government, addressed to the embarrassed Aberdeen. Palmerston, no doubt highly amused, arranged to have copies of his former adversary's pamphlet distributed to the other European courts.[114] Gladstone's awakening to the politics of patriotism showed how tempting it was in the years after 1848 to assert England's mission abroad against 'un-English' practices – especially for an ambitious politician.

## NAPOLEON III, PALMERSTON, GLADSTONE AND DEFENCE

Despite Palmerston's ability to exploit popular dislike of continental regimes, he had not yet succeeded in challenging the lack of political will to remedy defensive shortcomings. The blunt refusal of Parliament and public to support Russell's proposed defence increases of 1848, together with the fall in expenditure between 1848 and 1850, made the defence issue potentially explosive. Though the new French republic's internal problems in 1848 made an aggressive policy less likely in the short term, there was no guarantee that the French regime would not eventually – as in 1793 – be drawn into an ideological or expansionary war, given the number of potential flashpoints on France's borders. The technological threat continued: in 1850 the screw-propelled ship *Napoleon*, superior to any British model, was finished. The fashionable perception of the 1850s, that time was moving more rapidly, a consequence of the boom in railway travel and of evolutionary theory, contributed to the psychology of panic by underscoring the rapidity with which the French could attack. In 1850 the former soldier and colonial administrator Sir Francis Head created a storm when he published *On the defenceless state of Great Britain*, arguing for a great increase in the home army and Channel Fleet. Minor fortification works and the strengthening of harbours of refuge at Dover, Portland and the Channel Islands continued – Russell told Palmerston in 1850 that we are 'fortifying as quickly as the public will allow' – but there was not enough money to implement a step change either in fortifications or in steam ship building.[115] Nor was there any chance of re-establishing the regular militia, though Palmerston reopened the campaign for this in January 1851, warning about France's 'disciplined army'.[116]

Yet once the association between military spending and 'aristocratic' government had been broken, the defence issue would be much more attractive.

---

[114] R. Shannon, *Gladstone: I: 1809–1865* (London, 1982), pp. 240–1.
[115] Partridge, *Military planning*, p. 13.    [116] Ibid., p. 132.

It could win support from Conservatives and could divide Radicals, since many of them saw the value of a powerful navy, both as a safeguard for free trade and as a symbol of English freedom dating back to King Alfred. More generally, the victory of free-trade principles had underlined the notion that naval invincibility was the key to Britain's greatness. When the Queen had a sailor suit made for the infant prince of Wales in 1846, modelled on the dress of the royal yacht crew, she inaugurated what was to be one of the greatest and most enduring fashion sensations of all time, driven by a combination of patriotism and status-seeking.

It was Louis Napoleon's *coup d'état* of December 1851 that made defence a front-rank issue, even though, paradoxically, it led to Palmerston's temporary dismissal. In 1849–51 most British criticism of foreign powers had been directed at Austria and Russia rather than the post-revolutionary regime in France, especially once Louis Napoleon had become president in December 1848. France's naval expenditure in 1851 was the lowest since 1839. Louis Napoleon – who had acted as a special constable during the Chartist demonstration in London in 1848 – was widely seen in Britain as the only man who could keep the army and the socialists in check, and business confidence in him was high: over two million francs were invested in the first month of his presidency. Even when Napoleon effected his *coup d'état*, in order to shore up his crumbling power base, there was considerable sympathy for him. Palmerston, most of the political elite, and many businessmen considered his move the best chance for France to recover stability and tranquillity. The only alternatives in such an excitable country seemed to be anarchy or socialism.[117]

But in many other ways the coup seemed very worrying. Its unconstitutionalism was the most immediate concern. The violence and bloodshed associated with it, so close to British shores, suggested that he had no interest in representative principles (though he later restored universal suffrage). There was particular shock that fourteen people were shot when hiding behind a carpet that only a few months previously had been admired by the Queen herself at the Great Exhibition. Like many who had friends in the Parisian intelligentsia, Dickens never forgave 'the cold-blooded scoundrel at the head of France – or on it', and his *A tale of two cities* (1859) can be seen as a commentary on the dehumanising effects of French state oppression.[118] Napoleon seemed to have no respect for constitutional traditions or press

---

[117] F. C. Palm, *England and Napoleon III: a study of the rise of a utopian dictator* (Durham, NC, 1948), pp. 22, 30, 55, 60–73.
[118] 14 Jan. 1852, Storey *et al.*, *Letters of Dickens*, vol. VI, p. 575.

and personal liberties. Charles Wood commented in a public speech that 'such a despotism never prevailed in France'.[119] The *Illustrated London News* saw the outcome as an 'iron tyranny, without parallel in European history'; France had moved decisively 'out of the alliance and brotherhood of constitutional states'. David Masson wrote that the whole of the Continent was now 'virtually or really under Russian influence'.[120]

The growth of Napoleon's power after the coup raised the spectre of his uncle's autocracy. It suggested that his power base was fragile and insecure and that, as a result, he could prosper only by invoking his ancestry and pursuing a glorious and successful policy abroad. Could his oft-claimed desire to remain on good terms with England be trusted, when his political image depended on doing something different? Ultimately, he was bound to want, and need, to avenge the great humiliation of Waterloo.[121] The founding of the Second Empire, with his assumption of the title Napoleon III in November 1852, added to this perception. Behind it was psychological fear of French invasion, the legacy of the intense wartime propaganda of the 1800s which warned that Napoleon Bonaparte's invading French mobs would sweep away private property, individual freedom and Protestant religion in an orgy of criminality and uncontrolled animal passion.[122] British public life in the 1850s was dominated by men over whose youth the original Bonapartist shadow had fallen.

For all these reasons, the coup of 1851 created enormous shock waves in British politics. It heightened the sense that Britain was the only defender of liberty in Europe, and that its values were themselves in peril of attack from continental autocracy. Tennyson, Poet Laureate, wrote several poems after the coup, expressing the view that now that Napoleon had overthrown freedom by murder and lies, Britain was left with 'the one voice in Europe' and 'we *must* speak'.[123] A. V. Kirwan asserted that Napoleon could hold 'absolute power' in France only by attempting to corrupt or destroy the spirit of liberty in England.[124] This was a fevered response, but it reflected a feeling that England's position as the defender of liberty both required her to act and placed her in a position of vulnerability against a resurgently

---

[119] For the fuss about this, see *Hansard*, 124:83–5, 14 Feb. 1853.
[120] *Illustrated London News*, 20 Dec. 1851, pp. 721–2; D. Masson, 'The doctrine of non-intervention', *British Quarterly Review*, 15 (1852), 282–3.
[121] [F. Greenwood *et al.,*] *The Napoleon dynasty: or, history of the Bonaparte family* (London, 1853), p. 610.
[122] S. Cottrell, 'The devil on two sticks: Franco-phobia in 1803', in R. Samuel (ed.), *Patriotism: the making and unmaking of British national identity* (3 vols., London, 1989), vol. 1, pp. 267–8.
[123] 'The third of February, 1852', in C. Ricks (ed.), *The poems of Tennyson* (London, 1969), pp. 1000–1, and more generally pp. 997–1017.
[124] 'The coup d'état in France', *Fraser's Magazine*, 45 (1852), 125.

autocratic Continent. Many politicians shared the widespread alarm and believed either that an invasion was possible, or that Napoleon would seek to hit Britain's power elsewhere, perhaps by taking Egypt.[125]

The result was a defence panic, which led almost immediately to the fall of the Russell government in February 1852, at the hands of Palmerston. Russell hurriedly introduced a compulsory militia scheme costing £200,000 per annum. It was opposed by an unholy but successful combination of opponents: those Conservatives and Liberals for whom it did not go far enough joined uneasily with Cobden and the traditional critics of militarism and high spending. The government's attempts to minimise libertarian objections by restricting the militia to a local rather than national ('regular') basis allowed Palmerston – a long-term advocate of a regular militia – to charge that the scheme was inefficient. Russell's defeat was obviously inspired by Palmerston's desire for revenge, and the government could hardly have survived for long in any event. Nonetheless, it was now impossible to ignore the defence issue.

The medium-term upshot of the panic was to damage seriously both Conservatives and Cobdenite Radicals, and to allow a marriage of political convenience between Palmerston and propertied economical Liberals. In various guises, this was to dominate British politics for the next dozen years, on a patriotic, non-'aristocratic' agenda combining firm defence and classless finance.

The Conservatives suffered badly from the fact that in 1852 they took office as a minority government at a time of high tension with France. This meant that they would suffer whether they pursued an economical or an aggressive policy. Disraeli was a vigorous advocate of cheap defence and good relations with Napoleon III because it would help his aim, as Chancellor, to produce a budget that would offer tax benefits to the various social classes and thus rid the Conservatives of their sectional and backward-looking protectionist image.[126] Moreover he did not want Conservative MPs to be portrayed as self-interested lobbyists for military or colonial interests. But other Conservatives, especially from the older generation or military backgrounds, overruled him, with the crucial support of Prime Minister Derby. This was partly due to military pressure, but also because the panics were founded on the perception that Parliamentary government was vulnerable in the face of continental autocracy.[127] Therefore a weak government needed to overcompensate by a show of naval vigour, especially

---

[125] *Stanley*, p. 97; Gardiner, *Harcourt*, vol. I, p. 65.    [126] Parry, 'Disraeli and England', 711–12.
[127] See e.g. Greville to Clarendon, 21 Oct. 1852, Maxwell, *Clarendon*, vol. I, p. 350.

since the Conservatives were already being accused by Radical journals of defending the 'despotic system throughout the Continent' in their foreign policy.[128] The case for increased spending was also strengthened by the emotion surrounding the funeral of the duke of Wellington, the great Conservative chief and vanquisher of Bonaparte, watched by one and a half million spectators. The Conservatives had to increase defence estimates by £800,000. And this forced Disraeli into a budget that Liberals could combine to oppose because the search for extra revenue alienated too many interests. The government fell on the issue in December 1852.

The other losers were the Radicals, especially the Cobdenites. They were damaged for two reasons: their association with the cause of peace at a time of anxiety about defence, and the ease with which their opponents could accuse them of an anti-patriotic commercialism. Napoleon's coup and the fear of French attack dealt a severe blow to Cobden's arguments for international cooperation and peace.[129] His attacks on the militia seemed tired, tasteless and unpatriotic. If Europe had fallen under autocratic control, then England could not afford to neglect its own defences or to pursue a selfish isolationist foreign policy. Commentators who fuelled the panic alleged that commercial class preference for taxpayer benefit over national virtue and honour had infected British public life in recent decades and weakened Britain's ability to cope with the illiberal continental threat. The Peace Society, having been revivified in 1848, took years to recover from the negative publicity of 1851–3, as the invasion scare was followed rapidly by the Crimean crisis. It looked either naïve or materialistic. Indeed the defence panic involved a deliberate attack on the values of commercialism or 'Manchesterism'. Henry Reeve of *The Times* justified his scaremongering writings by arguing that 'this nation is a good deal enervated by a long peace, by easy habits of intercourse, by peace societies and false economy'. Though regretting the extent of the panic, Clarendon admitted that it was right to 'rouse our countrymen from the apathetic habits and utilitarian selfishness engendered by a long peace'.[130] Tennyson, bemoaning the lack of pluck exemplified by the House of Lords' views on defence, asked whether the 'manly strain of Runnymede' had become a 'fallen nobility', swayed by the bawling of the 'niggard throats of Manchester'. 'Too much we make our Ledgers, Gods.'[131]

---

[128] *Stanley*, p. 71.    [129] M. Taylor, *British Radicalism*, pp. 216–18.

[130] Laughton, *Reeve*, vol. I, pp. 251–3, 258. Though no scaremonger, Disraeli emphasised from now until his death the damage done to a patriotic foreign policy by the dominance of 'the commercial principle' in English public life: Parry, 'Disraeli and England', 716–23.

[131] 'The third of February, 1852', and 'Hands all round!', *Poems of Tennyson*, pp. 1001–3.

And so a Liberal–Peelite coalition was formed in December 1852, under Aberdeen – in which Palmerston, barred from the Foreign Office by Court and Peelite agreement, was Home Secretary. It was dominated by Peelites and by Liberals who sympathised with their primary aim of strengthening government's reputation for disinterested, businesslike financial administration. This was certainly the objective of Gladstone's famous budget of 1853, which announced a programme of abolishing or reducing import duties, and diminishing direct taxation over the next few years, with the aim of lightening the fiscal burden on all classes and establishing fairness between urban and rural interests. The budget was designed to signal the classlessness, efficiency and libertarianism of the free-trade state, in contrast to high-taxing continental despotism. It signalled the peculiar relationship between the Peelites and Palmerston. In many ways, particularly on foreign policy, their priorities were very different, and the tensions between them were to become apparent in the build-up to and early stages of the Crimean War. But at another level this uncomfortable marriage was the basis for Liberal political success. A strong liberal defence and foreign policy and a reputation for fair classless finance were the two principles on which Liberal dominance in Victorian Britain over the next twenty years was founded.

This was so, firstly, in terms of what it appeared to oppose: a selfish and extravagant old Tory Protectionist financial policy based on class interests, tariffs and colonial preference. The Liberals, by contrast, claimed to stand for global free trade and the defence of liberal principles in Europe and beyond. The Aberdeen coalition sped ahead with the development of responsible government in the white settler colonies.

Secondly Gladstone's budget was a success because its rhetoric faced in a different direction from its real effect. He talked of abolishing the income tax by 1860, he promised further tariff cuts and he nodded towards the Radicals who favoured differentiation between 'temporary' and 'permanent' incomes (by reforming the succession duties). All this suggested that a system of high and inequitable taxation was defunct. Through its visionary talk of tax reductions, the budget gave the impression of planning economies for many years ahead. This was useful in keeping Radicals on side, but also in reconciling Gladstone himself to the unpleasant task in hand, which was to increase taxes in the short term in order to deliver the defence expenditure increases that Palmerston wanted. The result was the highest naval establishment since 1815: 45,500 seamen.[132] Continuous

---

[132]  Bartlett, *Britain and sea power*, p. 290.

service was extended throughout the fleet from five to ten years. Work had begun in 1852 on forts on the Isle of Wight and to the west of Portsmouth. Palmerston, as Home Secretary, now started meetings to plan defence operations with the Admiralty and War Office. Gladstone found the extra money needed in 1853 but also suggested – rather optimistically, as it turned out – that Britain was so well governed that economic policy could soon move steadily and rationally in the direction of tax reductions. Confidence in the nation's economic and defence strength would prevent future expensive panics, while reductions in tariffs would benefit international trade and global cooperation.

Thirdly, and at the most general level, Gladstone and Palmerston articulated the two strongest bases of an 'English' policy: on the one hand, an equitable fiscal arrangement and businesslike competence in place of aristocracy, sectionalism and Whig drift; on the other, a liberal mission abroad. The only way to avoid the slur that a low-tax policy attractive to commercial opinion was Cobdenite and materialist was to justify it by a patriotic politics expressing an uplifting national purpose. The only way to get the Radicals to agree to the smack of firm executive government was to peddle Gladstone's agreeable fantasy that England, uniquely, was so skilled at self-government that in the medium term it would be able to function without either income tax or tariffs. The only way for Palmerston to get his defence increases was to reassure businessmen that he would still work for peace and good relations with France. Indeed this was also the only way for Palmerston to reconcile the two halves of his game-plan: to maintain the French entente, so as to make Britain count in Europe, and yet to build up domestic popular support for his foreign and defence policy, so as to maintain British naval supremacy over France and his own increasing supremacy over his political rivals.

## TOWARDS A WAR OF VALUES

By 1853 suspicion of continental autocracy, a strong sense of England's global greatness and an uneasy coalition between Palmerstonian and Peelite strategies were the three leading themes in British politics. They were also the main causes of British entry into a major European war in the Crimea in 1854, as the ally of Napoleon III, the man against whom there had been an invasion panic in 1852. One long-standing interpretation of the path to war asserts that 'Russophobia' was a major feature of mid-nineteenth-century culture.[133] This interpretation, however, which dates from 1950,

---

[133] Gleason, *Genesis of Russophobia.*

was a product of the Cold War, and depends on a very selective reading of the material. Russia had not been the central concern in English discussion of foreign policy before or since 1848; nor was Russia yet the threat to India that it became after the Central Asian advances of the 1860s.[134] Britain's European fleet was organised on the assumption that France, rather than Russia, was the most immediate threat. English discussion was directed not against or for particular foreign countries, but on the distinctiveness and duty of *Britain* in the global struggle between liberalism and autocracy. Russia, as head of the autocratic side, was one major anxiety. But the problems caused by the restlessness of Napoleon III, and an enhanced sensitivity about Britain's honour, were equally important in explaining the outbreak of war.

In 1853 the Russians were widely believed to be trying to carve out a sphere of influence in the Balkans, in preparation for a break-up of the Ottoman empire. The Tsar's vision of a partition of Ottoman lands, conveyed to the British Ambassador in January 1853, created major alarm in Britain when published. In the spring, Russia demanded that Turkey should accept its claim to protect the welfare of all Orthodox Christians within Ottoman boundaries. This claim, rejected by Turkey, led the British and French to move their fleets to Besika Bay, off Constantinople, as a gesture of sympathy with Turkey in June 1853. Undaunted, the Russians occupied the Principalities of Moldavia and Wallachia, the Turkish territory north of the Danube, as a declaration of intent to threaten the Sultan further. They had done this on previous occasions, but in the circumstances of post-1848 politics this act seemed to presage a Russian drive to bolster its dominance in eastern Europe by territorial expansion. During his 1851 visit Kossuth had told an open-air meeting in Islington: 'Do not give a charter to the Tsar to dispose of the World.'[135] By 1853 it was becoming fashionable to argue that if the Russians took Constantinople, the consequences would be fatal to constitutionalism across much of Europe. This view became a major staple of wartime rhetoric. 'Were Russia crippled and overthrown,' W. R. Greg wrote, 'the difference would be felt in every village in Germany, in every dungeon in Italy, at every hearth-stone and in every heart from the Baltic to the Mediterranean.'[136] Nonetheless, at the outset, the Eastern crisis of 1853 need have been no more sinister for England than

---

[134] H. Strachan, 'Soldiers, strategy and Sebastopol', *Historical Journal*, 21 (1978), 303–4.
[135] A. Palmer, *The banner of battle: the story of the Crimean War* (London, 1987), p. 10.
[136] 'The significance of the struggle', *North British Review*, 24 (1855–6), 269. See also J. Martineau, 'International duties, and the present crisis', *National Review*, 1 (1855), 227–8, for his view on the consequences of a Russian advance for Greece, Austria, Naples, Spain and Germany.

the previous Russo-Turkish tensions of the 1820s and 1830s. In its early stages the government felt that Napoleon III was mostly to blame for its emergence.[137]

The Aberdeen coalition wished to be friendly to Napoleon. As usual, Britain needed to work with France in order to maximise its own international influence, to check Napoleon's impetuosity, to stop him gaining special concessions in the area, and to restrain Russia. Moreover, calming the panic was the prerequisite of an effective financial policy at home. Napoleon, for his part, was anxious to uphold a British entente. However, he showed every sign of wishing to use the crisis to gain personal prestige and influence in the eastern Mediterranean. He sent the French fleet to Salamis in March 1853 and at later stages of the crisis showed frustration whenever British policy-makers were divided or urged delay. His disdain for the constraints of traditional Concert diplomacy and his anxiety to show his support for the Turk were potentially destabilising factors in diplomatic negotiations.

The Russian occupation of Turkish territory, together with domestic jitters about the Tsarist threat to liberty, created another problem – the perceived insult to its honour if Britain were to do nothing while the Russians advanced towards Constantinople. This was not so much because of sympathy for the Turks – which was patchy and grudging at best – as because the fleet was already present in the eastern Mediterranean.[138] It was on this issue that the 'forward party' in the cabinet emerged, led by Palmerston, who from March 1853 advocated a vigorous naval response as a warning to Russia, usually with support from Russell and Lansdowne. Foreign Secretary Clarendon, who eventually and reluctantly joined them, argued that, if Turkey was abandoned, 'we make her the prey of Russia which Austria would then join'.[139] Willingness to protect Turkey was partly a matter of keeping in line with Napoleon, but the more fundamental consideration was British prestige. Russell claimed that to desert the Turks, having moved the fleet near Constantinople to protect them, would 'be felt as deep disgrace and humiliation by the whole country'.[140] The perception that British public opinion would not condone such a desertion significantly influenced the forward party, as Clarendon suggested several times.[141] Press criticism of the Russian aggression had been growing throughout the

---

[137] Schroeder, *Austria*, p. 39.
[138] For views on Turkey in 1853, see e.g. M. Taylor, *British Radicalism*, pp. 223–9.
[139] Schroeder, *Austria*, p. 61.    [140] 27 Sept. 1853, ibid., p. 87.
[141] 5 July 1853, quoted in G. B. Henderson, *Crimean War diplomacy and other historical essays* (Glasgow, 1947), p. 198; Schroeder, *Austria*, pp. 62–4, 67–8, 79–80.

summer.[142] When Turkey declared war on Russia in October 1853 there were mass meetings in London, Glasgow and the North denouncing Tsarist inhumanity in Poland and Hungary. If the Russians advanced on Constantinople while the allied fleets dithered in the eastern Mediterranean then Britain would be humiliated.

This dilemma also forced the British government to react sceptically to attempts by the Russians or Austrians to settle the issue by the use of 'Concert' diplomacy. Though some cabinet members wanted to treat these in good faith, ultimately it proved impossible for Britain to accept the legitimacy of a 'Concert' approach because in the climate of 1853 the Concert looked like the tool of autocratic Europe. In August 1853 the Turks protested at the major initiative of the Concert, the Vienna Note – which required them to consent to administrative reforms for the benefit of the Balkan Christians. As long as the Russian occupation infringed their sovereignty, they were unwilling to accept a form of words for defusing the crisis that was acceptable to Russia: to submit to Russian pressure threatened riots in Constantinople and the overthrow of the Sultan's government. The Turks' obstinacy and eventual declaration of war were encouraged by their confidence that British and French fleets would not abandon them. Once the Turks had rejected the Vienna Note, Britain effectively undermined it, as it later did with the Olmütz proposals in the autumn. Palmerston, Russell and Clarendon felt that 'Concert' diplomacy was too closely aligned with Austrian and Russian interests. They believed that Russia was manoeuvring to put Turkey in the wrong, so as to justify its occupation of the Principalities. Russia had indicated that it would not accept the Turks' requested amendments to the Vienna Note.

Therefore to support the Concert against the Turks seemed tantamount to siding with Russian policy; this was the moment, in September, at which Russell came out decisively for supporting the Turkish case.[143] The 'forward party' were also suspicious of Austria, traditionally the lynchpin of the Concert. It was widely known that Russia's aggression on Turkey had been planned on the assumption that Austria would acquiesce in it and in important ways support it. Indeed the Tsar envisaged that as part of a new Eastern settlement Russia and Austria would jointly control and garrison

---

[142] For the press, see e.g. *Daily News* and *Morning Herald*, quoted in K. Martin, *The triumph of Lord Palmerston: a study of public opinion in England before the Crimean War* (London, 1963 edn), p. 118.

[143] Scherer, *Russell*, pp. 225–6. Schroeder, *Austria*, is a distinguished account of the crisis, but takes a very pro-Austrian view and does not recognise Parliamentary and popular constraints on British policy.

the Straits.[144] The most generous interpretation of Concert diplomacy was that it was aiming to find solutions that were acceptable enough to Russia to allow it to retreat gracefully. Even so, the leading British players felt that the Russians were too aggressive at crucial points in the discussions: for example when Nesselrode's interpretation of the Vienna Note was leaked, implying that Russia still intended to operate a sphere of influence in Balkan Turkey, or when the Russians destroyed the Turkish fleet at Sinope at the end of November 1853.[145] Such events created the public impression in Britain that Russia harboured plans to reshape the area in its own interests. Members of the 'forward' party repeatedly suggested that Russia could not be trusted to withdraw its claims.[146]

If it was dishonourable for Britain to bully Turkey into submission, Russia must be persuaded to back down. Since the Concert was not a reliable instrument for this work, the 'forward party' argued that Britain and France must try to force Austria and then Russia to accept the need for a Russian retreat. If this were successful, it would win a much-needed diplomatic victory for home audiences in both countries to savour. It would also show that the might of European autocracy had been weakened by British influence (and would defuse domestic suspicion of France). One of Palmerston and Clarendon's consistent concerns in 1853 was to show that London and Paris, not Vienna, were the arbiters of Europe. These tactics had occasional success, as far as Austrian willingness to compromise with the allies was concerned, but they failed in their ultimate objective of forcing Russia to withdraw, because Russia's own pride was too heavily involved.

One reason for their failure was that, though the 'forward party' had a greater public following than the 'peace' grouping, they never had a majority in cabinet – only four of the twelve ministers had voted with Palmerston on Don Pacifico in 1850. In particular, Prime Minister Aberdeen, the leader of the 'peace party', was disinclined to threaten the Tsar or to disrupt the Concert. Britain's policy throughout the summer and autumn of 1853 thus fell between two stools, and the Tsar seems to have doubted that it would ever go to war against him. Critics of the 'forward party' argued, then and since, that a more cooperative style of diplomacy, less intent on embarrassing Russia, might have worked. However, a peace settlement which left

---

[144] Schroeder, *Austria*, p. 29; A. D. Lambert, *The Crimean War: British grand strategy, 1853–56* (Manchester, 1990), p. 11.

[145] Schroeder, *Austria*, pp. 67–70, 116, 123; see Martin, *Triumph of Palmerston*, p. 133 on the effect of the Nesselrode leak on the press.

[146] Schroeder, *Austria*, pp. 51, 81.

Russia and Austria more influential in the East, and in Europe generally, would have damaged national honour. Alternatively, had Britain hesitated, leading Napoleon III to tire of his allies and to befriend the Turk on his own, Russia and France might have fought until they agreed a partition of Ottoman lands to mutual benefit, strengthening both countries at Britain's expense.

Moreover, any outcome that constrained or humiliated Britain abroad would almost certainly have radicalised domestic politics significantly, bearing in mind that most blame would have been attached to the conservative Peelites in the cabinet. The political tables were turning: the dominance of foreign-policy issues was now making *them* more vulnerable to charges of selfish oligarchical behaviour than Russell. Aberdeen's noble lineage, coroneted image in cartoons and reputation as the Tory Foreign Secretary who had arranged to betray Mazzini's correspondents to the Austrians in 1843–4 did not make him popular. There was much press criticism of those who seemed unwilling to use the fleet to do anything to stop the Russian threat to Constantinople. James Martineau, the Unitarian preacher, later reminisced about the nation's 'measured' and 'reasonable indignation', not just at 'the Russian Autocrat' but at the 'languid and half-hearted tone of Ministers' who lacked a clear view and decisive will. 'To wait till the fleet of Sebastopol was at the Golden Horn, beneath the eyes of the Russian army on the southern slopes of the Balkan, would be to let the future of Europe go by default.'[147] In domestic politics it was not just the Aberdeen coalition that was at stake; it was the whole reputation of propertied government. Palmerston and Russell were concerned, among other things, to prop it up. Both also had grievances against the Aberdeen coalition. At its outset Palmerston had been stripped of the Foreign Office by Peelite and Court pressure. Russell had been given to understand by Aberdeen that he would resign in his favour as Prime Minister, but the foreign crisis made Aberdeen change his mind. If either had resigned at any point after the summer of 1853, the coalition would have fallen, and this gave them great strength.

In identifying themselves with an assertively liberal and 'manly' policy, Palmerston and Russell were manoeuvring at the domestic level as well as the international. They were mobilising against the Peelites but also struggling against each other for the leadership of Liberal MPs. Their mutual refusal to be outbid by the other in formulating a patriotic policy ran parallel to the British and French determination not to be outbid by the other in the

---

[147] Martineau, 'International duties', 210, 227.

Near East. In December 1853 Palmerston temporarily resigned, in protest at the cabinet's support for Russell's Reform bill, by which the latter was seeking to rally Liberal MPs and reassert his own popularity. Simultaneously there was a crisis over Eastern policy, as the Russians destroyed the Turkish fleet at Sinope. Palmerston told Clarendon that the 'Stain' of Sinope on *Britain*'s honour must be wiped away.[148] Russell, similarly, had for days been telling Aberdeen that, as Leader of the House of Commons, he could not be expected, when Parliament reassembled, to defend Britain's failure to respond to this attack, which 'must tarnish the British name throughout the East' given the British fleet's presence nearby. Moreover, he believed that the Russians would shortly cross the Danube deeper into Ottoman territory, endangering Constantinople. If Russia forced Turkey to a humiliating peace settlement, 'our reputation in the world would be severely affected'.[149]

Had Palmerston based his resignation on anger at Aberdeen's weakness in the East, Russell would have followed, the government would have fallen and an enervating national political crisis would have ensued. By resigning instead over Reform, he separated himself from Russell but still forced Aberdeen to beg him to return.[150] Most of the press took Palmerston's side, tending to treat Sinope as evidence that the Russians were bent on war at all costs, aiming at Constantinople and the humiliation of Britain. Even *The Times*, formerly the most prominent supporter of peace, changed its mind and suggested that probably only war was now compatible with honour. When Palmerston resigned, his newspaper sympathisers immediately interpreted it as a protest at Aberdeen's failure to make a manly response to the Russians. Moreover the *Morning Post*, widely believed to speak Palmerston's sentiments, declared that he had been pushed out by the same cause as in 1851 – a '*rapprochement* between the Courts of Vienna and England'.[151] The *Morning Advertiser* claimed that German influences at Court were 'synonymous with Russian' ones, and were undermining Britain's free institutions; what it called the 'German conspiracy' had struck again. Extraordinary rumours over the next month, beginning in the cheap press but eventually picked up by the more respectable, claimed that a great struggle between patriotic and foreign interests at Court had ended with Prince Albert being committed to the Tower of London on a charge of high treason.[152]

---

[148] 13 Dec. 1853, quoted in Palmer, *Banner of battle*, p. 32.
[149] Scherer, *Russell*, pp. 228–9; Schroeder, *Austria*, p. 112.
[150] There is a discussion of this manoeuvre in Brown, *Palmerston and foreign policy*, pp. 183–90.
[151] Martin, *Triumph of Palmerston*, pp. 172–8.
[152] Williams, *Contentious Crown*, pp. 100–2, 161–3; Martin, *Triumph of Palmerston*, pp. 178–86.

An internationally inactive coalition bereft of Palmerston and Russell and opposed by most of the press could not have lasted a fortnight after Parliament reassembled in early 1854. Aberdeen gave way; Palmerston returned to office, his position greatly strengthened against both his rivals; Reform was sidelined; Napoleon III was pacified; the British and French fleets entered the Black Sea. Once there, they were bound to try to restrict Russian naval movements in ways that the Russians would find unacceptable. War was more or less inevitable and came in March 1854.

The Crimean War was an aberration in British policy and, in hindsight, a clear mistake. Britain was unprepared for it and could identify no obvious benefits from it. Carlyle alleged that the war was all the work of 'the idle population of editors'.[153] But in fact British interests made it very difficult to avoid. The pressure of public opinion on a divided cabinet played its part, but essentially the war was caused by the breakdown of the traditional understandings between the powers in the ideologically strained aftermath of 1848. In the context of that breakdown, Britain's role as the defender of liberty, progress, fairness and self-government against brute aggression seemed obvious to most onlookers, who overwhelmingly saw the war as a fight for justice against brute aggression. Very many churchmen and Nonconformists justified the conflict as one for freedom and law in Europe – leading Cobden to fulminate against the vulgar crusading Protestantism of the '"Saint" party'. Cobden put much more blame for the war on the clamour of misguided Radicals than on the government. Maurice hoped that the war would prevent a Russian 'universal empire'; Radicals such as George Holyoake saw it as an opportunity to liberate Italy, Hungary and Poland.[154] The more racially inclined pundits suggested that aggressive conquest was a 'physiological necessity' for Russia, inherent in its people and justified by Panslavist doctrine.[155] And many moralist intellectuals regarded Britain's entry into war as an act of national moral purification. Kingsley wanted it to sweep away 'the dyspeptic unbelief, the insincere bigotry, the effeminate frivolity which paralyses our poetry as much as it does our action'. Tennyson's 'Maud' caught that mood powerfully with its suggestion that war might erode the selfish materialism of the previous decade; critical

---

[153] Journal, spring 1854, J. A. Froude, *Thomas Carlyle: a history of his life in London* (2 vols., London, 1884), vol. II, p. 151.

[154] Anderson, 'Reactions of Church and Dissent', 211–13. For the pro-war sentiments of the young R. W. Dale and the leading Nonconformist Baines, and for Cobden's anger at the latter, see Larsen, *Friends of religious equality*, pp. 213–14. For Cobden's blame, see McCord, 'Cobden and Bright', p. 105.

[155] See the Carlylean David Masson, 'Peace and its political duties', *North British Review*, 25 (1856), 270–1.

opinion, though ambivalent about many aspects of the poem, generally approved of that ambition.[156] Maurice, again, believed that the war had created an unprecedented degree of 'national heart and godliness amongst us'.[157] The attempt to infuse Liberal politics with ethical righteousness had won its first victory – a war that was to kill over half a million people.

By the end of the 1840s the hopes of the 1830s, that an alliance between constitutional governments in Britain and France could spread peace and liberalism throughout Europe, had been dashed.[158] The disappointments of 1848–9 made Britain seem the sole reliable guardian of liberty. The libertarian image of the British state, meanwhile, was strengthened as a result of a series of clashes in and after 1848, particularly on financial, Irish and colonial policies. The image of the leading Whig aristocratic dynasties, the Greys and Russells, was badly damaged, and a more inclusive tone was propagated, emphasising efficiency and economy on the one hand and straightforward manliness on the other. Throughout the 1850s, Whig moralistic interventionism continued to be criticised as 'un-English'.

But this knee-jerk suspicion of state intervention was not an adequate basis for party politics; it meant paralysis in many domestic policy areas. Once the image of the state had been cleansed, the inadequacies of *laissez-faire* as a political creed (as opposed to an economic one) became obvious. It was easy to associate it with a selfish concern by materialist ratepayers and taxpayers to cut charges at all costs. Anxiety about national defence had already led to increasing criticisms of Cobdenism or 'Manchesterism' as anti-social – one reason for the enthusiasm for a vigorous Eastern policy in 1853–4. As chapter 2 noted, Unitarian and free-thinking provincial elites, as well as Russellite Whigs, were especially keen to challenge complacent anti-interventionism on social issues. Therefore, the politicians who triumphed in the power struggles of the early 1850s did not establish a lasting settlement – not least because of the tensions between Palmerston and the Peelites, which were apparent all the way through the Aberdeen coalition and erupted spectacularly in 1855. Though the coalition of 1852 was the strongest basis on which a government could stand, and though Palmerston was undoubtedly the most popular of elite politicians, support for him was fragile, based on antagonism to continental values rather than

---

[156] C. Hibbert, *The destruction of Lord Raglan: a tragedy of the Crimean War 1854–55* (London, 1961), p. 25; E. F. Shannon, Jr, 'The critical reception of Tennyson's "Maud"', *Publications of the Modern Language Association of America*, 68 (1953), 402–3.
[157] Maurice, *Maurice*, vol. II, p. 250.
[158] T. C. Grattan, 'Lord Palmerston and his policy', *Westminster Review*, 1 n.s. (1852), 591.

any domestic agreement on policy. It was logical that a cabinet crisis over the conduct of the war in early 1855 should lead to his own elevation to the premiership after the resignation of Aberdeen, because he was indispensable to any government. But his indispensability was the result of the break-up of the old party system, together with the emphasis on international affairs after 1848. His appeal was to a lowest common denominator, to a patriotic style which was a *sine qua non* of political success without supplying a coherent medium-term policy. He did not want the Liberals to reunite around a strong party programme, based on constitutional or religious reform; if they did they would prefer Russell as their leader. He was an appropriate Liberal leader for the mid-1850s because English Liberalism was organised around the rejection of values that seemed alien to England: patronage-ridden exclusiveness at home, autocracy and repression abroad. After the Crimean War it became clear that such an appeal was not enough. National pride must have an ethical content if it was to engage Liberals, especially those marginalised in the early 1850s. This was a natural response to the disappointments of war, but also to the post-war European climate, in which questions of ethics and national purpose became highly pertinent.

# CHAPTER 5

# Italian unification and the search for an ethical nationhood

The years 1859 and 1868 were crucial in the history of the Liberal party. On both occasions the party rallied against a minority Conservative government, demonstrating in the process a degree of purpose and unity, and a range of support, that no Liberal government had been able to muster since the 1830s. In 1859 the immediate cause was Italy, in 1868 Ireland. The Italian issue associated the party with global strength and an international mission on behalf of constitutional, religious and commercial liberty. Success there appeared to represent a conclusive victory for English constitutional values in Europe over the forces of autocracy. The Conservatives could be presented as friends of oppression and clericalism, or at least too feeble in the struggle against these. In 1868 the Irish issue offered many of the same benefits for the party, and its significance is best appreciated in the light of the Italian debates. Different groups of Liberals welcomed the proposal to disestablish the Irish Church for different reasons, but with underlying agreement that – on analogous principles to the Italian case – it was the best route to the reassertion of British authority and values in Ireland against the twin 'foreign' threats of repressive papal clericalism and violent secular republicanism. Disraeli's alternative was unacceptably unpatriotic.

In a sense, therefore, the claim was that Italy and Ireland could be won for Britain, and this aspiration demonstrates the enormous national self-confidence of the decade. However, not all Liberals viewed these policies in a narrowly chauvinistic light. The dominance of the Italian and Irish issues demonstrates that, with constitutionalism more secure, political debate in the 1860s was increasingly concerned with how to build national communities in a post-autocratic age. Most assumed that successful nations could only be built on pluralist foundations. This awareness of the need to tolerate a variety of local customs was shaped by growing Liberal familiarity with foreign cultures (particularly Italy, Germany and the United States), an enhanced distaste for the vulgarity and meanness of Little Englandism, and an interest in historicism. Much Liberal thought of the 1860s, typified by Mill and Arnold, stressed the benefits of drawing from the strengths of other cultures, and synthesising them to create a higher unity. One consequence was a recognition that, to some extent, Britain needed to be more tolerant than in the 1850s about how to govern the Catholic peoples of Ireland – though this did not make the earlier Whiggish continental ideas any more acceptable to the Liberal coalition. A compromise between 'English' and traditional Irish customs would best consolidate a pluralist kingdom, the most liberal and progressive kind of state. It would be a natural development of the British model of constitutional inclusiveness and could be Britain's legacy to the world now that autocracy was on the wane. In promoting a political model for the age, Britain, the liberator of Italy, would be the new Rome.

This interest in nation-building, together with the reaction against the chauvinist *laissez-faire* assumptions of the 1850s, was also influenced by a consciousness that Britain itself would benefit from an active social policy designed to bind the national community together. By the mid-1860s it was no longer possible to ignore class tension, agitation for Parliamentary reform, and the enfeebling political consequences of middle-class materialism. By the time of Palmerston's death in 1865 there was a stronger feeling that the Liberals needed to be galvanised into more decisive and positive legislative action, stimulated in part by continental models.

Reaction against ignoble *laissez-faire* was paralleled in the foreign-policy field by a certain amount of discontent with the lack of opportunities for morally inspiring interventions in European affairs. For a long time this discontent was marginalised, because in the early 1860s it was generally assumed that the triumph of constitutional liberalism and international peace would be a natural consequence of economic and social progress. This complacency fitted with the general optimism of the period about the smoothness of social and biological evolution. However, uncertainty about Britain's international role now that autocracy appeared to have been defeated grew during the continental crises of the mid-1860s. Should Britain rely on free trade and economic progress, or resort to military and diplomatic intervention? Did it still need colonies? Should Britain spread its values by firm rule or by setting an example of toleration and respect for conscience? On occasion, these questions could not be ignored – for example over trade policy, Canadian defence and, as discussed in the Introduction, the Jamaican revolt of 1865. After 1867 the need to redefine the English mission intensified. This was partly because of the extension of the franchise at home, and partly because of the success of nation-building abroad in the 1860s. By 1869 Prussia and the United States, in particular, were more forceful international players, while growing international tension made Napoleon III's France all the more restless. The traditional simple British Liberal perspective, of a world divided between liberalism and autocracy, was now being replaced by one of strong competing nation-states. This was bound to lead to insecurity in Britain about the predominance of its interests and values. In the late 1860s this insecurity was largely disguised by continuing complacency that the world was going Britain's way, though there were already tensions about the status of its colonies. That complacency would not last much longer.

## ITALY, LIBERTY AND NATIONALITY, 1859–60

The establishment of an independent constitutional Italian regime in 1859–60 was an enormously symbolic moment for Victorian Liberalism. It resonated loudly in domestic politics because it was a victory against the four faces of autocracy with which the British were most familiar – Austria, Russia, Napoleon III and the Pope. And in the context of the Crimean War this victory seemed complete and permanent, opening a vista of unstoppable progress for English values. Moreover, it was accompanied by a powerful show of British naval supremacy, and by a triumph for free-trade principles – which might now dominate Europe. Autocracy had buckled in the face of more civilised values, economic and social as well as constitutional, and without significant bloodshed. Northern Italy had rebelled against the rule of those 'inferior in refinement' and 'intelligence', as Gladstone put it.[1] In future, political, economic and ethical progress might make headway without much need for military conflict. In the first half of the 1860s it seemed so self-evident that the world was following Britain's lead that it was not necessary to consider too closely how far Britain might still need to intervene navally or diplomatically to maintain its position. Different Liberals could see the victory in Italy as a victory for subtly different principles; hence its fruitful political ambiguity.

At the end of the Crimean War in 1856 autocracy had clearly been damaged, but there was no consensus that it had yet been destroyed. Russia no longer posed a naval threat to Turkey, British ships dominated the Mediterranean, and the check to Russian power in Europe was real enough. But the war never became the full-blooded crusade for European liberties – in Italy, Poland and Hungary – for which Palmerston at one stage hoped.[2] The cost,

---

[1] 'Foreign affairs – war in Italy', *Quarterly Review*, 105 (1859), 549–50.
[2] Lambert, *Crimean War*, pp. 89–90, 93, 300–1.

the cabinet, Napoleon III, the Austrians and the Prussians had all conspired against this idea. Gains from the war were limited, essentially to the demilitarisation of the Black Sea and autonomy for Moldavia and Wallachia. It did nothing for European stability, undermining the old diplomatic status quo by weakening Austria, while Russia yearned for revenge for its defeat and Napoleon III was more restless than ever. British politicians widely – and correctly – assumed that Napoleon would no longer be content to play second fiddle to Britain in their entente. Indeed the war had shown British military failings relative to the French ally. As early as April 1856 there was a major steam review of the navy, a statement of naval power, directed at France. From 1855 the Court was planning a major dynastic alliance against France, a marriage between the Queen's eldest daughter Victoria and the Crown Prince of Prussia, which was celebrated in January 1858. Suspicion of Napoleon's intentions was intense. There had been Radical disquiet even at the wartime alliance with him. Those who regarded the ending of the war as premature tended to blame Napoleon for it. He was also generally held at fault for the failure to carry through a joint Anglo-French protest at miscarriages of justice by the autocratic King of Naples in 1856.[3]

In the late 1850s, with the Russian threat reduced, Napoleon came to define more particularly the threat to Britain, physical, constitutional and ideological. The catalyst of the anti-Bonapartist alarm of 1858–9 was the attempted assassination of him in January 1858 by the Italian patriot Felice Orsini, using bombs that he had had made in England. Napoleon demanded that Britain should act to prevent subversive activities by its refugees, and some French colonels petitioned Napoleon to take military action against the dens of conspirators that they believed existed across the Channel. With the British army preoccupied with the task of restoring order after the Indian Mutiny, Palmerston's government decided to mollify the Emperor by tightening the law on conspiracy to commit murder. But this prompted anti-French demonstrations outside Parliament, which Palmerston's opponents in the Commons used to obstruct the bill by nineteen votes and bring down his government. Russell, Gladstone, Roebuck, A. W. Kinglake, Bright, Milner Gibson and W. J. Fox were among the Liberals and Peelites who voted against him. Many cast aspersions on Palmerston's domestic liberalism: no true Liberal would restrict English liberties at the behest of a foreign autocrat. Gladstone claimed that to sacrifice such 'an important principle of English law' would 'establish a moral complicity between us and those who seek safety in repressive measures', would betray England's 'responsibility' to defend the 'sacred cause' of liberty and would be 'a blow and discouragement to that sacred cause in every country in the world'.[4] The *Daily News* asked if England was to be annexed for police purposes to France. William Harcourt, then a young polemicist, declared that England, 'the last hope and refuge of Europe', must stand firm in order to keep alight the 'sacred beacon . . . athwart the dark waters of illimitable despotism'.[5]

Moreover, press fever soon intensified, on the completion of the enormous French naval base at Cherbourg, and the building of the first French iron-clad battleship, *La Gloire*. As with steam in the 1840s, this looked like a revolution in naval warfare for which the British fleet was unprepared. The inaugural celebrations at Cherbourg in August 1858, witnessed by Victoria, Albert and a hundred MPs, seemed designed to warn the British of Napoleon's power.[6] Certainly this was the message taken home by aggressive Radical observers such as Roebuck, who put himself forward as 'Tear'em' the watchdog to guard the free British against threats of invasion by 'a despot'.[7] Napoleon's arrest of the Anglophile Montalembert for publishing a pamphlet on the superiority of English institutions and political culture also became a *cause célèbre*, which suggested that the Emperor seemed to have no respect for constitutional traditions or press and personal liberties. His apparent determination to challenge England led to much criticism of his 'Imperialism', which seemed dangerously unstable. Unlike a British politician accountable to Parliament, it appeared impossible for him to be straightforward and 'manly', because his need to secure dynastic survival led to a concentration on foreign adventure and prestige as a distraction from domestic taxes and oppression. This expensive policy disrupted trade and increased expenditure, thus requiring ever more desperate throws of the foreign-policy dice.[8] The system of 'personal rule' was unchecked, arbitrary

---

[4] *Hansard*, 148:1819–20, 19 Feb. 1858. See Porter, *Refugee question*, pp. 177–87. For extra-Parliamentary Radical support for foreign refugees against their governments, see also Finn, *After Chartism*, pp. 177–86.

[5] Urban, *British opinion*, p. 103; 3 Feb. 1858, Gardiner, *Harcourt*, vol. I, p. 93; Storey *et al.*, *Letters of Dickens*, vol. VIII, p. 522.

[6] Salevouris, 'Riflemen form', pp. 39–40; *The Times*, 9 Aug. 1858, pp. 6, 8; Urban, *British opinion*, pp. 107–8.

[7] R. E. Leader, *Life and letters of John Arthur Roebuck* (London, 1897), p. 272.

[8] See Salisbury in 1860 and 1871: P. Smith, *Lord Salisbury on politics: a selection from his articles in the Quarterly Review, 1860–1883* (Cambridge, 1972), pp. 129–30; marquess of Salisbury, 'Political lessons of the war', *Quarterly Review*, 130 (1871), 256–86.

and self-indulgent; it lacked principle, scruple and public spirit; it spawned materialism and false national pride.[9] Imperialism seemed the antithesis of the widespread participation in a political community that secured stability and strengthened man's moral integrity. Much of the British commentary on Napoleon's regime took the form of a comparison with the most famous of empires, the Roman empire, the decay of which was generally blamed on decadence, public extravagance and the pursuit of false glory. After the Montalembert affair, the *Daily Telegraph* called him 'the Tiberius of the Tuileries'.[10]

The other concern about Napoleon was that he would fall back on a standard French expansionist strategy by declaring sympathy for radical ideas: nationalism and the human brotherhood. This might destabilise Europe – and Ireland. Therefore his first aggression, in Italy, was particularly alarming. He began to foment Piedmontese challenges to Austrian rule in Lombardy and Venetia in the winter of 1858–9. *The Times* remarked that for the second time in the century a despot was planning to conquer, devastate and pillage 'in the name of the "Rights of Man"'.[11] Austria declared war on Piedmont-Sardinia in late April 1859 and Napoleon placed 200,000 men in Italy in eight weeks. In late April *The Times* also revealed that in the previous month he had signed a secret treaty with Russia, apparently leaving him free to attack England at will. This created a crisis in the City of London, and a great panic about the inadequacy of defence, exacerbated by Indian commitments. Volunteer corps began to be formed up and down the country, authorised by the War Office on 12 May, while Tennyson published (anonymously) a famous poem in *The Times* on 9 May, 'Storm! Storm! Riflemen form!' aimed at rallying opinion against the threat of attack by Napoleon. The Volunteer movement grew rapidly to about 120,000 men between the summer of 1859 and the autumn of 1860.[12]

In politics, this situation meant a repeat of the events of 1852–3. Once again a strong and vigorous response was needed, an assertion of British power. Once again, there was a minority Conservative government in office which was a sitting duck for allegations of feebleness, both because it lacked

---

[9] A. V. Kirwan, *Modern France: its journalism, literature and society* (London, 1863), p. vii; [F. Greenwood et al.,] *The Napoleon dynasty: or, history of the Bonaparte family* (London, 1853); F. D. Maurice to Hare, 31 Dec. 1851, in Maurice, *Maurice*, vol. II, p. 97; *Spectator* and *The Times*, 1870, quoted in D. Raymond, *British policy and opinion during the Franco-Prussian War* (New York, 1921), p. 74.
[10] 26 Nov. 1858, p. 4.    [11] Urban, *British opinion*, p. 119.
[12] Cunningham, *Volunteer Force*, p. 15.

enthusiasm for liberalism and because of its minority status in Parliament.[13] It attempted to overcompensate for this weakness by raising taxes for a panicky increase in defence spending. Disraeli, the Conservative Chancellor of the Exchequer, saw his plans to woo public opinion with tax reductions collapse; in February 1859 defence estimates were raised by £1 million. Yet this opened the government to Liberal charges of incompetence and vested-interest favouritism. Moreover, the government was in a weak position on Italy, because no effective Italian policy was possible while Austria and France were at loggerheads. The Austrian aggression against Piedmont revived anti-Austrian sentiment. The Liberal press placed an indignant emphasis on Conservative partiality to Austria and on Court pressure for a pro-Austrian policy. The government was blamed for not warning Austria and France more effectively against entering the war.[14] By its weakness, it had damaged Britain's position, encouraged Austrian aggression and introduced the risk that, if Napoleon went too far, the British might have to fight against him for an unpopular cause.[15] Investors wanted an honourable peace; the government seemed unable to provide it. There were also allegations that the Tories were in league with the Catholic powers of Europe to safeguard the Pope's temporal power (and to win much-needed Commons support from Irish Catholics).[16] Indeed the papacy made clear its preference for the Conservatives at the 1859 election, and the party gained eight seats in Ireland.

Criticism of Conservative feebleness allowed the Liberals to rally. Palmerston and Russell buried their differences of 1857–9, leading to the famous Liberal party meeting at Willis's Rooms and the defeat of the Conservative government in a no-confidence debate in early June. They needed to come to an understanding on Parliamentary reform, since it was the issue on which their supporters had differed the most. But the main reason for their agreement was foreign policy. However, it was less an agreement on the details of an Italian policy than a belief that Britain must have a majority (and therefore a Liberal) government and must assert a strong image abroad

---

[13] See e.g. Hatherton to Reeve, 5 Mar. 1859, Laughton, *Reeve*, vol. II, p. 13; Herbert to Graham, 10 Jan. 1859, Lord Stanmore, *Sidney Herbert Lord Herbert of Lea: a memoir* (2 vols., London, 1906), vol. II, p. 166.

[14] Urban, *British opinion*, pp. 190–1, 205–6, 221n145; D. Beales, *England and Italy 1859–60* (London, 1961), pp. 52–3; A. I. Dasent, *John Thadeus Delane editor of 'The Times': his life and correspondence* (2 vols., London, 1908), vol. I, p. 310.

[15] See various speakers (e.g. Bury, Palmerston, Bright, Russell) in the debate on the Address, *Hansard*, 154:98, 193, 297, 7, 9, 10 June 1859.

[16] Urban, *British opinion*, p. 222.

and a calming influence on the panic at home. Palmerston had written to Russell on 18 May that the Liberals must return to power so that 'this country and other countries should know in the present state of the world . . . the organ of Great Britain is a government . . . that . . . may have . . . weight . . . authority and . . . independence of action'.[17] The aim was to secure an honourable neutrality and peace, which would appeal to commercial, as well as anti-Austrian, Radicals – hence the symbolic willingness of the leading Cobdenite Milner Gibson to serve in the new cabinet. To achieve this, men were more important than measures. When Palmerston returned as Prime Minister, Russell himself took the Foreign Office in order to keep out Clarendon or Granville, either of whom would have adopted a very much less assertive policy in Italy.[18] Moreover the Peelites were now able to advertise their patriotism more successfully than in 1853–5. Herbert, particularly, urged vigorous defence measures and became War Secretary in the new cabinet.

Luck was with the new ministers. In opposition, the Liberals had not been united about Italy, partly because they differed on how far to encourage nationalist challenges to the ideological status quo in Europe, but mainly because of anxieties about the damage that Napoleon III might do to the balance of power if he put himself at the head of European nationalism. And any change that weakened Austria would thrust it back into the Russian camp. Fortunately, within weeks of their return to power, the Austrian defeat at Solferino, which ensured the loss of Lombardy to Piedmont, was followed by the signing of the treaty of Villafranca by Austria and France. This treaty, a betrayal by Napoleon of Piedmont's further ambitions, sought to defend as much of the status quo as possible elsewhere in Italy. In the eyes of the Liberal press, it revealed Napoleon in his true colours as an autocrat who shared with Austria the concern to prop up the Pope and the forces of reaction and repression.[19] It greatly damaged his reputation in Italy as a friend of liberal nationalism.

The Franco-Austrian pact meant that, for the first time in years, the British could encourage Italian liberalism without playing into the hands of one or other of their rivals. In the summer of 1859 there were risings in north-central Italy against the existing pro-Austrian regimes, opening the prospect that they would join liberal Piedmont in an independent state. Conservatively minded policy-makers in all countries wanted an international

---

[17] Steele, *Palmerston and Liberalism*, pp. 90–1. See also the emphasis on foreign policy in *The Times'* report of the Willis's Rooms meeting on p. 93.

[18] Russell to Herbert, 21 May 1859, Stanmore, *Herbert*, vol. II, p. 187; Scherer, *Russell*, p. 265.

[19] See, for example, the cartoon, 'Free Italy (?)', in *Punch*, 23 July 1859, p. 37.

congress to find a workable compromise to the central Italy question. Pressured by the quietist majority and by the Queen, who worked together to try to keep Britain on the same wavelength as the continental powers, the cabinet advocated the policy of military non-intervention in the area by all powers. However, Palmerston and Russell (sometimes with the vacillating Napoleon III) succeeded in frustrating the conservatives' agenda. They wanted instead to allow the Italians in Parma, Modena and Tuscany to settle their own future by plebiscite. Russell told a mass audience at Aberdeen in September that England 'held a beacon on high which might yet save the rest of the world'.[20] This strategy antagonised the Austrians so much that there was a risk of armed intervention in the central Italian states to prevent the plebiscites. In December 1859 and January 1860 the 'two dreadful old men' tried and failed to persuade the cabinet to accept an Anglo-French alliance to protect Italy from the risk of Austrian intervention (and to restrain Napoleon III and keep him on side).[21] Only Gladstone fully supported them, on the basis that the principle of safeguarding Italian liberties against foreign interference was 'a peculiarly English principle'.[22] The cabinet deadlocked and nearly fell. Palmerston and Russell were forced to retreat, partly owing to non-interventionist instincts in cabinet, but more from a fear that joint action might be construed aggressively, as an ideological alliance to upset the existing boundaries of Europe, instead of as a peace-keeping mission. Yet in fact they achieved their main goal, because the hint of an alliance was enough to make Austria commit itself against intervention. All powers accepted the policy of Italian self-determination, and the states concerned all voted for absorption into Piedmont-Sardinia.[23]

A further panic in the spring of 1860 also ended by helping the promoters of a large liberal state in Italy. Napoleon III persuaded Piedmont to accept that Savoy and Nice should be annexed by France as compensation for the absorption. Most English newspapers waxed indignant at this act of 'spoliation'. It weakened Napoleon's claim to be a disinterested supporter of Italy, and raised the fear that he was embarking on a policy of pursuing 'natural boundaries' for France, all the way to the Rhine. In an extraordinary speech which won much press sympathy Russell gave vent to the 'choler of the British nation', warning Napoleon that in the event

---

[20] C. T. McIntire, *England against the papacy 1858–1861: Tories, Liberals, and the overthrow of papal temporal power during the Italian Risorgimento* (Cambridge, 1983), p. 150.

[21] As Victoria famously later described Palmerston and Russell: to Leopold, 25 Feb. 1864, *LQV 1862–78*, vol. I, p. 168.

[22] 7 Jan. 1860, *GD*, vol. v, p. 453.

[23] See Beales, *England and Italy*, pp. 115–30, for an account of the cabinet discussions.

of further acts of aggression Britain would act with other powers to preserve the European settlement against him.[24] The uproar against Napoleon
enabled Palmerston to get his defence increases through cabinet and damaged his Cobdenite critics, particularly when a Parliamentary outburst by
Bright suggested that he was more concerned with manufacturers' profits
than with national honour.[25] When Garibaldi turned the Sicilian revolt of
April 1860 into a Sardinian campaign to overthrow the Kingdom of Naples,
the French suggested that the two powers should blockade the Straits of
Messina to stop him. The British declined. Russell and Palmerston allowed
a British Legion of Volunteers, organised by the Radical George Holyoake
and others, to leave England to fight for Garibaldi, despite the terms of
the Foreign Enlistment Act; Palmerston claimed that they were excursion-
ists to Mount Etna.[26] Ideally, the British would have preferred to retain
the Kingdom of Naples as a second Italian kingdom – were it not for the
fact that Napoleon III wanted a united Italy even less than they did. The
result of Garibaldi's march was the virtual unification of Italy (excepting
Venetia and Rome). Russell sent a famous dispatch praising the Italians for
building up their own liberties in the spirit of 1688 – a warning to Prussia,
Austria and Russia, meeting in Warsaw, that they should not intervene
against the Piedmontese.[27] The former papal territories were annexed to
Piedmont in November 1860. Garibaldi wrote to the people of Glasgow
that 'England was the representative of God' in the battle against 'tyranny
and evil priests'.[28]

   The Italian issue therefore allowed Liberals to combine national assertiveness with the defence of oppressed peoples, and to marry a commitment to
constitutional liberalism with a triumphant hostility both to the untrustworthy Napoleon and to the more traditional conservative forces of Austria
and the papacy. Though no British politician had intended a new liberal
Italian state in 1859, and many in the cabinet had feared the disruption
to the status quo that it might cause, the outcome seemed a great victory

---

[24] *Hansard*, 157:1257–8, 26 Mar. 1860; Scherer, *Russell*, pp. 274–6: given as 'cholar'.

[25] Bright, fearing that the panic would increase expenditure and derail Cobden's commercial treaty,
notoriously declaimed 'perish Savoy' rather than increase tension with France at such a moment.
This remark was immediately exploited both by the Conservatives (Manners noted that 'at any rate
France is not unrepresented in our body') and by 'manly' Liberals such as Kinglake and Roebuck. The
Conservatives nearly managed to delay the Commercial Treaty as a result, and the threat that they
posed over this issue gave Palmerston the perfect opportunity to push for higher defence spending.
See *Hansard*, 156:2170, 2171, 2 Mar. 1860 and 2229, 2248–50, 5 Mar. 1860.

[26] J. McCabe, *Life and letters of George Jacob Holyoake* (2 vols., London, 1908), vol. I, pp. 311, 313.

[27] Earl Russell, *Selections from speeches 1817 to 1841 and from despatches 1859 to 1865* (2 vols., London,
1870), vol. II, p. 282. See Odo Russell in Walpole, *Russell*, vol. II, pp. 325–8.

[28] McIntire, *England against the papacy*, p. 219.

against autocracy and clericalism, increasing opportunities for British commercial and naval influence. And the influence of the British Court in foreign policy had, for the moment, been checked. Russell and Palmerston regarded this as an important victory for liberalism after Albert's assertiveness and Victoria's obstinacy in the 1850s.[29] Moreover, the Pope's rule over most of the central Italian territories (Romagna, the Marches and Umbria as well as the area around Rome) had been ended. In 1859, when Austrian troops withdrew from the Romagna, papal power there was overthrown, and locals pressed for plebiscites on annexation by Piedmont, as in the more northerly Italian states. The British government not only supported this but also led the international pressure for the ending of papal government in the rest of central Italy. In a dispatch of August 1859 Russell attacked the 'effete despotism' of papal rule and demanded that it be limited to a small area around Rome.[30] In September 1860 he got his way when the Piedmontese invaded Umbria and the Marches in support of the movement against papal control in those regions. The anti-liberal tendencies of the Pope after 1848, the re-establishment of the hierarchy in England in 1850, and a stream of stories about corruption and misgovernment in the Papal States in the early 1850s had all contributed to a strong English critique of the degeneracy of papal rule. In Gladstone's eyes, recent declarations by Catholics across Europe defending papal pretensions, including in 1851 and 1859 in the United Kingdom, posed 'something of a challenge to all governments'.[31]

An Italy 'resting on constitutional monarchies', as Russell put it, seemed to mark a victory for English political values much more than a victory for nationalist ones.[32] In that sense it was a reassuringly conservative outcome, especially since Italy's settled borders and emerging liberal institutions made it unlikely that it would be an expansionist or troublesome power. Having originally viewed unification as potentially unpleasant Sardinian imperialism, Gladstone was suddenly converted to it because the Italians had demonstrated their respect for 'the English way'. They had shown their constitutional and moral maturity, their ability to marry the defence of local liberties with a respect for authority. England's mission was to continue to educate European public opinion into a respect for these

---

[29] When the Queen repeatedly objected to one of Russell's flamboyant dispatches on Italy in August 1859, he complained: 'we might as well live under a despotism': Granville to Argyll, 31 Aug. 1859, in Lord E. Fitzmaurice, *The life of Granville George Leveson Gower second Earl Granville 1815–1891* (2 vols., London, 1905), vol. I, pp. 356–7.

[30] McIntire, *England against the papacy*, pp. 119, 136.    [31] 7 Jan. 1860, *GD*, vol. v, p. 454.

[32] Draft to the Queen, 8 Dec. 1859, quoted in McIntire, *England against the papacy*, p. 150.

values.[33] Palmerston also claimed that a free Italy would develop according to English political patterns, with a 'great Whig party' dominant over both republicans and 'arbitrary and despotic' Tories.[34] The consensus was that, under Cavour, Piedmont-Sardinia had embraced 'English institutions': liberal constitutional monarchy, free-trade ideas and competent finance. They were the 'English of Italy'.[35]

Perhaps, then, Italy was becoming more English. And perhaps Britain was the new Rome, shouldering the task of spreading values of civilisation and human dignity through the known world.[36] If so, it was not surprising that Italy became such an attractive cultural symbol for the British in the 1860s. From 1864, Thomas Cook's tours encouraged the idea that its tourist centres were spaces which the British could, in effect, colonise. The Risorgimento gave the impression that modern Italy, with English assistance, was rediscovering its ancient or early modern principles of civic virtue: the discipline of self-government, the worth of measured liberty. Many Britons already identified with aspects of the Italian past. The prosperous mercantile elites of provincial Britain often saw their towns as modern-day equivalents of Florence or Venice.[37] To model the Manchester Free Trade Hall of 1853 on a sixteenth-century palazzo made the claim – in the era of free trade – to dominate the seas as powerfully, and to govern as liberally, as the mercantile republics had done. So did the Palladian design for the new Foreign Office, in support of which Palmerston picked a timely fight with the Conservatives (and many architects) in 1858–9; he claimed that their Gothic alternative was churchy, gloomy and 'not an English style of architecture'.[38] And Ruskin's *The stones of Venice* (1851–3) conveyed to evangelical, and lapsed evangelical, Victorians a profoundly congenial fantasy – that the Italian city-states had been inspired by a devout, personal, lay religious spirit not so far removed from that of a serious nineteenth-century Protestant. Ruskin's writings were enormously influential in persuading middle-class British people that Italian travel was a respectable pursuit. By the 1860s not just the aristocracy, the university-educated upper-middle classes, and

---

[33] See D. M. Schreuder, 'Gladstone and Italian unification, 1848–70: the making of a Liberal?', *English Historical Review*, 85 (1970), 484, 488–9. Gladstone later commented that he had expected Italy to be 'the most conservative power in Europe': 28 Oct. 1881, *Derby diary, 1878–93*, p. 368.

[34] *Hansard*, 155:578, 28 July 1859.

[35] W. C. Cartwright, 'Count Cavour', *Edinburgh Review*, 114 (1861), 272–3; F. P. Cobbe, 'Women in Italy in 1862', *Macmillan's Magazine*, 6 (1862), 364.

[36] J. Pemble, *The Mediterranean passion: Victorians and Edwardians in the South* (Oxford, 1987), p. 64.

[37] See e.g. the comments in the history of Bradford (1866) quoted in Lees, *Cities perceived*, p. 51. The Bradford Town Hall (1869) was designed with a Tuscan campanile.

[38] *Hansard*, 155:932, 4 Aug. 1859; for the background, see I. Toplis, *The Foreign Office: an architectural history* (London, 1987), chs. 10, 11, 13.

louche expatriates, but also many earnest provincial Dissenters and their ladies were familiar with the past and present life of Florence, Venice and Rome.

In some quarters it even became fashionable to argue that if the ordinary Italians of the past had had spiritual and moral sincerity, the same was or could be true of their modern equivalents. This argument should not be taken too far: they, particularly southerners, were still widely seen as backward and superstitious.[39] It was not admiration for Italians but admiration for Britain and hostility to Austria, France and the Pope that made unification so attractive. However, among a minority there was a view that Britain could learn from present as well as past Italian culture. Ever since the 1840s Mazzini, then the most charismatic Italian refugee in England, had divided Liberal opinion, some admiring his ethical earnestness, humanity and vision (eight hundred influential figures in the London literary and political world banded together at his suggestion to create the Friends of Italy in 1851) while others regarded him as a conspirator, a revolutionary and an anarchist.[40] For most traditional Liberals, the new monarchy in Italy strengthened ordered constitutional progress in *opposition* to the wilder theories of Mazzinian nationalism (especially if backed by the unreliable Napoleon III). However, some Radicals could see it as a victory for ethical nationalist principles and ideas of the brotherhood of man. They hoped that Italian unification would set a course for European liberalism.[41] Moreover the swiftness of the Italian triumph suggested that these values could be projected peacefully through the Continent by the force of aroused, enlightened public opinion.

In other words, 'Italy' was the best sort of political issue because different Liberals could adopt it for diverse reasons: its ambiguities greatly helped to strengthen and widen the Liberal coalition. There was a similar ambiguity on the associated issues that grew out of Anglo-French tensions in 1859–60. British naval supremacy was reasserted spectacularly, while there was a major advance towards lower tariff levels throughout Europe.

Just as in 1853, the invasion scare of 1858–9 allowed a marriage between Palmerstonian defence strategy and Gladstonian finance – a marriage that, though tense in private, was publicly ideal. Palmerston regarded Cherbourg, the iron-clad *La Gloire* and Napoleon's Italian adventures as part of a bid

---

[39] W. R. Greg, 'The kingdom of Italy', *Edinburgh Review*, 113 (1861), 270–2; E. Dicey, 'The Naples question', *Macmillan's Magazine*, 4 (1861), 503.
[40] See D. Mack Smith, *Mazzini* (New Haven, 1994), pp. 89–90, 94, 145.
[41] J. Morley, *Recollections* (2 vols., London, 1917), vol. II, p. 135.

for diplomatic equality with England, and he was determined to defeat it. In this he was aided by the continuation of very high levels of public alarm. Napoleon's behaviour over Italy showed his willingness to 'make war for an idea';[42] Villafranca was widely seen as a plot to leave him free to attack England; then the Savoy and Nice scare of March 1860 demonstrated his thirst for territory. The Continent seemed in a state of suspended warfare; Britain must be better prepared to deal with it. If the French controlled the Channel and captured British ships, they could paralyse British commerce.[43] In November 1859 Palmerston told Russell that he was losing his earlier confidence that Napoleon did not plan such an attack. In response he demanded stronger fortification of naval arsenals and dockyards, extra ship-building, and subsidies to the Volunteers (in July 1859 the government had agreed to provide weapons for one-quarter of the members of each club). Herbert, War Secretary, argued that fortifications were the best way of defusing a real panic about the defenceless state of Britain, which would lead to demands for much greater spending.[44] A Royal Commission report proposed an outlay of £11.85 million, to be spread over four years; Gladstone entered a lengthy protest, and seemed on the verge of resigning from the cabinet. Palmerston settled on a £8.7 million programme, and after months of resistance, strong anti-French opinion eventually forced Gladstone to give in. Palmerston airily told the Queen that 'it would be better to lose Mr Gladstone than to run the risk of losing Portsmouth or Plymouth'.[45] Four more iron-clads were planned in November 1859, to make six in all, at an additional cost of £2.5 million in the 1860 estimates. The plan was to restore supremacy at sea and make it clear to Napoleon that it would be suicidal for France to attempt to challenge that supremacy. By 1861 England had a clear superiority in ships of the line, and once the Admiralty was convinced of the reliability of iron-clads the French lead in these was also overhauled.[46] Napoleon never challenged British naval supremacy again and diverted his attention to the Rhine. Defence spending rose from £20.7

[42]  Herbert to Gladstone, 23 Nov. 1859, quoted in Salevouris, *'Riflemen form'*, p. 95.
[43]  In September 1856, Nassau Senior argued that continental despotism required Britain to maintain a large military force: Simpson, *Many memories*, p. 253. See also Clarendon, 28 Mar. 1859, in A. L. Kennedy (ed.), *'My dear duchess': social and political letters to the duchess of Manchester 1858–1869* (London, 1956), pp. 49–50; B. Ranft, 'Parliamentary debate, economic vulnerability, and British naval expansion, 1860–1905', in L. Freedman, P. Hayes and R. O'Neill (ed.), *War, strategy and international politics: essays in honour of Sir Michael Howard* (Oxford, 1992), pp. 78–9.
[44]  Salevouris, *'Riflemen form'*, pp. 94–6.
[45]  Steele, *Palmerston and Liberalism*, p. 99; H. C. F. Bell, *Lord Palmerston* (2 vols., London, 1966 edn), vol. II, p. 262.
[46]  Salevouris, *'Riflemen form'*, ch. 5.

million in 1858/9 to £29.1 million in 1861/2, not helped by a range of global problems for British forces to contend with, from China to India and the United States. The proportion of government spending devoted to defence was higher in 1861–5 than in any other nineteenth-century peacetime quinqennium.[47]

A strong navy was undoubtedly popular. Though Cobden loathed the popular notion that Palmerston was 'the vigilant guardian of the national safety', even he accepted that the requirements of British commerce dictated British naval supremacy.[48] Radical and Liberal supporters of spending on the navy and the Volunteers argued that effective national self-defence would not only guard against the threat of invasion and 'render us independent alike of the friendship or the enmity of all or any of the potentates of Europe'; it would also keep army expenditure down and frustrate militarist scaremongers.[49]

One reason for this popularity was that at the same time Gladstone resumed his programme of tariff cuts and promised future tax reductions. He found the necessary money for defence increases by raising income tax. But he criticised the high spending of recent years and vowed to reduce estimates in future, promising economical and efficient government in place of Conservative extravagance. This promise was borne out: the end of the French threat made spending cuts possible, while unprecedented economic prosperity allowed major reductions in both income tax (from 10d to 4d) and duties on items of everyday consumption between 1860 and 1865. This was the basis of Gladstone's great reputation for fiscal prudence.

Meanwhile the lowering of tariffs in Europe by the 1860 Anglo-French Commercial Treaty, worked out by Cobden and Chevalier with support from Gladstone and Russell, further reassured Radicals. Originally conceived as a Cobdenite alternative to Palmerston's arms race with Napoleon, it became more widely attractive once Napoleon had been put in his place. Almost all Liberals could agree that British influence in Europe should be geared to promoting peace and liberalism, and indeed that France, once

---

[47] H. C. G. Matthew, 'Disraeli, Gladstone, and the politics of mid-Victorian budgets', *Historical Journal*, 22 (1979), 633.

[48] *Hansard*, 168:1103, 1 Aug. 1862; 167:380, 3 June 1862. For Bright, similarly, see Steele, *Palmerston and Liberalism*, p. 99.

[49] Elcho, *Hansard*, 155:411, 25 July 1859; T. Hughes, 'The Volunteer's catechism, with a few words on butts', *Macmillan's Magazine*, 2 (1860), 192; W. H. G. Armytage, *A. J. Mundella 1825–1897: the Liberal background to the Labour movement* (London, 1951), p. 29.

disciplined, could play an important role in that. As Clarendon remarked, 'nothing will go well in Europe if England and France are supposed to be pulling different ways'.[50] The Treaty seemed to confirm that Britain's role was to spread the gospel of free trade and commercial intercourse to more benighted parts of Europe. *Punch* showed the schoolmistress Dame Cobden teaching little Napoleon, in shorts, how to spell the word 'F-R-E-E'.[51] Napoleon's embrace of free trade increased his popularity in the City and suggested to the more supercilious Englishmen that he was willing to accept English tutelage more generally.[52] France negotiated tariff reduction treaties with eleven other countries between 1861 and 1866, and these established something like a common European market, especially because of the operation of the most-favoured-nation clause, by which the signatories became entitled to the lowest duties previously agreed by the other party. The result was a substantial lowering of European tariffs.

Liberal confidence in the power of free trade to improve international relations was undoubtedly genuine and widespread, but it disguised a significant division of opinion about commercial diplomacy. Cobden and Gladstone had embarked upon the French Treaty for political purposes: to prevent panic and high spending. Cobden feared that Anglo-French war would hand economic supremacy to the United States. Peace and trade, on the other hand, would ensure harmony between the peoples of Britain and France, 'God's own method of producing an entente cordiale'.[53] As unilateral free traders, they were less interested in the commercial consequences of the 1860 Treaty; indeed, disliking bargaining counters, they insouciantly abolished almost all Britain's protective tariffs in the Treaty. They felt that haggling over sectional protective tariffs would ruin the state's reputation for neutrality as between economic interest groups. Gladstone, with typical lack of self-doubt, claimed that the logic and example of free trade would in any case conquer 'every country of the civilized world'.[54] These views were shared by Lowe, his Chancellor in the government of 1868, and by the Liberal ministers in charge of the Board of Trade in the 1860s, the Cobdenites Milner Gibson and Bright. After the French made treaties with Belgium, Italy, Prussia and Austria, Britain was forced to follow suit, but was

---

[50] Clarendon to Reeve, 6 Apr. 1864, Laughton, *Reeve*, vol. II, p. 103.
[51] *Punch*, 28 Jan. 1860, p. 37.
[52] The *Daily News* remarked of the passages on the papacy in Napoleon's New Year letter of 1860 that he 'takes a liberal, statesmanlike, and we may add, thoroughly English view of the whole question': Urban, *British opinion*, pp. 348, 351.
[53] Cobden: Marsh, *Bargaining on Europe*, p. 10; Schwabe, *Cobden*, p. 309.
[54] 1853: Matthew, *Gladstone 1809–74*, p. 116.

rarely able to get benefits beyond the extension of the arrangements already made by France's treaties, because Britain lacked bargaining tools. Moreover, the tensions surrounding these negotiations created ill-will. All this hardened the view of Gladstone and Lowe that reciprocity treaties were a mistake.[55]

Others, however, believed that commercial negotiations were exercises in manipulative diplomacy, and that Britain must take an active part in this game, so as to outwit the French. Napoleon intended his twelve treaties of the early 1860s as the means by which France could establish a European tariff network that would be shaped to its own commercial needs. W. E. Forster, recently elected MP for Bradford, became the Parliamentary leader of a push for a more assertive policy of commercial diplomacy in order to defend particular interests, supported by Bradford and other Chambers of Commerce. As befitted a young Radical, the superficial target of Forster's campaign was the aristocratic, effete Foreign Office, which he said had given France valuable victories by not empathising sufficiently with commercial needs or working well enough with the Board of Trade. In 1864 he secured a Select Committee which recommended increasing the role of the latter, and establishing a Commercial Division of the Foreign Office in order to fight better for British industry. But his underlying enemy was non-interventionist Cobdenism, which he fumed was 'impractical and un-English'. Britain was 'essentially a commercial country', and its ministers needed to assist commerce as much as other European governments did.[56] Because of British economic success in the 1860s, this remained a small-scale dispute, but its significance lay in the future. In the 1880s Forster emerged as the champion of a coherently assertive approach to foreign and imperial policy, founded on a mixture of economic, strategic and ethical arguments. As chapter 7 shows, Forster, son of a Quaker missionary, was to reinvigorate the movement for moralistic interventionism: the 'Saint' party, Cobden's long-standing *bête noire*.

The events of 1859–60 strengthened the idea that natural forces – trade and public opinion – would do more than armies to shape European progress. There was an increasing assumption that, with autocracy vanquished, force need no longer play much part in Britain's policy. But though such talk mollified Cobdenite Radicals, it is not correct to suggest – as

[55] J. W. T. Gaston, 'Trade and the late Victorian Foreign Office', *International History Review*, 4 (1982), 323–5; Marsh, *Bargaining on Europe*, p. 71.
[56] Searle, *Entrepreneurial politics*, pp. 171–4, 193–5; Gaston, 'Trade', 319–21; Forster, 1863, in T. W. Reid, *Life of the right honourable William Edward Forster* (2 vols., London, 1888), vol. 1, p. 362; Forster, *Hansard*, 177:1852–3, 17 Mar. 1865.

many did then and since – that this talk marked a victory for them against Palmerston or a turn towards isolationism.[57] Cobden's bold claim of 1864, in the wake of the Schleswig-Holstein crisis, that 'non-intervention is the policy of all future Governments in this country', was aspiration, not fact.[58]

To the extent that non-interventionist language became fashionable, it reflected a complacent and insular confidence that the world was naturally moving Britain's way: not the end of arrogance but its zenith. The less doubt there was about Britain's power, the less pressure there was to assert it. As Disraeli remarked in 1866, 'the abstention of England from any unnecessary interference in the affairs of Europe is the consequence, not of her decline of power, but of her increased strength'.[59] He had an ulterior motive for saying that, since the incoming minority Conservative government wanted to prevent a large rise in military estimates in order to avoid controversy in the Commons which might unseat it. But it is very telling that in 1866, in contrast to 1852 and 1859, the conjunction of the Austro-Prussian War and a minority government did *not* create a panic about Britain's military weakness. In the first half of the 1860s, in fact, there was often an excess of confidence. *The Times*, observing the Volunteer review before Queen Victoria in June 1860, remarked that it was proof that England was 'at heart a military nation'.[60] Gladstone noted in 1859: 'The English piously believe themselves to be a peaceful people; nobody else is of the same belief.'[61] There was also no shortage of interest in foreign policy at this time.[62] There was, for example, a revived enthusiasm about the triumph of constitutional principles in Greece, especially when the Greeks overthrew the pro-Russian King Otho and, in late 1862, offered Victoria's son Alfred

---

[57] Historians often suggest that Britain retreated into isolationism in the 1860s, especially as a result of the Danish crisis. E.g. Beales, *England and Italy*, p. 173; A. J. P. Taylor, *The trouble makers: dissent over foreign policy 1792–1939* (London, 1957), pp. 64–5 (Cobden was 'the real Foreign Secretary of the early eighteen-sixties'); R. W. Seton-Watson, *Britain in Europe 1789–1914: a survey of foreign policy* (London, 1937), esp. p. 465 and ch. 12; Prest, *Russell*, p. 398, who claims that the decision against intervention over Schleswig-Holstein in 1864 was 'decisive for British foreign policy in the nineteenth century'; Krein, *Last Palmerston government*.

[58] To Chevalier, 5 Nov. 1864, Morley, *Cobden*, vol. II, p. 450. See *Nonconformist*, 20 July 1864, quoted in Larsen, *Friends of religious equality*, p. 208, for a similar view. It is worth noting that in 1862 there was still no chance of Parliament granting Cobden a pension: Vincent, *Formation of the Liberal party*, p. 72n.

[59] Monypenny and Buckle, *Disraeli*, vol. IV, p. 467.

[60] *The Times*, 25 June 1860, quoted in Salevouris, 'Riflemen form', p. 186.

[61] Gladstone to Herbert, 28 Nov. 1859, Stanmore, *Herbert*, vol. II, p. 233.

[62] Cobden and Disraeli both noted that it dominated discussion: Cobden to Potter, 10 May 1864, Morley, *Cobden*, vol. II, p. 447n; *Stanley*, p. 203 (1 Dec. 1863).

their throne. Though it was diplomatically necessary to decline this offer, the princess of Wales's Danish brother took the throne instead, with British approval.

It was increasingly argued that constitutional government and free trade would slowly triumph without the need for expensive wars. The collapse of the old Concert created the impression that the reactionary powers could no longer obstruct the growth of progress. The apparent victories for constitutionalism in Greece and Italy allowed the government to end British military occupation of the Ionian Islands in 1863 and give them to Greece, arguing that this symbol of force in the regional fight against autocracy was no longer necessary.[63] Moreover, war was even less in Britain's interests than ever: Britain desired no territorial acquisitions in Europe, and war threatened trade and endangered the 'English' balance of liberty and order. Russell remarked in 1859 that 'every war in Europe has a tendency to become revolutionary'.[64]

So a virtuous struggle for liberalism against the odds was no longer so urgent abroad – or, with Palmerston's career ambitions sated, at home. The old certainties in European politics were collapsing, and continental struggles could not be packaged in simple ideological terms. Thus it was often not clear, to politicians or public, how Britain should respond to them.[65] Britain did not want to see 'liberalism' advance in Poland if it was a device for giving Napoleon ascendancy on the Continent. Nor did it want Napoleon to be humiliated by the Eastern powers. Britain normally tried to mediate in European disputes – over Poland in 1862–3, the Danish–Prussian quarrel over Schleswig-Holstein in 1863–4, and the Austro-Prussian War of 1866 – on the basis of upholding the principles of public law and fair play, but won little support from other countries. None of the other powers were keen on a concerted approach; in particular, Napoleon repeatedly shied away from the idea of joint action with Britain. Much of the original anxiety to defend the Poles and Danes in 1862–3 came from the press and from public meetings, and government felt obliged to respond to it.[66] A remark of Palmerston's in July 1863, regarded by some diplomatic historians

[63] Palmerston made it clear that this was a military outpost to suit the needs of 1815, not 'part of the dominions of the British Crown': *Hansard*, 169:127–8, 5 Feb. 1863. For the background, see B. A. Knox, 'British policy and the Ionian Islands, 1847–1864: nationalism and imperial administration', *English Historical Review*, 99 (1984), 503–29.

[64] Scherer, *Russell*, p. 271.

[65] A. H. Layard, 'England's place in Europe', *Saint Paul's: a monthly magazine*, 1 (1867–8), 284–5.

[66] See Kutolowski, 'Mid-Victorian public opinion', 86–110; W. E. Mosse, 'England and the Polish insurrection of 1863', *English Historical Review*, 71 (1956), 33–4.

as a blustering pledge to Denmark, was not, and was not seen as such at the time.[67] Once it had proved impossible to find allies, the government's reluctance to go to war was well known and popular at home, all the more so in 1864 in view of increasing Danish intransigence.[68] There was no internal dissent: only one non-Catholic Liberal MP voted against the government in the crucial Parliamentary vote on the Danish issue.[69]

Nonetheless, the British failure to resolve these crises did not help Palmerston's government. Russell's moralistic hectoring looked artificial. In fact the confusion of 1864 really marked the end of the Palmerstonian era, in which opposition to autocracy had dominated British political language. It now seemed outdated. An unprecedented 22 per cent of the record of Parliament in 1864 was taken up with foreign themes; but from now on, attention turned away to domestic politics.[70]

Even so, this was not a long-lasting rejection of an active foreign politics, for two reasons. First, Britain's main objective in the 1860s – to check Napoleon's expansionist plans – was achieved.[71] Unless tightly confined, a continental land war pursued by England and France would have benefited Napoleon much more than England and given him the parity (if not more) that it was Palmerston's great object to avoid. The Polish crisis broke up an emerging understanding between France and Russia that might have led to tension in the Balkans and on the Rhine. And Napoleon's support for the Poles, which seemed so self-interested, contributed significantly to the waning of the traditional Radical enthusiasm for them. Moreover the cabinet did not reject intervention on principle during the Danish crisis. In June 1864 a slight majority of them, and the Queen, seem to have been willing to send the British fleet to Copenhagen had the Prussians gone so far as to menace it.[72]

Secondly, one effect of 1864, and the five preceding years, was to stimulate a debate about the future of Liberal foreign policy. Indeed Forster's pressure for a more active commercial diplomacy should be seen as part of that debate. It was an unhurried discussion, owing to the extraordinary complacency of the decade. However, irritation quickly arose at those who seemed to argue for a completely 'non-interventionist' policy towards

---

[67] K. A. P. Sandiford, *Great Britain and the Schleswig-Holstein question 1848–64: a study in diplomacy, politics, and public opinion* (Toronto, 1975), p. 59.
[68] Kutolowski, 'Mid-Victorian public opinion', 102–3; Scherer, *Russell*, p. 286; see e.g. Palmerston to Russell, 13 Feb. 1864, Ashley, *Palmerston*, vol. II, pp. 247–8.
[69] Sandiford, *Great Britain*, p. 160.     [70] The figures are in A. J. P. Taylor, *Trouble makers*, p. 64.
[71] Even Roebuck by 1865 claimed that Napoleon and England were at peace: Leader, *Roebuck*, p. 309.
[72] Scherer, *Russell*, p. 319.

Europe. Many influential liberal commentators agreed that such a policy was too ignoble, selfish and depressing, and that the nation had a duty to act on behalf of justice and against oppression.[73] The very fact that nations were now cooperating better in pursuit of progress made an 'utterly selfish and isolated policy' unacceptable for a country that should be leading that progress.[74] In his sermon on the death of Palmerston in 1865, the Birmingham Nonconformist R. W. Dale maintained that Britain's world power was 'not granted us by the Providence of God merely that we might be able to protect our commerce [and increase] our already almost boundless wealth'. Rather, the nation should be prepared to protect a people's freedom and independence against alien tyranny, and it should act against slavery.[75]

This debate was part of the more general concern of the mid-1860s with enhancing the morality and cohesion of the *domestic* community, paralleling Dale and Dawson's critique of selfishness in local politics discussed in Part I. John Morley, one of those who regarded non-intervention as 'immoral', suggested that 'deep want of moral harmony at home and want of moral power abroad are twin results of a common antecedent': a lack of 'vivid *national* impulse'. The key to revitalising foreign policy was therefore the same as for internal policy: the extension of the franchise.[76] Rather similarly, some official Liberals interpreted the ministry's quarrels and weakness over Schleswig-Holstein as demonstrating that executive government had lost the capacity either to educate and lead the public mind or to discipline the Queen's 'Continental Advisers' – 'Leopold & other intriguing potentates' – who 'don't act on English principles of policy'. A stronger party system would allow a more decisive and liberal foreign policy, independent of both the Court and the insular quietists in the Commons.[77] On all these counts, there was a need to infuse some unifying and uplifting purpose into Liberal foreign policy, just as there was, simultaneously, a need to galvanise party and nation on internal issues. As usual, domestic and international objectives were so intimately linked as to be almost inseparable.

---

[73] J. S. Mill, 'A few words on non-intervention', *Fraser's Magazine*, 60 (1859), 766–76; W. R. Greg, 'Principle and no-principle in foreign policy', *National Review*, 13 (1861), 241–73; G. Smith, *The empire: a series of letters published in 'The Daily News', 1862, 1863* (Oxford, 1863), pp. ix–x; Layard, 'England's place in Europe'; M. E. G. Duff, *A glance over Europe: being an address delivered at Peterhead on the 19th December 1867* (Edinburgh, 1867), p. 57; J. Morley, 'England and the European crisis', *Fortnightly Review*, 1 (1867), 621–9.

[74] Goschen, seconding the Queen's speech, *Hansard*, 173:81, 4 Feb. 1864.

[75] A. W. W. Dale, *Dale*, pp. 251–2.   [76] Morley, 'England and the European crisis', 625, 628.

[77] *Kimberley*, pp. 130–1, 136, 197, 8 Apr., 26 May 1864, 16 Feb. 1867.

## THE NATIONAL COMMUNITY

The continuing potency of the Italian issue was evident during Garibaldi's visit to England in 1864, when Liberals of all social classes welcomed him. His exploits in 1860 and his attempt on Rome in 1862 showed him to be a manly opponent of Bourbon, French and papal influence in the peninsula. Though his personal religion was hardly orthodox, evangelicals gave him copies of the Bible and the *Pilgrim's progress* and spoke of his great practical religion.[78]

Garibaldi's popularity demonstrated the variety of ways in which Italy resonated in English politics. One important element of his appeal was as a symbol of the dignity of man – a representative of political virtue, humanity and brotherhood, all the more striking given his simplicity and low birth.[79] Italy could not teach England anything about constitutions and politics, but many British visitors regarded it as freer of class conflict, irreligion and working-class vulgarity than their own country. J. R. Green wrote that unlike Teutonic (i.e. English institutional) democracy, the philosophy of the new Italy implied 'a development of the whole man – political, intellectual, religious and artistic'.[80] Rome was the setting for George Eliot's memorable depiction, in *Middlemarch* (1872), of Dorothea's awakening to the claims of her fellow-men, and escape from her spiritually, socially and sexually narrow and insular English life. Eliot later claimed that in the early 1860s 'ideas were with fresh vigour making armies of themselves, and the universal kinship was declaring itself fiercely'.[81] Admiring Liberals and Radicals found in Garibaldi and in Mazzini uplifting exemplars of social brotherhood and altruism – especially once Italy had safely rejected the latter's republican political views in favour of 'English' institutions. For Mazzini, nationality was an ideal expression of what drew men together, at family, civic and universal level as much as at the national one. He depicted social harmony as a realisation of God's will for the human race and as an antidote to secular philosophies like socialism. As such, he appealed to freethinkers (Mill, John Morley) and academic Liberals (T. H. Green, Goldwin Smith) but also to incarnationalist broad churchmen such as Benjamin Jowett, and Unitarian advocates of the 'civic gospel' such as Dawson and Jesse Collings in Birmingham and the young Liberal politician James Stansfeld. Morley subsequently reminisced that Mazzini was 'the moral genius that

---

[78] Beales, 'Garibaldi in England', p. 185.
[79] Harvie, *Lights of Liberalism*, p. 103.   [80] Pemble, *Mediterranean passion*, pp. 143–8.
[81] G. Eliot, *Daniel Deronda* (1876; Harmondsworth, 1967 edn), ch. 11, p. 159.

spiritualised politics, and gave a new soul to public duty in citizens and nations'.[82]

Therefore the cult of the Italian heroes reflected a more general interest at this time in the challenges of building a true nation and nationhood. The American Civil War seemed to demonstrate, firstly, the Americans' political immaturity in failing to keep their nation together, then the ability of the seceding Southerners to 'make a nation', in Gladstone's famous phrase, and finally the achievement of the northern republicans in reconstituting the nation on a higher ethical plane, abolishing the inhumane institution of slavery. Most importantly, in Britain itself, Parliamentary reform was becoming a pressing issue, as noted in chapter 1: many Liberals were expressing concerns about class cohesion and the need to make working men feel part of the political nation. In 1866 Gladstone claimed that the Northern victory in America had shown the benefits of an enlarged franchise: 'augmented power can be marshalled on behalf of the government and increased energy given to the action of a nation'.[83] The assumption gained ground that British politics needed infusing with social and civic values, in reaction to the insular and celebratory *laissez-faire* assumptions that had been so powerful in the previous decade.[84] The harsh rhetoric of *laissez-faire* purists, that resistance to state intervention protected English character against continental threats, was increasingly lampooned now that those threats seemed less frightening. The growth of free trade and constitutionalism in Europe made the continental regimes appear less threatening. So did increased opportunities to receive foreign news instantly owing to newspapers' use of Reuters' telegraph service from 1859. Thomas Cook claimed that his package tours to France (successfully from 1861), Switzerland and Italy (1863), and the United States (1866) broke down 'partition walls of prejudice'.[85] Satires on the narrowness of the chauvinist mind achieved some success, including Mr Podsnap in Dickens's *Our mutual friend* (1865).

In the 1860s, therefore, those commentators who believed that Britain could benefit from lessons from other countries on social and cultural practices – on how to become a *society* – became less marginal. Two writers who

---

[82] *Recollections*, vol. 1, p. 75.

[83] April 1866, quoted in R. Quinault, 'Gladstone and Parliamentary reform', in D. W. Bebbington and R. Swift (eds.), *Gladstone centenary essays* (Liverpool, 2000), p. 83.

[84] In 1849 Matthew Arnold had gloomily written of 'the union of invincibility and speculative dulness [*sic*]' in the England of 1815 and of the present: C. Y. Lang (ed.), *The letters of Matthew Arnold: I: 1829–1859* (Charlottesville, VA, 1996), p. 148.

[85] 1860, quoted in J. Buzard, *The beaten track: European tourism, literature, and the ways to culture, 1800–1918* (Oxford, 1993), p. 49. For the reporting of foreign news, see D. Read, *The power of news: the history of Reuters 1849–1989* (Oxford, 1992), pp. 22–6.

made this point particularly vigorously – J. S. Mill and Matthew Arnold – were both influenced by the argument of the French historian Guizot, that, while the English were better at practical civilisation, the French were better at social civilisation. Both Mill and Arnold argued that greater social unity depended on developing a common culture. In *Culture and anarchy* (1869) Arnold famously defined culture as 'the best that has been thought and said in the world'. In contrast, English philistinism stemmed from a lack of taste, refinement and appreciation of beauty, a shortage of cross-class social pursuits and an inability to appreciate the benefits of education. In the 1860s Arnold – who later claimed that, in France, if a cultivated man met a peasant he could feel that he was 'talking with an equal' – urged educational reform in Britain, using the French lycée as his model for a system of publicly aided and inspected secondary schools. He maintained that the decline of aristocratic influence and the advance towards democracy made this necessary in order to raise the cultural and ethical standards of the middle classes, the new governing classes. He similarly lauded the *Académie française* as a model for the defence and propagation of the ideal of culture by an elite clerisy. But he neither wanted nor expected Britain to import French institutions wholesale. France, for him, was a useful symbol of something broader and more abstract: Hellenism – the classical notion of civilisation as the harmonious development of man's faculties. The French had cultivated Hellenic qualities more than the English, and the English could learn from the French about the merits of rectifying the balance. Similarly the Germans had reworked their Hellenic inheritance so as to place more emphasis on the role of the state as the agency that would acculturate and elevate all their people, and the English could learn from that too. Arnold was a great admirer of Goethe and the German Enlightenment for their emphasis on intellectual inquiry to promote improvement and social unity.[86]

Interest in Germany was an important strand of the thought of many of the more intellectual Liberals in the 1860s. But, again, not many considered that the Germans had much to teach the English about *politics*, on account of their authoritarian political tradition and, in reaction, their overly

---

[86] Arnold's first significant commentary on these themes was in *The popular education of France* (London, 1861), especially the introduction, 'Democracy'. A good introduction to this and his other writings on education in the 1860s is G. Sutherland (ed.), *Matthew Arnold on education* (Harmondsworth, 1973). For this paragraph, see also F. J. W. Harding, *Matthew Arnold the critic and France* (Geneva, 1964), pp. 128, 174, and Varouxakis, *Victorian political thought* (also for Mill). There is an interesting discussion of Arnold and Germany in F. E. Faverty, *Matthew Arnold the ethnologist* (Evanston, IL, 1951), ch. 4.

speculative and impractical political and religious thought. More attractive were the domestic virtues that derived particularly from German religion and industry, and the spirituality and reverence associated with the less avant-garde German cultural icons such as the late-lamented Mendelssohn. Germanisers, particularly intellectual Unitarians, broad churchmen and young academic Liberals, tended to be keen on the development of a more complete education system and the increased involvement of the state in it. They argued that this would strengthen national unity by building a shared attachment to culture, morality and a truly spiritual religion.[87]

An important aspect of the 'Germanist' movement in the 1860s was admiration for Switzerland – now a favourite destination for English travellers – because it was a model of what Germany might become politically if it could become a proper nation and slough off its Prussian authoritarianism. The Swiss, like the Germans, had a strong historic identity based around participatory political citizenship, reinforced by the virtues deriving from a peasant proprietorship. Unlike much of Germany, Switzerland had not succumbed to autocracy, nor had it followed the intolerant French democratic-nationalist model. Instead it was an example, like England, of the successful mixing of nations, religions and languages in a liberal state.[88] Its long and prosperous political history seemed complemented by its pure and healthy air and its divinely created mountain scenery. Surely the experience of living so directly under the hand of God, in a 'region of eternal liberty . . . where only those who never will be slaves find themselves at home', had taught the Swiss godliness, 'patriotism and manly independence'.[89] The fashion for historicism, the scholarly interest in discovering and asserting collective cultural identities through language, history and customs, pointed to the deep roots of English, German and Swiss constitutional traditions and the common ground that they shared. This historicism also had a positive effect on Radical self-confidence because it bolstered the argument that English liberties derived from ancient customs rather than needing to be taught to the people by Whig aristocrats.

---

[87] I have learned a lot about these themes from my student M. C. Ledger-Lomas, 'The idea of "Germany" in early and mid-Victorian social, cultural and educational thought' (University of Cambridge PhD, 2005).

[88] J. E. E. D. Acton, 'Nationality', *Home and Foreign Review*, 1 (1862), 21.

[89] G. C. Swayne, 'Mountaineering – the Alpine Club', *Blackwood's Magazine*, 86 (1859), 457; J. B. Atkinson, 'Aesthetics among the Alps', *Blackwood's Magazine*, 81 (1857), 269; Bryce in *Essays on Reform* (London, 1867), pp. 261–2.

Many Radicals also admired the civic republicanism of the Northerners in the American Civil War. They saw them as committed to the fight against slavery and to an unstratified democratic society, but also keen defenders of constitutionalism, self-government, and Protestantism, and opponents of French Radical socialism. It was common for young academic and Nonconformist Liberals, up-and-coming Radicals like Dilke and Chamberlain, and working-class leaders, to contrast English political and social values unfavourably with this American ideal. When some Liberal university men published an influential volume of *Essays on Reform* in 1867 to accompany the debates on franchise extension, one reviewer commented that they seemed more content with Swiss and American institutions than with English ones. After the war, Radicals claimed that the lack of British upper-class sympathy with the American North and with the abolition of slavery revealed the anti-democratic and unethical sentiments of the British governing classes, and the superior virtue of working men – thus proving that the tone of British politics would improve after a further instalment of Parliamentary reform. British reaction to the American Civil War played an important part in developing the myth that academic Liberals, Nonconformists and virtuous working men were united in promoting the cause of humanity and challenging the rule of class snobbery and lazy amorality. What Morley called 'the party of active humanity, of political initiative, of the republic in its true sense' used American comparisons to try to moralise British public debate.[90]

All these various foreign examples could be used to suggest the benefits of political and social change in Britain. However, it is also important to understand the limitations of this admiration for other countries. Even Mill and Arnold had enormous respect for British political and social values. They sought a higher civilisation, synthesising the best of existing national cultures, and thus achieving the highest potential of humanity. Arnold lamented the fact that since the Reformation England had continuously developed the 'Hebraic' qualities of earnestness, piety and energy much more strongly than the 'Hellenic' ones of the European Renaissance. The resulting middle-class Nonconformist suspicion of state activity was a liability in the task ahead, the education of the democracy into citizenship. But, as he said when attacked, he only recommended strengthening the power of the state because English libertarian vigour and moral rectitude

---

[90] J. Morley, 'England and the war', *Fortnightly Review*, 8 (1870), 479–80. For this paragraph, see Harvie, *Lights of Liberalism*, pp. 97, 105–13; G. Smith, 'The experience of the American Commonwealth', in *Essays on Reform*, and e.g. T. Hughes, 'Opinion on American affairs', *Macmillan's Magazine*, 4 (1861), 416.

were easily powerful enough to restrain it. His mission was not to make England like France, but to supplement the 'native independence and indi-vidualism of the English character' with 'an ideal of high reason and right feeling'.⁹¹ Notwithstanding his criticisms, he called the Puritan middle classes of Britain the 'best stuff in the nation', complementing the 'hon-estest upper class which the world has ever seen'. The French, meanwhile, lacked Hebraic morality, self-control, seriousness and spiritual endeavour, while their sensuality was responsible for the doctrine of the Rights of Man.⁹² Both men became progressively more depressed at the willingness of the French to submit to Napoleon III. Mill, in particular, once an admirer of French politics, doubted after 1851 that they would ever be weaned off the grandeur of centralised government. He so disliked the illiberal French yearning to impose views on others that he would have preferred an Aus-trian victory to a French one in Italy in 1859.⁹³ Arnold urged England to take the lead in the Italian question so as to establish 'moral predominance' in both Italy and Europe for English rather than French values.⁹⁴

Criticism of the political overcentralisation and immorality of Napoleon's regime was the norm in British debate. James Bryce consid-ered that the absence of local democratic institutions in France had made government since 1789 'a tremendous engine of despotism'.⁹⁵ There was a long-standing tradition of associating French culture with sensuality, profli-gacy and effeminacy, which the tendencies of the Second Empire reinforced. Napoleon's power seemed to rest on unscrupulous flatterers; there were too few men of 'public virtue'.⁹⁶ It was generally believed that his government gave favours and lavish contracts to businessmen and stockjobbers, while taxpayers' money was wasted on superficial embellishments to the capital. Such extravagance did not promote solid prosperity; the unrestrained and impatient materialism of the Parisians created a culture of conspicuous con-sumption, of 'luxury and profligacy', and their city became the 'paradise of the *nouveau riche* and the *demi-monde*'.⁹⁷ Depraved Paris – described by

⁹¹ Arnold, *Popular education of France*, pp. xxxi–xxxii; P. Smith and G. Summerfield (eds.), *Matthew Arnold and the education of the new order* (Cambridge, 1969), pp. 20–1.
⁹² Smith and Summerfield, *Arnold*, pp. 11–12; Sutherland, *Arnold on education*, p. 80; Harding, *Arnold and France*, p. 11; Varouxakis, *Victorian political thought*, pp. 13–14, 128.
⁹³ Varouxakis, *Victorian political thought*, pp. 21, 127–8, 153–4.
⁹⁴ M. Arnold, *England and the Italian question*, ed. M. M. Bevington (Durham, NC, 1953 edn), p. 49.
⁹⁵ *Essays on Reform*, pp. 258–9.
⁹⁶ *The Times*, 11 Jan. 1873, p. 8; Gladstone, 'Germany, France, and England', *Edinburgh Review*, 132 (1870), 578.
⁹⁷ A. Hayward, 'The personal history of imperialism in 1870', *Fraser's Magazine*, 2 (1870), 638–9; Salisbury, 'Political lessons of the war', 261; A. V. Dicey, 'Louis Napoleon: 1851 and 1873', *Fortnightly Review*, 13 (1873), 197–204.

E. A. Freeman as 'a collection of shops and stuck-up people, with the Tyrant's house in the middle' – imposed a tone on the country. Luxury, mixed with egalitarian ideology, 'brutified' the public sphere and, by 1870, destroyed discipline in the army.[98] Dislike of French morals was ingrained in Britain: the satirist Wilkie Collins shrewdly observed that 'the morality of England is firmly based on the immorality of France'.[99] It was all the more alarming, then, that sensual and materialist French values might be mounting a cultural invasion of British life. The more philistine of the upper classes, the potential leaders of England, seemed tempted by the immorality of Paris, which, as Carlyle succinctly put it, was 'nothing but a brothel and a gambling hall'.[100] Looking back in 1870, Queen Victoria regretted the effects of 'horrid Paris' on her sons, and concluded that Napoleon's 'frivolous and immoral court did frightful harm to English society'.[101] The French Sunday was also a potentially 'demoralizing' force, especially given the intensity of the 'commercial energy' of the British middle classes. If the law allowed businessmen to open their shops and theatres on Sunday, their urge for profit would make them unable to resist the idea, thus exploiting their workmen, disrupting their own family life and diminishing the place for reflection, religion and culture in society.[102]

American society was also frequently criticised for its materialism and lack of civilisation and ethics, which were widely attributed to the absence of Church Establishments and of propertied political leadership. The United States was identified with economic swagger, selfish protectionist tendencies, vulgarity and bullying. Gladstone commented on America's 'self-love'.[103] The collapse of the Union in 1860–1 was widely blamed on the lack of an altruistic patriotism, on the one hand, and the constitutional failings of a federal republic, which did not give adequate legitimacy to one designated authority, on the other. The impeachment of President Johnson, after the war, added to the latter criticisms. Such a constitution could only be maintained by a 'wise, calm and generous temper' – but the North had

---

[98] Freeman, 1861: W. R. W. Stephens, *The life and letters of Edward A. Freeman* (2 vols., London, 1895), vol. I, pp. 295–6; Kirwan, *Modern France*, p. 356; Hayward, 'Personal history of imperialism', 640; W. R. Greg, 'Suum cuique: the moral of the Paris catastrophe', *Fraser's Magazine*, 4 (1871), 127.

[99] To Dickens: R. Gibson, *Best of enemies: Anglo-French relations since the Norman Conquest* (London, 1995), p. 225.

[100] R. Christiansen, *Tales of the new Babylon: Paris, 1869–1875* (London, 1994), p. 17.

[101] R. Fulford (ed.), *Your dear letter: private correspondence of Queen Victoria and the Crown Princess of Prussia 1865–1871* (London, 1971), p. 300.

[102] W. Arthur, *'The people's day': an appeal to the rt. hon. Lord Stanley MP against his advocacy of a French Sunday* (5th edn, London, 1855), pp. 14–15, 37.

[103] At Newcastle, *The Times*, 9 Oct. 1862, p. 7. This paragraph benefits particularly from D. A. Campbell, *English public opinion and the American Civil War* (Woodbridge, 2003).

behaved with typical American arrogance in suppressing the constitutional rights of the South.[104] In the early stages of the war many Englishmen – not just from the upper classes – defended the South from what they regarded as Northern dictation, bullying and economic greed. A division of the country might, as Arnold suggested, make it more culturally diverse and less materialistic.[105] It might also reduce the threat to British North America and the West Indies. The Trent affair created strong anti-American feeling in Britain. There was in fact great confusion and diversity of opinion in Britain about the American Civil War, at least until it was clear that the South was facing defeat. Critics of Parliamentary reform in Britain played on fears that franchise extension would 'Americanise' British culture.[106] And, though some of the Radical sympathy with the American North was primarily concerned to point up the shortcomings of the British governing classes, it was also a way of stressing traditions that the Anglo-Saxon polities had in common, and that Britain merely needed to be more confident in embracing fully.[107]

So, despite a belief that Britain would be a better-balanced country if it took note of some aspects of French and American political culture, few seriously proposed a radical shift. France and the United States had failed in the most important of tasks, that of maintaining a stable, healthy and virtuous political community, and had succumbed to the evils of materialism. Meanwhile the aspects of German culture that were most widely admired in England were the ones that the English shared (morality, Protestantism and energy) while the English were clearly more experienced at sustaining a libertarian political community. Emphases on Teutonic or American liberty were statements about the depth of the civic tradition in Britain, not a call to uproot it. Germany did not even exist as a nation, while Prussia was hardly a symbol of constitutional liberty and decentralisation; there was no guarantee that the speculative, abstract Germans could make one work.

It followed that only England could lead the world. As Mill wrote in 1861, England was 'the Power which, of all in existence, best understands

---

[104] Reeve, 'The disunion of America', *Edinburgh Review*, 114 (1861), 560–4, 577–8.

[105] Vaughan was one interesting case: see *Robert Vaughan, D. D.: a memorial* (London, 1869), p. 24. For Arnold, see Varouxakis, *Victorian political thought*, p. 12.

[106] H. F. Dubrulle, ' "We are threatened with . . . anarchy and ruin"; fear of Americanization and the emergence of an Anglo-Saxon confederacy in England during the American Civil War', *Albion*, 33 (2002), 583–613; Lewis to Head, 20 Jan. 1859, Lewis, *Letters of Lewis*, p. 363; Aberdeen to Clarendon, 2 Nov. 1858, Maxwell, *Clarendon*, vol. II, p. 167.

[107] J. M. Ludlow, 'The American crisis', *Macmillan's Magazine*, 4 (1861), 176. M. Gerlach, *British Liberalism and the United States: political and social thought in the late Victorian age* (Basingstoke, 2001), pp. 8–11, offers a useful discussion of Harcourt's sympathy with the North.

liberty – and . . . has attained to more of conscience and moral principle in its dealings with foreigners, than any other great nation'.[108] Since Mill and Arnold were widely criticised for their lack of patriotism, it is easy to see that there was no shortage of confidence in the English global mission in the 1860s.[109] Mill proclaimed that the whole European elite believed that 'the safety, and even the power of England, are valuable to the freedom of the world, and therefore to the greatest and most permanent interests of every civilized people'.[110] Intellectual debate about the values that England needed to absorb was shaped by the general belief that it had a clear mission to guide the world towards a higher civilisation. What Acton called 'the English system' of constitutional pluralism was surely the best way of maintaining successful nation-states in future.[111] Behind the 'ethical turn' and 'continental turn' in Liberal discourse lay an intense patriotism, and a Liberal–Radical discussion about the purpose of British global leadership in a post-autocratic world. Expressions of praise for classical and Christian values, civic republicanism and the power of the Hebraic conscience were all part of a dialogue on how best Britain should deploy its responsibilities for world progress.

## GLADSTONE AND PATRIOTISM

One of the coming men of the 1860s who was most concerned that Britain should play an ethical global leadership role and develop a stronger community at home was W. E. Gladstone, Liberal leader from 1867. Gladstone frequently argued that Britain had a responsibility to avoid an arrogant, dictatorial governing style abroad, and these views inevitably had a major impact on the debate about the future direction of Liberal foreign policy. However, he was no isolationist. Moreover, though much of his rhetoric stressed the value of European cooperation, in none of his policies did he think that he was betraying the interests of England. Gladstone was in fact an intense British nationalist, as his interventions in foreign-policy discussions in 1851, 1858 and 1859–60 should already have made clear. His attitudes were also affected by his extremely strong religious conscience, as befitted a politician who had come to maturity during the moral revival of

---

[108] *CWM*, vol. XIX, p. 565.
[109] For criticisms, see J. Stapleton, 'Political thought and national identity in Britain, 1850–1950', in S. Collini, R. Whatmore and B. Young (eds.), *History, religion, and culture: British intellectual history 1750–1950* (Cambridge, 2000), pp. 248–9; Smith and Summerfield, *Arnold*, p. 20; S. Coulling, *Matthew Arnold and his critics: a study of Arnold's controversies* (Athens, OH, 1974), pp. 160–2.
[110] *Hansard*, 189:880, 5 Aug. 1867.
[111] J. E. E. D. Acton, 'Nationality', *Home and Foreign Review*, 1 (1862), 15–17.

the 1840s. In 1880 he declared that the 'two most powerful motives that act upon nations' were 'religion' and 'patriotism'.[112] He believed that Britain had a divinely inspired global purpose to struggle against sinfulness. Moreover, he felt a personal, as well as a national, responsibility to promote that purpose.

In the 1860s Gladstone's main domestic theme was the importance of class harmony and the duty of the politician to maintain it. His financial policy as Chancellor was designed to withdraw the state from controversial economic territory and to reduce tax burdens equitably on all classes, so that popular confidence was maintained in its lack of bias. The two most obvious examples of vested-interest pressure, to him, were military expenditure at the behest of particular knots and groups and classes, and Protection, which sheltered 'the most selfish instincts of class against the just demands of the public welfare', contrary to 'nature, liberty, and justice'.[113] The main theme of Gladstone's politics was to assert a common national interest instead of these sectional ones. He distinguished between a national and a continental approach to government; in the latter, states bribed particular interests (rich and poor) by grants and doles. He spoke vehemently against the 'Continental system of feeding the desires of classes and portions of the community at the expense of the whole'.[114] He argued that 'the old British constitution', 'liberal sentiments' and class harmony had prevailed, until the 'lamentable excesses of the first French Revolution' had infected English life and had created, by 'terrible re-action', mistrust between class and class which had been mitigated by 1832 and fully laid to rest after 1846.[115] Fortunately the great gift of free commerce had led to increased wealth, comfort and closer union between classes, 'mistrust and alienation' fading away 'like mists before the rising sun'.[116]

The modern politician, Gladstone felt, had a duty to check sectional pressures by teaching more Englishmen the discipline of the historic national policy of self-government. Modestly extending the franchise, from time to time, was one way of teaching and reinforcing that discipline; widespread political participation would help to check the inevitable human tendency to self-interest and class interest.[117] But active, disinterested leadership and

---

[112] At Penicuik, 25 Mar. 1880, W. E. Gladstone, *Political speeches in Scotland March and April 1880* (Edinburgh, 1880), p. 291.

[113] 'Free trade, railways, and the growth of commerce', *Nineteenth Century*, 7 (1880), 377.

[114] E.g. at Leigh, *The Times*, 21 Oct. 1868, p. 8.      [115] *Hansard*, 175:322–3, 11 May 1864.

[116] At York, *The Times*, 13 Oct. 1862, p. 4; Parry, *Rise and fall*, p. 169.

[117] *Hansard*, 183:144, 27 Apr. 1866. 'Self-command, self-control, respect for order, patience under suffering, confidence in the law, regard for superiors' were the qualities that fitted people for the vote: *Hansard*, 175:325, 11 May 1864.

popular morality were at least as important in this task. The moral qualities of the English had been crucially enhanced by Christianity; their struggle against the ambitions of the Pope had kept them free and maintained a vigorous and pure religion. One great motto of his Liberalism, from the mid-1860s, was 'trust the people', but the people were to be trusted because voting, as he was to make very clear to them, was an act of individual responsibility before God. Without a strong sense of Christianity in the nation, the future of politics would ultimately be bleak.[118] The growth of materialism – of plutocracy – threatened to divide class from class, just as in America. The 'rapid creation and extension of wealth' jeopardised 'the foundations of national character'.[119] The effective antidotes were an attachment to nation and community and a sense of Christianity. In 1871 Gladstone felt that England, like fifteenth-century Italy, almost needed a Savonarola.[120] The people must be kept aroused for good. For Gladstone, like Russell, Reform was really a device to stimulate more virtuous government.

So voters should be educated to play their part in the mechanism that kept the state unbiased as between classes. True patriotism meant being on constant watch against the sinfulness and corruption of vested interests, and endorsing the policy of economy, vigour and purity of patronage that kept those interests under control and preserved English politics from continental infection.[121] The virtuous political leader should encourage that alertness by beneficial activity: Gladstone commented that his political motto was 'keep moving', in order to check the 'dangerous powers and tendencies' of lapse, decay and corruption which were 'in sleepless operation'.[122] A constant diet of legislation was needed to prevent Parliament from setting the wrong tone. The basis of his admiration for evangelical Nonconformists was their agreement about the need for a virtuous purifying passion in politics. The two political parties should be counteracting parts of the machine of state, the Liberals invigorating and dynamic and the Conservatives providing steadiness and a link to tradition. The Liberal party, therefore, was the 'instrument' by which the work of righteousness could be carried on. Palmerston had failed to lead it in this direction, thus

---

[118] Gladstone to Acland, 12 Apr. 1864, A. H. D. Acland, *Memoir and letters of the right honourable Sir Thomas Dyke Acland* (London, 1902), p. 229.

[119] February 1876, quoted in D. Bebbington, *The mind of Gladstone: religion, Homer, and politics* (Oxford, 2004), p. 282. See Parry, *Democracy and religion*, p. 168 for several instances of his alarm.

[120] To Houghton, 13 Sept. 1871, *GD*, vol. VIII, p. 36.

[121] Parry, *Democracy and religion*, pp. 170–1.

[122] At Newton, 22 July 1865, W. E. Gladstone, *Speeches and addresses delivered at the election of 1865* (London, 1865), p. 30.

stimulating indiscipline, sectionalism and public amorality.[123] Party was a valuable disciplinary mechanism, which would dragoon Parliament into constructive activity rather than factional and selfish whims or idleness. However, and crucially, party was a mere device; he did not accept its moral right to steer his own action if Providence dictated otherwise. Like Disraeli, but for a very different ultimate purpose, Gladstone believed that heroic leadership was necessary in order to create an uplifting national unity through politics.[124]

For Gladstone, this national unity and vigour served a divine purpose. Providence had bestowed particular favours on England – its geographical position and resources, and the 'resolution, energy, skill, perseverance, and good faith' of the English character, which had given it the elements of industrial greatness.[125] England's commercial enterprise, its morality and capacity for self-government had ensured its global power, and these Providential blessings gave it a special responsibility to use that greatness. The world was designed to develop towards a 'wonderful consummation', unity in God, and political leaders were duty-bound to assist that process.[126] Britain's politicians must try to promote the international unity of man, as well as the unity of the kingdom. In October 1864 he proclaimed that Providence had assigned Britain the task of teaching 'the great lesson to mankind that their happiness and their glory lies in union and in attachment of one towards the other'.[127] This was a very sober duty. At Greenwich in 1871 he announced that Britain would be 'acquitted' or 'condemned' on the question of 'having turned to account, or having failed to turn to account, the powers, the energies, the faculties, which mark the people of this little island as among the small and select company of great nations that [have been] gifted with the qualities that mark the leaders of mankind'.[128]

This mission was to be achieved in a number of ways. It was a 'special design of Providence' that Britain should use its economic power to encourage open commerce, since the exchange of commodities would not only add to general standards of wealth and comfort but would encourage

---

[123] To Granville, 23 May 1877, A. Ramm (ed.), *The political correspondence of Mr Gladstone and Lord Granville 1876–1886* (2 vols., Oxford, 1962), vol. I, p. 42; R. Shannon, 'Peel, Gladstone and party', *Parliamentary History*, 18 (1999), 321–2.

[124] Gladstone to Graham, 29 Nov. 1856, Parker, *Graham*, vol. II, p. 292; Parry, 'Disraeli and England', 726–8.

[125] *The Times*, 10, 11 Oct. 1862, both p. 7.

[126] Gladstone, 'Universitas Hominum; or, the unity of history', *North American Review*, 145 (1887), 589–602.

[127] *Proceedings at the opening of Farnworth Park . . . with a report of the oration delivered by W. E. Gladstone, M. P.* (Bolton, 1865), p. 42.

[128] *Bassett*, p. 425.

international harmony.[129] Its equally Providential island status – the 'streak of silver sea' – was an 'exceptional and peculiar bount[y]' of God, safeguarding Britain from sinful aggressive temptation and allowing it to act as a trusted mediator in Europe.[130] Peace would diminish the spirit of militarism which created artificial political interest-groups, bloated European debts, checked economic growth and kept many men in barracks, underemployed and prey to immoral occupations.[131] England should not withdraw from Europe; rather, it should 'seek to found a moral empire upon the confidence of the nations', intervening on the principle of 'Public Right', which was set to become 'the governing idea of European policy'.[132]

Gladstone very frequently spoke of intervention for specific beneficial purposes as a policy in line with the highest intentions of European civilisation, and hence sanctioned by a 'Concert of Europe'. His 'Concert' was a moralised version of Aberdeen's old idea of the European system. It was an abstract conception of an international moral order, based on the Christian and Hellenic traditions. But it was not a real coalition of real states, and Gladstone's idea did not require him to be more internationalist in practice than his contemporaries. He assumed that if England fulfilled its Providential destiny, it would 'win the prize' as 'the foremost among the nations'.[133] It must act according to conscience, with whatever other powers would be supportive.[134] It is quite clear – rather clearer than most historians have been willing to recognise – that Gladstone believed that England understood duty, responsibility and conscience better than other nations and must take the lead in urging a course of action on them. In his distrust of European cabals, he was a Canningite. In his extraordinary article of 1870, described by the *Saturday Review* as a bid to 'sermonize the world', he criticised not just the military prodigality of most continental states but also Napoleon III's 'rash and unscrupulous ambition' and constant error, and the greed and unscrupulousness of the Prussian King William and Bismarck; Prussia had yet to 'prove her civilisation'. He remarked that

---

[129] 1870, quoted in A. Howe, 'Gladstone and Cobden', in D. W. Bebbington and R. Swift (eds.), *Gladstone centenary essays* (Liverpool, 2000), p. 121; at Liverpool, *The Times*, 14 Oct. 1864, p. 7.

[130] 'Germany, France, and England', 588–93.

[131] 'The new Parliament and its work', *Quarterly Review*, 101 (1857), 581.

[132] 'Germany, France, and England', 592–3.

[133] Ibid., p. 593. Vast amounts have been written about Gladstone's 'European sense': some of the literature is summarised by K. A. P. Sandiford, 'Gladstone and Europe', in B. L. Kinzer (ed.), *The Gladstonian turn of mind: essays presented to J. B. Conacher* (Toronto, 1985), p. 177n1. One splendid essay properly emphasises Gladstone's concern with hard-headed national interests in foreign policy: P. W. Schroeder, 'Gladstone as Bismarck', *Canadian Journal of History*, 15 (1980), 163–95.

[134] For an early example of this view (1856), see Beales, *England and Italy*, p. 27.

there was a 'deep & wide difference between England & ruling German ideas on the first principles of free Polity'. His views about Austria were even less charitable.[135]

Indeed he explicitly contrasted his belief in Britain's Providential mission with the 'continental' policy of self-seeking, prestige and competition with other powers.[136] England's God-given separateness and economic power prevented it from needing to squabble for tangible and intangible benefits in that way. Therefore in Gladstone's eyes it was Palmerston who was sometimes un-English in his tendency 'to bluster and to intimidate' in the search for 'that temporary substitute for strength which is termed *prestige*'.[137] In reaction to this, on occasion he self-consciously distanced himself from a bullying approach to foreign governments. When four British travellers in Greece were murdered in 1870, with the possible connivance of Greek politicians, he argued that it would be premature to blame the Greeks for their maladministration; it was the legacy of centuries of Turkish rule.[138] This was clearly an attempt to strike a different note from Palmerston on Don Pacifico. But his criticism was of Palmerston's chauvinistic tone – and the arrogance that it encouraged in the *British public* – rather than of the policy of moral interference in other countries *tout court*. As long as Britain itself remained vigilant against arrogance and vanity, it had the right to protest against worse examples of complacency abroad. Even at his most critical, in the Don Pacifico speech in 1850, Gladstone acknowledged that Britain sometimes had a 'duty' to encourage the development in other countries of 'institutions akin to those of which we know from experience the inestimable blessings'.[139] His visit to Naples later in 1850, when he found the Neapolitan liberal intellectual and anti-Romanist Carlo Poerio languishing in the dungeons of Naples as a political prisoner, was a jolting insight into the practices of a continental state. It drove him to protest against 'the negation of God erected into a system of government' – a standing rebuke to Christian principles, poisoning the historic heart of Christian Europe.[140] In 1851–2, and especially in 1859–60, the Italian issue was crucial in making Gladstone aware of England's unique international

---

[135] 'Germany, France, and England', 580, 583; to Max Müller, 26 Feb. 1871, *GD*, vol. VII, p. 455. See also Fitzmaurice, *Granville*, vol. II, pp. 200–1, and Sandiford, 'Gladstone and Europe', p. 185. For the *Saturday Review*, see Raymond, *British policy*, p. 221.

[136] See his comments of 1876 in Shannon, *Bulgarian agitation*, p. 6.

[137] 'Prospects political and financial', *Quarterly Review*, 101 (1857), 254; 'The declining efficiency of Parliament', *Quarterly Review*, 99 (1856), 556.

[138] *Hansard*, 201:1157, 20 May 1870.       [139] *Hansard*, 112:582, 27 June 1850.

[140] W. E. Gladstone, *Two letters to the earl of Aberdeen, on the state prosecutions of the Neapolitan government* (London, 1851).

responsibility to crusade against unconstitutional and inhumane principles of state.

Similarly, Gladstone never changed his early view that the colonies – and Ireland – were a great 'moral responsibility' for Britain to govern well.[141] This meant a traditionally English recipe of a disinterested local executive, a benevolent propertied leadership, an energised electorate and a transparent financial system in which taxpayers sought no special favours. The un-English model – which had unfortunately grown up as a result of governing-class selfishness – was lazy, complacent and extravagant rule of these free communities from distant London. The solution to the Irish question lay in replacing an arrogant and chauvinistic governing mentality with a moralised one, in line with God's will. In 1868 he told the voters that it was a disgrace that the realm appeared 'to the world as a divided country'. His self-proclaimed task was to address a 'great evil . . . the estrangement of the minds of the [Irish] people from the law, from public authority, from this country'. It was a 'libel upon Providence' and a violation of 'the whole order of the world' to suggest that a civilised people like the Irish should prefer turbulence to peace; therefore it was the fault of misgovernment from London, for which the country must atone.[142] Indeed Gladstone instructed British voters that the enlargement of the franchise now made it *their* responsibility. As a 'Christian people', they had to decide whether to 'take upon yourselves the responsibility and the scandal of continuing to drag Ireland behind the chariot wheels of Great Britain, as if she was a captive country' – a responsibility of which he personally vowed to 'have no part'.[143]

In the 1860s he was absolutely confident that he could provide a disinterested and economical government that would bind the Irish to Britain. By the 1880s he could not evade responsibility for the continuing state of Ireland; too much power was still exercised in London, and the Irish still lacked political maturity. It is not surprising that, in the circumstances, the idea of increased self-government attracted him – as a way of imposing that maturity. He had long seen practical self-government for the settler colonies as the proper historic foundation of English world power.[144] He

[141] 1835, in R. Hyam and G. Martin, *Reappraisals in British imperial history* (London, 1975), p. 91.
[142] At Wavertree, *The Times*, 16 Nov. 1868, p. 5; at Liverpool, 14 Oct. 1868, *Speeches of the right honourable William Ewart Gladstone, MP in south-west Lancashire, October, 1868* (Liverpool, 1868), p. 25.
[143] At Bootle, *The Times*, 14 Nov. 1868, p. 10; at St Helens, 5 Aug. 1868 and Warrington, 12 Oct. 1868, *Speeches of Gladstone in 1868*, pp. xv, 14.
[144] See ch. 7 below. Colonial subjects 'made a first breach in my Toryism': 1892, *PMP*, vol. 1, p. 43.

was attracted by the idea of suzerainty, by which self-governing local entities would acknowledge membership – and the abstract supremacy – of a larger entity representing desirable values. Ideally, the British empire could become like this, like the universal Catholic Church in the religious sphere.[145] So his was not an anti-imperial vision; rather, it reflected his confidence that the English-speaking peoples would increasingly shape the direction of the world, a subject on which he was enthusiastic by the late 1870s. However, his vision of Ireland as a colony depended on the realisation that the Union of 1801 was illegitimate, a view that he reached only in 1885. In 1868 he was a devoted and great Unionist, believing that it was his mission to bind the whole United Kingdom together on proper principles of integrated, economical, unprejudiced government in the patriotic tradition.

### IRELAND

It was indeed Ireland that supplied the Liberal party with its great unifying crusade and ethical mission in 1868–9, after its embarrassments over the 1867 Reform Act. Gladstone reunited the party in support of the disestablishment of the Irish Church and secured a large majority at the 1868 election. Church disestablishment then took up most of the 1869 session, and Irish land was nearly as prominent in 1870. The centrality of Ireland to Liberal politics in the late 1860s is best understood by considering it in relation to the issues about Italy, ethics and national unity that this chapter has discussed so far. The rise of Fenian nationalism, Napoleon III's tendency to indulge in nationalist enthusiasms, the assertiveness of the papacy, and the legacy of the American Civil War all highlighted the need to repress potentially 'foreign' movements in Ireland that were challenging British sovereignty. The threats from secular republicanism and Ultramontane clericalism reminded Liberals of the Italian analogy, and the apparent success with which both had been checked was encouraging. The best chance of securing Ireland for British constitutional monarchy surely seemed to lie in a pluralist approach, more tolerant of local practices and traditions than arrogant Englishmen had previously been, in order to defeat the nationalist and papist alternatives to an 'English' Ireland. It was particularly helpful for Liberals that Disraeli, whose patriotism was suspect anyway, could be

---

[145] H. C. G. Matthew, 'Gladstone, Vaticanism and the question of the East', in D. Baker (ed.), *Studies in Church History*, 15 (1978), 427, 441.

accused of the opposite policy, of strengthening the papacy. Conservative illiberalism in Ireland, as inappropriate as Austrian misgovernment of
northern Italy, provided the Liberal party with a magnificent rallying-cry.

One potentially alien influence in Irish politics remained the Ultramontane Catholic hierarchy. Almost all Liberals were suspicious of papal
power, seeing it as oppressive and foreign. In the 1860s the maintenance
of the Pope's temporal power around Rome, and the Vatican's Syllabus of
Errors of 1864, excited considerable Liberal criticism, which badly damaged
Liberal–Catholic relations.[146] Gladstone had a particularly intense hostility
to the political ambitions of popes, whom he saw as the main agents of
schism in the universal Church. He maintained that the Church of England
had kept its doctrine so pure by consistently resisting papal aggression, as
well as foolish modern continental thinking.[147] By his attempts to intervene
in European and Irish politics, Pius IX had done 'wider & deeper mischief
than any other living man', hindering spiritual unity and mental, moral
and political freedom. In Italy he had strengthened autocracy and foreign
occupation by Austria and France, and by reaction had encouraged a lot of
Italians into scepticism.[148] Gladstone hoped that the destruction of papal
temporal power might revive a historic, Dantesque individualist Christian
political and spiritual consciousness in Italy. In Britain and Ireland too, the
Pope still threatened to interfere with the independence of the individual
believer. Gladstone was inclined to see Irish Catholic opposition to his
policies as a papist challenge to government authority. After the Vatican
Council of 1870 he felt that the Pope's demands for influence over the
mental freedom and moral conscience of the Catholic flock damaged 'the
title of her obedient members to the enjoyment of civil rights'.[149] But if it
was crucial that British policy in Ireland should attack Ultramontanism, it
should also avoid traditional Whig erastianism: these were the twin errors
of the continental regimes in handling religion. Gladstone thought that
it was quite visionary to hope that English government could control the
Irish religious temperament through heavy-handed state endowment and
influence over the various sects. So Catholic resistance to such interference was in his eyes quite understandable. Instead, the state should defend

---

[146] D. A. Quinn, *Patronage and piety: the politics of English Roman Catholicism, 1850–1900* (Houndsmills, 1993), p. 12–13; S. Gilley, 'The Garibaldi riots of 1862', *Historical Journal*, 16 (1973), 697–732.

[147] 'German philosophy has added but little to the stock of our knowledge of the mind & nature of men, if indeed it has added anything': to Manning, 16 Feb. 1873, *GD*, vol. VIII, p. 287.

[148] The quotation is to Russell, 8 Dec. 1873, *GD*, vol. VIII, p. 422. For Gladstone and Ultramontanism, see Parry, *Democracy and religion*, p. 156 and Bebbington, *Mind of Gladstone*, pp. 118–20.

[149] To Odo Russell, 3 Mar. 1874, *GD*, vol. VIII, p. 470.

Catholics' rights to receive their own instruction. Catholicism was the faith of the bulk of Irishmen; it was 'the school of character and belief, in which Providence has placed them'.[150]

A more immediate threat to British rule was Irish-American Fenianism. After an abortive Fenian rising in March 1867, the leaders were imprisoned in England, and in September a prison officer was killed during a rescue attempt on Manchester jail. Three men – inevitably dubbed the 'Manchester martyrs' – were hanged for this offence in November 1867. In December the use of explosives in a further attempt on Clerkenwell prison killed four bystanders and injured dozens. Fenianism represented a republican Irish nationalism, based in America and funded by American money, which was particularly easy to raise because of the tension with Britain during the Civil War. But Gladstone always recognised that its animosity to British government had 'its root & seat in Ireland itself'. He later described the Fenian uprising as prompting an awakening of 'the national judgment and conscience' about Ireland.[151] Such a movement could not be ignored, bearing in mind the Liberal emphasis on self-determination in Italy. In fact Fenianism had emerged in 1858–9, stimulated mainly by the example of Mazzinian republicanism and French intervention in Italy. Liberals always claimed that British rule in Ireland, unlike Austrian rule in Italy, was progressive and beneficial; the Fenian agitation now required them to justify this. Even before it, Gladstone argued that the English could not say that 'duty to the [Irish] people has been discharged', which was all the more awkward because 'we . . . have gone about preaching to others that they ought to have regard to national rights, feelings, and traditions'.[152] Mill wrote that to hold Ireland by force without tackling obvious Irish grievances would place England 'in a state of open revolt against the universal conscience of Europe and Christendom'.[153] Moreover the agitation raised profound issues about threats to national territory. Napoleon III might exploit Irish dissatisfaction with British rule, while the newly enfranchised British democracy might not be as willing as the old electorate to impose a coercive regime on Ireland. But above all there was fear of a simultaneous rising of Fenians in Ireland, and of Fenian sympathisers, either in Canada, or against

[150] Parry, *Democracy and religion*, p. 175; memorandum, 13 Feb. 1844, *PMP*, vol. II, p. 233.
[151] To Manning, 26 Aug. 1872, *GD*, vol. VIII, p. 201; to D. H. Macfarlane, 28 Nov. 1880, *GD*, vol. IX, p. 624.
[152] *The Times*, 15 Oct. 1864, pp. 7–8. For the Italian and American context to Fenianism, see R. V. Comerford, *The Fenians in context: Irish politics and society 1848–82* (Dublin, 1985), pp. 46–64.
[153] E. D. Steele, 'J. S. Mill and the Irish question: reform, and the integrity of the empire, 1865–1870', *Historical Journal*, 13 (1970), 436.

Canada from the United States. Cuts in British defence of Canada made it even more vulnerable to American aggression than before. For the British to repress a simultaneous major rising on the American continent and in Ireland would be impossible; to lose control in either Canada or Ireland would be a great humiliation.[154]

How should these threats be met? In December 1867 at Southport, Gladstone said that Ireland could be governed well only by appreciating 'the traditions, the views, and the ideas' of the Irish. His aim was a pluralist governing strategy, fusing Irish and British approaches. He privately denied that his legislation was *founded* on 'Irish ideas', though he acknowledged that it was influenced by 'Irish circumstances' and 'Irish history'.[155] In particular, he sought to recognise Ireland's historic attachment to its Catholicism and to its landholding traditions, to which historicist scholarship was now drawing attention. By the 1860s, owing to the shifts charted in the Introduction, it was difficult to deny that the Irish were culturally and politically different from the English in ways that no government could quickly remedy. They were more rural, more superstitious, more emotional and less self-disciplined.[156] When Lord Lieutenant there, the future Lord Kimberley hoped that 'fair just Government' would produce 'slow but certain improvement', though he also acknowledged that 'laws however good can only very slowly mould national character'.[157] Gladstone appreciated that the British needed to rule Ireland more sensitively, but he did not doubt the justice of British rule. At this apogee of liberal confidence in the power of English values to guide progress, the obvious solution was for government policy to acknowledge Irish circumstances in order to create a stronger kingdom. Arnold and Mill argued that the union of the complementary cultural qualities of Saxon and Celt was a natural development and would enhance the quality of British civilisation.[158] Russell wrote in 1868 that England, Scotland and Ireland were closely connected, 'governed by a mixed race of Norman, Saxon, and Celt' and 'destined to form . . . a community, or, if you will, an empire, distinguished by its high spirit,

---

[154] Gladstone to Fortescue, 11 Dec. 1867, quoted in E. D. Steele, 'Gladstone, Irish violence, and conciliation', in A. Cosgrove and D. McCartney (eds.), *Studies in Irish history presented to R. Dudley Edwards* (Dublin, 1979), p. 268.

[155] Parry, *Democracy and religion*, p. 266; to Argyll, 5 Jan. 1870, *GD*, vol. VII, p. 212.

[156] See e.g. G. Smith, *Irish history and Irish character* (Oxford, 1861), p. 18; M. Arnold, *On the study of Celtic literature* (London, 1867); Acton, 1859, quoted in Varouxakis, *Victorian political thought*, pp. 122–3; Kimberley to Spencer, 12 Jan. 1869, in J. Powell (ed.), *Liberal by principle: the politics of John Wodehouse 1st earl of Kimberley, 1843–1902* (London, 1996), pp. 115–17.

[157] 1 Apr. 1866, *Kimberley*, p. 185; to Currie, 15 April 1870, Powell, *Liberal by principle*, p. 121.

[158] *CWM*, vol. XIX, p. 552; Arnold, *Celtic literature*.

its freedom, and its civilisation'.[159] Gladstone's public recognition that different solutions were appropriate for different nations within the United Kingdom helped to consolidate the Liberal hold not only on Ireland but also on Wales and Scotland at the 1868 election.

The Liberals' political strategy was also shaped by their vehement rejection of the alternative Irish policy set out by Disraeli and the Conservative party. Irish Catholic MPs' irritation with Liberal anti-papalism had led to closer ties with the Conservative party since 1859; there were informal alliances in Commons votes on foreign policy and Church-rate bills. Disraeli, frustrated in opposition, wanted to build on this cooperation to recover power. As so often in his career, his fertile mind concocted a strategy combining low Parliamentary tactics and grand philosophy. He conceived an alliance of Anglicans and Catholics in defence of organised religion against destructive 'cosmopolitan' enemies – unbelief, German theological scholarship and continental revolutionary ideas. Indeed in 1870 he was to set out some high-flown ideas about Anglicanism's mission to synthesise the highest ideals of mankind, the Hebraic religious conscience (represented by the Pope) and the secular Hellenic admiration for humanity (manifest in Mazzinianism and other republican movements), which were fighting for dominance of the European mind.[160] In 1864 he refused to meet Garibaldi on his triumphant visit to Britain; he declared that the temporal power of the Pope was a bulwark against revolution. He hoped that the Irish Catholic MPs, aware of their weak political position, might be attracted into an alliance of institutional religions, accepting state regulation of their Church. This would demonstrate their institutional attachment to the Crown while also safeguarding the position of the Anglican Church Establishment in Ireland. But already in 1865 some Liberal politicians sought to make capital out of this emerging Conservative policy of maintaining Church rates and Anglican and Catholic clerical privileges in education. Milner Gibson charged the Tories with pursuing an illiberal and un-English alliance with Ultramontanism. Shaw-Lefevre made the analogy between Disraeli and the Pope, complaining that the former was laying down an 'encyclical' enforcing particular forms of religion and using 'ministers of religion as a means of governing'.[161]

Disraeli became Prime Minister in February 1868, on the retirement of Derby, at just the time that Ireland emerged centre-stage in British

---

[159] John, Earl Russell, *A letter to the right hon. Chichester Fortescue, MP on the state of Ireland* (2nd edn, London, 1868), p. 93.

[160] In *Lothair*. Parry, 'Disraeli and England', 713–14.

[161] Quinn, *Patronage and piety*, pp. 186–7nn47 and 48.

politics. His minority Conservative government could only stay in power if it retained the support of the Irish Catholic MPs. His Irish Secretary Mayo planned a scheme that would prop up the Church Establishment in Ireland while conciliating the Catholics. Mayo aimed to get Catholic support for the continuation of the Anglican Establishment in Ireland by conceding a Charter to the Catholic University, allowing it to grant degrees as the bishops had requested; he personally also supported their request for state endowment of the University. Meanwhile the Church Establishment would be maintained in a reformed state, under plans to be announced by a Royal Commission. The Conservatives announced their support for a Charter in March. Six days later, Gladstone went on the attack, turning Ireland into a second Italian question.

From the moment that he became Prime Minister, Disraeli was a target for ruthless Liberal abuse of his 'un-Englishness'. Liberals alleged that, as in 1859, the Conservatives were upholding the forces of oppression and clericalism – in a disastrous Disraelian pact between the Anglican and Roman Catholic Churches. Lacking an Englishman's understanding of liberty, patriotism or religion, Disraeli by this scheme would damage all three of these concepts. He would perpetuate the Irish Church Establishment, 'the memorial of every past mischief and oppression' by the British; he would therefore divide the Irish from England when they should be reconciled to it.[162] He would strengthen the Catholic Church; he would increase the attractiveness of the two anti-British movements which the Irish found most seductive, Ultramontanism and Fenianism. His scheme maintained the husk of a Protestant Establishment in Ireland, but this merely made Protestantism there more unpopular by associating it with state coercion. Protestantism might well be benefited by disestablishment, since Irish Protestants would be forced to become more effective ministers of and propagandists for Christ. But even if this did not happen, it would help to weaken Romanism. Most Liberals assumed that the ecclesiastical grievance was the main reason for the hold of the priests over the Irish lay political conscience, and that disestablishment would help to set the Catholic laity free from the potential political oppression of Rome.[163] That was why Disraeli's Catholic university scheme attracted such revulsion in the Liberal party – because it checked that natural progressive development in Ireland which already appeared to be happening in Italy and instead sacrificed the laity to the Romanists.[164] Most Liberals of the 1860s (unlike

[162] Address, 9 Oct. 1868, *Speeches of Gladstone in 1868*, pp. iv–v.
[163] At Southport, 21 Oct. 1868, ibid., pp. 60–1.     [164] Parry, *Democracy and religion*, pp. 268–9.

Gladstone) placed inordinate hopes in the capacity of a liberal higher education to create a modern-minded gentlemanly elite and believed that the best
hope of the regeneration of Ireland lay in the emergence of a well-educated
propertied laity through a reformed university system. In fact Disraeli saw
the political danger of advocating state endowment of a denominational
Catholic University and refused to be committed to Mayo's idea. But it
made no difference as far as Liberals were concerned. Right up to the 1868
election they charged that this was in fact his policy. Gladstone, presum-
ably thinking that Disraeli was in league with the Pope, quoted the Vatican
newspaper *L'Osservatore Romano* as evidence of the premier's intentions.
He alleged that the Conservative policy of multiple establishments and a
Catholic University was 'wholly foreign and opposed to the general and
deliberate decisions of the people of this country'.[165]

In other words, the Irish Church Act of 1869 proceeded on the basis that
the most liberal religious policy in a *Catholic* country was to undermine
the close connection between religion and the state. The model for Irish
ecclesiastical politics was not to be England, since the Anglican Establishment in Ireland could not claim, as the English one could, to be a national
institution. Disestablishment, instead, was reminiscent of the Italians' cry
of 'a Free Church in a Free State'. The separation of Church and state
would greatly weaken the chances of papal interference in politics, but
would also protect religion from the anger of secular liberals and the threat
of a secularised national culture. It would purify Catholicism and build
up a native, living variant of it as a barrier against Ultramontanism and
atheism. The Free Church doctrine for Ireland – and Italy – was attractive
to a broad swathe of Liberals who supported Church Establishments in
England, as well as to those ethical freethinking Radicals (such as John
Morley) who did not.[166] J. R. Green thought that Italy needed a Reformation, a revitalised religion to avoid the danger of 'Young Italy . . . growing
up Godless, indolent, spiritless, with little love for anything but lounging
and billiards'.[167]

Moreover, Disraeli's attempt to woo the Irish Catholic MPs failed, and
most of them supported disendowment. In December 1864 Irish laymen
and priests had founded the National Association to press for the disestablishment and disendowment of the Church of Ireland along with two other

[165] At Leigh and Southport, 20 and 21 Oct. 1868, *Speeches of Gladstone in 1868*, pp. 44, 60–1; Parry,
*Democracy and religion*, pp. 272–3. This charge was followed by other candidates: A. L. Thorold,
*The life of Henry Labouchère* (London, 1913), p. 79.
[166] See Morley, 1868: J. Morley, *Critical miscellanies: II* (London, 1905), p. 337.
[167] Pemble, *Mediterranean passion*, p. 148.

issues. They were concerned, not least, to keep hold of the leadership of lay Catholic opinion against the secular and revolutionary Irish-American Fenian movement, by focusing on religious topics. Since 1856, O'Neill Daunt, one of the National Association leaders, had been corresponding with the secretary of the Nonconformist Liberation Society on this and other issues.[168] British Nonconformist activists naturally welcomed disestablishment, and the eagerness and enthusiasm with which Gladstone took up the policy in 1868–9 won him their admiration and enthusiasm.[169]

The power of the argument for the complete separation of Church and state ended the chances of the old Whig Irish policy – concurrent endowment of all the religious sects. When Russell raised the Irish Church issue in 1867, he hoped that the removal of the offensive Irish Establishment could be accompanied by some version of this policy. He, Grey and other Liberal peers continued to advocate it, right up to July 1869 – helping to explain why the Irish Church Bill nearly foundered in the Lords. Their argument remained that concurrent endowment would bolster Protestantism in Ireland while giving the Catholic clergy financial benefits and thus an interest in the state and in order.[170] These arguments still appealed to intellectuals such as Matthew Arnold, who claimed that Irish Catholics were 'a thousand times more superstitious and unprogressive' than Catholics in Germany because of the lack of endowment for Catholic clergy and universities.[171] But since the 1840s they had appeared too 'continental', oppressive and Romanist for British tastes. By contrast, the disestablishment and disendowment option allowed the Liberals to fight the 1868 election by an indirect appeal to anti-Catholicism. They contrasted Disraeli's supposed plan to endow a Catholic University with their own refusal to give any money to the priests, and their withdrawal of all state funding from Irish religions, including the controversial Maynooth grant which had excited anti-Catholic opposition for twenty-five years. On the hustings in Lancashire Gladstone called himself an 'ardent Protestant' – using the term, apparently, for the first time since 1836.[172] As a result, the Liberals won most Irish Catholic votes, yet prevented Disraeli from rallying anti-Catholic opinion against them (outside bitterly sectarian Lancashire). This was political ambiguity of a high order.

[168] E. R. Norman, *The Catholic Church and Ireland in the age of rebellion, 1859–1873* (London, 1965), chs. 4, 7; P. M. H. Bell, *Disestablishment in Ireland and Wales* (London, 1969).

[169] *Nonconformist*, 25 Jan. 1871, p. 73.     [170] Parry, *Democracy and religion*, pp. 131–3, 274, 283–4.

[171] Preface, 2nd edn, *Higher schools and universities in Germany* (1874), in R. H. Super (ed.), *The complete prose works of Matthew Arnold* (11 vols., Ann Arbor, MI, 1960–72), vol. VII, p. 102.

[172] Parry, *Democracy and religion*, p. 272.

The policy of disestablishment and disendowment was so attractive because, though 'Italian', it was also the most 'English' available: anti-state-continentalist, anti-Ultramontane and anti-Fenian. It aimed to neutralise the political power of religious vested interests, just as Corn Law repeal and the Peel–Gladstone fiscal strategy had sought to neutralise the political power of economic ones. Dismantling the connection between a minority Anglican Church and the state would strengthen both, and thus the Union, because the government would lose the sectional image that had damaged its reputation in Ireland, while Anglicans would no longer attract the odium associated with political favourites.

Gladstone's commitment to take Irish ideas into account but to pursue an essentially 'English' policy was equally apparent in the 1870 Irish Land Act. It sought to distance the government from past 'oppression' – the memory of historic landlord confiscations. It was founded on the notion that a disinterested British government could find an equitable social contract between landlord and tenant and hence guide the Irish towards stable political and social relations. And it took some account of the strong Irish attachment to customary occupancy rights, which secured tenure, and the right to sell the land on, as long as a fair rent was paid. In 1869–70 recognition of fixity of tenure as a *legal principle* was politically impossible, because it was seen in cabinet, Parliament and the press as unacceptably democratic and socialist. In any case Gladstone disliked the principle, fearing that it would discourage landlords' investment and threaten their position. But he aimed to offer much of the *practice*, by building his proposals on local customary traditions underpinning tenure – especially the 'Ulster custom'. Understanding of the historical basis of these traditions had spread in the 1860s, not least with the translation of the Brehon Law in stages from 1865. One of the editors of the Brehon Law, W. N. Hancock, helped to shape the 1870 bill. This increasing awareness of cultural distinctions made it fashionable to argue that contractual approaches to property were less well suited to peasant societies than to advanced ones, and that in dealing with backward rural cultures government should pay more attention to indigenous communal traditions.[173] Gladstone's plan in 1870 was to extend 'Ulster custom' throughout Ireland. However, propertied opposition in and outside the cabinet made it clear that this would not be acceptable to British political opinion. So in its final form the Act only gave legal recognition to customary tenants' rights wherever they could be proved to exist. Elsewhere, the tenant would be allowed certain rights, safeguarded by the authority of a

---

[173] Dewey, 'Celtic agrarian legislation', 56–61.

court, in order to re-establish a working relationship between landlord and tenant, in which both recognised the property rights of the other as under the old customary arrangements.

Gladstone presented this as a restitution and atonement for the earlier confiscations and as a highly conservative proposal, a specific amendment of property rights on Burkean principles of historical legitimacy.[174] Moreover, in basing his legislation on specific *Irish* customs, he was also denying the applicability of these ideas about tenants' rights to British landowning arrangements. In fact, the Act upheld a lot of 'English' assumptions about the importance of land-ownership in promoting social improvement. Moreover, it gave only very limited support to the European model of tenant land purchase. Bright urged Irish land reform on Prussian principles in 1866, and, as the leading advocate of these ideas in cabinet, suggested an examination of the Prussian reforms in 1869. He managed to insert some provisions into the 1870 Act which empowered the Treasury to loan up to two-thirds of the purchase money for peasants who wished to buy their holdings. But Gladstone disliked this reversion to the 'continental policy' of government loans, claiming that it would make 'the State a great Land Jobber', and the clauses were ineffectual, creating only 870 owners by 1881.[175]

So Gladstone's Irish reforms of 1869–70 sought to recognise Irish cultural distinctions, but with the ultimate aim of checking anti-British sentiment, unifying the kingdom and continuing the civilising and Providential mission of Britain in Ireland. Moreover he spent relatively little energy on negotiating with any Irish politicians. He put much less emphasis than Russell on patronage as a political tool; stress on this was incompatible with his high-minded notions of executive neutrality and rigid economy. Indeed the rejection of concurrent endowment itself – the strategy of keeping both Protestants and Catholics acquiescent by state grants – pointed to the low opinion that the new ministers had of the political significance of patronage. In fact, one initial influence on the Home Rule movement which emerged in 1870 was that Gladstone's government was paying insufficient attention to local Irish interests. Gladstone was unworried. Having passed his measures of conciliation and, in his own mind, ended oppressive government, he denied that there was still 'national dissatisfaction' in Ireland.[176] It naturally followed that he blamed a foreign influence, the

[174] Steele, *Irish land*, pp. 252–4.
[175] Gladstone to Granville, 24 May 1869, *Ramm 1868–76*, vol. I, p. 22; Steele, *Irish land*, p. 102.
[176] Mar. 1874: see Steele, 'Gladstone, Irish violence', p. 270.

Ultramontane priests, for the breakdown in sympathy between Ireland and England after 1870, as chapter 6 reveals.

## 1868–70: NATIONAL EDUCATION AND RELIGION; EMPIRE AND ECONOMY

For Russell and Gladstone the other great benefit of the Irish issue was that it would promote their major objective after Palmerston's death in 1865 – to restore a strong principle-based party system, revitalising and purifying politics, and giving a lead to opinion. By the end of Palmerston's life there was a widespread view that the Liberals must develop a greater coherence as a party, with some sort of legislative agenda. Kimberley, for example, liked the Irish Church initiative of 1868 since it gave the chance of 'a better tone to politics, and some strength to the Executive'.[177] When Russell finally became Prime Minister in 1865, Parliamentary reform was obviously the first, crucial step to make the Liberals a party again and galvanise Parliament into more virtuous activity. Despite the setback of 1866 on Reform, Russell used his last months as Liberal leader, after the 1867 Act was passed, to publicise the two issues which he was most anxious for the party to rally around: Irish Church reform and elementary education.[178] Gladstone then fought the 1868 election on a focused, purifying agenda, concentrating on Ireland and on a campaign for economy and efficiency in government. Though his government of 1868–74 was to pursue a large legislative programme, reflecting pressure from various elements within the party to respond to the task of governing a broader political nation, the core problems, as far as the leadership were concerned, were Ireland, education and economy.[179] In fact the dominance of the Irish issue in 1868 hid some tensions on even these other two topics. Since these were to become so important to patriotic politics from 1870, as chapter 6 explains, some initial exploration of them is necessary here.

Elementary education was now the key domestic question for those Liberals who wanted to improve the social and moral tone of the nation. The 1867 Reform Act made it possible to conceive, for the first time, that the state could legitimately compel local authorities to provide education – partly

---

[177] 4 Apr. 1868, *Kimberley*, p. 217.
[178] See his motion on the Irish Church, *Hansard*, 188:354, 24 June 1867; his *A letter to the right hon. Chichester Fortescue, MP on the state of Ireland* (2nd edn, London, 1868); and his motion on education, in *Hansard*, 190:493, 2 Dec. 1867.
[179] For an analysis of the various categories of legislation pursued in 1868–74, see J. P. Parry, 'Gladstone, Liberalism and the government of 1868–1874', in D. W. Bebbington and R. Swift (eds.), *Gladstone centenary essays* (Liverpool, 2000), pp. 94–112.

because of the greater legitimacy of the state, partly because of propertied anxiety about uneducated voters. Education suddenly became the question of the day. But what should be the relative roles of government, Church and clerisy in directing that process? Differences of opinion about the role of conventional religious teaching in a national education system had prevented progress towards it in the past. Moreover, the Conservatives had adopted the idea of Church defence, goading Radical Liberals to adopt a vigorously anti-clerical position, and opening the door for Churchmen to defect to Conservatism if they managed to implement it.

The campaign for a *uniform* national system was headed by the most rigorous anti-clericals, driven by animosity to the Church and to the perceived political consequences of its educational dominance. The National Education League was set up in 1869 to argue that the proper basis for a national system was elected local-authority control and a secular approach to the religious problem. Leaguers won support from Millite intellectuals, the more advanced Nonconformists and many trade union leaders, but also from civic activists who took a positive pride in the capacity of local government to act for the interests of the community and develop communal values. Such men – George Dawson in Birmingham being a particularly charismatic example – were often influenced by admiration for the civic republicanism associated with Mazzini and the United States and believed that the urban community could create a more vibrant patriotism than an intellectually and socially restrictive religious body. Education should be based on secular and civic ideals, with no support for specific religious denominations. This, applied to Ireland, would also secure lay dominance of education there against the Catholic priests who were demanding more control over schools. The League thus stood for a new type of ethical relationship between government and people across the United Kingdom. In 1869 controversy forced it to use the vaguer word 'unsectarian' rather than secular to describe its attitude to the teaching of religion, suggesting that Bible reading, for example, might be permitted. Nonetheless, many Churchmen remained extremely suspicious about the idea of 'national' education on these lines, seeing it as a challenge to the national Church. In 1869 a rival body, the National Education Union, was established to defend the place of religion in education. This included not just Conservatives but many Liberal Churchmen, plus Wesleyans and indeed some evangelical Nonconformists, such as Baines of Leeds. It rejected the political values of Birmingham Radicalism; symbolically, it was founded in the other centre of provincial Liberalism, Manchester.

Manchester had dominated the lobby for education legislation since the early 1850s and provided the alternative vision which had much more influence on the 1870 Elementary Education Act. The educational needs of the town made the introduction of local-authority support for education a high priority, while the heavy involvement of Anglican and Roman Catholic priests in local schooling led to a recognition that their interests should be taken into account in any scheme. Moreover, the Liberal elite was socially grander, better established and more attuned to anxieties about social order than in Birmingham. Since 1857 moderate Manchester Anglicans had reached a compromise with Radicals and Unitarians, by which they advocated a system of schools funded by local rates and supporting religious education. In 1867 and 1868 bills were introduced (by Bruce and Forster, the rising Liberal social reformers) which were based on the Manchester plans. They allowed local authorities to levy a rate for the support of existing schools or building new ones, but required them to give some form of religious instruction, with a conscience clause permitting parents who objected to it to withdraw their children.[180] These bills were motivated by an elitist and moralistic concern that the local poor should learn order, discipline and sound economic and moral principles. Several influential educational reformers pointed to the benefits for economic and social harmony in Germany that had resulted from an educated workforce. Indeed Forster, who as Gladstone's education minister was to be the architect of the 1870 Act, argued that 'civilised communities throughout the world are massing themselves together', and he looked forward to strengthening 'our national power' by 'increasing the intellectual force of the individual'.[181]

When Forster introduced a 'national' education system in 1870, he meant two things by it. Firstly, the state should take responsibility to ensure that localities provided effective education across the country. His bill gave the state the power to require a locality to elect a school board wherever it deemed accommodation for children inadequate. But voluntary educational agencies were given a 'year of grace' (in fact reduced to five months) to build schools to ward off the threat of a board. Schools funded by the various religious agencies would still provide most of the education. Forster welcomed this, secondly, because he wanted a national recognition of Christianity. He was determined to oppose discrimination against

[180] A. J. Marcham, 'Educating our masters: political parties and elementary education 1867 to 1870', *British Journal of Educational Studies*, 21 (1973), 184–5.
[181] Forster, *Hansard*, 188:1351, 10 July 1867; 199:465–6, 17 Feb. 1870.

existing denominational schools, and to encourage religious teaching in the new board schools. Church schools provided three-quarters of school accommodation, while the Church Establishment seemed to Forster to be 'a great engine of good'.[182] Catholics and Wesleyans also maintained substantial numbers of schools, as did the British and Foreign Schools Society, historically patronised by Whigs and moderate Nonconformists and providing undenominational religious teaching.

Forster's insistence on religious teaching was partly for political reasons: he wanted to settle the issue quickly without raising complaints from Churchmen, ratepayers or anti-centralisers. At Greenwich in October 1871 Gladstone claimed that one great principle of the 1870 Act was that 'we should trust . . . as little as possible to the central Government, and as much as possible to the local authorities and the self-governing power of the people'.[183] But Forster's emphasis on a Christian education system also reflected his Liberal Anglican view that institutional religion would support social order and national community. To 'make a man moral', he must first be made 'religious'. He told an audience at Leeds that 'religion is the motive power', whereas human faculties were just 'machines' which were 'useless' without it, and that what was wanted was a 'John Wesley exciting religious fervour in the minds of the masses'.[184] De Grey, the cabinet minister responsible for the bill, was similarly hostile to secularism, on principles learned from F. D. Maurice.[185] After some input by Gladstone, the 1870 bill gave school boards the choice of allowing any degree of religious instruction in funded schools, subject only to the operation of a conscience clause. Since in practice hardly any English board appeared likely to confine itself to a secular solution, the political significance of this was that it gave *carte blanche* to any religious interests to teach as much religion as they wanted.

The problem was that in the eyes of very many Nonconformists and Radicals, religious teaching provided by the Church Establishment was sectarian, not national. It quickly became widely argued – including by many Manchester reformers – that the government had given too many concessions to the Church. In March and April 1870 there were massive protests from the League and from Dissenters against the proposal not to restrict the freedom of Church schools to teach their own religion, which they said would set up

---

[182] At Bradford, *The Times*, 12 Aug. 1868, p. 8.     [183] *Bassett*, p. 413.
[184] *Hansard*, 188:1355, 10 July 1867; *Nonconformist*, 26 May 1869, pp. 490–1.
[185] Indeed his vehemence on the subject probably explains his astonishing conversion to Catholicism in 1874: Denholm, *Ripon*, p. 107.

a new Establishment, especially in rural areas. Many Liberal backbenchers complained about the protection given to denominational education, and eventually forced an amendment (the Cowper–Temple clause), which significantly restricted the amount that could be given in board schools. Meanwhile, Anglican lobby groups mobilised both against this Liberal–Radical pressure and against those provisions of the bill that restricted the Church's freedoms. In June the government attempted to end the crisis by setting up the so-called 'Dual System', under which existing voluntary schools would be funded not from the rates, like the board schools, but from the Privy Council.[186] This compromise relieved the consciences of Nonconformists, but it also gave Anglican and Catholic schools more protection from local Radical attacks. Thus it destroyed the vision of many educational reformers, of integrating board and denominational schools in one locally accountable rating system: a true communal enterprise as opposed to a clerical vested interest.[187] The Radical junior minister – and fervent Italophile – G. O. Trevelyan resigned in protest, having fought the 1868 election on the principle of rejecting 'the public endowment and recognition of creeds', for England as well as Ireland.[188] The attempt to preserve a religious identity for the state meant damaging the nationality of the system. The disputes of 1870 also revealed that the unexpectedly far-reaching nature of the 1867 Reform Act had increased the sense of vulnerability felt by various social and religious groups that the increased power of the state might be used against them.

Defensive economy also posed problems. In his 1868 campaign, Gladstone focused on economy in order to win the confidence of voters in the state's efficiency, disinterestedness and good housekeeping. He severely criticised the Conservative government's increase of £3 million in general expenditure – in addition to the spiralling costs of their Abyssinian war. He claimed that Disraeli's ministry had pandered to 'knots and groups, and even classes' who aimed to 'feed . . . themselves upon the produce of the public industry'.[189] Once in office, he paid particular attention to defence expenditure. He relied on the traditional identification of the Liberals with strength abroad to reduce expenditure without engendering panic. Good relations with other powers, the decline of the French naval threat, and the

---

[186] Parry, *Democracy and religion*, pp. 301–6.

[187] Francis Taylor, chairman of the Manchester Education Bill Committee, to *The Times*, 4 Dec. 1871, p. 8.

[188] G. M. Trevelyan, *Sir George Otto Trevelyan: a memoir* (London, 1932), p. 91.

[189] At Warrington, 12 Oct. 1868, *Speeches of Gladstone in 1868*, pp. 5–13.

end of the need to patrol against the slave trade, all helped. Scientific innovation, such as Captain Cowper Coles's revolutionary turret-ship, seemed likely to ensure continued British naval supremacy at less cost. The non-European fleet was cut by a fifth in the 1869 Estimates, and 24,000 troops were brought back from the colonies in 1869–70. Overall spending was dramatically reduced, by about £6 million, back to previous Liberal levels. Gladstone, at the height of his powers, was determined to demonstrate the purity of the Liberal state.

These reductions should be seen as symbols of the self-confidence of the 1860s, not of disdain for the colonies. J. S. Mill, for example, thought that overseas possessions were very useful for national 'prestige', which was, 'in the present state of the world, a very great advantage to mankind'.[190] There was hardly any interest in colonial separation, and a general hostility to the idea of allowing them to fall into rival hands, as a debate about Canadian defence during the American Civil War had demonstrated. Palmerston asserted that the idea that the colonies were 'an encumbrance and an expense . . . is not the opinion of England, and it is not mine'.[191] Bright and Cobden decided not to call for Canadian independence unless the Canadians asked for it. Gladstone argued that, until they did, Britain had a duty to maintain the connection.[192] There was, as before, a *theoretical* willingness to accept Canadian and Australian independence as eventually natural. But the writer who argued this most strongly, Charles Dilke in *Greater Britain* (1868), presented it as a necessary preliminary to making a 'virtual confederation of the English race' by strengthening ties with the United States, Britain's natural ally in the task of 'imposing English institutions on the world'. Dilke maintained that it was absurd for Britain to pay money to defend indolent French-Canadians, 'the only true French colony in the world', against the spread of a vigorous Anglo-Saxon culture.[193] Such arguments indicated an increasing Liberal–Radical interest in the idea that Britain and the United States should henceforth lead the world. *The Times* coined the phrase 'Pan-Saxonism' in 1869 to denote the potential global reach of Anglo-Saxon values.[194]

---

[190] To J. E. Cairnes, 15 June 1862, *CWM*, vol. xv, p. 784.

[191] To Russell, July 1864, Stembridge, *Parliament*, p. 33.

[192] Ibid., pp. 21–8, 81–8; see Kimberley, 8 May 1869, *Kimberley*, p. 234. The Colonial Laws Validity Act of 1865 specifically reiterated the right of the Westminster Parliament to legislate for those colonies which had their own legislatures.

[193] C. W. Dilke, *Greater Britain: a record of travel in English-speaking countries during 1866 and 1867* (2 vols., London, 1868), vol. i, pp. 69–70, 73–5, vol. ii, pp. 150, 157.

[194] F. Harcourt, 'Gladstone, monarchism and the "new" imperialism', *Journal of Imperial and Commonwealth History*, 14 (1985), 34.

It is, however, significant that the arrival of an economising Liberal ministry immediately caused widespread concern that the government *was* now indifferent to the colonies. In 1869 the New Zealand government requested a loan for £1.5 million for military assistance against the Maoris, in view of the impending withdrawal of the British garrison. When Britain refused, the New Zealanders made representations among their friends in London, with the result that the affair was paraded as evidence of anti-colonial official feeling. The government had to agree to a loan of £1 million. And the Liberal MP R. R. Torrens asked for a select committee on the colonial question in April 1870, worried at indications of a lack of official commitment to Canada as well as New Zealand.[195] The sense that separatist notions were in the ascendant led to the establishment of a bipartisan Colonial Society in March 1869, to promote the colonial connection. Russell protested about the snub to New Zealand and the reductions in Canadian defence, seeing this as a threat to the empire, and as a matter of personal honour given his commitments to both colonies in 1839–41.[196]

At root, this concern to bolster the colonial connection was inspired by two factors. The first was a fear about the tone of domestic policy after 1867, a sense that the weight of materialist, plutocratic, insular sentiment in Parliament was now greater. This was assisted by Bright's presence in cabinet, as a representative of the Manchester School and long-term critic of defence spending and the empire. Those with a particular attachment to the colonies could see Gladstone's cuts not as a purifying measure but as deferring to a narrowly commercial view of the state's global responsibilities. The *Pall Mall Gazette* lamented the effect on colonial policy of the 'timid shop-keeping spirit' of commercial Liberalism.[197] It was also significant that the lobbying on the New Zealand affair was pursued in conjunction with a demand for state aid for emigration to the colonies. This indicated a broader opposition to *laissez-faire* social policy within the Liberal party. Rising poor-rates stimulated concern about pauperism and overpopulation in the late 1860s, reflected in the foundation of the Charity Organisation Society, and there was a strong feeling that state-aided emigration would not only strengthen colonial ties but would also prevent severe social problems at home. The imperial enthusiast and Radical Edward Jenkins, writing in *Fraser's* in April 1871, thought that the only alternative to emigration was contraception, which would 'inoculate English society with French vices',

[195] *Hansard*, 200:1817–36, 26 Apr. 1870; R. Koebner and H. D. Schmidt, *Imperialism: the story and significance of a political word, 1840–1960* (Cambridge, 1964) pp. 95–102.
[196] Russell, *Selections from speeches*, vol. I, pp. 151–2.    [197] Harcourt, 'Gladstone, monarchism', 34.

'destroy our unique home-life and home-ideas' and clip the strength of the English race.[198]

Secondly, anxiety was fuelled by the international situation. Partly this was due to the success of the nation-building of the 1860s. One element of Forster's concern for education was the competition posed to Britain from so many growing and confident powers. A major feature of Russell's anxiety about the colonies was the threat that France, the United States and Russia might annex anything that Britain discarded.[199] Animosity between Bismarck's increasingly powerful Prussia and Napoleon's excitable France mounted from 1867, while the Pope declared his infallibility at the Vatican Council in 1870. Could British supremacy in Europe and the world still be assumed? Gladstone's choices as Foreign Secretary, Clarendon and then Granville, were deliberately chosen to provide a change of tone from Palmerstonian posturing against continental autocracy, but their preference for quiet and agreeable diplomacy with other powers might be a liability if the European situation worsened.

So there were disquieting signs, both at home and overseas. There is no doubt that by 1870 many Liberals wanted domestic and foreign policy to project a greater sense of responsibility for national and international development. But on the whole, up to 1870, there was palpable optimism about their ability to govern on a broad, inclusive and progressive basis. England had for nearly twenty years been blessed with class harmony and prosperity, apparently by Providence. More than ever, after the passage of another Reform Act, England seemed a strong ethical community. In the summer of 1867 Edward Dicey wrote that the spread of prosperity, culture, education and communication would increase popular awareness of being 'part and parcel of that grand entity which we call a nation' and yet would also lead to closer bonds with other peoples.[200] After the murder of the four Englishmen in Greece in 1870, there were press demands for the government to defend British honour and interests there in some way. But it is striking that Gladstone was able to defuse the main demand, for changes to the 1864 constitution, by pointing out that this would be a retrograde step for Britain's cause in Greece – the cause of 'popular institutions' – and that time must be given for them to mature.[201] On the first day of the 1869 session, Granville, the Liberal leader in the Lords – the same man whom Radicals had ridiculed as the Queen's lapdog in 1851 – walked

[198] E. Jenkins, 'Two solutions', *Fraser's Magazine*, 3 (1871), 451–6.
[199] Russell, *Selections from speeches*, vol. 1, p. 153.
[200] 'War and progress', *Macmillan's Magazine*, 16 (1867), 171–2.
[201] *Hansard*, 201:1123–60, 20 May 1870. See R. Jenkins, *The Dilessi murders* (London, 1961), ch. 5.

hand-in-hand from cabinet to Parliament with John Bright, to symbolise the alliance between the Liberal aristocracy and the Radical conscience. In early July 1870, as the new Foreign Secretary, he told the House of Lords that his chief civil servant had never known 'so great a lull in foreign affairs'.[202] He was not to know quite what an extraordinarily ill-timed remark this was.

[202] Fitzmaurice, *Granville*, vol. ii, p. 33n.

# CHAPTER 6

# The Franco-Prussian War and the destruction of the first Gladstone government, 1870–1874

In the long history of the British left, no collapse has been more spectacular than that experienced by Gladstone's government between 1870 and 1874. Only once since 1832 had the Conservative party won a general election, and that was before the Liberal cause was so greatly strengthened by the events of 1846 and 1848. A similar Conservative victory, so soon after the 1867 Reform Act, was widely regarded as almost inconceivable. Yet it happened, in February 1874 – after an unprecedented twenty-four by-election defeats for the government in England (out of fifty-one Liberal seats vacated between 1870 and 1873). Historians of this government, myself included, have failed to consider that the events of 1870–1 in Europe, mostly flowing from the Franco-Prussian War, which began in July 1870, could have had much to do with the Liberals' loss of direction. This chapter argues that they had an enormous amount to do with it. Indeed it is scarcely credible that Britain would be untouched by the swift Prussian victory in the war, the fall of Napoleon III, the unification of Germany, the Russian démarche in the Black Sea, the Paris Commune, the Vatican Council, the destruction of the Pope's temporal power, and the sense of an all-out ideological conflict between the forces of clericalism and their opponents in every country in western Europe.

These events had such an effect on Liberalism because of the party's reliance on the themes traced in chapter 5. Its success in the 1860s had reflected its ability to project Britain's global power while promoting free trade and low taxation. The incoming Gladstone government of 1868 believed that it was possible to continue the policy of economy while upholding national honour and developing an ethical mission abroad. Meanwhile it followed a domestic strategy of shaping the enlarged electorate into a stronger community of sentiment by interventionist 'improving' educational and social legislation and by an inclusive pluralistic policy in Ireland. This chapter argues that all these policies were undermined by the continental crisis of 1870–1. The first and most obvious effect was to ruin the government's financial, defence and international strategy. With French power destroyed, and no other allies, Britain was unable to act effectively in the new European situation, creating severe embarrassment – and another defence panic. Divided in their response, Liberals could not avoid looking feeble, unpatriotic, and vulnerable to the charge of self-interested commercial materialism. The contradictions within the uplifting rhetoric of the 1860s were laid bare. Moreover, in domestic affairs, influential Radicals urged that Britain should respond to the new political climate at home and abroad by developing an uplifting civic republican agenda, but this proved extremely unpopular with more conventional opinion. The second half of the chapter traces how, at the same time, the government's careful balancing-act on educational and Irish matters collapsed spectacularly for much the same reason: different groups of Liberals clung more vehemently to their own, conflicting ideas of the policies that would best promote 'English' values. Worse, many of them, fired with patriotic and anti-Catholic zeal, disastrously lost sight of the need to incorporate Irish opinion in their national vision.

These policy disputes were all affected by clamour to assert British distinctness from the Continent. In 1870–1 Europe presented three images, none of which was at all appealing to British Liberalism. One was symbolised by the might of the Prussian army, supplied with modern technology and mass popular backing, and directed by an all-powerful central autocracy. The French alternative was hardly more alluring: an effete, corrupt and luxurious imperial regime, undermined by its own materialist excesses and giving way to a bloody democratic anarchy in the 1871 Commune. Thirdly, the rise of secular republicanism and socialism encouraged the resurgence of Romanism across Europe, in a desperate reaction. All three images were strongly at odds with Liberal ideas of 'Englishness'. Since there was less confidence than after 1848 that Britain could defeat these foreign threats on the international stage, it was all the more important to try to reassert the right values, and defeat the wrong ones, at home. This intensified the anxiety about popular political education which was already resulting from the major extension of the franchise in 1867 – much broader than most propertied Liberals had wanted. But after 1870 it became clear that there was not enough agreement on the way forward in practice. By 1874 there was hardly any policy on which the Liberal party could unite.

## FOREIGN AFFAIRS AND DEFENCE

Duped by Bismarck, a neurotic Napoleon III declared war on Prussia in July 1870 and within six weeks France had been humiliated by the speed

and efficiency of the Prussian advance. After the great defeat at Sedan, on 1
September, Napoleon III fell and later fled to England. The Second Empire
was at an end. But the war lasted for five more months. It devastated much
of eastern France and only ended with the forced cession of Alsace and
Lorraine to the new German empire which was proclaimed at Versailles on
18 January 1871. Prussian aggression had resulted in German unification.
It also allowed Russia to assert power in the Near East and created the
conditions for a revolutionary regime in Paris. The Pope's temporal power
over Rome was overthrown: would he now unleash his spiritual power
more vigorously as a reaction? The balance of forces in Europe had changed
decisively, and not in Britain's favour.

The process of responding to these events opened up major differences
of opinion within the Liberal party. Divisions between economisers and
Palmerstonians could no longer be disguised. There was naturally still a
strong party, headed by Gladstone himself, in favour of keeping defence
costs low and defining England's mission abroad as mainly ethical and
humanitarian. For them, low expenditure also promoted the progressive
agenda at home. Bright warned Gladstone that 'every man added to the
forces and every ship put in Commission strengthens your opponents'.
His brother Jacob charged that for two hundred years military intervention had caused 'poverty, misery and crime' at home. Harcourt thought
it was retrograde to allow foreign affairs to dominate political debate.[1]
Rylands, Potter and White held the Cobdenite flame aloft in the Commons. So, outside it, did the Cobden Club (founded in 1866, shortly after
Cobden's death), with its motto of 'Free Trade, Peace, Goodwill among
Nations'. Many Radicals and Nonconformists urged Britain to continue
with its 'disinterested' mission of promoting such ideals abroad, by, for
example, encouraging the referral of disputes to international mediation or
arbitration.[2] After all, Napoleon's impulsive declaration of war in July 1870
seemed to show clearly the shortcomings of decision-making in an 'imperial'
regime.

But in the 1860s economy had seemed compatible with a high British
global profile. The legacy of Palmerston ensured considerable sympathy
within the party for the language of national 'honour' and 'duty'. And the
rising young cabinet ministers of the 'Volunteer' generation – Hartington, Kimberley, Ripon and Goschen – tended to be vigorous upholders

---

[1] 17 Nov. 1870, G. M. Trevelyan, *Bright*, p. 418; *Nonconformist*, 8 Feb. 1871, p. 126; *Illustrated London
News*, 7 Jan. 1871, p. 18; Gardiner, *Harcourt*, vol. 1, pp. 233–5.

[2] M. M. Robson, 'Liberals and "Vital Interests": the debate on international arbitration, 1815–72',
*Bulletin of the Institute of Historical Research*, 32 (1959), 38–55; *Nonconformist*, 14 Dec. 1870, p. 1195.

of the national interest and strong defence.[3] If England were humiliated abroad, how could it preach its progressive gospel? If it were ill-prepared against attack, how would it stand up to autocratic or any other threatening powers? Some of those Liberals who urged a strong foreign or defence policy (and it was possible to advocate the latter without the former) had been 'manly' Radical critics of upper-class effeteness in the 1840s and 1850s. Two vigorous spokesmen for these views in the media were J. A. Froude, the historian and editor of *Fraser's Magazine*, and James Fitzjames Stephen. Froude still blamed aristocratic ineptitude for delaying military efficiency and for attempting to uphold rank and hierarchy in the colonies instead of the spirit of entrepreneurial freedom that suited the Englishman's character. But he and Stephen loathed the penny-pinching commercial spirit and felt it essential that British politics should rediscover a strain of masculine liberal patriotism. Robert Lowe, Chancellor of the Exchequer, shared some of these views, particularly on strong defence. So did Frederick Greenwood, the editor of the *Pall Mall Gazette*. Froude, Stephen and Greenwood were increasingly unsympathetic to the drift of Liberalism because they robustly opposed humanitarian sentimentalism, thinking that it prevented the efficient pursuit of the national interest at home and abroad just as much as 'Old Corruption' had done. Instead they cultivated a hard-headed, modern-minded professional attitude to government – as did Lowe, Hartington, Kimberley and Goschen.[4]

Moreover, newspapers and pamphleteers (particularly but not only Conservative ones) contributed to the pressure on government to uphold the national honour. Especially successful were two fictional publications. One, *The fight at Dame Europa's school*, by the Anglican clergyman H. W. Pullen, told the story of the Franco-Prussian War as a fight between two monitors, Louis and William, over a disputed area of the school garden. John (Bull), head of school, was prevented from stopping the fight by his fag Billy (Gladstone), who advised him that he could not afford to intervene. Dame Europa blamed the fight on John's cowardice and told him that 'you were placed in authority in order that you might act'. The story, of

---

[3] Ripon, reflecting his strong religious sense (Christian Socialism converting to Catholicism), was more sensitive to humanitarian and ethical considerations than the others.

[4] See J. A. Froude, 'England's war', *Fraser's Magazine*, 3 (1871), 135–50; J. Stapleton, 'James Fitzjames Stephen: liberalism, patriotism, and English liberty', *Victorian Studies*, 41 (1998), 243–63. Greenwood's *Pall Mall Gazette* still claimed to stand for 'true Liberalism' in 1874 (Parry, *Democracy and religion*, p. 409) but Greenwood soon became a strident Tory. Lowe argued that if Britain had a properly trained militia of 400,000 men, it would not need to worry about the drift of continental diplomacy: 21 Aug. 1870, Lady Burghclere (ed.), *A great lady's friendships: letters to Mary, marchioness of Salisbury, countess of Derby 1862–1890* (London, 1933), pp. 276–7.

which originally only five hundred copies were printed, sold 189,000 by February 1871 and spawned over fifty ripostes and spin-offs, roughly equally divided for and against intervention.[5] The other story, originally published in *Blackwood's Magazine* for May 1871 and quickly reprinted as a sixpenny pamphlet was *The Battle of Dorking*, by G. T. Chesney, an Indian army veteran, officer with the Royal Engineers, and future Conservative MP. Its subject was a Prussian invasion of England, a ruthless and technologically sophisticated advance through the familiar and beautiful scenery, crushing the ill-trained English Volunteers who were left to defend the country while the overstretched and undermanned army was deployed elsewhere in the world. *The Battle of Dorking* sold eighty thousand copies in a month and invented a new genre, that of the invasion story.[6]

Two strands of non-Cobdenite Radical opinion were also politically significant over the next few years. Those particularly sympathetic to the democratic and humanitarian ideals of 1789 tended to argue that, with France prostrate but free from Napoleon, it was England's duty to take up the advocacy of these ideas, both as the basis on which to build a broader political community at home, and as the foundation-stone of its international policy. For them, France symbolised the republican idea, the idea of progress, the idea of humanity struggling against feudal oppression. Sympathy with a popular French republic should be the essence of the foreign policy of an advanced liberal state. This view was popular among Francophile intellectuals such as John Morley, Ludlow, George Meredith, Algernon Swinburne and the positivist circle around E. S. Beesly and Frederic Harrison. Their indignation was roused by the prolonged misery inflicted on the French by the Prussian armies between September 1870 and January 1871, which was designed to force the cession of Alsace and Lorraine as a condition of peace. Harrison and Ludlow both pointed out that England could only matter in Europe by working in concert with a liberal France.[7] As the extent of the French collapse became clear, there was also interest in the idea of a citizen army to defend England against the threat of Prussian militarism.[8] However, this call to arms generated fierce debate among intellectual Radicals. Mill approved, but Morley and Russell's son Amberley did not.[9]

[5] F. Madan, '*The fight at Dame Europa's school' and the literature associated with it* (London, 1882), p. 6.
[6] I. F. Clarke, 'The Battle of Dorking, 1871–1914', *Victorian Studies*, 8 (1965), 308–28.
[7] F. Harrison, 'The effacement of England', *Fortnightly Review*, 9 (1871); J. M. Ludlow, 'The reconstitution of England', *Contemporary Review*, 16 (1871).
[8] J. E. Cairnes, 'Our defences: a national or a standing army?', *Fortnightly Review*, 9 (1871), 167–98.
[9] Russell and Russell, *Amberley papers*, vol. II, p. 399.

A second group of Radicals, typified by Dilke and Trevelyan in Parliament and Joseph Chamberlain and Edward Jenkins outside it, attempted to create a new popular Liberalism around a vigorous patriotism. They maintained that the honour of democratic England and its democratic colonies must be defended as symbols of Anglo-Saxon political virtue. Critical of both non-interventionist Manchesterism and of aristocratic complacency, these men looked forward to developing a communal republican ethos at home inspired by that of the United States. They had no doubt that the English and Americans were 'incomparably the finest people in the world'.[10] Trevelyan was a meritocratic enthusiast for army reform who offended the Queen and the duke of Cambridge when he was a junior minister in January 1869 by referring to the 'tremendous influence of the Court' as an obstacle to it.[11] He and Dilke were both self-consciously 'manly' admirers of the Volunteers and athleticism. Dilke came into the Commons in 1868 advocating 'peace, but a peace more dignified than that which has of late prevailed'.[12] He loathed the Manchester school, attacked government weakness towards Russia over the Black Sea in 1871 and became a supporter of national enrolment and home drill. In 1873 Dilke and Chamberlain were working towards a Radical programme of free schools, free church, free land, free labour: an attack on remaining feudal restrictions on working-men's freedom in English society, and a nod to the free labour, free soil tradition of the American Republicans.

The effect of international turbulence in 1870–1 was to divide the party on the question of Britain's diplomatic and military response. Should Britain assert itself abroad, improve its defences or retrench? There were so many calls for a 'resolute' and 'manly' approach, but so much pressure also for economy and restraint, that the Liberal coalition inevitably split. Moreover, though the government took a middle course between these camps, the changed European situation and Britain's lack of allies ensured that it would appear to fail to uphold national honour.

At first the outbreak of the Franco-Prussian War seemed to hold few political dangers for Gladstone's ministry. Napoleon III rushed into war so quickly that there was no way of stopping him through mediation. There was a consensus that Britain should supply humanitarian aid and try to restore peace as soon as possible, but there was also pleasure that Britain was

[10] Trevelyan, 1880: G. M. Trevelyan, *Trevelyan*, p. 106.
[11] P. Guedalla, *The Queen and Mr Gladstone 1845–1879* (London, 1933), p. 147.
[12] Memoirs, Dilke papers, B. L. Add. Mss. 43931, f.2. For his satire on the Cobdenite Rylands, see ibid., f.60.

now too progressive a state to tolerate the presence of two such mighty military machines as those possessed by France and Prussia. Neutrality was obviously the most sensible course economically and strategically. Assuming that Belgium was not invaded, intervention on either side would have been impossible to justify. Many defenders of national honour, backed by the Queen, believed that, if Britain were to retain the world's respect, it must assert its commitment, of 1839, to protect Belgium from attack by either side. This nearly led to an awkward cabinet split, which was prevented by the publication in *The Times* of a draft treaty of 1867, in which the French proposed to Prussia a French protectorate of Belgium. The mood in the Commons now made it necessary to conclude treaties with both contenders guaranteeing that Britain would fight against either if they invaded Belgian neutrality. Parliament granted £2 million in a vote of credit for the naval and military services and the government was given permission to add twenty thousand men to the army, without which it was generally agreed that the army could not mount an expedition to Antwerp if necessary. Some of the cabinet had been urging strong action of this sort, but Bright came to the verge of resignation at the prospect of spending 'English blood & treasure for purposes which I do not deem to be English'.[13]

At this stage, opinion was clearly anti-French, comprising suspicion of the politics and aggressive behaviour of Napoleon III, some admiration for German cultural values, and the hope that political and economic liberalism would spread in German lands. The rapid collapse of Napoleon seemed a natural consequence of his own misgovernment and inveterate plotting over two decades. Having based his regime on Caesarism, overriding the educated part of the population, he had had to appeal to the average Frenchman's lust for prestige. Gladstone felt that he had overreached himself and rightly fallen. Untrained in the beneficent principles of self-government, the French could not grasp 'the principles of mutual respect, and moral independence, which must regulate a well-ordered family of nations'. Napoleon had lost the war because overcentralisation and corruption had killed French public spirit.[14] Many moralistic Liberals saw the conflict as one of values:

---

[13] Bright to Gladstone, 3 Aug. 1870, Bright papers, B. L. Add. Mss. 43385, f.97. See Gladstone to Bright, 1 Aug. 1870, *GD*, vol. VII, pp. 336–7. De Grey (Ripon) felt that the cabinet would incur the 'gravest responsibility' if it did not increase the undermanned army: to Hartington, 27 July 1870, Ripon papers, B. L. Add. Mss. 43565, f.17.

[14] Gladstone, 'Germany, France, and England', 576–80. See also e.g. Raymond, *British policy*, pp. 73–5, 149; A. Hayward, 'The personal history of imperialism in 1870', *Fraser's Magazine*, 2 (1870); H. Reeve, 'France', *Edinburgh Review*, 133 (1871), 10–18; *The Times*, 11 Jan. 1873, p. 8; Varouxakis, *Victorian political thought*, p. 94 (Bagehot).

discipline, domesticity and morality against disorder and sensuality. The inherently domestic and non-aggressive Germans were fighting for hearth and home – for 'national unity'.[15] Anglo-Saxonists like Dilke argued that 'our true alliance' lay 'with men who speak our tongue, with our brothers in America, and our kinsmen in Germany and Scandinavia'.[16] Perhaps Germany was ripe for the triumph of Liberal values over Prussian Junkerdom: 'a Liberal party, composed of the best of the landowners and the best of the bourgeoisie, will have it all its own way in the end'. Gladstone felt that the decline of Austrian influence in Germany would improve its prospects of constitutionalism.[17] Moreover at first sight Napoleon's fall was a repeat of the overthrow of Louis Philippe in February 1848, which had lessened pressure for high defence expenditure in Britain. In September 1870 the Home Secretary, Bruce, suggested that the danger to Britain was now reduced.[18]

But the war did not end there. Bismarck demanded the unacceptable: the annexation of Alsace and Lorraine. The damage inflicted on France as it held out against siege in the following five months, combined with its ultimate capitulation, was a great embarrassment for Britain, as the self-proclaimed defender of fair play between nations. Britain failed to mediate between the combatants and failed to protect the forced annexation of two provinces without a plebiscite of the inhabitants. After the fall of Napoleon the public mood in Britain changed significantly: it did not 'understand why H. M. G. can do nothing but look on' while Paris was bombarded and starved.[19] The enfeeblement of France by Prussia would also obviously threaten Britain's influence in European affairs. But the cabinet was paralysed into inaction by a false reading of the Schleswig-Holstein crisis of 1864. Gladstone, initially, and Granville, throughout, were obsessed by the notion that Britain's attempt on that occasion to lay down 'general principles, when nobody will attend to them' had lost it 'moral weight' abroad.[20] Granville feared that a British initiative would offend Prussia and encourage it to support the Russian desire to reoccupy the Black Sea, while

---

[15] Lady W. Russell, in K. Urbach, *Bismarck's favourite Englishman: Lord Odo Russell's mission to Berlin* (London, 1999), p. 47; Earl Russell, *The foreign policy of England 1570–1870: an historical essay* (London, 1871), pp. 92–3; Gladstone, 'Germany, France, and England', 564; Harcourt, 18 Oct. 1870, Gardiner, *Harcourt*, vol. I, pp. 222–3.

[16] Millman, *Franco-Prussian War*, p. 177.

[17] M. E. Grant Duff, *Studies in European politics* (Edinburgh, 1866), pp. 250–1; Gladstone, 'Germany, France, and England', 558–60.

[18] Bagehot came to his support: St John Stevas, *Bagehot: VIII*, p. 65.

[19] O. Russell, in Urbach, *Bismarck's favourite Englishman*, p. 51.

[20] 7 Oct. 1870, *Ramm 1868–76*, vol. I, p. 139; *GD*, vol. VII, p. 358.

also giving the Americans the chance to attack British shipping.[21] Gladstone changed his mind and twice tried to persuade the cabinet to approach the other powers to make a protest against the Prussian annexation but could not overcome the usual quietist cabinet majority. This was ironic: he himself had insisted on cabinet control of foreign policy, in a deliberate break from the policy of Palmerston and Russell, so that the concerns of Commons Liberals about taxation and expenditure could be given weight. Gladstone had to content himself with the thought that Germany was the real loser by the annexation because it had forfeited the 'sympathy' of the 'Liberal party in England', and the higher sentiment of Europe, for twenty years.[22]

Granville was proved wrong: British inaction over Alsace and Lorraine did not prevent Russia, in November 1870, from abrogating the neutralisation of the Black Sea, which had been agreed in the Treaty of Paris signed at the end of the Crimean War. This single-handed declaration undid the main Crimean achievement and reopened the threat to Constantinople and the Mediterranean. It was, after all, an event in the Black Sea, the massacre of Sinope, that had made British opinion willing to go to war in December 1853. The sense that national honour was at stake led to press uproar, especially from *The Times*, the *Telegraph*, the Palmerstonian *Morning Post* and the Conservative *Standard*. Even the *Daily News* warned that for Britain not to challenge the Russian declaration would mean 'once and for ever to abandon her position among European powers'.[23] Granville urged a strengthening of the Mediterranean fleet, but was overruled by Gladstone, who was trying unsuccessfully to prevent the Quaker Bright from resigning from the cabinet (claiming ill-health) and who felt that the arrangement of 1856 was too impractical to uphold. Gladstone could see no special British interest in the Black Sea, while French weakness made Britain less vulnerable in the Mediterranean.[24] But Kimberley believed that the country 'does not agree with him in his ultra-pacific, anti-Turkish policy'.[25] Arthur Otway, Granville's deputy at the Foreign Office, resigned, warning that the choice was 'humiliation or war'.[26] The embarrassment

---

[21] Millman, *Franco-Prussian War*, pp. 212–17.

[22] Urbach, *Bismarck's favourite Englishman*, pp. 109–10.

[23] W. E. Mosse, 'Public opinion and foreign policy: the British public and the war scare of November 1870', *Historical Journal*, 6 (1963), 41–3, 53–5.

[24] *Ramm 1868–76*, vol. I, pp. 143–4, 156, 160–1. There was also Liberal pressure to avoid the folly of another Crimean War, and the Queen was anxious to lower the tension: Mosse, 'Public opinion', 46–9, 55.

[25] To de Grey, 20 Feb. 1871, Powell, *Liberal by principle*, pp. 124–5.

[26] Otway: *GD*, vol. VII, p. 410n4. See also Granville, 30 Mar. 1871, *Ramm 1868–76*, vol. I, pp. 230–1.

was reduced by the unauthorised behaviour of Odo Russell, ambassador to Prussia, who used the press fever to give Bismarck the quite erroneous impression that Britain was planning to go to war with Russia with or without allies.[27] Bismarck therefore consented to the calling of a conference of the powers to review the Treaty. But he knew full well that it would uphold Russia's claims in the Black Sea, which it did in March 1871. Dilke complained that Britain's acceptance of a conference signalled an intention to abandon treaty obligations at the behest of the Eastern powers, setting a dreadful precedent for the future. His Parliamentary motion of protest after the event was only symbolic, but the government still had to declare a vote of confidence in order to prevent widespread Liberal dissension.[28]

These two setbacks seriously damaged government authority. Everything that the Liberals had said against the Conservatives for lacking the authority to prevent the Italian war of 1859 was now turned against them – and this was a graver crisis. As had been demonstrated in the past, public opinion might forgive foreign embarrassments if accompanied by rousing liberal rhetoric and the impression of activity. By eschewing such rhetoric, Britain lost much more 'moral weight' than it had done in 1864. Political and media opponents called for a 'resolute' and 'manly' policy – satisfyingly vague terms. They lamented the policy of 'selfish isolation' which had betrayed national honour and left Britain 'despised' in Europe, and they blamed the dominance of selfish manufacturing interests, concerned only with tax cuts, in the reformed Parliament.[29] Gladstone was ridiculed for the complacency and insularity of his remarks about 'happy England', separated by a 'streak of silver sea' from the dangers and hardships of the Continent, in his supposedly anonymous *Edinburgh Review* article that autumn. The contrast with the age of Palmerston was exploited, not least in a famous *Punch* cartoon of Gladstone as 'injudicious bottle-holder' being lectured by the ghost of Palmerston on the need to stand up to the Russians in order to get them to back down.[30] Gladstone's perceived weakness abroad, combined with his High Anglican tendencies, unstraightforward

---

[27] Urbach, *Bismarck's favourite Englishman*, pp. 61–4.    [28] *Hansard*, 205:894, 30 Mar. 1871.

[29] For selfishness, see Sir R. Peel, *Hansard*, 204:397, 17 Feb. 1871. For manliness, see Mosse, 'Public opinion', 41. For the derision of Europe, see Peel, *Hansard*, 204:399, 17 Feb. 1871; Froude, 'England's war', 135; Anon., 'England's place among the nations', *Macmillan's Magazine*, 23 (1871), 358–9; marquess of Salisbury, 'The terms of peace', *Quarterly Review*, 129 (1870), 556. The complaint of deference to commercial sentiment was shared by, for example, Salisbury, 'Terms of peace', 556; Harrison, 'Effacement of England', 166.

[30] *Punch*, 25 Feb. 1871, pp. 76–7. For responses to the Gladstone article, see Raymond, *British policy*, pp. 220–3.

language and unpredictable enthusiasms, encouraged critics to portray him as unmanly.[31] Kimberley noted how restlessly 'John Bull chafes under his policy of non-intervention . . . It is lucky for Europe we are not armed to the teeth like the Continental powers.'[32] Ludlow asserted that the ministry had 'practically foundered' because of the stigma of meeting a European emergency with an inadequate army and a complete lack of policy.[33]

Of course, there were still many Liberals optimistic about the future of European liberalism and hopeful that the establishment of constitutional government in France and Germany would make it easier to settle future disputes by arbitration.[34] But the underlying problem was the changed state of Europe. Peace depended on good relations between Germany and Russia. An informal understanding between them and Austria now left Britain marginalised more than at any time since the 1840s, if not the 1820s.

These events created a new panic about the inadequacy of home defence. It rested on two main planks. The first was a revival of alarm about the contrast between feeble government at home and autocratic power abroad. The speed and proficiency of the Prussian triumph over France had been awesome. It was attributed to the most dynamic and potentially threatening forces of the age: machine power complementing a mass of men inspired by an idea, organised with clinical efficiency by an apparently omnipotent central government.[35] The idea that a state could gain such strength by harmonising these awesome forces was naturally alarming to a country which prided itself on its decentralisation and libertarianism. The second was excessive pressure for retrenchment from a dominant commercial class. Its insularity and selfishness and growing political influence were the real targets of both Pullen's *Fight at Dame Europa's school* and Chesney's *Battle of Dorking*. Chesney's argument was that blinkered commercial men's unwillingness to pay for proper defence was fatally counterproductive. His story started from the assumption that global overstretch had scattered the British army and navy too thinly, leaving the country in the hands of the Volunteers, who were untrained because drill would interfere with

---

[31] Parry, *Democracy and religion*, pp. 141–3; more work could be done on this theme.

[32] To H. Wodehouse, 14 Sept. 1870, Powell, *Liberal by principle*, p. 122.

[33] 'The reconstitution of England', 506–7.

[34] Some of the 'John' stories were similarly optimistic about future peaceful international cooperation, e.g. *The fight ended* (London, 1871); *Dame Europa's school fifty years hence* (London, 1871); *After the fight at Dame Europa's school* (London, 1871); *The true story about the fight at Dame Europa's school* (London, 1871).

[35] By e.g. Gladstone, 'Germany, France, and England', 563, and an invasion story, *The carving of Turkey* (1874), quoted in I. F. Clarke, *Voices prophesying war 1763–1984* (London, 1966), p. 48.

industrial productivity. Once they were outclassed by a silent, ruthlessly efficient German military machine, British commerce was the great loser – the taxpayer was burdened with reparations, while trade was redirected to German rather than British factories, thus destroying British prosperity. Commercialism was an easy target not only for military and Conservative critics, but also for disaffected anti-*laissez-faire* writers like Froude and Ludlow. They lamented that 'patriotism has become a jest'. Ludlow argued that only by building communal pride and embracing a statist policy could Britain reconstitute Europe against 'brutal, rapacious, German militarism' and 'rapacious, crafty, Russian despotism'.[36]

The invasion panic led to many calls for Britain to develop a defence force more similar to the Prussian or Swiss ones. J. E. Cairnes suggested a standing army of trained citizens in place of the current system of idle officers and inefficient soldiers. In a letter to *The Times*, the aged Russell called for a force of 200,000 'disciplined' regular and militia troops, and extensive army reform, in order to defend coast and colonies, and to uphold national treaty obligations, honour and interests. *The Times* launched a movement for compulsory militia service; it also ran a campaign to expose Volunteer inefficiency and to demand better integration with the regular army.[37] In December 1870 Kimberley thought the newspapers had gone 'stark mad' in their panic.[38] But there was further derision in the summer of 1871 when the Berkshire manoeuvres – the first attempt to get the regular army, the militia and the Volunteers together to practise the arts of war – were cancelled because the War Office noted that there was a risk of rain, in which case encampment on arable land might be objectionable to the soldiers. The *Annual Register* drily remarked that 'few more severe criticisms could be passed upon an army than to pronounce it incapable of encountering the risk of the rain and wind of an English autumn in a southern county'.[39]

The invasion scare itself did not last long; there was less reason for it than in 1859, given the lack of continental interest in invasion. (By 1874 the British navy was twice the size of the French.) More persistent, however, were the underlying concerns about penny-pinching in defence policy. The navy suffered a series of embarrassments. In order to demonstrate British naval strength both to the contending parties in the Franco-Prussian War and to domestic opinion, a great display had been organised in the Atlantic for September 1870. The highlight was the maiden voyage of HMS *Captain*,

---

[36] Froude, 'England's war', 135–7, 149; Ludlow, 'The reconstitution of England', 506–7, 517.

[37] Cairnes, 'Our defences'; Russell, *The Times*, 21 Jan. 1871, p. 5; Russell, *Foreign policy*, pp. 93–4; Cunningham, *Volunteer Force*, pp. 88–9.

[38] 14 Dec. 1870, *Kimberley*, p. 255.  [39] *The Annual Register for the year 1871* (London, 1872), p. 99.

the very symbol of a modern Liberal naval strategy. Its novel design featured a large number of heavy turret guns which could be rotated flexibly to meet the source of danger. *The Times*, Cobden and the economy-minded Admiralty minister Childers had all praised it as a victory of technology and cheapness over reactionary military objections. In a phrase that became notorious, a subsequent official report stated that the *Captain* had been 'built in deference to public opinion'.[40] Unfortunately this top-heavy ship overturned in a moderate gale in the Bay of Biscay; only 18 of the 499 people on board survived. The bad news for the Admiralty did not end there. Two more ships, the *Agincourt* and the *Megaera*, ran aground in the summer of 1871. In each case the court-martial blamed the parsimony and inefficiency of the Admiralty in failing to keep them in good repair.[41] In August 1871 E. J. Reed, who had resigned as Chief Constructor of the navy after a dispute with Childers in 1870, claimed that Childers had not listened to warnings about the unseaworthiness of some ships. Reed and the Controller of the Admiralty, Sir Spencer Robinson, the two leading technical experts on ship design in the Admiralty, had always maintained that the *Captain* was too low in the water to be safe. Both men were scientifically minded professionals and Liberals; they now became high-profile government critics and stood as by-election candidates.

Their supporters in the press charged that the failings at the Admiralty were the consequence of Childers arrogating power to himself in order to pursue his Gladstonian campaign for economy and 'business methods'. He had ignored the naval experts on the old five-man Admiralty Board and concentrated power in his own civilian hands.[42] Whigs and Conservatives joined forces in the Lords and the Commons to criticise the economy mania and demand greater professionalisation in naval administration.[43] Themes of naval maladministration and complacent timidity abroad were prominent in the celebrated but quickly banned theatrical satire on the Gladstone government, *The happy land* (March 1873). The Gladstone character remarked that, when their country had to 'submit to an unparalleled series of humiliations in the eyes of surrounding nations', the best response was to put a retired solicitor who knew nothing about ships in charge of the

---

[40] S. Sandler, ' "In deference to public opinion": the loss of HMS *Captain*', *Mariner's Mirror*, 59 (1973), 64. The quotation, from the court-martial report, remains prominent on the memorial to the drowned men in St Paul's Cathedral.

[41] N. McCord, 'A naval scandal of 1871: the loss of HMS *Megaera*', *Mariner's Mirror*, 57 (1971), 115–34.

[42] N. A. M. Rodger, 'The dark ages of the Admiralty, 1869–85: Part I, "Business methods", 1869–74', *Mariner's Mirror*, 61 (1975), 334–8.

[43] *Hansard*, 204: 295, 16 Feb. 1871, and 205:1280, 18 Apr. 1871.

navy.[44] The co-author was W. S. Gilbert – who thus created the prototype of *HMS Pinafore*'s Sir Joseph Porter.

It was already obvious at the end of 1870 that the government needed to recover a reputation for professionalism in defence. But it misjudged the situation. War Secretary Cardwell's awareness that the 'English public [were] in a growling humour' encouraged him to press ahead with the proposal to abolish the purchase of army commissions that was being urged by Wolseley and Baring within the War Office and recommended by a Royal Commission report of 1870.[45] It was seen as leading the way to a more disciplined and technically aware officer corps and to regimental reorganisation. The purchase of commissions had been criticised for many years, not least because, though theoretically regulated by Royal Warrant, a shortage of them, especially in the best regiments, had driven prices up to 'over-regulation' levels. Cardwell seized on the report and persuaded a reluctant Gladstone that the ministry should take up the idea of purchase abolition. This was a miscalculation. The cost of compensating officers who had bought their commissions expecting to sell them on was variously estimated at £8–12 million. Gladstone doubted that backbench feeling in favour of meritocratic reform was strong enough to welcome such expenditure, and so it proved.[46] On the second reading of the abolition bill, several Liberals as well as many Conservatives protested at the cost: four criticised the payment of over-regulation prices in compensation.[47] The public seemed indifferent: no petitions at all were presented in favour of the bill. Moreover, not a few Liberal MPs identified with the classes which were happy to buy commissions for their sons – especially as many officers now came from commercial and professional rather than aristocratic backgrounds. Northbrook said that there was hardly a Liberal MP who did not have a relation in the army; Cardwell complained about the effect of 'Plutocracy' on backbench reforming zeal.[48]

Secondly, the international turbulence of 1870–1 allowed Conservatives, military Liberals and Radical reformers all to argue that purchase abolition was a sideshow and that the more urgent issue, after the Prussian victory, was the creation of a more professional army, with a coherent system of appointment, promotion and reserve forces. Though Cardwell's bill also

---

[44] F. Tomline [W. S. Gilbert] and G. A'Beckett, *The happy land: a burlesque version of 'The wicked world'* (London, 1873). I have treated this issue at greater length in 'Gladstone, Liberalism', pp. 103–8.

[45] Cardwell to Gladstone, 26 Dec. 1870, B. L. Add. Mss. 44119, f.181.

[46] 8 Mar. 1871, *GD*, vol. VII, p. 460.     [47] Rylands, Muntz, Headlam, Anderson.

[48] T. F. Gallagher, '"Cardwellian mysteries": the fate of the British Army Regulation Bill, 1871', *Historical Journal*, 18 (1975), 333–4, 336, 342, 344.

sketched out changes in policy on enlistment and auxiliaries, these were easily attacked as imprecise and inadequate political gestures, cobbled together
in a hurry. He was jeered when he claimed that his reforms would guarantee 'perfect security and independence'.[49] The broader debate about army
reform was unhelpful to the Liberal party because there was no agreement
about the solution. The party contained some keen defenders of the army,
such as Anson, Bury and Grosvenor, most of whom were hereditary rather
than progressive Liberals, from great families. Some reformers, meanwhile,
wanted a thoroughgoing modernisation of the military bureaucracy. These
included Trevelyan, but he had a more particular grievance. This was the
power of the Commander-in-Chief, the duke of Cambridge, over selection procedure, which he saw as the major obstacle to meritocracy. However, his campaign against the Queen's cousin was obviously an attempt to
win a democratic reputation and was criticised by more mainstream army
reformers.[50] Moreover, all the advocates of professional reform were usually
at odds with those who wanted to create a more 'popular' army by extending military service, perhaps to the point of universal instruction in arms
and compulsory training in the reserve for a few weeks every year. This
would be a 'school of equality' and health and vigour, a republican system
based on a universal notion of patriotism, breaking down class divisions.
A more popular army would no longer be a marginal and unfamiliar force
in British society but one, like the Swiss and German armies, reflecting the
moral and intellectual qualities of the whole nation. Mundella hoped that
it could become a 'University', as in Germany.[51] But other Liberals were
appalled at the idea of spreading military values so widely in a free society.[52]
Once again Liberal reformers were divided on how far it was appropriate
to follow continental models.

Internal Liberal dissension helped the Conservatives to make the bill
into a major trial of strength, dominating the 1871 session and crowding
out most other legislation. In the end the Lords refused to pass the bill and
the government had to resort to royal warrant to terminate the purchase
system, which they could have done from the beginning. But to impose

---

[49] *Hansard*, 205:125, 16 Mar. 1871.
[50] His motion of February 1871 to alter the tenure and powers of the Commander-in-Chief won eighty-
three votes, but he was criticised for his personal grudge and 'family mania' against Cambridge by
several Liberals: see *Hansard*, 204: 621–6 (Bury), 640 (Osborne), 1410 (Colonel White), 21 Feb., 6
Mar. 1871.
[51] Cairnes, 'Our defences'; E. A. Freeman, 'The panic and its lessons', *Macmillan's Magazine*, 24 (1871),
7–9; Herbert and Mundella, *Hansard*, 204:1947, 205:470, 13, 23 Mar. 1871.
[52] E.g. W. R. Greg, 'Popular *versus* professional armies', *Contemporary Review*, 16 (1871), 351–73.

this burden on taxpayers after Parliament had protested against the government's motives for most of the session was criticised as contrary to the
spirit of the constitution by several Whig peers. Veteran army reformers
Russell and Grey also chided the government's superficial approach and
lack of interest in systematic professionalism.[53] The Liberals were unable to
raise a storm of popular indignation against the Lords' behaviour because
it did not look manifestly more unpatriotic than that of the government.
Abolition left the army no less aristocratic than before; Gladstone toyed
with a more radical reform but did not want to act precipitately during
the panic, while the experience of 1871 hardly suggested that the Commons
would be agreeable to further discussions once the panic subsided.[54]

Anxiety about defence also made economy a controversial subject. Government spending was rising, owing to compensation for the abolition
of purchase, the military spending of August 1870 and the central grants
to voluntary schools, to be followed in 1872 by the compensation payment for the *Alabama* claims. Gladstone justified all these to himself, but
they intensified the need to find savings from elsewhere. After the fall
of Napoleon, he quickly tried to decelerate Palmerston's fortification programme. He felt a personal responsibility to pursue spending reductions,
especially on defence, in order to rally the party, give effect to his electoral
pledge of 1868, encourage peace abroad and strengthen class relations at
home.

The resulting battle for spending cuts created enormous strain within
the cabinet right up to the 1874 election, and difficulties in Parliament,
beginning in April 1871 when the government was humiliated over its budget. Chancellor Lowe's initial idea was to spread the extra military costs
between the social classes by combining a penny increase in the income
tax with a stamp tax on boxes of matches and a doubling of succession
duties on estates. The last two proposals met with impassioned opposition, from match girls on the one hand and propertied MPs on the other.
The government had to drop both proposals and to increase the income
tax by 2d instead. The nature of the clamour – street demonstrations and
'plutocratic' class pressure in Parliament – suggested that the executive's
ability to suppress class tension was declining. Several Radicals protested
about the weakness of the government in face of demands from the London clubs and the metropolitan press for increased military spending, and
they complained that the pledges of 1868 had not been met. The income

---

[53] See e.g. Russell, *Hansard*, 207:1679–90, 14 July 1871.     [54] *GD*, vol. VII, pp. 380–3, 494, 501–2.

tax increases made them more determined; as in 1848, popular resentment would surely follow.[55] At Whitby that autumn Gladstone also blamed army and 'club influences' for the invasion scare and warned that the revival of class tension, rather than inadequate army provision, was the greatest threat to the nation's power.[56] He used the Radicals' criticism to urge his military ministers to agree to defence cuts.

But even Cardwell, a creature of Gladstone's, was only able to deliver a portion of his demands: though army spending fell from £14.7 million in 1871–2 to £13.5 million in 1873–4, this was higher than the £12.1 million of 1870–1. And naval spending rose from £9.0 million in 1870–1 to £10.1 million in 1873–4. Goschen, who succeeded Childers at the Admiralty, had been 'PallMallish' in urging a naval demonstration in the Mediterranean at the time of the Black Sea crisis. He resisted pressure for naval cuts, pleading an increase of prices, the costs of protecting commerce and anti-slave-trade missions, and the state of the public mind.[57] The *Nonconformist* complained at the lack of Parliamentary and public interest in economy.[58] Cabinet support for it was also lukewarm, especially since Childers and Bright were absent ill. The Liberal peers and Lowe were not reliable allies. The latter was an advocate of a strong navy and a large militia, and of the retention of the income tax as a great engine of finance; Gladstone considered him 'wretchedly deficient' in controlling expenditure.[59] In 1873 he took advantage of an error of Lowe's to remove him as Chancellor and take the job himself, aiming to reinvigorate his government with a great scheme of finance. But he discovered that the War and Colonial Offices were hard nuts to crack: he complained that he could not interfere in the decision to send a military expedition to the Gold Coast in 1873 because the War Office would not let him know the facts.[60] He reverted to his desire of the 1850s to abolish the income tax. But he could not get the defence departments to give him the £1 million extra that he needed to finance this. This drove him to dissolve Parliament in January 1874 and to make a dramatic appeal to the electorate for income tax abolition, over

[55] See e.g. *Hansard*, 205:465, 494, 495, 23 Mar. 1871 (Mundella, Dixon, Jacob Bright), and 205:1585–90, 24 Apr. 1871 (White, Rylands).

[56] *Nonconformist*, 6 Sept. 1871, pp. 876, 881; *GD*, vol. VIII, pp. 36, 76–7.

[57] 20 Nov. 1870, *Ramm 1868–76*, vol. I, p. 161; Goschen to Gladstone, 19 Sept. 1871, Gladstone papers, B. L. Add. Mss, 44161, f.177. See Rodger, 'Dark ages', 340–2, and A. R. D. Elliot, *The life of George Joachim Goschen first Viscount Goschen 1831–1907* (2 vols., London, 1911), vol. I, pp. 115–18.

[58] 5 Mar. 1873, pp. 236–7.

[59] Burghclere, *Great lady's friendships*, pp. 276–7; 14 Dec. 1871, *GD*, vol. VIII, p. 77; 9 Sept. 1873, *Ramm 1868–76*, vol. II, p. 407.

[60] Matthew, *Gladstone 1809–1874*, p. 190.

their heads.[61] Driven by his own evangelical impulse to purify politics, Gladstone had exaggerated public interest in economy, which was limited by the buoyant economy and previous tax reductions.

One reason for the failure of the economy card was an increasing interest in the colonies and the ethical and philanthropic mission against slavery and native misgovernment in Africa and the Pacific. As chapter 5 showed, already in the late 1860s there was anxiety that supposedly dominant 'Manchester' commercial values would undermine the colonial connection. Now, with Russia and Germany, and indeed the United States, so large, unfriendly and threatening, attachment to the colonies grew. Froude argued that they offered a way of 'recovering the esteem of the world' and a solution to domestic unemployment through emigration.[62] A conference was held to urge Imperial Federation at the Westminster Palace Hotel in July 1871. Federalism itself was very much a minority view, generally seen as impractical and unnecessary. But even so, critics of it, like the *Nonconformist*, believed that 'every true Englishman . . . must desire to see welded together the scattered fragments which constitute the British Empire' and unite 'the great Anglo-Saxon family'. Moreover, the extension of civilisation to backward regions was 'marked out' by Providence as England's destiny.[63] Disraeli attempted to exploit the colonial cry, but in fact so many Liberals were anxious to uphold the imperial mission that he failed to get much benefit from it. The two responsible government ministers, Kimberley and Knatchbull-Hugessen, both made strong defences of Britain's task in the undeveloped world.[64]

Already in 1870–1 the government had been forced to abandon its plan of relinquishing the Gambia to the French in exchange for concessions elsewhere. MPs from both parties protested, claiming that the people were 'all Protestants' who did not want to be handed over, that Britain had a duty to protect the natives from the slave trade, and that French rule there would be unacceptably military.[65] In 1872–3 Parliamentary and public pressure also drove the government to act against the slave trade in East Africa, assisted by media coverage in 1872 of Stanley's discovery of David Livingstone and of the latter's virtuous exploits. To Gladstone, the rhetoric

[61] W. H. Maehl, 'Gladstone, the Liberals and the election of 1874', *Bulletin of the Institute of Historical Research*, 36 (1963), 53–69.

[62] 'England's war', 144–6.    [63] 26 July 1871, pp. 737–8, 18 Dec. 1872, pp. 1289–90.

[64] Stembridge, *Parliament*, pp. 261–3.

[65] *Hansard*, 203:351, 365, 366, 15 July 1870 (Hay, Eastwick, Hughes). The new Colonial Secretary Kimberley then saw the benefits of retaining the territory: W. D. McIntyre, *The imperial frontier in the tropics, 1865–75* (London, 1967), pp. 106–9.

about protecting the natives from slavery and developing commerce in Africa was 'Bunkum'.[66] But in August 1872 the government announced its intentions to stamp out the trade; the *Nonconformist* claimed that this was the result of Livingstone's example. Naval pressure forced the Sultan of Zanzibar to sign a new anti-slave-trade treaty in 1873.[67] In 1873 the British public were further excited by the invasion of the Gold Coast by the Ashanti, who were demonised in the press as barbarous slavers. The War and Colonial Offices, with Wolseley on the spot, organised a march on the Ashanti capital Kumasi while the cabinet was in recess. Gladstone was 'aghast' at the expenditure, and the Gold Coast inevitably became a Crown Colony, but he admitted that a failure to act vigorously would have been very damaging.[68]

Anxiety about the drift of continental events and increasing concern to defend Britain's global position meant that Anglo-American relations also posed problems. Many Liberals wanted to cultivate good relations with America in order to reduce spending and as a symbol of Anglo-Saxon solidarity. In early 1871 the cabinet agreed to negotiate a treaty with the United States conceding that the long-running *Alabama* dispute should be settled by international arbitration. The Americans had claimed compensation for the damage done to Northern shipping during the Civil War by the Confederate steamer the *Alabama*, which the government had (unknowingly) allowed to leave Liverpool stacked with arms in 1862. The decision to go to arbitration was welcomed in some quarters as a commitment to the peaceful resolution of disputes. However, Britain had traditionally seen itself as the fair-minded arbitrator of the disputes of other less reasonable powers. Many Englishmen did not feel that the government – Palmerston's government – had a case to answer over the *Alabama*. And it was not principle but international weakness that had led to the acceptance of arbitration. American sponsorship of Irish Fenianism was one concern, while fear that Britain might have to go to war with Russia in late 1870 opened the prospect of a reverse *Alabama*, an opportunistic American attack on British shipping. In May 1869 the American demagogue Sumner had requested the cession of Canada as compensation for the indirect losses incurred by the North owing to the prolongation of the war, which he claimed was the fault of

[66] 21 Oct. 1873, *Ramm 1868–76*, vol. ii, p. 418.
[67] *Nonconformist*, 14 Aug. 1872, p. 840. See R. J. Gavin, 'The Bartle Frere mission to Zanzibar, 1873', *Historical Journal*, 5 (1962), 122–48.
[68] Harcourt, 'Gladstone, monarchism', 39–42; Powell, *Liberal by principle*, pp. 135–6; McIntyre, *Imperial frontier*, pp. 140–51.

the *Alabama*. Focusing once more on Canadian defence would reverse the cuts of the late 1860s.

There was, in fact, no alternative to arbitration, so cabinet ministers who felt that a resort to it would involve 'national dishonour' were outvoted.[69] Unfortunately the arbitration was bedevilled by rows with the United States, which demanded massive indirect claims. Only in June 1872, after many months of tension, when the affair was on the verge of collapse, was a way found of getting the indirect claims withdrawn. Kimberley, one of the 'national honour' party in the cabinet, felt that Gladstone and Granville were both too weak and that but for resistance in cabinet 'they would long ago have utterly disgusted the country'.[70] In September 1872 the arbitrators found against Britain to the tune of $15.5 million. This larger-than-expected award was an embarrassment, on grounds of economy and honour.[71] It was undoubtedly awkward to be bested by a 'democratic' ex-colony that had only just stopped tearing itself apart. The process also confirmed the fear that international opinion was unfriendly to Britain. Significantly, in 1873, Gladstone firmly distanced himself from those Radicals who wanted to make compulsory arbitration a permanent part of the international system, arguing that it would deny nations the chance to uphold their own interests and honour.[72] Though the settlement of the claims much reduced Anglo-American tension for the future, the intense disputes of 1871–2 revived the Civil-War-era English dislike of American assertiveness and added to British insecurity. Gladstone himself called the indirect claims something that 'no people with a spark of spirit [would] submit to at the point of death'.[73]

Coming on top of the European and African problems, the *Alabama* affair showed that international turbulence after 1870 had the same effect as in 1848, increasing Britain's sense of distinctness and suspicion of foreign regimes. One aspect of this was a noticeable panic about republicanism. Suspicion of it owed something to dislike of the demotic politics of Sumner's United States, but much more to the descent of defeated France into the confusion, misery and slaughter of the Commune between March and May 1871. Once again the French had veered from one political extreme to another; once again they dreamed of a socialist utopia; once again the

[69] Morley, *Gladstone*, vol. II, p. 403.    [70] 20 June 1872, *Kimberley*, p. 269.

[71] Some government ministers admitted their displeasure in public: Coleridge, *Nonconformist*, 30 Oct. 1872, p. 1107; Lowe, *Ramm 1868–76*, vol. II, p. 358. Gladstone and Granville were both disappointed; *Ramm 1868–76*, vol. II, pp. 341–2.

[72] *Hansard*, 217:73–82, 8 July 1873.    [73] *Hansard*, 209:86–7, 6 Feb. 1872.

overcentralised nature of the regime put France at the mercy of Parisian workers. Once again the eventual upshot was terrible bloodshed, as French troops reconquered the city and exacted revenge. Once again the inhumanity and immaturity of French politics lay revealed.[74] A vigorous republican movement in Spain and the revival of social unrest in Ireland added to the sense that Europe was witnessing a battle between authoritarian traditions in political and ecclesiastical affairs and the egalitarian values of republicanism and socialism. Argyll told Gladstone that the 'devilry' in Paris was 'a mockery of "civilisation" [and] a warning as to the real character of the modern forms of European Republicanism'.[75] The Commune stimulated a reaction of the propertied classes in Britain against democratising tendencies in British life, colouring their response, for example, to the strikes of 1872 and the trade union legislation of 1871. It increased the anxiety about overpopulation and unemployment at home – and thus strengthened the case for the colonies. It pointed up the evils of overcentralisation and socialism. The anti-Communard prejudices of the London clubs roused the wrath of the earnest young Millite Radical Amberley. But his more temperate cousin Arthur Russell pointed out that they 'after all contain all the political, legal, scientific & literary ability of England'.[76]

However, as Amberley's anger indicates, there was also some Radical sympathy with the aspirations of the Communards. Such sympathy was more limited than in 1848 and rarely unqualified; Mazzini, for example, felt that their sectional parochialism had betrayed the cause of real nationhood. Still, they had secured the French republic, and religious and civil liberty, against 'sacerdotal tyranny and monarchical selfishness'; they had defended local vitality after the overcentralisation of previous regimes; they had shown more patriotism than the French ruling classes.[77] The Commune played a small part, and the continuing influence of Mazzini and the dynamism of post-war America played a larger one, in stimulating artisan interest in republicanism in Britain. Republican clubs began to be founded, eighty-five in all by 1874, and the movement was supported by Bradlaugh and other high-profile Radical figures. At its most intellectual level, the republican movement was an attempt to revitalise progressive politics by creating a more civic-minded and egalitarian national tone. That was

---

[74] Raymond, *British policy*, pp. 387–95.
[75] Argyll to Gladstone, 30 May 1871, B. L. Add. Mss. 44102, f.26.
[76] 22 July 1871, Russell and Russell, *Amberley papers*, vol. II, p. 475.
[77] T. Wright, 'The English working classes and the Paris Commune', *Fraser's Magazine*, 4 (1871), 64; J. Mazzini, 'The Commune in Paris', *Contemporary Review*, 17 (1871), 307–18; W. T. M. Torrens, 'Localism and centralism', *Contemporary Review*, 17 (1871), 409–13.

certainly one attraction of it to Radical MPs like Dilke, Auberon Herbert and the Mazzinian P. A. Taylor. At the popular level, republicanism was often a shorthand all-purpose cry for the better representation of working-class interests in politics in the aftermath of 1867 and the need for a new Liberal agenda.[78]

However, the issue which crystallised these abstract notions in a visible movement in 1870–1 was more specific. One strand of the old Radical tradition had depicted the royal family as parasites on the taxpayer: as 'able-bodied paupers' or 'Royal spongers'.[79] Such arguments were kept alive by the Queen's invisibility after the death of Albert. They were also helped by critical popular press coverage of extravagant upper-class gambling and loose morals, particularly the lifestyle and debts of the prince of Wales – 'an incessant round of frivolous amusement'.[80] In 1870 his denial in court of adultery with Lady Mordaunt was far from universally believed. Then in 1871 the Queen requested Parliamentary grants to support two of her children, as Prince Arthur came of age and Princess Louise married. Much extra-Parliamentary criticism resulted, which was strengthened by the allegation that the Queen had consistently saved money for her private use from her annual civil list entitlement – especially since her widowed seclusion – and that taxpayers should expect her to use that money to support her children. This allegation was set out at length in an well-publicised anonymous tract, called *What does she do with it?*, sometimes said to be by Trevelyan. Fifty-one Radical MPs voted to reduce the annuity proposed for Prince Arthur in July 1871, though both grants were approved easily.

In November, to a popular audience in Newcastle, Dilke criticised the cost of the monarchy and the 'political corruption' that hung around it; he implied that Victoria exercised considerable power, and he claimed that a republic was a matter of 'education and time'.[81] The monarchist and Conservative press seized the opportunity to raise the alarm about Liberal-Radical republicanism. In fact, they greatly exaggerated its extent. In Parliament, most Radical opponents of the grants merely wanted to show that the reformed Commons could pressure the monarchy to be more

---

[78] D. Craig, 'The crowned republic? Monarchy and anti-monarchy in Britain, 1760–1901', *Historical Journal*, 46 (2003), 183.

[79] T. Wright, 'English republicanism', *Fraser's Magazine*, 3 (1871), 755.

[80] *Reynolds's Newspaper*, 10 Dec. 1871, quoted in Williams, *Contentious Crown*, p. 41. His mother and Gladstone were both aware of the damage caused to the monarchy: Fulford, *Your dear letter*, p. 300; 21 Dec. 1871, *GD*, vol. VIII, pp. 81–4.

[81] *The Times*, 9 Nov. 1871, p. 6.

accountable and more 'national', performing a service commensurate with its cost. Dixon, who proposed reducing Arthur's annuity, saw it as an *anti-republican* move to reassure the taxpayer.[82] Thomas Wright remarked in 1871 that working-class republicanism would be better named 'Utilitarianism', since its preoccupation was with reducing the cost and unaccountability of the Court. There was little sense of urgency about constitutional republicanism, since the monarch did not appear to be obstructing the political process. In its openness to public opinion, the polity was often described as a disguised republic – all the more so since the death of Albert, and the 1867 Reform Act, which had revived party government and limited the scope for Court interference in politics. The Radical George Potter suggested that republicanism in Britain would remain largely a theoretical movement as long as the monarchy remained of good character and the Crown and its ministers remained impartial between classes.[83] Indeed some of the anxiety about the lack of active royal moral leadership was not republican in any sense, but instead represented an earnest lament at the materialism and frivolity of high society, and a wish for a better tone to ward off social dislocation and 'restore a common pulse'.[84]

Nonetheless, the republican movement developed a high enough profile in 1871 to ensure a powerful patriotic reaction against it. In May 1871 Derby had noted that the combination of domestic Radical activity and socialism in Paris had created 'something like a panic . . . among the upper and middle classes'.[85] For most propertied and middle-class people, the monarchy was still a central symbol of national identity. Despite her failings, no one was a better exemplar of moral propriety than the Queen. She had lived her whole adult life around the principle that the royal family must set a positive example rather than the extravagant, foppish and exclusive one associated with her uncles. As Ludlow put it in 1870, in the modern, rational age there was less instinctive devotion and loyalty to monarchy, but a great deal of 'respectful friendship' to the Queen. One million people had waited to see her open Blackfriars Bridge in 1869.[86] Her daughter's wedding was extremely popular, not least because, unusually, she was marrying a Briton (indeed the son of a Liberal cabinet minister, Argyll). The Queen had

---

[82] *Hansard*, 208:584–5, 31 July 1871.
[83] Wright, 'English republicanism', 757, 759; Mundella, *Hansard*, 210:312, 19 Mar. 1872; Potter, *Non-conformist*, 19 Apr. 1871, pp. 372–3.
[84] These were the views of the young Rosebery in 1871: McKinstry, *Rosebery*, pp. 60–4.
[85] 6 May 1871, *Derby diary 1869–78*, pp. 79–80. In proposing the grant for Louise, Gladstone defended monarchy by making a comparison with French instability: *Hansard*, 204:179–80, 13 Feb. 1871.
[86] J. M. Ludlow, 'Europe and the war', *Contemporary Review*, 15 (1870), 659–60; Harcourt, 'Gladstone, monarchism', 25.

become aware of the unpopularity of using taxpayers' money to support the usual marriage candidates, the 'small German princes' with a 'foreign view . . . on all subjects' – and aware also of the diplomatic and popular awkwardness of 'great foreign alliances'.[87]

One event then triggered an eruption of this loyal sentiment: the dangerous illness of the prince of Wales with typhoid in December 1871. This was the disease that was believed to have killed his father in 1861; indeed the final crisis of Bertie's illness occurred on the very anniversary of that dreadful event. This was Victorian melodrama of a high order, which gripped the nation. The mainstream media orchestrated a coming together of the national family to celebrate a leading member's return to health. Even those critical of his past behaviour could relish the thought that he had been saved for a purpose, so that he might become a dutiful national servant, a proper son to his dead father. His recovery symbolised a politically healthy nation, with a sound constitution. In early 1872 there was exuberant popular enthusiasm for a service of thanksgiving for the Prince's escape – an opportunity for public participation in the national drama. The newspapers promoted it as an exuberant display of 'patriotic zeal' and 'union', 'a nation's renewed homage to the glorious principles that have maintained that nation in the foremost place of the world'.[88] In his epilogue to *Idylls of the King* – an Albertian as well as an Arthurian epic – written soon afterwards and dedicated to the Queen, Tennyson wrote of 'that rememberable day [when] London roll'd one tide of joy thro' all Her trebled millions', in loyal celebration of empire and global greatness. England was a 'crown'd Republic', strong enough, if it kept its 'common-sense', to defeat the enemies of the age: unbelief, 'lust for gold', cowardice and immoral art 'stol'n from France'.

Here was a reminder of the fact that the English already enjoyed an open political system and did not need to experiment, continental-style, with new constitutions. Working-class Radicalism quickly returned to its more practical and limited concerns. Meanwhile in 1872 a motion by Dilke to inquire into the Queen's expenditure, with a view to establishing whether her civil list income was excessive, was seized on by his opponents as an attempt to promote the republican agenda; it gained two votes in Parliament. The

---

[87] Victoria to the prince of Wales, 29 Nov. 1869, *LQV 1862–78*, vol. 1, pp. 632–3. Princess Louise married the marquess of Lorne, a Liberal MP and the son of Argyll. The Birmingham Liberal MP Dixon said that the marriage was 'an attack on caste and privilege' and claimed that Argyll was so poor that he had had to 'put a son in trade'. Jacob Bright pointed out that Louise advocated the education of women: *Nonconformist*, 8 Feb. 1871, pp. 126, 134. For the wedding's popularity, see Williams, *Contentious Crown*, pp. 49, 207 and *Nonconformist*, 8 Mar. 1871, p. 241.

[88] Williams, *Contentious Crown*, pp. 171–2 (*The Times, Sunday Times, Illustrated London News, Daily Telegraph*).

*Nonconformist* lambasted Dilke's campaign for merely turning an impractical issue into a vehicle for Conservative reaction. It was quite right. When
the crowds at the thanksgiving service cheered not Gladstone but Disraeli
– who quickly took up the allegation that republicanism was an unpatriotic
trait widely held on the Liberal left – it was obvious that a change of major
significance had occurred.[89]

The fate of the Gladstone government was essentially decided in the
eighteen months between the outbreak of the Franco-Prussian War and the
thanksgiving service. Indeed the worst of the damage was done by April–
May 1871, when party unity was being ripped apart by half-a-dozen major
issues at the same time and the state of the Commons was 'indescribable'.[90]
The inability to cut a dash in Europe and the impertinence of the Americans
over the indirect claims were great shocks to national pride. The emergence
of Prussian and Russian militarism, the revival of the defence panic, and
the complaints about the dominance of Manchester materialism left the
government with a degraded reputation which it had no hope of shaking
off. The outbreak of the Commune contributed to a middle-class panic
about the rise of Radicalism and irreligion at home, and raised the spectre
of a Continent divided between autocracy and bloody socialism. It ensured
an anxiety to defend British uniqueness, but also divided opinion on how
to do this. The attempt by Gladstone to keep alive an economy agenda
was doomed by the strong prevailing hostility to Manchesterism among
the men of 'honour'. The bid on the Liberal left to develop a variant on it
around ideas of civic republicanism was defeated by a staunchly patriotic
rallying to the monarchy. The Liberal party lost its way on all these issues.
At the same time, it also did so on its educational and Irish policy.

## RELIGION, EDUCATION AND IRELAND

The Liberal concern to strengthen the nation through Irish and educational
reform had resulted in Acts to disestablish the Anglican Church in Ireland
in 1869, to introduce a system of elementary education in England in 1870
and to abolish restrictive clerical tests in the English universities in 1871.
But it quickly became clear that there was no consensus about the relation between religion and the state. At a time of intense concern to shape
the morality of the expanded electorate, this was a problem. The Pope's

---

[89] *Nonconformist*, 29 Nov. 1871, p. 1174. See also Harcourt, 'Gladstone, monarchism', pp. 31–3.
[90] 29 Apr., 22 Aug. 1871, *Derby diary 1869–78*, pp. 78, 87–8; 8 May, 16 June, 6 July 1871, T. A. Jenkins,
'Trelawny, 1868–73', 432, 435, 438–9.

spiritual assertiveness at the Vatican Council, the collapse of his temporal power and the upsurge of socialist republicanism in France all added to the sense that clerical and secular principles were fighting for contention in Europe. Relief that England seemed to be sheltered from the worst excesses of both sides in this dispute strengthened the view that it should hold fast to its own religious identity and ideally purify it further. However, Liberals disagreed vehemently on how to do this, as the fallout from the compromise Education Act of 1870 quickly showed. Moreover, all discussions of English education were overshadowed by their implications for Ireland. Ireland, unlike Britain, seemed to be following the European path – once more. Priestly and secular nationalist forces were both increasingly dominant, in ways which alarmed most English Liberals. Gladstone's party was faced by all these problems. Unsurprisingly, it could not cope with them.

These tensions are best traced in three stages. The 1870 Education Act led, firstly, to a vigorous challenge by Radical Nonconformists to Anglican power. Secondly, the interrelationship between the English educational issue and the Irish question needs to be explored. Finally, the quandary about Irish policy has to be assessed in the light of the Vatican Council, the *Kulturkampf* in Germany and the revival of political unrest in Ireland itself. These three conflicts each divided the Liberal coalition, so that Anglicans, Nonconformists and Catholics all had major grievances against the government by 1874.

Nonconformist dislike of the Anglican tendencies of the 1870 Education Act led to the so-called 'Nonconformist revolt'. This created great tension between Dissenting activists and the Gladstone government, and it badly weakened Liberal harmony and focus after 1870. In that respect, it was very damaging. Paradoxically, however, its *electoral* impact has been exaggerated in Liberal historiography. Nonconformist defections bore little responsibility for the defeat of the Liberals at the 1874 election. This was because Nonconformists launched a large number of local struggles to win political control against their enemies in the Church and the Conservative party, and to counteract the effects of what they saw as government weakness in the face of clericalism. As a result, Nonconformists strengthened their grip on local Liberal politics and made the party appear more hostile to the Church, alienating many Anglican voters.[91]

---

[91] Parry, *Democracy and religion*, pp. 396–9. I have discussed the themes of this section in more local detail in Parry, 'Nonconformity, clericalism', pp. 152–80.

Nonconformists were undoubtedly angry that the 1870 Act set up a 'new Establishment' and a 'new Church rate' and gave a great boon to priesthood and sectarianism. The National Society took advantage of the bill to raise £5 million to spend on erecting new Anglican schools, helped by government building grants. This allowed the Church to dominate education in many areas and deflect pressure for a school board. In 1880 there were nearly three times as many children at denominational schools as at board schools. The local disarray of anti-clerical forces, combined with the cumulative vote, permitted Anglican and Catholic representatives to do disproportionately well at the inaugural school board elections in 1870. Clericals dominated many boards, even in unexpected places such as Birmingham. On the boards, Churchmen and Catholics very frequently allied to protect the interests of existing denominational schools. In many towns they built few, if any, board schools, arguing that there was vacant accommodation in their own schools that should be filled up first. Moreover, Clause 25 of the 1870 bill allowed school boards to pay, from the rates, the fees of parents at any school of the parents' choice, if they were too poor to pay.[92] Nonconformists complained that clerical boards could use the measure to give substantial sums from the rates to Anglican schools, thus weakening further the case for board schools. Catholics could also benefit from the Clause; there was a strong Catholic presence in the three towns which made by far the most use of Clause 25 – Manchester, Salford and Liverpool – and so Catholic schools received about a third of the total amount paid under it.

Over the next few years, Nonconformists focused their campaign against clerical influence particularly on 'Clause 25'. The government, solicitous of parents' rights (and Anglican and Catholic pressure), refused to repeal the Clause, creating great frustration among backbenchers and Dissenting activists. In April 1872, 132 MPs supported Candlish's motion to abolish it. Of 425 Liberal candidates 300 supported repeal at the 1874 election, and the rest were mostly in counties or Lancashire boroughs where it would have been foolish to declare for it.

The primary effect of the campaign against Clause 25 was to rally the party at local level against clericals and Conservatives. Nonconformists created from it a host of virtuous local battles, alleging that Anglican and Catholic denominationalists were developing an unholy alliance of priestcraft. In most towns with a substantial Dissenting presence, they

[92] In fact Section 25, once the Act received Royal Assent, but it remained Clause 25 in Nonconformist mythology.

could use the issue to make life too uncomfortable for Churchmen on boards. They could ultimately refuse to pay rates for denominational support, as had the 'martyrs' in the struggles of the 1830s and 1840s against Church rates.[93] But in most places, boards quickly rejected sectarian controversy and deliberately sought compromise so that the constructive work of education could continue. So most boards never implemented Clause 25, while boards that did so usually paid the fees of only a very small number of pauper children.[94] The London School Board set an important trend in the autumn of 1871 when, after much agonising, it essentially decided not to pay fees to denominational schools. The London formula was adopted in many other towns.[95]

The campaigns against Clause 25 benefited Nonconformist and Liberal organisation. The reaction against the denominationalist school board majorities in Liverpool and Manchester led directly to the formation of Nonconformist Associations in both towns, in Liverpool in December 1870 and in Manchester in February 1871. These aimed to form a permanent lobby protecting Nonconformist interests and promoting the cause of religious equality. At the Birmingham school board election of 1870 the shock defeat of those hostile to the funding of sectarian religious teaching prompted a vigorous campaign against Clause 25 by the Central Nonconformist Committee, which persuaded many nearby towns to form Nonconformist Associations. Organisation of this sort ensured that the 1873 school board elections established unsectarian majorities in most of the northern and midland Liberal strongholds – not just in Birmingham and Rochdale but also in Bradford, Leeds and Nottingham. After those elections the *Nonconformist* pointed out that there were 'very few towns indeed' in which the Church would be able to implement Clause 25 unless aided by Catholics, as in the major Lancashire boroughs.[96] In most urban areas where Liberals were strong, Clause 25 had essentially been defeated by local political action – while in Lancashire it was a mixed blessing for the Conservative party, since the Anglican–Catholic coalition on fee

---

[93] By 1873 there were occasional reports of such protests, e.g. *Nonconformist*, 25 June 1873, p. 651.

[94] See e.g. Robert Newton, *Victorian Exeter 1837–1914* (Leicester, 1968), p. 222. In the year ending September 1873, school boards paid £5,850 for school fees, out of their total expenditure of £1,174,985. In 1872 Manchester school board paid £2,471, Salford paid £934, Liverpool paid £818 and Bristol paid £320. But no other English board paid more than £100, only three paid more than £50 and only eleven others paid more than £10. See *Parliamentary Papers*, 1873, vol. LII, p. 271, 1875, vol. LVIII, p. 411.

[95] *Nonconformist*, 1 Nov. 1871, p. 1073, and e.g. 15 Nov. 1871, p. 1123 (Pembroke), 13 Dec. 1871, p. 1221 (Croydon, Devonport).

[96] *Nonconformist*, 29 Mar. 1871, p. 300, 3 Dec., 31 Dec. 1873, pp. 1197, 1304.

payment weakened the party's ability to exploit the popular anti-Catholicism which had given it such success in 1868.[97] Even in Liverpool there was a potent 'Protestant' and anti-concurrent endowment reaction against the Anglican–Catholic alliance on the school board, leading to its defeat in 1873.[98]

In other words, though the 'Nonconformist revolt' was an expression of discontent ·with Liberal government policy, it also allowed Nonconformists to mount a moral political campaign against Church vested interests. This campaign integrated them more effectively with local Liberal parties during the expansion of party organisation after enlargement of the electorate in 1867. Significant numbers of candidates for northern and midland towns adopted Nonconformist rallying-cries in the run-up to the 1874 election.[99] It also crucially strengthened Nonconformists' commitment to local municipal control of education and effectively killed any remaining voluntaryist sympathies among them. It gave them confidence that virtuous politics could be popular and that public opinion would come right in the end. It demonstrated the superior rectitude of provincial England and its ability to harness popular enthusiasm to defeat government timidity and clerical vested interest. The vigorous battle against Clause 25 seemed too aggressively sectarian for some Anglican Liberals and for some freethinkers not very interested in religious issues, and it undoubtedly encouraged the Conservative reaction against the Liberal government among Anglican voters.[100] But it increased Nonconformist confidence that the urban communities of Britain could be secured for righteousness.

Even more damaging to Liberal unity and purpose was the second level of the Radical Nonconformist campaign on education. Feeling the need to propose an alternative basis for a national education scheme, they adopted the secular solution – the restriction of formal school teaching to secular subjects, but allowing the various denominations to provide their own doctrinal education to children of that faith at certain times of the week. This solution had the merit of ruling out state endowment both for denominational

---

[97] For Conservative awkwardness in Liverpool, see N. Collins, *Politics and elections in nineteenth-century Liverpool* (Aldershot, 1994), p. 141.

[98] Ibid., pp. 125, 141; *Nonconformist*, 26 Nov. 1873, p. 1172.

[99] Parry, *Democracy and religion*, pp. 399–401.

[100] See e.g. Fawcett's attack on Nonconformist selfishness: *Hansard*, 217:578–83, 17 July 1873. John Morley told Chamberlain that many Radicals agreed with Fawcett: 23 July 1873, Joseph Chamberlain papers, University Library, Birmingham, 5/54/4. More generally, see Parry, *Democracy and religion*, chs. 6, 7.

education in England and for Ultramontane Catholic teaching in Ireland. So it was not just an attempt to amend the 1870 English Act; it was also promoted as the only virtuous and just policy for all parts of the United Kingdom. It was claimed to be the only truly 'national' solution to the educational dilemma: a continuation of the 1860s strategy of binding Ireland to a truly liberal kingdom.

The Irish Catholic bishops were demanding a state-supported Catholic university or college in Ireland and denominationalist reforms to the Irish national system of elementary education, on the grounds that mixed education endangered the 'faith and morals' of Catholics. In October 1871 they asserted that Ireland had a right to state support on the same terms as English denominational schools, and that they would oppose Parliamentary candidates who would not advocate denominational education in Ireland.[101] The government was expected to introduce legislation on elementary and higher education in Ireland, because of Gladstone's pledges at the 1868 election and a Royal Commission report of 1870, which suggested that religious instruction for each denomination should be provided in Irish national schools. In the light of the English legislation of 1870, and the Pope's aggressive behaviour at the Vatican Council, Nonconformists awaited this legislation with trepidation. J. A. Picton told the Congregational Union that, applied in Ireland, Clause 25 would hand education over to the priests without check, something unacceptable in 'even comparatively benighted Austria'.[102] Most Nonconformists asserted that the Irish laity were content with the national schools and the mixed colleges – and indeed that the priests were losing control over the lay mind, explaining their increasingly desperate political assertiveness.[103] Cardinal Cullen's ideas were not 'Irish ideas' but 'Italian' ones; he was asking the British taxpayer for the funds necessary to 'turn every school into a Papal chapel'.[104] The Central Nonconformist Committee joined with the Liverpool and Manchester Associations to organise a nationwide Nonconformist campaign, culminating in a conference of 1885 delegates at Manchester in January 1872. This conference declared in favour of the secular solution throughout the United Kingdom – and vowed that Nonconformists should not in normal circumstances support Parliamentary candidates who were unsympathetic to this and to other changes to the 1870 Act. No disagreement was voiced

---

[101] *The Times*, 21 Oct. 1871, p. 3.     [102] *Nonconformist*, 24 May 1871, p. 529.

[103] *Nonconformist*, 6 Dec. 1871, p. 1201. The controversy surrounding priestly behaviour at the Galway by-election in early 1872 later strengthened these arguments: *Nonconformist*, 19 June 1872, p. 645.

[104] G. Payne Jarvis, in *Report of the general conference of Nonconformists, held in Manchester, January 23, 24, and 25, 1872* (Manchester, 1872), p. 224; *Nonconformist*, 24 January 1872, p. 93.

at the conference, and definite and genuine enthusiasm for the policy was expressed at scores of local gatherings afterwards.[105]

The swift adoption of the secularist policy was intended as a guide and warning to the government in framing its Irish educational policy, which was due to be unveiled in 1872. Dale was horrified that Gladstone appeared to be governing Ireland on 'Irish principles' instead of British ones. It was Ireland that preoccupied Dale the most in his ground-breaking lecture on *The politics of Nonconformity* in Manchester in November 1871, and it was the endowment of denominationalism in Ireland, not Clause 25, on which he then threatened that Nonconformists would break up the party. The Irish bishops' pretence to speak as 'divinely-constituted guardians of faith and morals' reminded him, he said, of the outrageous claims of the late-medieval Catholic Church. He asserted that the fight against them was no less urgent than the Reformation struggle in which the English people had first revealed their 'great qualities'.[106] As the *Daily News* correspondent wrote of the Manchester conference: 'Cardinal Cullen has taken his whip in hand and driven them over in a body to secular education.'[107] How else could the pretensions of the Catholic Church, especially in the educational field, be tackled? Most continental states had responded to Romanist assertiveness by repressive state tactics of endowment and control that were not acceptable to Nonconformists. Instead, religious equality and freedom must be asserted, on a genuinely national basis. One reason why it was urgent to end state endowment of denominational education in England was that Irish complaints that they were not getting the same privileges were stimulating a movement for Home Rule.

The secularist policy was also seen as a way of promoting true religion in Britain, against the threat from state and priestly activity and from secular democracy. Only through the free and earnest teaching of doctrinal Christianity could the 'barbarism' of modern society – 'the wildness of the passions' endangering civilisation – be tackled.[108] The secular solution marked the rejection of the compromise of officially backed 'undenominational' teaching, agreed as the basis of board school teaching in the 1870 Act. Earnest Nonconformists thought this hardly worth the name of religion, given the number of doctrinal compromises necessary to create

---

[105] *Nonconformist*, 8 May 1872, p. 487, 29 May 1872, pp. 568–9, 19 and 26 June 1872, pp. 638, 658, 14 August 1872, pp. 833–4.
[106] R. W. Dale, *The politics of Nonconformity: a lecture* (Manchester, 1871), pp. 25–9. See Dale's comments in *GD*, vol. viii, 66n5.
[107] *Daily News*, 24 January 1872, p. 3. See also *Nonconformist*, 21 February 1872, p. 186.
[108] H. W. Crosskey, 'The Nonconformist programme and policy', *Theological Review*, 9 (1872), 369.

something acceptable to such a wide variety of denominations. Dale argued that the 'new Establishment' of state-supported religious teaching was in some ways worse than the old one, because 'the necessity of having regenerate persons to teach Divine truth was ignored'. 'The training of the will to religious submission' could not be done by any state official; to help conquer sin, 'spiritual energy' was essential.[109] The continental educational systems showed the dangers of leaving religion to be taught by state functionaries. In France and Germany Voltairean 'bureaucrats' had been put in charge of religious education and, caring only to keep their state salaries, supplied mechanical and formulaic instruction. This had made Germany increasingly 'sceptical and infidel', while in France Christianity was presented in a 'perverted and debased form', with devastating effects on social cohesion. The 'evil working of the State–Church connexion' had led to the Commune.[110]

Not surprisingly, therefore, the educational furore also strengthened Nonconformist commitment to the principle of disestablishment of the Church of England, on the same principle – that it was the only way to preserve the vigour and purity of English religious life. In 1872 the veteran Liberation Society activist Edward Miall claimed that 'if Christianity is not to be killed by the Establishment, Christianity must kill the Establishment'.[111] The publicity given to Anglo-Catholic excesses within the Church alarmed Nonconformists further. A Judicial Committee ruling of 1872 (the Bennett judgment), and the movement to allow confession in the Church in 1873, suggested that the Established Church structure was not able to halt the spread of proto-Catholic doctrines and practices. The growth of ritualism also seemed to show the Church's inability to agree on the fundamental truths essential to a religious life. Dale told a Birmingham meeting of the Liberation Society in October 1872 that a 'comprehensive church' was 'a church which took everybody in'.[112] Ritualism demonstrated the same message as passionless erastianism or country-clergyman apathy: that the Church was a body more concerned with endowments and materialism than with the nation's spiritual salvation. In May 1873 the *Nonconformist* remarked that the conflict over disestablishment was one 'between the material and spiritual elements of English

[109] Dale at the Annual Meeting of the Liberation Society, *Nonconformist*, 2 May 1872, p. 454; R. W. Dale, 'The conference of Nonconformists', *British Quarterly Review*, 55 (1872), 520–2.

[110] *Nonconformist*, 2 May 1872, pp. 452 (Holden), 454 (Rogers), 19 June 1872, p. 636 (Richard); H. Allon, 'Why Nonconformists desire disestablishment', *Contemporary Review*, 17 (1871), 381.

[111] *Nonconformist*, 2 October 1872, p. 1005.

[112] *Nonconformist*, 9 October 1872, p. 1025. See also 19 June 1872, p. 633, 10 December 1873, p. 1213.

life'.[113] In 1871 Miall moved in the Commons for the disestablishment of all Churches in the United Kingdom, collecting eighty-nine votes. The Liberation Society then agitated the issue in the country, holding 222 meetings in 1872 and 269 in 1873. Miall introduced two more motions in 1872 and 1873, and in May 1873 the Crewe meeting of the main Nonconformist associations urged 'decided political action' to promote disestablishment, including 'every effort to return supporters of religious equality' at the next election.[114] In January 1873, the *Congregationalist* applauded this bout of Dissenting assertiveness against the feeble Whig tradition, seeing it as an overdue return to the Cromwellian era when 'our forefathers held sway in England'.[115]

Secularism and disestablishment also excited some ethically minded secular Radicals, keen to take a stand for intellectual freedom and desperate to find a cause to rally Liberals after the disasters of 1870–2. For them, these were the equivalents in religious policy of the constitutional interest in civic republicanism: a way of drawing on uplifting international radical ideals in order to build a humane community. John Morley, editor of the *Fortnightly Review*, believed that the development of a truly national education system on an elected local basis, free from religious control, was 'the greatest of public interests', the necessary foundation of an educated democracy. He was also particularly conscious of the need, across Europe, to find a way to preserve the freedom of the individual at the same time as the state was intervening more for the common good. He felt that secular education and religious freedom were the only bases on which this could be done. And, perhaps most importantly, national education would offer 'flaccid and aimless' Liberalism a great galvanising cause.[116] In 1873 Morley came together with Chamberlain to build up the National Education League as a modern equivalent of Cobden's Anti-Corn Law League. In 1873 the League fielded a candidate at the Bath by-election against the official Liberal. Secularism was the official policy of Chamberlain's Liberals in their successful campaign at the Birmingham school board elections in late 1873. In the same year Chamberlain, following Dilke, unfurled a broader American-influenced programme of 'Free Church, Free Land, Free Schools, Free Labour'.[117] But

---

[113] *Nonconformist*, 1 May 1873, p. 421. See Tillett at Ipswich, in *Nonconformist*, 22 October 1873, p. 1047.

[114] *Nonconformist*, 4 June 1873, p. 564, 18 June 1873, p. 611. S. M. Ingham, 'The disestablishment movement in England, 1868–74', *Journal of Religious History*, 3 (1964–5), 52.

[115] Cited in R. Howell, '"Who needs another Cromwell?": the nineteenth-century image of Oliver Cromwell', in R. C. Richardson (ed.), *Images of Oliver Cromwell: essays for and by Roger Howell, Jr* (Manchester, 1993), pp. 102–3.

[116] D. A. Hamer, *John Morley: Liberal intellectual in politics* (Oxford, 1968), pp. 92–107; J. Morley, *The struggle for national education* (London, 1873), pp. 108–9, 111.

[117] For Dilke, see *Nonconformist*, 15 Jan. 1873, p. 65.

for him and Morley, education and increasingly the broader question of disestablishment were to be the priorities. Such aspirations fuelled inevitable
allegations that English advocates of secularism had the same aims as foreign
freethinkers and republicans.[118]

This combination of a vigorous Nonconformist agitation for Church
disestablishment, and heterodox Radical demands for the removal of Bible
education from the official school timetable, created immense controversy. At a time of propertied and middle-class anxiety about working-class
morals, and about the health of national Protestantism, a profound reaction in favour of the institutional support of biblical Christianity was
inevitable. This was led by the Conservative party and the Church, but
Liberal opponents of secularism included most Liberal Anglicans and Wesleyan Methodists, and indeed significant numbers of the main Nonconformist sects. A group of the latter centred in London had organised a
protest against the secular policy in the early summer of 1872: 1,950 of
them eventually signed a petition against it, including famous preachers
such as Newman Hall and Charles Spurgeon.[119] The leading Unitarian
James Martineau said that secularism would play into the hands of priests
and parsons, while the teaching of the Bible was the best way to create a common basis for national Christianity.[120] As noted in chapter 2,
some Nonconformists were increasingly unenthusiastic about disestablishment now that Church and state were freer from aristocratic control and
corruption.

One Liberal (and Conservative) defence of Bible teaching in schools and
of a nationwide Church Establishment was that they were pillars of communal order and harmony, whereas secularism was a social dissolvent. They
emphasised moral duty and the importance of doing right; they helped
to keep men 'good Christians and therefore good citizens'. They upheld
law and order and respect for property; they introduced 'the principles of
Christianity into men's social and civil relations': they helped to moderate
warfare between class and class; they enhanced the sense of community
and interdependence; they made men less prone to gratify their selfish passions.[121] In all these ways they helped to discipline and guide the enlarged
electorate after 1867, and to civilise the poor. But this was not just a question

---

[118] E.g. *Spectator*, 6 July 1872, 842.

[119] *Nonconformist*, 15 May 1872, pp. 505, 509, 31 July 1872, p. 787; Parry, *Democracy and religion*, p. 336.
There were originally eight hundred signatures and so the group was often known as 'the eight
hundred'.

[120] *Nonconformist*, 29 May 1872, pp. 568–9. Scottish Liberals were even less inclined to accept secularism:
the overwhelming dominance of Presbyterian religion north of the border meant that there was a
general consensus on the value of religious teaching in schools.

[121] Parry, *Democracy and religion*, pp. 86, 98, 106–10.

of crude social control; it was also about sustaining a moral community of the sort that had made England great. It was Protestantism and individual responsibility that had driven England's economic success and global expansion and had ensured not only recent stability but the past Radical triumphs that underpinned that stability. Biblical Christianity had defined the nation's character and history. The Wesleyan William McArthur said that the Bible had 'made our nation what it was'.[122]

The Liberal Anglican view of the national Church was as a community defined by Parliament and public opinion. The Establishment kept Britain 'open to all the good influences which God is breathing through the world' – including the progress of the educated mind.[123] The national Church safeguarded Britain against the anti-social, narrowing, formalising tendencies of priestcraft. Priestcraft discouraged men and women from thinking and often gave them the impression that fidelity to particular practices, rather than a moral life, was the essence of true religion, thus justifying their selfish passions and pleasures – a trait intensified by the Catholic practice of confessing sins, which some high churchmen wished to introduce into the Church of England in the early 1870s. Clinging to such rituals also increased partisanship and sectionalism rather than unity in the Church and gave the impression that the priest had special access to divine truths which gave him superior powers. Hostility to the events unfolding at the Vatican Council had strengthened Liberal backbench interest in 'undenominational' education in the course of the debates on the 1870 Education Bill, leading to restrictions on the freedom of religious sects to teach their own doctrines in schools.[124] Liberal Anglicans argued that, by checking sectionalism and sacerdotalism, English political control of the Church had maintained the same balance between law and liberty as had operated in political life. A disestablished Church, however, would become more ecclesiastical and less political – less in tune with the nation's political development.[125] Secular education would drive the teaching of religion into the Sunday schools and into priestly hands, and it would create more sectarianism, less efficiency and the 'demoralisation and de-civilisation of the people'.[126] These arguments were equally attractive to pious but undoctrinaire broad churchmen and to modern-minded, anti-clerical and almost post-religious

---

[122] *Nonconformist*, 1 Mar. 1871, p. 202.
[123] J. Ll. Davies, 'Erastianism *versus* ecclesiasticism', *Contemporary Review*, 30 (1877), 164.
[124] Parry, *Democracy and religion*, pp. 301–6.     [125] Ibid., pp. 91–102.
[126] See Bishop Fraser, quoted in *Nonconformist*, 2 Oct. 1872, p. 1011; *The National Church: a monthly record of Church work and of the proceedings of the Church Defence Institution throughout the country*, 2:62 (March 1873).

men for whom the main attraction of an undenominational education was that it put the dangerous and divisive ecclesiastical temper firmly in its place.

Gladstone spoke very truly when in 1872 he remarked that advanced Nonconformists were mistaken to think that Englishmen's dislike of the papacy's assertiveness would have the same effect as on the Continent, that is, to make them more willing to take up the idea of Free Churches. Rather, the turbulent state of religio-political affairs abroad seemed more likely to have created a 'reaction' among Englishmen, increasing their attachment to the Church Establishment as an effective agent of social stability and symbol of national identity.[127] The Conservatives lost no time in exploiting this feeling, rallying Anglican and Wesleyan opinion in favour of national religion, morality and the status quo. The increasing success of Nonconformists in converting Liberal candidates in many northern and midland boroughs to the disestablishment cause seemed to be a sign of the way that Liberal politics were developing; their organised agitation, buttressed by the caucus, appeared likely to force the Liberal leadership to convert to its policies. Chamberlain's activism, and the caucus-inspired victory of the secularists at the Birmingham school board election, was a major propaganda coup for the Conservatives. The unpopularity of secularism as a policy for school boards in Britain quickly became apparent: Bright snapped to Chamberlain in August 1873 that it was abundantly clear that 'the public . . . are in favour of some religious teaching'.[128] The Conservative party benefited greatly from their twin cries of the 'Bible in the school' and 'the Church in danger'. After the 1874 defeat, Chamberlain admitted that even many Nonconformists had been 'carried over to the enemy by the "Bible" cry', though most of these were probably Wesleyans.[129] Gladstone's warning to Miall in the 1872 debate on disestablishment had been vindicated: that an immense number of long-standing social, family and propertied as well as religious interests were bound up with the Church Establishment and that it would be foolish to launch a premature attack on it.[130]

---

[127] *Hansard*, 212:576, 2 July 1872.

[128] J. L. Garvin, *The life of Joseph Chamberlain: I: 1836–1885* (London, 1932), p. 141. For the unpopularity of secularism (except in Wales), see J. Murphy, *Church, state and schools in Britain, 1800–1970* (1971), p. 69.

[129] A. Peel (ed.), *Letters to a Victorian editor: Henry Allon editor of the 'British Quarterly Review'* (1929), p. 43. On the Church defence issue at by-elections, the 1874 general election, and the 1873 London school board elections, see Parry, *Democracy and religion*, pp. 338–9, 404–7, and 'Nonconformity, clericalism'. For Wesleyan acceptance of the national system as a result of the controversy, see pp. 175–6.

[130] *Hansard*, 212:575, 2 July 1872.

Ireland cast a long shadow over British debates about education and Establishment in 1870–4. But it was even more problematic as a policy problem in its own right. As noted in chapter 5, the Liberal Irish reforms of the late 1860s aimed to bolster the integrity of the empire and to ward off the dual anti-British threats of Fenianism and Ultramontanism. Since this was a 'British' policy more than an 'Irish' one, tensions between British Liberals and Irish leaders would probably have revived in any event. But the international events of 1870–1 exacerbated those tensions, and the result was the destruction of not only the government's Irish policy but also Liberal unionism in most of Ireland.

The first problem for British opinion was that Irish disorder and political agitation did not die down on the passage of the Irish Church and Land Acts of 1869–70, requiring the British government to consider repressive legislation. A Peace Preservation Act had to be introduced in 1870, but Ribbonist agitation persisted in Westmeath. Worse, the continued imprisonment of Fenian prisoners, in the aftermath of the 1867 rising, strengthened secular Irish nationalism by romanticising the individual prisoners. Their fate seemed to belie the rhetoric of national integration. Nearly all Irish Liberal MPs joined the Amnesty Association, which argued that their release was necessary in order to show government trust of the Irish people. Though some prisoners were freed in February 1869, most of the leaders were not, and Isaac Butt led a revived campaign for their freedom from June 1869, involving forty monster meetings. The convict Rossa was sensationally elected to Parliament at the Tipperary by-election in late 1869.

The battle over the prisoners divided Gladstone from his Irish administration, especially after the outbreak of the Franco-Prussian War in 1870. Gladstone believed that releasing them would improve relations with the United States, lessen the risk to Canada and weaken American support for Fenianism. After the fall of Napoleon he was also alarmed that a new, extremist French regime might stimulate Irish republicanism, and he hoped that an early prisoner release would remove the main grounds for such a movement. Predictably, however, the same fear of a revival of republicanism in Europe made his Irish ministers and officials hostile to further releases. The French example raised fears of a revolution in Ireland and hardened British middle-class opinion against Irish radicalism. Gladstone gained a partial victory and it was decided to release all but eight prisoners in late 1870, but this was not a popular decision in Britain, especially when he followed it with a refusal to accept the recommendation of the Irish Office to suspend Habeas Corpus in Westmeath. Instead he insisted that Parliament should summon a select committee to determine whether such an act was needed. This demonstration of executive weakness in face of agitation was so unpopular in the metropolitan press and on the Liberal backbenches that Disraeli had to leave the Commons with fifty Conservative MPs in order to prevent the government being defeated on it.[131] Habeas Corpus was eventually suspended in Westmeath in June 1871, while the release of the remaining Fenians was now inconceivable before 1874.

Waning British sympathy for Irish liberties gave enormous impetus to Irish interest in increased self-government. The Home Government Association had been formed in 1870, originally as a constitutional forum for the expression of Irish opinion, in the hope of achieving greater input into British policy-making. It began as an elite cross-denominational organisation, reflecting some Protestant unease at Church disestablishment, a general wish for increased local powers, and a coolness towards rampant English Liberal free-trading progressive rhetoric. In 1871 it developed a popular momentum, as the cry of 'Home Rule' became a successful one at by-elections. Its leader, Isaac Butt, and three other MPs were all elected on that ticket in 1871, helped by their advocacy of the Fenian prisoner cause and tenant interests. However, they also identified with the Catholic demand for securities for denominational education.

Perhaps the most striking element of the emerging Home Rule movement was its ability to exploit the times by combining secular and Catholic grievances. Fenianism had been predominantly anti-clerical and the priests had often responded in kind, opposing its candidates at elections, but after 1870 tension of this sort between 'nationalist' and clerical politics abated in most areas. Some clergy sympathised with the Home Rule movement; some declined to contest its popularity; candidates, for their part, were generally ready to support Catholic demands in the battle against Protestant power.[132] One reason why Cullen, the leader of the bishops, was so determined to demand more securities for denominational education, at elementary and university level, was to keep religious issues at the forefront of Irish politics. This would maintain the Church's influence and check the rise of anti-clerical Fenian or Mazzinian nationalism in Ireland. He had some success: Fenianism lost ground to a broader Home Rule movement

---

[131] Parry, *Democracy and religion*, pp. 316–19, 372. Gladstone began to call for release immediately on hearing of Napoleon's defeat at Sedan: *GD*, vol. VII, pp. 352, 360–2. For middle-class opinion, see Raymond, *British policy*, p. 141.

[132] Inevitably local circumstances differed: see M. Hurst, 'Ireland and the Ballot Act of 1872', *Historical Journal*, 8 (1965), 336–40; D. Thornley, *Isaac Butt and Home Rule* (London, 1964), pp. 117–19; Comerford, *Fenians in context*, pp. 189–94; J. O'Shea, *Priest, politics and society in post-famine Ireland: a study of County Tipperary 1850–1891* (Dublin, 1983), pp. 160–3.

which appealed to Irish Catholic identity, and in 1873 the majority of the
Irish Republican Brotherhood decided that physical-force solutions were
now inappropriate. Believing that the institutions of religion and morality must be strengthened against democracy and irreligion across Europe,
Cullen was suspicious of the secularising influence of English rule as well
as Irish secular nationalism. His answer was uncompromising; in 1872 he
told the clergy of Dublin that the 'nationality of Ireland means simply the
Catholic Church'.[133]

Cullen and the bishops therefore became more intransigent in demanding support for denominationalism. But in British eyes this intransigence
seemed part of a European movement against liberalism, evident in the
Vatican Council and the Catholic Church's behaviour in Germany. So the
defence of 'mixed' education, at elementary and particularly at university
level, became a major issue for Liberal MPs. There was great backbench
sympathy with Henry Fawcett's proposal to abolish religious tests in the
Protestant Trinity College Dublin, thus creating two mixed universities in
Ireland (the other being Queen's) which would be beyond priestly control
and could educate the rising middle class. The abolition of religious tests in
the English universities in 1871 made this seem all the more logical a policy.
Moreover, British Conservatives also united around a policy of undenominational education in Ireland once the Protestants of Trinity themselves
decided to accept it as the best way of thwarting the Catholic threat.[134]
Thus Gladstone was caught in an extremely difficult situation. He believed
that Irish Catholics had a legitimate higher-education grievance owing to
the lack of good denominational provision. He wanted to use the issue
to defend all sects' right to receive their own religious teaching, and yet
to build up a lay Irish Catholic elite liberated from the papal yoke. Not
once but twice, in 1870 and 1872, Gladstone made Irish university policy
a question of confidence in the government, in order to prevent a massive backbench rebellion in favour of adopting Fawcett's motion. On both
occasions he did so with a remarkable outburst of ill-temper.[135]

His refusal to accept something like Fawcett's solution created a considerable stir. In September 1871 G. H. Whalley, Liberal MP for Peterbor-
ough, called a public meeting which demanded to know if Gladstone was

[133] H. Jenkins, 'The Irish dimension of the British *Kulturkampf*: Vaticanism and civil allegiance, 1870–
    1875', *Journal of Ecclesiastical History*, 30 (1979), 363; Norman, *Catholic Church*, p. 441; Comerford,
    *Fenians in context*, p. 203.
[134] For Liberal complaints, see Parry, *Democracy and religion*, p. 320, and Roebuck in H. Jenkins, 'Irish
    dimension', 353.
[135] Parry, *Democracy and religion*, pp. 180–1, 300, 347–8.

himself a Roman Catholic. The government minister most susceptible to Catholic pressure, Chichester Fortescue, caused a storm with a speech in October 1871 suggesting that the government was preparing concessions to the Catholics in Irish elementary education. The Irish Secretary, Hartington, a firm Protestant, had to quash this notion in an uncompromising address at Knighton in January 1872, denying that the government would hand the education of the Irish over to the priests. This speech in turn had serious consequences in Ireland, where it was primarily responsible for uniting clergymen and secular Radicals behind the victorious Home Rule candidates at the Kerry and Galway by-elections of February 1872. Irish feeling was even more enraged by the aftermath of the Galway election: Judge Keogh's swingeing criticisms of clerical morals and influence at the election, as he declared the Home Rule candidate Nolan unseated. On the publication of his evidence, Commons pressure, led by the vigorously 'Protestant' Liberal Henry James and by many Conservatives, forced the ministry to mount a disastrously unsuccessful prosecution of one Catholic bishop and twenty-three priests.[136] This prosecution united Irish opinion against the government; yet the rapid growth of Home Rule sentiment in Ireland increased alarm in Britain that Gladstone would make concessions to them in order to win their support in Parliament. The O'Keeffe affair – the dismissal of an Irish schoolmaster by the Commissioners of National Education after the Catholic Church hierarchy had suspended him as a priest – received wide publicity in Britain because it suggested that the bishops already controlled Irish education. One vehemently Protestant Liberal, Bouverie, asked whether the Commissioners had become 'the instruments of a foreign ecclesiastical power'.[137]

In such a climate, Gladstone's long-awaited Irish University Bill of February 1873 had no chance of success. He proposed a new national university examining board to which Trinity and any number of denominational Catholic colleges could affiliate, without state endowment. But the university would not be able to appoint professors, or examine, in philosophy or history, if this offended denominational scruples on these sensitive subjects, and all professors could be penalised if the authorities considered that they had offended religious sentiment (the so-called 'gagging clauses'). Cullen was alienated by the lack of endowment, by the temptation that the financial resources of Trinity would offer to a young Catholic layman, and by the fear that controversial evolutionists like Darwin or Huxley could be appointed to chairs at the university. The bishops duly declared against

---

[136] Ibid., pp. 326–7, 343, 349–50.    [137] Ibid., pp. 350, 370–1; *Hansard*, 213:516, 5 Aug. 1872.

the bill.[138] On the other hand, a lot of British opinion was alarmed by the possibility that denominational colleges with representation on the examining board could come to swamp the university, and by the restrictions on the teaching and examining of key subjects, which seemed contrary to the very purpose of a liberal university. In a bid to limit British opposition, the government panicked and declared that in committee it would not be bound to most of the details. The Irish revolt intensified, a hard core of British Protestants and intellectual Liberals still opposed the bill, and the government was sensationally defeated in March 1873 on the second reading.[139]

The immediate consequences of the defeat – the temporary resignation of the government and its forced return to office – were embarrassing enough: it never regained momentum or authority before the dissolution and electoral rout of early 1874. But the broader consequences were arguably worse. Firstly, it raised abstract Church–state issues that brought out divisions among British Liberals. Henry Reeve declared that 'the opposition of civil liberty to clericalism is in all parts of Europe the great principle of the age'.[140] In March 1872 *The Times* had agreed with Bismarck that the papacy was trying to rally European Catholics to overthrow the German empire as the new symbol of European Protestantism, though it was confident that the plot would be defeated.[141] But Liberals differed on how far state power should be used to oppose these Romanist presentations.

This was apparent in British reactions to Bismarck's *Kulturkampf* to discipline the Catholic Church in Germany. In one corner were erastians, like the aged Russell and A. P. Stanley, evangelicals (including some evangelical Nonconformists) and Carlylean advocates of the strong state such as Fitzjames Stephen and the writers on the *Pall Mall Gazette*. For all these men the Germans were quite correct to assert the right of the state to dictate the terms by which Catholic priests should operate.[142] Stephen believed that no compromise was possible: either the Church or the state must be supreme, and the state was the better defender of wisdom and reason, which were 'the best and highest authority we have'.[143] In the other corner were the Radical pro-disestablishment Nonconformists, the positivists,

---

[138] Spencer memo., 25 Feb. 1873, *Red Earl*, vol. I, pp. 104–6.

[139] Parry, *Democracy and religion*, pp. 353–66.

[140] 'The claims of Whig government', *Edinburgh Review*, 137 (1873), 575.

[141] F. A. Arlinghaus, 'British public opinion and the *Kulturkampf* in Germany, 1871–1875', *Catholic Historical Review*, 34 (1948–9), 386.

[142] Ibid., 391n24, 399–400.

[143] J. F. Stephen, 'Caesarism and Ultramontanism' [Part II], *Contemporary Review*, 23 (1873–4), 1016–17.

some other Radicals, and clerical advocates of ecclesiastical independence such as Gladstone. For these people, state interference with religious beliefs and practices was offensive and despotic, and the only way to defeat Romanism without encouraging materialism was by spiritual energy or intellectual counter-argument.[144] In the middle were many Liberals who were instinctively opposed to clericalism and were supportive of Establishment and law as a way of regulating potentially oppressive priestly behaviour, but who came to dislike the illiberalism of the Falk Laws, which substituted state for Church disciplinary authority and permitted the sacking of uncooperative priests. *The Times*, for example, started by arguing that Bismarck's policy was in harmony with 'the old German and the old English principles of national authority', seen at the Reformation, but by October 1873 decided that it would have been preferable to trust to 'English common sense to baffle the common enemy'. Most of the British press were hostile to the enforcement of the Laws. For the *Spectator*, Bismarck was an Orangeman not a Liberal. Even the Whiggish *Edinburgh Review* argued that, though a state undoubtedly had an abstract *right* to bring Churches within its dominion to heel, it was bad *policy* to place clergymen under what Odo Russell called 'military discipline'. It would be counterproductive, engendering sympathy for the Church, and, if it succeeded, it would lead to a growth of scepticism and 'the worship of money and force'.[145]

Moreover, the Conservatives exploited these tensions by taking up an issue that became a milder, English equivalent of the *Kulturkampf* – the question of how far to strengthen the Church of England's own hands to discipline ritualist High Anglican priests. The agitation against ritualism and its supposedly Catholicising influence on the Church was at its height in the early 1870s. Even Gladstone noted that the apparently increasing preference of the wealthy for ornate churches and ritualist services 'may represent not the spiritual growth, but the materializing tendencies of the age'.[146] The Queen and archbishop of Canterbury led those who wanted action to safeguard the Protestant nature of the Church of England. One of Disraeli's first acts as Conservative Prime Minister in 1874 was to acknowledge their pressure by giving time to the Public Worship Regulation Bill,

---

[144] See e.g. E. Jenkins, 'Bismarckism in England', *Contemporary Review*, 22 (1873), 107–25 for an attack on Stephen for not understanding true spirituality.

[145] Arlinghaus, 'British public opinion', 395–8; F. H. Geffcken and H. Reeve, 'Prince Bismarck and the Church of Rome', *Edinburgh Review*, 139 (1874), 363, 380–1; Urbach, *Bismarck's favourite Englishman*, p. 168.

[146] J. Bentley, *Ritualism and politics in Victorian Britain: the attempt to legislate for belief* (Oxford, 1978), p. 25.

which increased the bishops' powers to discipline ritualist priests. This was
part of his strategy to uphold the Church as a Protestant *via media* for the
defence of true faith in the Europe-wide battle between Catholicism and
secularism.[147] But, as Disraeli also realised, the bill badly divided Gladstone from most Anglican Liberals. Harcourt took the lead in supporting
it, arguing that Parliament must protest against Romish practices in the
national Church and stand firm against papal pretensions across Europe.
Gladstone, however, disliked state meddling with Church independence.
Radical Nonconformists tended to share his views, but did not help his
predicament by arguing that the logical consequence of his position was
to accept the disestablishment of the Church of England, the only just
solution to the great battle between Churches and states.[148] The rows of
the 1874 session played an important part in persuading him to resign the
Liberal leadership in 1875.

The controversy over Roman Catholic political ambitions also increased
British suspicion of Irish Catholicism. *The Times* felt that 'the Rome which
molests Germany and menaces its disruption . . . is the same Rome which
in these Isles fraternizes with every form of sedition and affiliates every
movement against the peace and union of the realm'.[149] Reeve announced
in the *Edinburgh Review* that the Irish Catholic clergy, already possessing
'a degree of freedom . . . which they certainly do not possess in any other
country', claimed to exercise 'a supreme control over civil rights', through
'the injunctions of the Pope and his agents'. To oppose this was to maintain 'the great principles of national independence', the very basis of the
constitution since the Reformation.[150] Many anti-clerical Liberals were
merely reverting to type in arguing such things – many had not sought
an alliance with Catholicism in the first place, and like Brand, Palmerston's chief whip, felt Irish Catholics to be 'the natural enemies of a Liberal
government'.[151]

Paradoxically, the Irish university defeat also caused a break between
Gladstone, the greatest defender of denominational claims in the government, and the Irish Catholics. Though to his anti-clerical critics within
the Liberal party Gladstone looked to be a defender of priesthood, his real
motivation had been opposition to state interference with the freedom of
believers in all sects to teach and receive Christian doctrine as they wished.
For the Irish Catholic priesthood he had little time, because of his fixed
belief that they themselves were driven not by patriotic but by Romanist

[147] Parry, 'Disraeli and England', 712–14.
[148] Parry, *Democracy and religion*, pp. 413–17; Bentley, *Ritualism*, p. 65.
[149] 16 Oct. 1873, Arlinghaus, 'British public opinion', 397.
[150] 'Claims of Whig government', 575–7.    [151] Parry, *Democracy and religion*, p. 263.

sentiment – and for the Pope, as noted in chapter 5, he had none at all. He now discerned 'one vast conspiracy' to plunge Europe into bloodshed in an attempt to restore the Pope's temporal power.[152] He interpreted the Irish bishops' opposition to his university scheme as part of this conspiracy, at the expense of government authority in Ireland. Therefore he became extremely hostile to the bishops and to the Home Rule agitation which he regarded, wrongly, as essentially their plaything. His *Vatican decrees* pamphlet, published a few months after his loss of office in 1874, was the result. It asserted that the Pope expected converts to the modern Roman Catholic Church to surrender their mental and moral freedom and to compromise their allegiance to the state, and that the British people were entitled to ask all Catholic laymen to pledge their loyalty afresh. It ended with the rallying-cry that however great 'the foreign influence of a caste', Britain would not be swayed 'from the accomplishment of its mission in the world'.[153] This astonishing production caused a sensation and sold 145,000 copies by the end of 1874. The *Dublin Review* claimed that he had 'offered a public insult' to the 'Catholic people' of Ireland.[154]

As a political statement, Gladstone's outburst was strikingly reminiscent of Russell's Durham Letter. Indeed it went further, casting aspersions on the patriotism of *lay* Catholics, which Whigs almost all assumed had been guaranteed by Emancipation in 1829.[155] It is only Gladstone's subsequent behaviour which has ensured that his reputation in Ireland is better than that of his predecessors. After five years as Prime Minister, both Russell and Gladstone, the only two nineteenth-century men who came to the premiership with the overt intention of pacifying Ireland, had resorted to a bitter attack on the 'anti-national' activities of the Irish priesthood. No doubt one reason was an awareness that in the strongly patriotic climate of 1851 or 1874 it was counterproductive on the mainland for a British Liberal party to bid for Roman Catholic votes, as Gladstone admitted to Granville.[156] A second was the need to quell the widespread suspicion that both men were too favourable to Catholicism – that Gladstone, indeed, was on the brink of conversion. But, most importantly, Gladstone, like Russell, could not accept that Romanist clerics had the right to dictate an Irish policy to a liberal British state. And both men were remarkably unconcerned about the possibility of an Irish separatist movement. They assumed that there

---

[152] 2 Nov. 1874, *Ramm 1868–76*, vol. II, p. 458.
[153] *The Vatican decrees in their bearing on civil allegiance: a political expostulation* (London, 1874), pp. 7–8, 23–4, 65–6.
[154] J. P. Rossi, *The transformation of the British Liberal party: a study of the tactics of the Liberal opposition, 1874–1880* (Philadelphia, PA, 1978), p. 14.
[155] Parry, *Democracy and religion*, p. 425.     [156] 25 Nov. 1874, *Ramm 1868–76*, vol. II, p. 460.

was no scope for a successful Irish politics except in association with British Liberal leadership. The priests were trying to fill that vacuum but must not be allowed to do so. In 1877 Gladstone commented that if only a proper Irish leader would emerge, it would not be difficult to settle the country.[157] But both Russell and Gladstone had such clear prejudices about what Ireland ought to want that they might well not listen even if a leader did emerge. Too often Gladstone regarded Irish leaders, secular and religious, as distorting elements within the political machine. The responsibility to maintain right relations between the component parts of the kingdom lay instead with the executive government. As he said of the Catholics and the Irish university question in 1870, 'we *know* what we ought to give them whether they will take it or not'.[158]

Gladstone was so blinded by his concerns about the 'anti-national' plots of the Pope and the priesthood that he failed to observe the realities of Ireland. Neither the bishops nor the Pope were in the van of Irish political development. Indeed at the 1874 election the former were occasionally embarrassed and defeated when they supported candidates who were not sufficiently sympathetic to Home Rule, such as in Limerick and Louth. More commonly, there was no great tension between the priests and the Home Rule cause: nearly all successful candidates in Catholic areas paid lip-service both to the religious and to the political grievances. Fifty-nine MPs were returned under the Home Rule banner, though for many it was a flag of convenience. Several influences contributed to that success, but the desire to assert a distinctive Irish Catholic identity, against apparent English hostility, was the main one.[159] The key fact about the 1874 election in Catholic Ireland was that it was hardly possible to be elected on a ticket of Liberal unionism. Neither British party was interested in courting the Irish; Disraeli criticised Gladstone for governing too much on 'Irish principles'.[160] In their desperation to reflect the Protestantism and Englishness of the national character, both parties had alienated the bulk of Irish political opinion. It was not until the economic depression of the late 1870s and the emergence of Parnell that they woke up to what they had done.

Goschen remarked in 1872 that, in view of the number of panics recently agitating the public mind, it seemed 'as if this old country's nerves were shattered'.[161] The Conservatives' revival, culminating in victory at the 1874

---

[157] 20 Nov. 1877, in Ramm, *1876–86*, vol. I, p. 58.
[158] To Fortescue, 19 Aug. 1870, *GD*, vol. VII, p. 346.     [159] Comerford, *Fenians in context*, p. 197.
[160] *Inaugural address delivered to the University of Glasgow* (2nd edn, London, 1873), p. 56.
[161] At Bristol, Elliot, *Goschen*, vol. I, p. 128.

election, was due to a combination of overlapping fears about class, property, religion, morality, order and traditional values, all stimulated by the newly democratic tone of post-1867 politics. The basis of their appeal was to those whose familiar moral universe was threatened by the prospect of large-scale popular or anti-clerical movements. At Glasgow in 1873 Disraeli claimed that ministers had attacked every class and institution by their assaults on religious endowments, their harassing interventionist measures, their mismanagement of the army and navy, and their contempt for the professions. His regular refrain was that the Liberal party had betrayed English values.

What concerns us is not so much the defeat itself but the collapse of the Liberal agenda. Well before 1874 the Liberal coalition had lost its way, owing to the interaction of domestic anxieties and global events. The events of 1870–1 made Europe and indeed the world look a more threatening place, and the government seemed too weak in defending Britain's interests and values. This led to an invasion scare and a series of damaging disputes about military preparation. The authority of the government was destroyed from the winter of 1870–1. By spring 1871 it was assailed by a dozen different crises, from which it never truly recovered. The result was a paralysing loss of direction, a flow of by-election losses, a sensational election defeat and the destruction of Liberal unionism in Catholic Ireland. All the major Liberal political strategies – a vigorously Palmerstonian foreign policy; the moralistic social reform platform of Russell, Bruce and Forster; Gladstone's intense economising drive; the strong state envisaged by Froude and the *Pall Mall Gazette*; the philosophical Radicalism of Mill; the activist Nonconformists' vision of a free-church polity; a Catholic–Liberal alliance in Ireland – had run into the sand.

Instead of agreement on policy, one persistent theme was now anxiety about national unity, in the face of sectionalism and materialism. The Conservative victory seemed to demonstrate the failure of the Liberal attempt at a cross-class ethical politics. It appeared to be due mainly to middle-class selfishness, false religion and false patriotism – exemplified by what Frederic Harrison called 'the sleek citizens, who pour forth daily from thousands and thousands of smug villas round London, Manchester and Liverpool'.[162]

Of course different Liberals defined the party's problem in different ways. Some were not too upset by the defeat because they felt that the party had itself succumbed to sectionalism, faddism and penny-pinching. Military men, aristocrats and socially well-connected littérateurs claimed that Liberalism was infected by Cobdenite commercialism, particularly given the

---

[162] 'The Conservative reaction', *Fortnightly Review*, 15 (1874), 305.

growth of plutocracy and the perceived increase of shopkeeper influence in
Parliament after the 1867 Reform Act. The crisis of 1874 terminally weakened the attractiveness of non-interventionism at home and abroad. As
chapter 7 will show, an uplifting domestic and foreign policy became *de
rigueur* for Liberals after 1874. But Mazzinian Radicals, Christian Socialists,
broad-church Anglicans and Nonconformists could also be heard pointing
to a depressing lack of class and community spirit because of the worship
of money, and urging an assault on it, whether by a stronger social policy
or a bolstering of true religion or republican virtue.

One particularly powerful critique of this modern English materialism
was delivered by the Palmerstonian Liberal and failed Parliamentary candidate, Anthony Trollope, in his massive novel of 1873–4, *The way we live now*.
This was a sustained lament at the infection of traditional English politics
and social life by dishonesty and money-grubbing. The central villain of
the book is Felix Carbury, the symbol of a decadent ruling class that is no
longer loyal to a gentlemanly culture of community leadership but instead
combines a selfish thirst for consumption and wealth with an inability to
work to earn it morally. He and others in his class demonstrate their corruption by their willing involvement with financial tricksters, all of whom have
come from abroad: American railroad speculators and the shady continental financier Melmotte. These degrading foreign presences loomed large in
Trollope's mind because of American and French involvement in real-life
scandals and swindles of the early 1870s.[163] The ease with which Melmotte,
mysterious foreigner, unprincipled Jew and vulgar materialist, exploits this
deep-seated moral disease for his personal benefit suggests that London
society is now defined by money. He even briefly becomes a Conservative
MP. Indeed it is irresistible to speculate that Trollope was partly warning
about the real-life Jewish figure who was the beneficiary of the moral crisis
of Liberal Britain in 1873–4: Disraeli, the undisputed victor of the 1874
election. As Mrs Gladstone so graphically wrote to her son, with reference
to the outgoing government's financial surplus of over £5 million, 'Is it not
disgusting after all Papa's labour and patriotism and years of work to think
of handing over his nest-egg to that Jew?'[164] But the unpalatable fact was
that the depraved voters had delivered themselves up to him. And in that
fact lay not only the crisis of Liberal Britain, but also its salvation.

[163] A. Trollope. *The way we live now*, ed. J. Sutherland (Oxford, 1982 edn), pp. xviii–xxi.
[164] G. Battiscombe, *Mrs Gladstone: the portrait of a marriage* (London, 1956), p. 158.

# The Eastern question and its consequences, 1875–1886

Overseas and Irish affairs dominated British politics in the dozen years after 1874. Between 1875 and 1878, and again in 1882, the Eastern question could not be avoided – the question of the legitimacy of Ottoman rule in the Balkans and Egypt, and the responsibilities of Britain in both of these areas. These debates were strongly influenced by memories of the previous Near Eastern crises of 1840 and 1853. Continuities were also apparent in 1879–80, when the Liberals' attack on Disraeli's foreign and domestic policy, culminating in their victory at the 1880 election, was a restatement of thirty years of constitutional and patriotic argument, against Disraeli's 'imperialism', his apparent rejection of English political values.

The use of this word did not, however, mean that Liberals were hostile to the global assertion of British power. Many of them, conscious of the bad publicity given to non-intervention in the previous ten years, took advantage of the emphasis on foreign policy after 1875 to create a more uplifting overseas agenda for the party. They sought to combine patriotism with a vigorous defence of constitutional and Christian principles, in order to rally the party, to educate the electorate, and to recover a reputation for world leadership on Liberal terms. They saw this as a counter-strategy to Disraeli's confused and artificial attempt at national aggrandisement.

Then, after 1880, Liberal government was very concerned to uphold the duties and status of England against any threat that might emerge – and several did emerge in the 1880s. In particular, Africa became a place of tension between the great European powers. This ensured that ministers could not avoid becoming caught up in the struggle for extra territory if they were not to lose face abroad and at home. Suspicion of French, German and Russian intentions was rife in the media. Secondarily, there was horror at the challenge posed by Arab 'lawlessness' to civilised British values. Imperial assertiveness was also necessary for domestic political reasons, given the rising challenge from the Conservative party. Moreover, the coming men of Radicalism, Dilke and Chamberlain, presented a vigorous foreign policy as proof that a truly national and representative Parliament, bolstered in 1884–5 by further Parliamentary reform, could defend national interests better than effete aristocrats had in the past – in the same way as it could legislate more effectively in domestic matters.

However, this forward policy had damaging consequences for defence spending and for diplomatic flexibility. Moreover, not all Liberals found it easy to square England's territorial expansion with the Liberal commitment to the spread of constitutional principles, particularly self-government. Gladstone, especially, disliked it – though he himself had been a strong upholder of British rights, and the rule of law, both in Egypt and in Central Asia. His declaration in favour of Home Rule for Ireland was in large part an attempt to counteract imperialism by an older, purer notion of England's global mission, on the basis of economy, accountability and justice, which would set the tone for domestic and international politics. In the circumstances of the mid-1880s, however, Gladstone's move struck other Liberals as a suicidal blow to British power.

## THE DISRAELIAN THREAT, 1874–80

It is often claimed that Disraeli stole the language of patriotism from Palmerstonian Liberalism for the Conservative party, through his bold foreign initiatives.[1] He was certainly attempting to do this: the search for a patriotic political agenda dominated his career. He hoped to secure his place in history as the man who revived English greatness after it had been weakened by wrong-headed policies and Cobdenite materialism since the 1840s. And he was keenly aware of the politician's duty to forge a sense of national unity, for which foreign policy was ideal.[2]

But Disraeli never succeeded in this task. His racial background and opinions placed great obstacles in his way, and he faced bitter Liberal criticism on account of his 'un-Englishness'. Anthony Wohl has recently exposed the virulence and racial intolerance lying behind the Liberal denigration of him in the late 1870s. Even before the Eastern crisis began, cartoonists loved to emphasise his Jewish characteristics and his wizardry.[3] From 1876 his Jewishness became an important aspect of the Liberal explanation for his willingness to condone the rule of the un-Christian and Asiatic Turk over European Christians. Gladstone himself deplored the effect of

---

[1] Following the famous argument of Cunningham, 'Language of patriotism'.
[2] Parry, 'Disraeli and England'.
[3] A. S. Wohl, '"Dizzi-Ben-Dizzi": Disraeli as alien', *Journal of British Studies*, 34 (1995), 375–411.

'Judaic sympathies' on government policy.[4] This Liberal critique varied in the overtness of its racial reference. A few writers were unscrupulously and vehemently anti-Semitic, most notably Freeman and Goldwin Smith, who raised the question of whether Jews could be patriots in the *Nineteenth Century* in 1878. Slightly more subtly, cartoonists could not resist depicting Disraeli as an Asiatic, Oriental figure, and Liberal politicians, needing to personalise and simplify the issues, pointed to Disraeli's own admiration for 'Asiatic' principles of autocratic and theocratic government in his 1847 novel *Tancred.*[5] Though anti-Semitism was certainly a sub-text of Liberal language, it should also be said that for some Liberals – including those impressed by Jewish moral values – the problem was that Disraeli had *cast off* his Jewish faith without acquiring another: hence his rootlessness, moral emptiness and lack of convictions.[6] It is better to say that Liberals criticised his policy for its irresponsible lack of Christian humanitarianism. However, Jewishness was far from being the only 'other' in British political debate.[7] Liberal criticism was not just aimed at Disraeli but at the Foreign Office and a whole set of traditional and 'aristocratic' prejudices in foreign policy-making. Moreover, those who talked of 'Asiatics' and 'Orientals' were making a constitutional point at least as much as a racial one – and also contrasting Western energy and progress with Eastern passivity and stagnation. From 1878, especially, the Liberals were able to mount a broader attack on Disraelian 'imperialism', which rested on both constitutional and ethical grounds. They charged that Disraeli's government had betrayed English political institutions and true English interests abroad – because he could not understand and empathise with 'the moral and intellectual wellbeing of the nation'.[8]

When the Turks massacred thousands of Bulgarians in 1876, in their attempt to keep the lid on Balkan insurgency, a popular agitation arose in Britain, powered mainly by Nonconformist and other Liberal grass-roots opinion. One impetus was a humanitarian horror at finding barbarous Turkish practices alive in Europe. Turkey was 'a modern Sodom &

---

[4] In a letter made public in October 1876, and on several other occasions: ibid., 399–400.
[5] Ibid., 396–9; marquess of Hartington, *Election speeches in 1879 and 1880 with address to the electors of north-east Lancashire* (London, 1880), p. 229; H. Dunckley, 'The progress of personal rule', *Nineteenth Century*, 4 (1878), 792–3.
[6] G. Smith and G. A. Smith, *Whom to follow: William Ewart Gladstone, MP, or the earl of Beaconsfield* (Edinburgh, 1879), pp. 82–6, 105.
[7] I disagree with Wohl's argument that Jewishness was seen as Disraeli's '*whole* characteristic' and that 'Anglo-Jewry' was stereotyped as the only 'Other': 'Dizzi-Ben-Dizzi', 377, 401.
[8] Smith and Smith, *Whom to follow*, p. 96. The most nuanced and perceptive treatment of these issues is D. Feldman, *Englishmen and Jews: social relations and political culture, 1840–1914* (London, 1994), ch. 4.

Gomorrah'; Sir Thomas Fowell Buxton claimed that the Turkish system of government was based on 'slavery and the slave trade'.[9] Yet the main point was that responsibility lay not just with the Turk but with the British government. The agitators maintained that the massacres could have been prevented had the European powers been able to carry out the wishes of enlightened international opinion and to impose real changes in Turkish administration. The reason why this had not happened was the sloth of the Western powers over a long period of time and especially the encouragement recently given to the Turkish Sultan by the Disraeli government in the face of pressure for reforms from Russia, Austria and Germany. This was a great simplification of a complicated diplomatic position, but it was true that Disraeli had resented the fact that the three powers seemed to be taking Britain for granted in their plans for European Turkey. The British fleet had been moved to Besika Bay, west of Gallipoli, in a move that could be construed as support for the Sultan. Disraeli incensed the agitators by first denying the seriousness of the atrocities and then discussing them with apparent flippancy. Such complacency, on top of existing suspicion of his perceived lack of political morals, intensified their feeling that Britain must cleanse its reputation on the European stage.

In the eyes of the agitators, moral iniquity was shared by past as well as present British governments, because they were responsible for the continuing Turkish presence in Europe. At the root of the agitation was the demand that Britain should recognise, and atone for, *its own* guilt for Turkish misgovernment of its Christian European provinces. That was why religious figures were so prominent in the agitation – mainly Nonconformists, but also many Anglo-Catholics; it looked inward much more than outward. W. T. Stead, a committed evangelical Nonconformist, played a particularly large role in organising the agitation through the columns of his paper the *Northern Echo*; he considered himself inspired by the 'clear call of God's voice'. Hundreds of thousands of soldiers had been killed in the Crimean War – and the effect had been to prop up the rule of the Turks in Europe. British policy was responsible for their presence; the British people, by condoning this policy, had 'been the unwitting means of destroying' those massacred in Bulgaria. Atonement was necessary. Stead proposed a day of national mourning and humiliation as a memorial of 'our national repentance'.[10]

---

[9] Wohl, 'Dizzi-Ben-Dizzi', 387; Shannon, *Bulgarian agitation*, pp. 30, 103.
[10] Shannon, *Bulgarian agitation*, pp. 71, 136–7.

In arguing for this memorial (unsuccessfully), Stead was not just pointing the finger at sinful policy; he was also setting out his vision of an ideal political community in which prayer and righteous action would play the crucial part. He – and others – maintained that in fervently condemning the atrocities they were following in Cromwell's footsteps when he protested against the slaughter of the Vaudois Protestants by Catholic forces in 1655. This protest, famously celebrated by Milton – and now by a Ford Madox Brown painting of 1877 – had passed into Dissenting legend as a heroic assertion of the English Protestant conscience, but also of English power in Europe. It set an example of the virtuous foreign policy that a true religious commonwealth could follow. For Nonconformists, at any rate, the emphasis was on England's particular responsibility – much more than on that of Europe in general. Stead's comparison with the heroic days of Cromwell was a claim that the agitators spoke for the historic soul of England: he was confident about summoning up among the people a sense of 'citizenship' and a proper 'English patriotism'.[11] The agitation involved a criticism of the Established Church, on whose apathy the failure of the idea for a day of repentance could be blamed. But it also directed Nonconformist activity away from the disestablishment cause – which, in England, was never again to be as virile as in the first half of the 1870s. In the struggle to boost the nation's spiritual health, disestablishment seemed less efficacious than a vigorous global mission.

In addition, the agitation was a criticism of the amorality of those who controlled foreign policy: the Foreign Office, the Court, the aristocracy. Evangelical Nonconformists were, on the whole, optimistic that their values were taking root in domestic politics, local and national. But in foreign affairs they had made little mark. Thus the agitation struck at the most visible remaining outposts of class privilege and declared that here too the nation's conscience should now determine policy, rather than a privileged and selfish clique. The electorate would thus be 'a new force in the arena of Europe'.[12] The days of aristocratic effeteness – particularly *non-interventionist* aristocratic effeteness – must be terminated.

The Bulgarian cause also enthused some other, less evangelical, Liberals, who had already decided on constitutional-humanitarian grounds that Turkish rule in Europe must end. Harcourt said that the Turks' atrocities were much worse than those perpetrated by the government of Naples in

---

[11] W. T. Stead (ed.), *The M.P. for Russia: reminiscences and correspondence of Madame Olga Novikoff* (2 vols., London, 1909), vol. I, p. 280.

[12] Stead, Sept. 1876, quoted in A. P. Saab, *Reluctant icon: Gladstone, Bulgaria, and the working classes, 1856–1878* (Cambridge, MA, 1991), p. 53.

the 1850s, against which the English had so nobly protested. Lord Edmond Fitzmaurice lamented that Disraeli's England would be 'convicted before the eyes of Europe of having tried to check the enfranchisement of an oppressed people'. Evelyn Ashley invoked Palmerston and the idea of a 'spirited foreign policy . . . on behalf of oppressed nationalities'.[13] Ruskin, Carlyle and T. H. Green, though not conventional evangelicals, all had sufficient residual sympathy with the evangelical conscience to applaud the arousal of the people in a good cause. Hutton and Morley valued the humanitarianism of the agitation as a sign of 'moral healthiness' in the nation and an antidote to materialism. A few, like Freeman, had a learned enthusiasm for the cause of ethnic Balkan nationality, while Anglo-Catholics looked forward to the renaissance of the Eastern Church in the region, even at Santa Sophia itself. Some were less interested in the religious aspects than in the critique of governing-class morals, as in the Governor Eyre case.[14] Disraeli's own acceptance of an earldom in the summer of 1876 implied that he was concerned with status, rank and ambition and not with principle and earnestness. Attitudes to the agitation reflected its class edge: it won few admirers from the world of the London clubs and metropolitan press, but attracted many working men.

Gladstone, like the aroused Nonconformists, was drawn to the agitation by a sense of personal and national responsibility. He remained sensitive to his position as a member of the cabinet that had declared war on Russia in 1854. He always defended that decision: the determination of Europe to check Russian aggression represented 'an advance in civilisation'.[15] The powers still had an obligation to prevent renewed aggression against the Ottoman empire, and its integrity and independence should be upheld until they could agree on a better solution. But they had also entered into commitments, in 1856, to protect the subject peoples of the Ottoman empire. So Gladstone felt that his 'old Crimean responsibilities forced me forward' to defend them in 1876. Moreover he agreed with the agitators that the English people generally had to acknowledge, and repent of, their collective 'moral complicity with the basest and blackest outrages upon record'.[16] Gladstone had on several occasions since 1856 sketched out the view that the natural way to reconcile these various responsibilities was for the concession of autonomy to the Balkan provinces under the nominal suzerainty of the

[13] *Hansard*, 231:168, 1088, 1136, 31 July 1876, 11 Aug. 1876; see also M. E. G. Duff, *Foreign policy* (London, 1880), p. 16.
[14] Shannon, *Bulgarian agitation*, pp. 26, 29, 80, 190, 206–9.
[15] 'The history of 1852–60, and Greville's latest *Journals*', *English Historical Review*, 2 (1887), 291.
[16] Shannon, *Bulgarian agitation*, pp. 50–2, 124; Saab, *Reluctant icon*, pp. 90–3.

Ottomans. That remained his position in 1876, though somewhat extravagantly expressed in the phrase that Turkish officials should clear 'bag and baggage' out of Bulgaria. How to achieve this, though, was a more vexed issue, and in 1876 his main concern was simply to press the government to accept its duty to work with the other powers to achieve a solution. The indignant tone of his famous pamphlet of September 1876, *Bulgarian horrors and the question of the East*, was caused not by any enthusiasm for a radical solution but by the iniquity of Disraeli. English power abroad had been wrongly used, because Disraeli sought merely to 'flatter the . . . narrow, selfish, epicurean humour' of the British public. It was an 'absolute and imperative duty' to arouse the nation to press for a nobler course, to teach the government its responsibilities – to Christianity, humanitarianism and constitutionalism.[17] Gladstone feared that Disraeli's plan was to frustrate the other powers' attempts to save the Ottoman empire and instead to speed its break-up so that Britain could take Egypt. The newly gazetted earl of Beaconsfield could then end as duke of Memphis.[18] But he remained reluctant to agitate in the autumn of 1876, and he hoped that the agitators' National Conference of 8 December would strengthen the hand of Salisbury, the British delegate at the Constantinople Conference (opening on 14 December), which sought to get European agreement on a scheme for Balkan autonomy.

Gladstone's emphasis on a need for a collective European response to the Eastern crisis was not the result of any special 'European sense' in him, or of any particular enthusiasm for internationalism. Since the risings in Bulgaria, and indeed in Bosnia and Herzegovina in 1875, it had been generally assumed that civilised continent-wide opinion would not allow Turkish rule to endure in Europe any longer, and that the collective pressure of the European powers must solve the issue. Indeed, it had been obvious since 1840 that European states would have to be jointly involved in any readjustment of Ottoman territory. For Liberals to emphasise the European dimension was useful in criticising Disraeli's isolationist policy, and in protecting themselves from the charge of sympathy with Russia. It was also a way of resurrecting the optimistic language of the 1860s while disguising a commitment to any more detailed solution. It allowed them to avoid the vexed issue of how far to give self-government to the warring ethnic groups within the Balkans. Moreover, Gladstone's particular notion of the 'Concert of Europe' weakened the idea in practice. For him, the Concert was

[17] W. E. Gladstone, *Bulgarian horrors and the question of the East* (London, 1876), esp. pp. 17–18, 61–2.
[18] To Argyll, Morley, *Gladstone*, vol. II, p. 551.

a religious concept, a symbol and expression of Europe's Christian culture. His sense of his duty to interpret God's purpose ensured that he would define particular roles for the Concert that would probably conflict with the practical agenda of the powers. Like the Liberal party, the Concert was merely an instrument that helped Gladstone to do God's work. For example, the Treaty of Berlin of 1878 was a product of great power diplomacy, yet Gladstone condemned it bitterly. His own idea of the Concert as a moral force hardly ever included Austria and Russia and was ambivalent about the intentions and moral rectitude of Bismarck's Germany and of France.

So the Bulgarian agitation was in origin a limited and inward-looking movement, drawing on traditions of Liberal patriotism. The problem for the Liberal Parliamentary leadership – Hartington, Forster, Harcourt, Childers and the Whig peers – was that extra-Parliamentary feeling developed during 1877 in ways that were increasingly divisive for the party. After the Turks refused to accept the terms of the Constantinople Conference, the European powers could not stop the Russians declaring war on Turkey in April 1877. From that point, some Liberal agitators were increasingly concerned to maintain British neutrality, against the threat that Disraeli might move against Russia. Non-interventionist organisations such as the Peace Society and the Workmen's Peace Association became active in the campaign, which turned more and more on the immorality of re-fighting the Crimean War. This made some people erroneously assume that Gladstone himself was a non-interventionist. Moreover, the difficulties of maintaining a coherent position amid the diplomatic tensions of 1877 meant that there was nothing like the intense campaign of 1876 on the details of foreign policy itself.

Instead, the issue became mixed up with the drive by Liberal party organisers to enlist the urban working-class electorate and to fight Tory domination of the counties. This was a crucial time in the development of national large-scale party organisation, and party workers found personalities to be very helpful in engaging the interest of humble voters; for Liberal activists, Gladstone became a model of a moral, humane and democratic approach to politics, and Disraeli the opposite. This image of Gladstone depended much less on the finer points of the Eastern question than on his appeals to extra-Parliamentary opinion to condemn the Establishment's foreign policy. Increasingly alarmed by Disraeli's anti-Russian tone, he took to describing the forces pressing for war as the society clubs and militarist classes of London, and 'English millionaires, who preferred to invest capital resulting from your labours in Turkish Bonds' – a striking statement from someone who only a few months previously had himself invested £45,000 in Egyptian bonds.[19] In the long run, the creation by party activists and propagandists of a heroic People's William had enormous consequences for Gladstone's career and reputation. But to seek to rally any party by mounting a popular agitation against the whole tenor of foreign policy over the previous two decades, and on the ticket of opposition to war against Russia, was a fatally flawed strategy, especially because of the risk that Russia might attack Constantinople. A few days after the war began, Gladstone introduced a package of Commons resolutions demanding that until Turkey improved its handling of its subject peoples it would lose all claim to British support, and that Britain should work instead for reforms to bring liberty and self-government to Turkey's European provinces. The party could not agree on them and he suffered a humiliating reverse.[20]

Most of the Liberal Parliamentary leadership remained detached from these popular pressures. It is often said that this was because they did not approve of basing foreign policy on moral rather than 'national interest' considerations. But this is not quite true. Undoubtedly there was a section of the party that subordinated moral to hard-headed strategic or commercial concerns. However, that approach was taken mainly by Conservatives and military men – or by those who drifted away from the Liberals because they disapproved of the moral fervour of 1876–80, as quite a few propertied people and financiers did.[21] The more common Liberal response was to refuse to see a distinction between national interests and a progressive ethical policy. They wanted in principle to be associated with the extension of constitutional principles to the East, and they attacked Conservative talk about separate 'British interests' as merely selfish, materialist and vainglorious.[22] Britain, they said, had no interests separate from the general interest: to promote European peace, prosperity and liberty by active diplomacy and mediation. Harcourt and Childers argued that it was quite wrong to see Disraeli's feeble, 'flaccid' and isolated policy as following Palmerston's.[23] Already by 1875 it was generally recognised that the Ottoman empire governed its subject peoples on principles that were unacceptable to the liberal European mind. While Europe was developing materially and morally, Turkey was manifestly stagnating. So Britain should never again fight to

---

[19] Public letter, May 1877, quoted in Saab, *Reluctant icon*, p. 137; H. C. G. Matthew, *Gladstone 1875–1898* (Oxford, 1995), p. 14n.

[20] See Swartz, *Politics of foreign policy*, p. 58.     [21] Parry, *Rise and fall*, p. 276.

[22] See e.g. Dilke and Goschen in *Hansard*, 233:1152, 1166, 13 Apr. 1877. British interests were instead 'the common interest of nearly the whole of Europe': Duff, *Foreign policy*, p. 15.

[23] Harcourt, *Hansard*, 231:1136, 11 Aug. 1876; Gardiner, *Harcourt*, vol. 1, pp. 324–5; Childers, *Childers*, vol. 1, p. 251.

uphold Turkey's place in Europe as in 1854. In 1874 Russell commented that 'I tried myself, with Palmerston's aid and sanction, to improve the Turks. They are unimprovable, and I give them up.'[24]

Nonetheless, most of the front bench were uneasy about the agitation, because of the difficulties of applying abstract principles in the Balkans, and its consequences for the balance of power within the Liberal party itself. Hartington believed that the European powers must cooperate to impose effective guarantees for the Christians' liberties, but that complete autonomy would be impracticable and counterproductive given the mixture of religions and races.[25] Politically there was also a great risk to the Liberal party's reputation for patriotism if British agitation against the Turk encouraged the Russians to think that they could take Constantinople unopposed, bearing in mind renewed criticism that Liberal preference for peace was driven by money-lust and laziness.[26] Already at the National Conference on the Eastern question in December 1876 Freeman had made the same blunder as Bright had done in early 1860 over Savoy, declaiming 'Perish [England's] dominance in India' rather than that England should strike a blow for the defence of Turkey.[27] These were all gifts to the Conservatives. Moreover some Liberals, such as Joseph Cowen and Harrison, still held the traditional Radical view that Russia was the inveterate enemy of European liberal nationalism, capable of imposing 'Imperial despotism' on Europe. To the extent that working-class jingoism had an ideological basis, it drew on these traditions. Russia could still be demonised as an enemy of civilisation or as the agent of revolutionary pan-Slavist principles in south-east Europe.[28]

So the Parliamentary leadership refused to rule out the possibility of supporting a war against Russia in any circumstances, while consistently trying to bolster those moderates in the Conservative cabinet, led by Derby, who were discouraging warlike pressure and urging a joint settlement of the issue. Harcourt was furious with Gladstone for proposing his resolutions

---

[24] Walpole, *Russell*, vol. II, p. 450n.
[25] B. Holland, *The life of Spencer Compton eighth duke of Devonshire* (2 vols., London, 1911), vol. I, pp. 181–8.
[26] E.g. *The latest row in Dame Europa's school and what the new masters said* (London, n.d. [1876]); *Dame Europa in trouble again* (London, 1877).
[27] Saab, *Reluctant icon*, p. 121.
[28] Cowen, *Hansard*, 237:1435–6, 11 Feb. 1878; Shannon, *Bulgarian agitation*, pp. 217, 230. G. H. Mac-Dermott's music-hall song of 1878, which created the concept of 'jingoism', included reference to the struggles of the Circassians against Russian oppression in the 1830s, a combat that had been publicised by the Radical David Urquhart until the 1850s. This language, then, was hardly fresh. The duke of Sutherland, one of the most enthusiastic of Garibaldi's English backers in the 1860s, also became a keen Turcophile in 1877–8.

of April 1877, arguing that his 'mischievous egotism and folly' would make middle-ground opinion angry, playing into the hands of the Disraeli faction in cabinet and weakening the moderates.[29]

Despite the Liberal divisions of 1877, the government was in a worse position. The cabinet was badly split on how far to resist Russia, not least because many ministers felt that a war would be both a strategic and a domestic political disaster. Yet Disraeli was driven on by a fear that he would be more badly humiliated than Aberdeen had been in 1853 if the Russians took Constantinople or came close to doing so. Even if the other powers eventually acted to stop this happening, they rather than he would get the credit for having done so.

It was only in 1878, when he managed to marginalise cabinet opposition to a forward strategy, that the Liberals were faced with the prospect of embarrassing decisions. In February 1878 false rumours circulated of a Russian march on Constantinople. Forster withdrew his amendment criticising the government for asking for money for possible military action – dividing the Liberal party in the process. Over the next few months, Disraeli rode a temporary high, as he claimed to have played a crucial part in ending the war, settling the crisis and bringing 'peace with honour'. At the Congress of Berlin it did indeed appear as if he had won a great patriotic triumph. Yet the Conservatives were wise not to dissolve Parliament. Though foreign-policy embarrassments could help to lose elections, foreign-policy successes were less likely to win them, in the teeth of a bad economic recession and tax rises.[30]

Moreover the Liberals were increasingly able to unite in arguing that Disraeli, both at Berlin and afterwards, was pursuing a novel and irresponsible aggressive policy. This process began with the settlement of 1878. By a secret Anglo-Turkish convention, Britain acquired Cyprus from the Sultan, mainly in order to defend the route to India against Russia. Disraeli also pledged a protectorate over Asia Minor in order to improve financial administration and to safeguard it from instability and possible attack. Liberals alleged that this 'mad undertaking' involved an 'immense military responsibility' and committed Britain to a 'new and most hazardous policy in Asia Minor', which was not in its interest and brought it into direct contact with the Russian frontier. The protectorate threatened to entangle Britain in internal Turkish politics and in a Russian war.[31] Many Liberals

---

[29] Gardiner, *Harcourt*, vol. I, p. 318; see also Childers, *Childers*, vol. I, p. 243.

[30] Parry, 'Disraeli and England', 722.

[31] Gladstone, *Hansard*, 242:692–3, 30 July 1878; Lowe, 'Imperialism', *Fortnightly Review*, 24 (1878), 464.

also felt that the acquisition of Cyprus did not make sense from a strategic point of view – though, tellingly, some of those with ministerial experience of Indian or military affairs disagreed.[32] Critics charged that India was now being given a 'disproportionate importance' in British policy. The justification of British rule in India was that it was done well. Currently it was being done badly – taxes were too high, revenue was stagnant, and defence and security were growing problems. But instead of addressing these problems conscientiously, the government was advertising India as the jewel of the empire. Gladstone feared that the 'alien' Disraeli was trying to reposition Britain as an 'Asiatic' rather than a liberal power.[33]

These arguments, half-formed in the summer of 1878, were given real force when the government found itself conducting a war against Afghanistan in the autumn, owing to the policy of its Indian viceroy Lytton. The Afghan war was instrumental in forcing Disraeli's former Foreign Secretary Derby out of the Conservative party and towards a partnership with Liberals. It overthrew the traditional policy of reserve, of keeping Afghanistan independent but friendly, which had been championed by governments of both parties since the 1840s. Like the Asia Minor protectorate, it departed from the conventional policy that buffer states were valuable in preventing tension and an arms race with Russia. The aim now seemed to be to expand until 'natural boundaries' were reached (a phrase associated with Napoleon III). The war badly weakened Indian finances, alienated one Amir and met its nemesis at Kabul in 1879 with the murder of the new British Resident Cavagnari.

In Liberal eyes, the Afghan disaster demonstrated Disraeli's foolishness and extravagance in carelessly opening new fronts for risky expansion. Former Liberal viceroy Northbrook insisted that the real security of India rested not on this utopian quest but on good and economical government in India itself.[34] Disraeli's policy could be explained only as a bid for popularity among the new voters, to disguise the economic downturn at home and the lack of real achievement at Berlin, in what Harcourt called a 'servile imitation of the imperialism of the Second Empire'. He sought to use taxpayers' money to flaunt Britain's status in the face of other European powers, like a vulgar 'Bourgeois Gentilhomme': this was something 'unbecoming

---

[32] On Childers and Halifax, see Rossi, *Transformation of the Liberal party*, pp. 73–4.

[33] Duff, *Foreign policy*, p. 51; Shannon, *Gladstone 1865–1898*, pp. 214, 221; Gladstone, 'England's mission', *Nineteenth Century*, 4 (1878), 580. For Disraeli's attempt to make Britain an Asiatic power see also G. Carslake Thompson, *Public opinion and Lord Beaconsfield 1875–1880* (2 vols., London, 1886), vol. I, p. 41.

[34] At Falmouth, 1879: B. Mallet, *Thomas George earl of Northbrook: a memoir* (London, 1908), p. 148.

English gentlemen', in Lowe's eyes.[35] Rome and Napoleon had both fallen because of imperial overextension. Similarly, reckless expansion now would have damaging consequences for both the economy and political morality, increasing defence expenditure and creating a swaggering military-imperial ruling class. For Gladstone, who was already clear that Britain's global duties exceeded its strength and that it was necessary to rest its international influence as far as possible on self-government and economy, it was obvious that those like Disraeli who exaggerated Britain's continental commitments and set up 'fictitious interests' for it to pursue, must by definition be behaving unpatriotically. They must logically be in league with 'such Continental friends as practise upon our credulity and our fears for purposes of their own'.[36]

It appeared, then, that Disraelian imperialism rested on a 'forward' policy in Asia (and in southern Africa) and on the un-English idea of 'prestige': the desire for military glory, new territory and Napoleon's idea of universal domination.[37] Liberal comparisons between the Asiatic Disraeli and the absolutism of Roman and Bonapartist emperors became very common.[38] Disraeli did not understand that an *English* attitude to global responsibilities was the reverse of 'imperialist' and was based on a husbanding of its material resources. The growth of constitutional and religious liberties, self-government, education and free trade, at home and in the colonies, constituted England's real power. The direction of European politics had been moving in the direction of England, and 'freedom', since 1848. But Disraeli had betrayed the cause of Balkan liberties in various ways, left ambitions in the region unsettled and kept Turkish corruption alive; this had therefore given Russia more claim to interfere in future.[39]

Gladstone claimed that the Treaty of Berlin had weakened the moral reputation on which Britain's international stature depended, by ranging it on the 'side of servitude, of reaction, and of barbarism'. Disraeli and Salisbury had spoken in the 'tones of Metternich, and not in the tones of Mr. Canning,

---

[35] Harcourt, *Hansard*, 243:767–8, 13 Dec. 1878; Hartington, *Election speeches*, p. 218; Lowe, *Hansard*, 237:853–4, 1 Feb. 1878. See also Duff, *Foreign policy*, p. 47.

[36] Gladstone, 'Kin beyond sea', *North American Review*, 127 (1878), 190.

[37] For Gladstone's attack on prestige as a 'sham production', see *Hansard*, 237:937, 4 Feb. 1878.

[38] Dunckley, 'Progress of personal rule'. When the government transferred seven thousand Indian army troops to Malta at a time of great tension with Russia in spring 1878, claiming that this did not require the authority of Parliament, Liberal critics pointed to the Roman empire's use of subject races to provide its military strength in its decadence: *Spectator*, cited in N. Vance, *The Victorians and ancient Rome* (Oxford, 1997), p. 230; Harcourt, *Hansard*, 240:335, 20 May 1878. For Disraeli's 'Roman triumph' on returning from Berlin, see Laughton, *Reeve*, vol. II, p. 267.

[39] Hartington, *The Times*, 8 Feb. 1879, p. 10 and *Election speeches*, p. 69; Duff, *Foreign policy*, p. 16.

or of Lord Palmerston, or of Lord Russell'.[40] The 1878 settlement set up
an unworkable state in Eastern Rumelia, depriving Bulgaria of important
territory, and encouraged Austria to exercise its 'traditions of Latinism and
domination' over Slav lands by annexing Bosnia and Herzegovina and damaging Montenegro.[41] It was also offensive to Greece, the Balkan country
most advanced in self-government and most sympathetic to English values.
The Greeks had asked for Thessaly and Epirus from the Turks but a com-
pact by Britain, Austria and Turkey had frustrated this at Berlin. In June
1878 Dilke set up a Greek committee, hoping to make the cause of Greek
expansion another Italy for Liberals.[42] Moreover the secret Anglo-Turkish
Convention of 1878, agreeing the concession of Cyprus, defied past treaties
by which the powers had settled Ottoman affairs jointly; it was a rebuke
to the principle of open discussions between European powers.[43] It was
doubly offensive for not being ratified by Parliament. It was not that Parliament necessarily had a right to dictate a foreign policy to the executive –
the more executive-minded Liberals, including Gladstone, did not want
this – but that the government had departed from English policy norms
without public accountability. Indeed one Liberal MP, Dillwyn, moved in
1879 that the royal prerogative over foreign policy should be curtailed.[44]

Dillwyn's motion reflected Liberal backbench insecurity about Disraeli's
attempt to strengthen Crown power at the expense of Parliament. Liberals
charged that, like Napoleon III, he tended towards 'personal government'
or 'personal rule', denying national liberties and fiscal traditions.[45] One
campaign song of Leeds Liberals in 1880 was 'The Despot! Lord B!' to
the tune of 'Bonnie Dundee'.[46] The main way in which Parliament had
traditionally managed to influence foreign policy was in voting supplies
only for specific purposes. Accordingly there was great Liberal ill-feeling at
the government's demand for a vote of credit at the time of the war scare
of February 1878, which did not detail the cause of expenditure. As the
economic situation worsened in the late 1870s, Liberals commonly charged

[40] Gladstone, 'England's mission', 562; *Hansard*, 242:683, 30 July 1878.
[41] Harcourt, *The Times*, 8 Feb. 1879, p. 6; Gladstone, 'Liberty in the East and West', *Nineteenth Century*,
   3 (1878), 1173–4, and 'Russia and England', *Nineteenth Century*, 7 (1880), 549.
[42] For the unsatisfactory outcome of Dilke's endeavours for a larger Greece over the next three years,
   see P. L. Hionidis, 'The Greek kingdom in British public debate, 1862–1881' (University of London
   PhD, 2002), ch. 6.
[43] Childers, *Childers*, vol. 1, p. 256.      [44] *Hansard*, 246:242, 13 May 1879.
[45] See Hartington, *Election speeches*, pp. 33, 218; Thorold, *Labouchère*, p. 130; Duff, *Foreign policy*, p. 22;
   Mundella at Sheffield, *The Times*, 3 Sept. 1878, p. 6; Jacob Bright, 1878, in Williams, *Contentious
   Crown*, p. 132.
[46] C. Binfield, ' "I suppose you are not a Baptist or a Roman Catholic?": Nonconformity's true confor-
   mity', *Proceedings of the British Academy*, 78 (1992), 90.

that Disraeli had used foreign policy as a diversion from his incompetent domestic policy. Between 1874 and 1880 expenditure rose by £7 million, £1.5 million of which went on the army, and income tax tripled from 2d to 6d in a vain attempt to meet a ballooning deficit. Over fifteen thousand trade bankruptcies were reported in both 1878 and 1879. In a replay of the arguments of 1868 Liberals called for retrenchment and disinterested finance, claiming that high taxes were aggravating the depression. The Rothschilds – old friends of Disraeli – had collected an enormous commission of £150,000 for arranging the purchase of the Suez Canal shares in 1875. Such things were reminiscent of 'the worst finance of the demoralised French Empire'.[47] The government's drift towards interference in Egypt could also be blamed on bondholders who sought the maintenance of their interest payments after the bankruptcy of 1875.[48] Here was further evidence of the dominance of plutocratic rather than civic values.[49]

In place of Parliament, Disraeli seemed to be reinforcing the power and status of the Crown in the popular imagination. Gladstone detected interference by the Queen in foreign policy, a 'corruption . . . due to Lord Beaconsfield'.[50] The Royal Titles Act of 1876 – known to be the Queen's personal wish – made her Empress of India, bestowing on her a foreign title which seemed to reflect the imperial claim to be above the law rather than the respect for free institutions which was expected of a modern constitutional monarch. The title of Empress suggested the 'sham-Caesarism' of Napoleonic France, and the aggressions of Germany and Russia. It was the style of a 'military, autocratic, irresponsible, and arbitrary power'; was there not a danger of changing 'the character of the Government' to match?[51] The Queen's displays of partisanship, notoriously her visit to Disraeli's house at Hughenden during the Eastern crisis in December 1877, added to Liberal complaints. Some feared that the government, colluding with Victoria, had a plan to recreate popular awe for the Crown – 'Oriental adulation' – in order to diminish the constitutional checks on it.[52]

---

[47] Smith and Smith, *Whom to follow*, p. 9; Hartington, *Election speeches*, p. 27; Lowe, 'Imperialism', 454–7. 230 MPs supported Rylands's motion for reduced expenditure: *Hansard*, 245:987, 24 April 1879.

[48] See e.g. the debate initiated by Goldsmid, *Hansard*, 249:681, 11 Aug. 1879 (one of several).

[49] For Gladstone and Lowe on plutocracy, see e.g. W. E. Gladstone, 'The county franchise and Mr Lowe thereon', *Nineteenth Century*, 2 (1877), 554.

[50] Shannon, *Gladstone 1865–1898*, pp. 220–1.

[51] *Daily News*, in Williams, *Contentious Crown*, p. 126; Cowen, *Hansard*, 228:503, 23 Mar. 1876. See also Samuelson, *Hansard*, 227:1729, 9 Mar. 1876; Pease, *Hansard*, 228:313, 20 Mar. 1876.

[52] Dunckley, 'Progress of personal rule', 803; see Verax [H. Dunckley], *The Crown and the cabinet* and *The Crown and the constitution* (both Manchester, 1878).

Such sentiments indicate the continuing Whiggish suspicion of the Crown's political ambitions. Derby, who was personally deeply worried by the behaviour of both Victoria and the prince of Wales, blamed the extent of the criticism of Crown activity on the fact, 'partly known, partly suspected', that the Queen had pushed Disraeli towards war with Russia. He also feared that Court influence was steering the government and fashionable society towards a hostility to the French Third Republic which would end in an illiberal Anglo-German alliance. In this context, royal favours to Napoleon III's son the Prince Imperial threatened to imperil good relations with Paris.[53] When the Prince Imperial was killed fighting one of Disraeli's wars in South Africa in 1879, Liberal backbenchers turned the issue of his memorialisation into a protest against government and Court Bonapartism. They led a successful movement against the idea of erecting a monument to him in Westminster Abbey, arguing that to celebrate such a person in the 'national Walhalla' would be deeply offensive, not least because the monument was to be placed 'right over the tomb of Oliver Cromwell'.[54] These arguments appealed to the civic republican tradition. But they also reflected alarm that Disraeli's 'Imperialism', by being 'distasteful to the English imagination' and a 'symbol of despotism', would destroy the appeal of constitutional monarchy and drive people to real republicanism. To Harcourt, shared admiration for English institutions 'constituted a national spirit' and generated 'patriotism and loyalty' which was now being threatened. As another pamphlet put it, the breaking of the bond between monarchy and the multitude that Disraeli was attempting 'had caused French Imperialism to fall and American Democracy to corrupt'.[55]

The Napoleonic system also failed to educate and guide the electors and instead pandered to the acquisitive thirst of a jingo mob. The creator of household suffrage in 1867 made no attempt to teach the people he had enfranchised the 'lessons of self-denial and self-restraint' which had traditionally conserved England's global strength – let alone to found his policy on Christian conceptions of morality. Gladstone asserted that the great duty of government, especially in foreign affairs, was to 'soothe and tranquillize the minds of the people' and wean them off 'the baleful spirit of domination'. Yet Disraeli's foreign policy had been driven by the goal

---

[53] *Derby diary 1878–93*, pp. 10, 35, 88, 103, 176. For another suggestion of the Queen's influence on foreign policy, see Dunckley, 'Progress of personal rule', 800–1.

[54] *Hansard*, 249:531, 536, 8 Aug. 1879, 254:698, 16 July 1880.

[55] Forster and Harcourt, *Hansard*, 228:150–1, 105–6, 16 Mar. 1876; Cowen, *Hansard*, 228:509, 23 Mar. 1876; Smith and Smith, *Whom to follow*, p. 132.

of 'dazzl[ing] the unthinking'.[56] 'Imperialism' or 'sham-Caesarism' seemed an apt description of a system in which influence was exercised by an alien conspirator, a class-bound Court, a selfish plutocracy and an unrepresentative, un-Christian, spendthrift mob rather than by rational public debate and a respect for freedom. Disraeli had abandoned the prudent restraint of the English governing classes for the vulgar extravagance of the *nouveaux riches*. His reckless, wasteful foreign policy was eroding real British power abroad, just as their gambling and selfishness was undermining respect for English gentlemen at home. The Conservatives were 'the materialists of politics'. France had been weakened and corrupted that way; England must not be.[57] Disraeli's habitual 'depreciation of Parliamentary institutions' threatened to erode the basis of England's greatness, the 'habit of self-government', and to make a great empire 'little'. As Gladstone said at Midlothian, 'what we are disputing about is a whole system of Government'.[58]

The impression is often given that Gladstone single-handedly masterminded the Liberal critique of Beaconsfieldism in 1879–80. But this is to confuse substance and tone. The essential arguments were neither created nor argued by him alone. They could unite the vast Liberal coalition for one final time, because they spoke to principles of patriotism and constitutionalism deep in the party. With the aid of Whig landlords, the Liberals made thirty-eight gains in English and Scottish county seats. The combination of depression, high taxation, an embarrassingly unsuccessful foreign policy, and the recovery of Liberal political and organisational unity ensured Conservative defeat. The speeches of 1879–80 recapitulated the whole history of the Liberal party. Disraeli stood accused of betraying the principles of constitutionalism and fiscal responsibility at home and in the empire, and the glorious line of moral intervention in Europe from Canning to Palmerston and Russell that had helped to give freedom to Belgium, Spain, Portugal, Italy and Greece.

The emphasis on the perils of overextension and arrogance reassured non-interventionists in the party, but 1880 was certainly no victory for them. Gladstone went out of his way to assure voters that the next Liberal government would not follow the 'great and serious error' of the Manchester school, since there were times when an assertive and even warlike policy

[56] W. E. Gladstone, *Midlothian speeches 1879*, ed. M. R. D. Foot (Leicester, 1971 edn), p. 37; Duff, *Foreign policy*, p. 52.
[57] Duff, *Foreign policy*, pp. 50–3; Gladstone, 'England's mission', 569–70.
[58] F. Seebohm, 'Imperialism and socialism', *Nineteenth Century*, 7 (1880), 727; Gladstone, 'England's mission', 584; Gladstone, *Midlothian speeches*, p. 50.

was required, based on principles of justice or faith.[59] He wanted to avoid
the excessive commitments that would disturb Britain's fiscal machinery
(and class relations in consequence), and to avoid the disturbance of the
international machinery that kept the peace. But, as Grant Duff argued,
it was *Disraeli* who had adopted a mean 'isolated position', out of kilter
with the responsibilities of a progressive European power.[60] Hence the
uplifting Liberal talk of a Concert of Europe, even though this ran parallel
with obvious distrust of the role in practice of Turkey, Russia, Austria and
Germany. Where Liberals were not so ambivalent was in their admiration
for Anglo-Saxon virtues and Anglo-American friendship. This was one of
the great themes of the late 1870s, following the amicable celebrations of
the centenary of 1776, with their paeans to the strength of the libertarian
constitutional tradition, and the British tours of the American evangelists
Moody and Sankey in 1874 and 1875. The more unsatisfactory the state
of European politics, the more reassuring it was to think that English
expansion overseas offered some guarantee for continued global progress.[61]

It was the tone, more than the substance, of his Midlothian campaign
which was distinctively Gladstonian. Gladstone's mode of presenting his
argument appealed particularly to two constituencies and to two moral
traditions, both continuing from the Bulgarian agitation, which henceforth
gave his career great popular appeal and momentum. The first was the
language of atonement, of acceptance of individual responsibility for past
sins, in order to keep society alert and virtuous. Gladstone told the nation
that the election was an occasion for each 'inner conscience, before God and
before man' to declare whether 'a great and a free people' would condone or
condemn the government and Parliament that had perpetrated the horrors
of the last four years.[62] This emphasis on responsibility appealed not just to
the evangelical conscience but to working men proud of the right to vote.

---

[59] 17 Mar. 1880, W. E. Gladstone, *Political speeches in Scotland: March and April 1880* (Edinburgh, 1880),
pp. 30–1. On the perils of arrogance, see Gladstone, *Midlothian speeches*, p. 37.

[60] Duff, *Foreign policy*, p. 15.

[61] See M. J. Sewell, 'Public sentiment and public men: the Anglo-American relationship in the late
nineteenth century' (University of Cambridge PhD, 1987), pp. 76–7, 142–3; M. Sewell, '"All the
English-speaking race is in mourning": the assassination of President Garfield and Anglo-American
relations', *Historical Journal*, 34 (1991), 673–7; H. Tulloch, *James Bryce's American Commonwealth: the
Anglo-American background* (Woodbridge, 1988), pp. 35–8, 49; J. Coffey, 'Democracy and popular
religion: Moody and Sankey's mission to Britain, 1873–1875', in E. F. Biagini (ed.), *Citizenship and
community: Liberals, Radicals and collective identities in the British Isles, 1865–1931* (Cambridge, 1996),
pp. 93–119; Gladstone, 'Kin beyond sea'; Gerlach, *British Liberalism*, pp. 48–57.

[62] Gladstone, *Midlothian speeches*, pp. 57–8. 'Politicus' from Manchester envisaged a 'day of wrath'
being visited on Beaconsfield for his abuse of power, his wars, his over-taxation and his inhumanity:
*The apparition of the late Lord Derby to Lord Beaconsfield* (Manchester, n.d.), p. 16.

So, secondly, did the focus on 'our common humanity'.[63] From now on, humanity was to become a much more important aspect of his language than the Whig-Liberal emphasis on constitutional freedoms. One did not need to be deeply religious to be moved by Gladstone's rhetoric, simply to feel a sense of human concord. At Midlothian, Gladstone later said, the nation 'broadly recognised the brotherhood of man'. Humanity would surely reject the responsibility for the 'frivolous' policy that had driven women and children from burnt Afghan hill-villages 'to perish in the snows of winter', and that had slaughtered the Zulus who had done 'the duties of patriotism' by offering 'their naked bodies to the terribly improved artillery and arms of modern European science'.[64] One Unitarian minister argued that Disraeli had 'put a false meaning' on patriotism, which historically meant a concern with 'national integrity . . . justice and honour . . . keen moral sensibility and . . . the grand humanities of life'.[65] This mixture of evangelical and humanitarian appeal, and of reason and emotion, inspired Nonconformists and many working men. Gladstone's apparent ability to communicate moral ideals to ordinary voters justified Hartington in ceding the commission to form a government to him when the Queen invited him to become Prime Minister after the 1880 election.

### FRANCE, GERMANY AND AFRICA

On returning to power in 1880, Gladstone's government aimed to root out the errors of Beaconsfieldism in three ways: by restoring an economical and equitable fiscal settlement; by extending the constitutional principles and practice of urban England to the counties; and by asserting England's Providential world mission to extend freedom, peace and good government, as opposed to artificial and selfish posturing. These objectives all had the same dual purpose: at the mundane level, to consolidate Liberal electoral popularity; at the more abstract, to reiterate inclusive, participatory cross-class political ideals that would underpin continued social stability at home and provide a foundation for a better international order.

In these years the assertion that Britain's mission involved an organic process of spreading its values and its people through the world became a Liberal commonplace, as a counter-argument to Disraeli's 'Oriental' conception of imperialism. A free association of English-speaking peoples in the

[63] At Blackheath, *The Times*, 11 Sept. 1876, p. 10.
[64] *PMP*, vol. i, p. 113; Gladstone, *Midlothian speeches*, pp. 91–2.
[65] J. C. [J. Cuckson], *Earl Beaconsfield: a political sketch* (Birmingham, 1880), p. 18.

settler colonies and the United States would be complemented by imperial rule over more backward peoples on responsible principles of trusteeship, humanity and philanthropy. The Gladstone government was determined to revert to constitutional liberalism in Jamaica, where a representative government and broad suffrage were restored in 1884. Derby, a prize seceder from Disraeli's Conservative party, who became Colonial Secretary in 1882, made it clear that the reason for the Jamaican reforms was that 'we should do our duty'.[66] In opposition, Gladstone had emphasised that Britain's role in India must be that of benevolent trustee rather than exploiter, and Ripon's reforms as Viceroy from 1880 aimed to increase local powers of taxation, spread ideas of fiscal responsibility and guarantee the rights of qualified Indian magistrates to try Europeans – encountering strong criticism at home. As in Jamaica, the object was not to prepare these territories for independence in the foreseeable future, but to reassert proper and exemplary principles of government from which the world would learn.

This was part of a more general mission. In 1884 Gladstone declared that it was 'among the most patent and palpable facts of the condition of the world, that God Almighty has given to the people who inhabit these islands a great function and a great duty of colonization'.[67] The Liberal historian Seeley argued in his well-received book *The expansion of England* (1883) that it was mistaken and demeaning to describe the British empire in 'the language of Oriental bombast'. The 'self-supporting' settlements at its heart were not the sort of empire which should be feared, as likely to damage domestic political values or finance. Rather, Greater Britain was a naturally developing 'world-state', 'with the sea for streets'.[68] Similar arguments were enthusiastically propagated by the Americanophile W. T. Stead through the *Pall Mall Gazette*, which he had taken over. Gladstone placed increasing stress on the benefits of Anglo-American friendship for world peace and development and made a number of pro-American speeches. It was after urgings from him that the rising Ulster Liberal politician James Bryce wrote his book, *The American Commonwealth* (1888), praising the strength, efficiency, libertarianism, nobility and civilising power of American constitutional arrangements, founded on English governing principles.

In 1880 it did not seem necessary to extend Britain's territorial responsibilities as part of this mission. But the Liberal critique of Disraeli had not included any denial of the *principle* of extending them, and when

---

[66] Bolt, *Victorian attitudes to race*, pp. 91, 107.     [67] At Edinburgh: *GD*, vol. x, p. lxiii.
[68] J. R. Seeley, *The expansion of England: two courses of lectures* (London, 1884), pp. 288, 293–304. The book sold eighty thousand copies in two years.

Gladstone's government of 1880–5 was forced to take on new commitments, particularly in Africa, most Liberals had no great difficulty in condoning this. Some did so by reference to traditional themes of constitutionalism and ethics; others claimed that it was a short-term duty reluctantly done in support of local and international order. There was nothing surprising or hypocritical about the development of a Liberal imperial policy so soon after the appeals of Midlothian; its practitioners believed that they conducted it in a very un-Disraelian tone. In any case, the main reason for the new commitment was an entirely traditional one: hostility to and suspicion of other European powers. Africa became an inescapable issue because it became one of the major sites of continental power politics, a new field for British alarm at French and German intentions.

A major reason for the growing anxiety about international rivalry was the economic depression and the return of protectionism on the Continent: tariff walls started rising in Austria, Germany and Russia between 1878 and 1880. The effect was to weaken significantly the previous confidence that British economic values would naturally spread through Europe with the passage of time. Between 1879 and 1882 this was powerfully shown by the failure of the attempt to renegotiate the Anglo-French commercial treaty, which had already nearly foundered on an earlier bout of French protectionism in 1871–2. Now, commercial lobbies at home, such as the Bradford wool interest, pressed the government to demand that France should lower import duties on their goods, while the French asked the British to lower wine duties. Neither request was acceptable to the other side. From 1882 Anglo-French commercial relations were conducted on a most-favoured-nation basis – as indeed were British relations elsewhere in Europe. This arrangement meant not only that Britain was no longer the driver of a movement towards lower tariffs across the Continent, but also that it was at the mercy of increasing protectionist pressures in other countries over the next ten years. This became clear as early as 1883 when new arrangements became necessary for Anglo-Italian trade. A further depression in 1884–6 intensified suspicion at home of foreign governments' commercial intentions. At the 1885 general election some Tories urged 'Fair Trade', exploiting ill-feeling at Spain's refusal to accept Britain's proposed tariff package. It was telling that Chamberlain, an aggressive commercial Liberal, had already suggested a policy of retaliation against Spain in 1882, as well as calling for the establishment of a Ministry of Commerce to give better government protection to national commercial interests.[69]

---

[69] D. W. R. Bahlman (ed.), *The diary of Sir Edward Walter Hamilton 1880–1885* (2 vols., Oxford, 1972), vol. I, p. 310, 21 July 1882. Generally, see Marsh, *Bargaining on Europe*, chs. 6 and 7.

Emerging anxieties about Britain's diplomatic and economic clout on the Continent encouraged the right-wing press and the Conservative party to be more aggressive in upholding British prestige. They celebrated Britain's imperial might and the symbols of national virility – the monarchy, the armed services, the globe coloured red. Though the Conservatives lost the 1880 election, the voting seemed to suggest that their imperial appeal was increasingly attractive in London, many boroughs and most of the Home Counties. The army was now more popular and better integrated into society. By 1882 a new annual London event, a military tournament to raise money to support soldiers' widows, had become popular; enjoying extensive royal patronage, it became the Royal (Military) Tournament in 1884. Disraeli's government had encouraged military drill in schools, while by 1880 the number of Volunteers was back up at 200,000 after a dip in the mid-1870s, and they were keener to adopt military uniform and be associated with the regular army.[70] Press coverage of the Afghan and South African conflicts between 1878 and 1881 romanticised the conflicts and the valorous military commanders, Roberts and Wolseley, who had rescued the situation after earlier humiliations. As the London music-hall became more sanitised and open to a broader social clientele, it developed a reputation for 'jingo' celebrations.[71] By the mid-1880s there was an identifiable market for adventure novels celebrating the pluck of English soldiers in dangerous parts of the world, such as G. A. Henty's *By sheer pluck* (1884), his celebration of the 1873 Ashanti campaign. The Queen's title of Empress of India became increasingly accepted, as a symbol of British power against the Russian Tsar and the German Emperor. By 1880 advertisements were appearing for 'Empress Brand' condensed milk, including her picture.[72] The identification of Disraeli with imperial patriotism began a year after he was safely dead, in 1881: the Indian administrator Sir George Birdwood suggested in a letter to *The Times* that the anniversaries of his death should be observed as Primrose Day, and this practice was soon widely adopted.

The Conservative opposition could use the language of prestige to exploit any Liberal weakness on empire issues. The new government's decision to

---

[70] P. L. Binns, *The story of the Royal Tournament* (Aldershot, 1952), chs. 1 and 2; Cunningham, *Volunteer Force*, pp. 93–6.

[71] D. Russell. '"We carved our way to glory": the British soldier in music hall song and sketch, c 1880–1914', in J. M. Mackenzie (ed.), *Popular imperialism and the military 1850–1950* (Manchester, 1992), pp. 57–8; G. S. Jones, *Languages of class: studies in English working class history, 1832–1982* (Cambridge, 1983), p. 231.

[72] R. Opie, *Rule Britannia: trading on the British image* (Harmondsworth, 1985), p. 43.

stabilise the Afghan situation by retreating from Kandahar was controversial, in the light of the press coverage of Roberts's heroic march to take it. Similarly, after the British army was embarrassingly defeated by the Boers at Majuba Hill in 1881, the press and the opposition blamed Liberal unmanliness for the refusal to retaliate. In the posthumous Disraeli cult, his (Russellite) phrase 'Peace with honour' was used to imply a contrast with Gladstone's alleged weakness abroad.[73] In fact, the Liberal approach in Afghanistan, South Africa, Jamaica and India was not as weak-minded as Conservative criticism suggested: the goal, instead, was the better extension of English influence. Afghan policy reverted to the traditional assumptions about buffer states and Indian budgetary stability. Boer self-government in the Transvaal was accompanied by informal British suzerainty over external relations, in an attempt to safeguard the Crown's sway in southern Africa. Most Liberals had no difficulty in justifying British rule in India for the foreseeable future, on the grounds of their ethical responsibility to give justice and protection to the Indians.

Nonetheless, Liberals were put on the defensive by these developments. Moreover, international tension ensured that the defence of empire and British prestige would be important themes. The increasingly frosty international economic climate led to commercial rivalry around the coasts of Africa in the late 1870s and 1880s.[74] Trading firms and entrepreneurial adventurers from Britain and from other European countries sought to exploit the supposed wealth of the African interior, by competing for influence on the Niger delta, the Congo river and the Zanzibar coast. They needed protection, from the natives and from rival traders. The French government was increasingly assertive in promoting its citizens' activities in the Congo and in Madagascar from the late 1870s. Commercial demands for a similar degree of British government protection were paralleled by pressure from religious groups for the state to tackle the evil of the slave trade. All these elements contributed to the 'Scramble for Africa'. They were not the only factors influencing policy on the ground: recent historical writing has rightly stressed both the additional role of local issues, and the reluctance and caution of European governments in practice.[75] But the

---

[73] See the report of a Leeds meeting, in *Yorkshire Post*, 4 Oct. 1884, quoted in M. Roberts, 'W. L. Jackson, Leeds Conservatism and the world of Villa Toryism, c.1867–c.1900' (University of York PhD, 2003), p. 242.

[74] For this theme, see W. G. Hynes, *The economics of empire: Britain, Africa and the new imperialism 1870–95* (London, 1979), esp. pp. 23, 33–4, 43, 57–83.

[75] See e.g. D. M. Schreuder, *The scramble for southern Africa, 1871–1895: the politics of partition reappraised* (Cambridge, 1980).

emphasis here is on the African issue as it played out in domestic politics, where fears of foreign competition, and commercial and religious pressures for a forward policy, predominated.

The point at which Liberal policy came up against these new realities was the decision to occupy Egypt in the summer of 1882. The British navy – assisted by American marines – intervened to restore 'order', ostensibly on behalf of the great powers. Gladstone presented the occupation in terms of England's duty as a spokesman for 'European' principles of good government, fiscal rectitude, justice and humanity. But as usual his notion of 'European principles' was bound up with his assessment of British needs. Egypt was undoubtedly a European interest. It was one of the last remaining 'buffer' regions of the European theatre, originally including the Low Countries and northern Italy, which had been monitored since 1815 in order to prevent instability which might allow aggrandisement either by France or its enemies. However, the great ambiguity over the occupation of 1882 arose from the fact that, in the case of Egypt, France's main enemy was Britain. Was Britain acting for Europe or for itself? For Britain, the most important concern in 1882, as at every point since the 1790s, was not, as is so often suggested, a non-European one; it was, rather, to prevent Egypt from falling into French hands. It was essential to maintain order so as to guard against an unpredictable instability which would probably jeopardise Britain's ability to exercise power both in the Mediterranean and on the route to India.[76] Public opinion was also deeply critical of the apparent weakness of British policy in the months before the intervention, which seemed humiliating. Concerns about British trade and investment naturally played their part in the public anxiety that order should be restored in Egypt, as did a specific alarm about the Suez Canal, but the influence of particular vested interests on policy can easily be overstated.[77] This was a political crisis, in which

[76] R. T. Harrison, *Gladstone's imperialism in Egypt; techniques of domination* (Westport, CT, 1995), argues convincingly that all British governments would tend to interfere to preserve Britain's influence in the Near East and that the behaviour of Gladstone's government in 1882 reflected this tendency much more than pressure from men on the spot.

[77] The argument that economic interests played the dominant part in the intervention is principally associated with P. J. Cain and A. G. Hopkins, *British imperialism, 1688–2000* (Harlow, 2002 edn), pp. 312–17. In fact the Cain and Hopkins account is more equivocal and tentative than the general argument of their book might suggest. They repeatedly run political and economic explanations together and do not suggest that 'policy-makers were in the hands of the bond-holders', so the conclusion appears to be merely that policy-makers 'recognised the need to defend Britain's substantial economic interests in Egypt' among other more political factors. As I argue below, it was politically essential *not* to appear to be in the bondholders' pockets. Cain and Hopkins themselves perhaps

questions of national authority, honour and international rivalry remained dominant.

Since the days of Napoleon and Nelson, Egypt had been a contested sphere of influence between Britain and France in their battle for global dominance. At every stage after 1875 the problem for Britain in Egypt was, just as in 1853–4 at the Straits, that it could not allow the French to become more deeply committed in the area than Britain was. The Khedive's declaration of bankruptcy in 1875 created a financial and increasingly a political crisis which the French took the lead in tackling, not least on behalf of the international bondholders. After a military revolt in February 1879, Disraeli and Salisbury wished that Britain had more troops to spare from South Africa so that it could make some initial plans for intervention in Egypt – in order to warn the French off intervention themselves.[78] In 1879 French pressure brought about the Dual Control, a tightening of the Anglo-French grip over Egyptian public finance and government in the hope of restoring solvency and stability. Both countries wanted to preserve the status quo and to avoid antagonising the other, particularly after Bismarck came to terms with Austria and Russia in 1881.

But the growing turmoil in Egypt created a situation in which the status quo could not be maintained. After 1878 Turkish rule everywhere looked extremely fragile and in any case the Liberal government of 1880 had very little influence at Constantinople. The Dual Control and the inadequacies of Khedive Tewfik made matters worse by weakening the Egyptian government's authority. Dual Control efficiency at collecting money increased Egyptian taxpayers' perception of heavy imposts, which Moslem activists could blame on the European presence. In such a situation, Anglo-French tension mounted. Many Britons suspected that French policy in Egypt would be influenced by the concerns of the bondholders, and a willingness to work with Moslem forces to undermine British interests. Just as Disraeli in 1877–8 was driven by fear that the Russian occupation of Constantinople would humiliate and destroy his government, so in 1882 the Liberal cabinet could not look with equanimity on the possibility of a French-dominated

---

dismiss the Canal factor too swiftly (pp. 316–17): it was a major concern for Hartington, as India Secretary, and for some of the strongest advocates of intervention, who were eventually able to use the crisis to make sure that it was protected. However, in the first crucial stages, the cabinet explicitly rejected action on those grounds: see memo, 21 June 1882, *GD*, vol. x, p. 284; Bahlman, *Hamilton*, vol. 1, p. 299, 7 July 1882; Swartz, *Politics of foreign policy*, p. 136.

[78] Swartz, *Politics of foreign policy*, p. 130.

Egypt. Moreover there was a school of thought that assumed that the Ottoman empire was breaking up and that each of the powers should get some part of it. This was particularly well represented in the press and the Conservative party, but the India Secretary Hartington, for example, also quickly adhered to it. For these people, Egypt was naturally Britain's to claim, because of the route to India and the fact that four-fifths of Suez Canal shipping was British, while the French should take Syria and Palestine as well as Tunis – which it had already occupied in 1881, adding to British suspicions. If Britain did not secure the route to India, this would strengthen Russia's hand appreciably. The Palmerstonian Hartington was committed to a vigorous and unsentimental defence of British interests, both in the Mediterranean and on the route to India, and was willing, like his mentor, to work either with France or against it to that end.

Arabi's military revolt of autumn 1881 made ministers more alarmed that Egypt might fall under nationalist control or French occupation claiming to defend the bondholders. Either way, the Canal might be closed to British commerce and troops in wartime. But the British government was very reluctant to extend its formal responsibilities or to appear to be acting in the interests of the bondholders. So it began by following the age-old strategy of working with France in order to restrain it and keep it under control. This bore fruit in the Joint Note of January 1882, assuring the Khedive of both powers' support for the existing regime. But this was a compromise: Hartington and Dilke (who only joined the cabinet later in the year) saw it as the prelude to a strong joint policy, while Gladstone remained opposed to any intervention in Egypt that did not take place under the aegis of the Sultan, the nominal overlord of the country. The latter idea was unacceptable to the French, who suspected that Britain preferred Turkish or international action in order to marginalise them. Then Gambetta, who had been willing to consider Anglo-French intervention, fell from power in Paris and French political instability increased. His successors were less keen on French action and no keener on Turkish. They would consent to an international conference, but the other European powers would not intervene to bring this to pass. Bismarck had no desire for a rapid solution that would extricate Britain from its difficulty; instead he used the crisis to drive a wedge between Britain and France. The consequence was drift until June, and ministerial anger at the French for shirking their responsibility to maintain order in the country. Dilke, who had favoured intervention in Egypt since 1878, complained that they had 'completely sold us, and we once more realised the fact that they are not pleasant people to go tiger-hunting with'. Hartington argued that imperial interests were being jeopardised by cabinet indecision, and that Britain should prepare to take action, firstly in the hope of forcing the French to see their duty, and secondly to intervene alone if necessary.[79]

Criticism that Anglo-French authority was collapsing then intensified after the rioting of 11–12 June in which fifty Europeans, including several Britons, were killed in Alexandria. Dramatised by the British press, the affair created a major outcry at home. It was a Don Pacifico moment, raising the old question of British responsibility for its citizens: the *Saturday Review* argued that 'the safety of Englishmen in various countries abroad depends on the general conviction that England will avenge them if they are massacred'. Dilke noted: 'Our side in the Commons are very Jingo about Egypt. They badly want to kill somebody. They don't know who.'[80] Chamberlain and most of the cabinet peers now became predisposed to action, though initially no good reason presented itself. However, British (and French) warships had been in Alexandrian waters since May, and Admiral Seymour reported that Arabi was reinforcing shore batteries, which could be viewed as provocation, or even preparation for an attack on the fleet. The cabinet sent an ultimatum to him to stop the building; it was ignored, and the city was bombarded on 11 July. Order collapsed in Alexandria; there were reports of widespread looting and burning. The government, forced to pursue the logic of its earlier policy, then secured a vote of credit for troops to check Arabi's growing influence. The Suez Canal was seized in mid-August.

Though some Liberal MPs were privately and indeed publicly appalled by the intervention, the majority of the party rallied to it as a necessary act in defence of stable government and British interests and honour. Radical opposition was muted and essentially confined to the (uncharitably dubbed) 'peace-at-any-price' party led by Henry Richard and Wilfrid Lawson. Only eight Liberal MPs voted against the vote of credit. Though Bright resigned from the cabinet on the issue, he never spoke in public on it. The Cobden Club declined to take up a position. The Anti-Aggression League, founded a few months earlier to uphold the principles of Midlothian, and including thirty-six MPs, collapsed in confusion on considering the issue, and the normally outspoken Radical Labouchère, and Stead and

---

[79] D. Nicholls, *The lost Prime Minister: a life of Sir Charles Dilke* (London, 1995), pp. 80–1, 101; S. Gwynn and G. M. Tuckwell, *The life of Sir Charles W. Dilke* (2 vols., London, 1918), vol. 1, p. 464; R. Robinson and J. Gallagher, *Africa and the Victorians: the official mind of imperialism* (London, 1961), pp. 107–8.

[80] *Saturday Review*, 15 July 1882, p. 71; 14 June 1882, Gwynn and Tuckwell, *Dilke*, vol. 1, p. 460. See Swartz, *Politics of foreign policy*, pp. 135–6.

John Morley, the editorial influences on the *Pall Mall Gazette*, all supported the government.[81]

Intervention was so widely condoned because any alternative policy appeared unacceptably weak, jeopardising British global power, prestige and image. The killings of June, on top of months of confusion and economic uncertainty, seemed an affront to Western and specifically British status, undermining its influence and damaging trade. Tories and others were claiming that England was 'the laughing-stock of Europe'.[82] The continuing preference of the French and the Turks for negotiation with Arabi, together with France's growing unwillingness to intervene against him, strengthened the belief that they were potentially treacherous allies concerned with upholding their own vested interests and quite possibly working with Arabi himself. If Britain would not act, France would get more licence in the area, and passage through the Canal might soon be merely 'by sufferance of France' as the *Pall Mall Gazette* put it.[83] There was also the danger of a Bismarck-led initiative, further weakening Britain's position. Finally, the intervention crucially improved the government's standing in the Commons, at a time of severe crisis over Ireland. Four days before the bombardment the government had been defeated by a rebellion on the Crimes Bill, while Whiggish backbenchers disliked its Arrears Bill. The Tories were in high hopes that Liberal divisions on Irish policy would force the government into a dissolution and election. The escalating military action in Egypt and the increasing sense of public relief meant that the Conservative leader's 'golden opportunity' was lost.[84] As Wolseley's campaign against Arabi progressed in the summer, culminating in the victory of Tel-el-Kebir in September, the London public seemed to gloat over 'every cannon shot' – as the Irish nationalists pointed out with satirical relish. Childers felt that it had gained the government 'an authority which years of Parliamentary and diplomatic victories could not confer on a Ministry'.[85]

---

[81] M. E. Chamberlain, 'British public opinion and the invasion of Egypt, 1882', *Trivium*, 16 (1981), 18–20.

[82] Bahlman, *Hamilton*, vol. I, p. 292, 25 June 1882; W. S. Blunt, *Secret history of the English occupation of Egypt* (London, 1907), pp. 336, 339, 348, 374n. On the pathetic image created by Anglo-French indecision, see 'The Neddy of the Nile', *Punch*, 24 June 1882, p. 295, and contrast with the celebration of successful *sole* British activity: 'A lion in the path!', *Punch*, 15 July 1882, p. 19; 'The lion's just share', *Punch*, 30 Sept. 1882, pp. 150–1. *Punch's* hostility to the French is evident also at 29 July, 5 Aug. 1882, pp. 43, 55.

[83] Chamberlain, 'British public opinion', 15–16. Derby also suspected underhand French activity: see *Derby diary 1878–93*, p. 471.

[84] Swartz, *Politics of foreign policy*, p. 141.

[85] J. V. Crangle, 'The British peace movement and the Anglo-Egyptian War of 1882', *Quarterly Review of Historical Studies*, 15 (1975–6), 146; Childers to Wolseley, 15 Sept. 1882, Childers, *Childers*, vol. II, p. 128.

The threat – the 'other' – which forced the occupation of Egypt was Arab 'savagery' as well as European rivalry. The intervention was justified to domestic Liberal opinion as a mission on behalf of law and good government against violence, fanaticism and vested interests. It was essential to present Arabi as the symbol of lawlessness rather than legitimate popular sentiment. Men on the spot fed the press stories about his militarist proclivities and lack of popular following. Accounts of the violence of Arabi's troops allowed most British Radicals to demonise the revolt as an unpleasant combination of militarism and the 'fanaticism of the East'. Gladstone asserted that the object of Arabi's 'military despotism' was to 'sell to the Sultan, in return for his support, the acquired liberties of that country, and to replace it under the Turkish yoke'.[86] Arab rule in Egypt also suggested that slavery would continue, ending the prospects of its abolition by 1886 as laid down in an Anglo-Egyptian Slave Convention of 1877. In these presentations of Arabi's revolt, there was undoubtedly some use of stereotypes of Oriental barbarism, but the basis of the charge was not specific to his race: it was that Arabi was the latest in a long line of global foes of liberal ideas of order, justice and progress. The media was especially sensitive to reports of 'lawlessness' and 'rebellion' in Egypt because of the recent sensational coverage of the 'outrages' against British law in Ireland, culminating in the extremely hostile press reaction to the Phoenix Park murders on 6 May. Few Liberals sympathised with the 'nationalism' of Arabi, any more than they did with the Irish variety. In the context of 1882 both ideals seemed to offend 'English' values of good government. Gladstone defended intervention as a response by those who 'represent the civilised world' to 'sheer military violence'.[87] Yet the demonisation of Arabi could also fit with support for Egyptian self-determination. After all, as English history demonstrated, military oppression was incompatible with constitutionalism. Gladstone and Chamberlain both told the Commons that the British action in Egypt was the *precursor* to 'liberating the national sentiment'. Dilke claimed that Arabi 'holds the Egyptian nationality by the throat'.[88] This optimism was highly convenient politically for all three men. Once Gladstone had convinced himself of the Providential legitimacy of England's crusade against

---

[86] Gladstone to Bright, 14 July 1882, *GD*, vol. x, p. 298, and draft to Richard, 31 Aug. 1882, ibid., p. 324. See A. Schölch, 'The "Men on the Spot" and the English occupation of Egypt in 1882', *Historical Journal*, 19 (1976), 773–85.

[87] Gladstone to Bright, 14 July 1882, *GD*, vol. x, p. 298.

[88] Gladstone, *Hansard*, 272:1590, 24 July 1882; Garvin, *Chamberlain*, pp. 447–8, 450; M. E. Chamberlain, 'Sir Charles Dilke and the British intervention in Egypt in 1882: decision-making in a nineteenth-century cabinet', *British Journal of International Studies*, 2 (1976), 241. For the English comparison, see 'An English resident in Egypt', 'Egypt and constitutional rule', *Contemporary Review*, 41 (1882), 555, 559.

Arabi, his enthusiasm knew no bounds, and he insisted on a loud official celebration of Tel-el-Kebir in the London parks.[89]

The government repeatedly pledged that British intervention would be merely temporary; therefore it should cause no prolonged diplomatic ructions. Gladstone hoped to settle Egypt by international conference, and to disengage. By August 1883 there were only 5,000 troops there as against 35,000 in late 1882. However, withdrawal was impossible for three reasons: the weakness of independent local administration in Egypt, unwillingness to upset British public opinion, and fear of benefiting France. In Gladstone's mind, an Englishman could confront continuing instability in Egypt in only one way, by encouraging the capacity for self-government: the need, therefore, was 'to plant solidly western & beneficient institutions in the soil of a Mahomedan community' before withdrawing, in order to prevent future chaos.[90] But he so desperately wanted withdrawal that he was willing to convince himself that Egypt could already govern itself. Yet in early 1884 he and Granville were the only cabinet ministers who claimed that Egypt could, while scepticism about this was also strongly held in the press. Derby, though intellectually predisposed to withdrawal, reluctantly concluded that the absence of reliable local authority made it essential for Britain 'to recognise our responsibilities as rulers of Egypt'.[91] Meanwhile, the defeat of Hicks Pasha's army in the Sudan in 1883 damaged British prestige by association, and the need to assert that prestige in the Sudan made withdrawal much more unpalatable.

By 1885 the dictates of British 'responsibility', combined with continuing hostility to France, ensured that the cabinet stayed in Egypt. Chamberlain and Dilke, though for a long time keen to play the Radical self-government card by advocating 'Egypt for the Egyptians', were even keener that, as long as a European presence was necessary, Britain must not lose out to the French. Their desire to tell 'the French to go to the Devil' created an implicit Whig–Radical agreement in cabinet against Gladstone whenever he mooted a plan for British disengagement.[92] In the spring of 1884 France was pressing for a British commitment to future withdrawal and for an international conference to agree a common European policy on the management of the Egyptian debt. But Gladstone could not get cabinet approval for an agreement with France on these points. His private secretary, Eddy

[89] Gladstone to Childers, 15 and 16 Sept. 1882, *GD*, vol. x, pp. 333, 335.
[90] To Rosebery, 15 Nov. 1883, *GD*, vol. xi, p. 59.
[91] *Derby diary 1878–93*, pp. 636, 640, 13, 25 Feb. 1884. For the press, see P. Auchterlonie, 'From the Eastern question to the death of General Gordon: representations of the Middle East in the Victorian periodical press, 1876–1885', *British Journal of Middle Eastern Studies*, 28 (2001), 18.
[92] Chamberlain, Jan. 1885, quoted in Cooke and Vincent, *Governing passion*, p. 183.

Hamilton, was struck by the depth of 'the old anti-French feeling of John Bull' in London society. In any case, there were strict limits to Gladstone's own willingness to make concessions to the French, and Hamilton himself felt that the revival of the Dual Control must be averted.[93] The Queen, Hartington and Rosebery thought similarly. There was also the fear that a concessionary agreement in mid-1884 would offer a great chance for the Conservatives to defeat the government and kill the Reform Bill then in the Commons. A provisional understanding collapsed in August to general relief. The English press opposed concessions; the French would not agree to a reduction of the bondholders' interest payments; Bismarck would not exert himself to settle the feud between his rivals. In January 1885 Hartington, Northbrook, Childers and Selborne were on the verge of resigning from the cabinet over new proposed concessions to France. These resignations were averted when Gladstone agreed to object to the French proposal of an international commission of inquiry into Egyptian finance. Instead the powers agreed to give Egypt two years to put its finances in order, and an international loan, under British occupation. This international settlement kept open the possibility of British withdrawal in theory, but it was now a political impossibility in practice, especially after the news of Gordon's murder at Khartoum.

Chamberlain's change of mind, in the face of the French threat, was particularly revealing, since a major theme of his Egyptian rhetoric had been that British policy in Egypt must not be driven by vested financial interests, in the shape of the bondholders. Before 1880 many Liberals had claimed that Conservative, as well as French, policy in Egypt favoured the bondholders' interests. In 1882 most English periodicals continued to be very critical of bondholder greed.[94] Moreover, in 1884–5 fringe Conservatives – Churchill and the Fourth Party – were charging that Liberal policy on Egypt was being directed by two members of the great Baring finance house, the Consul-General Evelyn Baring and the cabinet minister Northbrook. It was essential for a Liberal government not to be seen to side with the bondholders. In 1885, with Northbrook dissenting, it agreed to cut their interest rates by half of one per cent. Putting them in their place allowed the cabinet to unite around the continuing occupation of Egypt.

After one of the many inconclusive, fractious cabinet discussions of 1884, Derby noted that the cabinet 'do not know our own minds about Egypt'.[95]

---

[93] Bahlman, *Hamilton*, vol. II, pp. 618, 625.
[94] Crangle, 'British peace movement', 141; Auchterlonie, 'Eastern question', 16.
[95] 6 Aug. 1884, *Derby diary 1878–93*, p. 694.

The reason for this was that staying and leaving would both create huge problems, of a size that no government had faced for years. In a devastating memorandum in November Harcourt warned his colleagues that Egypt, quite unlike India, was 'practically a European province', and that attempting to hold it would bring 'all the evils of becoming a Continental state'. 'You will have European interference at any moment. You must defend it against the Powers. It is an affair of many millions a year.'[96]

The occupation was indeed a defining moment for British foreign policy; in fact it ended the conditions under which the Liberal strategy had thrived. When Britain lacked continental territorial interests, it could afford to play the powers off against each other. Its diplomatic and defence strategy now had to change. The rupture with France was serious, and Britain badly needed new friends in Europe. This was as Bismarck had intended. Gladstone assumed that England's unique position allowed it 'to be exempted from many necessities incumbent upon other European Powers'.[97] His idea of the Concert of Europe was that it would do Britain's will, at minimum expense. Bismarck thought differently: 'I do not see why an English interest must become a European interest.'[98] He had consolidated his power by the Dreikaiserbund of 1881 with Russia and Austria, while Gladstone had failed to bully the other powers into accepting that the 'Concert' should force the Ottomans to give substantial extra territory to Montenegro and Greece. After 1882 Bismarck used the 'Scramble for Africa' to heighten Anglo-French tension and to win an African position for Germany. It took twenty-two years for Britain to repair the damage done to French relations by the Egyptian occupation, and then by an entente which made Britain dependent on France's goodwill in the Mediterranean, implying a commitment to France elsewhere which was to have truly disastrous consequences.

In the meantime Britain was forced to pay much more attention to defence, in order to protect its position in the Mediterranean and to cope with increasing international rivalry. Over the next twenty years the enormous cost of this destroyed the Gladstonian financial system based on minimal taxation on all classes. In the medium term the most serious

---

[96] 16 Nov. 1884, Gardiner, *Harcourt*, vol. I, pp. 601–6; 22 Mar. 1884, *Derby diary 1878–93*, p. 648. Similarly, Salisbury lamented in 1887 that, had Britain not gone into Egypt, 'we could snap our fingers at all the world': to Wolff, quoted in E. D. Steele, 'Britain and Egypt 1882–1914: the containment of Islamic nationalism', in K. M. Wilson (ed.), *Imperialism and nationalism in the Middle East: the Anglo-Egyptian experience* (London, 1983), p. 12.

[97] 2 Oct. 1884, Bahlman, *Hamilton*, vol. II, pp. 694–5.

[98] 1881: P. Hayes, *Modern British foreign policy: the twentieth century 1880–1939* (London, 1978), p. 7.

development was the 1889 Naval Defence Act, based on the principle that the British navy must be as strong as those of any two other powers. This was the natural consequence of the Mediterranean Agreements of 1887 with Italy and Austria, which Britain made in order to guard against a probable Franco-Russian alliance. The naval spending increases of the 1890s, to secure Britain's position against the reality of this alliance, were responsible for Gladstone's final retirement in 1894 and for great strain on the low-tax policy, which was finally demolished by the Boer War. But already in the 1880–5 government the alarm bells were sounding. France became seen as a naval and military threat to Britain for the first time since 1859. A defence panic ensued. And, as in 1871, the Liberals bore its brunt.

In this period the main fear was of French attacks on British commercial shipping. Britain imported four-fifths of its food and was increasingly reliant on cheap food imports from the United States and the colonies, while its trade with Europe was becoming progressively less important than its trade outside. The *Jeune Ecole* of French naval strategists argued for a strategy of torpedo-boat and cruiser attacks on British trading vessels in order to create panic and higher insurance premiums and thus undermine Britain's economy. Already in 1880 a number of naval experts warned about French superiority in cruisers and torpedo-boats, and the threat to commerce and colonial links, but Gladstone was initially set on retrenchment.[99] The anxiety of the naval defence lobby intensified in 1881–2. One reason was the amount of what it considered to be naïve Cobdenite optimism in Liberal circles about international goodwill. A Liberal MP, the railway magnate Sir Edward Watkin, began diggings for a Channel Tunnel, arguing that it would cultivate Anglo-French communication, commerce and friendship, and check the Continent's recent drift back to tariffs. Many local trade associations and some trade unions supported the Tunnel scheme on such grounds.

But in early 1882 influential opinion in Britain suddenly mobilised against the Tunnel project. Childers noted government surprise at the 'explosion of hostile feeling', considering that the project had been publicly discussed for ten years. The reason was the growth of tension with France over Egypt and the trade treaty negotiations. The War Office, and especially Wolseley, led the opposition to the scheme. He argued that 200,000 men would be needed to guard the English end, destroying all the benefits of England's island status. By raising constant doubts about England's capacity

[99] J. C. R. Colomb, *The defence of Great and Greater Britain* (London, 1880), pp. 1–19; P. H. Colomb, *Memoirs of Admiral the right honble Sir Astley Cooper Key* (London, 1898), ch. 17.

to defend itself, the Tunnel would make it necessary to employ a standing army, placing 'us under those same conditions that have forced the Powers of Europe to submit to universal service'.[100] Wolseley was not alone in his doubts. The editor of the *Nineteenth Century*, James Knowles, quoted Shakespeare on 'this scepter'd isle . . . This fortress built by Nature for herself against infection and the hand of war'. Knowles organised a petition against the Tunnel scheme signed, among others, by twenty-six MPs, fifty-nine generals, seventeen admirals and two hundred clergymen.[101] A number of invasion stories appeared, suggesting, for instance, that the French could infiltrate a military force into Dover disguised as waiters and pastrycooks, and capture the English end of the Tunnel.[102] John Bright, defender of the Cobdenite legacy, expressed surprise that military lobbyists doubted that eight million adult males could protect a hole twenty feet wide, but the cabinet lost confidence and stopped the project in 1883. Opposition to the Tunnel rested on three grounds. One was pride and faith in Britain's historic and natural island status, combined with a critique of the 'selfish, mercenary, and unpatriotic' motives of Cobdenite materialists like Watkin and his shareholders. A second was suspicion of France, in the light of the Egyptian crisis and the failure of the tariff negotiations. The third was that a Tunnel, by stimulating an understandable public anxiety about invasion, would periodically inflame an agitation for extra military expenditure. Only if 'the streak of silver sea' still protected Britain would it be free from the need to spend massively to rival the standing armies of the Continent.[103]

The rejection of the Tunnel prevented this need, but the effect was to highlight the crucial role in national defence played by the navy. In the context of increased tension with France, Bismarck's schemes to entrap Britain in continental alliances, and growing anxiety about the protection of British commerce, a strong navy was a necessity. It was the best means of preserving Britain's traditional freedom of manoeuvre. By 1884 there was great pressure for naval expansion on these 'blue water' grounds. At first this was expressed particularly by Admiralty lobbyists and imperial enthusiasts, including Forster and his adopted son Hugh Arnold-Forster. Then in 1884 their hands were strengthened by French press discussion of

---

[100] To Roberts, 17 Mar. 1882, Childers, *Childers*, vol. II, p. 78; K. Wilson, *Channel Tunnel visions 1850–1945: dreams and nightmares* (London, 1994), p. 22. See this book and T. Whiteside, *The tunnel under the Channel* (London, 1962), chs. 3 and 4, for background.

[101] *Nineteenth Century*, II (1882), 493–500.       [102] Clarke, *Voices prophesying war*, pp. III–13.

[103] Bright at Birmingham, *The Times*, 16 June 1883, p. 10; *Nineteenth Century*, II (1882), 496–7; Gwynn and Tuckwell, *Dilke*, vol. I, p. 427; Garvin, *Chamberlain*, p. 432.

*Jeune Ecole* ideas, and by a whole series of African tensions with France and Germany. There was talk of a Franco-German maritime league, which in terms of first-class ships would outnumber the British navy. Stead took up the cause in the *Pall Mall Gazette* in September 1884. He announced that 'the scramble for the world has begun in earnest', that France and Germany would take existing British possessions as well as new ones of their own, and that England, which 'alone among the Great Powers of the older world . . . stands for liberty', should be prepared to accept an extra penny on the income tax to defend it.[104] As noted in chapter 2, there was a simultaneous Dissenting anxiety about a possible French *cultural* invasion, infecting morals. The Tories also took up the navy issue, and Tennyson, veteran of invasion scare poetry, and nominally a Liberal peer, penned a verse warning Admiralty minister Northbrook that 'on you will come the curse of all the land, if that Old England fall, which Nelson left so great'.[105] Most of the Liberal press took up the cry as well, as Childers, now Chancellor, pointed out to an angry Gladstone. The cabinet had to give into the pressure and Northbrook introduced a £5.5 million spending programme over five years for ships and coaling stations, including fifteen cruisers specifically to protect trade. The Admiralty and the press had asked for more, but Gladstone, 'really the sole obstacle' to defence expenditure increases in Kimberley's opinion, prevented it.[106]

By the time of the 1885 budget Childers had to face not only the increased costs of the naval programme but also significant extra expenditure on the imperial problems discussed below: Bechuanaland, the Sudan and Pendjeh. In April 1885, £11 million had to be raised for the last two by vote of credit. Indeed there was a further naval panic in spring 1885, when it seemed that the European powers might exploit Britain's difficulties in Africa and Asia.[107] Such were the unavoidable demands of being an imperial power. Childers had to impose £6 million of new taxation, including increases in beer, spirit and succession duties and the income tax – to 8d. This strong financial package may have helped to defuse the Pendjeh incident by demonstrating Britain's commitment to imperial defence and therefore encouraging Russia to back down. But it also raised income tax one-third

---

[104] R. L. Schults, *Crusader in Babylon: W. T. Stead and the Pall Mall Gazette* (Lincoln, NE, 1972), pp. 91, 93.

[105] Clarke, *Voices prophesying war*, p. 114.

[106] Childers to Gladstone, 18 Dec. 1884, Childers, *Childers*, vol. 1, p. 170; 2 Dec. 1884, *Kimberley*, p. 350.

[107] S. R. B. Smith, 'Public opinion, the navy and the City of London: the drive for British naval expansion in the late nineteenth century', *War and Society*, 9 (1991), 29–50; W. E. Forster, 'A few more words on imperial federation', *Nineteenth Century*, 17 (1885), 552.

higher than it had been left by the great Satan himself, Disraeli, in 1880. Gladstone's restorative financial mission had failed.

The Egyptian conundrum – the desire to withdraw on the one hand, and the growing awareness of Britain's responsibilities in the area on the other – had a further damaging effect by complicating policy towards Egypt's Sudanese dependency. Any intervention there implied a commitment to Egypt; any attempt to deny responsibility raised questions about national honour and ethics. The result was a policy paralysis and the greatest public relations disaster of the Gladstone government.

In November 1883 an Egyptian army was slaughtered in the Sudan when it attempted to suppress the uprising of the Mahdi. The ten thousand casualties included its commander Hicks Pasha and two other British officers. How should the British respond? On the one hand, attempting to police the Sudan would be a great drain on resources and would further embroil Britain in an area from which Gladstone was desperately trying to extricate it. On the other, the domestic authority of the British-supported Egyptian government depended on a vigorous policy against the rebels, and it refused to evacuate the area. Moreover, though this was not formally a British army, British newspapers naturally still called for revenge. In any case it was necessary to rescue the remnants of Hicks's army.

Forster, since 1882 a disaffected ex-cabinet minister, and Stead became prominent in the ensuing debate. Since his resignation over government weakness in Ireland, Forster had been publicising the existence of slavery in Egypt and urging a British campaign against it, arguing that it was morally irresponsible to strip natives of the protection of the British mantle. As MP for Bradford, a major exporting city, and son of an anti-slavery campaigner, he was consistently active in all the contentious African issues of 1882–5: Egypt, the Sudan, the Congo, the Transvaal and Bechuanaland. He argued that intervention in these places would protect native freedoms and uphold British honour and conscience, as well as promote commercial interests. In particular, he urged British action against Arab slave-traders in Egypt and the Sudan, and to protect the native tribes in southern Africa against Boer oppression. In March 1883 he called for the British occupation of Bechuanaland, to this end.[108] Many Nonconformists and Anglican evangelicals were interested in an Anglo-American ethical mission against slavery, inspired above all by the example of Livingstone, who had become

---

[108] D. M. Schreuder, *Gladstone and Kruger: Liberal government and colonial 'Home Rule' 1880–5* (London, 1969), p. 331.

an icon of the anti-slavery cause after his martyr's death in Africa in 1873. Missionaries returning from Africa publicised the plight of the natives and the sinfulness of tolerating this savagery. There was also a repeat of the Nonconformist horror of 1876 at the rape and sexual immorality that Orientals – in this case Arab slave-traders – were capable of inflicting. In any Commons debates on Africa, there was a danger that the Conservative opposition would be joined by Liberal advocates of what Gladstone called 'Forsterism'.[109]

Forster and Stead joined forces to urge the Liberal party to adopt a Cromwellian policy of righteous assertiveness based on imperial duty and Anglo-American global domination. Stead saw crusading journalism as a way of articulating and mobilising the individual responsibility that was needed to maintain the moral vigour of British public life; it certainly gave him a great platform for the exhibition and promotion of his own ego and power. One American journalist remarked in 1890 that between 1884 and 1888 Stead 'came nearer to governing Great Britain than any other one man in the kingdom'.[110] In his desire to stimulate the popular imagination and conscience – and the circulation of the *Pall Mall Gazette* – he imported the interview from American journalism. Forster was his first subject.

In January 1884 Stead interviewed Charles Gordon, the evangelical soldier who had become a religious hero as an opponent of the East African slave trade while Governor-General in the region in the 1870s. Stead used the interview to urge his dispatch to Khartoum, in order to rescue the soldiers, treat with the Mahdi and do his best to save the natives from oppression. This idea was quickly taken up by evangelical-humanitarian opinion, which argued that evacuation from the Sudan meant abandoning women and children there to 'rape and slaughter', since the Anglo-Egyptian Slave Convention, under which slavery in the Sudan was rather optimistically marked down for abolition in 1889, would be unenforceable. The cabinet needed to find a man to lead the expedition to rescue the garrisons, not least in order to prop up the Egyptian government and prevent direct British rule in Cairo. A group of ministers, aware of Gordon's local knowledge, seized the opportunity to put him in charge. Gladstone exploited his media popularity, calling him 'a Christian hero' and a 'genius' in 'his dealings with Oriental people'.[111] Bearing in mind the many difficulties on the spot, genius was certainly required. In March, Gordon's problems

---

[109] To Bright, 28 May 1884, *GD*, vol. XI, p. 151.
[110] F. Whyte, *The life of W. T. Stead* (2 vols., London, 1925), vol. I, p. 114.
[111] *Hansard*, 284:722, 12 Feb. 1884.

were made worse by another eruption of anti-slavery opinion at home: the Anti-Slavery Society and its Commons supporters protested against a plan to make Zobeir, a charismatic local chief, Governor-General of the Sudan, on the grounds that he was a notorious slaver (brought to the public's attention by Gordon himself in the 1870s). The government had to give way, in order to avoid a vote of censure, but this was a tragedy for Gordon since Zobeir was the strongest counter-weight to the Mahdi and best placed to keep order in the territories through which he would have to return from Khartoum.

As this showed, the Gordon affair was always intensely political. Tories and disaffected Liberals sought to use the affair to make broader points about the government's lack of 'responsibility', 'humanity' or 'honour' in international proceedings. A *Punch* cartoon showed Gordon giving Gladstone and 'responsibility' a piggyback through Africa.[112] From March onwards, the crucial question became whether the government had a duty to assemble a further expedition to reinforce Gordon, as Gordon himself, Baring in Cairo, Wolseley and the Queen all demanded, in order to prevent the local tribes from gravitating to the Mahdi. Gladstone refused to budge, fearing the implications for his Egyptian exit strategy. The cabinet not only declined to sanction an expedition but withdrew the bulk of the other military force in the region, at Suakin, to the irritation of both the prestige party and the Forsterites (since Suakin was the outlet for the Red Sea slave trade as well as a safeguard of British naval dominance in the Red Sea). Hartington, the War Secretary, and Wolseley at the War Office both pressed strongly for a relief expedition, arguing that public opinion would not accept any other plan.[113] For Stead, the affair became a trial of strength between the press, representing the English popular conscience, and irresponsible official bureaucracy.

On three occasions in the 1884 session the Conservatives proposed censure motions on government policy in the region, hoping to overthrow it and to come into office to carry their own Reform bill. On 12 May they argued that ministers had sent Gordon out to save their own skins, but were now denying responsibility for his safety, which was despicable in itself and gave a helping 'hand to the progress of barbarism over civilization, and . . . Mahomedanism over Christianity'.[114] In cabinet, Dilke supported Hartington's call for an expedition, while insisting that he wanted a quick British

---

[112] *Punch*, 2 Feb. 1884, p. 55.
[113] See Wolseley and Hartington letters, Holland, *Devonshire*, vol. 1, pp. 441–6.
[114] Baron H. de Worms, *Hansard*, 288:92, 12 May 1884.

evacuation in Egypt and the establishment of self-government there. He and Chamberlain felt that this package was necessary to prevent Forster and the other dangerous ex-cabinet minister, Goschen, from allying with the Conservatives to bring down the government.[115] It survived the May censure debate by twenty-eight votes with the help of a pledge by Hart-ington to save Gordon; he admitted that 'it would be indelible disgrace' to neglect to do so. Forster and Goschen both deliberately abstained, lac-ing their speeches with attacks on the government's failure to exercise its 'responsibility' for Gordon and for order at Khartoum.[116]

But Gladstone believed that a Forsterite Sudanese policy must be defeated because of its consequences for Egypt and Britain. Where was Britain's 'pub-lic right' to interfere in the Sudan? Occupation would deliver to Egyptian oppression a people who were 'struggling rightly to be free' and would impose a burden on the Egyptian treasury which would imperil its own future independence.[117] Moreover, he was appalled by the initial estimates of the cost of an expedition, particularly the Hartington/Wolseley idea of a railway across country from Suakin to Berber, which would be a perma-nent symbol of English conquest. The situation was resolved only by the combination of Hartington's threat to resign (which would mean the fall of the government without settling Parliamentary reform or Egypt) and the collapse of the London conference on Egypt, bolstering continued British rule there. Gladstone unbent far enough to agree to Northbrook's idea of a vote of credit for £300,000 (a 'ridiculous' sum in Hartington's eyes) so that preparations for an expedition could be made if necessary. This, together with the dispersal of the cabinet for the summer, allowed the War Office to take charge of the situation. By 9 September Wolseley's small force was in Cairo. On 5 February 1885 the news reached London that he had arrived at Khartoum too late to save Gordon and his men, and that the Mahdi's forces had raped and slaughtered many civilian women and children in the city.

The British reaction to Gordon's death was both immense and pre-dictable. In a large section of the media he was painted as a Christian martyr, whose object had been the protection of native races, and who had stuck to his duty despite terrible odds. Some evangelicals saw the loss as an assumption by Gordon of the sins of the nation, or at least as a visitation of God's displeasure on a materialist country. Conservatives maintained that the government did not understand the need to uphold

---

[115] 2 Apr. 1884, Gwynn and Tuckwell, *Dilke*, vol. II, pp. 47–8.
[116] *Hansard*, 288:207–20, 260–72, 13 May 1884.     [117] *Hansard*, 288:55, 224, 12, 13 May 1884.

national 'honour'. Wolseley taught his dog to growl at every mention of the word 'Gladstone'. Public clamour for the reassertion of British military prestige was irresistible. The cabinet quickly agreed to a campaign to stamp out the Mahdi's rebellion and the separate one by Osman Digna, and to begin the Suakin-Berber railway. Hartington pledged to reverse the 'spectacle of British civilization retiring before a barbarous form of Mohamedan fanaticism': this was necessary on behalf of the people of Egypt, the powers, Britain's Moslem subjects, the Indian empire, and 'the name, the credit, and the honour of England'.[118] Gladstone now proposed the assassination of Osman Digna in order to stop his revolt and bring stability prior to a withdrawal from the region.[119] That was impossible, owing to the lack of military resources in the Sudan. The railway to Berber was begun on 13 March, but Osman Digna was not captured; after a defeat, he retreated into the mountains. It quickly became clear that a major expedition would be necessary to take Berber and to safeguard the building of the railway, let alone to capture Khartoum or the Mahdi.

But what would be the point, since neither Gladstone nor Hartington wanted a long-term British occupation of Khartoum? Almost no one claimed that there were major British strategic or commercial interests in the Sudan. To the man in the street, Khartoum was geographically and culturally remote. No European rival sought to humiliate Britain by taking it. It was more important to see off French pressure on Egypt herself. The Mahdi's threat to Cairo had collapsed; he was retreating southwards from Khartoum, challenged by rivals. Wolseley, in the Sudan, advised that the attempt to vanquish him would cost millions and do little good where it mattered, 'in the eyes of the world'. 'Let the Turk into the Soudan, and re-establish your prestige in some less fruitless manner.'[120]

The need was indeed to demonstrate British prestige, in front of the European powers on the one hand and Britain's Moslem subjects on the other. And, as if Providentially, a chance arose almost immediately to do this, owing to the Russian advance on Pendjeh on the Afghan border. This was a shrewd attempt to embarrass Britain by forcing it to keep its Indian army on the subcontinent when regiments of it were badly needed in North Africa. It brought home to politicians the extent of imperial overstretch and Britain's vulnerability to attack from any of the great powers. Rosebery reflected that, if Britain were to conduct a major campaign on both the Sudanese and Afghan fronts, 'with both our arms bound . . . we

---

[118] *Hansard*, 294:1703, 27 Feb. 1885.      [119] To Hartington, 16 Feb. 1885, *GD*, vol. XI, p. 297.
[120] 1 Apr. 1885, Bahlman, *Hamilton*, vol. II, p. 827.

should be exposed to endure what any Power might choose to lay upon us, and be compelled to forgo all voice or share in the destinies of the world'.[121] Gladstone also noted that Britain could not struggle with France, Russia and the Sudan at the same time and must concentrate its resources where it had clear responsibilities.[122] The Gordon affair made it politically impossible to abandon Egypt to international control, but that made it easier to terminate operations in the Sudan. Childers and Hartington, conscious of the British blood shed there, and, in Hartington's case his personal pledges to Parliament, were reluctant to join the new consensus for withdrawal but eventually did so. The Conservatives were unable to make much of the abandonment of the Suakin-Berber railway, or of Dongola, because of the media anxiety over Central Asia: 'the "man in the street" has transferred his ardour from the Soudan to the confines of India'.[123]

As soon as British prestige in Asia was threatened, imperial strategists and the press were all but united that this was an arena far more important than the Sudan. Hartington himself, when India Secretary in 1880–1, had guaranteed the Afghan frontier against unprovoked attack, a decision that had been politically essential in order to head off allegations of Liberal weakness against the Russians. The Russian advance could be seen as an attack on the common-sense Hartington–Ripon policy on the north-west frontier from one extreme, just as the Disraeli–Lytton attack had been from the other. In a masterly Commons performance, Gladstone described it as the breaking of an agreement, the reopening of a question that his own government had settled in 1880–1 and that therefore intimately involved its own honour. 'Certainly one of his grandest triumphs,' recorded his private secretary Hamilton: 'there was hardly a man who could not help cheering'.[124] Russia backed down without a fight. Pendjeh demonstrated that Gladstone retained considerable skill on foreign-policy issues, but also that the international and domestic climate had changed dramatically and that a strong national policy would now always be necessary against the various rival European powers. Over the next ten years the British military establishment in India nearly doubled.

The Sudan affair showed that ethical 'Forsterism' was a problem for the government, because of its common ground with the Conservative opposition. However, it also showed that threats to British imperial interests

---

[121] Rosebery to Ponsonby, 24 Apr. 1885, G. E. Buckle (ed.), *Letters of Queen Victoria, second series* (London, 1928), vol. III, pp. 640–2.
[122] 13 Apr. 1885, *Derby diary 1878–93*, p. 773.    [123] 11 Apr. 1885, Bahlman, *Hamilton*, vol. II, p. 833.
[124] 27 Apr. 1885, ibid., pp. 850–1.

from foreign powers had a greater political impact. The development of the 'Scramble' for territory in southern and coastal Africa between 1883 and 1885 also demonstrated both points very well. Forsterism had some influence in forcing the government forward, but international rivalry had more. In fact, the powers eventually resolved the tensions of the 'Scramble' fairly amicably. Arguably, therefore, its greatest effect for domestic politics was that Dilke and Chamberlain used it to set out a patriotic Radicalism that changed the balance of power within the Liberal party. They saw how they could work with Hartington and the Palmerstonians in the hope of strengthening their own position, marginalising the Little Englanders, minimising the threat from the Conservatives and adjusting to the new realities of global imperialism.

There had always been scope for 'Forsterism' in relation to southern Africa. Though the incoming Gladstone government was determined to reverse the Conservatives' annexation of the Boer lands in the Transvaal, it was sensitive to the dangers of renewed Boer insurgency against the Tswana tribes in Bechuanaland. Gladstone's policy of suzerainty, ratified in October 1881, was designed to give the Transvaal self-government in practice while not relinquishing British influence, thus in theory safeguarding the rights of the native tribes, as well as the defence of South Africa against European rivals. Threats to the Tswana continued, and John Mackenzie, missionary and anti-slavery activist, held a series of provincial meetings from 1882 calling on Britain to protect them. He won support from influential spokesmen for the Liberal conscience such as Stead, Dale of Birmingham and Wemyss Reid of the *Leeds Mercury* – as well as from evangelical Tories like the City banker Fowler. But lobbying on behalf of natives was rarely able to change policy in southern Africa by itself – though it played a part in the decision of 1883 to take control in Basutoland from a discredited Cape administration.[125] In March 1884 Kimberley asked the cabinet to increase the British protectorate over Zululand, but to no avail: 'I see the cabinet do not want more niggers.' In 1883 *The Times* commented, in discussing Bechuanaland, that 'we must cease to pose as the defenders of the weak against the strong all over the world'.[126] For its part, the Colonial Office was reluctant to be assertive, since its prime goal was to get the Cape government to accept its local responsibilities.

---

[125] Schreuder, *Scramble for southern Africa*, pp. 103–9.
[126] Gwynn and Tuckwell, *Dilke*, vol. II, p. 86; *The Times*, 14 Apr. 1883, quoted in A. Sillery, *John Mackenzie of Bechuanaland 1835–1899: a study in humanitarian imperialism* (Cape Town, 1971), p. 77.

However, when these issues came to the fore again in 1884–5, they did so in the context of increasing public anxiety about foreign-power competition for commercial and strategic benefits around most of the coast of Africa. Lobby groups of merchants proliferated in the trade depression from 1883: African sections of both the Liverpool and London Chambers of Commerce in 1884 were founded in order to influence government policy, while Manchester merchants established the Manchester Geographical Society in 1885 in order to study new opportunities for the export of cotton. Imperial consolidation was a popular theme for the Chambers: Birmingham took up the cry in 1885, while London called for a 'new colonial movement' in 1884. Simultaneously, the French and Germans were developing interests in African ports. Significant tension had arisen over the mouth of the Congo, where both countries were upset by the British attempt to negotiate a treaty with Portugal maintaining informal British primacy, which had been ruthlessly established by Palmerston in the decade after 1846. And the Germans were annoyed by Britain's refusal either to agree to protect German traders at Angra Pequena on the coast of south-west Africa or to consent to Germany doing so. Bismarck, pressed by a colonial party at home, regarded this disdainful response as an 'affront to our national self-esteem' and in August 1884 declared Angra Pequena German.[127] He exploited French displeasure at British policy in Egypt to persuade them of the value of a conference at Berlin to settle contested African coastal tensions. There he forced Britain to accept German claims in Africa and New Guinea in return for helping to settle Egypt. The Berlin conference resolved the Congo issue (satisfactorily from a British viewpoint), and British trade interests were in most cases well protected. It laid down the doctrine that effective occupation, rather than informal paramountcy, should determine future European rights to African territory. It helped to ensure that the 'partition of Africa' was conducted according to understandings between the powers, forestalling future serious tension between them in this new theatre. The partition could also be seen as a joint European operation to check the expansion of militant Islam.[128]

The domestic significance of the great power rivalries of 1883–5 that preceded the Berlin conference was that they allowed Dilke and Chamberlain to become unapologetic imperialists. They became the two most consistent

[127] For commercial pressures, see Hynes, *Economics of empire*, pp. 57–83, and B. M. Ratcliffe, 'Commerce and empire: Manchester merchants and West Africa, 1873–95', *Journal of Imperial and Commonwealth History*, 7 (1979), 308–11. For the Angra Pequena affair, see Schreuder, *Scramble for southern Africa*, ch. 3.

[128] Hyam, *Britain's imperial century*, p. 216.

and assiduous advocates of commercial interests in Africa and of a policy of challenging French and German claims to African territory. They insisted that the promotion of commerce was not just a legitimate task of government but also one of the most appropriate ways in which to pursue a patriotic politics. This allowed them to defend the national interest while remaining loyal to their theoretical Radical commitment to self-government for Africans. Dilke was a major promoter of the Congo treaty. Both men had wanted Britain to set up a protectorate in the Cameroons in 1882, following pressure applied by John Holt and other Liverpool and London merchants. They criticised the Foreign Office for timidity and bureaucracy in delaying intervention until it was too late and the Germans had taken the area. Dilke was similarly angry about Colonial Secretary Derby's public renunciation of interest in Madagascar in 1882, an area where British and American missionaries were active; he thought Derby too anxious to avoid offending the French, who subsequently occupied it. After the failure in Cameroon, Chamberlain vowed in March 1885 that commercial interests would never forgive the government if it did not secure the lower Niger against French rivalry. He proposed that a charter, awarding large-scale commercial rights in the area, should be given to George Goldie's National African Company; this was awarded in 1886, and the Lower Niger was recognised as a British sphere.[129] In East Africa, Dilke and Chamberlain were anxious about German ambitions in the Zanzibari hinterland. So were the influential shipping magnate William Mackinnon, the Manchester Chamber of Commerce, the town's MP Jacob Bright, and Lord Aberdare (former Home Secretary Bruce and chairman of the National African Company). Gladstone scorned the idea of establishing a British protectorate over it, and it took a great deal of official and commercial lobbying to get an agreement with Germany dividing the territory, which was done in 1885–6 with the British taking the northern portion (later Kenya).[130] There were similar tensions with Germany in the Pacific, over Samoa and New Guinea, in 1884–5. Chamberlain commented: 'I don't care the least about New Guinea and I am not afraid of German colonisation, but I don't like to be cheeked by Bismarck or anyone else.'[131]

Radical pressure for assertiveness also influenced policy on southern Africa in 1884–5, since the Germans were interested in south-west Africa and in St Lucia Bay in the south-east, and the fear emerged that the Boers

---

[129] Cooke and Vincent, *Governing passion*, p. 206; Garvin, *Chamberlain*, pp. 294–5.

[130] Nicholls, *Dilke*, p. 93; M. E. Chamberlain, 'Clement Hill's memoranda and the British interest in East Africa', *English Historical Review*, 87 (1972), 533–47.

[131] To Dilke, 29 Dec. 1884, Garvin, *Chamberlain*, p. 497; see *Derby diary 1878–93*, pp. 685, 695.

would make an alliance with them to subvert British power at the Cape. In mid-1884 Chamberlain, Dilke and Hartington began to criticise Derby and the Colonial Office for failing to protect British interests in southern Africa. The cabinet had consented to the German occupation of Angra Pequena in return for German help on the Egyptian question. Then in September the Boers occupied large parts of Bechuanaland. Chamberlain now urged action on behalf of the Tswana; Hartington felt that Britain's simultaneous feebleness against Germany over South Africa and against France over Egypt was weakening it in both disputes rather than allowing it, as in the days of Palmerston, to play its rivals off against each other. There was support for action of some sort from a wide spectrum of opinion, from old Earl Grey to anti-slavery Dissenters. Derby regarded the force of press lobbying as 'irresistible'. Thus the cabinet came to sanction an expedition to Bechuanaland. The Colonial Office and Gladstone hoped that this action and the threat of German–Boer consolidation would encourage the Cape to make its own arrangements to defend the area. However in the event, in 1885, the British themselves had to annex Bechuanaland, as well as territory on the south-east coast, against the fear of 'German encroachment'.[132]

These imperial crises allowed Dilke and Chamberlain to position Radicalism as a strongly patriotic movement. They saw an assertive extra-European policy as a declaration of national pride but with attractively Radical, particularly commercial, connotations, given the interest of merchants in the potential of African markets. Government had a responsibility to support commercial interests abroad, just as it did to protect Englishmen's lives and property. Kimberley observed that 'the neo-Radical is more often a "jingo" than not'.[133] A strong foreign policy, promoting Anglo-American liberal principles throughout the world, demonstrated the democracy's superior vitality to the effete world of the Foreign and Colonial Offices. These aristocratic establishments could be attacked for not seeing that the promotion of British commercial interests was essential for a strong nation in a competitive world, reflecting the vigour of a politically articulate, libertarian and entrepreneurial people. Dilke and Chamberlain ridiculed Granville's tenure of the Foreign Secretaryship and Derby's rule at the Colonial Office. They saw both men as indecisive, spineless and dilatory figures, instinctive appeasers for the sake of a quiet life, who lacked any clear conception of international politics. 'Old Granny'

---

[132] Garvin, *Chamberlain*, pp. 491–3; Grey in *The Times*, 14 Oct. 1884 ('bold & English': N. E. Johnson (ed.), *The diary of Gathorne Hardy, later Lord Cranbrook, 1866–1892: political selections* (Oxford, 1981), p. 541); 11 Jan. 1884, *Derby diary 1878–93*, pp. 624–5.

[133] To Ripon, 15 Feb. 1884, Powell, *Liberal by principle*, p. 169.

was ignominiously moved away from the Foreign Office on the formation of the 1886 government, while 'Dawdling Derby' was an easy target because of the image of indecisiveness that he had acquired when Conservative Foreign Secretary in the 1870s. Derby was especially blamed for the handling of the London Convention of February 1884 with the Boers (to review the 1881 settlement), because he omitted Britain's claim of 'suzerainty' over them, thus facilitating their subsequent incursions into the grazing lands of Bechuanaland. Moreover, Granville and Derby had been responsible, almost continuously, for the sorry conduct of British foreign relations since the death of Palmerston. This attack on the bumbling and inefficient world of the diplomatic bureaucracy was reminiscent of the Bulgarian agitation and the Administrative Reform Association of 1855. It was a campaign with clear Radical undertones and class objectives.

This vigorous strategy also helped the two Radicals' broader political aims in the party. It helped them to work together with the leading Whigs against Cobdenite Radicals and Gladstone, yet it allowed them to compete with the Whigs for the patriotic mantle, just as Palmerston and Russell had worked together, yet also in rivalry, in the 1850s. Hartington, far more than Disraeli, was Palmerston's political heir. He combined Palmerston's liberal-constitutional language with his concern to maintain Britain's strategic and military strength – and his belief that this was the way to marginalise the political challenge from the Conservatives. As India and then War Secretary between 1880 and 1885, he was particularly concerned with the defence of India and with the general issue of British prestige. He was the leading Liberal advocate of a policy of imperial assertiveness in Egypt, the Sudan and Persia, and also a supporter of a forward policy in South Africa. He was also Gladstone's inevitable successor as leader of the Liberal party, and it was almost universally assumed at the beginning of 1885 that Gladstone would retire as soon as the Redistribution Bill was passed in the spring. The crucial question for the future of the party would be the relationship between Hartington and Dilke and Chamberlain. The party must be held together against a reviving Conservative threat, by a strong defence of national greatness. But the latter were also determined, once their hands were strengthened by the Third Reform Act, to demand a high price for accepting Hartington as Prime Minister. And by denying his claim to be the only true representative of the Palmerstonian tradition, they might underline his dependence on their support.

These three men were also conscious that a well-presented imperial policy would appeal to, yet neutralise, the Forsterite wing of Liberalism. None of them had much time for an overtly religious or sentimental political language; all considered themselves to be modern-minded, essentially post-religious politicians. After Gordon met Hartington, he commented that he needed a Bible.[134] But they were aware that Forster's language attracted many strongly patriotic evangelicals.[135] It had a broader appeal too. In 1884–5 Forster and Stead took up Earl Grey's idea of a Colonial Council in London, in order to flesh out the idea of imperial federation.[136] This would strengthen British power against rivals, by improving coordination between the metropolis and the colonies, acting as a lobby group for imperial needs and evolving a joint defence strategy (a particular problem in the light of Australian criticisms of British insensitivity over the German threat to New Guinea). Another reason for urgency, for many federalists, was the impending extension of the franchise, which was likely to intensify the drift and lack of vision in British colonial policy, and the dominance of insular and sectional domestic pressures either for lower taxes or for expenditure on other causes. A permanent structure for empire offered the prospect of withstanding these democratic instincts. Moreover, for federalists of Liberal views, a federated empire would act as a symbol of the vigorous, manly, self-supporting values that characterised the settler colonies, and of the mission to spread these values over the world; it was important to teach the new democracy about both.[137] At a time when Britain's domestic and foreign future hung in the balance – 'the present outlook is dark and stormy', Forster wrote in 1885 – federation offered the prospect of creating a true Cromwellian 'commonwealth'. The young Scottish Liberal peer Rosebery – another admirer of Cromwell – coined the phrase 'commonwealth of nations' when speaking in Adelaide during a world tour in 1883–4.[138]

In itself, imperial federation was too abstract and impractical to be a successful movement. However, with a few exceptions, such as Harcourt and Morley, by 1885 the balance of forces among the coming men in the Liberal party clearly favoured those who were happy to play the imperial card. Rosebery's extraordinarily rapid rise in the party in the 1880s was

---

[134] J. Pearson, *Stags and serpents: the story of the House of Cavendish and the dukes of Devonshire* (London, 1983), p. 167.

[135] Including some evangelical Dissenters: Bebbington, *Nonconformist conscience*, pp. 110, 112–15.

[136] Whyte, *Stead*, vol. 1, p. 106.

[137] I have benefited from discussions on the imperial federation movement with Duncan Bell and from his thesis, 'The debate about federation in empire political thought, 1860–1900' (University of Cambridge PhD, 2004).

[138] Forster, 'A few more words', 552; Koebner and Schmidt, *Imperialism*, p. 182. Forster, in fact, had used the term first, in 1876: McKinstry, *Rosebery*, p. 121. Rosebery advocated Cromwell's 'patriotism' and 'imperialism' as exemplary, because they rested on his 'faith . . . in God and in freedom, and in the influence of Great Britain as promoting, as asserting, both'; Lord Rosebery, *Cromwell: a speech delivered at the Cromwell Tercentenary Celebration 1899* (2nd edn, London, 1900), pp. 23–4.

mostly due to his identification with imperial (but also Scottish) issues. His world tour was planned in order to gain a strategic view of the empire and Britain's world role as a progressive, constitutional force, something that he assumed would be essential for a future Liberal leader. For him as for Hartington, Dilke and Chamberlain, empire was a way of defending national interests against rising foreign threats, and spreading Anglo-Saxon constitutional and entrepreneurial values in a modern, essentially secular, manly and vigorous way. Granville and Derby, by contrast, were busted flushes after 1885. Both were taken aback by what Granville called 'wild and irrational' press clamour for imperial expansion.[139]

Liberal supporters of imperialism were also aware that by 1885 the Conservative party posed a greater threat to Liberalism than at any time in their adult lives, and that any weakness abroad would be mercilessly contrasted with the 'honest, manly, straightforward' imperial policy of Conservatives.[140] Conservatives could increasingly compete for the patriotic mantle with Liberals, for a number of reasons. The Church and the army, the institutions with which they were best identified, now appeared more 'national' and less exclusive than of old, not least because of Liberal reforms of them. Alarm at atheist and foreign threats encouraged the perception of their value. Bright noted as early as 1877 that the Church's position was becoming unassailable.[141] The army was much more integrated into national life by the 1880s, partly owing to press and music-hall celebrations of imperial victories, and partly because the 1880–5 government strengthened the territorial system and the links with the Volunteers. Childers, the architect of the reforms, subsequently expressed his pleasure at the 'rising local sentiment' in the army.[142] But it was now more difficult to present it as a sinister force, soaking up money and threatening liberties.

Meanwhile Liberals could now be attacked for their un-Englishness, over the 'American' caucus, for example, which seemed to transfer power to 'wirepullers', or over the 'socialism' of their rate and land policies. Conservatives could also claim that the Liberal party was now a sectional rather than national party, on account of its 'faddism'. The variety of competing

---

[139] Dec. 1884, quoted in Robinson and Gallagher, *Africa and the Victorians*, p. 207. Derby was in fact more 'forward' in colonial affairs than his reputation suggested. But the Liberal peers got a bad press: apart from Hartington, the imperialist Rosebery was the only acceptable candidate as Liberal Foreign Secretary in 1886. Even Kimberley's appointment would have been met by a 'chorus of newspaper denunciations': *Kimberley*, p. 364, 3 Feb. 1886.

[140] *Yorkshire Post*, 25 Sept. 1885, quoted in M. Roberts, 'W. L. Jackson, exemplary manliness and late-Victorian popular Conservatism', in M. McCormack (ed.), *Public men: political masculinities in modern Britain* (forthcoming).

[141] *Derby diary 1878–93*, p. 46.          [142] Childers, *Childers*, vol. II, pp. 60–1, 65.

agendas did in fact make it difficult for the 1880–5 cabinet to impose a legislative programme, which in reaction allowed Chamberlain to urge a move towards a systematic programmatic politics. In 1885 Chamberlain damaged the party not primarily by his detailed policy proposals, on which he hastily back-pedalled once the Conservatives began to gain from criticising them, but by his alarmingly 'provincializing and Americanizing' assault on the Westminster political ethos – class-conscious, brash, threatening to property and the Church, and deliberately shocking to English political establishment conventions.[143]

Moreover, once the Disraelian threat had disappeared, Liberals were finding it more and more difficult to create a distinctively *liberal* patriotism on policy issues. Fundamentally this was because of a waning confidence that traditional liberal values could surmount class tensions at home, any more than they could surmount great power rivalry abroad without a much more vigorous assertiveness. Though there was large-scale Liberal support for the 1884 Reform Act, there was also considerable anxiety about its effects on the existing balance of class power. Liberals had always emphasised the deliberative and integrative function of Parliament as a national assembly. Yet there were increasing doubts that the Commons could bind together the nation and create a stable consensus – not least because of the obstruction campaign of the Irish Nationalist MPs, which paralysed the legislative programme and led to the implementation of the *clôture* to curtail Parliamentary debate in 1882.[144] It could no longer be said that the British constitution was obviously more effective than those of other Western countries. In particular, though the French Third Republic was not yet entirely stable, it was much more successful than previous regimes. Lawlessness – as in the international nihilist movement and other terrorist organisations – was a general problem, and it became apparent that European states needed to work together against it, just as they did in Africa against Islamic uprisings. In 1881 the British government prosecuted the German immigrant editor of an anarchist magazine for praising the assassination of Tsar Alexander II. The prosecution against *Freiheit*, which was successful, marked a new attitude to the political activities of foreign refugees in England, very different from the defence of them that was common in Liberal–Radical politics in the 1840s and 1850s. Gladstone's government wanted to cooperate with

---

[143] J. A. Spender, *The public life* (2 vols., London, 1925), vol. 1, p. 80. For the debate of 1878–83 on whether the caucus was an Americanising force, see P. Pombeni, 'Starting in reason, ending in passion: Bryce, Lowell, Ostrogorski and the problem of democracy', *Historical Journal*, 37 (1994), 325–7, and Gerlach, *British Liberalism*, pp. 61–3.

[144] On the use in practice of the closure and the guillotine, see Parry, *Rise and fall*, pp. 254–5, 310n.

other states to defend the forces of law, not least because of its own bid for the assistance of the United States authorities against American promoters and funders of the Clan-na-Gael bombing campaign which began in Lancashire and London in early 1881. Strikingly, it was Home Secretary Harcourt, formerly a flamboyant libertarian and youthful assailant of Napoleon III, who led the new tough policy, not just over the *Freiheit* prosecution but also by ordering regular police surveillance of refugees in England from this time.[145]

In all these ways, the power of a specifically liberal patriotic language seemed to be waning. This was one reason why so many leading Liberals were attracted to a liberal imperialism. But for others, particularly Gladstone, imperial language was becoming alarmingly nationalistic. When Rosebery told him of his plans for a world tour he was 'stunned'. He thought imperial federation 'little short of nonsensical', and showed no interest in the finer points of the Scramble for Africa.[146] In his eyes, a cult of territorial acquisition and international rivalry overburdened the Treasury, unbalanced the machinery of state and of foreign relations and inculcated the wrong values in the people. In 1877 he had ridiculed the idea of a British occupation of Egypt, on the grounds that it would alienate France, add to international tension and force Britain to govern a Moslem people, something for which it had no talent. Further acquisitions of this sort would 'compromise British character in the judgment of the impartial world', and prevent the tackling of domestic ills. They would be too great a burden, economically and morally, for a nation that already had more responsibilities than the Roman empire. The desire to extend the realm of British conquest stemmed from materialist lusts: states could be swayed by 'the sudden flush of wealth and pride' more easily than individuals, because the accountability of the individual conscience was suppressed.[147] Political pressures had forced Gladstone to support intervention in 1882, but by 1885 he was clearly furious at the financial, diplomatic and moral costs of the continuing occupation, and by the rising clamour from the press and the Conservative party for an extension of imperial assertiveness. The upshot was his election address of September 1885, perhaps the most astounding ever written by a Prime Minister. He attempted to turn the contest into a virtuous crusade against Conservative-style nationalist imperialism. In

---

[145]  B. Porter, 'The Freiheit prosecutions, 1881–1882', *Historical Journal*, 23 (1980), 833–56.

[146]  To Rosebery, 29 July 1883, *GD*, vol. XI, pp. 10–11; 19 Nov. 1884, Bahlman, *Hamilton*, vol. II, p. 737. See Chamberlain, 'Clement Hill's memoranda', 538–42.

[147]  Gladstone, 'Aggression on Egypt and freedom in the East', *Nineteenth Century*, 2 (1877), 150–2, 161–2.

order to do so, he admitted that the policy to which his own government had been driven both in Egypt and the Sudan was a 'grave political error', a 'war against nature', and that 'the Providential order commonly allots . . . retribution' to such errors. Britain must follow its withdrawal from the Sudan with a withdrawal from Egypt, thus restoring the 'perfect independence and salutary influence' in Europe 'given us by the Almighty'.[148]

It was, then, the duty of a God-fearing statesman to reassert the right view of England's mission, based on the Providential principles of economy, restraint and self-government. Moreover, the chance to do so immediately occurred in Ireland – demonstrating once more how intimately linked were the underlying issues in domestic and foreign policy.

### HOME RULE, DEMOCRACY, EMPIRE AND NATIONHOOD

The devastating split in the Liberal party in 1886 over Gladstone's scheme of Home Rule for Ireland involved a great many issues and considerations and has been exhaustively analysed. Here there is only room to consider those aspects which are directly related to the themes discussed already. It now appears clear that Gladstone was *not* converted to Home Rule by the result of the autumn 1885 election, which left the Irish Nationalists holding the balance of power. His interest in it was not originally sparked by the need to bid for their support. Instead, as he later recalled, he had been persuaded of the cause by reading a newspaper report of a speech by the Irish MP William O'Brien, on 1 March 1885. The speech convinced him that the Union of 1801 was illegitimate and not morally binding on the Irish.[149]

The date was deeply significant. There was nothing novel in O'Brien's speech, nothing that Gladstone would not have heard dozens of times before from Irish MPs. His sensitivity to the argument about the illegitimacy of the Union was surely aroused by the two dominant political issues of February–March 1885: the far-reaching Parliamentary reform legislation for Britain and Ireland, and the controversies over British imperial activity in Africa. In deciding that Home Rule was a necessary act of justice, Gladstone wanted to instruct the newly emerging democracy, in Britain and Ireland, about the responsibilities of both governments and voters. Both must exercise their consciences and demonstrate civic selflessness if

[148] *The Times*, 19 Sept. 1885, p. 8.
[149] J. Loughlin, *Gladstone, Home Rule and the Ulster question 1882–93* (Dublin, 1986), p. 36; Shannon, *Gladstone 1865–1898*, pp. 352, 356.

right relations were to be maintained within the polity. He also wanted
to assert the right view of empire – a mid-century vision of a group of
predominantly white settler colonies, exemplifying this self-disciplined,
'English' self-governing practice. Conversely, the opposition that he stirred
up, and that so disastrously divided the Liberal party when he launched
his scheme in early 1886, was largely driven by a sense that it would teach
the wrong values at home and be fatal to Britain's global standing as an
imperial power. Gladstone's urgency in promoting Home Rule in 1885–6
stemmed from an insistence that his conception of England's Providential role must be maintained against a false view, and that God would not
release him from politics until this was done. (Conveniently, it would also
indicate his irreplaceability as a leader.) Rather than a piece of heroic progressivism, it was a desperate stand against unsavoury aspects of the modern
world.

Gladstone was not a man to do the bidding of Irish Nationalist MPs. In
1883 he compared them to 'vermin about a man's person' – a nuisance, but
not likely to deflect him from a righteous course. As throughout his career,
he took little notice of them and was disdainfully reluctant to negotiate
with them. In 1878 he had rebuked them for their lack of sympathy with
the Balkan people who had 'suffered oppression a hundredfold deeper and
crimes a hundredfold blacker' than the Irish.[150] He made little of the problems of Ireland at Midlothian in 1879–80 – he believed that his government
had resolved the historic Irish grievances and that this was one area where
Disraeli had not undermined his legacy. Gladstone rejected the premise of
the more explicit Nationalist rhetoric that emerged from the late 1870s –
that English imperial rule could legitimately be compared to Turkish or
Austrian misrule elsewhere. (The nature of the connection between the
imperial turn in British political discourse and the radicalisation of Irish
Nationalism between 1878 and 1882 is worthy of further study.) British
guidance, he felt, had had a civilising effect. He considered most Nationalist MPs unscrupulous and ungentlemanly; one great aim of his Home
Rule scheme was to undermine their appeal and restore the leadership of
a civic-minded propertied Irish elite. In principle he had no difficulty in
justifying his government's coercive legislation to uphold law and order;
he also believed that Irish dislike of the British could easily be exaggerated.
He saw Parnell's Nationalists as a danger; unless legitimate Irish grievances
were met, their power would grow, so a strong policy was needed to nip

---

[150]  8 Oct. 1883, *Derby diary 1878–93*, p. 594; to Hartington, 30 May 1885, *GD*, vol. XI, p. 349; Shannon,
      *Gladstone 1865–1898*, p. 215. See Chamberlain's complaint of 1882: Garvin, *Chamberlain*, p. 352.

their support in the bud.[151] He had expected a majority at the 1885 election, which would allow him the freedom to explore the Irish government problem and to show the capacity of the British executive for disinterested action. Nationalists themselves rued Gladstone's Home Rule declaration as counterproductively premature.[152]

However, Gladstone, like everyone else, was naturally aware in the months leading up to the 1885 election that, as the first to be fought on a mass franchise in Ireland, it would indicate great popular support for the Nationalists. He recognised that government had a duty to respond to a cry of this magnitude. When he reflected on what had gone wrong in Anglo-Irish relations, he was drawn to the removal of the Irish Parliament at the Union of 1801. He considered that its continued existence would have forced landlords to sympathise with the people, and to provide responsible leadership. Right relations between government and people had been disturbed by the force and fraud of the Act of Union, never properly legitimised. It was, like some more recent British imperial aggressions, a grasping, domineering, un-Christian act. 'A great National sin had been committed.' Britain should atone for it by removing the distortion that it had introduced into the political machinery. The Irish Parliament should be restored.[153]

Gladstone's presentation of the Irish problem therefore concentrated less on the abstract rights of Irishmen than on the selfishness of British rule. Some years beforehand he had commented that the state of Ireland was 'a warning & a judgment for our heavy sins as a nation: for broken faith, for the rights of others trampled down, for blood wantonly and largely shed'. In June 1886 he wrote of the 'baseness and blackguardism' of the means by which the Union was carried.[154] For many evangelical Dissenters too, the Home Rule cause taught England a moral lesson: the need to get 'down in the very dust' and confess past iniquities and injustices.[155] In repentance, England would now offer justice and humanity. One great attraction of Home Rule was that it offered the new democracy in Britain an uplifting morality tale. The advent of a wider electorate made it crucial to educate the voters of the United Kingdom into the principles of humility, and of

---

[151] E. D. Steele, 'Gladstone and Ireland', *Irish Historical Studies*, 17 (1970), 78–9; to Bankes, 7 Apr. 1882, *GD*, vol. x, p. 233; 28 Feb. 1882, *Derby diary 1878–93*, p. 404.

[152] Healy: Shannon, *Gladstone 1865–1898*, p. 366.

[153] The quotation is from a conversation with Kimberley: Elliot, *Goschen*, vol. i, p. 316. See Loughlin, *Gladstone, Home Rule*, pp. 186–7.

[154] 31 Dec. 1880, *GD*, vol. ix, p. 656; 17 June 1886, *Derby diary 1878–93*, p. 835. See also his comments of 1886 on England's misdeeds, quoted in Shannon, *Bulgarian agitation*, p. 280.

[155] J. E. Butler, *Our Christianity tested by the Irish question* (London, 1888), p. 61.

mutual obligations between classes, interest groups and nations. Gladstone convinced himself that this was God's mission for him. This would allow him to construct democratic politics on an ethical platform rather than one pandering to materialism and class tension. Ideals of humanitarianism and sympathy with other peoples would offer an antidote to class jealousy and to amoral press-generated imperial fervour which was corroding British voters' moral and liberal sensibilities. This element of Gladstone's language was indeed very attractive outside Parliament. Some of Gladstone's strongest supporters over Home Rule, such as John Morley, advocated it on essentially Mazzinian principles, as did many Radical working men.[156]

Unlike some Liberals, Gladstone had no difficulty in recognising the existence of an Irish nationality, attributable principally to a shared historical-cultural memory, afforced by ethnicity and religion. However, nationality was only significant for him up to a point. He frequently argued that the Scots were also a nation, with a discernible set of cultural values, but they were fully assimilated into the United Kingdom and accepted rule from Westminster. There was no reason in principle why the Irish should be different. Though he frequently expressed his theoretical willingness to legislate on a different basis for Scotland, Wales and England, and to consider limited devolution, this desire was not driven by an appreciation of an urgent national grievance, but by an executive politician's anxiety to improve the general efficiency and accountability of British government.[157] Therefore he did not want to tackle the Irish problem through a scheme of United Kingdom federalism. Similarly he did not believe that Protestant Ulster had a specific historic nationality which required a separate political arrangement. The need, instead, was to make restitution for the error of the Union, and to supply the conditions for good government. As a result, all Irishmen would benefit, and those Irish Protestant gentry who behaved responsibly would recover their rightful position of political leadership.[158] So the scheme of 1886 sought to repeal the Union in favour of a new, freer arrangement: a looser suzerainty from Westminster over an Irish Parliament, comparable to that which the British were also operating over the Transvaal. Gladstone's vision of the future of Ireland was based on his long-standing conception of the settler colonies. They had all begun as bodies of

---

[156] Parry, *Democracy and religion*, pp. 444–6.
[157] See e.g. Steele, 'Gladstone and Ireland', 86. On his greater enthusiasm for Scottish and Welsh identity than for Irish, see J. R. Vincent, 'Gladstone and Ireland', *Proceedings of the British Academy*, 63 (1977), 230–1.
[158] D. G. Boyce, 'In the front rank of the nation: Gladstone and the Unionists of Ireland, 1868–1893', in D. W. Bebbington and R. Swift, *Gladstone centenary essays* (Liverpool, 2000), pp. 185–201.

'free men' who had sought to establish new communities 'upon principles of freedom analogous to our own'. They should be seen as self-governing 'municipal corporations', whereas the tragedy of nineteenth-century imperial and Irish policy was that that perspective had been rejected in favour of an overly assertive and high-taxing 'executive government' approach from the centre, enfeebling local vigour.[159]

Nonetheless, most advocates of Home Rule were desperate to argue that the scheme would safeguard some British influence in Ireland, particularly control of external and defence policy, and London's ability to overrule the Dublin Parliament *in extremis*. There was great controversy about how far the plan was compatible with the maintenance of the United Kingdom. This ambiguity was compounded by the government's indecision about whether Irish MPs were or were not still to sit at Westminster. Ambiguity arose because the constitutional framework was not the crucial issue for Gladstone. Essential for him was that Ireland must remain loyal to the monarchy and within the sphere of British defence, but these things were also true of British colonies which had hardly any formal ties to Westminster. Gladstone's concern was to win Irish hearts and to instil the right political values by restoring the historic relationship between Britain and its overseas territories. He repositioned Ireland as a British outgrowth, as deserving as Canada and the Australian states of the responsible government awarded them in the 1840s and 1850s by his generation of colonial reformers. The best way to develop Irish stability, and loyalty to Britain, was by developing the same basis of effective citizenship that all self-governing 'English' communities should practise. Home Rule was a declaration that English global influence should be based on ethics, humanity and sympathy with 'the great human brotherhood' rather than on the traditional imperial practices of aggression, domination and ill-treatment.[160] Some Liberals who were hostile to the extension of Britain's imperial commitments, such as Harcourt, may have supported Home Rule mainly from approval of this alternative definition of the nation's mission.[161]

Gladstone hoped that his scheme would educate the Irish voter – like the British voter – to understand the principles of self-government and electoral and fiscal responsibility, the absence of which had 'lacerated other great and distinguished nations'.[162] By restoring the former Irish Parliament, Home

---

[159] He had set this idea out best in *Hansard*, 121:951–61, 21 May 1852.

[160] Gladstone, 8 June 1887, *PMP*, vol. IV, p. 86. See Butler, *Our Christianity tested*, pp. 28–9.

[161] See P. Jackson, *Harcourt and son: a political biography of Sir William Harcourt* (Madison, NJ, 2004), pp. 146–7.

[162] At Dublin, *The Times*, 8 Nov. 1877, p. 7.

Rule would create for the first time an Irish electorate and political class that would be mature enough to grasp those principles. Irish MPs had been able to bribe the Treasury into giving particular local interest-groups special benefits and doles. They had been able to undermine the imposition of law and the working of the British Parliament, because there was no general acceptance of the discipline and mutual obligations that made good government work. The result was 'economical and moral demoralisation' in all classes in Ireland: 'every new loan [is] a new danger'.[163] In Gladstone's eyes, the divine plan for the government of the world sought a balance between authority and public conscience: the law disciplined the people to understand the proper functions of government, while an aroused public conscience was required in order to check the sinfulness of those in authority. The propertied classes were the natural rulers of society, but the processes of political participation, party and public accountability were necessary to prevent their rule from turning into vested-interest and narrow class government. This machinery had been disrupted in Ireland. In 1871 he lamented the enfeebling there of 'those principles of self-reliance, those powers of local action, that energy and public spirit which are the inherited possessions of this country'. In 1882 he remarked on the 'miserable & almost total want of the sense of responsibility for the public good & public peace in Ireland'.[164] Local control over taxation would strengthen pressure for retrenchment and a fair distribution of revenues.

In other words, Gladstone wanted to give Ireland the blessings of self-government in order to make it more English. A second house in the Irish Parliament, favouring peers and gentry, would allow the 'moral repatriation' of the Anglo-Irish peerage, educating them 'to nationality, to love of country, to popularity'. Police numbers would fall if local Irish gentlemen started to play their proper role in their communities. The distressing need for an un-English coercion policy would lapse. Decentralisation and individual responsibility would check the demand for French *préfets*.[165] Gladstone had consistently fought against the 'continental' policy of state assistance for peasant proprietorship, not least because it would allow Irish landlords to neglect their political and social responsibilities. Although in 1886 political pressures forced him to accompany the Home Rule Bill with a half-hearted

---

[163] 24 May 1883: Bahlman, *Hamilton*, vol. II, p. 439; Trevelyan, 30 Dec. 1882, *Derby diary 1878–93*, p. 488.
[164] At Aberdeen, Sept. 1871, quoted in Vincent, 'Gladstone and Ireland', 235; to Forster, 12 Apr. 1882, *GD*, vol. X, p. 238.
[165] Boyce, 'In the front rank', 197–8; *GD*, vol. IX, p. 602. For the desire for French *préfets*, see *Red Earl*, vol. I, p. 19.

measure to extend land purchase, he hoped to minimise its offensiveness by forcing the Irish to pay the bulk of the burden themselves.[166]

Home Rule was the culmination of Gladstone's attempts to challenge the two principal foreign influences in Ireland: popery and American-Irish republicanism. The 1886 bill explicitly forbade the Irish Parliament to endow popery – earning Matthew Arnold's contempt.[167] Gladstone and his evangelical supporters claimed that, by establishing a constitutional voice for Ireland, the bill would finally defeat the power of the Pope, which he felt had contributed to his own downfall in 1873–4. Josephine Butler maintained that the Coercion Acts had driven the Irish to look to Rome, and that the establishment of self-government and liberty would remove 'all danger of subserviency to a foreign ecclesiastical power'.[168] For most people, terrorists and American money were by now a greater threat. Contacts and money from across the Atlantic sustained both Davitt's New Departure and Parnell's National League; the bombing campaign of Clan-na-Gael, now the main American-Irish political organisation, operated sporadically in Britain between 1881 and 1885. Stead argued for Home Rule partly on the grounds that, by approximating to American ideas of government, it would satisfy most Irishmen in America and destroy Parnell's financial base, the true threat to the Union. More importantly, it would weaken sympathy for American-based organisations in Ireland. He quoted Macaulay on Jewish emancipation: 'foreign attachments are the fruit of domestic misrule'; if government was 'tolerably good', 'the feeling of patriotism' was 'certain' to develop.[169]

Therefore Home Rule would also strengthen the legitimate authority of government, in Ireland and in the United Kingdom as a whole. This was particularly important given the onset of fuller democracy in 1885. A coercive policy was a symbol of weakness not strength; government legitimacy properly rested on participation and decentralisation. Indeed, it was in the hope of reasserting respect for the executive authority of Dublin Castle that the two most influential past Liberal Viceroys of Ireland, Kimberley and Spencer, reluctantly acquiesced in Home Rule. In particular they were pessimistic that, with the advent of more complete democracy on the mainland, the British Parliament would have the discipline to maintain a resolute Irish order policy. The Commons was now too unreliable,

---

[166] A. Warren, 'Gladstone, land and social reconstruction in Ireland 1881–1887', *Parliamentary History*, 2 (1983), 167–9; 23 Dec. 1885, *GD*, vol. XI, p. 458.
[167] 'The nadir of Liberalism', *Nineteenth Century*, 19 (1886), 659–60.
[168] Parry, *Democracy and religion*, pp. 445–6; Butler, *Our Christianity tested*, p. 8.
[169] Whyte, *Stead*, vol. I, pp. 227–8.

too inconsistent and too prone to party, sectional and populist whims. Self-government, therefore, offered the best chance of authoritative rule in Ireland.[170] Morley and Bryce similarly felt that a British democracy would not be willing to apply a consistent coercive regime. The result would be, more than ever, a 'policy of vacillation'. 'A democracy can only govern on democratic principles.'[171] Home Rule, on the other hand, would allow the restoration of legislative vigour not just in Ireland but also in the House of Commons, removing a sectional cause of obstruction that had jammed the machinery of state. There would be less need for the foreign checks on Parliamentary independence, the *clôture* and guillotine, that had had to be introduced in 1882. By ending drift, division and confusion, the concession of Home Rule would invigorate executive government in Britain and give a better tone to its leadership of the democracy. And a stable and peaceful Ireland would make it easier for Britain to assert itself abroad – morally and, if necessary, militarily.

Therefore there were sound constitutional and patriotic reasons for supporting Home Rule. But the politically crippling fact about the issue was that almost exactly the same arguments could also be made against it. In the early 1880s, disorder, boycotting and agitation in Ireland, bombing on the mainland and obstruction in Parliament created a very widespread conviction in the British press and in public opinion that the Irish were undisciplined, irresponsible and lawless. It was easy to argue that Irishmen lacked respect for the law, the constitution and the rights of property. Frederick Greenwood contrasted this with 'the ingrained English love of order, insistence on obedience to law, what we used to brag of as "law-abidingness"'. In October 1880 Chamberlain noted British workmen's annoyance at Parnell: they 'do not like to see the law set at defiance'. A year later, Derby was similarly aware of the unanimity of English opinion. Indeed Morley felt – just like Russell in 1848 – that the difficulties in Irish policy were 'due to the British public'.[172] The government, picking up on this mood, presented Parnell as a threat to Parliamentary government and the Land League as the antithesis of constitutionalism, allowing it to get general support for a Coercion Act in 1881. Home Secretary Harcourt used the supposed

---

[170] Nov. 1880, *GD*, vol. IX, pp. 620–2; Powell, *Liberal by principle*, p. 184.
[171] Harvie, *Lights of Liberalism*, p. 226; Morley, Bryce, *Hansard*, 304:1274, 305:1228–9, 9 Apr., 17 May 1886.
[172] J. W. R. Scott, *The story of the Pall Mall Gazette* (London, 1950), p. 257; 27 Oct. 1880, Gwynn and Tuckwell, *Dilke*, vol. I, pp. 345–6; 19 Oct. 1881, *Derby diary 1878–93*, p. 365; Whyte, *Stead*, vol. I, p. 88.

American input into the agitation as one justification for coercion. When the Land League leaders and Parnell challenged the authority of the Land Court of 1881, Gladstone saw this as 'the most immoral, the most wicked assault not only on law and order but on private rights'.[173] Chamberlain, another convert to coercion, considered Parnell's behaviour as insulting to British pride as he found Germany's in 1885. Such perceptions were assisted by the climate of alarm at international terrorism and anarchism, especially after the assassination of the Russian Tsar in March 1881.

Few Liberals had wanted to make Ireland a priority again in 1880. It was Parnell who put it back on the agenda, but the alien practices that made him impossible to ignore also made the idea of conceding to him instinctively unpalatable to many Englishmen. There were serious disputes within the cabinet about how best to contain Parnell's influence, one of which led to Forster's resignation in 1882. On that occasion the cabinet rejected his demand that Parnell should be made to renounce violence, not because they wished to pander to him, as Forster thought, but because they thought that such a declaration would suggest that they regarded Parnell as the ringmaster of Irish stability.[174] This episode was quickly followed by the Phoenix Park murders, which made the introduction of a stringent Crimes Act for three years politically necessary.

In 1886, therefore, it was easy to dispute the claim that the Irish were immediately fit for virtually complete self-government. This argument was compatible with a Radical constitutional perspective. Indeed from a Radical point of view the most weighty Liberal Unionist arguments were made by Bright, who insisted that the average Irishman had shown a lack of the constitutional maturity and the manly moral independence that had fitted the English to govern themselves. This was clear from the widespread support that they gave to 'revolutionists' and to Nationalist MPs who were bankrolled 'by the enemies of this country' in the United States, in opposition to the lawful authority of a democratic Parliament.[175] The problems in imposing law and trial by jury, the influence of the priesthood, and the weakness of the middle class were all frequently cited as evidence that the Irish character crucially lacked self-reliance.[176]

Such anxieties also demonstrate a growing gloom about the state of Ireland, dissipating a good deal of the former Liberal optimism about the prospects for improving it. In December 1885 Hartington, Northbrook

---

[173] Warren, 'Gladstone, land', 159.
[174] Gwynn and Tuckwell, *Dilke*, vol. I, p. 439; Kimberley, 1 May 1882, *GD*, vol. x, p. 247.
[175] G. M. Trevelyan, *Bright*, pp. 446, 448; at Birmingham, *The Times*, 2 July 1886, p. 10.
[176] Parry, *Democracy and religion*, pp. 443–4.

and Harcourt could be found reflecting bleakly on the inevitability of a
civil war in order to maintain British rule there.[177] Much of the British
press comment on Irish unrest, and depiction of Irish behaviour, used
racial stereotypes to explain Irish violence.[178] Social Darwinist ideas encouraged the development of racialist sentiment, particularly on the Tory side.
But though most Liberals had no doubt that the Irish were more backward than the English and held a different view of government and individual responsibility, it did not follow that they were unimprovable. By
1880 there was little illusion and much pessimism about the extent of the
backwardness: 'turbulence and disrespect of law have been bred in them
for generations till they have become part of the Irish nature'. But, as Kimberley went on, 'That is no reason for not taking measures to improve
the breed, but it is a reason for unlimited patience. Coercion by itself is
of little use.'[179] There was no shortage of Liberals who still argued in the
1880s that Britain's responsibility in Ireland was to act as a trustee for the
imposition of law and pursuit of progress. It is significant that one of the
few Victorian Liberal intellectuals who enthusiastically embraced racialist language, E. A. Freeman, was a supporter of Home Rule so as to rid
Britain of the Irish problem.[180] For most, the real issue in the 1880s was not
the precise racial qualities of the Irish; it was the duties and problems of
Britain.

Viewed from a *British* perspective, the Irish problem was intractable
because no Liberal government could survive if it maintained that coercion
was enough: constitutional solutions must be applied in Ireland, just as
elsewhere in the United Kingdom. It was particularly intractable in the
1880s because the impending extension of the franchise made it especially
necessary to assert that Liberalism embraced principles of popular consent.
The Irish question was so central to British politics between 1882 and 1886
because the lack of progress towards constitutional reform in Ireland could
be easily exploited by some Liberal MPs, by the dissident Conservatives
of the 'Fourth party', and by the Parnellites. Radicals used the Irish local
government issue as a political football to demonstrate that their liberalism
was purer than that of the Whigs. Gladstone mooted local government
reform from time to time, though without much urgency, and mainly in
order to defeat proposals for land purchase, by using the argument that
the former must precede the latter. Chamberlain's proposal of 1885, for
a central board scheme, was widely distrusted as part of his struggle to

---

[177] K. R. M. Short, *The dynamite war: Irish-American bombers in Victorian Britain* (Dublin, 1979),
    p. 228.
[178] See the debate discussed in Introduction, n. 54.     [179] 8 Nov. 1880, *Kimberley*, p. 319.
[180] Harvie, *Lights of Liberalism*, p. 222.

seize control of the political agenda, and for giving too little power to the localities while offering a springboard for Irish agitators and socialists.[181] But all advocacy of constitutional change was half-hearted because it was politically impossible in the climate of 1882–5, given the Phoenix Park murders, the mainland bombing campaign, the alarmism of British public opinion, and the paralysis in cabinet caused by Whig–Radical tension in advance of 1885 and Gladstone's expected retirement. Hartington, whose brother had been assassinated in Phoenix Park, made it plain in early 1883 that this was not the time for the government to lose its responsibility for Irish order, and the cabinet readily agreed.[182]

Nonetheless, it was quite clear that any new Liberal government after 1885 would have to accept Irish local government reform and land purchase in some form, just as it would have to accept county councils and land reform in Britain. Hartington, for one, recognised this.[183] In fact, most landlords now welcomed land purchase, and many Whigs and Radicals, though not Gladstone, could also have cooperated on a policy of more active state involvement in the Irish economy, to encourage capital investment, for example in railways and tramways.[184] Moreover, the coercion policy was destroyed in the run-up to the 1885 election by political manoeuvrings between factions within Gladstone's dying cabinet, and then by the incoming minority Conservative ministry, which decided not to renew it as part of a policy of accommodating Parnell. Kimberley commented ruefully that the whole 'edifice of order' built up by Spencer had been destroyed by a 'faction fight'.[185]

Therefore one question for Liberals in 1886 was whether the reforms that a democratic British Parliament would propose would be sufficient to create a workable political and social relationship with the Irish. Opponents of Gladstone's scheme argued that it was too early to abandon the attempt to do this. Chamberlain, for example, claimed that strong democratic government could secure Ireland for the Union. When he heard that Spencer was supporting Home Rule in the hope of restoring strong executive authority to Ireland, he observed that because the aristocrat Spencer could not govern Ireland he arrogantly assumed that no one else could either. Chamberlain, by contrast, maintained that British rule in Ireland had hitherto been as feeble as aristocratic rule everywhere else.[186] With the full support of the

---

[181] Cooke and Vincent, *Governing passion*, pp. 226–7, 231.
[182] Holland, *Devonshire*, vol. I, pp. 384–5. See Bahlman, *Hamilton*, vol. II, pp. 392–3, 395.
[183] On future local government reform, see *Hansard*, 304:1251–2, 9 Apr. 1886.
[184] See Bahlman, *Hamilton*, vol. II, pp. 439, 452.
[185] Kimberley to Grant Duff, 5 Mar. 1886, Powell, *Liberal by principle*, p. 182.
[186] *Red Earl*, vol. II, p. 109n.

British democracy, Irish landlord sectionalism could be broken, while the extension of the franchise and of representative institutions in Ireland itself would smash Parnell's power. (Chamberlain's preferred ideas for constitutional development in Ireland drew on the American federal or Canadian provincial assembly models.)[187] Bright and Leatham similarly argued that, since 1884–5 had only just created a fully representative national system, it was perverse to divide a people so recently united.[188]

But more fundamental to Liberal opposition to Home Rule was the more negative argument that the scheme would weaken British power. They presented it as a concession to a campaign based on lawlessness and outrage, which suggested to all voters that disobedience of the law would bring political benefits. An Irish Parliament was being demanded by lawless means for particular purposes – to seize property, avoid rent, and damage minorities. It would be a sectional rather than a liberal body, not able to protect all interests equally, in contrast to the historic function of the Westminster Parliament to maintain throughout the length and breadth of the empire 'the undisputed supremacy of the law'.[189] The scheme gave the imperial Parliament no practical power to veto unfair acts, and its legitimacy in Ireland would be reduced further because of the exclusion of the Irish MPs from it. It could not be a final settlement, because Irish Nationalists would not accept the reservation of defence, foreign affairs and trade powers to Westminster, would not tolerate the payment of taxes to that end and would lobby for complete separation.[190] Like the white settler colonies, Ireland would go its own way, levying tariffs against Britain just as Canada and Australia had done. Brodrick claimed that Home Rulers were in alliance with men who 'receive their instructions and draw their pay from the foreign enemies of Great Britain' – whether these were Irish-American terrorists or the Pope.[191] The retention of Ireland was essential to the integrity and status of the United Kingdom in a way that the retention of Canada, say, was not. Home Rule could also be presented as damaging to the imperial ideal, privileging the local and sectional over the communal. National unity was the only way to teach opinion at home and abroad the benefits of strong government and British global power. At a time of major threats abroad, the concession of self-government to Ireland would have a great effect on our 'moral position, material position, political position,

---

[187] J. L. Garvin, *The life of Joseph Chamberlain: II: 1885–1895* (London, 1933), pp. 145, 188; *Hansard*, 306:697, 1 June 1886.

[188] *Hansard*, 305:1012, 13 May 1886; Bright, *The Times*, 2 July 1886, p. 10.

[189] Hartington, *Hansard*, 304:1262–3, 9 Apr. 1886.     [190] Parry, *Rise and fall*, pp. 298–300.

[191] G. C. Brodrick, *Unionism: the basis of a national party* (Oxford, 1888), p. 6.

imperial position'.[192] And this assertion of global power appeared to be the only strategy capable of seeing off the growing threat from the Conservatives. A vigorous policy, at home and abroad, was the basis of Chamberlain's vision for the post-Gladstonian Liberal party. Probably his deepest frustration at Gladstone's Home Rule scheme was that it was clearly designed to head off both elements of his own vision for the future of Liberalism: an interventionist, redistributive social policy, and international assertiveness.

In 1886, then, most Liberals on both sides thought primarily about how to uphold particular *English* values with which they had long been associated. Among supporters of Home Rule, some were primarily concerned to instil principles of economy and fiscal responsibility into the Irish, some had a commitment to popular constitutional and religious rights or to Mazzinian principles of nationality, and some were at root concerned to find a better basis for government authority. Among opponents, some were primarily anxious about Britain's imperial strength, some were above all concerned to uphold the rule of law and rights of property, and some were particularly attached to an organicist view of the nation. Many were pulled in both directions, because they found elements of the arguments on either side attractive, and of course political motives determined the path that a number of these chose. The issue was so divisive because these were all legitimate positions for Liberals to adopt. The progress of democracy highlighted the problems of treating turbulent Ireland as a normal part of the United Kingdom, but nor was it possible for a Liberal party to agree on treating it on any other basis. A lot of the tensions were specific to the peculiar circumstances of 1885–6: the challenging domestic and international context and the personal tensions and ambitions generated by the assumption that Gladstone was about to retire.

Therefore the abstract fitness of the Irish for self-government was not, in fact, the main cause of the split. Indeed the fundamental reason for its extent was that Gladstone polarised politics on Home Rule, calling an election and turning it into a referendum on his scheme. Gladstone was driven, not by accountability to party, but by an overpowering sense of a personal commitment to God and by a deeply old-fashioned vision of Irish and British political relationships. This behaviour struck his Liberal opponents as a dictatorial demand for the party to display a blind loyalty

---

[192] Goschen, quoted in E. Stokes, 'Milnerism', *Historical Journal*, 5 (1962), 48–9; A. R. D. Elliot, *Hansard*, 305:1384, 18 May 1886; see also R. Lowe, 'What shall we do for Ireland?', *Quarterly Review*, 124 (1868), 260.

to him, replacing the more traditional approach of maturing policy by rational and independently minded discussion. By launching this personal crusade, he not only wrecked the Liberal party but did more than anyone since George III to make a solution to the Irish question impossible. He ensured Conservative dominance of British politics for twenty years, on condition that they clung to defence of the Union, making concessions towards Home Rule impossible for them or their Liberal Unionist allies. Yet this polarisation should not obscure the impetus that still existed in the Liberal party (and to some extent in the Conservative party) in favour of the principle of constitutionalism in Ireland. If the Liberals had remained united under a new leader, they would surely have moved towards a significant extension of local self-government in Ireland within a few years of 1885. Sensitivity to Irish grievances and commitment to civil liberties and political participation would have been impossible to repress. It would have required political finesse and patience to lead the party slowly to this conclusion, given the anxieties about law, property and national strength. How painlessly this would have happened would have depended on the state of relations between Hartington and Chamberlain, and on the electoral and Parliamentary situation, which would have determined how far a Liberal government could act independently of Parnellite pressure.

This is not to say that any Liberal constitutional solution for Ireland would have been far-reaching enough to solve or postpone crisis there – not least because, like every other Liberal plan for Ireland, it would have reflected the image and identity of England more effectively than it engaged with Irish politics. Moreover, pessimism about the prospects for liberal English values in Ireland was undoubtedly growing in the 1880s. In 1881 Derby noted that for the first time it was widely acknowledged in England that 'we are holding Ireland against the wishes of the Irish'.[193] This was part of a broader anxiety about the power of liberal England. For most of the past fifty years, it had seemed relatively easy to reconcile order and executive vigour with a claim to be politically inclusive in Britain and Ireland, and to demonstrate Britain's power to spread liberal constitutional and economic ideas overseas, at low cost. In the 1880s, increasingly, it did not. The crisis over the government of Ireland was one of the most spectacular examples of that increasing difficulty, but, as before, the Irish problem was best understood when placed in a wider context.

---

[193]  19 Feb. 1881, *Derby diary 1878–93*, p. 308.

# Conclusion: Liberalism, state and nation

Nineteenth-century political history is often written without any reference to the fact that most propertied Britons considered their country to be the greatest power that the world had ever seen and expected that status to be maintained. It is almost always written without reference to the widespread belief that Providence had given Britain its great position and required duties in return. And it is invariably written without enough reflection on the connection between Britain's global policy and the domestic dominance of the Liberal party between 1830 and 1886. This book has argued that for most of that period the Liberal party was successful at identifying with the values that seemed to have made Britain a uniquely successful polity and a major force in the progress of the world. Liberal leaders constructed a series of patriotic discourses around the themes of constitutionalism, tolerance, fiscal accountability, free trade and Christian humanitarianism. By studying the period 1830–86 as a whole, and by concentrating on how those discourses connected domestic, Irish and foreign themes, it is possible, on the one hand, to get a clearer sense of the nature and timing of British political shifts, and, on the other, to see that the most effective political language was one that was both liberal and nationalistic. By emphasising the pre-Gladstonian history of British Liberalism, a better picture emerges both of the character and success of the Liberal party, and of the prevailing political values of the nineteenth century, before the brief swing to imperialism of the 1880s and 1890s. Another point to emerge is that for Liberals, European themes mattered much more in this period than imperial ones (even as late as the occupation of Egypt in 1882), while Ireland's problems were seen primarily in terms of tensions between English and continental values (rather than in terms of Irish racial backwardness).

The overall effect is to place more emphasis than is usual on the nationalism, rather than the internationalism, of the Liberal tradition, and on the progressive dimension to national identity politics.

There has been a tendency to equate mainstream Liberal approaches to foreign affairs with an idealistic anti-imperialist 'internationalism', which, in their different ways, Cobden and Gladstone are supposed to have represented. Cobden's cast of mind may have been genuinely internationalist, and he suffered politically for it, but it is far more problematical to apply that label to Gladstone. Much nineteenth-century Liberal thought, in addition to his, included aspirations towards greater international cooperation and harmony, and approval of some foreign practices. But the vast majority of those who took these positions, including Gladstone, were first and foremost vigorous patriots and were primarily concerned with the status, honour and role of Britain. It is similarly misleading to see nineteenth-century Nonconformity as primarily internationalist. In the 1840s, in particular, many Nonconformists became involved in international movements for peace and against slavery as part of a general political crusade against un-Christian, reactionary and feudal forces at home and abroad. But this focus was never to be as marked subsequently, mainly because after that intensely Radical and dissatisfied decade, most Nonconformists accepted the argument that British elites were more progressive than those of most other regimes. The notion that divine Providence gave Britain a blessed role in the world's development towards Christian perfection took the sting out of the earlier stress on the need for the righteous of all nations to work together against sinfulness. The one people with whom Nonconformists generally continued keen to cooperate were the Americans, especially after the victory of the anti-slavery forces in the Civil War, but this is better seen as an instance of Anglo-Saxon Providentialism than of genuine internationalism.

The emphasis here, instead, has been on the centrality of patriotic themes to the identity of the Victorian Liberal party. In an era still dominated politically by the propertied and commercial classes, the successful defence of the national interest gave governments great strength, while perceived weakness significantly damaged them. For most of this period, and particularly in the 1850s and 1860s, the party was usually able to turn British global power to its benefit. Liberals generally argued that there was no contradiction between patriotism and internationalism – that there was a neat fit between British interests and general world interests. The spread of liberal constitutionalism and free trade would encourage peace and international commerce, to Britain's particular benefit as the world's greatest trading power. It would also facilitate the exchange of civilised ideas and practices. Britain's constitutional and economic strength and its concomitant naval power were presented as its trademarks; if other countries were able to adopt the British model, they would benefit both themselves and Britain.

In European affairs, these trademarks often allowed Britain to punch above its military weight. At home, continental crises were usually seen in terms of the prospects they offered for the spread of British as opposed to alien values – which were associated with the other powers, particularly France, Russia, Austria and the papacy. To win this international battle of interests and values, Liberal leaders usually suggested that a manly and vigorous approach to policy was needed, rather than effete complacency. Theirs was the only party that could defend and promote Britain's real interests abroad with sufficient energy and commitment, because of the firm constitutional basis, and classless financial basis, of their regime at home, and the public confidence that derived from that. From Wellington onwards, the Conservative party seemed too feeble and passive in foreign and domestic policy, until Disraeli began his artificial and confused attempt at an 'imperial' alternative.

There was thus an intimate connection between Liberals' language on domestic and on foreign issues. Liberal politics involved a constant and usually fairly successful search for a national and public rather than a sectional and class-ridden political image. The basis of their claim to govern was that under them the British constitution was open and inclusive, and (after 1846) that financial policy was disinterested as between classes. The emphasis was on maintaining and promoting the health and vigour of the national community. A state founded on these principles would be strong both at home and in its global operations. The constant articulation of pride in the values that Britain projected to the world helped to define its purpose and underpin state legitimacy to a broader public at home. This was a major reason why foreign affairs were so prominent in Liberal discourse during this half-century. The same rhetoric had equally valuable effects in the shorter term, at a high political level, in the perpetual battle to keep a large Liberal coalition united and focused on an uplifting cross-class agenda. An overseas cause could do that all the more effectively if, like the Italian one, it could appeal to different groups of Liberals for slightly different reasons. The dominant languages of Liberalism were constitutional, fiscal-economic, and ethical – the last being shorthand for an amalgam of humanitarian, Protestant and Providential arguments. A really successful issue would strike chords with each of these elements in some way or other. It would embody particular sets of values which were widely attractive and which seemed to sum up the success and harmony of Liberal England.

One key component of the Liberal agenda was always the defence of liberty from oppression by an over-mighty state or by powerful political, economic or religious vested interests. That was why opposition to continental autocracy was so marked, and why there was such self-satisfaction at the decentralisation of power in nineteenth-century Britain, which gave considerable scope for independent action by local authorities, voluntary agencies and private enterprise. Inevitably, therefore, there was a very strong strand of Liberalism that sought to keep the power of the *British* state within bounds, and one core element of Liberal electoral popularity was the sense that the party stood for low taxes and the defence of individual independence and dignity.

However, one theme of this book has been that, beyond the economic sphere, where there was broad acceptance of them, the centrality of *laissez-faire* ideas to Liberal political argument can easily be exaggerated. Before 1885 Parliament was overwhelmingly composed of propertied individuals, so debates about what it might do could usually be conducted without serious worries that the interventions proposed would destroy property rights. In order to understand elite Liberal thought and action, we need to factor in the importance of concern for social order, political authority and moral improvement, or, to put it another way, ideas of social duty and Christian responsibility. In the same way, though there was an inclination against intervening in European quarrels, on fiscal, military and ideological grounds, there were also strict limits to the appeal of a non-interventionist foreign policy. It often did not seem compatible with Liberal notions of national honour and status, or of England's Providential mission for world improvement.

This book has argued that the political attractiveness of a complete rejection of an interventionist state policy was greater at some times than others – at times when there seemed a particular need to assert that libertarianism was the essence of Englishness. This was the case in the 1840s, building up to the crisis of 1847–51, and to some extent through the 1850s and early 1860s. Moreover, these arguments predominated, more or less simultaneously, in domestic, colonial and Irish affairs, because the underlying issue in each case was about the values that the British state should project and reject. The unique capacity of the British for 'self-government' was celebrated, in contrast to the failings of continental regimes. This meant that it was easier to argue against Parliamentary, social, educational and Irish reform. The cult of low taxes and political freedom seemed to justify extending self-government in the colonies, to the detriment of earlier Whiggish and evangelical ideas of responsibility for colonial development and native protection.

However, at other times these libertarian themes were subordinated to a countervailing argument, which stressed the urgent responsibility of politicians to take action to defend and promote English constitutional and ethical values, and to protect and develop the unity and health of Britain as a political nation and social community. These arguments played an important part in domestic Liberal discourse in justifying Parliamentary, educational and social reform in the 1830s, 1860s and 1880s, which seemed necessary in order to tackle class disharmony and might also overcome an embarrassing state feebleness. The search for a vigorous executive politics, engaging enthusiasm in and beyond Parliament, was a persistent theme of Liberal party leaders: it was the only way of disciplining an independently minded House of Commons; it helped to create a sense of communal public participation in politics; and it checked the power of the Court and of disruptive sections of Liberal opinion.

Arguments about state responsibility also justified the special efforts made in the 1830s, 1860s and 1880s to bind Ireland more effectively into the United Kingdom. Theoretically this would not be too difficult, since a basic principle of Liberalism was constitutional pluralism. The argument ran that successful nations and empires rose above, rather than relied on, a crude ethnic nationalism. Instead, they secured the loyalty of different religions and races to the constitution and the rule of law through a political strategy of equal citizenship and a recognition of their distinct grievances. The problem, however, was that any successful Liberal strategy required some arrangement with Irish Roman Catholicism. The Whiggish version of this, in the 1830s, focused on the use of political patronage and taxpayers' money to win Catholics' loyalty, in both secular and ecclesiastical spheres. The Radical Nonconformist version, which was fully articulated in the 1860s and early 1870s, was the opposite, rejecting any official or financial link between the state and any religion: an extension of the politics of disinterestedness from the fiscal to the religious sphere. Each was superficially attractive, since a great need of Liberal politics in Ireland was to offer the Catholics some constitutional benefits rather than just repression. But each failed, partly because Irish policy was always determined so much by 'English' political assumptions that it was never 'Irish' enough to please many Catholics, and partly because, despite this, each version clashed with a major facet of English Liberal identity. The former was unpopular for its overbearing 'continental' ethos and the second denied a religious aspect to the state. In the 1840s and 1870s, therefore, Liberal Irish policy fell between two stools, pleasing neither Irish Catholics nor many patriotic Britons.

How did foreign and defence issues fit with the waxing and waning of the libertarian non-interventionist theme? The crisis of 1847–51 entrenched a low-tax policy which seemed likely to keep defence spending down and strengthened British self-satisfaction that it had escaped the errors into which the continental states had fallen, suggesting the benefits of avoiding European quarrels. Superficially, therefore, the era seemed to favour Cobdenite non-interventionism. However, more importantly, the sense of a continent-wide ideological battle between constitutionalism and autocracy led first to a sense of vulnerability about defence and then to an aggressively patriotic insistence on standing up for liberty abroad, culminating in the Crimean War. Both movements were fuelled by widespread distaste at the perceived dominance at home of insular commercial materialism, which seemed to care too little for higher political and social objectives. For most of the 1850s the active defence of liberty abroad against the autocratic threat was a crucial theme in politics, paralleling a heightened emphasis on British identification with it at home. This arrangement suited Palmerston and some other Liberals who did not want the revival of a Liberal party organised on principles of domestic activism.

Success for liberal constitutionalism in Italy, and for free-trade principles, in 1859–60 seemed to suggest that autocracy was in terminal decline and that the spread of English values in Europe would no longer be contested. Now, finally, there seemed real scope for the Cobdenite argument that further diplomatic and naval activity by the state was unnecessary and indeed counterproductive, since economic forces would naturally promote international commerce and harmony. Non-interventionist arguments thus became more influential in the early 1860s. However, there was a continuing resistance to them from those who considered them irresponsible and demeaning. Such people regarded an ethical English international mission as essential, because it suggested a commitment to world progress, and because it celebrated more elevated values than mere money-grubbing. An uplifting international agenda seemed one essential element of an attractive and morally improving image to place before the domestic electorate.

For most of the 1860s these debates about Britain's international mission in a post-autocratic world proceeded on largely abstract principles, owing to general contentment with the global status quo. But from the late 1860s the international situation changed to Britain's disadvantage, at roughly the same time that, owing to the 1867 Reform Act, the domestic political scene also altered significantly. A new order of assertive states arose, with global aspirations. By 1871 Germany had united and the United States had recovered from civil war. Russia may have had less scope to interfere in places of interest to Britain in Europe – except in the Balkans – but instead extended its ambitions in Central Asia, apparently threatening India. The effect was to make the international arena a lot more menacing to British interests, and to change the tone of domestic debate about it. The comprehensive defeat of France in 1870 weakened France's and Britain's influence in Europe. The domination of European politics by Germany and Russia and the threat from the United States made it impossible for Gladstone's government to uphold national honour to the extent that the public had come to expect. This severely damaged its reputation.

Pessimism about the health of British values abroad, together with divisions about the direction which the British mission should take, was paralleled by a loss of direction and control in domestic and Irish policy in the early 1870s. As a result, some Liberals advocated an insistent libertarianism and Protestantism at home, while others did not. By the time of the defeat of 1874 there was little on which Liberals seemed to agree. However, that defeat, combined with the shock to British complacency about its world standing, and the decline in Radical suspicion of domestic state activity which is considered below, made it possible to begin to rediscover a sense of Liberal purpose around the principles of Parliamentary and social reform and a more active and assertive foreign policy. This was necessarily a slow process as far as domestic policy was concerned, but the foreign aspect was made much easier by the behaviour of Disraeli, whose 'un-English' conception of the nation's international mission allowed a great rallying of Liberals in defence of traditional constitutional and ethical principles, at home and abroad, at the election of 1880.

The virtuous Liberal foreign-policy rhetoric of 1878–80 developed into a more vigorous interventionism in government after 1880. The main reason for this was a shift in global and domestic realities. The pace of international rivalry was increasing: most of Britain's rivals were raising tariff walls to protect their commerce and sought new markets and imperial prestige across the world, principally in Africa. The debates about the course that Britain should follow *vis-à-vis* rivals in Africa and Asia in the 1880s were now mainly conducted in terms of simple national interest and prestige. France and Germany were now more difficult to portray as autocracies (and British political arrangements were less distinctively liberal), but they were significant threats in themselves. One reason for defending Britain's honour was the need to see off a rising threat from a vigorously patriotic Conservative party, which tended to argue in these non-ideological terms. But the constitutional and ethical dimensions of Liberal argument by no means disappeared. Traditional stereotypes of alien authoritarianism still

cropped up in a few debates. A more common rhetorical gambit was the
ethical argument about Britain's duty to protect African natives from slavery
or Boer oppression, which played an important subsidiary role in explaining
Britain's involvement in Africa in 1880–5. That involvement in turn had
a major impact on domestic economic policy, by escalating considerably
the cost of defence against other powers. For that reason, and because of
the generally unethical (or, he felt, hypocritically ethical) tone in which
overseas assertiveness was now celebrated in domestic politics, Gladstone
determined to stand against it, and to promote an older, purer idea of the
British mission. Irish Home Rule was his way of doing that, as part of his
response to the urgent crisis of political legitimacy in Ireland that he saw
resulting from the extension of the franchise in 1885, which he felt required
a properly English policy of 'self-government' to be forced on the Irish.

During the period of this book, some of those Liberals who advocated a
strong overseas policy, such as Palmerston and his political heir Hartington,
justified it mainly in terms of honour, status and interests, though even they
brought a significant ideological tinge to their language. However, this book
has paid particular attention to three other strands of self-consciously patriotic Liberalism, exemplified by Russell, Forster and Chamberlain, which
found an ideologically coherent way of linking foreign assertiveness to state
activism in domestic policy.

   No one can hope to make sense of elite Victorian Liberalism without
understanding the fusion of Whig constitutionalism and Liberal Anglican moral interventionism that shaped the mind of Lord John Russell.
Despite his dogmatism and naïveté, and despite the strong rejection of
some aspects of the Whig notion of the state in the late 1840s, more
of his policy approaches survived than perished: a latitudinarian Church
Establishment, an undenominational national education system, a moralistic social policy, and great pride in the values of the settler colonies.
One reason for that was the substantial overlap between his views and the
self-righteously robust liberal evangelical and commercial Liberalism symbolised particularly by Forster. Forster revived the alliance of 'Saints' and
Whigs that had powered the anti-slavery movement in the 1820s and 1830s,
first to impose a national education system in 1870, and then to push the
state into supporting commercial and philanthropic endeavour in Africa.
His blunt imperialism and strong defence of the rule of law in Ireland
made him a dangerous figure in the early 1880s, a potential ally of Conservatives and a forefather of Liberal Unionism. While Forster represented
one style of vigorous commercial Liberalism, Chamberlain stood for a less

religious alternative. Whereas Forster advocated Anglo-American partnership primarily for the democratic Protestant zeal that it could unleash, Chamberlain saw the United States as the model for a secular civic republicanism which could galvanise British politics and create a more harmonious and powerful domestic and international community. In his eyes, once again, social reform at home was the natural parallel of an assertive policy abroad. Moreover, in the 1880s, both Forster and Chamberlain dwelt on the notion of Anglo-American solidarity in order to revitalise the traditional Liberal claim that British constitutional and ethical principles could dominate the world.

Both men also contrasted the vigour of their own democratic politics with the feebleness of aristocrats who lacked both their personal manliness, and the confidence in the benefits of state action that stemmed from popular backing. This revived a common Liberal theme through the years, which can be traced back at least as far as Palmerston's assaults on Wellington in 1828–30. Indeed the careers of Palmerston, Forster and Chamberlain in particular remind us how important a role in Liberal self-projection was played by the concept of manliness, with its inclusive connotations of enterprise, energy, individual responsibility and self-discipline. These themes were not incompatible with a quietist foreign policy – indeed Bright successfully projected a powerfully manly identity – but they sat particularly well with a vigorous one.

In other words, the common ground between Russell, Forster and Chamberlain helps us to understand not only the connections between domestic and foreign arguments, but also the number of elements within Liberal political argument that remained resistant to a *laissez-faire* approach either at home or abroad. Moreover, one underlying theme of the book has been the connection between the popularity of an active domestic and foreign policy and the amount of Liberal–Radical confidence in the fairness of the constitution.

While many traditional Whigs always valued state authority as much as liberty, at the heart of early nineteenth-century Radicalism was suspicion of the malevolent power of a state that seemed to be in the grip of exclusive vested interests. Before 1850 it was easy to mobilise Radical sentiment against specific examples of misbehaviour by an over-mighty and sectional regime. The Church, the army, the monarchy and the civil and colonial service were all regarded by Radicals with wariness, as institutions which relied on their connection with aristocracy and government to win political and financial favours for themselves at the expense of the citizen and taxpayer. This created much tension with Whig-Liberals. After 1850, however, it became more difficult to identify examples of vested-interest misgovernment that were gross enough to stimulate a widespread Radical campaign against them. This difficulty became greater after the extension of the franchise in 1867, because it made the argument that the state was still in the hands of an unrepresentative elite much more problematical.

However, traditional Radicalism remained very potent at first after 1867, adding to the confusion of those few years. Some Nonconformists identified continuing elite misgovernment and entertained the idea of mobilising the popular conscience in virtuous crusades against it. Some Radicals regarded Church disestablishment, republicanism, and/or major expenditure cuts on the army and the colonies, as the next stepping-stones towards a truly disinterested state. Indeed Radical intellectuals like Mill and Morley asserted that it was the Whig alternatives of a moralistic latitudinarian Establishment and a strictly constitutional monarchy which were illogical compromises that showed the irrationality of the English political mind. So in the early 1870s the 'Whig' and 'Radical' agendas diverged sharply. Nonetheless, the 'irrational' compromises advocated by the former eventually won out. The extended franchise, adding further to the perceived legitimacy of the state, weakened the attractiveness of traditional Radical cries of 'Old Corruption', which now instead fuelled a rapid middle-class reaction in favour of the Conservatives. The result was that Church, monarchy, army, civil service and colonies all survived the brief crisis of 1869–73 and prospered as more identifiably 'national' entities in the late nineteenth century, in a triumph for Whiggish Liberal approaches. All of them benefited from the logic of a more representative politics.

After the divisions and confusions of the early 1870s had died away, Radical energies gradually began to concentrate more on using the power of the state, and of popular participation in local authorities, for more positive ends. This naturally altered the tone and content of late-Victorian Liberal domestic politics in ways that are well known. Increasing interest in communal social action prefigured the so-called New Liberalism of the twentieth century, which only appears as a sharp break from nineteenth-century practice if nineteenth-century practice is misconceived as dominated by principles of *laissez-faire* rather than constitutional inclusiveness. And, from the 1880s, at central and local level, Liberal activity and 'meddling' pushed the party far enough away from its former emphasis on individual liberty to allow the Conservative party to win a lot of electoral advantage, particularly but not only among the middle classes, by snatching the libertarian mantle.

Across the nineteenth century, however, it is no less misleading to portray Liberalism as a statist than as a narrowly libertarian movement. It always found it easiest to rally against the suggestion of Tory 'oppression' or 'vested interest' unfairness, and since the Conservative party was in power for most of the 1874–1905 period, it had plenty of practice at this. Before then, it left enormous freedom to individual initiative, even at its most interventionist. In fact, as a political movement, it gained success when it projected the images of responsibility and freedom simultaneously. The Liberal party needed to find a set of appeals and images that transcended divisions and smoothed over potential differences by highlighting common purposes. Multi-faceted patriotic rhetoric helped greatly here. As this book has shown, there were a number of different strategies for reconciling commitment to low taxes and undictatorial government with a confident and effective profile abroad. It was more difficult to do at some times than others. This book has identified a number of moments at which shifting variables required an adjustment of political priorities, since, in politics, success is always short-term. In general, however, it can be said that this was regularly a viable strategy during the period.

There were a number of peculiarities about the period that made the pursuit of a liberal constitutional patriotism possible. The international dominance of British trade and naval power facilitated the spread of free trade at relatively low cost. The drift of events in Europe seemed to be favourable to the Liberal cause until at least the late 1870s: in the 1830s and 1840s there was a general assumption that the collapse of autocratic power was merely a matter of time, while Protection did not become seen as a major threat to British commerce until the very end of the period. The fact that most serious mid-European disputes took place in countries with coasts made it easier for Britain to win influence by flexing its naval and diplomatic muscles. It was usually able to play a significant diplomatic role without needing to spend money to compete with the continental standing armies, and without needing to restrict its flexibility by entering formal alliances. All this kept the tax burden down at home. So did the preference of both the landed and commercial classes to maintain the decentralised nature of the British state, which was not effectively challenged. Above all, there was a broad confidence, between the 1850s and 1880s, that general economic prosperity and the growth of working-class savings would continue to keep taxes and interest rates low, minimise the appeal of class resentment and socialism, and underpin social stability.

But in the 1880s, by contrast, there was less scope for optimism on most of these fronts. British commercial dominance was facing challenges, particularly from Germany and the United States. Britain's reliance on food imports made its merchant marine particularly vulnerable to enemy attack. This, and more urgently the occupation of Egypt, increased defence spending significantly. Liberal narratives of the inevitability of global progress towards liberal constitutionalism and free trade were beginning to seem naïve. Racial attitudes in society were becoming harsher. Britain no longer looked obviously more liberal politically than other Western countries and, to the extent that it was, this was no longer so widely applauded. The fourfold increase in the franchise in twenty years between 1866 and 1886 raised many questions about how to guide and discipline the democracy and to prevent sectional and disintegrative pressures on domestic and foreign policy. It was no longer so easy to see the empire as a demonstration of British Christian and libertarian values in white settler communities when Britain had occupied a Moslem country in 1882 against the wishes of the people and the powers of Europe. It was no longer so easy to justify rule in Ireland when a Nationalist party dominated the country and Irishmen were bombing in London. The most obvious way of asserting a patriotic appeal by the mid-1880s was an unsentimental defence of British prestige and British strategic and commercial rights against other powers and other races. This also encouraged a greater emphasis on the importance of the 'Asiatic' or 'Oriental' empire, particularly India, and the need for firm rule over it. These tendencies all fitted better with the Conservative than the Liberal conception of Britain's global mission.

The root problem for Liberals was a waning of consensus and confidence about the ability of liberal constitutional values to bind the nation together in a common domestic and global purpose. In 1888 Meredith Townsend of the *Spectator* wrote that Englishmen 'have become uncertain of themselves, afraid of their old opinions, doubtful of the true teaching of their own consciences. They doubt if they have any longer any moral right to rule anyone, themselves almost included.'[1] In the light of the brash Tory imperialism of the 1890s, this appears an odd remark, but it is less odd when applied to the Liberal tradition which this book has featured. This was so not only abroad but also at home. It was much less clear how Liberals could continue to reconcile the classes and maintain the influence of property, intellect and morality. General uncertainty about the British mission sparked disagreements on the future direction of domestic Liberalism, exacerbating both faddism and divisions over whether interference with individual liberty was 'socialist'. The spread of free-thought raised the question of how the

[1] M. Townsend, 'Will England retain India?' (1888), reprinted in Townsend, *Asia and Europe* (London, 1901), p. 115.

individual conscience could be trained into the morals and discipline necessary to make its owner a fully responsible member of the political community. And it was increasingly easy for the Conservatives to compete with Liberals on equal terms for the patriotic high ground. They could claim to be the 'national' party, the party of both 'honour' abroad and 'liberty' at home, at least as plausibly as Liberals. And Liberal reforms to the army, the Church and the county elites had made these bastions of Conservatism appear less sinister than Radicals had traditionally claimed them to be.

Of course optimism about the future was not completely undermined, nor was Liberalism fatally wounded. The split of 1886 killed neither the party nor the Liberal tradition in British political life, which in fact it helped to disseminate through all three main twentieth-century parties. A Conservative party guided by three Chamberlains, Churchill, Baldwin, Butler and Macmillan owed an enormous amount to Liberal Unionism. And in 1906 the Liberals were able to win a crushing election victory because they discovered once again how to project a cross-class appeal, marrying traditional constitutional and fiscal arguments with a strong attack on the sectionalism and false patriotism of a divided, feeble, tariff-reforming Conservative party. However, twenty years is a long time in politics, during which much changed. A. V. Dicey was right: the 1880s and 1890s witnessed 'that singular phenomenon which is best described as the disintegration of beliefs or, in other words, the breaking up of established creeds, whether religious, moral, political, or economical'.[2]

This, in other words, was the end of an era in which the sense that liberty, constitutionalism and ethics were central to national identity had, more often than not, given focus and dynamism to a broad coalition of British Liberals and had enabled them to lay down the law to Europe. By setting British politics in a European context, it is possible to appreciate better the international, but more particularly the insular, objectives of British Liberalism during that half-century. Perhaps there is, after all, some relevance in Kipling's line of 1891: 'What should they know of England, who only England know?'

---

[2] A. V. Dicey, *Lectures on the relation between law and public opinion in England during the nineteenth century* (2nd edn, London, 1914), pp. 438–9.

# Abbreviations and select bibliography

This bibliography is of the biographies, memoirs, collections of letters and secondary works that I have found most useful or that appear frequently in the text. The book also relies on many contemporary sources not listed below, mostly newspapers, periodical articles, pamphlets and other writings. Where those contemporary sources are cited in the footnotes, the reference is given in full on the first mention in *each chapter*. Works which appear in this bibliography are cited in full only on their first appearance in the *whole book*, except for a few items in the first section below, which have been abbreviated consistently throughout in the form here given.

## ABBREVIATED WORKS

*Bassett*          A. T. Bassett (ed.), *Gladstone's speeches: descriptive index and bibliography* (London, 1916).

*CWM*          F. E. L. Priestley, J. M. Robson *et al.* (eds.), *The collected works of John Stuart Mill* (33 vols., Toronto, 1963–91).

*Derby diary 1869–78*          J. R. Vincent (ed.), *A selection from the diaries of Edward Henry Stanley, 15th earl of Derby (1826–93) between September 1869 and March 1878* (London, 1994).

*Derby diary 1878–93*          J. R. Vincent (ed.), *The diaries of Edward Henry Stanley, 15th earl of Derby (1826–93) between 1878 and 1893: a selection* (Oxford, 2003).

*GD*          H. C. G. Matthew *et al.* (eds.), *The Gladstone diaries* (14 vols., Oxford, 1968–94).

*Gooch*          G. P. Gooch (ed.), *The later correspondence of Lord John Russell, 1840–1878* (2 vols., London, 1925).

*Hansard*          *Hansard's Parliamentary debates* (3rd series unless stated otherwise in footnotes).

*Kimberley*          A. Hawkins and J. Powell (eds.), *The journal of John Wodehouse first earl of Kimberley for 1862–1902* (London, 1997).

*LQV 1837–61*          A. C. Benson and Viscount Esher (eds.), *The letters of Queen Victoria . . . between the years 1837 and 1861* (3 vols., London, 1908).

| | |
|---|---|
| *LQV 1862–78* | G. E. Buckle (ed.), *The letters of Queen Victoria second series: . . . between the years 1862 and 1878* (2 vols., London, 1926). |
| *PMP* | J. Brooke and M. Sorensen (eds.), *The Prime Ministers' papers series: W. E. Gladstone* (4 vols., London, 1971–81). |
| *Ramm 1868–76* | A. Ramm (ed.), *The political correspondence of Mr Gladstone and Lord Granville, 1868–1876* (2 vols., London, 1952). |
| *Red Earl* | P. Gordon (ed.), *The Red Earl: the papers of the fifth Earl Spencer 1835–1910* (2 vols., Northampton, 1981–6). |
| *Stanley* | J. R. Vincent (ed.), *Disraeli, Derby and the Conservative party: journals and memoirs of Edward Henry, Lord Stanley, 1849–69* (Hassocks, 1978). |

## BIOGRAPHIES, MEMOIRS, LETTERS, SPEECHES

Acland, A. H. D., *Memoir and letters of the right honourable Sir Thomas Dyke Acland* (London, 1902).

Anglesey, marquess of, *One-leg: the life and letters of Henry William Paget first marquess of Anglesey* (London, 1961).

Armytage, W. H. G., *A. J. Mundella 1825–1897: the Liberal background to the Labour movement* (London, 1951).

Ashley, E., *The life of Henry John Temple, Viscount Palmerston: 1846–1865* (2 vols., London, 1876).

Auchmuty, J. J., *Sir Thomas Wyse 1791–1862: the life and career of an educator and diplomat* (London, 1939).

Bahlman, D. W. R. (ed.), *The diary of Sir Edward Walter Hamilton 1880–1885* (2 vols., Oxford, 1972).

Baines, E., *The life of Edward Baines late MP for the borough of Leeds* (London, 1851).

Battiscombe, G., *Shaftesbury: a biography of the seventh earl 1801–1885* (London, 1988 edn).

Bebbington, D., *The mind of Gladstone: religion, Homer, and politics* (Oxford, 2004).

Bell, H. C. F., *Lord Palmerston* (2 vols., London, 1966 edn).

Blakiston, G. (ed.), *Lord William Russell and his wife, 1815–1846* (London, 1972).

Bourne, K. (ed.), *The letters of the third Viscount Palmerston to Laurence and Elizabeth Sulivan 1804–1863* (London, 1979).

Bourne, K., *Palmerston: the early years 1784–1841* (London, 1982).

Boyd, C. W. (ed.), *Mr Chamberlain's speeches* (2 vols., London, 1914).

Broughton, Lord, *Recollections of a long life* (6 vols., London, 1911).

Bulwer, Sir H. L., *The life of Henry John Temple, Viscount Palmerston* (2 vols., London, 1870).

Bunsen, F., *A memoir of Baron Bunsen* (2 vols., London, 1868).

Burghclere, Lady (ed.), *A great lady's friendships: letters to Mary, marchioness of Salisbury, countess of Derby 1862–1890* (London, 1933).

Carpenter, J. E., *James Martineau, theologian and teacher: a study of his life and thought* (London, 1905).

Childers, S., *The life and correspondence of the right hon. Hugh C. E. Childers 1827–1896* (2 vols., London, 1901).

Chitty, S., *The beast and the monk: a life of Charles Kingsley* (London, 1974).

Clive, J., *Macaulay: the shaping of the historian* (New York, 1975 edn).

Cobden, R., *Speeches on questions of public policy* (2 vols., London, 1870).

Coleridge, E. H., *Life and correspondence of John Duke Lord Coleridge* (2 vols., London, 1904).

Connell, B., *Regina v. Palmerston: the correspondence between Queen Victoria and her Foreign and Prime Minister 1837–1865* (London, 1962).

Dale, A. W. W., *The life of R. W. Dale of Birmingham* (London, 1898).

Dale, R. W., *The life and letters of John Angell James* (London, 1861).

Dasent, A. I., *John Thadeus Delane editor of 'The Times': his life and correspondence* (2 vols., London, 1908).

Denholm, A., *Lord Ripon 1827–1909: a political biography* (London, 1982).

Doughty, Sir A. G. (ed.), *The Elgin–Grey papers 1846–1852* (4 vols., Ottawa, 1937).

Edsall, N. C., *Richard Cobden: independent Radical* (Cambridge, MA, 1986).

Elliot, A. R. D., *The life of George Joachim Goschen first Viscount Goschen 1831–1907* (2 vols., London, 1911).

Fitzmaurice, Lord E., *The life of Granville George Leveson Gower second Earl Granville 1815–1891* (2 vols., London, 1905).

Froude, J. A., *Thomas Carlyle: a history of his life in London* (2 vols., London, 1884).

Fulford, R. (ed.), *Your dear letter: private correspondence of Queen Victoria and the Crown Princess of Prussia 1865–1871* (London, 1971).

Gardiner, A. G., *The life of Sir William Harcourt* (2 vols., London, 1923).

Garvin, J. L., *The life of Joseph Chamberlain: I: 1836–1885* (London, 1932).

Greville, C. C. F., *A journal of the reigns of King George IV, King William IV and Queen Victoria*, ed. H. Reeve (8 vols., London, 1896 edn).

Guedalla, P., *The Queen and Mr Gladstone 1845–1879* (London, 1933).

Gwynn, S. and Tuckwell, G. M., *The life of Sir Charles W. Dilke* (2 vols., London, 1918).

Hardcastle, Mrs, *Life of John, Lord Campbell* (2 vols., London, 1881).

Hewett, O. W., '. . . and Mr. Fortescue': a selection from the diaries of Chichester Fortescue, Lord Carlingford, 1851–62* (London, 1958).

Hodder, E., *The life and work of the seventh earl of Shaftesbury* (3 vols., London, 1886).

*The life of Samuel Morley* (London, 1887).

Holland, B., *The life of Spencer Compton eighth duke of Devonshire* (2 vols., London, 1911).

Huxley, L., *Life and letters of Thomas Henry Huxley* (2 vols., London, 1900).

Jackson, P., *Education Act Forster: a political biography of W. E. Forster (1818–1886)* (Madison, NJ, 1997).

*Harcourt and son: a political biography of Sir William Harcourt* (Madison, NJ, 2004).

Jenkins, T. A. (ed.), 'The Parliamentary diaries of Sir John Trelawny, 1868–73', *Camden Miscellany*, 32 (1994).

Johnson, G. W. and L. A. (eds.), *Josephine E. Butler: an autobiographical memoir* (Bristol, 1909).

Kennedy, A. L. (ed.), *'My dear duchess': social and political letters to the duchess of Manchester 1858–1869* (London, 1956).

Kriegel, A. D. (ed.), *The Holland House diaries 1831–1840: the diary of Henry Richard Vassall Fox, third Lord Holland* (London, 1977).

Laughton, J. K., *Memoirs of the life and correspondence of Henry Reeve* (2 vols., London, 1898).

Leader, R. E., *Life and letters of John Arthur Roebuck* (London, 1897).

Lever, T. (ed.), *The letters of Lady Palmerston* (London, 1957).

Lewis, Sir G. F. (ed.), *Letters of the right hon. George Cornewall Lewis, Bart, to various friends* (London, 1870).

Longford, E., *Victoria R.I.* (London, 2000 edn).

McCabe, J., *Life and letters of George Jacob Holyoake* (2 vols., London, 1908).

McKinstry, L., *Rosebery: statesman in turmoil* (London, 2005).

Mack Smith, D., *Mazzini* (New Haven, 1994).

Mallet, B., *Thomas George earl of Northbrook: a memoir* (London, 1908).

Matthew, H. C. G., *Gladstone 1809–1874* (Oxford, 1986).

*Gladstone 1875–1898* (Oxford, 1995).

Maurice, F., *The life of Frederick Denison Maurice, chiefly told in his own letters* (2 vols., London, 1884).

Maxwell, Sir H., *The life and letters of George William Frederick fourth earl of Clarendon* (2 vols., London, 1913).

Miall, A., *Life of Edward Miall* (London, 1884).

Monypenny, W. F. and Buckle, G. E., *The life of Benjamin Disraeli earl of Beaconsfield* (6 vols., London, 1910–20).

Morley, J., *The life of Richard Cobden* (2 vols., London, 1896 edn).

*The life of William Ewart Gladstone* (3 vols., London, 1903).

*Recollections* (2 vols., London, 1917).

Nicholls, D., *The lost Prime Minister: a life of Sir Charles Dilke* (London, 1995).

Parker, C. S., *Sir Robert Peel from his private papers* (3 vols., London, 1899).

*Life and letters of Sir James Graham* (2 vols., London, 1907).

Paton, J. L., *John Brown Paton: a biography* (London, 1914).

Powell, J. (ed.), *Liberal by principle: the politics of John Wodehouse 1st earl of Kimberley, 1843–1902* (London, 1996).

Prest, J., *Lord John Russell* (London, 1972).

Ramm, A. (ed.), *The political correspondence of Mr Gladstone and Lord Granville 1876–1886* (2 vols., Oxford, 1962).

Reed, A. and Reed, C., *Memoirs of the life and philanthropic labours of Andrew Reed* (London, 1863).

Reid, S. J., *Lord John Russell* (London, 1895).

Reid, T. W., *Life of the right honourable William Edward Forster* (2 vols., London, 1888).

Russell, B. and Russell, P. (eds.), *The Amberley papers: the letters and diaries of Lord and Lady Amberley* (2 vols., London, 1937).

Russell, John, Earl, *Selections from speeches 1817 to 1841 and from despatches 1859 to 1865* (2 vols., London, 1870).

*Recollections and suggestions 1813–1873* (2nd edn, London, 1875).

Ryland, J. E., *The life and correspondence of John Foster* (2 vols., London, 1846).

St John Stevas, N. (ed.), *The collected works of Walter Bagehot: Volume VIII* (London, 1974).

Scherer, P., *Lord John Russell: a biography* (Selinsgrove, 1999).

Schults, R. L., *Crusader in Babylon: W. T. Stead and the Pall Mall Gazette* (Lincoln, NE, 1972).

Schwabe, Mrs Salis, *Reminiscences of Richard Cobden* (London, 1895).

Shannon, R., *Gladstone: I: 1809–1865* (London, 1982).

*Gladstone: heroic minister, 1865–1898* (London, 1999).

Simpson, M. C. M., *Many memories of many people* (London, 1898).

Smith, E. A., *Lord Grey 1764–1845* (Oxford, 1990).

Southgate, D., *'The most English minister . . .': the policies and politics of Palmerston* (London, 1966).

Stanley, A. P., *The life and correspondence of Thomas Arnold* (2 vols., London, 1880 edn).

Stanmore, Lord, *Sidney Herbert Lord Herbert of Lea: a memoir* (2 vols., London, 1906).

Steele, D., *Lord Salisbury: a political biography* (London, 1999).

Stephen, C. E. (ed.), *Sir James Stephen: letters* (privately printed, 1906).

Stephens, W. R. W., *The life and letters of Edward A. Freeman* (2 vols., London, 1895).

Storey, G. et al. (eds.), *The letters of Charles Dickens* (12 vols., Oxford, 1965–2002).

Taylor, M. (ed.), *The European diaries of Richard Cobden, 1846–1849* (Aldershot, 1994).

Thompson, D., *Queen Victoria: gender and power* (London, 2001 edn).

Thornley, D., *Isaac Butt and Home Rule* (London, 1964).

Thorold, A. L., *The life of Henry Labouchère* (London, 1913).

Trevelyan, G. M., *The life of John Bright* (London, 1914).

*Sir George Otto Trevelyan: a memoir* (London, 1932).

Trevelyan, G. O., *The life and letters of Lord Macaulay* (1876; Oxford, 1978 edn).

Urbach, K., *Bismarck's favourite Englishman: Lord Odo Russell's mission to Berlin* (London, 1999).

Walpole, S., *The life of Lord John Russell* (2 vols., London, 1889).

Whyte, F., *The life of W. T. Stead* (2 vols., London, 1925).

Wilson, W., *The life of George Dawson* (Birmingham, 1905).

## SECONDARY WORKS

Anderson, O., 'The Janus face of mid-19th century English Radicalism: the Administrative Reform Association of 1855', *Victorian Studies*, 8 (1965), 231–42.

'The reactions of Church and Dissent towards the Crimean War', *Journal of Ecclesiastical History*, 16 (1965), 209–20.

*A liberal state at war: English politics and economics during the Crimean War* (London, 1967).

'The growth of Christian militarism in mid-Victorian Britain', *English Historical Review*, 86 (1971), 46–72.

Arlinghaus, F. A., 'British public opinion and the *Kulturkampf* in Germany, 1871–1875', *Catholic Historical Review*, 34 (1948–9), 385–413.

Arnstein, W. L., *The Bradlaugh case: a study in late Victorian opinion and politics* (Oxford, 1965).

Auerbach, J., *The Great Exhibition of 1851: a nation on display* (New Haven, 1999).

Bartlett, C. J., *Great Britain and sea power 1815–1853* (Oxford, 1963).

Beales, D., *England and Italy 1859–60* (London, 1961).

'Garibaldi in England: the politics of Italian enthusiasm', in J. A. Davis and P. Ginsborg (eds.), *Society and politics in the age of the Risorgimento: essays in honour of Denis Mack Smith* (Cambridge, 1991), pp. 184–216.

Bebbington, D. W., *The Nonconformist conscience: chapel and politics, 1870–1914* (London, 1982).

Belchem, J., 'Britishness, the United Kingdom and the revolutions of 1848', *Labour History Review*, 64 (1999), 143–58.

Bell, Q., *The schools of design* (London, 1963).

Bendiner, K., *The art of Ford Madox Brown* (University Park, PA, 1998).

Bensimon, F., *Les Britanniques face à la révolution française de 1848* (Paris, 2000).

Biagini, E. F., *Liberty, retrenchment and Reform: popular Liberalism in the age of Gladstone, 1860–1880* (Cambridge, 1992).

Binfield, C., *So down to prayers: studies in English Nonconformity, 1780–1920* (London, 1977).

Black, R. D. C., *Economic thought and the Irish question, 1817–70* (Cambridge, 1960).

'Economic policy in Ireland and India in the time of J. S. Mill', *Economic History Review*, 2nd ser., 21 (1968), 321–36.

Bolt, C., *Victorian attitudes to race* (London, 1971).

Brent, R., *Liberal Anglican politics: Whiggery, religion and reform, 1830–1841* (Oxford, 1987).

'The Whigs and Protestant Dissent in the decade of reform: the case of Church rates, 1833–1841', *English Historical Review*, 102 (1987), 887–910.

Bristow, E., 'The Liberty and Property Defence League and individualism', *Historical Journal*, 18 (1975), 761–89.

*Vice and vigilance: purity movements in Britain since 1700* (Dublin, 1977).

Brown, D., *Palmerston and the politics of foreign policy 1846–55* (Manchester, 2002).

Buckner, P., *The transition to responsible government: British policy in British North America, 1815–1850* (Westport, CT, 1985).

Buzard, J., *The beaten track: European tourism, literature, and the ways to culture, 1800–1918* (Oxford, 1993).

Cain, P. J., 'Capitalism, war and internationalism in the thought of Richard Cobden', *British Journal of International Studies*, 5 (1979), 112–30.

Campbell, D. A., *English public opinion and the American Civil War* (Woodbridge, 2003).

Chamberlain, M. E., 'Clement Hill's memoranda and the British interest in East Africa', *English Historical Review*, 87 (1972), 533–47.

  'Sir Charles Dilke and the British intervention in Egypt in 1882: decision-making in a nineteenth-century cabinet', *British Journal of International Studies*, 2 (1976), 231–45.

  'British public opinion and the invasion of Egypt, 1882', *Trivium*, 16 (1981), 5–28.

Charmley, J., *Splendid isolation?: Britain, the balance of power and the origins of the First World War* (London, 2000).

Claeys, G., 'Mazzini, Kossuth and British Radicalism, 1848–1854', *Journal of British Studies*, 28 (1989), 225–61.

Clarke, I. F., 'The Battle of Dorking, 1871–1914', *Victorian Studies*, 8 (1965), 308–28.

  *Voices prophesying war 1763–1984* (London, 1966).

Comerford, R. V., *The Fenians in context: Irish politics and society 1848–82* (Dublin, 1985).

Conway, S., 'The politicization of the nineteenth-century Peace Society', *Historical Research*, 66 (1993), 267–83.

Cook, S. B., *Imperial affinities: nineteenth century analogies and exchanges between India and Ireland* (London, 1993).

Cooke, A. B. and Vincent, J. R., *The governing passion: cabinet government and party politics in Britain, 1885–6* (Brighton, 1974).

Coulling, S., *Matthew Arnold and his critics: a study of Arnold's controversies* (Athens, OH, 1974).

Cragoe, M., *Culture, politics and national identity in Wales, 1832–1886* (Oxford, 2004).

Cunningham, H., *The Volunteer Force: a social and political history 1859–1908* (London, 1975).

  'The language of patriotism, 1750–1914', *History Workshop Journal*, 12 (1981), 8–33.

Curtis, L. P., *Apes and angels: the Irishman in Victorian caricature* (Newton Abbot, 1971).

  'Comment: the return of revisionism', *Journal of British Studies*, 44 (2005), 134–45.

Dawson, G., *Soldier heroes: British adventure, empire and the imagining of masculinities* (London, 1994).

de Groot, E., 'Contemporary political opinion and the revolutions of 1848', *History*, 38 (1953), 134–54.

de Nie, M., *The eternal Paddy: Irish identity in the British press* (Madison, WI, 2004).

Dewey, C., 'Celtic agrarian legislation and the Celtic revival: historicist implications of Gladstone's Irish and Scottish Land Acts, 1870–86', *Past and Present*, 44 (1974), 30–70.

Dreyer, F. A., 'The Whigs and the political crisis of 1845', *English Historical Review*, 80 (1965), 514–37.

Ellens, J. P., *Religious routes to Gladstonian Liberalism: the Church rate conflict in England and Wales, 1832–1868* (University Park, PA, 1994).

Fay, C. R., *Palace of industry, 1851: a study of the Great Exhibition and its fruits* (Cambridge, 1951).

Feldman, D., *Englishmen and Jews: social relations and political culture, 1840–1914* (London, 1994).

Finn, M. C., '"A vent which has conveyed our principles": English Radical patriotism in the aftermath of 1848', *Journal of Modern History*, 64 (1992), 637–59.
  *After Chartism: class and nation in English Radical politics, 1848–1884* (Cambridge, 1993).

Foster, R. F., *Paddy and Mr Punch: connections in Irish and English history* (London, 1993).

Gallagher, T. F., '"Cardwellian mysteries": the fate of the British Army Regulation Bill, 1871', *Historical Journal*, 18 (1975), 327–48.

Gaston, J. W. T., 'Trade and the late Victorian Foreign Office', *International History Review*, 4 (1982), 317–38.

Gerlach, M., *British Liberalism and the United States: political and social thought in the late Victorian age* (Basingstoke, 2001).

Gilley, S., 'The Garibaldi riots of 1862', *Historical Journal*, 16 (1973), 697–732.
  'English attitudes to the Irish in England, 1780–1900', in C. Holmes (ed.), *Immigrants and minorities in England* (London, 1978), pp. 81–110.

Gleason, J. H., *The genesis of Russophobia in Great Britain: a study of the interaction of policy and opinion* (Cambridge, MA, 1950).

Goldman, L., *Science, reform, and politics in Victorian Britain: the Social Science Association 1857–1886* (Cambridge, 2002).

Gray, P., *Famine, land and politics: British government and Irish society, 1843–1850* (Dublin, 1999).
  'National humiliation and the Great Hunger: fast and famine in 1847', *Irish Historical Studies*, 32 (2000), 193–216.

Greaves, R. W., 'The Jerusalem bishopric, 1841', *English Historical Review*, 64 (1949), 328–52.

Griffin, B., 'Class, gender, and Liberalism in Parliament, 1868–1882: the case of the Married Women's Property Acts', *Historical Journal*, 46 (2003), 59–87.

Hall, C., *White, male and middle-class: explorations in feminism and history* (Cambridge, 1992).
  '"From Greenland's icy mountains . . . to Africa's golden sand": ethnicity, race and nation in mid nineteenth-century England', *Gender & History*, 5 (1993), 212–30.

*Civilising subjects: metropole and colony in the English imagination, 1830–1867* (Oxford, 2002).

Hamer, D. A., *The politics of electoral pressure: a study in the history of Victorian reform agitations* (Hassocks, 1977).

Hanham, H. J., 'Political patronage at the Treasury, 1870–1912', *Historical Journal*, 3 (1960), 75–84.

Harcourt, F., 'Gladstone, monarchism and the "new" imperialism', *Journal of Imperial and Commonwealth History*, 14 (1985), 20–51.

Harding, F. J. W., *Matthew Arnold the critic and France* (Geneva, 1964).

Harling, P., *The waning of 'Old Corruption': the politics of economical reform in Britain, 1779–1846* (Oxford, 1996).

'The centrality of locality: the local state, local democracy, and local consciousness in late-Victorian and Edwardian Britain', *Journal of Victorian Culture*, 9 (2004), 216–34.

Harrison, B., 'The Sunday trading riots of 1855', *Historical Journal*, 8 (1965), 219–45.

*Drink and the Victorians: the temperance question in England 1815–1872* (London, 1971).

Harrison, R. T., *Gladstone's imperialism in Egypt; techniques of domination* (Westport, CT, 1995).

Harvie, C., *The lights of Liberalism: university Liberals and the challenge of democracy 1860–86* (London, 1976).

Hempton, D., *Methodism and politics in British society 1750–1850* (London, 1984).

Henderson, G. B., *Crimean War diplomacy and other historical essays* (Glasgow, 1947).

Hicks, G., 'Don Pacifico, democracy, and danger: the Protectionist party critique of British foreign policy, 1850–1852', *International History Review*, 26 (2004), 515–40.

Hilton, B., *The age of atonement: the influence of evangelicalism on social and economic thought 1785–1865* (Oxford, 1988).

Hoppen, K. T., *The Mid-Victorian generation 1846–1886* (Oxford, 1998).

'Riding a tiger: Daniel O'Connell, Reform, and popular politics in Ireland, 1800–1847', *Proceedings of the British Academy*, 100 (1999), 121–43.

Howe, A., *Free trade and Liberal England, 1846–1946* (Oxford, 1997).

'Gladstone and Cobden', in D. W. Bebbington and R. Swift (eds.), *Gladstone centenary essays* (Liverpool, 2000), pp. 113–32.

Howe, S., *Ireland and empire: colonial legacies in Irish history and culture* (Oxford, 2000).

Hurd, D., *The Arrow War: an Anglo-Chinese confusion 1856–1860* (London, 1967).

Hyam, R., *Britain's imperial century, 1815–1914: a study of empire and expansion* (2nd edn, Basingstoke, 1993).

Hyam, R. and Martin, G., *Reappraisals in British imperial history* (London, 1975).

Hynes, W. G., *The economics of empire: Britain, Africa and the new imperialism 1870–95* (London, 1979).

Jackson, A., 'Ireland, the Union, and the empire, 1800–1960', in K. Kenny (ed.), *Ireland and the British empire* (Oxford, 2004), pp. 123–53.

Jenkins, H., 'The Irish dimension of the British *Kulturkampf:* Vaticanism and civil allegiance, 1870–1875', *Journal of Ecclesiastical History*, 30 (1979), 353–77.

Jenks, L. H., *The migration of British capital to 1875* (London, 1963 edn).

Jones, G. S., *Outcast London: a study in the relationship between classes in Victorian society* (New York, 1984 edn).

Jones, H. S., *Victorian political thought* (Houndsmills, 2000).

'The idea of the national in Victorian political thought', *European Journal of Political Theory*, 5 (2006), 12–21.

Kahan, A., *Liberalism in nineteenth-century Europe: the political culture of limited suffrage* (Basingstoke, 2003).

Kamenka, E. and Smith, F. B. (eds.), *Intellectuals and revolution: socialism and the experience of 1848* (London, 1979).

Keller, U., *The ultimate spectacle: a visual history of the Crimean War* (Amsterdam, 2001).

Kerr, D. A., *Peel, priests and politics: Sir Robert Peel's administration and the Roman Catholic Church in Ireland, 1841–1846* (Oxford, 1982).

'A nation of beggars'? Priests, people, and politics in famine Ireland, 1846–1852* (Oxford, 1994).

Knights, B., *The idea of the clerisy in the nineteenth century* (Cambridge, 1978).

Koebner, R. and Schmidt, H. D., *Imperialism: the story and significance of a political word, 1840–1960* (Cambridge, 1964).

Kofas, J. V., *Financial relations of Greece and the Great Powers, 1832–1862* (Boulder, CO, 1981).

Krein, D. F., *The last Palmerston government: foreign policy, domestic politics, and the genesis of splendid isolation* (Ames, IA, 1978).

Kriegel, A. D., 'A convergence of ethics: Saints and Whigs in British antislavery', *Journal of British Studies*, 26 (1987), 423–50.

Kutolowski, J. F., 'Mid-Victorian public opinion, Polish propaganda, and the uprising of 1863', *Journal of British Studies*, 8 (1969), 86–110.

Lambert, A. D., *The Crimean War: British grand strategy, 1853–56* (Manchester, 1990).

Larsen, T., *Friends of religious equality: Nonconformist politics in mid-Victorian England* (Woodbridge, 1999).

Lawrence, J. and Taylor, M. (eds.), *Party, state and society: electoral behaviour since 1820* (Aldershot, 1997).

Lees, A., *Cities perceived: urban society in European and American thought, 1820–1940* (Manchester, 1985).

Lorimer, D. A., *Colour, class and the Victorians: English attitudes to the negro in the mid-nineteenth century* (Leicester, 1978).

Loughlin, J., *Gladstone, Home Rule and the Ulster question 1882–93* (Dublin, 1986).

Lubenow, W. C., *Parliamentary politics and the Home Rule crisis: the British House of Commons in 1886* (Oxford, 1988).

'The Liberals and the national question: Irish Home Rule, nationalism, and their relationship to nineteenth-century Liberalism', *Parliamentary History*, 13 (1994), 119–42.

McCord, N., 'Cobden and Bright in politics, 1846–1857', in R. Robson (ed.), *Ideas and institutions of Victorian Britain: essays in honour of George Kitson Clark* (London, 1967), pp. 87–114.

'Some difficulties of Parliamentary reform', *Historical Journal*, 10 (1967), 376–90.

*The Anti-Corn Law League 1838–1846* (London, 1968 edn).

Machin, G. I. T., *Politics and the Churches in Great Britain 1832 to 1868* (Oxford, 1977).

McIntire, C. T., *England against the papacy 1858–1861: Tories, Liberals, and the overthrow of papal temporal power during the Italian Risorgimento* (Cambridge, 1983).

McWilliam, R., *Popular politics in nineteenth-century England* (London, 1998).

Mandler, P., *Aristocratic government in the age of reform: Whigs and Liberals, 1830–1852* (Oxford, 1990).

'"Race" and "nation" in mid-Victorian thought', in S. Collini, R. Whatmore and B. Young (eds.), *History, religion, and culture: British intellectual history 1750–1950* (Cambridge, 2000), pp. 224–44.

Marsh, P., *Bargaining on Europe: Britain and the first common market, 1860–1892* (New Haven, 1999).

Martin, K., *The triumph of Lord Palmerston: a study of public opinion in England before the Crimean War* (London, 1963 edn).

Matthew, H. C. G., 'Gladstone, Vaticanism and the question of the East', in D. Baker (ed.), *Studies in Church History*, 15 (1978), 417–42.

Millman, R., *British foreign policy and the coming of the Franco-Prussian War* (Oxford, 1965).

Mitchell, L. G., *Holland House* (London, 1980).

'Britain's reaction to the revolutions', in R. J. W. Evans and H. Pogge von Strandmann (eds.), *The revolutions in Europe 1848–1849: from reform to reaction* (Oxford, 2000), pp. 83–98.

Morris, R. J., 'Samuel Smiles and the genesis of self-help: the retreat to a petit bourgeois Utopia', *Historical Journal*, 24 (1981), 89–108.

Morton, G., *Unionist nationalism: governing urban Scotland, 1830–1860* (East Linton, 1999).

Mosse, W. E., 'England and the Polish insurrection of 1863', *English Historical Review*, 71 (1956).

'Public opinion and foreign policy: the British public and the war scare of November 1870', *Historical Journal*, 6 (1963).

Müller, F. L., *Britain and the German question: perceptions of nationalism and political reform, 1830–1863* (Basingstoke, 2001).

Murphy, J., *The religious problem in English education: the crucial experiment* (Liverpool, 1959).

Norman, E. R., *The Catholic Church and Ireland in the age of rebellion, 1859–1873* (London, 1965).

Palm, F. C., *England and Napoleon III: a study of the rise of a utopian dictator* (Durham, NC, 1948).

Palmer, A., *The banner of battle: the story of the Crimean War* (London, 1987).

Parry, J., *Democracy and religion: Gladstone and the Liberal party, 1867–1875* (Cambridge, 1986).

*The rise and fall of Liberal government in Victorian Britain* (New Haven, 1993)

'Past and future in the later career of Lord John Russell', in T. C. W. Blanning and D. Cannadine (eds.), *History and biography: essays in honour of Derek Beales* (Cambridge, 1996), pp. 142–72.

'Disraeli and England', *Historical Journal*, 43 (2000), 699–728.

'Gladstone, Liberalism and the government of 1868–1874', in D. W. Bebbington and R. Swift (eds.), *Gladstone centenary essays* (Liverpool, 2000), pp. 94–112.

'The impact of Napoleon III on British politics, 1851–1880', *Transactions of the Royal Historical Society*, 6:11 (2001), 147–75.

'Nonconformity, clericalism and "Englishness"; the United Kingdom', in C. Clark and W. Kaiser (eds.), *Culture wars: secular-Catholic conflict in nineteenth-century Europe* (Cambridge, 2003), pp. 152–80.

'Liberalism and liberty', in P. Mandler (ed.), *Liberty and authority in Victorian Britain* (Oxford, 2006), pp. 71–100.

'Palmerston and Russell', in D. Brown and M. Taylor (eds.), *Palmerston studies* (2 vols., Southampton, forthcoming), vol. 1, ch. 7.

'Whig monarchy, Whig nation: the representative function of modern monarchy since 1780', in A. Olechnowicz (ed.), *The monarchy and the British nation, 1780–2005* (Cambridge, forthcoming, 2007).

Partridge, M. S., *Military planning for the defense of the United Kingdom, 1814–1870* (New York, 1989).

Paz, D. G., *The politics of working-class education in Britain, 1830–50* (Manchester, 1980).

Peatling, G. K., 'The whiteness of Ireland under and after the Union', *Journal of British Studies*, 44 (2005), 115–34.

Pemble, J., *The Mediterranean passion: Victorians and Edwardians in the South* (Oxford, 1987).

Petrie, G., *A singular iniquity: the campaigns of Josephine Butler* (London, 1971).

Porter, B., *The refugee question in mid-Victorian politics* (Cambridge, 1979).

'The Freiheit prosecutions, 1881–1882', *Historical Journal*, 23 (1980), 833–56.

'"Bureau and barrack": early Victorian attitudes towards the Continent', *Victorian Studies*, 27 (1983–4), 407–33.

Quinault, R., '1848 and Parliamentary reform', *Historical Journal*, 31 (1988), 831–51.

'The French revolution of 1830 and Parliamentary reform', *History*, 79 (1994), 377–93.

Quinn, D. A., *Patronage and piety: the politics of English Roman Catholicism, 1850–1900* (Houndsmills, 1993).

Raymond, D., *British policy and opinion during the Franco-Prussian War* (New York, 1921).

Roberts, M. J. D., 'Morals, art, and the law: the passing of the Obscene Publications Act, 1857', *Victorian Studies*, 28 (1985), 609–29.

Robinson, R. and Gallagher, J., *Africa and the Victorians: the official mind of imperialism* (London, 1961).

Robson, M. M., 'Liberals and "Vital Interests": the debate on international arbitration, 1815–72', *Bulletin of the Institute of Historical Research*, 32 (1959), 38–55.

Rodger, N. A. M., 'The dark ages of the Admiralty, 1869–85: Part I, "Business methods", 1869–74', *Mariner's Mirror*, 61 (1975), 331–44.

Rossi, J. P., *The transformation of the British Liberal party: a study of the tactics of the Liberal opposition, 1874–1880* (Philadelphia, PA, 1978).

Royle, E., *Radicals, secularists and republicans: popular freethought in Britain, 1866–1915* (Manchester, 1980).

Saab, A. P., *Reluctant icon: Gladstone, Bulgaria, and the working classes, 1856–1878* (Cambridge, MA, 1991).

Salevouris, M. J., *'Riflemen form': the war scare of 1859–1860 in England* (New York, 1982).

Samuel, R. (ed.), *Patriotism: the making and unmaking of British national identity* (3 vols., London, 1989).

'The discovery of Puritanism, 1820–1914: a preliminary sketch', in J. Garnett and H. C. G. Matthew (eds.), *Revival and religion since 1700: essays for John Walsh* (London, 1993), pp. 201–47.

Sanders, C. R., *Coleridge and the broad church movement* (Durham, NC, 1942).

Sandiford, K. A. P., *Great Britain and the Schleswig-Holstein question 1848–64: a study in diplomacy, politics, and public opinion* (Toronto, 1975).

'Gladstone and Europe', in B. L. Kinzer (ed.), *The Gladstonian turn of mind: essays presented to J. B. Conacher* (Toronto, 1985), pp. 177–96.

Schleunes, K. A., *Schooling and society: the politics of education in Prussia and Bavaria 1750–1900* (Oxford, 1989).

Schreuder, D. M., *Gladstone and Kruger: Liberal government and colonial 'Home Rule' 1880–5* (London, 1969).

'Gladstone and Italian unification, 1848–70: the making of a Liberal?', *English Historical Review*, 85 (1970), 475–501.

*The scramble for southern Africa, 1871–1895: the politics of partition reappraised* (Cambridge, 1980).

Schroeder, P. W., *Austria, Great Britain and the Crimean War: the destruction of the European Concert* (Ithaca, NY, 1972).

'Gladstone as Bismarck', *Canadian Journal of History*, 15 (1980), 163–95.

*The transformation of European politics, 1763–1848* (Oxford, 1994).

Searle, G. R., *Entrepreneurial politics in mid-Victorian Britain* (Oxford, 1993).

*Morality and the market in Victorian Britain* (Oxford, 1998).

Seed, J., 'Unitarianism, political economy and the antinomies of liberal culture in Manchester, 1830–50', *Social History*, 7 (1982), 1–25.

Semmel, B., *The Governor Eyre controversy* (London, 1962).

Shannon, R. T., *Gladstone and the Bulgarian agitation 1876* (London, 1963).

'John Robert Seeley and the idea of a national Church', in R. Robson (ed.), *Ideas and institutions of Victorian Britain: essays in honour of George Kitson Clark* (London, 1967), pp. 236–67.

Simon, A., 'Church disestablishment as a factor in the general election of 1885', *Historical Journal*, 18 (1975), 791–820.

Smith, P. and Summerfield, G. (eds.), *Matthew Arnold and the education of the new order* (Cambridge, 1969).

Stanley, B., 'Christian responses to the Indian Mutiny of 1857', in W. J. Sheils (ed.), *The Church and war: studies in Church history, volume 20* (Oxford, 1983), pp. 277–89.

Steele, E. D., 'Gladstone and Ireland', *Irish Historical Studies*, 17 (1970).

'J. S. Mill and the Irish question: reform, and the integrity of the empire, 1865–1870', *Historical Journal*, 13 (1970), 419–50.

*Irish land and British politics: tenant-right and nationality 1865–1870* (Cambridge, 1974).

'Gladstone, Irish violence, and conciliation', in A. Cosgrove and D. McCartney (eds.), *Studies in Irish history presented to R. Dudley Edwards* (Dublin, 1979), pp. 257–78.

*Palmerston and Liberalism, 1855–1865* (Cambridge, 1991).

Stembridge, S., *Parliament, the press and the colonies, 1846–1880* (New York, 1982).

Strachan, H., 'Soldiers, strategy and Sebastopol', *Historical Journal*, 21 (1978), 303–25.

Super, R. H. (ed.), *The complete prose works of Matthew Arnold* (11 vols., Ann Arbor, MI, 1960–72).

Swartz, M., *The politics of British foreign policy in the era of Disraeli and Gladstone* (London, 1985).

Taylor, A., 'Palmerston and Radicalism, 1847–1865', *Journal of British Studies*, 33 (1994), 157–79.

Taylor, A. J. P., *The trouble makers: dissent over foreign policy 1792–1939* (London, 1957).

Taylor, M., 'John Bull and the iconography of public opinion in England, c 1712–1929', *Past and Present*, 134 (1992), 93–128.

*The decline of British Radicalism, 1847–1860* (Oxford, 1995).

'The 1848 revolutions and the British empire', *Past and Present*, 166 (2000), 146–80.

Tosh, J., 'Gentlemanly politeness and manly simplicity in Victorian England', *Transactions of the Royal Historical Society*, 6:12 (2002), 455–72.

Urban, M. F., *British opinion and policy on the unification of Italy 1856–1861* (New York, 1938).

Vance, N., *The sinews of the spirit: the ideal of Christian manliness in Victorian literature and religious thought* (Cambridge, 1985).

*The Victorians and ancient Rome* (Oxford, 1997).

Varouxakis, G., *Victorian political thought on France and the French* (Basingstoke, 2002).

Vernon, J., *Politics and the people: a study in English political culture, c. 1815–1867* (Cambridge, 1993).

Vincent, J., *The formation of the British Liberal party, 1857–1868* (Harmondsworth, 1972 edn).

'Gladstone and Ireland', *Proceedings of the British Academy*, 63 (1977), 193–238.

Wahrman, D., *Imagining the middle class: the political representation of class in Britain, c. 1780–1840* (Cambridge, 1995).

Ward, J. M., *Colonial self-government: the British experience* (London, 1976).

Warren, A., 'Gladstone, land and social reconstruction in Ireland 1881–1887', *Parliamentary History*, 2 (1983), 153–73.

Watts, R., *Gender, power and the Unitarians in England, 1760–1860* (London, 1998).

Williams, R., *The contentious Crown: public discussion of the British monarchy in the reign of Queen Victoria* (Aldershot, 1997).

Wilson, K., *Channel Tunnel visions 1850–1945: dreams and nightmares* (London, 1994).

Wohl, A. S., '"Dizzi-Ben-Dizzi": Disraeli as alien', *Journal of British Studies*, 34 (1995), 375–411.

Worden, B., 'The Victorians and Oliver Cromwell', in S. Collini, R. Whatmore and B. Young (eds.), *History, religion, and culture: British intellectual history 1750–1950* (Cambridge, 2000), pp. 112–35.

# Index